The Children of Ishmael

CRITICAL PERSPECTIVES ON JUVENILE JUSTICE

Authors Krisberg and Austin take a different view from most standard
juvenile delinquency texts concerning the causes and solutions to
juvenile delinquency and the effectiveness of the present-day juvenile
justice system. They point out that traditional explanations of delinquency rarely give due emphasis to racism, economic exploitation,
poverty, sexism and political repression as contributing factors. They
also claim that delinquent behavior is widespread throughout the
social structure and is not primarily a lower-class phenomenon, and
that the juvenile court system today is a bureaucratic nightmare in
which due process and legal safeguards are virtually nonexistent.

The reason for their book, then, is to "restore a sense of balance to
the study of juvenile delinquency"; to review traditional explanations
and theories and offer several alternative hypotheses. In the process
they provide extensive historical material, which gives students important new insights into how political, social, and legal currents shaped
the juvenile justice system.

In addition to major original contributions by the authors, this book
contains contributions from leading figures of contemporary criminology, including many proponents of the New Criminology.

Mayfield Publishing Company

Now Sarah Abraham's wife bare him no children: and she had an hand-maid, an Egyptian, whose name was Hagar.

And Sarah said unto Abraham, Behold now, the Lord hath restrained me from bearing: I pray thee, go in unto my maid; it may be that I may obtain children by her. And Abraham hearkened to the voice of Sarah.

And Sarah Abraham's wife took Hagar her maid the Egyptian, after Abraham had dwelt ten years in the land of Canaan, and gave her to her husband Abraham to be his wife.

And he went in unto Hagar, and she conceived: and when she saw that she had conceived, her mistress was despised in her eyes.

And Sarah said unto Abraham, My wrong be upon thee: I have given my maid into thy bosom; and when she saw that she had conceived, I was despised in her eyes: the Lord judge between me and thee.

But Abraham said unto Sarah, Behold, thy maid is in thy hand; do to her as it pleaseth thee. And when Sarah dealt hardly with her, she fled from her face.

And the angel of the Lord found her by a fountain of water in the wilderness, by the fountain in the way to Shur.

And he said, Hagar, Sarah's maid, whence camest thou? and whither wilt thou go? And she said, I flee from the face of my mistress Sarah.

And the angel of the Lord said unto her, Return to thy mistress, and submit thyself under her hands.

And the angel of the Lord said unto her, I will multiply thy seed exceedingly, that it shall not be numbered for multitude.

And the angel of the Lord said unto her, Behold, thou art with child, and shalt bear a son, and shalt call his name Ishmael; because the Lord hath heard thy affliction.

And he will be a wild man; his hand will be against every man, and every man's hand against him; and he shall dwell in the presence of all his brethren.

And she called the name of the Lord that spake unto her, Thou God seest me: for she said, Have I also here looked after him that seeth me?

Wherefore the well was called Baerlahairoi; behold, it is between Kadesh and Bered.

And Hagar bare Abraham a son: and Abraham called his son's name, which Hagar bare, Ishmael.

And Abraham was fourscore and six years old, when Hagar bare Ishmael to Abraham.

Genesis 16: i-xvi

The Children of Ishmael

CRITICAL PERSPECTIVES ON JUVENILE JUSTICE

A Text with Readings

COMPILED BY BARRY KRISBERG AND JAMES AUSTIN

 MAYFIELD PUBLISHING COMPANY

To our parents, and especially for Ruthie, Karen, and Moshe

Library of Congress Catalog Card Number: 77-089919
International Standard Book Number: 0-87484-387-1

Manufactured in the United States of America
Mayfield Publishing Company
285 Hamilton Avenue, Palo Alto, California 94301

This book was set in IBM Century Medium by Libra
Cold Type and Typ Art and was printed and bound by
the George Banta Company. Sponsoring editor was
Alden C. Paine, Carole Norton supervised editing, and
John Hamburger was manuscript editor. The text and
cover were designed by Nancy Sears and Michelle Hogan
supervised production. The New York House of Refuge
scenes originally appeared in *Appleton's Journal* of
March 18, 1971; scenes on pages 6, 290, and 388 by
permission of The Bettmann Archive. Cover photo
© James Motlow 1973, by permission of Jeroboam.

CONTENTS

viii

CHAPTER 9
THE AMBIGUITY OF SOCIAL REFORM   567

PREFACE

The humanistic potential of sociology can be realized only if the necessary knowledge is transmitted to people seeking intellectual and political liberation. C. Wright Mills referred to this in his book, *The Sociological Imagination*, and exemplified in his own professional life how a scientist can contribute to social change and human liberation. His highest goal was to assist fellow humans in developing the critical perspective necessary to understand their world, and thus participate in shaping it. Mills's "sociological imagination" involves translating "the personal problems of milieu" into the "public issues of social structure." By making people aware of the larger social forces that impinge upon their lives, they may be able to break down the imprisoning ideologies used to justify social injustice. Though this requires great personal sacrifice, the therapeutic results will be more successful than traditional therapies.

This book was inspired by Mills, and his hope for "the sociological imagination." The aim of *The Children of Ishmael* is to challenge the thoughtful student, and to promote critical thinking in the area of juvenile justice. Although our terminology may shock readers accustomed to the complacent neutrality of standard juvenile delinquency texts, we believe our approach to be heuristic, timely, and intellectually honest. This text shares the New Criminology perspective of such American writers as Richard Quinney, Charles Reasons, and William Chambliss, as well as British authors, Ian Taylor, Paul Walton, and Jock Young. Several works by the New Criminologists are reprinted in various chapters. Despite our sympathies, we have not ignored the works of scholars of different viewpoints, and the material presented offers a balanced review of available data and theory. In this review we search for the hidden biases, and have consciously attempted to delineate our own assumptions throughout. We cannot say for sure that our biases are superior to others, but we offer the reader an opportunity to judge issues of fact and theory based upon the best assembled evidence.

For this purpose we have chosen a mixed format of narrative and readings. Original chapters summarize such subjects as the history and structure of the juvenile justice system in order to provide an easily accessible synthesis of the literature. In other cases, excellent articles enrich our presentation and allow the reader to conduct an independent evaluation of existing data. Some of the articles have never previously appeared in print, many have never appeared in an anthology, and all represent significant, current research, drawn from a variety of academic fields. *The Children of Ishmael* provides material encompassing the broad range of issues surrounding juvenile justice and delinquency. This information is organized within a coherent theoretical framework, including theories of etiology, the sociology of juvenile justice, as well as discussions of public policy. We have made a special effort to present an extensive historical perspective in chapter 2, and to focus throughout the text on the interrelation of theory and practice.

Our text is sharply critical of the contemporary juvenile justice system. Courses emphasizing field experiences and internships are invaluable, and we encourage students to follow up our analysis with visits to juvenile court agencies and institutions. Where feasible, we have endeavored to offer meaningful alternatives to current juvenile justice practices. Our intent is neither to immobilize the student with cynicism, nor to encourage a superficial utopianism concerning the potential for social change. It is our hope that students realize that social institutions are both comprehensible and capable of being changed by constructive reform efforts.

We wish to acknowledge the help of friends who read early drafts of various chapters and contributed thoughtful suggestions, including Ruth Austin, Karen McKie, Isami Waugh, Dexter Waugh, Wayne Lawrence, and Melanie Fong. Marc Hofstadter, Karen Bailey, and Josie Ibrahim provided help in typing and assembling the manuscripts. The authors also wish to express their appreciation to Alden Paine and the staff at Mayfield for helping us move from concept to reality.

New York House of Refuge on Randall's Island, 1871

THE NEED FOR A CRITICAL PERSPECTIVE

CHAPTER 1

Anyone who hates children and dogs can't be all bad.

—W. C. FIELDS

The late Mr. Fields would not have looked askance at the way children are treated in America. Despite public utterances of our love for children, the young occupy a peculiarly ambivalent position in a society controlled by adults. Young people form a subservient class, alienated, powerless, and prone to economic manipulation. In an economic system based on the refinement of technology and profit making youth are often exploited. Economic institutions view youth as a lucrative but unsophisticated market, and considerable corporate effort is expended in marketing, producing, and advertising goods directed toward children. Young people are subjected to a barrage of huckstering of nutritionally worthless foods, dangerous recreational products, and useless health and cosmetic aids. Since youth rarely participate in defining their consumer needs, they become frustrated in their roles of non-producers, acting merely as "conspicuous consumers" generating profits.

Politically, young people are excluded from full participation in structuring and governing society. They have no organized lobbies, limited voting power, and hold few positions of authority. Youth

1

are, however, subject to controlling forces by the state. Virtually all aspects of young lives are regulated and determined through state-enforced rules and intervention. Some observers argue that the educational system is constructed to channel youth into predetermined adult roles. Their education does not fully equip the young to deal with a social structure fraught with group conflict and institutionalized violence. Schools train children to uncritically accept the prevailing values and ideologies of an unequal society.

The plight of youth is even more apparent for those who have contact with the juvenile justice system. *Juveniles* are neither children nor adults; the term is a legal construction. Their rights, privileges, and even identities are delineated by those who make and enforce laws. Those processed by the juvenile courts confront additional prejudices since they are typically poor and from third world groups.

The juvenile justice system was ostensibly created to provide individual guidance and protection to children heading toward a life of adult criminality. But many observers of the court believe that it has amounted to little more than a social control institution, offering second-class justice to wayward youth. Critics assert that the court often arbitrarily removes youngsters from their homes and communities via routine court procedures, making a mockery of the concept of justice. The juvenile justice system, operating in support of the dominant society, controls youth from the poorer classes, especially those unwilling to conform to the mores of society. The concepts of juvenile and juvenile delinquency thus reinforce the subservient condition of lower-class youth.

THE NATURE AND EXTENT OF DELINQUENCY

Although there is consensus among criminologists that delinquent behavior is widespread and increasing, precise definitions of delinquency do not exist. There is so much variation among state laws that almost any form of misbehavior or nonconformity can be construed as delinquent. Vague phrases such as "incorrigibility," "in need of supervision," "leading an idle life," "waywardness," or "beyond parental control" are typical of the legal definitions of delinquency. Delinquent behavior under the court's jurisdiction ranges from *juvenile status offenses*, which would not be criminal if committed by adults, to more serious crimes, such as burglary, larceny, and assault. In addition, the juvenile court handles cases of neglected, abused, and dependent children. Many diverse kinds of parental or youth behavior may justify judicial control over a child's life even to the extent of long-term incarceration. The result of this wide latitude is that police, probation officers, and judges may simultaneously become the arbiters and interpreters of moral behavior. The juvenile justice system, reflecting the structure of power within society, is rarely responsive to the needs of victims and offenders, children and parents.

There are few legal safeguards for children due to the vagueness of juvenile court statutes and the informal nature of juvenile court proceedings. If similar conditions prevailed in adult criminal courts, they would be challenged as violations of constitutional rights guaranteeing due process and equal protection of law. In much the same way that definitions of delinquency are ambiguous, the age during which a person is considered a juvenile is subject to considerable variation. The maximum age during which juvenile court intervention is permissible ranges from age fifteen through twenty-one, and some states leave the age criteria open and provide no statutory provisions.

In 1974, over 27 percent of all arrests made in the United States, or nearly 1.7 million, were of persons under eighteen.[1] If only index crimes—homicide, rape, robbery, aggravated assault, burglary, larceny, and auto theft—are considered, juveniles represent 45 percent of those arrested. In the past five years juvenile arrests have increased over 15 percent. These figures are high despite the fact that the controversial status offenses are not included. National figures are difficult to obtain on the number of juveniles arrested for status offenses such as truancy, incorrigibility, curfew violations, or running away. In California, where figures are available, over 25 percent of all juvenile arrests involve status offenses.[2] President's Commission on Law Enforcement and the Administration of Justice has estimated that one of every five or six males will be referred to juvenile court by his eighteenth birthday.[3] A Philadelphia study reported that approximately 35 percent of all males born in 1945 had at least one official police contact by age eighteen.[4] So little is known about female delinquency that estimates have not been made. It is clear that the juvenile justice system exercises considerable influence over the lives of American youth.

Policy makers, academicians, and juvenile justice officials have responded to the accelerating delinquency rates with conflicting reform measures. Although there is consensus that the juvenile system has failed to curb delinquency, there is little agreement on how to best correct its failures. Bolstered by studies that suggest rehabilitation does not work, some call for more punitive and deterrence-oriented approaches. Others argue that children must be protected from the harmful labelling effects of the juvenile justice system. This has led to recent legislation that combines both conservative and liberal interests. California's Juvenile Justice Reform Act (AB 3121), effective in 1977, stipulates more severe dispositions for delinquents charged with felony-type offenses, and, at the same time, reduces state control over status offenders.

THE NEED FOR A CRITICAL PERSPECTIVE

Traditional texts on juvenile delinquency have generally assumed that social policy is based on a consensus of accepted values, with the juvenile court operating in this context. Although both delinquency and the juvenile justice system have been described in detail these descriptions have often been insensitive to sociopolitical realities, and have lacked historical perspective. Most writers on juvenile justice underestimate the significance of social inequities rooted in the basic organization of our society. While proposing modest reforms, conventional textbooks usually lend support to the existing character of the juvenile justice system, and encourage their readers to become mere technicians. Traditional explanations of delinquency rarely emphasize racism, economic exploitation, poverty, sexism, and political repression. They assume that deviant behavior is judged solely by legal norms, without discussing the social environment in which laws are created and administered.

A new critical approach to juvenile justice is needed, since the traditional perspective has not been adequate. This view is partially motivated by the political and social milieu of the last two decades. Watergate, political assassinations, revelations of FBI and CIA criminal activities, and other corporate and governmental scandals have cast doubt on both our leaders and our political processes. Moreover, the civil rights and the women's rights movements, the protests against the Vietnam War and the worldwide struggles against colonialism have led many Americans to question conventional values and existing social arrangements. We can no longer uncritically accept official wisdom without questioning the assumptions on which it is based.

This critical reexamination will provide a historical perspective on juvenile justice; a review of traditional explanations and theories; and will offer several alternative hypotheses. For instance, although the juvenile court has been traditionally portrayed as a way of providing more humane treatment of wayward youth, there is evidence to support a less benevolent view of its origins. Many authorities assert that the juvenile justice system acts in the child's best interest, providing individualized and humane dispositions. But under close scrutiny, the juvenile court appears a bureaucratic nightmare in which due process and legal safeguards are virtually nonexistent. Research shows that juveniles are subject to arbitrary and often unfair decisions by court personnel. While officials claim that the system converts delinquents into productive and law-abiding citizens, research on a wide range of rehabilitation projects is not encouraging. Juvenile delinquency theorists have assumed that, since there is a preponderance of lower-class juveniles in our courts and penal institutions, serious youthful misconduct is primarily a lower-class phenomenon. Empirical evidence reveals that, on the contrary, delinquent behavior is widespread throughout the social structure.

Through a critical perspective we seek to restore a sense of balance to the study of juvenile delinquency. We wish to reexamine traditional theories that have been responsible for legitimating and perpetuating inequities in the treatment of juveniles. Juvenile justice is inextricably tied to the broader problems of social justice, and to contradictions within the social structure. Advances in theory and practice in the study of delinquency will depend on our understanding of the effect of age bias and other forms of social oppression.

Psychologist Erik Erikson has observed: "Childhood . . . is the model of all oppression and enslavement, a kind of inner colonization, which forces grown-ups to accept inner repression and self-restriction."[5] A detailed study of the various forms of juvenile oppression by official agencies echoes Erikson's view. A critical perspective on the oppression of children may enlighten us about the artificial restrictions and inequitable limits placed upon our social lives.

NOTES

1   Clarence Kelly, *Uniform Crime Reports 1975.*
2   California Department of Justice, *Crime and Delinquency in California, 1974.*
3   President's Commission on Law Enforcement and the Administration of Justice, *The Challenge of Crime in a Free Society.*
4   Marvin Wolfgang, Robert Figlio, and Thorsten Sellin, *Delinquency in a Birth Cohort.*
5   Erik H. Erikson and Huey P. Newton, *In Search of Common Ground*, p. 52.

BIBLIOGRAPHY

California Department of Justice, Bureau of Criminal Statistics. *Crime and Delinquency in California, 1974.* Sacramento, Calif., 1975.

Erikson, Erik H., and Newton, Huey P. *In Search of Common Ground.* New York: W. W. Norton, 1973.

Kelly, Clarence. *Uniform Crime Reports 1975.* Washington, D.C.: Federal Bureau of Investigation, 1975.

President's Commission on Law Enforcement and the Administration of Justice. *The Challenge of Crime in a Free Society.* Washington, D.C.: U.S. Government Printing Office, 1967.

Wolfgang, Marvin; Figlio, Robert; and Sellin, Thorsten. *Delinquency in a Birth Cohort.* Chicago: University of Chicago Press, 1974.

Rescue of Children from a Drunken Mother

HISTORY OF THE CONTROL AND PREVENTION OF JUVENILE DELINQUENCY IN AMERICA

CHAPTER 2

The first specialized institution for the control of juvenile delinquency in America was the New York House of Refuge, founded in 1825. But specialized treatment of wayward youth has a much longer history—one tied to changes in the social structure of medieval Europe. These same changes prompted the colonization of the New World and led to attempts to control and exploit the labor of African, European, and Native American children.

Virtually all aspects of life were in a state of flux for the people of Europe in the later Middle Ages (sixteenth and seventeenth centuries). The economy was being transformed from a feudal system based on subsistence agriculture to a capitalistic, trade-oriented system focusing on cash crops and the consolidation of large tracts of land. In religious matters, the turmoil could be amply witnessed in the intense struggles of the Reformation. Politically, power was increasingly concentrated in the hands of a few monarchs, who were fashioning strong centralized states. The growth of trade and exploration exposed Europeans to a variety of world cultures and peoples.

For the lower classes of European society, these were "the worst of times." The rising population density as well as primitive methods of agricultural production led to a virtual exhaustion of the

8

land. Increasing urban populations created new demands for cheap grain, and landlords responded by increasing the fees paid by peasants who worked the land. Large numbers of peasants were displaced from the land to permit the growth of a capitalist pasturage system. The standard of living of the European peasantry dropped sharply and this new, displaced class streamed into the cities and towns in search of means of survival. The workers and artisans of the cities were deeply threatened by the prospect that this pauper class would drive down the general wage level. Most European towns experienced sharp rises in crime, rioting, and public disorder.

To control and defuse the threat of this new "dangerous class," the leaders of the towns enacted laws and other restrictions to discourage immigration and contain the movement of the impoverished peasantry. Poor Laws were passed, preventing the new migrants from obtaining citizenship, restricting their membership in guilds, and often closing the city gates to them. Vagrancy laws were instituted to control and punish those who seemed a threat to the social order. Certain legislation, such as the Elizabethan Statute of Artificers (1562), restricted access into certain trades, forcing the rural young to remain in the countryside.

Urban migration continued despite most attempts to curtail it. The collective units of urban life, the guild and the family, began to weaken under the pressure of social change. Children were often abandoned or released from traditional community restraints. Countless observers from this period tell of bands of youths roaming the cities at night, engaging in thievery, begging, and other forms of misbehavior.[1]

At this time family control of children was the dominant model for disciplining wayward youth. The model of family government, with the father in the role of sovereign, was extended to those without families through a system of *binding out* the young to other families. Poor children or those beyond parental control were apprenticed to householders for a specified period of time. Unlike the apprenticeship system for the privileged classes, the binding out system did not oblige the master to teach his ward a trade. Boys were generally assigned to farming tasks and girls were brought into domestic service.

As the problem of urban poverty increased, the traditional modes of dealing with delinquent or destitute children became strained. Some localities constructed institutions to control wayward youth. The Bridewell (1555) in London is generally considered the first institution specifically designed to control youthful beggars and vagrants. In 1576 Parliament passed a law establishing a similar institution in every English county. The most celebrated of these early institutions was the Amsterdam House of Corrections (1595), which was viewed as an innovative solution to the crime problem of the day.[2] The houses of correction combined the principles of the poorhouse, the workhouse, and the penal institution. The youthful inmates were forced to work within the institution, and thus develop habits of industriousness. Upon release they were expected to enter the labor force, so house of correction inmates were often hired out to private contractors. Males rasped hardwoods used in the dyeing industry, and when textile manufacturing was introduced to the houses of correction, this became the special task of female inmates.

The early houses of correction, or so-called *Bridewells*, accepted all types of children including the destitute, the infirm, and the needy. In some cases, parents placed their children in these institutions because they believed the regimen of work would have a reformative effect. Although it is debatable whether the houses of correction were economically efficient, the founders of such institutions clearly hoped to provide a cheap source of labor to local industries. The French institutions, called *hospitaux generaux*, experimented with technological improvements and different labor arrangements. This often brought charges of unfair competition from guilds, fearing the demise of their monopoly on labor, and businessmen, who felt threatened by price competition at the marketplace. Some writers stress the economic motive of these early penal institutions: "The institution of the houses of correction in such a society was not the result of brotherly love or of an official sense of obligation to the distressed. It was part of the development of capitalism."[3]

The enormous social, political, and economic dislocations taking place in Europe provided a major push toward colonization of the Americas. People emigrated for many reasons—some to get rich, some to escape political or religious oppression, and some because they simply had nothing to lose. Settlement patterns and the resulting forms of community life varied considerably. In the Massachusetts Bay Colony, for example, the Puritans attempted to establish a deeply religious community to serve God's will in the New World. The Puritans brought families with them, and from the outset made provisions for the care and control of youths.

In contrast, the settlement of Virginia was more directly tied to economic considerations. There were persistent labor shortages, and the need for labor prompted orders for young people to be sent over from Europe. Some youths were sent over by *Spirits*, who were agents of merchants or shipowners. The Spirits attempted to persuade young people to emigrate to America. They often promised that the New World would bring tremendous wealth and happiness to the youthful immigrants. The children typically agreed to work a specific term (usually four years) in compensation for passage across the Atlantic and for services rendered during the trip. These agreements of service were then sold to inhabitants of the new colonies, particularly in the South. One can imagine that this labor source must have been quite profitable for the plantations of the New World.

Spirits were often accused of kidnapping, contractual fraud, and deception of a generally illiterate, destitute, and young clientele.

Other children coming to the New World were even more clearly coerced. For example, it became an integral part of penal practice in the early part of the eighteenth century to transport prisoners to colonial areas. Children held in the overcrowded Bridewells and poorhouses of England were brought to the Americas as indentured servants. After working a specified number of years as servants or laborers, the children were able to win their freedom. In 1619 the colony of Virginia regularized an agreement for the shipment of orphans and destitute children from England.

That same year, Africans, another group of coerced immigrants, made their first appearance in the Virginia colony. The importation of African slaves eventually displaced reliance on the labor of youthful poor because of greater economic feasibility. The black chattels were physically able to perform strenuous labor under extreme weather conditions without adequate nutrition. These abilities would finally be used to describe them as beasts. Also, the high death rates experienced under these conditions did not have to be accounted for. The bondage of Africans was soon converted into lifetime enslavement, which passed on through generations. The southern plantation system, dependent on the labor of African slaves, produced tremendous wealth, further entrenching this inhuman system.[4] Racism, deeply lodged in the English psyche, provided the rationale and excuse for daily atrocities and cruelties.[5]

Studies of slavery often overlook the fact that most slaves were children. Slave traders thought children would bring higher prices. Accounts of the slave trade emphasize the economic utility of small children, who could be jammed into the limited cargo space available. Children were always a high proportion of the total slave population because slave owners encouraged the birth of children to increase their capital. Little regard was paid by slave owners for keeping families together. African babies were a commodity to be exploited just as one might exploit the land or the natural resources of a plantation, and young slave women were often used strictly for breeding. A complete understanding of the social control of children must include an examination of the institution of slavery, comparing this to the conditions faced by children in other sections of the country.[6]

Another group of children who are often ignored in discussions of the history of treatment of youth in America are Native Americans. In 1609 officials of the Virginia Company were authorized to kidnap Native American children and raise them as Christians. The stolen youths were to be trained in the religion of the colonists, as well as in their language and customs. The early European colonists spread the word of the gospel to help rationalize their conquests of lands and peoples. But, an equally important motivation was their interest in recruiting a group of friendly natives to assist in trade negotiations and pacification programs among the native peoples. The early Indian schools resembled penal institutions, with heavy emphasis on useful work, Bible study, and religious worship. Although a substantial amount of effort and money was invested in Indian schools, the results were considerably less than had been originally hoped:

> Missionaries could rarely bridge the chasm of mistrust and hostility that resulted from wars, massacres and broken promises. With so many colonists regarding the Indian as the chief threat to their security and the Indians looking upon the colonists as hypocrites, it is little wonder that attempts to win converts and to educate should fail.[7]

Unlike attempts to enslave children of African descent, early efforts with Native Americans were not successful. Relations between European colonists and Native Americans during this period centered around trading and the securing of land rights. These contrasting economic relationships resulted in divergent practices in areas such as education. Although there was general support for bringing "the blessings of Christian education" to the Native American children, there was intense disagreement about the merits of educating African slaves. While some groups, such as the Society for the Propagation of the Gospel, argued that all heathens should be educated and converted, others feared that slaves who were baptized would claim the status of freemen. There was concern among whites that education of slaves would lead to insurrection and revolt. As a result, South Carolina and several other colonies proclaimed that conversion to Christianity would not affect the status of slaves.[8] Many southern colonies made it a crime to teach reading and writing to slaves. A middle-ground position evolved, calling for religious indoctrination without the more dangerous education in literacy.[9]

In the early years of colonization, the family was the fundamental mode of juvenile social control, as well as the central unit of economic production. Even in situations where children were apprenticed or indentured, the family still served as the model for discipline and order. Several of the early colonies passed laws requiring single persons to live with families. The dominant form of poor relief at this time was placing the needy with other families in the community.[10] A tradition of family government evolved in which the father was empowered with absolute authority over all affairs of the family. Wives and children were expected to give complete and utter obedience to the father's wishes. This model complemented practices in political life, where absolute authority was thought crucial to the preservation of civilization.

Colonial laws supported and defended the primacy of family government. The earliest laws concerning youthful misbehavior prescribed the death penalty for children who disobeyed their parents. For example, part of the 1641 Massachusetts *Body of Liberties* reads as follows:

> If any child, or children, above sixteen years of age, and of sufficient understanding, shall CURSE or SMITE their natural FATHER or MOTHER, he or they shall be putt to death, unless it can be sufficiently testifyed that the Parents have been very unchristianly negligent in the education of such children: so provoked them by extreme and cruel correction, that they have been forced thereunto, to preserve themselves from death or maiming: *Exod* 21:17, *Lev* 20:9, *Exod* 21:15.[11]

Although there is little evidence that children were actually put to death for disobeying their parents, this same legal principle was used to justify the punishment of rebellious slave children in the southern colonies. Family discipline was typically maintained by corporal punishment. Not only were parents held legally responsible for providing moral education for their children, but a Massachusetts law of 1642 mandated that parents should teach their children reading and writing. Later, in 1670, public officials called tithingmen were assigned to assist the selectmen (town councilmen) and constables in supervising family government. The tithingmen visited families who were allegedly ignoring the education and socialization of their children. Although there are records of parents brought to trial due to their neglect of parental duties, this manner of supervising family government was not very successful.

The family was the central economic unit of colonial America. Home-based industry, in which labor took place on the family farm or in a home workshop, continued until the end of the eighteenth century. Children were an important component of family production, and their labor was considered valuable and desirable. A major determinant of a child's future during this time was the father's choice of apprenticeship for his child. Ideally the apprenticeship system was to be the stepping stone into a skilled craft, but this happy result was certain only for children of the privileged classes. As a consequence, children of poor families might actually be *bound out* as indentured servants. The term of apprenticeship was generally seven years and the child was expected to regard his master with the same obedience due natural parents. The master was responsible for the education and training of the young apprentice and he acted *in loco parentis*, assuming complete responsibility for the child's material and spiritual welfare. While apprenticeships were voluntary for the wealthier citizens, for the wayward or destitute child they were unavoidable. The use of compulsory apprenticeships was an important form of social control exercised by town and religious officials upon youths perceived as troublesome.[12]

The industrial revolution in America, beginning at the end of the eighteenth century, brought about the gradual transformation of the labor system of youth. The family-based productive unit gave way to an early factory system. Child labor in industrial settings supplanted the apprenticeship system. As early as the 1760s there were signs that the cotton industry in New England would transform the system of production, and by 1791 all stages in the manufacture of raw cotton into cloth were performed by factory machinery. The Samuel Slater factory in Providence, Rhode Island, employed one hundred children aged four to ten years in cotton manufacture. Here is a description of the workplace environment:

> They worked in one room where all the machinery was concentrated under the supervision of a foreman, spreading the cleaned cotton on the carding machine to be combed and passing it through the roving machine, which turned the cotton into loose rolls ready to be spun. Most of the children tended the spindles, removing and attaching bobbins. Small, quick fingers were admirably suited for picking up and knotting broken threads. To the delight of Tench Coxe, a champion of American industry, the children became "the little fingers . . . of the gigantic automatons of labor-saving machinery."[13]

During the next two decades, the use of children in New England industrial factories increased, and children comprised 47 to 55 percent of the labor force in the cotton mills. The proliferation of the factory system transformed the lives of many Americans. On one hand, enormous wealth began to accumulate in the hands of a few individuals. At the same time, the switch from a family-based economy to a factory system where workers sold their labor meant that many families were displaced from the land. A large class of permanently impoverished Americans evolved. The use of child labor permitted early industrialists to depress the general wage level. Moreover, companies provided temporary housing and supplies to workers at high prices, so that they often incurred substantial debts rather financial rewards.

Increased child labor also contributed to the weakening of family ties, since work days were long and often competed with family chores. Children were now responsible to two masters—their fathers and their factory supervisors. Work instruction became distinct from general education and spiritual guidance as the family ceased to be an independent economic unit. Conditions of poverty continued to spread, and the social control system predicated upon strong family government began to deteriorate. During the first decades of the nineteenth century one could begin to observe a flow of Americans from rural areas to the urban centers. As increasing economic misery combined with a decline in traditional forms of social control, an ominous stage was being set. Some Americans began to fear deeply the growth of a dangerous class, and attempted to develop new measures to control the wayward youth who epitomized this threat to social stability.

THE HOUSES OF REFUGE (1825-1860)*

Severe economic downturns in the first two decades of the nineteenth century forced many Americans out of work. At the same time, increasing numbers of Irish immigrants arrived in the United States. These changes in the social structure, combined with the growth of the factory system, contributed to the founding of specialized institutions for the control and prevention of juvenile delinquency in America.[14]

As early as 1817, the more privileged Americans became concerned about the apparent connection between increased pauperism and the rise of delinquency. The Society for the Prevention of Pauperism was an early attempt to evaluate contemporary methods of dealing with the poor and suggest policy changes. This group also led campaigns against taverns and theaters they felt contributed to the problem of poverty. The efforts of several members of this group in New York City led to the founding of the first House of Refuge in 1825. The group conducted investigations, drew up plans and legislation, and lobbied actively to gain acceptance of their ideas. In other northeastern cities, such as Boston and Philadelphia, similar efforts were underway.

A number of historians have described these early nineteenth century philanthropists as *Conservative Reformers*.[15] These men were primarily from the wealthy, established families, and were often prosperous merchants or professionals. Ideologically, they were close to the thinking of colonial elite and later, to the Federalists. Popular democracy was anathema to them since they viewed themselves as God's elect, and felt bound to accomplish His charitable objectives in the secular world. Leaders of the movement to establish the first houses of refuge, such as John Griscom, Thomas Eddy, and John Pintard, viewed themselves as responsible for the moral health of the community, and they intended to regulate community morality through the example of their own proper behavior as well as through benevolent activities. The poor and the deviant were the objects of their concern and their moral stewardship.

While early nineteenth century philanthropists relied on religion to justify their good works, their primary motivation was protection of their class privileges. Fear of social unrest and chaos dominated their thinking.[16] The rapid growth of a visible impoverished class, coupled with apparent increases in crime, disease, and immorality, worried those in power. The bitter class struggles of the French Revolution and periodic riots in urban America signaled danger to the status quo. The philanthropy of this group was aimed at reestablishing social order, while preserving the existing property and status relationships. They were responsible for founding such organizations as the American Sunday School Union, the American Bible

---

*Historical data on the nineteenth century relies on the scholarship of Robert Mennel, Anthony Platt, Joseph Hawes, and the document collection of Robert Bremner et al. in *Children and Youth in America*.

Society, the African Free School Society, and the Society for Alleviating the Miseries of Public Prisons. They were often appointed to positions on boards of managers for lunatic asylums, public hospitals, workhouses for the poor, and prisons.

The idea for houses of refuge was part of a series of reform concepts designed to reduce juvenile delinquency. Members of the Society for the Prevention of Pauperism were dissatisfied with the prevailing practice of placing children in adult jails and workhouses. Some reformers felt that exposing children to more seasoned offenders would increase their chances of becoming adult criminals. Another issue was the terrible condition of local jails. Others worried that due to the abominable conditions of local jails, judges and juries would lean toward acquittal of youthful criminals to avoid sending them to such places. Reformers also objected that the punitive character of available penal institutions would not solve the basic problem of pauperism. The reformers envisioned an institution with educational facilities, set in the context of a prison. John Griscom called for "the erection of new prisons for juvenile offenders." A report of the Society for the Prevention of Pauperism suggested the following principles for such new prisons:

> These prisons should be rather schools for instruction, than places of punishment, like our present State Prisons where the young and the old are confined indiscriminately. The youth confined there should be placed under a course of discipline, severe and unchanging, but alike calculated to subdue and conciliate. A system should be adopted that would provide a mental and moral regimen.[17]

By 1824 the society had adopted a state charter in New York under the name of the Society for the Reformation of Juvenile Delinquents, and had begun a search for a location for the house of refuge.

On New Year's Day, 1825, the New York House of Refuge opened with solemn pomp and circumstance. A year later the Boston House of Reformation was started, and in 1828 the Philadelphia House of Refuge began to admit wayward youth. These new institutions accepted both children convicted of crimes and destitute children. Since they were founded as preventive institutions, the early houses of refuge could accept children who "live an idle or dissolute life, whose parents are dead or if living, from drunkenness, or other vices, neglect to provide any suitable employment or exercise any salutary control over said children."[18] Thus, from the outset, the first special institutions for juveniles housed together delinquent, dependent, and neglected children*—a practice still observed in most juvenile detention facilities today.

Delinquent children are those in violation of criminal codes, statutes, and ordinances. *Dependent children* are those in need of proper and effective parental care or control but having no parent or guardian to provide such care. *Neglected children* are destitute, are unable to secure the basic necessities of life, or have unfit homes due to neglect or cruelty.

The development of this new institution of social control necessitated changes in legal doctrines in order to justify the exercise of power by refuge officials. In *Commonwealth* v. *M'Keagy* (1831), the Pennsylvania courts had to rule on the legality of a proceeding whereby a child was committed to the Philadelphia House of Refuge on the weight of his father's evidence that the child was "an idle and disorderly person." The court affirmed the right of the state to take a child away from a parent in cases of vagrancy or crime. But since this child was not a vagrant, nor the father poor, the court ruled that the child should not be committed. Judicial officials did not wish to confuse protection of children with punishment, since this might engender constitutional questions as to whether children committed to houses of refuge had received the protection of due process of law.

The related question of whether parental rights were violated by involuntary refuge commitments was put to a legal test in *Ex parte Crouse* (1838). The father of a child committed to the Philadelphia House of Refuge attempted to obtain her release through a writ of habeas corpus. The state supreme court denied the motion, holding that the right of parental control is a natural but not inalienable right:

> The object of the charity is reformation, by training the inmates to industry; by imbuing their minds with principles of morality and religion; by furnishing them with means to earn a living; and, above all, by separating them from the corrupting influence of improper associates. To this end, may not the natural parents, when unequal to the task of education, or unworthy of it, be superseded by the *parens patriae*, or common guardian of the community? . . . The infant has been snatched from a course which must have ended in confirmed depravity; and, not only is the restraint of her person lawful, but it would have been an act of extreme cruelty to release her from it.[19]

The elaboration of the doctrine of *parens patriae* in the *Crouse* case was an important legal principle, used to support the expanded legal powers of the juvenile court. It is important to recognize the significance of both social class and hostility toward Irish immigrants in the legal determination of the *Crouse* case.[20] Since Irish immigrants were viewed at this time as corrupt and unsuitable as parents, it is easy to see how antiimmigrant feelings could color judgments about the suitability of parental control. As a result, children of immigrants comprised the majority of inmates of the houses of refuge.

The early houses of refuge either excluded blacks, or housed them in segregated facilities. In 1849 the city of Philadelphia opened a House of Refuge for Colored Juvenile Delinquents. Racially segregated refuges were maintained in New York and Boston only through the limited funds donated by antislavery societies. Since refuge managers viewed all female delinquents as sexually promiscuous with little hope for eventual reform, females also received discriminatory treatment.[21]

The managers of houses of refuge concentrated on perfecting institutional regimens that would result in reformation of juveniles. Descriptions of daily activities stress regimentation, absolute subordination to authority, and monotonous repetition:

> At sunrise, the children are warned, by the ringing of a bell, to rise from their beds. Each child makes his own bed, and steps forth, on a signal, into the Hall. They then proceed, in perfect order, to the Wash Room. Thence they are marched to parade in the yard, and undergo an examination as to their dress and cleanliness; after which, they attend morning prayer. The morning school then commences, where they are occupied in summer, until 7 o'clock. A short intermission is allowed, when the bell rings for breakfast; after which, they proceed to their respective workshops, where they labor until 12 o'clock, when they are called from work, and one hour allowed them for washing and eating their dinner. At one, they again commence work, and continue at it until five in the afternoon, when the labors of the day terminate. Half an hour is allowed for washing and eating their supper, and at half-past five, they are conducted to the school room, where they continue at their studies until 8 o'clock. Evening Prayer is performed by the Superintendent; after which, the children are conducted to their dormitories, which they enter, and are locked up for the night, when perfect silence reigns throughout the establishment. The foregoing is the history of a single day, and will answer for every day in the year, except Sundays, with slight variations during stormy weather, and the short days in winter.[22] *

Routines were enforced by corporal punishment as well as other forms of control. Houses of refuge experimented with primitive systems of classification based on the behavior of inmates. The Boston House of Reformation experimented with inmate self-government as a control technique. But despite public declarations to the contrary, there is ample evidence of the use of solitary confinement, whipping, and other bodily punishments.

Inmates of the houses of refuge labored in large workshops manufacturing shoes, producing brass nails, or caning chairs. Female delinquents were often put to work spinning cotton and doing laundry. It is estimated that income generated from labor sold to outside contractors supplied up to 40 percent of the operating expenses of the houses of refuge. The chief problem for refuge managers was that economic depressions could dry up the demand for labor, and there was not always sufficient work to keep the inmates occupied. Not only were there complaints that contractors improperly abused children, but such employment prepared youngsters for only the most menial work.

---

*This routine is reminiscent of the style of eighteenth century American Indian schools. It represents an attempt to recreate the ideal of colonial family life, which was being replaced by living patterns accommodated to industrial growth and development.

Youths were committed to the houses of refuge for indeterminate periods of time until the legal age of majority. Release was generally obtained through an apprenticeship by the youths to some form of service. The system was akin to the binding out practices of earlier times. Males were typically apprenticed on farms, on whaling boats, or in the merchant marine. Females were usually placed into domestic service. Only rarely was a house of refuge child placed in a skilled trade. Apprenticeship decisions were often made to ensure that the child would not be reunited with his or her family, since this was presumed to be the root cause of the child's problems. As a result, there are many accounts of siblings and parents vainly attempting to locate their lost relatives.

The founders of the houses of refuge were quick to declare their own efforts successful. Prominent visitors to the institutions, like Alexis de Tocqueville and Dorothea Dix, echoed the praise of the founders. Managers of the refuges produced glowing reports attesting to the positive results of the houses. Sharp disagreements over the severity of discipline required led to the replacement of directors who were perceived as too permissive. Elijah Devoe, a house of refuge assistant superintendent, wrote poignantly of the cruelties and injustices in these institutions.[23] There are accounts of violence within the institutions as well. Robert Mennel estimates that approximately 40 percent of the children escaped either from the institutions or from their apprenticeship placements. The problems that plagued the houses of refuge did not dampen the enthusiasm of the philanthropists, who assumed that the reformation process was a difficult and tenuous business at best.

Public relations efforts proclaiming the success of the houses of refuge helped lead to a rapid proliferation of similar institutions.[24] While special institutions for delinquent and destitute youth increased in numbers, the public perceived that delinquency was continuing to rise and become more serious. The founders of the houses of refuge argued that the solution to the delinquency problem lay in the perfection of better methods to deal with incarcerated children. Most of the literature of this period assumes the necessity of institutionalized treatment for children. The debates centered around whether to implement changes in architecture or in the institutional routines. Advocates of institutionalized care of delinquent and dependent youths continued to play the dominant role in formulating social policy for the next century.

THE GROWTH OF INSTITUTIONALIZATION AND THE CHILD SAVERS (1850-1890)

In the second half of the nineteenth century, a group of reformers known as the Child Savers instituted new measures to prevent juvenile delinquency.[25] Reformers including Lewis Pease, Samuel Gridley Howe, and Charles Loring Brace founded societies to save children from depraved and criminal lives. They created the Five Points Mission (1850), the Children's Aid Society (1853), and the New York Juvenile Asylum (1851). The ideology of this group of reformers differed from that of the founders of the houses of refuge only in that this group was more optimistic about the possibilities of reforming youths. Centers were established in urban areas to distribute food and clothing, provide temporary shelter for homeless youth, and introduce contract systems of shirt manufacture to destitute youth.

The Child Savers criticized the established churches for not doing more about the urban poor. They favored an activist clergy that would attempt to reach the children of the streets. While this view was somewhat unorthodox, they viewed the urban masses as a potentially dangerous class that could rise up if misery and impoverishment was not alleviated. Charles Loring Brace observed:

> Talk of heathen! All the pagans of Golconda would not hold a light to the ragged, cunning, forsaken, godless, keen devilish boys of Leonard Street and the Five Points. . . . Our future voters, and President-makers, and citizens! Good Lord deliver us, and help them![26]

Brace and his associates knew from first-hand experience in the city missions that the problems of poverty were widespread and growing more serious. Their chief objection to the houses of refuge was that long-term institutionalized care did not reach enough children. Moreover, the Child Savers held the traditional view that family life is superior to institutional routines for generating moral reform.

Brace and his Children's Aid Society believed that delinquency could be solved if vagrant and poor children were gathered up and *placed out* with farm families on the western frontier. *Placing out* as a delinquency prevention practice was based on the idealized notion of the American farm family. Such families were supposed to be centers of warmth, compassion, and morality; they were "God's reformatories" for wayward youth. Members of the Children's Aid Society provided food, clothing, and sometimes shelter to street waifs, and preached to them about the opportunities awaiting them if they migrated westward. Agents of the Children's Aid Society vigorously urged poor urban youngsters to allow themselves to be placed out with farm families. Many believed that western families provided both a practical and economical resource for reducing juvenile delinquency. The following passage from a Michigan newspaper gives a vivid picture of the placing out process:

> Our village has been astir for a few days. Saturday afternoon, Mr. C. C. Tracy arrived with a party of children from the Children's Aid Society in New York. . . .
> Sabath day Mr. Tracy spoke day and evening, three times, in different church edifices to crowded and interested audiences. In the evening, the children were present in a body,

and sang their "Westward Ho" song. Notice was given that applicants would find unappropriated children at the store of Carder and Ryder, at nine o'clock Monday morning. Before the hour arrived a great crowd assembled, and in two hours *every child was disposed of*, and more were wanted.

We *Wolverines* will never forget Mr. Tracy's visit. It cost us some tears of sympathy, some dollars, and some smiles. We wish him a safe return to Gotham, a speedy one to us with the new company of destitute children, for whom good homes are even now prepared.[27]

Contrary to the benevolent image projected by this news story, there is ample evidence that the children were obliged to work hard for their keep, and were rarely accepted as members of the family. The Boston Children's Aid Society purchased a home in 1864, which was used to help adjust street youth to their new life in the West. The children were introduced to farming skills and taught manners that might be expected of them in their new homes.

Another prevention experiment during the middle part of the nineteenth century was the result of the work of a Boston shoemaker, John Augustus. In 1841, Augustus began to put up bail for men charged with drunkenness, although he had no official connection with the court. Soon after, he extended his services to young people. Augustus supervised the youngsters while they were out on bail, provided clothing and shelter, was sometimes able to find them jobs, and often paid court costs to keep them out of jail. This early probation system was later instituted by local child-saving groups, who would find placements for the children. By 1869 Massachusetts had a system by which agents of the Board of State Charities took charge of delinquents before they appeared in court. The youths were often released on probation, subject to good behavior in the future.

These noninstitutional prevention methods were challenged by those who felt an initial period of confinement was important before children were placed out. Critics also argued that the Children's Aid Societies neither followed up on their clients, nor administered more stringent discipline to those who needed it. One critic phrased it this way:

The "vagabond boy" is like a blade of corn, coming up side by side with a thistle. You may transplant both together in fertile soil, but you will have the thistle still. . . . I would have you pluck out the vagabond first, and then let the boy be thus provided with "a home," and not before.[28]

Many midwesterners were unsettled by the stream of "criminal children" flowing into their midst. Brace and his colleagues were accused of poisoning the West with the dregs of urban life. To combat charges that urban youths were responsible for the rising crime in the West, Brace conducted a survey of western prisons and almshouses to show that few of his children had gotten into further trouble in the West.

Resistance continued to grow against the efforts of the Children's Aid Societies. Brace, holding that asylum interests were behind the opposition, maintained that the longer a child remains in an asylum, the less likely he will reform. (The debate over the advantages and disadvantages of institutionalized care of delinquent youth continues to the present day.) Brace continued to be an active proponent of the placing out system. He appeared before early conventions of reform school managers to present his views and debate the opposition. As the struggle continued over an ideology to guide prevention efforts, the problem of delinquency continued to grow. During the nineteenth century poverty, industrialization, and immigration, as well as the Civil War helped to swell the ranks of the "dangerous classes."[29]

Midway through the nineteenth century, state and municipal governments began taking over the administration of institutions for juvenile delinquents. Early efforts had been supported by private philanthropic groups with some state support. But the growing fear of class strife, coupled with increasing delinquency, demanded a more centralized administration. Many of the newer institutions were termed *reform schools* to imply a strong emphasis on formal schooling. In 1876, of the fifty-one refuges or reform schools in the U.S., nearly three-quarters were operated by state or local governments. By 1890, almost every state outside the South had a reform school, and many jurisdictions had separate facilities for male and female delinquents. These institutions varied considerably in their admissions criteria, their sources of referral, and the character of their inmates. Most of the children were sentenced to remain in reform schools until they reached the age of majority (eighteen years for girls and twenty-one for boys), or until they were reformed. The length of confinement, as well as the decision to transfer unmanageable youths to adult penitentiaries, was left to the discretion of reform school officials.

Partially in response to attacks by Brace and his followers, many institutions implemented a cottage or family system between 1857 and 1860. The cottage system involved dividing the youths into units of forty or fewer, each with its own cottage and schedule. Although work was sometimes performed within the cottages, the use of large congregate workshops continued. The model for the system was derived from the practice of European correctional officials. There is evidence from this period of the development of a self-conscious attempt to refine techniques to mold, reshape, and reform wayward youth.[30]

During this period, a movement was initiated to locate institutions in rural areas, since it was felt that agricultural labor would facilitate reformative efforts. As a result, several urban houses of refuge were relocated in rural settings. Many rural institutions used the cottage system, since it was well suited to agricultural production. In addition, the cottage system gave managers the opportunity to segregate children according to age, sex, race, school achievement, or "hardness." Critics of the institutions, such as Mary Carpenter, pointed out that most of the presumed benefits of rural settings were artificial, and that the vast majority of youths who spent time in these reform schools ultimately returned to crowded urban areas.

The Civil War deeply affected institutions for delinquent youth. Whereas prisons and county jails witnessed declines in population, the war brought even more youths into reform schools. Institutions were strained well beyond their capacities. Some historians believe that the participation of youths in the draft riots of northern cities produced an increase in incarcerated youths. Reform schools often released older youngsters to military service, in order to make room for additional children. Due to the high inflation rates of the war, the amount of state funds available for institutional upkeep steadily declined. Many institutions were forced to resort to the contract labor system to increase reform school revenues in order to meet operating expenses during the war and in the postwar period.

Voices were raised in protest over the expansion of contract labor in juvenile institutions. Some charged that harnessing the labor of inmates had become the raison d'être of these institutions, rather than the reformation of youthful delinquents. There were growing rumors of cruel and vicious exploitation of youth by work supervisors. An 1871 New York Commission on Prison Labor, headed by Enoch Wines, found that refuge boys were paid thirty cents per day for labor that would receive four dollars a day on the outside. In the Philadelphia House of Refuge, boys were paid twenty-five cents a day, and were sent elsewhere if they failed to meet production quotas. Economic depressions throughout the 1870s increased pressure to end the contract system. Workingmen's associations protested against the contract system, since prison and reform school laborers created unfair competition. Organized workers claimed that refuge managers were making huge profits from the labor of their wards.

> From the institutional point of view, protests of workingmen had the more serious result of demythologizing the workshop routine. No longer was it believable for reform school officials to portray the ritual as primarily a beneficial aid in inculcating industrious habits or shaping youth for "usefulness." The violence and exploitation characteristic of reform school workshops gave the lie to this allegation. The havoc may have been no greater than that which occasionally wracked the early houses of refuge, but the association of conflict and the contract system in the minds of victims and outside labor interests made it now seem intolerable.[31]

The public became aware of stabbings, fighting, arson, and attacks upon staff of these institutions.

All signs pointed toward a decline of authority within the institutions. The economic troubles of the reform schools continued to worsen. Additional controversy was generated by organized Catholic groups, who objected to Protestant control of juvenile institutions housing a majority of Catholics. This crisis in the juvenile institutions led to a series of investigations into reform school operations.[32] The authors of these reports proposed reforms to maximize efficiency of operation, and increase government control over the functioning of institutions in their jurisdictions. One major result of these investigative efforts was the formation of Boards of State Charity. Members of these boards were appointed to inspect reform schools and make recommendations for improvements, but were to avoid the evils of the patronage system. Board members, who were described as "gentlemen of public spirit and sufficient leisure," uncovered horrid institutional conditions, and made efforts to transfer youngsters to more decent facilities. Men such as Frederick Wines, Franklin Sanborn, Hastings Hart, and William Pryor Letchworth were among the pioneers of this reform effort.

Although it was hoped that the newly formed boards would find ways of reducing the proliferation of juvenile institutions, such facilities continued to grow, as did the number of wayward youths. These late nineteenth century reformers looked toward the emerging scientific disciplines for solutions to the problems of delinquency and poverty. They also developed a system to discriminate among delinquents, so that "hardened offenders" would be sent to special institutions such as the Elmira Reformatory. It was generally recognized that new methods would have to be developed to restore order within the reform schools, and to make some impact upon delinquency.

Juvenile institutions in the South and the Far West developed much later than those in the North or East, but essentially along the same lines. One reason for this was that delinquency was primarily a city problem, and the South and Far West were less urbanized. In the South, black youths received radically different treatment from whites. While there was toleration for the misdeeds of white youth, black children were controlled under the disciplinary systems of slavery. Even after Emancipation, the racism of southern whites prevented them from treating black children as fully human, and worth reforming. The Civil War destroyed the prison system of the South. After the war, southern whites used the notorious Black Codes, and often trumped up criminal charges to arrest thousands of impoverished former slaves, placing them into a legally justified forced labor system. Blacks were leased out on contract to railroad companies, mining interests, and manufacturers. Although many of these convicts were children, no special provisions were made because of age. Conditions under the southern convict lease system were miserable, and rivalled the worst cruelties of slavery. Little in the way of specialized care for delinquent youth was accomplished in the South until well into the twentieth century. The convict lease system was eventually replaced by county road gangs and prison farms, characterized by grossly inhumane conditions of confinement. These were systems of vicious exploitation of labor and savage racism.[33]

JUVENILE DELINQUENCY AND THE PROGRESSIVE ERA

The period from 1880 to 1920, often referred to by historians as the Progressive Era, was a time of major social structural change in America. The nation was in the process of becoming increasingly urbanized, and unprecedented numbers of European immigrants were migrating to cities in the Northeast. America was becoming an imperialist power, and was establishing worldwide military and economic relationships. Wealth was becoming concentrated in the hands of a few individuals, seeking to dominate American economic life. Labor violence was on the rise, and the country was in the grip of a racial hysteria affecting all peoples of color. The tremendous technological development that was occurring reduced the need for labor.[34]

During the Progressive Era, those in positions of economic power feared that the urban masses would destroy the world they had built. Internal struggles developing among the wealthy heightened the tension. From all sectors came demands that new action be taken to preserve social order, and to protect private property and racial privilege.[35] Up to this time, those in positions of authority had assumed a laissez-faire stance, fearing that government intervention might extend to economic matters. While there was general agreement of the need for law enforcement to maintain social order, there was profound skepticism about attempts to alleviate miserable social conditions or reform deviant individuals. Some suggested that if society consisted of a natural selection process in which the fittest would survive, then efforts to extend the life chances of the poor or "racially inferior" ran counter to the logic of nature.

Others during this era doubted the wisdom of a laissez-faire policy, stressing that the threat of revolution and social disorder demanded scientific and rational methods to restore social order. The times demanded reform, and before the Progressive Era ended, much of the modern welfare state and the criminal justice system were constructed. Out of the turmoil of this age came such innovations as widespread use of the indeterminate sentence, the public defender movement, the beginning of efforts to professionalize the police, extensive use of parole, the rise of mental and I.Q. testing, scientific study of crime, and ultimately the juvenile court.

Within correctional institutions at this time, there was optimism that more effective methods would be found to rehabilitate offenders. One innovation was to institute physical exercise training, along with special massage and nutritional regimens. Some believed that neglect of the body had a connection with delinquency and crime. Those who emphasized the importance of discipline in reform efforts pressed for the introduction of military drill within reform schools. There is no evidence that either of these treatment efforts had a reformative effect upon inmates. But it is also easy to understand why programs designed to keep inmates busy and under strict discipline would be popular at a time of violence and disorder within prisons and reform schools. As institutions faced continual financial difficulties, the contract labor system came under increasing attack. Criticism of reform schools resulted in laws in some states to exclude children under twelve years old from admission to reform schools. Several states abolished the contract labor system, and efforts were made to guarantee freedom of worship among inmates of institutions. Once again, pleas were made for community efforts to reduce delinquency, rather than relying solely upon reform schools as a prevention strategy. The arguments put forth were reminiscent of those of Charles Loring Brace and the Child Savers. For example, Homer Folks, president of the Children's Aid Society of Pennsylvania, articulated these five major problems of reform schools in 1891:

1   The temptation it offers to parents and guardians to throw off their most sacred responsibilities. . . .
2   The contaminating influence of association. . . .
3   The enduring stigma . . . of having been committed . . .
4   . . . renders impossible the study and treatment of each child as an individual.
5   The great dissimilarity between life in an institution and life outside.[36]

One response was to promote the model of inmate self-government within the institution's walls. One such institution, the George Junior Republic, developed an elaborate system of inmate government in 1893, in which the institution became a microcosm of the outside world. Self-government was viewed as an effective control technique, since youths became enmeshed in the development and enforcement of rules, while guidelines for proper behavior continued to be set by the institutional staff. The inmates were free to construct a democracy, so long as it conformed to the wishes of the oligarchic staff.[37]

The populist governments of several southern states built reform schools, partly due to their opposition to the convict lease system. But these institutions too were infused with the ethos of the Jim Crow Laws, which attempted to permanently legislate an inferior role for black Americans in southern society. One observer described the reform school of Arkansas as a place "where white boys might be taught some useful occupation and the negro boys compelled to work and support the institution while it is being done."[38] Black citizens, obviously displeased with discrimination within southern reform schools, proposed that separate institutions for black children should be administered by the black community. A few such institutions were established, but the majority of black children continued to be sent to jail, or were the victims of lynch mobs.

Growing doubt about the success of reform schools in reducing delinquency led some to question the wisdom of applying an unlimited *parens patriae* doctrine to youth. In legal cases, such as *The People* v. *Turner, State* v. *Ray* and *Ex parte Becknell*, judges questioned the quasi-penal character of juvenile institutions and wondered whether there ought not to be some procedural safeguards for children entering court on delinquency charges.[39]

The state of Illinois, which eventually became the first state to establish a juvenile court law, had almost no institutions for the care of juveniles. Most early institutions in Illinois had been destroyed in fires, and those that remained were regarded as essentially prisons for children. Illinois attempted a privately financed system of institutional care, but this also failed. As a result, progressive reformers in Chicago complained of large numbers of children languishing in the county jail, and pointed out that children sometimes received undue leniency due to a lack of adequate facilities.

A new wave of Child Savers emerged, attempting to provide Chicago and the state of Illinois with a functioning system for handling wayward youth.[40] These reformers, members of the more wealthy and influential Chicago families, were spiritual heirs of Charles Loring Brace, in that they too feared that social unrest could destroy their authority. But through their approach, they hoped to alleviate some of the suffering of the impoverished, and ultimately win the loyalty of the poor. Reformers such as Julia Lathrop, Jane Addams, and Lucy Flower mobilized the Chicago Women's Club on behalf of juvenile justice reform. Other philanthropic groups, aligning with the powerful Chicago Bar Association, helped promote a campaign leading to the eventual drafting of the first juvenile court law in America. Although previous efforts had been made in Massachusetts and Pennsylvania to initiate separate trials for juveniles, the Illinois law is generally regarded as the first comprehensive child welfare legislation in this country.

The Illinois law, passed in 1899, established a children's court that would hear cases of delinquent, dependent, and neglected children. The *parens patriae* philosophy, which had imbued the reform schools, now extended to the entire court process. The definition of delinquency was broad, so that a child would be adjudged delinquent if he or she violated any state law, or any city or village ordinance. In addition, the court was given jurisdiction in cases of incorrigibility, truancy, and lack of proper parental supervision. The court had authority to institutionalize children, send them to orphanages or foster homes, or place them on probation. The law provided for unpaid probation officers, who would assist the judges and supervise youngsters. In addition, the law placed the institutions for dependent youth under the authority of the State

Board of Charities, and regulated the activities of agencies sending delinquent youth from the East into Illinois.

The juvenile court idea spread so rapidly that within ten years of the passage of the Illinois law, ten states had established children's courts. By 1912 there were twenty-two states with juvenile court laws; and by 1925 all but two states had established specialized courts for children. Progressive reformers proclaimed the establishment of the juvenile court as the most significant reform of this period. The reformers celebrated what they believed to be a new age in the treatment of destitute and delinquent children. In *Commonwealth* v. *Fisher*, the Pennsylvania supreme court defended the juvenile court ideal in terms reminiscent of the court opinion in the *Crouse* case of 1838:

> To save a child from becoming a criminal, or continuing in a career of crime, to end in maturer years in public punishment and disgrace, the legislatures surely may provide for the salvation of such a child, if its parents or guardians be unwilling or unable to do so, by bringing it into one of the courts of the state without any process at all, for the purpose of subjecting it to the state's guardianship and protection.[41]

Critics, pointing to the large number of children who remained in jails and detention homes for long periods, expressed doubt that the court would achieve its goal. Some judges, including the famous Judge Ben Lindsey of Denver, decried the seemingly unlimited discretion of the court. With so much diversity among jurisdictions in the United States, it is difficult to describe the functioning of a typical court. As the volume of cases in the urban areas soon overwhelmed existing court resources, judges became unable to give the close personal attention to each case advocated by the reformers. As little as ten minutes was devoted to each case as court calendars became increasingly crowded. Similarly, as caseloads soared, the quality of probationary supervision deteriorated and became perfunctory.

It is important to view the emergence of the juvenile court in the context of changes taking place in American society at that time. Juvenile court drew support from a combination of optimistic social theorists, sincere social reformers, and the wealthy, who felt a need for social control. The juvenile court movement has been viewed as an attempt to stifle legal rights of children by creating a new adjudicatory process based on principles of equity law. This view misses the experimental spirit of the Progressive Era by assuming a purely conservative motivation on the part of the reformers.

Although most reformers of the period understood the relationship between poverty and delinquency, they responded with vastly different solutions. Some reformers supported large-scale experimentation with new social arrangements, such as the Cincinnati Social Unit Experiment, an early forerunner of the community organization strategy of the War on Poverty of the 1960s.[42] Other reformers looked to the emerging social science disciplines to provide a rational basis for managing social order. During the Progressive Era, there was growth in the profession of social work, whose members dealt directly with the poor.[43] Progressive reformers conducted social surveys to measure the amount of poverty, crime, and juvenile dependency in their communities. They supported social experiments to develop new behavior patterns among the lower classes to help them adjust to the emerging corporate economy. The development of mental testing became crucial in defining access to the channels of social mobility, and for demonstrating, to the satisfaction of the white ruling class, their own racial superiority. Moreover, biological explanations of individual and social pathology rationalized the rise in crime and social disorder, without questioning the justice or rationality of existing social arrangements.

The thrust of Progressive Era reforms was to found a more perfect control system to restore social stability while guaranteeing the continued hegemony of those with wealth and privilege. Reforms such as the juvenile court are ideologically significant because they preserved the notion that social problems (in this case delinquency, dependency, and neglect) could be dealt with on a case-by-case basis, rather than through broad-based efforts to redistribute wealth and power throughout society. The chief dilemma for advocates of the juvenile court was to develop an apparently apolitical or neutral system, while preserving differential treatment for various groups of children. The juvenile court at first lacked a core of functionaries who could supply the rationale for individualized care for wayward youth, but soon these needs were answered by the emergence of psychiatry, psychology, and criminology, as well as by the expanding profession of social work.

THE CHILD GUIDANCE CLINIC MOVEMENT

In 1907, Illinois modified its juvenile court law to provide for paid probation officers, and the Chicago Juvenile Court moved into new facilities with expanded detention space. The Juvenile Protective League, founded by women active in establishing the first juvenile court law, was intended to stimulate the study of the conditions leading to delinquency. The members of the Juvenile Protective League were especially troubled that large numbers of wayward youth repeatedly returned to juvenile court. Jane Addams, a major figure in American philanthropy and social thought, observed, "At last it was apparent that many of the children were psychopathic cases and they and other borderline cases needed more skilled care than the most devoted probation officer could give them."[44]

But the new court facilities did provide an opportunity to examine and study all children coming into the court. The Juvenile Protective League promised to oversee this study of delinquency, and Mrs. Ellen Sturges Dummer donated the necessary money to support the effort. Julia Lathrop was chosen to select a qualified psychologist to head the project. After consulting with William James, she selected one of his former students, Dr. William A. Healy. Healy proposed a four- to five-year study to compare some five hundred juvenile court clients with patients in private practice. The investigation, according to Healy, "would have to involve all possible facts about heredity, environment, antenatal and postnatal history, etc."[45]

In 1909, the Juvenile Protective League established the Juvenile Psychopathic Institute, with Healy as its first director, and Julia Lathrop, Jane Addams, and Judge Julian W. Mack on the executive committee.* The group, in its opening statement, expressed its plans

> to undertake . . . an inquiry into the health of delinquent children in order to ascertain as far as possible in what degrees delinquency is caused or influenced by mental or physical defect or abnormality and with the purpose of suggesting and applying remedies in individual cases whenever practicable as a concurrent part of the inquiry.[46]

Jane Addams added her concern that the study investigate the conditions in which the child lives, as well as the mental and physical history of his ancestors.

Healy held an M.D. degree from the University of Chicago, and had served as a physician at the Wisconsin State Hospital. He had taught university classes in neurology, mental illness, and gynecology, had studied at the great scientific centers of Europe, and was familiar with the work of Freud and his disciples. The major tenet of Healy's scientific credo was that the individual was the most important unit for study. Healy argued that the individualization of treatment depended upon scientific study of individual delinquents.

Healy and his associates published *The Individual Delinquent: A Textbook of Diagnosis and Prognosis for All Concerned in Understanding Offenders* in 1915. This book, based on a study of one thousand cases of repeat juvenile offenders, was intended as a practical handbook. The methodology involved a study of each offender from social, medical, and psychological viewpoints. Healy even did anthropometric measurements,† suggested by Lombroso and his followers, although Healy doubted that delinquents formed a distinctive physical type. But Healy was never able to locate a limited set of causes for delinquency through empirical observation. He stressed the wide range of potential causes of delinquency, including the

---

*There were a few earlier clinics that specialized in care of juveniles, but these had mostly dealt with feebleminded youngsters.

†Anthropometric measurements assess human body measurements on a comparative basis. A popular theory of the day was that criminals have distinctive physical traits that can be scientifically measured.

influence of bad companions, the love of adventure, early sex experiences, and mental conflicts. At this stage Healy adopted an eclectic explanation of delinquency: "Our main conclusion is that every case will always need study by itself. When it comes to arraying data for the purpose of generalization about relative values of causative factors we experience difficulty."[47] Despite exhaustive researches, Healy and his associates could not find distinctive mental or physical traits to delineate delinquents from nondelinquents.

Later, in 1917, Healy advanced his theory of delinquency in *Mental Conflict and Misconduct*. In this work, Healy stressed that while the individual may experience internal motivation toward misbehavior, this usually results in his merely feeling some anxiety. When mental conflict becomes more acute, the child may respond by engaging in misconduct. These ideas were heavily influenced by the work of Adolf Meyer, whose interpretation of Freud had a major influence on American psychiatry. Healy agreed with Meyer that the family was a crucial factor in delinquency. "The basis for much prevention of mental conflict is to be found in close comfortable relations between parents and children."[48] Healy's emphasis on the family was well received by those in the delinquency prevention field who had traditionally viewed the family as God's reformatory.

The significance of Healy's work cannot be overemphasized, since it provided ideological rationale to defend the juvenile court. Healy's work gave legitimacy to the flexible and discretionary operations of the court. Although some used Healy's emphasis on the individual to minimize the importance of social and economic injustice, there is evidence that Healy understood that delinquency was rooted in the nature of the social structure.

> If the roots of crime lie far back in the foundations of our social order, it may be that only a radical change can bring any large measure of cure. Less unjust social and economic conditions may be the only way out, and until a better social order exists, crime will probably continue to flourish and society continue to pay the price.[49]

Healy's work also gave support to the concept of professionalism in delinquency prevention. Since juvenile delinquency was viewed as a complex problem with many possible causes, this rationale was used to explain the increased reliance on "experts." In the process, the juvenile court became insulated from critical scrutiny by its clients and the community. If actions taken by the court did not appear valid to the layman, this was because of a higher logic, known only to the experts, which explained that course of action. Moreover, the failure of a specific treatment program was often attributed to the limits of scientific knowledge, or the failure of the court to follow scientific principles in its dispositions.

After his work in Chicago, Healy went to the Judge Harvey Baker Foundation in Boston to continue his research, where he began actual treatment of youths. Healy became a proselytizer for the child guidance clinic idea. Working with the Commonwealth Fund and the National Committee for Mental Hygiene, Healy aided the development of child guidance clinics across the nation. These efforts were so successful that by 1931, there were 232 such clinics in operation. There is even a report of a traveling child guidance clinic that visited rural communities in the West to examine children. The child guidance clinic movement became an important part of a broader campaign to provide mental hygiene services to all young people. The clinics were initially set up in connection with local juvenile courts, but later some of them became affiliated with hospitals and other community agencies.

In Sheldon and Eleanor Glueck's classic delinquency research they evaluated the success of Healy's Boston clinic. In *One Thousand Delinquents: Their Treatment by the Court and Clinic* (1934), the Gluecks found high rates of recidivism among children treated at the clinic. Healy, though deeply disappointed by the results, continued his efforts. The Gluecks continued, in a series of longitudinal studies,* to search for the causes of delinquency and crime. Like Healy, they maintained a focus on the individual, and they increased efforts to discover the factors behind repeated delinquency. The work of the Gluecks reflected a less optimistic attitude about the potential for treatment and rehabilitation than that found in Healy's work. They emphasized the importance of the family, often ignoring the impact of broader social and economic factors. It is ironic that the thrust of delinquency theories in the 1930s should be toward individual and family conflicts. Since 20 percent of the American people were unemployed, the effects of the depression of the thirties must have been apparent to the delinquents and their families, if not to the good doctors who studied them with such scientific rigor.

THE CHICAGO AREA PROJECT

The Chicago Area Project of the early 1930s is generally considered the progenitor of large-scale, planned, community-based efforts with delinquent youth. The Area Project differed from the dominant approaches of the time, which relied on institutional care and psychological explanations for delinquent behavior. The Area Project, conceived by University of Chicago sociologist Clifford Shaw, was an attempt to implement a sociological theory of delinquency in the delivery of preventive services. The theoretical heritage of the project is found in such works as *The Jack-Roller* (1930), *Brothers in Crime* (1936), and *Delinquency and Urban Areas* (1942), all by Shaw and his associates. They attributed variations in delinquency rates to demographic or socioeconomic conditions in different areas of cities.

---

*Longitudinal studies analyze a group of subjects over time.

This ecological approach assumed that delinquency was symptomatic of social disorganization. The adjustment problems of recent immigrants, together with other problems of urban life, strained the influence on adolescents of traditional social control agencies such as family, church, and community. Delinquency was viewed as a problem of the modern city, which was characterized by the breakdown of spontaneous or natural forces of social control. Shaw contended that the rapid social change that migrant rural youths are subjected to when entering the city promotes alienation from accepted modes of behavior:

> When growing boys are alienated from institutions of their
> parents and are confronted with a vital tradition of delinquency
> among their peers, they engage in delinquent activity as part
> of their groping for a place in the only social groups available
> to them.[50]

The Chicago Area Project thus viewed delinquency as "a reversible accident of the person's social experience."

The project employed several basic operating assumptions. The first was that the delinquent is involved in a web of daily relationships. As a result, the project staff attempted to mobilize adults in the community, hoping to foster indigenous neighborhood leadership to carry out the programs with delinquent youth. The second assumption was that people participate only if they have meaningful roles; therefore the staff attempted to share decision making with neighborhood residents. In order to maximize community participation, staff members had to resist the urge to direct the programs themselves. The final premise of the Area Project was that within a given community there are people who, when given proper training and guidance, can organize and administer local welfare programs. A worker from within the community, with knowledge of local customs, who can communicate easily with local residents is more effective in dealing with delinquency problems. The project staff believed that placing community residents in responsible positions would demonstrate the staff's confidence in the ability of residents to solve their own problems.

The Area Project was overseen by a board of directors, responsible for raising and distributing funds for research and community programs. In several years, twelve community committees developed in Chicago as "independent, self-governing, citizens' groups, operating under their own names and charters."[51] The neighborhood groups were aided by the board in obtaining grants to match local funds. Personnel from the Institute for Juvenile Research at the University of Chicago served as consultants to local groups. The various autonomous groups pursued such activities as the creation of recreation programs, or community improvement campaigns for schools, traffic safety, sanitation, and law enforcement. There were also programs aimed directly at delinquent youth, such as visitation privileges for incarcerated children, work with delinquent gangs, and volunteer assistance in parole and probation.

Most observers have concluded that the Chicago Area Project succeeded in fostering local community organizations to attack problems related to delinquency.[52] There is also evidence that delinquency rates decreased slightly in areas affected by the project, but these results are not conclusive. Shaw explained the difficulty of measuring the impact of the project as follows:

> Conclusive statistical proof to sustain any conclusion regarding the effectiveness of this work in reducing the volume of delinquency is difficult to secure for many reasons. Trends in rates for delinquents for small areas are affected by variations in the definition of what constitutes delinquent behavior, changes in the composition of the population, and changes in the administrative procedures of law enforcement agencies.[53]

The Illinois State Division of Youth Services took over all thirty-five staff positions of the Area Project in 1957. It appears that this vibrant and successful program was quickly transformed into "a rather staid, bureaucratic organization seeking to accommodate itself to the larger social structure, that is, to work on behalf of agencies who came into the community rather than for itself or for community residents."[54]

The Chicago Area Project, with its grounding in sociological theory and its focus on citizen involvement, contrasts sharply with other delinquency prevention efforts of the thirties. Its focus on prevention in the community raised questions about the continued expansion of institutions for delinquent youth. Although some attributed support of the project to the personal dynamism of Clifford Shaw, this ignores the basic material and ideological motivation behind it. It would be equally shortsighted to conclude that child saving would not have occurred without Charles Loring Brace, or that the child guidance clinic movement resulted solely from the labors of William Healy. Certainly Shaw was an important advocate of the Chicago Area Project approach, and his books influenced professionals in the field, but the growth of the project was also a product of the times.

Since there is no detailed history of the founding and operation of the project, we can only speculate about the forces that shaped its development. We do know that Chicago at that time was caught in the most serious economic depression in the nation's history. Tens of thousands of people were unemployed, especially immigrants and blacks. During this period, a growing radicalization among impoverished groups resulted in urban riots.[55] The primary response by those in positions of power was an expansion and centralization of charity and welfare systems. In addition, there was considerable experimentation with new methods of delivering relief services to the needy. No doubt, Chicago's wealthy looked favorably upon programs like the

Area Project, which promised to alleviate some of the problems of the poor without requiring a redistribution of wealth or power. Both the prestige of the University of Chicago and the close supervision promised by Shaw and his associates helped assuage those with wealth or power. Shaw and his associates did not advocate fundamental social change, and project personnel were advised to avoid leading communities toward changes perceived as too radical.[56] Communities were encouraged to work within the system, and to organize around issues at a neighborhood level. Project participants rarely questioned the relationship of urban conditions to the political and economic superstructure of the city.

Later interpreters of the Chicago Area Project did not seem to recognize the potentially radical strategy of community organization within poor neighborhoods. Its immediate legacy was twofold: the use of detached workers, who dealt with gangs outside the agency office; and the idea of using indigenous workers in social control efforts. While detached workers became a significant part of the delinquency prevention strategy of the next three decades, the use of indigenous personnel received little more than lip service, since welfare and juvenile justice agencies hired few urban poor.

The success of the Area Project depended upon relatively stable and well-organized neighborhood's with committed local leaders. Changes in the urban structure that developed over the next two decades did not fit the Chicago Area Project model. The collapse of southern agriculture and mass migration by rural blacks into the cities of the North and West produced major social structural changes. This movement to the North and West began in the twenties, decreased somewhat during the depression years, and later accelerated due to the attraction provided by the war industry jobs. During this same period large numbers of Puerto Ricans settled in New York City and other eastern cities. While economic opportunity attracted new migrants to the urban centers, there was little satisfaction for their collective dreams. Blacks, who left the South to escape the Jim Crow Laws, were soon confronted by de facto segregation in schools, in the work place, and in housing. Job prospects were slim for blacks and Puerto Ricans, and they were most vulnerable to being fired at the whims of employers. In many respects, racism in the North rivalled that of the South. The new migrants had the added difficulty of adapting their primarily rural experiences to life in large urban centers.[57]

Racial ghettos became places of poverty, disease, and crime. For the more privileged classes, the situation paralleled that of sixteenth century European city dwellers who feared the displaced peasantry, or that of Americans at the beginning of the nineteenth century who feared the Irish immigrants. During this period, riots erupted in East St. Louis, Detroit, Harlem, and Los Angeles. To upper-class observers, these new communities of poor black and brown people were disorganized collections of criminals and deviants.

Racism prevented white observers from recognizing the vital community traditions or the family stability that persisted despite desperate economic conditions. Moreover, the label *disorganized communities* could be used ideologically to mask the involvement of wealthy whites in the creation of racial ghettos.[58] A liberal social theory was developing, which, though benign on the surface, actually blamed the victims for the conditions in which they were caught. Attention was focused upon deviant aspects of community life, ascribing a culture of poverty and violence to inner-city residents, and advocating remedial work with individuals and groups to solve so-called problems of adjustment. The following quote from the National Commission on the Causes and Prevention of Violence is illustrative of this posture:

> The cultural experience which Negroes brought with them from segregation and discrimination in the rural South was of less utility in the process of adaption to urban life than was the cultural experience of many European immigrants. The net effect of these differences is that urban slums have tended to become ghetto slums from which escape has been increasingly difficult.[59]

Delinquency theorists suggested that lower-class communities were becoming more disorganized, since they were not characterized by the stronger ties of older ethnic communities.

> Slum neighborhoods appear to us to be undergoing progressive disintegration. The old structures, which provided social control and avenues of social ascent, are breaking down. Legitimate but functional substitutes for these traditional structures must be developed if we are to stem the trend towards violence and retreatism among adolescents in urban slums.[60]

Irving Spergel, leading authority on juvenile gangs, suggests that social work agencies made little use of indigenous workers after World War II because delinquency had become more aggressive and violent. Welfare and criminal justice officials argued that only agencies with sound funding and strong leadership could mobilize the necessary resources to deal with the increased incidence and severity of youth crime.

The movement toward more agency involvement brought with it a distinctly privileged-class orientation toward delinquency prevention. Social service agencies were preeminently the instruments of those with sufficient wealth and power to enforce their beliefs. The agencies were equipped to redirect, rehabilitate, and, in some cases, control those who seemed most threatening to the status quo. Workers for these agencies helped to perpetuate a conception of proper behavior for the poor, consistent with their expected social role. For example, the poor are told to defer gratification and save for the future, but the rich are often "conspicuous consumers." While poor women are expected to stay at home and raise their families, the same conduct is not uniformly applied to wealthy women. The well-to-do provide substantial funding for private social service agencies, and often become members of the boards that define policies for agencies in inner-city neighborhoods. The criteria for staffing these agencies during the two decades following World War II included academic degrees and special training that were not made available to the poor or people of color.

Social agencies, ideologically rooted and controlled outside poor urban neighborhoods, were often pressured to respond to "serious" delinquency problems. During this period, the fighting gang, which symbolized organized urban violence, received the major share of delinquency prevention efforts. Most agencies, emphasizing psychoanalytic or group dynamic approaches to delinquency, located the origin of social disruption in the psychopathology of individuals and small groups. The consequence of this orientation was that special youth workers were assigned to troublesome gangs in an attempt to redirect the members toward more conventional conduct. Little effort was made to develop local leadership, or to confront the issues of racism and poverty.

Detached worker programs emphasized treatment by individual workers, freed from the agency office base, operating in neighborhood settings. These programs, with several variations, followed a basic therapeutic model. Workers initially entered gang territories, taking pains to make their entrance as inconspicuous as possible. The first contacts were made at natural meeting places in the community such as poolrooms, candy stores, or street corners.

> Accordingly, the popular image of the detached worker is a young man in informal clothing, standing on a street corner near a food stand, chatting with a half dozen rough, ill-groomed, slouching teenagers. His posture is relaxed, his countenance earnest, and he is listening to the boys through a haze of cigarette smoke.[61]

The worker gradually introduced himself to the gang members. He made attempts to get jobs for them, or arranged recreational activities, while at the same time persuading the members to give up their illegal activities. Manuals for detached workers explained that the approach would work because gang members had never before encountered sympathetic, nonpunitive adults, who were not trying to manipulate them for dishonest purposes. A typical report states: "Their world (as they saw it) did not contain any giving, accepting people—only authorities, suckers and hoodlums like themselves.[62] This particular account even suggests that some boys were willing to accept the worker as an *idealized father.* The worker was expected to influence the overall direction of the gang, but if that effort failed, he was to foment trouble among members and incite disputes over leadership. Information that the workers gathered under promises of confidentiality was often shared with police gang-control officers. Thus, despite their surface benevolence, these workers were little more than undercover agents whose ultimate charge was to break up or disrupt groups that were feared by the establishment. These techniques, which focused on black and brown youth gangs in the fifties, were similar to those later used with civil rights groups and organizations protesting the Vietnam War.

There were many critics of the detached worker programs. Some argued that the workers actually lent status to fighting gangs, and thus created more violence. Other critics claimed that the workers often developed emotional attachments to youthful gang members, and were manipulated by them.[63] Community residents often objected to the presence of detached workers, since it was feared they would provide information to downtown social welfare agencies. Although studies of the detached worker programs did not yield positive results, virtually all major delinquency programs from the late forties to the sixties used detached workers in attempts to "reach the fighting gang."

THE MOBILIZATION FOR YOUTH

During the late 1950s economic and social conditions were becoming more acute in the urban centers of America. The economy was becoming sluggish, and unemployment began to rise. Black teenagers experienced especially high unemployment rates, and the discrepancy between white and black income and material conditions grew each year. Technological changes in the economy continually drove more unskilled laborers out of the labor force. Social scientists such as Daniel Moynihan and Sidney Wilhelm view this period as the time in which a substantial number of blacks became permanently unemployed.[64] Social control specialists for the privileged class surveyed the problem, and sought ways to defuse the social danger of a surplus labor population.

The Ford Foundation was influential during this period in stimulating conservative local officials to adopt more enlightened strategies in dealing with the poor.[65] Once again there was an ideological clash between those favoring scientific and rational government programs, and those who feared the growth of the state, demanded balanced government budgets, and opposed liberal programs to improve the quality of life of the poor. The Ford Foundation, through its Grey Areas projects, spent large amounts of money in several American cities to foster research and planning of new programs to deal with delinquency and poverty.

The most significant program to develop out of the Grey Area projects was the Mobilization for Youth, which began in New York City in 1962 after five years of planning. It aimed to service a population of 107,000 (approximately one-third black and Puerto Rican), living in sixty-seven blocks of New York's Lower East Side. The unemployment rate of the area was twice that of the city overall, and the delinquency rate was also high.

The theoretical perspective of the project was drawn from the work of Richard Cloward and Lloyd Ohlin:

" . . . a unifying principle of expanding opportunities has worked out as the direct basis for action." This principle was drawn from the concepts outlined by the sociologists Richard Cloward and Lloyd Ohlin in their book *Delinquency and Opportunity*. Drs. Cloward and Ohlin regarded delinquency as the result of the disparity perceived by low-income youths between their legitimate aspirations and the opportunities— social, economic, political, educational—made available to them by society. If the gap between opportunity and aspiration could be bridged, they believed delinquency could be reduced; that would be the agency's goal.[66]

The Mobilization for Youth project involved five areas: work training; education; group work and community organization; services to individuals and families; and training and personnel. But the core of the Mobilization was to organize area residents to realize "the power resources of the community by creating channels through which consumers of social welfare services can define their problems and goals and negotiate on their own behalf."[67] Local public and private bureaucracies became the targets of mass protests by agency workers and residents. The strategy of the Mobilization for Youth (MFY) assumed that social conflict was necessary in the alleviation of the causes of delinquency. Shortly after the MFY became directly involved with struggles over the redistribution of power and resources, New York City officials charged that the organization was "riot-producing, Communist-oriented, left-wing and corrupt."[68] In the ensuing months, the director resigned, funds were limited, and virtually all programs were stopped until after the 1964 presidential election. After January 1965, the MFY moved away from issues and protests toward more traditional approaches to social programming, such as detached-gang work, job training, and counselling.

Another project, Haryou-Act (Harlem Youth Opportunities Unlimited), which was developed in the black community of Harlem in New York, experienced a similar pattern of development and struggle. The Harlem program was supported by the theory and prestige of psychologist Kenneth Clark, who suggested in *Dark Ghetto* that delinquency is rooted in feelings of alienation and powerlessness among ghetto residents. The solution, according to Clark, was to engage in community organizing to gain power for the poor. Haryou-Act met sharp resistance from city officials, who labelled the staff as corrupt and infiltrated by Communists.

Both the MFY and Haryou-Act received massive operating funds. The Mobilization for Youth received approximately $2 million a year; Haryou-Act received about $1 million a year; and fourteen similar projects received over $7 million from the federal Office of Juvenile Delinquency.* It was significant that for the first time the

---

*By comparison, the Chicago Area Project operated on about $283,000 a year.

federal government was pumping large amounts of money into the delinquency prevention effort. Despite intense resistance to these efforts in most cities because local public officials felt threatened, the basic model of the Mobilization for Youth was incorporated into the community action component of the War on Poverty.

In 1967, when social scientists and practitioners developed theories of delinquency prevention for President Johnson's Crime Commission, the Mobilization was still basic to their thinking.[69] Their problem was to retain a focus upon delivery of remedial services in education, welfare, and job training to the urban poor without creating the intense political conflict engendered by the community action approach. The issue was complicated because leaders such as Malcolm X and Cesar Chavez, and groups like the Black Muslims and the Black Panther party articulated positions of self-determination and community control. These proponents of ethnic pride and "Power to the People" argued that welfare efforts controlled from outside were subtle forms of domestic colonialism. The riots of the mid-sixties dramatized the growing gap between people of color in America and their more affluent "benefactors."

It is against this backdrop of urban violence, a growing distrust of outsiders, and increased community-generated self-help efforts that delinquency prevention efforts of the late sixties and early seventies developed. A number of projects during this period attempted to reach the urban poor, who had been actively involved in ghetto riots during the sixties. In Philadelphia, members of a teenage gang were given funds to make a film and start their own businesses. Chicago youth gangs such as the Black P. Stone Nation and the Vice Lords were subsidized by federal funding, the YMCA, and the Sears Foundation. In New York, a Puerto Rican youth group, the Young Lords, received funds to engage in self-help activities. In communities across the nation there was a rapid development of summer projects in recreation, employment, and sanitation to help carry an anxious white America through each potentially long, hot summer. Youth patrols were even organized by police departments to employ ghetto youths to *cool out* trouble that might lead to riots. Few of the programs produced the desired results, and often resulted in accusations of improperly used funds by the communities. Often financial audits and investigations were made to discredit community organizers, and accuse them of encouraging political conflicts with local officials.

One proposed solution that offered more possibility of controlled social action to benefit the young was the Youth Service Bureau.[70] The first Youth Service Bureaus (YSBs) were composed of people from the communities, and representatives of public agencies who would hire professionals to deliver a broad range of services to young people. The central idea was to promote cooperation between justice and welfare agencies and the local communities. Agency representatives were expected to contribute partial operating expenses for the programs, and, together with neighborhood representatives, decide on program content. Proponents of the YSB approach stressed the need for diverting youthful offenders from the criminal justice system, and for delivering necessary social services to deserving children and their families. Ideally, the YSBs were designed to increase public awareness of the need for more youth services.

The Youth Service Bureaus generally met with poor results. There was often intense conflict between community residents and agency personnel over the nature of program goals, and YSBs were criticized for not being attuned to community needs.[71] Funds for these efforts were severely limited in relation to the social problems they sought to rectify. In some jurisdictions YSBs were controlled by police or probation departments, with no direct community input. These agency-run programs temporarily diverted youths from entering the criminal justice process by focusing on services, such as counseling.

The most important aspect of the YSBs was their attempt to operationalize the diversion of youth from the juvenile justice process, although its success seems highly questionable. Some argue that diversion programs violate the legal rights of youths, since they imply a guilty plea. Others warn that diversion programs expand the welfare bureaucracy, since youths who once would have simply been admonished and sent home by police are now channelled into therapeutic programs. Still others believe that diversion without social services does not prevent delinquency. In any case, there has been a major shift from the community participation focus of the Mobilization for Youth to a system in which community inputs are limited and carefully controlled. This change in operational philosophy is often justified by the need to secure continued funding, as well as by claims of increasing violence by delinquents. But it is important to remember that these same rationales were used to justify a move away from the community organizing model of the Chicago Area Projects of the 1930s. Whenever residents become involved in decision making, there are inevitably increased demands for control of social institutions affecting the community. Such demands for local autonomy question the existing distributions of money and power, and thus challenge the authority of social control agencies.

INSTITUTIONAL CHANGE AND COMMUNITY-BASED CORRECTIONS

Correctional institutions for juvenile delinquents were subject to many of the same social structural pressures as community prevention efforts. For instance, there was a disproportionate increase in the number of youths in correctional facilities, as blacks migrated to North and West. In addition, criticism of the use of juvenile inmate labor, especially by organized labor, disrupted institutional routines.

But throughout the late thirties and the forties increasing numbers of youths were committed to institutions. Later on, the emergence of ethnic pride and calls for Black and Brown Power would cause dissension within the institutions.

The creation of the California Youth Authority (CYA) just prior to the Second World War centralized the previously disjointed California correctional institutions.[72] During the forties and fifties, California, Wisconsin, and Minnesota developed separate versions of the Youth Authority concept. Under the Youth Authority model, criminal courts committed youthful offenders from sixteen to twenty-one years old to an administrative authority, which determined the proper correctional disposition.* The CYA was responsible for all juvenile correctional facilities, including the determination of placements, and parole. Rather than reducing the powers of the juvenile court judge, the Youth Authority streamlined the dispositional process in order to add administrative flexibility. The Youth Authority was introduced into California at a time when detention facilities were overcrowded, institutional commitment rates were rising, and the correctional system was fragmented and compartmentalized.

The Youth Authority model was developed by the American Law Institute, which drew up model legislation, and lobbied for its adoption in state legislatures. The American Law Institute is a non-profit organization, seeking to influence the development of law and criminal justice. The institute is oriented toward efficiency, rationality, and effectiveness in legal administration.

The treatment philosophy of the first Youth Authorities was similar to the approach of William Healy and the child guidance clinic. John Ellingston, formerly chief legislative lobbyist for the American Law Institute in California, related a debate between Healy and Clifford Shaw over the theoretical direction the new Youth Authority should follow. The legislators, persuaded by Healy's focus on diagnosis of individual delinquents, ensured that the clinic model became the dominant approach in California institutions.

Sociologist Edwin Lemert attributed the emergence of the California Youth Authority to the growth of an "Administrative State" in America. In support of this assertion Lemert noted the trend toward more centralized delivery of welfare services and increased government regulation of the economy, together with the "militarization" of American society produced by war. Lemert, however, did not discuss whether the purpose of this "Administrative State" was to preserve the existing structure of privilege. The first stated purpose of the California Youth Authority was "to protect society by substituting training and treatment for retributive punishment of young persons found guilty of public offenses."[73]

---

*California originally set the maximum jurisdictional age at twenty-three years, but later reduced it to twenty-one. Some states used an age limit of eighteen years, so that they dealt strictly with juveniles. In California, both juveniles and adults were included in the Youth Authority model.

42

The centralization of youth correction agencies enabled them to claim the scarce state delinquency prevention funds. In-house research units publicized the latest treatment approaches. In the 1950s and the 1960s psychologically oriented treatment approaches, including guided-group interaction and group therapy, were introduced in juvenile institutions. In this period of optimism and discovery many new diagnostic and treatment approaches were evaluated. Correctional administrators and social scientists hoped for a significant breakthrough in treatment, but it never came. Although some questionable evaluation studies claimed successes, there is no evidence that the new therapies had a major impact on recidivism. In fact, some people began to question the concept of enforced therapy, and argued that treatment-oriented prisons might be more oppressive than more traditional institutional routines.[74] Intense objections have been raised particularly against drug therapies and behavior modification programs. Takagi views this as the period when brainwashing techniques were first used on juvenile and adult offenders.*

Another major innovation of the sixties was the introduction of community-based correctional facilities. The central idea was that rehabilitation could be more effectively accomplished outside conventional correctional facilities. This led to a series of treatment measures such as group homes, partial release programs, halfway houses, and attempts to decrease commitment rates to juvenile institutions. California was particularly active in developing community-based correctional programming. The Community Treatment Project, designed by Marguerite Warren in California, was an attempt to replace institutional treatment with intensive parole supervision and psychologically oriented therapy. Probation Subsidy involved a bold campaign by CYA staff to convince the state legislature to give cash subsidies to local counties to encourage them to treat juvenile offenders in local programs. Probation subsidy programs were especially oriented toward strengthening the capacity of county probation departments to supervise youthful offenders.[75]

Proponents of the various community-based programs argued that correctional costs could be reduced and rehabilitation results improved in a community context. Reducing state expenditures became more attractive as state governments experienced the fiscal crunch of the late 1960s and the 1970s.[76] It was also thought that reducing institutional populations would alleviate tension and violence within the institutions. But, it appears that these community alternatives have created a situation in which youngsters who are sent to institutions are perceived as more dangerous, and, as a result, are kept in custody for longer periods of time.

---

*Paul Takagi, in "The Correctional System," cites Edgar Schein, "Man Against Man: Brainwashing," and James McConnell, "Criminals Can Be Brainwashed—Now," for candid discussions of this direction in correctional policy.

The ultimate logic of the community-based corrections model was followed by the Department of Youth Services in Massachusetts, which closed all of its training schools for delinquents. Youngsters were transferred to group-home facilities, and services were offered to individual children on a community basis.[77] The Massachusetts strategy met intense public criticism by juvenile court jûdges, correctional administrators, and police officials. There have been some recent attempts to discredit this policy, and to justify continued operation of correctional facilities. But the Massachusetts strategy has influenced a move to de-institutionalize children convicted of status offenses—those considered crimes only if committed by children, such as truancy, running away, or incorrigibility. In 1975, the federal government made $15 million available to local governments that developed plans to de-institutionalize status offenders.

At the moment, the forces opposing institutionalized care are making ideological headway, due to past failures of institutional methods in controlling delinquency. But previous experience suggests that the pendulum is likely to swing back in favor of the institutional approaches. Already there is increased talk about the "violent" delinquent and the alleged increases in violent youth crime; these words have always signalled the beginning of an ideological campaign to promote more stringent control measures and extended incarceration or detention. It is also significant that most states are not firmly committed to community-based treatment. Most jurisdictions still rely on placement in institutions, with conditions reminiscent of reform schools a hundred years ago. Children continue to be warehoused in large correctional facilities, receiving little care or attention. Eventually they are returned to substandard social conditions to survive as best they can.

CHANGES IN JUVENILE COURT LAW

In the late 1960s, the growing awareness of the limitations of the juvenile justice system resulted in a series of court decisions that altered the character of the juvenile court. In *Kent* v. *U.S.* (1966) the Supreme Court warned juvenile courts against "Procedural arbitrariness"; and in *In re Gault* (1967) the Court recognized the rights of juveniles in such matters as notification of charges, protection against self-incrimination, the right to confront witnesses, and the right to have a written transcript of the proceedings. Justice Abe Fortas wrote: "Under our Constitution the conditions of being a boy does not justify a kangaroo court."[78] The newly established rights of juveniles were not welcomed by most juvenile court personnel, who claimed that the informal humanitarian court process would be replaced by a junior criminal court. Communities struggled with methods of providing legal counsel to indigent youth, and restructuring court procedures to conform to constitutional requirements.

The principles set forth in *Kent* and later in the *Gault* decision offer only limited procedural safeguards to delinquent youth.[79] Many judicial officers believe that the remedy to juvenile court problems is not more formality in proceedings, but more treatment resources. In *McKiever* v. *Pennsylvania* in 1971, the Supreme Court denied that jury trials were a constitutional requirement for the juvenile court.[80] Many legal scholars believe that the current Supreme Court has a solid majority opposing extension of procedural rights to alleged delinquents. The dominant view is close to the opinion expressed by Chief Justice Warren Burger in the *Winship* case:

> what the juvenile court systems need is less not more of the trappings of legal procedure and judicial formalism; the juvenile court system requires breathing room and flexibility in order to survive the repeated assaults on this court. The real problem was not the deprivation of constitutional rights but inadequate juvenile court staffs and facilities.[81]

It may be that we are entering a period of dramatic changes in the nature of the juvenile justice process.[82] There will continue to be an ideological struggle between advocates of more formal legal doctrine and proponents of a return to the *parens patriae* doctrine. Some jurisdictions may abolish juvenile status offenses, and there will continue to be an expansion toward diversion programs to replace formal court processing.

SUMMARY

We have traced the history of the juvenile justice system in America in relation to significant population migrations, rapid urbanization, race conflicts, and transformations in the economy. These factors continue to influence the treatment of children. The juvenile justice system has traditionally focused on the alleged pathological nature of delinquents, ignoring how the problems of youths relate to larger political and economic issues. Both institutional and community-based efforts to rehabilitate delinquents have been largely unsuccessful. Those with authority for reforming the juvenile justice system have traditionally supported and defended the values and interests of the well-to-do. Not surprisingly, juvenile justice reforms have inexorably increased state control over the lives of the poor and their children. The central implication of this historical analysis is that the future of prevention and control of delinquency will be largely determined by ways in which the social structure evolves.[83] It is possible that this future belongs to those who wish to advance social justice on behalf of young people rather than to accommodate the class interests that have dominated this history.[84] But one must be cautious about drawing direct inferences for specific social reforms from this historical summary. William Appleman Williams reminds us: "History offers no answers per se, it only offers a way of encouraging people to use their own minds to make their own history."[85]

NOTES

1   Wiley B. Sanders, *Juvenile Offenders for a Thousand Years*, pp. 3-52.

2   Thorsten Sellin, *Pioneering in Penology* provides an excellent description of the Amsterdam House of Corrections.

3   Georg Rusche and Otto Kirchheimer, *Punishment and Social Structure.*

4   Kenneth M. Stamp, *The Peculiar Institution*; and Norman R. Yetman, *Voices from Slavery.*

5   This issue is well treated by Winthrop Jordan, *The White Man's Burden.*

6   Sources of primary material are Yetman, *Voices from Slavery*; and Gerda Lerner, *Black Women in White America*; another fascinating source of data is Margaret Walker's historical novel, *Jubilee.*

7   Robert Bremner et al., *Children and Youth in America: A Documentary History*, vol. 1, p. 72.

8   Ibid., p. 97.

9   Ibid., pp. 316-39; and Thomas Gossett, *Race: The History of an Idea in America.*

10   David Rothman, *The Discovery of the Asylum*, pp. 3-56.

11   Joseph Hawes, *Children in Urban Society: Juvenile Delinquency in Nineteenth Century America*, p. 13.

12   Bremner et al., *Children in America*, vol. 1, pp. 572-83.

13   Ibid., p. 146.

14   Robert Pickett, *House of Refuge*; Hawes, *Children in Urban Society*, pp. 27-60; and Robert Mennel, *Thorns and Thistles*, pp. 3-31.

15   Mennel, *Thorns and Thistles*; and W. David Lewis, in *The Development of an American Culture*, eds. Stanley Coben and Lorman Ratner.

16   Mennel, *Thorns and Thistles*, pp. 6-9.

17   Ibid., p. 11.

18   Bremner et al., *Children in America*, p. 681.

19   *Ex parte Crouse*, 4 Wharton (PA) 9 (1838).

20   A good description of anti-Irish feeling during this time is provided by John Higham, *Strangers in the Land.*

21   The preoccupation with the sexuality of female delinquents continues today. See Meda Chesney-Lind, "Juvenile Delinquency: The Sexualization of Female Crime."

22   Bremner et al., *Children in America*, p. 688.

23   Elijah Devoe, "The Refuge System, or Prison Discipline Applied to Delinquency."

24   David Rothman, *The Discovery of the Asylum.*

25   Anthony Platt, *The Child-Savers, The Invention of Delinquency*; Hawes, *Children in Urban Society*, pp. 87-111; and Mennel, *Thorns and Thistles*, pp. 32-77.

26   Mennel, *Thorns and Thistles*, p. 34.

27   Ibid., p. 39.

28   Ibid., p. 46.

29   The term "dangerous classes" was coined by Charles Loring Brace in his widely read *The Dangerous Classes of New York and Twenty Years Among Them.*

46

30 Hawes, *Children in Urban Society*, pp. 78-86.

31 Mennel, *Thorns and Thistles*, p. 61.

32 The classic of these studies is that of E. C. Wines, *The State of Prisons and Child-Saving Institutions in the Civilized World*, first printed in 1880.

33 Blake McKelvey, *American Prisons*, pp. 172-89.

34 William Appleman Williams, *The Contours of American History*, pp. 343-412; and James Weinstein, *The Corporate Ideal in the Liberal State*.

35 Thomas Gossett, *Race: The History of an Idea in America*, pp. 54-369.

36 Mennel, *Thorns and Thistles*, p. 111.

37 Hawes, *Children in Urban Society*, pp. 153-57.

38 Mennel, *Thorns and Thistles*, p. 12.

39 *The People v. Turner*, 55 Illinois 280 (1870); *State v. Ray*, 63 New Hampshire 405 (1886); *Ex parte Becknell*, 51 California 692 (1897).

40 Platt, *The Child-Savers*, pp. 101-36; and Hawes, *Children in Urban Society*, pp. 158-90 provide the most thorough discussions of the origins of the first juvenile court law.

41 *Commonwealth v. Fisher*, 213 Pennsylvania 48 (1905).

42 Anatole Shaffer, "The Cincinnati Social Unit Experiment," pp. 159-72.

43 Roy Lubove, *The Professional Altruist* is a good discussion of the rise of social work as a career.

44 Hawes, *Children in Urban Society*, p. 244.

45 Ibid., p. 250.

46 Ibid., pp. 250-51.

47 Mennel, *Thorns and Thistles*, p. 165.

48 Hawes, *Children in Urban Society*, p. 255.

49 William Healy, Augusta Bronner, and Myra Shimberg, "The Close of Another Chapter in Criminology."

50 Solomon Kobrin, "The Chicago Area Project: A Twenty-five Year Assessment," p. 579.

51 Ralph Sorrentino quoted in Dale Sechrest, "The Community Approach to Delinquency," p. 6.

52 Solomon Kobrin, "The Chicago Area Project: A Twenty-five Year Assessment"; and Short, "Preface," in *Delinquency in Urban Areas*, eds. Shaw and McKay.

53 Clifford Shaw quoted in Helen Witmer and E. Tufts, *The Effectiveness of Delinquency Prevention Programs*, p. 16.

54 Sechrest, "The Community Approach," p. 15.

55 See Richard Cloward and Francis Fox Piven, *Regulating the Poor*.

56 Saul Alinsky, *Reveille For Radicals*.

57 Oscar Handlin, *The Newcomers*; and Robert Coles, *Children of Crisis: A Study of Courage and Fear*.

58 William Ryan, *Blaming the Victim*.

59 National Commission on the Causes and Prevention of Violence, *To Establish Justice, To Ensure Domestic Tranquillity*, p. 30.

60 Cloward and Piven, *Regulating the Poor*, p. 211.

61 Malcolm Klein, "Gang Cohesiveness, Delinquency, and a Street-Work Program," p. 143.

62 Paul Crawford, Daniel Malamud, and James R. Dumpson, "Working with Teenage Gangs," p. 630.

63 Hans Mattick and W. S. Caplan, "Stake Animals, Loud-Talking and Leadership in Do-Nothing and Do Something Situations."

64   Daniel Moynahan, *Maximum Feasible Misunderstanding*; and Sidney Wilhelm, *Who Needs the Negro?*

65   Peter Morris and Martin Rein, *The Dilemmas of Social Reform*, pp. 7-32; and Daniel Moynahan, *Maximum Feasible Misunderstanding*, pp. 21-37.

66   Harold Weissman, *Community Development in the Mobilization for Youth*, p. 19.

67   George Brager and Francis Purcell, *Community Action Against Poverty*, p. 247.

68   Weissman, *Community Development*, pp. 25-28.

69   President's Commission on Law Enforcement and the Administration of Justice, *Challenge of Crime in a Free Society*.

70   Sherwood Norman, *The Youth Service Bureau: A Key to Delinquency Prevention*.

71   Elaine Duxbury, *Youth Service Bureaus in California: Progress Report #3*; and U.S. Department of Health, Education, and Welfare, *National Study of Youth Service Bureaus—Final Report*.

72   John Ellingston, *Protecting Our Children from Criminal Careers* provides an extensive discussion of the development of the California Youth Authority.

73   Edwin Lemert, *Social Action and Legal Change*, pp. 49-50.

74   Thomas Mathieson, *The Defences of the Weak*.

75   Paul Lerman, *Community Corrections and Social Control* is a provocative evaluation of the Community Treatment Project and Probation Subsidy.

76   See James O'Connor, *The Fiscal Crisis of the State* for a discussion of the causes of this fiscal crunch.

77   Yizak Bakal, *Closing Correctional Institutions*.

78   *In re Gault*, 387 U.S. 1 (1967).

79   Nicholas Kittrie, *The Right To Be Different*, pp. 113-53.

80   *McKiever v. Pennsylvania*, 403 U.S. 528 (1971).

81   *In re Winship*, 397 U.S. 358 (1970).

82   In 1975 the American Bar Association released part of a major report, dealing exclusively with procedural reforms of the juvenile justice system.

83   This perspective is similar to that of Rusche and Kirchheimer in their criminological classic, *Punishment and Social Structure*.

84   Alexander Liazos, "Class Oppression and the Juvenile Justice System"; and Barry Krisberg, *Crime and Privilege*.

85   William Appleman Williams, *The Contours of American History*, p. 480.

BIBLIOGRAPHY

Alinsky, Saul. *Reveille For Radicals*. Chicago: University of Chicago Press, 1946.

Bakal, Yizak. *Closing Correctional Institutions*. Lexington: Lexington Books, 1973.

Brace, Charles Loring. *The Dangerous Classes of New York and Twenty Years Among Them*. New York: Wynkoop and Hallenbeck, 1872.

Brager, George, and Purcell, Francis. *Community Action Against Poverty*. New Haven: College and University Press, 1967.

Bremner, Robert, *et al*. *Children and Youth in America: A Documentary History*. Cambridge: Harvard University Press, 1970.

Chesney-Lind, Meda. "Juvenile Delinquency: The Sexualization of Female Crime." *Psychology Today*, July 1974, pp. 43-46.

48

Cloward, Richard, and Piven, Francis Fox. *Regulating the Poor*. New York: Pantheon, 1971.

Coles, Robert. *Children of Crisis: A Study of Courage and Fear*. Boston: Little, Brown and Co., 1967.

Crawford, Paul; Malamud, Daniel; and Dumpson, James R. "Working with Teenage Gangs." In *The Sociology of Crime and Delinquency*, edited by Norman Johnson *et al*. New York: John Wiley and Sons, 1970.

Devoe, Elijah. "The Refuge System or Prison Discipline Applied to Juvenile Delinquency." New York, 1848. From the Sprague Pamphlet Collection, Cambridge: Harvard Divinity School.

Duxbury, Elaine. *Youth Service Bureaus in California: Progress Report #3*. Sacramento: California Youth Authority, 1972.

Ellingston, John. *Protecting Our Children from Criminal Careers*. Englewood Cliffs, N.J.: Prentice-Hall, Inc., 1955.

Gossett, Thomas. *Race: The History of an Idea in America*. New York: Schocken, 1965.

Handlin, Oscar. *The Newcomers*. New York: Doubleday, 1959.

Hawes, Joseph. *Children in Urban Society: Juvenile Delinquency in Nineteenth Century America*. New York: Oxford University Press, 1971.

Healy, William; Bronner, Augusta; and Shimberg, Myra. "The Close of Another Chapter in Criminology." *Mental Hygiene* 19 (1935): 208-22.

Higham, John. *Strangers in the Land*. New York: Atheneum, 1971.

Jordan, Winthrop. *The White Man's Burden*. New York: Oxford University Press, 1974.

Kittrie, Nocholas. *The Right To Be Different*. Baltimore: Johns Hopkins Press, 1971.

Klein, Malcolm. "Gang Cohesiveness, Delinquency, and a Street-Work Program." *Journal of Research on Crime and Delinquency* (July 1969): 143.

Kobrin, Solomon. "The Chicago Area Project: A Twenty-five Year Assessment." In *The Sociology of Crime and Delinquency*, edited by Norman Johnson *et al*. New York: John Wiley and Sons, 1970.

Krisberg, Barry. *Crime and Privilege*. Englewood Cliffs, N.J.: Prentice-Hall, 1975.

Lemert, Edwin. *Social Action and Legal Change*. Chicago: Aldine Publishing Co., 1970.

Lerman, Paul. *Community Connections and Social Control*. Chicago: University of Chicago Press, 1975.

Lerner, Gerda. *Black Women in White America*. New York: Random House, Vintage, 1973.

Lewis, W. David. In *The Development of an American Culture*, edited by Stanley Coben and Lorman Ratner. Englewood Cliffs, N.J.: Prentice-Hall, 1970.

Liazos, Alexander. "Class Oppression and the Juvenile Justice System." *Insurgent Sociologist* 1 (1974): 2-23.

Lubove, Roy. *The Professional Altruist: The Emergence of Social Work as a Career, 1880-1930*. Cambridge: Harvard University Press, 1965.

Marris, Peter, and Rein, Martin. *The Dilemmas of Social Reform*. New York: Atherton Press, 1967.

Mathieson, Thomas. *The Defences of the Weak*. London: Tavistock, 1965.

Mattick, Hans, and Caplan, W. S. "Stake Animals, Loud-Talking and Leadership in Do-Nothing and Do Something Situations." In *Juvenile Gangs in Context*, edited by Malcolm Klein. Englewood Cliffs, N.J.: Prentice-Hall, 1967.

McConnell, James V. "Criminals Can Be Brainwashed—Now." *Psychology Today*, April 1970.

McKelvey, Blake. *American Prisons*. Montclair, N.J.: Patterson Smith, 1972.

Mennel, Robert. *Thorns and Thistles*. Hanover: The University of New Hampshire Press, 1973.

Moynahan, Daniel. *Maximum Feasible Misunderstanding*. New York: Free Press, 1969.

National Commission on the Causes and Prevention of Violence. *To Establish Justice, To Ensure Domestic Tranquillity*. Washington, D.C.: U.S. Government Printing Office, 1969.

Norman, Sherwood. *The Youth Service Bureau: A Key to Delinquency Prevention*. Hackensack, N.J.: National Council on Crime and Delinquency, 1972.

O'Connor, James. *The Fiscal Crisis of the State*. New York: St. Martin's Press, 1973.

Pickett, Robert. *House of Refuge: Origins of Juvenile Justice Reform in New York, 1815-1857*. Syracuse: Syracuse University Press, 1969.

Platt, Anthony. *The Child-Savers, The Invention of Delinquency*. Chicago: University of Chicago Press, 1968.

President's Commission on Law Enforcement and the Administration of Justice. *Challenge of Crime in a Free Society*. Washington, D.C.: U.S. Government Printing Office, 1967.

Rothman, David. *The Discovery of the Asylum*. Boston: Little, Brown and Co., 1971.

Rusche, Georg, and Kirchheimer, Otto. *Punishment and Social Structure*. New York: Russell and Russell, 1968.

Ryan, William. *Blaming the Victim*. New York: Random House, 1971.

Sanders, Wiley B. *Juvenile Offenders for a Thousand Years*. Chapel Hill: University of North Carolina, 1970.

Schein, Edgar H. "Man Against Man: Brainwashing." *Corrective Psychiatry and Journal of Social Change* 8 (1962): 2.

Sechrest, Dale, "The Community Approach to Delinquency." Berkeley: University of California, School of Criminology, 1970.

Sellin, Thorsten. *Pioneering in Penology*. Philadelphia: University of Pennsylvania Press, 1944.

Shaffer, Anatole. "The Cincinnati Social Units Experiment." *Social Service Review* 45 (1971): 159-71.

Short. "Preface" to *Delinquency in Urban Areas*, edited by Shaw and McKay, 1969.

Stamp, Kenneth M. *The Peculiar Institution*. New York: Random House, Vintage, 1956.

Takagi, Paul. "The Correctional System." *Crime and Social Justice* 2 (1974): 82-87.

U.S. Department of Health, Education, and Welfare, Youth Development and Delinquency Prevention Administration. *National Study of Youth Services Bureaus—Final Report*. Prepared by the California Youth Authority. Washington, D.C., 1973.

Walker, Margaret. *Jubilee*. New York: Bantam, 1969.

Weinstein, James. *The Corporate Ideal in the Liberal State*. Boston: Beacon Press, 1968.

Weissman, Harold. *Community Development in the Mobilization for Youth*. New York: Association Press, 1969.

Wilhelm, Sidney. *Who Needs the Negro?* Cambridge, Mass.: Schenkman, 1970.

Williams, William Appleman. *The Contours of American History.* New York: New Viewpoints, 1973.

Wines, E. C. *The State of Prisons and Child-Saving Institutions in the Civilized World.* Montclair: Patterson Smith, 1880.

Witmer, Helen, and Tufts, E. *The Effectiveness of Delinquency Prevention Programs.* Washington, D.C.: U.S. Government Printing Office, 1954.

Yetman, Norman R. *Voices from Slavery.* New York: Holt, Rinehart and Winston, 1970.

Boys at Skirt-Making, New York House of Refuge

THE CONTEMPORARY
JUVENILE JUSTICE SYSTEM:
ITS STRUCTURE AND OPERATION

CHAPTER 3

INTRODUCTION

Contrasting treatment of various youths dramatizes the contradictions inherent in current methods of regulating delinquent children in our society. Hundreds of thousands of American youths have direct contact with the juvenile justice system each year. In 1973 alone, nearly 1.5 million juvenile cases were formally processed by the juvenile courts.[1] This figure applies only to those children whose cases actually went to court; it gives no indication of the far larger numbers who passed through police and probation processing. Lemert[2] estimates that one out of every five children will have some official contact with the juvenile court,* and most will come from lower-class and Third World communities. In addition, recent research indicates that although delinquency is uniformly distributed throughout the social structure, the poor and disadvantaged are disproportionately represented in the juvenile justice process.[3] These findings suggest that the present system discriminates against disadvantaged segments of society.[4]

---

*Wolfgang and associates estimate that one-third of the children in a birth cohort will have some contact with police. Marvin Wolfgang, Robert Figlio, and Thorsten Sellin, *Delinquency in a Birth Cohort.*

The historical perspective of chapter 2 demonstrated how the *parens patriae* philosophy was used to justify funneling wayward children through a specially constructed court system, characterized by individualized and supposedly benevolent treatment. But despite this humane ideology, children who have never committed acts that would be judged criminal under adult criminal codes can still be placed for an indeterminate period in prisonlike settings. Such youths can remain imprisoned until reaching the age of majority without their cases ever being reviewed by the sentencing court, while receiving identical treatment to those who have committed more serious crimes. Conversely, youths with long records of felony-type crimes, including murder, may receive less severe punishment.[5] Such anomalies highlight the lack of uniformity that characterizes the juvenile system's processes and procedures. Indeed, many have concluded that the system is in reality little more than a collective of separate control agencies, all sanctioned under a broad legal framework, but each with its social climate and ethos.[6]

The previous chapter traced the historical development of the juvenile court in relation to changes in the structure of American society. In this chapter, we shall describe and analyze the diverse and often oppressive contradictions of the institutions that today attempt to control children who are officially perceived as troublesome or dangerous. In the process, it will be necessary to assess the various factors that foster these contradictions, including the influence of decision makers who play critical roles in the formulation of juvenile justice policy. The focus will be primarily on the working components of current juvenile justice processes, with special emphasis on the legal codes that structure and legitimate the system, as well as the agencies that enforce those codes. It is important that the reader understand how the various control agencies interact, and how certain critical areas of decision making or discretionary judgment promote differential treatment of delinquents.

Figure 1 depicts the procedural flow of cases moving through the juvenile justice system. The reader is encouraged to refer to this chart to become familiar with the sequential processing of children as various stages of the process are discussed.

The discussion is divided into two parts. First, a review of the juvenile codes establishes the generic framework by which individual jurisdictions have constructed their own juvenile justice systems. Issues such as definitions of delinquency, the structure and jurisdiction of the court, and the adjudicatory processes are examined in detail. Because legal codes comprise the cornerstone of the juvenile justice process, it is important to understand the functions of law and the legal profession within our society.[7] The second part of this chapter deals with the agents who uphold juvenile laws: police, probation intake officers, and related court personnel. Sociological studies centering on the influences of class and race in the operation of the juvenile justice system are reviewed toward building a critical perspective.

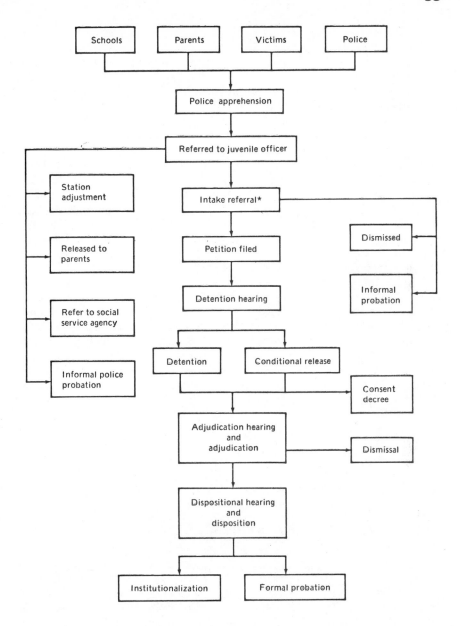

*In a few cases juveniles are referred directly to intake by schools, parents, or victims.

Figure 1
Juvenile justice system critical decision points

It is not our intention to generate a grand and novel theory to explain the operation of the juvenile justice system. We explore the influences of class and race because these factors have been largely ignored or deemphasized by social scientists writing about juvenile justice.* Our focus on workers in the juvenile justice system is not intended to blame the criminal justice practitioners for systemic inadequacies. The behavior of police, probation, and court personnel is circumscribed by the values and expectations inherent in the structure in which they work. Thus, although their functions help to perpetuate inequities, they must be viewed as victims as well as victimizers.[8] They are victimizers in the sense that they directly administer the inequitable and unjust practices of the system. But since they are often caught between public condemnation and administrative constraint, they must be considered victims. The rise of correctional and police unions is in part a reflection of their increasing awareness that they are being collectively exploited to preserve interests that are not necessarily their own.

The recognition that criminal justice workers are pawns in a much larger game is crucial to the development of a critical perspective on reform efforts. It is our contention that liberal reforms ignoring the influence of white privilege in our social institutions are destined to fail because they do not confront the root causes of the problems they seek to remedy. Such reforms as increased professionalism of juvenile justice personnel, improved training, upgraded facilities, and revised juvenile codes therefore can have only limited impact on the massive inequities of the juvenile justice system.[9]

PART ONE
THE JUVENILE LAWS AND PROCEDURES

At the foundation of the juvenile justice system are the respective legal codes of the fifty states. Although these codes attempt to standardize the processing of delinquent youth, they also seek to retain an atmosphere of individualized treatment and informality that is assumed to be essential to the success of the juvenile court. The result of this basic contradiction is a set of legal codes that afford only a quasi-legal framework to define state intervention.

---

*A notable exception is Wolfgang, Figlio, and Sellin in *Delinquency in a Birth Cohort,* who view race and class as the central variables in their delinquency research.

By 1932, all but two states had instituted juvenile codes patterned after the Illinois model adopted in 1899. Alluding to the doctrines of *parens patriae* and benevolence, the architects of these codes universally adopted models based on the adult criminal court system while eliminating most of the procedural safeguards protecting the constitutional rights of the accused. Many observers view this lack of procedural safeguards as the major proximal cause of inequitable and unjust treatment of children. Lemert claims that overreliance on the adult court model coupled with the absence of a true adversary system within the adjudication process has limited the system's to develop a viable approach to handle delinquent youths.[10] He notes that the persistence of these contradictions can be partially attributed to the powerlessness of the clients to make articulate demands on the court. We would argue that on the contrary, they persist because they continue to serve an important function. Unclear and contradictory codes appear to depoliticize the operations of the social control system while at the same time enabling it to selectively concentrate its power.

Let us turn now to the current status of juvenile laws, especially those relating to jurisdiction, detention, procedural rights, adjudication, and court structure.* On reviewing these laws, it will become apparent to the reader that most of what Lemert terms the "anomalies" that characterized juvenile justice in America in the nineteenth century remain with us to the present day. Apart from the limited reforms embodied in recent Supreme Court decisions in the *Kent, Gault,* and *Winship* cases, there has been little significant change in the legal framework that governs and determines the quality of justice for delinquent youth.

It is useful to begin the discussion of legal codes with an overview of the philosophics and processes that guided their creation, and still serve to maintain the traditional distribution of property and race privilege. Without such a perspective on law, one might conclude that the juvenile court system and its attendant legal configurations developed in a vacuum.

THE NATURE OF LAWS

Traditional theories of the nature of law in a democratic society have been grounded in the concept of pluralistic consensus. This

---

*Much of the data for this section on juvenile laws were taken from Mark Levin and Rosemary Sarri, *Juvenile Delinquency: A Comparative Analysis of Legal Codes in the United States.* This report was based on a national survey of existing juvenile codes as of January 1, 1972. It is probable that some laws have since changed. Data presented reflect legal codes and not state and local practices. Despite its limitations, we have relied on the Levin and Sarri report because theirs is the only available national survey of juvenile legal codes. One example of the limitations is that Levin and Sarri report that California prohibits the detention of juveniles in adult county jails. Our own research experience in 1976 showed that juveniles are routinely detained in at least one California county jail.

view suggests that laws—especially criminal laws—represent a negotiated consensus of the majority of the people. Society is viewed as
a relatively harmonious system in which various components act in
concert and are to some degree mutually dependent.[11] Perhaps the
best-known proponent of this consensus view of law is Roscoe
Pound, who argues that in a civilized society law reflects the cumula-
tive consciousness of the people.[12] In such a society, Pound reasons,
many individual interests can be peacefully accommodated, and any
conflicts that arise can be resolved through the existing legal system.
This state of order is possible because a legal system controlled by
the will of the people is assumed to forge fair and equitable laws.

Basic to the consensus perspective is the assumption that laws
are created in the interest of society as a whole, not in the interest
of the favored few. Those interests of highest priority are those that
seek to maintain the stability of society and perpetuate its ideals.
Change is expected only through the established legal framework,
and then only if change benefits the social system and accords with
the popular will.

> Looked at functionally, the law is an attempt to satisfy, to
> reconcile, to harmonize, to adjust these overlapping and often
> conflicting claims and demands, either through securing them
> directly and immediately, or through securing certain individual
> interests, or through delimitations or compromises of individual
> interests, so as to give effect to the greatest total of interests or
> to the interests that weigh most in our civilization, *with the
> least sacrifice of the scheme of interests as a whole* [emphasis
> added].[13]

The idealized view of law and society set forth by Pound is essentially
an ideological defense of the status quo. It fails to acknowledge that
the order constructed by the legal profession in fact mirrors the
perceptions and interests of a privileged segment of society. Access
to positions in the legal profession—to serve as lawyers and judges—
simply is not available to all segments of society. Indeed, it is a profession traditionally open only to those of relative affluence, whose
perspectives in turn have shaped its philosophies and procedures.
Pound's formulation further ignores the very existence of power
concentrations that have developed within our society.

An alternative view might portray society as a congeries of
interest groups, constantly competing with one another for benefits
within the distributive order. Each group is armed with a measure of
power, status, and resources, which enable it to withstand antagonists
and to pursue its own ends.[14] Such interest groups arise in all
segments of society, but owing to an imbalance in power, status, and
resources, only a few are capable of consistently winning their
struggles. For example, although groups such as the Black Panther
party, the NAACP, and the United Farm Workers may be viewed as
interest groups, their progress in the legal arena has been markedly
slow and arduous.

One means by which a segment of society develops and maintains dominance over others is by creating laws that legitimate the use of force on its own behalf. The formulation of criminal laws plays a particularly crucial role in this regard because criminal offenses are considered offenses against the community at large. (Adult criminal actions, for example, name the state as plaintiff.) Such actions are potentially punishable by the most severe societal sanctions. The class-biased origins of criminal laws against vagrancy, and the sale and use of drugs and alcohol have been well documented.[15] Our analysis, in chapter 2, of class bias in the history of delinquency prevention and control in America gains further dimension when we examine the groups most actively involved in the formulation of delinquency statutes. Typically, the main actors are judges, bar association's, and private foundations headed by executives from large corporations. These groups are supported by academicians, who impart an aura of scientific neutrality while generally advocating liberal but nonthreatening positions. Little or no credence is given in their deliberations to the views of the juveniles or parents who are ultimately affected by the structures they create.

Lemert in his analysis of changes in California juvenile court law attempts to minimize the role of powerful interest groups, but nonetheless unintentionally provides a good illustration of that role.[16] The key actors in the reformulation of the California juvenile laws were representatives of such agencies as the California Juvenile Officers' Association; the California Probation, Parole and Correctional Officers' Association; the California Youth Authority; and the Governor's Special Study Commission on Juvenile Justice. Although these representatives were by no means unified in all their recommendations, their disagreements arose almost exclusively over methods of control.

There are numerous examples of organizations influential in the control and structuring of juvenile justice that have strong interests in preserving the status quo. One such group, the National Council on Crime and Delinquency (NCCD), is an organization originally developed by probation and parole officers to improve their tenuous professional status. Wildeman, in his study "The Crime Fighters," points out that since its birth, NCCD has been dominated on its executive board by representatives from labor, government, and industry.[17] In Wildeman's view the reforms proposed by NCCD, such as its model penal code, have been formulated with a bias toward the primacy of private property over the alleviation of social injustices based on race, sex, and age.

The International Association of Chiefs of Police (IACP) has published a study on "Juvenile Justice Administration" in which they attempt to set forth standards "to relieve the injustices to our children caused by our justice 'system.'"[18] The Institute for Judicial Administration and the American Bar Association are formulating standards for juvenile justice relating to prevention, police, and detention. The consequence of the work of these groups has invariably been a limitation of the range of policy alternatives. They can subtly influence the course of juvenile justice without an overt exercise of power. The prospects for real change remain slight so long as influential groups insist on taking a narrow view of the possibilities of reform.

As Krisberg notes, academicians also play a central role in the legitimization of recommendations made by groups interested in social control.[19] Academic experts employed by large and influential universities invoke the image of "science" to defend the reasonableness and rationality of often oppressive policies.[20]

> Lawyers, social scientists, and psychologists and/or psychiatrists and social workers play a crucial role in maintaining the mythology that crime control activities are politically neutral, based upon scientific principles, and basically benevolent. . . . University-trained crime experts help develop and rationalize state crime policies while masking their ideological commitment through claims of scientific or professional neutrality.[21]

Law helps perpetuate the American myth that government represents the will of the people and that society exists peacefully without the need for conflict. Juvenile codes in particular reflect the intent of those in positions of power to maintain control over youth—especially those of poor and Third World families. Although we have been led to believe that the juvenile codes and the juvenile court were created to benevolently protect the young, the opposite result has occurred. The court, in asserting its legal role as guardian of the child, has too often become the enemy of youths in the lower economic and social strata.

JURISDICTION: THE RIGHT TO INTERVENE

One of the critical functions of the juvenile codes is to specify and delineate the conditions under which the state may legitimately intervene in a juvenile's life. A continuing concern of liberal reformers is the lack of systematic criteria to determine the behavioral circumstances necessitating state-sanctioned treatment and processing. State juvenile codes were adopted to eliminate the arbitrary character of juvenile justice within each jurisdiction. It was thought that the juvenile codes would enlarge the procedural safeguards for juveniles beyond those rights already afforded juveniles by the federal Constitution. The court ruled that since youths were not yet fully responsible for their actions, they should not be dealt with as harshly as their adult counterparts in the adult court. The logic of this argument is frequently cited in the 1955 case *In re Poff*:

> The original Juvenile Court Act enacted in the District of Columbia . . . was devised to afford the juvenile protections in addition to those he already possessed under the Federal Constitution. Before this legislative enactment, the juvenile

was subject to the same punishment for an offense as an adult. It follows logically that in the absence of such legislation the juvenile would be entitled to the same constitutional guarantees and safeguards as an adult. If this is true, then the only possible reason for the Juvenile Court Act was to afford the juvenile safeguards in addition to those he already possessed. The legislative intent was to enlarge and not diminish those protections.[22]

The historical perspective of chapter 2 showed the juvenile court developed in part out of changes in the economy and the need for more expedient, efficient, and economical means to process unruly children who were not properly socializing into the rapidly developing industrial society.[23] Barak argues that survival and proliferation of a corporate economy is predicated on developing viable means of social control.[24] Although the purported goal of the juvenile court and its accompanying legal framework was benevolent action on behalf of the child, there was a latent philosophy of social control to retain existing power structures. This argument takes on more meaning when one recognizes how the vagueness and ambiguity of current juvenile codes legitimate abuses within the system.

Narrowly defined, jurisdiction refers to the areas in which juvenile court has authority over an individual, based on geographic location, age, and behavior. In theory, the codes specify the types of behavior that are indicative of juvenile delinquency and thus warrant state intervention into a child's life. But defining behavior that points toward future delinquency is problematic indeed. The goal of prevention is realized by early detection of behavior that suggests tendencies toward more serious delinquent or criminal behavior. The role of the court is to discover youths exhibiting such patterns, and to treat them so their delinquent tendencies disappear. This legitimates the court's intervention in the lives of youth who may not have committed any crimes, but whose conduct may not reflect the expected behavior, norms, and values as defined by the more privileged segments of society. As Kittrie notes, there exists an almost unlimited range of juvenile court jurisdiction over children due to the rationalized need to intervene in the early stages of a delinquent career.[25]

> What power should society exercise over juveniles who drop out of school, leave home, form undesirable associations, and appear to progress towards crime, yet are short of it? When may society take preventive measures, and to what extent should social intervention depend on the availability of adequate treatment facilities?[26]

Current juvenile codes include three major categories of juvenile behavior in which the court has jurisdiction over the youth. First, the court may intervene in those instances where the youth has been accused of committing an act that would be defined as criminal for an adult, including misdemeanors and felony-type crimes. There is little controversy over the right of the court to intervene in such instances, owing to the seriousness of such behavior and the usual presence of a complainant.

Second, there are *status offenses*, which are currently the center of controversy among criminal justice practitioners and liberal reformers. Status offenses refer to acts that would not be defined as criminal if committed by an adult, including truancy, curfew violations, and running away. They are described in such phrases as "incorrigibility," "in need of supervision," "idling," "waywardness," "beyond parental control," or "unruly behavior." In 1974, police in California reported that 26.4 percent of all juvenile arrests were for status offenses, or, in state terminology, "delinquent tendencies."[27]

The third behavioral category of court intervention for delinquency involves dependency and neglect. In such instances the child is viewed by the court as being deprived of needed support and supervision from parental figures, and the family is judged incapable of resolving its insufficiencies. The rationale used for court intervention in dependency and neglect cases is that children need to be removed from the home for their own protection and well-being. Unfortunately, many children removed from unfavorable home environments may be placed in prisonlike settings, which can hardly be considered beneficial to their development.

Defenders of the juvenile justice system, recognizing some of the problems inherent in current definitions of court jurisdiction, have proposed narrower jurisdictional limitations on the juvenile court. Levin and Sarri cite a recently revised Ohio statute as an attempt, albeit ineffective, to relinquish some court control over youth:

> ... Ohio provides that the court may have jurisdiction over a child: (a) "who does not subject himself to the reasonable control of his parents, teachers, guardian, or custodian, by reason of being wayward or habitually disobedient; (b) who is habitually truant from home or school; (c) who so deports himself as to injure or endanger the health or morals of himself or others; (d) who is found in a disreputable place, visits or patronizes a place prohibited by law or associates with vagrant, vicious, criminal, notorious, or immoral persons."[28]

Such statutes serve to justify the state's intervention in a child's life regardless of the seriousness of his behavior or the potential for continued delinquency. The Ohio statute not only reflects current juvenile codes, but it is also typical of recent attempts to draft legislation to improve the juvenile justice system.

In 1959, the National Council on Crime and Delinquency adopted the Standard Juvenile Court Act, which was intended to serve as a model for states in standardizing their jurisdiction criteria:

> The court shall have exclusive original jurisdiction in proceedings: 1. Concerning any child who is alleged to have

violated any federal, state, or local law or municipal ordinance, regardless of where the violation occurred. . . . 2. Concerning any child . . . (b) whose environment is injurious to his welfare, or whose behavior is injurious to his own or others' welfare; or (c) who is beyond the control of his parent or other custodian.[29]

The broad and vague terms of this model legislation would probably be held unconstitutional if used as a basis for formulating adult criminal codes.

The International Association of Chiefs of Police, noting the problem of defining juvenile jurisdictions, in 1973 proposed equally vague standards to be used by states in developing model legislation:

(i) It is recommended that the term "juvenile delinquent" be applied only to a child who has committed a criminal offense and who is in need of supervision, treatment or rehabilitation.

(ii) It is recommended that the terminology "unruly" child be applied to children who: (a) Have committed an offense applicable only to a child (status offenders); (b) Are habitually disobedient of reasonable commands of parents or guardians and are ungovernable; (c) Are habitually truant from school; and (e) Are in need of treatment or rehabilitation for any of the foregoing.[30]

The above criteria for intervention appear on the surface to be reasonable and logical, but legal codes actually offer little protection from discriminatory and arbitrary decisions by police and court personnel. Since the basis for the police decision of whether or not to arrest the child is not well defined by law, there is even greater potential for abuse. We know from several research studies that the juvenile justice practitioners often make decisions based on social values, and those values are often imbued with class, race, and sexual biases.[31] A necessary prerequisite of justice for youth is the development of precise legal codes to delineate the jurisdiction of the court.

Sussman has dramatized the absence of precise criteria by compiling the following types of behavior that could qualify as juvenile delinquency under most juvenile statutes:

1 [A juvenile who] violates any law or ordinance;
2 [Who is] habitually truant;
3 [Knowingly] associates with thieves, vicious or immoral persons;
4 Incorrigible;
5 Beyond control of parent or guardian;
6 Growing up in idleness or crime;
7 So deports self as to injure self or others;
8 Absents self from home [without just cause] without consent;
9 Immoral or indecent conduct;

10 [Habitually] uses vile, obscene, or vulgar language [in public places];
11 [Knowingly] enters, visits house of ill repute;
12 Patronizes, visits policy shop or gaming place;
13 [Habitually] wanders about railroad yards or tracks;
14 Jumps train or enters car or engine without authority;
15 Patronizes saloon or dram house where intoxicating liquor is sold;
16 Wanders streets at night, not on lawful business;
17 Patronizes public poolroom or bucket shop;
18 Immoral conduct around school (or in public place);
19 Engages in illegal occupation;
20 In occupation or situation dangerous or injurious to self or others;
21 Smokes cigarettes (or uses tobacco in any form);
22 Frequents place the existence of which violates the law;
23 Is found [in place for permitting of which] adult may be punished;
24 Addicted to drugs;
25 Disorderly;
26 Begging;
27 Uses intoxicating liquor;
28 Makes indecent proposal;
29 Loiters, sleeps in alleys, vagrant;
30 Runs away from state or charity institution;
31 Found on premises occupied or used for illegal purposes;
32 Operates motor vehicle dangerously while under the influence of liquor;
33 Attempts to marry without consent, in violation of law;
34 Given to sexual irregularities.[32]

Starrs points out that juvenile laws were used during the civil rights movement in the South to disrupt and discourage protest efforts. He suggests that the juvenile court has in many instances merely become a governmental arm of racial segregation.

[Juvenile Court] can . . . intimidate civil rights demonstrators and their parents by long periods of inhuman confinement without recourse to bail. . . . On occasion, children have been adjudged delinquent when their parents, not they, were active civil rights workers.[33]

In 1965, the United States Civil Rights Commission concluded that the juvenile court had exercised its power in many cases simply to "curtail or penalize participation in constitutionally protected activities."[34] Our analysis of police and court personnel later in this chapter will demonstrate that the excessive latitude of the court results not in random intervention, but in selective intervention structured along distinct lines of race, sex, and class privilege. Kittrie concludes that where delinquency standards are vague, nonlegal variables such as race, class, and economic status exert significant influence on police and court decisions.[35] This argument is substantiated by the studies demonstrating that black children are typically sent to juvenile institutions at younger ages, for less serious offenses, and with fewer previous offenses than their white counterparts.[36]

Age is the most obvious criterion separating juvenile court from adult criminal court. Although there is a paucity of precise guidelines for juvenile court intervention based on behavior, one still might expect definitive age criteria to define court jurisdiction. Such is not the case. The codes exhibit wide variation in the age limitations placed on court procedures from state to state. Minimum age refers to the earliest age at which the court has jurisdiction over a child. Minimum age restrictions are stipulated in few of the codes, leaving individual courts to develop their own unwritten policies, or to rely on the common law dictum that no person can be held accountable for criminal behavior until the age of seven years. Maximum age limit refers to that age when a person is defined as an adult and is beyond the jurisdiction of juvenile court. While most states set the maximum limit for original jurisdiction at eighteen years, a substantial number have age limits of fifteen or sixteen years.* This variation is due in part to a difference of opinion among the juvenile justice experts concerning the age at which children mature. It is interesting to note that associations such as the National Council on Crime and Delinquency, the American Bar Association, the International Association of Chiefs of Police, and the American Institute for Judicial Administration all recommend that the maximum age limit be set at eighteen years for all states. If implemented, this would actually increase the length of jurisdiction over children beyond what is currently permitted in state codes.

Another age restriction in juvenile codes limits continuing jurisdiction, which defines the maximum age at which the court can retain control beyond the original age of jurisdiction. For example, if the case of a seventeen-year-old youth is heard by the juvenile court, it is possible in some states to retain control over that delinquent until the age of twenty-one. The youth cannot be tried again for the same crime once he has reached the age of eighteen, but it is possible for the court to retain its jurisdiction over the individual through probation, parole, or institutionalization. This legal loophole permits adult criminal courts to waive jurisdiction over a person charged with an adult offense if that person is still under juvenile court control. He can be remanded to the juvenile court, which can then inflict a stiffer sentence through continued incarceration or parole supervision stemming from a previous juvenile offense.

---

*Original jurisdiction refers to the age at which the juvenile court can initiate control over the youth. This is distinct from continuing jurisdiction, which is discussed later.

A further complication in delinquency cases is the method by which each state juvenile code calculates the official age of the youth. Most states (thirty-seven) place the age of the offender at the time the delinquent act was committed. Thus, in these states, a person who commits a delinquent act as a juvenile, but is not arrested until after he becomes an adult, can be returned to the juvenile court for adjudication and disposition. It is common practice for sophisticated youths familiar with the rules of court jurisdiction to lie about their age to police at the time of arrest, in order to gain entrance into adult criminal court. They seem confident that dispositions in adult court will be more lenient than those in juvenile court.

While most states (twenty-eight) specify in their codes that age is the sole determinant of court jurisdiction, other states introduce various conditions relating to the seriousness of the offense. For example, in Louisiana the juvenile court has no jurisdiction over youths more than fifteen years old, who have been charged with rape or other capital offenses.* But in Maryland, if a youth of the same age commits similar offenses, he or she is not protected from adult prosecution, since the maximum age of original jurisdiction there is fourteen years.

An additional jurisdictional question concerning age, the waiver or transfer of juveniles to the adult court, is undertaken in juvenile cases in which the offense is thought to be especially serious. In many states, the power to transfer a juvenile to the adult criminal court lies with the district attorney's office. The prosecutor's office is allowed to assume control over a juvenile case with or without the consent of the juvenile judge based on the judgment of the district attorney. Predictably, the guidelines used by the prosecutor in making such waivers or transfers are vague. Virginia, for example, permits the prosecutor at his discretion to transfer a youth out of juvenile court over the ruling of a juvenile judge, if the prosecutor views the youth as an habitual offender or if the offense carries a jail term of over twenty years. Nebraska allows the adult court to seize control of all juvenile offenders of fifteen years or older without specifying any rationale for such transfers.

This jurisdictional interface between adult and juvenile courts is widespread, since nearly all states give the judge the right in some cases to waive jurisdiction and transfer juveniles to adult court. The U.S. Supreme Court in the *Kent* decision attempted to ensure that juveniles could not be waived to adult criminal courts for trial without a formal hearing before a judge and with the assistance of a lawyer.[37] Critics of waivers argue that transferring juveniles to the adult court is in conflict with the juvenile court's treatment philosophy. A common reason given for transfer is that the juvenile court is unable to properly handle the juvenile, but there is no reason to conclude that the adult court is in a better position to provide the desired

---

*Capital offenses are those crimes punishable by death.

services. The basic intent of the waiver, despite liberal rhetoric to the contrary, is that adult court has more latitude to impose lengthy sentences than juvenile court, which in most cases must relinquish jurisdiction of offenders beyond the age of twenty-one. Conservative critics of the juvenile system, who complain that the court is too lenient, generally would like to see the use of waivers expanded.

Armed with the threat of transfer to adult court, juvenile authorities are in a strong position to influence a youth's decision to plead guilty to the alleged offense. It is a form of plea bargaining,* and serves as an incentive for a juvenile to relinquish his or her full due process rights.[38] One study uncovered three counties in one state that had established a policy of transferring to adult court any juveniles who refused to admit to the allegations presented in the delinquency petition. Authorities assumed that the reluctance of youths to admit guilt demonstrated incorrigibility and criminal sophistication.[39] Thus, to demand one's legal rights under the present juvenile system may increase the severity of punishment.

Despite the guarantees provided by the *Kent* decision, there is no assurance that in waiver hearings the case will be disposed of fairly. In many states, there is no requirement that the youth be present at such hearings, since the court is assumed to act in the best interests of the child. Some states provide that the judge in a waiver proceeding must consider the suitability of the youth for rehabilitation and the seriousness of the delinquent act, while others require only that the youth be deemed unsuitable for rehabilitation or treatment.† Frequently the transfer of a juvenile is based not on the merits of the individual case, but rather the discretion of court personnel. It is notable that some states guarantee the right of the juvenile to request transfer to an adult court. This alternative is typically used if the juvenile's lawyer feels that the disposition of the case would be more favorable in an adult court with a jury trial and its other constitutional safeguards.

A review of juvenile court laws gives one the impression that the court is empowered to gain control over virtually any youth, for whatever reasons it chooses. Kittrie warns that, in view of this enormous discretion, the juvenile court philosophy of *parens partiae* needs to be reexamined so that the court does not become overly zealous in its "therapeutic" actions.[40] This criticism is not novel, for as a California legislative commission's 1960 evaluation of California juvenile laws concluded:

> There is an absence of well-defined empirically derived
> standards and norms to guide juvenile court judges, probation,

---

*Plea bargaining involves an agreement whereby the defendant enters a plea of guilty in return for a promise from the district attorney that some charges will be dropped, or that the sentence will be less harsh. Most adult criminal cases are settled through plea bargaining.

†Most states do not require that the juvenile court establish "probable cause" that the youth is guilty of the alleged crime prior to transfer to adult court.

and law enforcement officials in their decision-making. Consequently, instead of a uniform system of justice, varied systems based upon divergent policies and value scales are in evidence. . . . Basic legal rights are neither being uniformly nor adequately protected under present juvenile court provisions.[41]

The diversity of court practices has led to injustices such as the plight of Gerry Gault, which resulted in the pivotal *In re Gault* decision. Gerry Gault was arrested at the age of fifteen for making obscene phone calls to a neighbor. He was subsequently convicted of the charge and placed in the Arizona State Industrial School for six years, during which time the court relinquished its jurisdiction over the case. The juvenile court judge who sentenced Gault stated that Gault was "habitually involved in immoral matters," and that the phone calls were tantamount to "disturbing the peace." Although the complainant in the case neither met with the judge nor attended the hearing, the judge felt justified in sentencing this fifteen-year-old to a penal institution for six years. If Gault had been tried as an adult in the same jurisdiction in Arizona, he would have been sentenced to not more than sixty days in prison with a maximum fine of fifty dollars. The Supreme Court decision that resulted was an attempt to provide basic procedural rights for juveniles, including rights to counsel, notice, cross-examination, and safeguards against self-incrimination.

The case of a fourteen-year-old youth in West Virginia is a further illustration of how current statutes encourage abuse. In this case, a youth had made a phone call to the local school and falsely reported the planting of a bomb on the premises. Because of the youth's age, he was tried in juvenile court, and was subsequently declared delinquent by the judge and committed to juvenile prison, where he remained for seven years until the age of twenty-one. Upon appeal to the state supreme court of appeals, the higher court affirmed the decision of the lower court. If the child had been sentenced in a West Virginia adult criminal court, the maximum sentence would have been thirty days in the local county jail.[42]

While some might conclude that statutory changes would remedy alleged abuses of court discretion, the *Gault* case demonstrated that law reform is not the entire answer. Soon after the Supreme Court's decision in the *Gault* case, many states rushed to develop ways of encouraging youths to voluntarily forfeit procedural safeguards, thereby bypassing the intended effect of the U.S. Supreme Court ruling. To be effective, reform of the juvenile court must be rooted in principles of *social justice* for children, not merely in easily circumvented procedural safeguards.

DETENTION: THE JAILING OF YOUTH

Detention refers to the period in which a wayward youth is taken into custody by police and probation prior to an adjudication hearing by the juvenile court. Various juvenile codes serve as standards for the selective use of detention. Although juvenile court was designed to protect children from the harmful effects of incarceration, the number of juveniles being incarcerated in detention facilities grows each year. The President's Commission on Law Enforcement and the Administration of Criminal Justice found, in 1965, that two-thirds of all juveniles apprehended by police were admitted to detention centers and detained for an average of twelve days. The projected national cost of this detention was $53 million. The Commission asserted that the excessive number of juveniles being detained was creating a serious social problem because in many jurisdictions juveniles were being housed in adult jails.[43] The Law Enforcement Assistance Administration (LEAA) reported that on the day of June 30, 1971, there were 11,748 juveniles in detention facilities.[44] NCCD has claimed that approximately half a million children are placed in detention each year, with the daily count approaching thirteen thousand.[45] In some states, detention is the most common treatment meted out by police in juvenile cases that are to be transferred directly to probation departments. For example, of the 239,060 juveniles referred by California police in 1974 to the probation intake unit, 153,746, or 73 percent of all cases, were first placed in detention.[46]

There is reason to believe that the use of detention has not diminished in the last several years, and may even be on the rise in certain jurisdictions. A review of recent jail surveys draws the following conclusion:

> In 1972 a survey of inmates in jails was made by the U.S. Bureau of Census (LEAA, 1974). That survey reported on 3,921 jails and 141,600 inmates, both numbers slightly below the 1970 Jail Census (LEAA, 1971). But it also reported the proportion of inmates 18 years of age or less at 9%, or a total of 12,744 youths. Unfortunately, the definition of "juvenile" varied between surveys so exact comparisons are not possible. However, it would appear that the number of youth in jail has not diminished since 1970, and it may well have increased substantially.[47]

Furthermore, a 1974 report by the Wisconsin Division of Family Services indicates that between 1961 and 1972 there was a 172 percent overall increase in the number of juveniles placed in Wisconsin's jails.[48] These data point to the obvious failure of the juvenile justice system to protect children from the evils of imprisonment.

In theory, detention of youth fulfills three primary objectives. (1) Youth are detained if there is reason to believe that in the absence of such external controls the juvenile would be free to commit additional serious crimes thereby posing a threat to the safety and security of the community. In this situation the child is incarcerated primarily for the benefit of the community. (2) Juveniles are also detained in cases where the bad influences of a home environment necessitate placing the child in a more protective setting. In this case, children are viewed as being endangered, and detention is construed as a temporary measure until a more permanent home placement can be arranged. (3) Detention parallels the function of the bail system in adult criminal court, and ensures the appearance of the youthful offender at subsequent court dates. This goal is consistent with the desires of court personnel who favor administrative techniques to expedite the processing of criminal matters at both adult and juvenile levels. It is exceedingly efficient and expedient for the court to have defendants readily available at all stages of the adjudication process. Unlike adult court, juvenile court does not necessarily provide an alternative similar to being released on one's own recognizance or on bail. In most states, the child must be released to the guardianship of parents or relatives, who must be willing to assume full responsibility for the child. Beyond these three official rationales for employing detention there is one additional function that is often ignored: punishment.[49]

The fact that status offenders make up a proportion of incarcerated juveniles weakens the argument that detention is used only in cases involving serious delinquent offenses.[50] A summary of many studies reveals that status offenders, especially females, are actually detained more often than those accused of committing crimes against persons or property.[51] Moreover, inasmuch as detained youths are typically from poor families and racial minorities, it is clear that the brunt of such punishment is borne by groups who do not have adequate resources to effectively resist such legal oppression.[52]

In most states, the power to detain rests with police and probation officers. Upon the arrest of a juvenile, police may transfer the child to a detention facility until screening procedures are completed by the probation or intake officer. Once the juvenile is received at the detention unit, the probation or intake officer may request that the juvenile be retained in custody for further investigation. If a delinquency petition has been filed, the youth can be detained until the adjudication and disposition hearings are completed, and even after disposition if there is a delay in placement. For instance, children waiting to be placed in foster homes are often detained several months until suitable homes are located.

Most states allow the child to be released to custody of parents or guardians so long as they promise to bring the juvenile to additional court appearances. However, police may not approve a release if they believe the child's home is incapable of providing their notion of proper supervision. Although a few states allow youths to be released upon their own signatures or through the posting of bail, this alternative is rarely exercised.

Once the initial decision has been made by law enforcement officials to incarcerate a child, it becomes the responsibility of the juvenile court to review the detention decision. Many states do not require a formal court hearing, and even in those states requiring a detention hearing there exist few guidelines for making the detention decision. Some states require mandatory hearings within twenty-four hours, while others merely suggest that the hearing be conducted "promptly." Indiana requires that unless the juvenile requests a hearing, the right to such judicial review is automatically waived. Tennessee, on the other hand, demands that detention hearings be conducted within three days of the custody date, or that a full adjudicatory hearing be held within seven days. If this requirement is not met, the youth is released from custody.[53] In those jurisdictions which have no statutory requirements for a hearing, one must presume that the detention decision is left to the discretion of judges, probation officers, or court referees. The relatively recent trend to mandatory detention hearings is largely a result of increased criticism of court procedure, coupled with recent Supreme Court decisions. These reform efforts have not proven adequate, since the child is in effect presumed guilty at the intake process. Statutes neither require the court to consider the factual merits of each delinquency petition, nor ensure that the authorities show probable cause to believe that the child committed a delinquent act.

Most states have no laws to regulate the duration of detention. In those few states that do provide standards, maximum lengths of detention range from three days to three months. Little is known about actual compliance with detention restrictions, since most states have no provisions for monitoring detention practices. Too often, those who are detained for the longest periods are children for whom it is difficult to locate suitable adult supervision. Thus, it is not true that those detention facilities for long periods of incarceration are the more serious offenders. More often, status offenders from broken homes are those who become the victims of detention for long periods of time.

Another important issue is that juveniles who are detained may be placed in adult county jails rather than specially designed juvenile institutions. This is of particular interest because the juvenile justice system was specifically intended to prevent the mixing of adult and juvenile offenders. In 1970, the National Jail Census showed that in all but four states, juveniles were incarcerated in adult jails. Sixty-six percent of the seventy-eight hundred juveniles in adult prisons were awaiting adjudication hearings, while 33 percent had been adjudicated as delinquent and were either awaiting court action or were serving jail sentences.[54] Only five states prohibited the placement of juveniles in adult jail facilities as of 1972.[55] Currently, only a small proportion of states provides for a review of the court's decision to transfer a child to an adult jail. In most states with no legal restrictions, the detention or jail transfer decision is left to the discretion of the court practitioner.

As in the area of jurisdiction, legal codes are generally inadequate to end the flagrant abuses in the jailing of juveniles. In fact, the absence of legal restrictions may actually encourage abusive detention practices. Not only is the number of children detained increasing, but the victims of detention are disproportionately selected from the poor and Third World communities.

Thus, the vast majority of the states' statutes do not specify as they do for adults, the availability of bail and other release procedures, the necessity of full judicial hearings on detention decision, or time controls on the duration of juvenile detention. These data leave little mystery as to why a far higher proportion of juveniles are detained than adults charged with the same behavior.[56]

Sarri estimates that the total number of youths placed in both adult jails and juvenile detention institutions approximates one million.[57] Comparing this statistic with the annual figure of 85,109 juveniles incarcerated in training institutions in the same year, one is led to conclude that detention is a serious national problem, even though the conditions in training schools often receive more publicity.[58]

STRUCTURING THE JUVENILE COURT

Following the initiative taken by Illinois in 1899, the states began, one by one, to design their own independent juvenile court systems. The result is that today there is a great diversity in both court structures and the roles of relevant participants. The right of appeal for juveniles was virtually ignored by states in fashioning their court systems due to their paternalistic philosophy. The judge was expected to be sensitive to the specialized needs of youthful offenders, thus assuming a paternal role. This ideology ignores appellate rights for the child, affirming the reluctance of court officials to reform juvenile codes to enable children to challenge court decisions.

Only a slight majority of states provide for appeal of juvenile court decisions to higher courts. In those states permitting appeals, some require that the case be tried *de novo*,* while others provide only for a review of the lower court's findings. Not only is there variation in appeal procedures among states, but one also finds inconsistencies within any given state. In Minnesota, for instance, the juvenile court takes two distinct forms. In most counties in the state, the probate court acts as the juvenile court, with appeals directed to the district court.[59] However, in two Minnesota counties, the district court has created specialized juvenile court structures, which forward all appeals directly to the state supreme court. While there is some question whether appellate decisions are more favorable to a youth when heard in a state supreme court rather than in a lower court, the decision will have greater impact at the supreme court level. If a state supreme court reverses a lower court's decision,

---

*Strictly defined, *de novo* refers to a rehearing of a case, in which new evidence and witnesses may be introduced.

this may establish a precedent that lower courts are obliged to follow. But if, on the other hand, a lower court reverses a case on appeal, the impact of such a decision on state court practice may be minimal. Dineen underscores the importance of varying appeal procedures:

> Since the appellate courts, particularly the highest court of any state, make the definitive interpretations of law in the state, issues and cases which do not progress past the inferior courts often are left unpublicized and with little value as precedent setting decisions. Juvenile law has long suffered from this condition of underdevelopment.[60]

While some states have uniform standards for juvenile courts, other states show considerable internal variation in juvenile court structure. Virginia, for instance, has an intrastate system allowing for the creation of "juvenile district courts" at city and county levels, and "regional [multi-county] juvenile and domestic relations courts," thereby permitting less populous cities and counties to establish widely diverse forms of juvenile court. Such disparities make it exceedingly difficult for the juvenile defense counsel to be aware of court procedures within a particular court. Some courts are far more rigid in their adherence to due process guidelines than others, and avenues for appealing lower court decisions often depend on local policies. In some jurisdictions, two juvenile courts may exist concurrently, with no formal provision to determine which court should initially hear the case. The confusion of juvenile court practice is for attorneys much like playing a high-stakes game without knowing either the rules or who makes them, and often discourages them from taking children's cases.

In view of the ambiguity of court structure, it is remarkable that states even concur that judges should preside over the courts and should possess law degrees. Several states in this respect exceed minimal requirements, specifying that juvenile judges be knowledgeable about family and child problems, or as Florida requires, "be selected with reference to experience in and understanding of problems of children and family welfare."[61] In spite of state codes requiring legal backgrounds for those serving in the court, statistics indicate that the codes have not been adhered to:

> A recent survey of juvenile court judges in the United States revealed that half had no undergraduate degree; a fifth had no college education at all; a fifth were not members of the bar.[62]

An examination of the process by which most juvenile judges are selected may lead one to question their supposed expertise. Since most states provide for the election of judges, justice is essentially linked to the political process. State election boards in many instances fail to indicate that a particular judicial position is on the juvenile court. Typically, a judge is elected to a position in an adult court, subsequently is transferred to the juvenile court by recommendation of senior members of the bench. In those few states that do not choose judges by election, they are appointed by the governor. Whether elected or appointed, judicial positions often represent political rewards for those who have supported the political party currently in power, and may have no relation to the candidate's skills. In some cases, judges may be transferred to the juvenile court as a penalty for incompetence or because of unpopular decisions.

> In some jurisdictions, for example, the juvenile court judgeship does not have high status in the eye of the bar, and while there are many juvenile court judges of outstanding ability and devotion, many are not.[63]

Due to heavy caseloads, as well as an unwillingness by local governments to provide adequate staffing for juvenile courts, some jurisdictions use referees in lieu of juvenile judges. Referees, too, are subject to political pressures, since they are appointed by juvenile judges and serve at the discretion of those judges. Not only do few states require that referees have law degrees, but only a slight majority of states specify *any* educational or professional criteria that referees must meet. In those states with educational requirements, they are so loosely worded that a referee need have no formal education or legal experience. Although referees' decisions are legally recommendations to the presiding judge, the heavy caseloads and the necessity of expediting juvenile justice results in virtual blanket approval, with an uncritical review and pro forma concurrence by the judges. The power of referees varies considerably from state to state. In California, the referee's final decision is binding although a discretionary appeal may be made to the juvenile judge. Mississippi's juvenile statutes provide that juvenile judges need only review the referee's decision in cases resulting in commitment to an institution. In states with no guidelines for referees, local policies are dictated by custom or the traditions of the individual juvenile courts.[64]

ADJUDICATION AND DISPOSITION

Once a child has been referred to the juvenile court, the court must determine the merits of the delinquency petition and see to disposition of the case. The adjudication hearing is the trial stage of the juvenile court process, in which information is presented before the court concerning the juvenile's alleged delinquent behavior. While adult criminal courts have such standards as restrictions on the introduction of hearsay evidence, protection against self-incrimination, the right to jury trial, the right to cross-examine witnesses, and the requirement of establishing guilt beyond a reasonable doubt, these safeguards are not built into the juvenile court.* The defense for

---

*One should not assume that adult courts are free of injustices merely because of more extensive procedural rules. See Robert Blauner, *Racial Oppression in America*, for an excellent discussion of institutional racism in the American justice system, particularly in the area of jury trials.

the absence of such protections in juvenile court is that the court is designed to protect children, and formalization would make the proceedings more like a junior criminal court.

The Supreme Court has not always shared this view. Recent Supreme Court decisions such as *In re Gault* and *In re Winship* provide minimal protection of the constitutional rights of juveniles, especially in adjudication hearings. In the *Winship* case, the Court ruled that juveniles could be judged delinquent only upon establishment of delinquency in a formal judicial hearing. Although juvenile courts initially used the principle of "a preponderance of evidence" to determine delinquency, the Supreme Court held in the *Winship* case that juvenile courts must establish delinquency "beyond a reasonable doubt." As of 1972, three states required that formal hearings be held only in cases where the facts are contested, while other states left formal hearings to the discretion of juvenile judges. Most states bar the public from attending court hearings, and five states permit judges to close hearings to the public at their discretion. Nearly all states empower the judges to determine which parties may be admitted to juvenile hearings.

In a recent decision, *McKiever* v. *Pennsylvania*, the Supreme Court ruled that juveniles do not have a constitutional right to trial by jury.[65] Jury trials for juveniles can be obtained only in those jurisdictions that specifically provide for them in state constitutions or statutes. At this writing, statutory right to a jury trial exists only in ten states, with Alaska providing for jury trial at the judge's discretion.

The type of evidence necessary for a court to reach a determination in a delinquency petition varies considerably from one state to another. Many juvenile codes require social investigations presented by the probation or intake officers. In many instances adjudications are premised on hearsay evidence contained in such investigations, and would not be admissible in an adult criminal court. Social investigations containing information concerning the child's family, school progress, peer associations, and attitudes, may have no bearing on the involvement in an alleged offense. Court personnel claim that such information is vital to a complete picture of the youth's situation and to selection of proper treatment. Although evidence may be presented by prosecutors, probation officers, or other court personnel, most states allow the judges to determine who argues for the delinquency petition. As a result of the *Gault* decision, juveniles have the right to counsel, notice of charges, cross-examination, and protection against self-incrimination. But the *Gault* decision does not provide for the right to choose an attorney independent of parents or guardians.

While recent Court decisions have provided minimal procedural safeguards to juveniles, there is still considerable resistance on the part of those responsible for the legal control of youths. The International Association of Chiefs of Police expressed fear that the juvenile court may be coming "dangerously close to complete adult court procedures."[66] The National Council of Juvenile Court Judges stated that the Supreme Court decisions have excessively formalized juvenile court hearings, thus reducing the possibility of individualized justice.[67] This view was best summarized by Supreme Court Chief Justice Warren Burger in his dissenting opinion in *Winship*:

> What the juvenile court systems need is not more but less of the *trappings* of legal procedure and judicial formalism; the juvenile system requires breathing room and flexibility in order to survive, if it can survive the repeated assaults from this court. . . .
> My hope is that today's decision will not spell the end of a generously conceived program of compassionate treatment intended to mitigate the rigors and trauma of exposing youthful offenders to a traditional criminal court; each step we take turns the clock back to the pre-juvenile court era. I cannot regard it as a manifestation of progress to transform juvenile courts into criminal courts, which is what we are well on the way toward accomplishing.[68]

Adult criminal proceedings are intended to be formal, adversarial hearings, open to the public, in which a judge or jury finds guilt or innocence, based on evidence pertaining directly to the offense in question. Adult defendants are assured the right to legal representation. In contrast, juvenile hearings are informal, and usually closed to the public and to news media. Such hearings are conducted by a referee or judge without a jury, and decisions may be based on information other than evidence related to the case.

If the youth is found delinquent at the adjudication hearing, a disposition hearing is then held. At this stage, the court determines if the youth is to be put on probation, fined, or placed in an institutional setting such as a foster home, a private institution, a boys' ranch, or a state training school. Disposition hearings are analogous to sentencing hearings in adult criminal courts.

But cases are increasingly handled informally prior to adjudication and dispositional hearings, often without consent of parent or child. Recommendation for "informal probation" is made by the probation officer investigating the case. Some observers believe that such informal court intervention results if there is insufficient evidence to support the delinquency petition. While some interpret the trend toward informal processing as a progressive step that will prevent labelling of youths by officials, there is an alternative explanation. That is that the court has been forced to sift out certain cases prior to the adjudication hearing in light of the *Gault* and *Winship* decisions, which require more extensive proof to establish the validity of a petition. In most cases, judicial approval of "informal probation" is contingent upon an admission of guilt by the youths. As a result, youths may admit to delinquent acts of which they are innocent because they fear being sent to a juvenile institution or feel powerless to assert their legal rights.

This informal probation procedure, even as statutorily limited, is of dubious merit. The voluntariness of the child's consent and the truthfulness of his confession are questionable, given the possibilities offered to the juvenile: fixed period of probation rather than possible institutionalization if he chooses the full hearing route. The child must gamble on asserting his rights.[69]

If the youth is found delinquent at the adjudicatory hearing, the juvenile judge may impose a sentence of formal probation, the most common disposition in the juvenile court. Most statutes leave the length of probation to the judge's discretion, supervision ending when the youth reaches twenty-one years of age. Most adult criminal courts set the probation terms at the time of sentencing. On the other hand, those few states requiring a fixed length of time for juvenile probation set a maximum of two years, with periodic review every two months.

If the judge does not choose formal probation, the other dispositional alternatives include placement in a foster home or private institution, commitment to a public juvenile training school, or fines and restitution. The latter sentencing alternatives, for cases involving property damage, clearly favor children from the wealthy families, whose parents are able to compensate victims for property losses. This same class bias is evident in commitments to private institutions, which are primarily available to delinquent children from financially secure families. For example, two boys from differing backgrounds might commit armed robbery. In the case of a wealthy child, his parents can afford to place him in a private institution, such as a prep school or a military academy. Another child, from a working-class home, cannot afford the high "tuition" costs, and may be placed in a state training school.

If youth is institutionalized, the court in most cases relinquishes control over the case, so that release is determined by the staff of the institution. Most states set the maximum length of incarceration at the age of twenty-one or the age of majority. Many states actually allow a youth to be transferred to an adult institution without consent of the juvenile court, requiring only that the youth be viewed as incorrigible prior to the transfer. In some states juvenile statutes permit children to be transferred directly to adult prisons without the court officials specifying reasons for the transfer.

Like other substantive areas of juvenile court law, the area of disposition is characterized by excessively vague guidelines. Judges and the other court personnel involved in these decisions have wide discretion in the sentencing of children. Cases are rarely reviewed, and dispositions are nearly always for indeterminate periods. Once incarcerated in a state institution, the child has few protections against arbitrary or capricious decisions by the institutional staff. There exists no right of appeal, the assumption being that treatment will be provided, even though it is rarely stipulated as a necessary element of incarceration.

The various state juvenile codes, which delineate the statutory provisions for the processing of youth, form the basis of the juvenile justice system. These codes ultimately sanction the decisions made by juvenile justice authorities. The inconsistency and ambiguity of juvenile codes suggest that states do not place a high value on the protection of children. Rather, state laws serve to legitimate pervasive social control over the lives of those children unfortunate enough to be caught in the web of the juvenile system.

PART TWO
THE PROCESSING OF YOUTH

In order to demystify the juvenile justice system, we must go beyond the inadequacies of the juvenile codes. In the following pages, we will examine those responsible for enforcing juvenile codes—police, probation officers, and court personnel. The conclusions of studies in this area are often contradictory. Our knowledge of the behavior of criminal justice practitioners is limited because only recently has significant attention been focused on the social reaction to delinquency.[70] The absence of scientific research in this area is partially due to the orientation of criminologists, who have studied delinquents without critically assessing the role of the police officers and juvenile judges in the creation of delinquent behavior.[71] We will also examine the role of criminal justice practitioners in controlling those members of society who have come to be viewed as "dangerous," due to economic or social status.

JUVENILES AND POLICE IDEOLOGY

Police are typically the first officials of the juvenile justice system a juvenile encounters. Since youths form impressions about the quality of justice they can expect to receive, based on this initial contact, the importance of police reaction to delinquency cannot be overemphasized. Police response ranges from a simple warning to arrest and detention. We will examine the complex of extralegal factors that interact to influence police response to youth.

Assuming the overriding *parens patriae* ideology, one might expect the police to have developed an especially sensitive approach for dealing with children. On the contrary, evidence suggests that youths are treated as harshly as their adult counterparts, with less respect for their constitutional rights. However, the theme of a unique police approach toward juveniles is supported by elite-dominated commissions studying police practices.[72]

> Underlying the special procedures devised for applying the constraints inherent in public authority against juvenile offenders is the hope that they can be rescued from a life of dissolution or crime. As a society, we mean to protect such children from adverse influences, give them a chance to avoid future mistakes and keep them from forever being branded and stigmatized. We treat them with consideration, taking into account their circumstances and the quality of the social response, including the family available to them. . . . Under juvenile law we have even refused to call a crime a crime on the theory that a juvenile has not achieved sufficient social maturity to be legally capable of a crime. And when a juvenile *is* arrested, we often call the arrest something else.[73]

But the expectation that police maintain order and law within society is in sharp conflict with this approach.

> Insofar as the police responsibility to the people of the community is concerned, they are expected to take aggressive and technically competent action to solve crimes—whether the perpetrators be adults or juveniles.[74]

In practice, these conflicting themes in police ideology, social service versus law enforcement, are usually resolved in favor of the more punitive approach. A former policeman has written that police recruits, when leaving the "ivory tower" atmosphere of the training academy, must make a crucial decision upon their first assignments in local precincts. They have to choose between the professional ideals taught in the academy, and the pragmatic stance characterized by a "lock-them-up" attitude.[75] Neiderhoffer found that police develop a cynical and authoritarian attitude toward their work as their length of service increases, and that they eventually reject the social service approach.

> The cynics deride the soft "do-gooder" social service philosophy. The authoritarian reliance on strong-arm methods is attractive to them because when respect for men and principles is absent, force is substituted.[76]

> Some police officials, recognizing this pervasive cynicism among police officers, have attempted to develop police specialists to deal solely with youth. But even with this trend, the fact remains that the vast majority of police-juvenile encounters occur between regular officers and youth. Police have generally been reluctant to support juvenile courts, since they view them as too permissive. One study of the juvenile justice system in California pointed out that police often abuse the civil rights of minors.

> The police are theoretically bound by the philosophy of the juvenile court law, but changes in the law in California have

come about because of abuses attributed to police. The
Governor's Special Study Commission on Juvenile Justice
(1960) in California led to many changes in the law, many of
which were designed to protect the minor's rights.[77]

Critics of police handling of juveniles attribute the tendency of
police to ignore the civil rights of youths to the conflict of controlling crime while attempting to maintain a benevolent treatment
approach.

But the professional orientation of the police department
emphasizes the repression and control of criminal activities
regardless of age and relies upon typified imputations of
"disorganized" or "bad" environments for seeking offenders.
For the police, "robbery" or "rape" has little to do with the
age of the offender or his life circumstances.[78]

Police often make no distinction between delinquents and adult
criminals, although children are not accorded the same legal rights.
Officers can utilize interrogation, search and seizure, and arrest
tactics that would clearly be illegal if used with adult offenders.
Police can take advantage of the fact that restrictions on evidence
and due process are not rigidly adhered to in the more informal
atmosphere of juvenile courts. Cicourel offers these conclusions:

The apprehension of juveniles involves an almost immediate
disregard for the procedures of criminal law; adult arrest, and
search and seizure rules are seldom followed. There are few
formal legal procedures followed, and the problem of evidence
seldom poses a serious issue, inasmuch as a presumption of
guilt is often an integral part of the investigative process. . . .
The police utilize a rather strict social control model for
juveniles they feel are guilty and repeaters; the juveniles are
handcuffed and treated as adults.[79]

There have been extensive efforts to educate rank-and-file police
officers to adopt enlightened approaches in handling juveniles, but
these efforts have had minimal impact. In fact, police officers have
spoken out strongly for more punitive approaches to delinquency.
In view of the historic role of police in controlling the poor segments
of society, there seems little hope that reform efforts can remedy
the situation.* Many people in poor and Third World communities

*The presence of professional and state-organized police forces is a recent
phenomenon. Until the middle of the nineteenth century, metropolitan areas in
America were guarded by contingents of community volunteers who worked in
a watch system. During the first decades of the nineteenth century industrialization expanded, triggering a massive migration of American workers from rural to
urban centers. Waves of European immigrants fulfilled the need for a ready
supply of cheap labor, thus adding to the rapid urbanization of America. It was
feared by those in the upper classes that traditional police tactics would be ineffective in controlling the large working-class sections of large cities. Protection
was felt necessary due to the possibility of increased militancy and insurrection

believe that the relationship of police to juveniles will improve only if there is greater community control over all aspects of policing.

ARREST AND ITS ALTERNATIVES

Only a small percentage of juveniles who are arrested or informally contacted by police are subsequently referred to probation intake, adjudicated, and disposed of by the juvenile court. The importance of the police in triggering the formal referral process is reflected in figure 2, which depicts the way juveniles were processed in California as of 1973. Note that the police were responsible for 87.7 percent of all juveniles referred to probation for further investigation and potential filing of delinquency petitions. Only 30.8 percent of the youths arrested actually had petitions filed in juvenile court. A small fraction of cases (0.2 percent) were sent to the juvenile institutions run by the California Youth Authority (CYA), while formal probation was the most common dispositional alternative of the court (17.8 percent of those arrested).

Data from the United States Children's Bureau indicates that 26.8 percent[80] of all children in juvenile court were charged with status offenses such as truancy, running away, curfew violations, and incorrigibility.† A study of juvenile training institutions found that while 25 percent of the boys had been incarcerated for status offenses, 75 percent of the girls were institutionalized for similar offenses. Sheridan found in a national survey of twenty juvenile training institutions that 30 percent of those incarcerated were committed for status offenses.[81]

Recent national estimates claim that 50 percent of all arrested juveniles are referred to juvenile court by police.[82] In addition, many contacts between police and youth are never formally recorded by state and federal crime reporting agencies, such as the Bureau of Criminal Statistics in California or the F.B.I. Informal contacts typically involve offenses such as curfew violations, running away, or trespassing, which usually result in a warning to the youth, although the police sometimes record these informal contacts for future use.

---

by workers. As Roscoe Pound noted in *An Introduction to the Philosophy of Law,* a central theme of progressive era reformers, which remains intact in current policy ideology, was the necessity for more effective social control forces to meet problems posed by society's increasing complexity and diversification. Professional police forces promoted the assimilation of the poor into the economic and social roles envisioned by those in power. The major concepts of police reform to emerge from the Progressive Era were centralization, crime prevention and deterrence, professionalism, the use of technology, and scientific approaches to law enforcement. For a detailed historical analysis of American police forces see *The Iron Fist and the Velvet Glove: An Analysis of the U.S. Police,* prepared by the Center for Research on Criminal Justice.

†Rosemary Sarri and Yeheskal Hasenfeld in *Brought to Justice? Juveniles, the Courts, and the Law,* p. 71, estimate that status offenses presently comprise almost 40 percent of all juvenile court referrals.

Sources from which delinquent juveniles were originally referred to California probation departments.

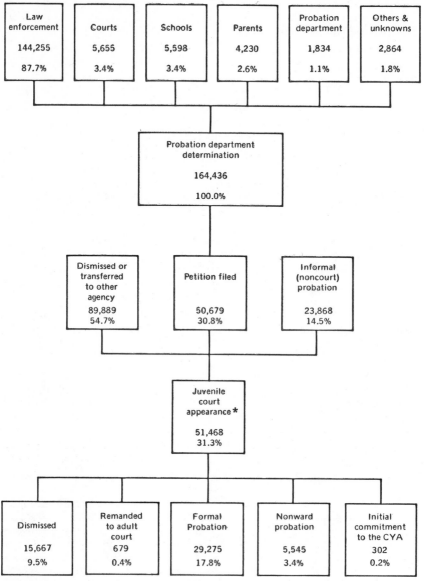

*The difference of 789 cases between the petition filed and juvenile court appearence figures is due to the varying time differential between filing and disposition.

Source: "Juvenile Probation in California, 1973," Bureau of Criminal Statistics, California Department of Justice, 1974.

Figure 2
Juvenile court process in California (based on 1973 data)

Police can use this data to compile a case history of a juvenile, which can be later used if the juvenile commits a more serious crime and the police wish to ensure that the child is judged delinquent.

A study of two police departments in California illustrates the use of such records in generating a history of the juvenile to defend the dispositional decisions of police and probation officers.

> I have focussed upon the significance of officers applying general policies or rules, based upon legal criteria and augmented by a sense of social structure and properties of the interaction scene, to designate acts of delinquency and criminal or ill character structure. The interrogation procedures and written reports constitute oral and written dossiers of juveniles, and provide the conditions for justifying evaluative and dispositional action.[83]

One empirical study reflecting the pervasiveness of unofficial police intervention with youth was Bordua's analysis of the Detroit police.[84] In 1964, the Detroit police department reported a total of one hundred six thousand contacts with juveniles. The youth bureau interviewed 25,645 youths, who were either arrested by them or referred by the patrol division. In addition, 10,157 interviews with minors were conducted for the purpose of gaining evidence. In contrast, the official police statistics recorded only 5,282 juvenile arrests, suggesting that in Detroit, police had informal contacts with youths nine times more frequently than they actually made arrests.[85] Police departments vary considerably in formal versus informal processing of youth. A 1971 survey by the International Association of Chiefs of Police (IACP) in three cities showed wide variations in informal processing of juveniles: the Kansas City, Kansas, police department handled less than 10 percent of its juvenile cases informally; the Topeka, Kansas, police department settled 20 to 30 percent informally; while in Des Moines, Iowa, the police settled 50 to 60 percent informally.[86]

Before discussing the factors that influence whether the police arrest or use other alternatives with youths, let us briefly review the possibilities available to police. There are five basic options once the police decide to intervene:

1 Release, accompanied by a warning to the juvenile.
2 Release, accompanied by an official report describing the encounter with the juvenile.
3 Station adjustment, which may consist of a) release to parent or guardian accompanied by an official reprimand; b) release accompanied by referral to a community youth services agency for rehabilitation; or c) release accompanied by referral to a public or private social welfare or mental health agency.
4 Referral to juvenile court intake unit, without detention
5 Referral to juvenile court intake unit, with detention.

Clearly these alternatives have significant ramifications for the child and his family. Given the wide range of possibilities, it is crucial to examine the factors influencing the selection of treatment alternatives by the police.

Packer points out that the police are confronted with two general models of law enforcement: the *due process* model, and the *crime control* model.[87] Faced with these two conflicting approaches, police tend toward the crime control model, in which their primary function is to deter and control crime by strict enforcement of criminal laws. In this model, police view themselves as forming a "thin blue line" between civilized society and total anarchy. In contrast, most policemen view the due process model, which protects the constitutional rights of all citizens, as an obstacle to law enforcement and the apprehension of criminals. In their eyes, search and seizure restrictions, limits on interrogation, and the legal presumption of innocence merely serve to protect sophisticated criminals from their just punishment. Skolnick summarizes this attitude:

> The ability of known "criminals" to frustrate and harass law enforcement, the commitment of the police department to structures for the apprehending of criminals, and the perceived demands of political superiors for the evidence of the policeman's ability and initiative, all combine, in the context of nontotalitarian norms about the initiative of workers, to bring the policemen to interpret procedural requirements as frustrating the efficient administration of criminal justice.[88]

Thus, the crime control model has become the working philosophy of most policemen, and helps justify violations of individual rights.

Coupled with this reliance on a crime control model, police tend to view themselves as self-confirmed experts or craftsmen in the field of law enforcement. The police appear convinced that they are the best qualified to determine whether an act is delinquent, when to release a youth rather than arrest him, when to detain a youngster, and when it is necessary to disregard certain individual rights in the interest of the community or the well-being of the delinquent.

> [The police officer] sees himself as a craftsman, at his best, a master of his trade. As such, he feels he ought to be free to employ the techniques of his trade, and that the system ought to provide regulations contributing to his freedom to improvise rather than constricting it.[89]

Police feel it would be impossible to catch criminals without an element of flexibility.

The problem of police discretion is not that police are hesitant to assume responsibility for their actions, but rather that they believe more specific guidelines would reduce the tools necessary for crime fighting. Attempts to restrict police discretion have not met with much success. In California, the revised Juvenile Court Law, which

Lemert cites as a revolutionary reform, offers the following ambiguous standard for police in decisions concerning the arrest of juveniles:[90]

> In determining which adoption of the minor he will make, the officer shall prefer the alternative which least restricts the minor's freedom of movement, provided such alternative is compatible with the best interests of the minor and the community.[91]

Within such a broad framework the officer maintains his freedom to act as he sees fit.

Additional examples of restrictions on the exercise of police discretion can be drawn from the training manuals of two metropolitan police departments:

> All other cases in which the youth officer feels that the court action is the most feasible disposition will be brought to the attention (referral or detain decision) of the court.[92]

> Juvenile officers are told to dispose of all juvenile offenders in the way that will be to the best interest of the offender and to society in general.[93]

Police guidelines and model standards do not specify the limits of police discretion, but merely advise the police to act in the best interests of youth and society. Law enforcement departments use this ideology to build public confidence that police will act in a fair and unbiased manner.

A large body of research, mostly conducted in the 1960s, attempted to isolate the factors influencing the selective nature of police arrests. These studies revealed that many police departments neither hire specialized youth officers, nor treat juveniles more benevolently than adult offenders. Since similar ideologies and tactics are used for both youths and adults, the results of studies pertaining to adult arrests also relate to police encounters with juveniles. In general, these studies (some of which are presented in the following sections) indicate that it is not the alleged delinquent behavior that best explains police arrest, but rather variables such as race, class, sex, and community toleration of deviance.

COMMUNITY

An important variable affecting police behavior is the character of the community in which the police operate. Police often make assumptions about communities described as lower class, impoverished, ghettos, or slums. First, such a community is assumed to fulfill what Cicourel terms the "background expectancies" of delinquency and crime. That is, since police have historically concentrated their activities in the lower-class neighborhoods, they have come to expect high crime rates to occur primarily in such areas. Secondly, poor neighborhoods are assumed to lack the local resources necessary to facilitate informal dispositions by police that would reduce the need for arrest, detention, and court referral. While resources for informal processing may or may not exist, police generally presume that poor communities contain only sources of social pathology. For example, although police often assume that one-parent families are inadequate for child-rearing in poor communities they do not necessarily reach similar conclusions about divorced or separated parents in suburbia.

Carter and Lohman, in a study of middle-class delinquency in California, found significant variations in police decisions to arrest or release informally in two middle-class communities when compared with police on a national basis.[94] They offer the following conclusion:

> These data clearly indicate that the "drop-out" rate, i.e., adjustments without the benefit of the formal agencies of juvenile justice, for the middle-class suburban youth at the law enforcement level is considerably above the national and state averages. Almost eighty per cent of the youth with residence addresses in Lafayette or Pleasant Hill had their delinquency disposed of in an informal fashion by the law enforcement agency. This phenomenon, which we will later refer to as "absorption," is also found at the probation department level and within the juvenile court structure.[95]

In this instance, the wealth of the community affects the police's decision to arrest and intervene in a youth's life, such that wealthier communities experience more leniency is the processing of youth than less affluent communities. Police, influenced by respect for members of privileged communities, are often hesitant to inform wealthy residents about the delinquency of their children.* Carter and Lohman evade the obvious conclusion that such an "absorption" of deviance is undemocratic, and that it represents a double standard of justice. They assume that this manner of handling troubled youth can, somehow, be extended to all segments of society without radical changes in the social structure.

A second study of police and probation practices in middle-income communities echoes the findings of Carter and Lohman.[96] In this study Cicourel analyzed how delinquent behavior is conceptualized by various agencies of social control. The research revealed that the wealth and public image of a family determines, to a large extent, the nature of the disposition of a juvenile's case. Middle- and upper-class families were in the best position to project appropriate images, and to provide alternatives such as private tutoring, professional counseling, and private institutionalization. Cicourel explains the exercise of class influence:

---

*Police in upper-class communities may avoid arresting juveniles because they know that adults in such communities have the power and money to influence dismissal of cases. The officers, who rarely reside in wealthy communities, can expect little support in conflicts with legitimate residents.

When parents challenge police and probation imputations of deviance, when parents directly question law enforcement evaluators and dispositions, law enforcement personnel find it difficult to make a case for the criminality in direct confrontation with the family resources and a "rosy" projected future. Imputations of illness replace those of criminality, or the incidents are viewed as "bad" but products of "things" done by "kids" today.[97]

Middle-income families, because of their fear of the stigma imputed to incarceration, mobilize resources to avoid this problem. The family's ability to generate or command resources for neutralizing or changing probation and court recommendations, as in adult cases, is a routine feature of the social organization of juvenile justice.[98]

Not only do class and status influence individual dispositions, but we can also observe how privileged communities succeed in informally handling juvenile cases.

RACE, CLASS, AND DEMEANOR

Several criminological studies have suggested that class, status, and race are of primary importance in selective enforcement of juvenile statutes.[99] This is not surprising, given the historical relationship of police to Third World and poorer communities. But even so, many academic experts and criminologists have failed to confront the integral role of racism and class in police behavior. Some writers have argued that race and class are not the essential factors, and instead stress the importance of the demeanor of the juvenile or the seriousness of the offense to explain how police behavior relates to the social background of the juvenile. For example, Gibbons's survey of studies on the attributes of delinquents makes the following conclusions:

However, there may be more to the picture than has been indicated. The results which we have examined thus far have been drawn from records of various kinds. They seem to show that demographic characteristics of offenders are related to police disposition, but this is because seriousness of offense is correlated with background characteristics. At the same time, we might find that more subtle social factors operate in police decision-making if we were to examine particular instances of officer-offender interaction.[100]

To support his view, Gibbons draws on significant but selective studies based on police records. Specifically, he refers to the works of Goldman, Terry, Bodine, and McEachern and Bauzer, all of which down-play the importance of class and race to explain police arrest decisions.[101] But there are also significant conflicting studies that utilize similar data and methodologies, but reach dissimilar conclusions. On both sides, findings are ambiguous, inconclusive, and contradictory, partially owing to the inadequacies of both data and methods employed. For example, Cicourel points out the weakness of quantitative delinquency research based solely upon police records in generating relationships and conclusions relevant outside academe.[102] While recognizing the limitations and difficulties inherent in such research, let us briefly examine some of the works that suggest that race and class are significant determinants in police arrest behavior and the subsequent processing of children. A number of studies of this issue are presented in their entirety in chapter 6.

A crucial study of race, class, and police-juvenile encounters is Terence Thornberry's comprehensive study "Race, Socioeconomic Status, and Sentencing in the Juvenile Justice System."[103] This study, considers all of the critical points in the juvenile intake process, from arrest to disposition. The data are based on a birth cohort of 9,601 cases collected in Philadelphia by Wolfgang, Figlio, and Sellin.[104] Holding constant both the seriousness of the offense and the number of previous juvenile offenses committed (recidivism), Thornberry found that the relationships of race and class to police disposition remained intact:

> But unlike the previous studies, the present study shows that when the two legal variables were held constant, the racial and SES differences did not disappear. Blacks and low SES subjects were more likely than whites and high SES subjects to receive severe dispositions. Although these differences were more noticeable at the levels of the police and the juvenile court than at the level of the intake hearing, they are generally observable at all three levels.[105]

Williams and Gold in their work entitled "From Delinquent Behavior to Official Delinquency," make an important distinction between delinquent behavior per se and delinquency that comes to the attention of juvenile authorities. In this work the authors compared the discrepancies between official reports and self-reported delinquent behavior in terms of sex, age, race, and socioeconomic status.[106] Although studies of self-reported delinquency have generally discredited the traditional assumption that delinquency is predominantly a lower-class phenomenon, this has been only minimally accepted by sociologists and law enforcement agencies.[107] The President's Commission on Law Enforcement and Administration of Justice, for instance, noted the results of self-report studies, but nonetheless concludes:

> There is still no reason to doubt that delinquency, and especially the most serious delinquency, is committed disproportionately by slum and lower class youth.[108]

Williams and Gold find that while race and class do not affect the incidence of delinquent behavior in self-report analyses, upper-class boys surprisingly appear to commit more serious offenses than their lower-class counterparts.

Comparing police action with various levels of decision making and referral, the same authors report that police do not behave in a racially discriminatory manner at the time of arrest. They find instead that the court intake unit tends to treat blacks more harshly than whites:

> Differential treatment [of blacks] at that point [intake referral] cannot be attributed to the greater seriousness of their offenses compared to whites; for the seriousness of offenses seems to matter little in the determination of court referrals.[109]

Williams and Gold suggest that discriminatory practices may reflect police response to background expectancies or stereotypes when assessing the adequacy of the juvenile's social milieu. They note that police and other social control agents tend to view poor, working-class families and communities as pathogenic and breeding grounds for crime.

In numerous studies of the impact of demeanor on police-juvenile encounters, the central issue is whether demeanor is independent of race and socioeconomic influences. Piliavin and Briar suggest that demeanor is closely associated with race, since they found that an "uncooperative demeanor" was recorded for more than one-third of black juveniles, compared to one-sixth of the white youths contacted by police.[110] Although it is conceivable that blacks may exhibit poor demeanors toward police, this should not be surprising considering the historical use of law enforcement in black communities. The reluctance of black youths to view police as nonthreatening and friendly allows the police to justify an over-zealous punitive approach toward blacks. Police beatings of black citizens have often resulted in victims being charged with "resisting arrest." In the words of one police official:

> If you know that the bulk of your delinquent problem comes from kids who, say, are from twelve to fourteen years of age, when you are out on patrol you are much more likely to be sensitive to the activities of juveniles in this age bracket than older or younger groups. This would be good law-enforcement practice. The logic in our case is the same except that our delinquency problem is largely found in the Negro community and it is these youths toward whom we are sensitized.[111]

The self-fulfilling prophesy of "poor demeanor" on the part of poor and Third World youths results because police are preponderant in their communities, and are prone to be overly sensitive about behavior that they view as hostile. Increasing resistance by the black community to police harrassment has helped to reinforce the prejudices of police as well as to intensify police intervention in such communities.

> These discriminatory practices—and it is important to note that they are discriminatory, even if based on accurate

statistical information—may well have self-fulfilling consequences. Thus it is not unlikely that frequent encounters with police, particularly those involving youths innocent of wrongdoing, will increase the hostility of these juveniles toward law enforcement personnel. . . . They thus serve to vindicate and reinforce officers' prejudices, leading to closer surveillance of Negro districts, more frequent encounters with Negro youths, and so on in a vicious circle.[112]

The interaction of race and demeanor helps explain the over-representation of blacks in official arrest figures, which police use to justify their attitudes toward Third World communities. The fact that police tend to view delinquency as strongly related to race was borne out by Kephart, who found in a survey of police officers in Philadelphia, that 75 percent of the officers overestimated the extent of arrests involving blacks within their precincts.[113] Although there are contradictory findings in the area of police behavior toward Third World communities, the relationship of race and class to police discretion should not be discounted, as some would suggest.

POLICE PROFESSIONALISM AND JUVENILE ARREST DECISIONS

The structure, policies, and political alliances of police departments affect the selective nature of police contacts with juveniles. But with the noted exception of James Q. Wilson's studies "The Police and the Delinquent in Two Cities" and *Varieties of Police Behavior*, little work has been done in this area. In both studies, Wilson examines arrest variations among police departments with respect to each department's structure and professional posture. These variables, which are often complex and contradictory, include the roles of police officers and administrators, community involvement, and political interference. For example, the concept of police specialization to create a distinct juvenile division may or may not alter arrest decisions. One might expect a professional juvenile officer with specialized social service training to be more understanding, lenient, and less discriminatory than a nonprofessional officer lacking such training. Wilson found, on the contrary, that specialized juvenile officers reacted with a more strict law enforcement approach, resulting in more arrests and court referrals made than expected. In another department studied, juvenile specialization created a more uniform approach to delinquency by stressing informal processing within the department.

Despite these contradictions, Wilson maintains that police professionalism is a significant factor in analyzing police departments. He notes that as police professionalism increases, there is a rise in the rates of juvenile arrests. Wilson explains this by arguing that officers in more specialized and professional departments have a more uniformly legalistic approach toward wayward youth. On one hand, more professional officers tend to view all acts of delinquency as requiring formal action, thereby resulting in higher arrest rates. But at the same time, professional officers seem less prone to discriminate against ethnic groups, particularly blacks. Wilson notes that while officers in the "fraternal" police department perceive blacks as especially prone to delinquency, officers in the more professional department were less apt to focus on ethnic background in determining the appropriateness of arrest. The main conclusion of Wilson's work is that merely professionalizing police, as liberal reformers of the progressive era had demanded, will not necessarily result in more humane treatment of wayward youth.

THE ROLE OF PROBATION INTAKE

Once police decide to refer a youth to the juvenile court rather than using the informal alternatives available at the time of arrest, the child is typically referred to an intake unit of the court usually staffed by probation officers. The sole function of intake units is to screen the cases referred by police or other individuals to determine whether a formal delinquency petition should be filed in the court. If a decision is made to file a petition, an investigation of the case is made to determine the validity of the allegations in the petition. The intake officer may decide that the allegations are without basis or that the case may be difficult to substantiate, and suggest that the juvenile be informally processed without further court intervention.

Most juveniles never go beyond the point of police contact, since police are influenced by the fact that cases are subject to the discretion of probation intake officers. Table 1 shows the two basic options of judicial and nonjudicial dispositions available to the intake

Table 1
Method of handling delinquency cases disposed of
by juvenile courts, United States, 1971*

Type of Court	Total	Judicial		Nonjudicial	
	Number	Number	Percent	Number	Percent
Total	1,125,000	475,000	42	650,000	58
Urban	717,000	320,000	45	397,000	55
Semiurban	331,000	110,000	33	221,000	67
Rural	77,000	45,000	58	32,000	42

Source: U.S. Department of Health, Education, and Welfare, Juvenile Court Statistics, 1971.

officers, and the frequency with which these alternatives are chosen. In 1971, 58 percent of all referred cases were disposed of by the intake officer in a nonjudicial manner, without formally filing a petition in court. In California in 1974, there were 178,332 youths referred to the intake unit by police, of which only 53,724 or 30 percent eventually resulted in the formal filing of a petition in juvenile court.[114] Based on data from New York, Mann estimates that 63 percent of juvenile cases are handled in a nonjudicial manner.[115]

There are three basic sources of referral to the intake unit, most commonly the police. Typically, when a juvenile is arrested, he is taken into custody, booked, and often transferred to a local detention unit to await further review by the intake officer. The detention facility can range from the local county jail where the youth may be mixed with adult offenders, to a specialized juvenile detention unit staffed with counselors and other specialists. According to California statistics, of 197,983 juveniles referred to probation intake units in 1972, 139,841 or 71 percent were transported to local juvenile halls or county jails.[116] This figure demonstrates the extent of the use of detention, despite widespread condemnation of such practices by academics and the more enlightened practitioners. In cases where the juvenile is referred to an intake unit, the probation officer must make an immediate decision whether to further detain the child or release him to the custody of an adult. It is significant that the police determine whether the child is referred directly to an intake unit or immediately detained. The result is that the intake unit has no direct control over the flow of referrals, and must rely to a large extent on the judgment of the arresting officer in determining the need for detention and court intervention.

A second referral alternative, the use of citations, is typically employed when the arresting officer believes that the child is a low security risk and can be safely returned home. The intake unit deals with such cases at a later stage.

A third possibility is for the juvenile to be directly referred to the intake unit via nonpolice agencies such as the juvenile court (usually in cases of revocations of probation), public school officials, parents, or the victims of undetected delinquent behavior. California data, which are also typical of other jurisdictions, show that only 13.3 percent of all referrals to intake in 1972 were from nonpolice agencies. Ignoring probation revocations in such referrals, the figure drops to 8.9 percent.[117] These data, coupled with the role of police in limiting the range of decisions open to probation intake officers and other court personnel, further underscore the pivotal role of police in processing juveniles.

JUVENILES AND PROBATION IDEOLOGY

Probation officers handle intake as well as postadjudication treatment. There is widespread belief that probation officers represent a more sophisticated or professionalized approach to juvenile delinquency than police. Juvenile probation officers, who are typically college-educated, are required to write numerous reports—essentially mini-legal briefs—arguing for dispositions that serve both the interest of the youth and that of the community. In order to present intelligent and persuasive arguments before the court, the probation officer must be aware of principles of law relating to jurisdiction, evidentiary restrictions, appeal motions, and dispositional alternatives. The officer must be a therapist able to diagnose the etiology of the delinquent's problem, and administer the appropriate assistance. While probation officers are expected to possess academic skills and broad knowledge, this professional image is invariably negated by the reality of most probation departments.

> The average probation officer's college degree gives him a broader base from which to claim professional status, but the organizational structure of the probation department leaves him few possibilities for change and little difference in pay. The probation department pyramids faster than the military-like police, so that a regular deputy probation officer is restricted in his internal mobility.[118]

Some have argued that probation officers at intake and post-adjudication stages function as highly paid clerical workers, whose primary responsibility is to facilitate the processing of juvenile cases with minimal delay. Probation officers are often burdened with excessive caseloads and departmental priorities emphasizing social investigations, court appearances, and report writing. Probation workers find that too much time is spent on clerical duties, leaving little for counseling and supervising juveniles. Newly recruited officers quickly realize that the professional status is rapidly lost in the monotonous task of churning out reports. Due to the constraints on their work, there is little evidence that probation workers are any more professional in approach than lower echelon criminal justice practitioners.

Some suggest that the probation officers view delinquency from a social work perspective, and thus act as a counter-force to the police approach of strict law enforcement. This view is misleading, since in reality probation departments experience internal conflict about work orientation. Quinney makes a distinction between the politically oriented officers and those with a social work orientation.

> These more recent [social work oriented] workers contrast with the older, politically oriented officers. Though professionally oriented workers are humanitarian and liberal in ideology, recognizing the dignity of the human personality, the older workers, drawing ideological support from a conservative middle-class philosophy of life, act as paternal counselors to the offender (delinquent). The professionally oriented officer, trained in the community by aiding the offender, while the politically oriented officers, relying upon

their common sense and experience, attempt to protect the community from the offender.[119]

Ohlin, Piven, and Pappenfort suggest, in a much earlier study, that there are three types of probation officers, each with its own distinct ideology.[120] One is the punitive officer, who reflects the image of a "frustrated policeman" and tends to view his work as law-enforcement oriented, much like the police ideology. In contrast to this type of probation officer is the "welfare worker," who adopts a social service approach. This type of officer, a relatively recent addition to probation departments, typifies the treatment approach that now pervades the juvenile justice system. Although "welfare workers" are trained in social work theory and often possess graduate social work degrees, they must make decisions that do not relate to a treatment perspective. Finally, there is the "protective" officer, who tends to vacillate between the approaches of the "welfare worker" and "frustrated policeman." This officer appears most concerned about not making any waves and remaining employed.

Despite what is known about probation, there have been suggestions that progressive changes in the juvenile system will originate and find support among probation officers. This view fails to recognize that while the perspective of probation officers differs from that of policemen, probation officers are still agents of control who enforce juvenile laws that preserve the status quo. Unwin, in his study of probation officers' attitudes in California—considered to be one of the more progressive states—found that probation workers favored increased use of detention:

> . . . only 4% of juvenile probation staff felt that minors were detained too often and 52% complained that they were not held as often as they should be. This variation is probably due to the fact that probation officers are the ones who request the detention hearing in the first place, but it does question the often-stated belief that probation officers are the most liberal or "soft-hearted" members of the criminal justice system.[121]

In order for their jobs to be manageable and tolerable, probation officers must work in concert with police. As a result, probation staff is influenced by the police perspective in handling juveniles, stifling the efforts of progressive reformers.

INTAKE ALTERNATIVES

Once juveniles have been referred to the intake unit, there are several alternatives available to the intake officer in disposing of cases. The range of alternatives varies from one jurisdiction to another depending upon factors such as community tolerance, the frequency of referrals, existing alternative resources, and resources available within the juvenile court itself. The latter includes access to detention facilities, probation resources, and the accessibility of juvenile court staff.

There are four basic disposition alternatives at the intake level: (1) dismissal, (2) the filing of a petition, (3) informal probation, and (4) referral to another agency. The most frequently chosen alternative is dismissal of the case: in California, in 1974 over 48 percent of all intake cases were closed by intake officers.[122] The cases of first offenders are sometimes dismissed because it is believed that the youths will not recidivate, while other cases may lack sufficient evidence to substantiate delinquency. Unwin, commenting on California's changing petitioning patterns, offers the following interpretation:

> While the percentage of cases granted informal supervision has remained substantially the same, the proportion of cases closed or referred to other agencies has risen from 46% to 57% and those on which petitions were filed have dropped from 42% to 28%. This probably reflects an increased awareness of the need to have strong "proof" of allegations due to the stronger role of defense attorneys and a tendency to keep as many offenders out of the system as possible.[123]

Unfortunately, we are unable to share Unwin's inference that probation intake units are naturally predisposed to exercise lenient judgments and minimize system penetration. This is similar to the police criticism that probation intake units are overly lenient in handling delinquents. Dismissal helps reduce the congestion of the juvenile court, and does not so much reflect a lenient intent as a need to quickly process large numbers of cases. It should be underscored that there is no empirical evidence that probation officers are more progressive as a result of high dismissal rates. In some jurisdictions, police rates of case dismissal are actually greater than that of probation intake.

The next most frequent probation intake alternative is filing a delinquency petition. In such cases the decision has been made that existing community resources or the youth's family are insufficient, and that the case must be resolved by formal adjudication. This decision often involves consultations with law enforcement agents, especially the district attorney's office, to determine whether the case can be prosecuted. The increased discussions with the district attorney's office reflects recent requirements that juvenile court proceedings insure the basic due process rights of youth. Questions are raised with the district attorney's office concerning the strength of the evidence and potential problems caused by police methods of arresting and detaining the youth. The impact of recent Supreme Court decisions on probation officers is viewed by Unwin as follows:

> The Gault and other decisions which have mandated many legal safeguards for juveniles, the tightening of rules of evidence and

the degree of proof necessary to make a finding, the provision almost routinely of defense counsel, and the general emphasis throughout society on protecting individual rights have vastly altered the traditional "parental" or equity nature of juvenile court to that of an adversary system which is, in many areas, almost identical to that of the criminal courts. The knowledge of the more stringent demands on "proving" a case to obtain a finding has doubtlessly influenced the decision making of the juvenile probation staff at every level.[124]

It should not be assumed that those juveniles who have petitions filed against them necessarily commit the most serious delinquent acts. Figures from California in 1972 reveal that youth charged with "delinquent tendencies" had petitions filed in 23 percent of the cases, whereas the filing rate for youths charged with specific crimes was only slightly higher at 34 percent.[125]

If the decision is made to file a petition, the court must decide whether to continue the youth in detention. The detention hearing is similar, in principle, to bail hearings in adult criminal court; the decision to release turns on the likelihood of the youth's appearing for subsequent court hearings. It is not uncommon for police to use the threat of informal detention to obtain a confession from the youth.[126] Probation officers may also rely on detention to gain additional information from a youth who would be less available if not in custody.

A third alternative in the intake process is informal probation, which essentially means resolving cases without formal court intervention. In California 14.6 percent of all juvenile cases referred to probation in 1974 were disposed of in this manner.[127] Informal probation can take on different meanings depending on the attitude of the local court and probation department. Under informal probation, the child is supervised by either police or probation for a designated period of time, ranging from a few months to several years.[128] The regulations of informal supervision may be just as stringent as the conditions of formal probation. If the youth fails to meet these obligations, it is possible to file a petition based on the original offense and begin the process again. One should not assume that informal probation is always geared to the best interests of the child. Police sometimes use it to develop a network of informers or to gain information to assist them in making further arrests.

Many critics feel that informal probation is an infringement on the youth's constitutional rights. The U.S. Children's Bureau, in its *Standards for Juvenile and Family Courts*, states that "no action which would deny or abridge the rights of a child or parent should be undertaken unless a petition is filed and a hearing held: probation has been defined as a legal status which to a certain extent limits the rights of the child and the parent and, therefore, should only be created by a formal court order."[129]

But a youth who has been placed on informal probation is still vulnerable to having a petition filed. This is particularly noteworthy since one of the primary conditions of informal probation is an admission of guilt. One study notes that most courts impose informal probation only for those children who admit to the offenses. Every case in which the juvenile denies guilt is automatically referred to formal adjudication or has a petition filed.[130] Thus, those children on informal probation have little defense available to them should they fail to meet the conditions of probation.

> Any child on informal probation, even under the model laws, faces the risk that for a considerable period of time formal court action on the original charge will be activated if he violates his probation conditions. Thus, under the present practices, a juvenile may be informally restricted for months, then taken to court on his original petition and again placed on probation or even committed to an institution.[131]

It is likely that commissions, such as the International Association of Chiefs of Police, will continue to recommend that informal probation be used less frequently due to potential infringement on juvenile rights.[132]

The intake alternative used least often is the referral of youth to non-law-enforcement or private agencies. In 1974, in California, only 7.1 percent of all cases were disposed in this fashion.[133] Although it is difficult to determine what types of cases are handled in this manner, one can assume that youth from more affluent families, who have the necessary resources, are more likely to be sent to such agencies.

With these diverse alternatives, the correct option is left largely to the personal preference of the intake officers. Few states provide statutes or written court policies to govern intake decisions. According to the President's Commission on Law Enforcement and Administration of Justice many intake units set policies via "word of mouth."[134] Because informal policies are not made public, there is a danger of arbitrary and unjust decisions, with few opportunities to review such probation determinations.

> Few formal guidelines are available to those who are responsible for exercising discretion in determining which youngsters should be sent deeper into the judicial process. Where these guidelines do exist, their relevance and justice is open to question. . . . Without a system for the periodic review and correction of criteria and decision-making practices in this area, such practices are infrequently refined and frequently arbitrary.[135]

Though one might conclude that the actions of the intake unit are random and contain no overall bias, racial and socioeconomic factors are key influences on intake decisions.

THE INFLUENCES ON INTAKE DECISIONS

As with the studies of police, research reveals correlations between the race and socioeconomic status of youth and juvenile court dispositions. Researchers in this area, however, are reluctant to attribute these relationships to racism or class biases, emphasizing instead intervening factors. In a review of the literature by Gibbons, which includes such studies as Lemert and Rosberg, Shannon, Terry, Axelrad, Cohn, Cross, and Alexander, the author acknowledges evidence that probation recommendations made at the intake level are based on the race or class position of the child.[136] But Gibbons qualifies this by stating that delinquent behavior itself is the key factor in such decisions.

> What are we to conclude from these studies of probation dispositions? . . . Youths who have been involved in offenses which arouse members of the community, who commit law violations which result in sizable financial suffering to the victims, and who are repeaters, are the ones who most often get placed on the transmission belt to the training school. Ethnic characteristics, sex, age, and other demographic variables seem to be related to dispositions through their interconnection with offense variances.[137]

Cohen in a study of dispositions of three juvenile courts draws a similar conclusion:

> Our study has yielded no empirical evidence to sustain the charge that [youth of] lower socioeconomic status are systematically accorded the most severe treatment by agents of the juvenile court. Similarly, there is no direct evidence to suggest minority youths are the objects of discriminatory treatment.[138]

But there are basic methodological problems inherent in such conclusions. Variables such as "demeanor" or the "seriousness of the offense" are inappropriately viewed as independent of race or class position, despite empirical evidence to the contrary. In addition, at the stage of juvenile court intervention one is left with a relatively homogeneous population with respect to race and socioeconomic status. As Cohen found in his study, it is statistically difficult to account for significant levels of intraclass variation in court dispositions. But, despite the problems associated with analysis of court decisions, there are studies that illustrate the relationship of race and class to intake dispositions. We shall briefly review several studies that discuss the role of nonlegal variables in intake dispositions.

Gibbons cites Cohn's study as an explanation for the absence of demographic variables in intake dispositions, but that study in fact reports that females and blacks were sent to institutions more often than white boys. Cohn explains that a high incidence of female sexual misconduct was responsible for their commitments, while blacks were institutionalized more often due to the seriousness of their delinquent acts and because they tended to be defined as coming from socially deprived backgrounds. Cicourel, and Harari and Chwast have shown that females, lower-class, and Third World youth are often stereotyped in such a way that they appear to social control agents as delinquents.[139]

Thomas and Sieverdes sought to clarify the confusion and contradiction resulting from studies of probation intake.[140] In their study of 346 juvenile case dispositions, they attempted to isolate the most significant legal and nonlegal variables affecting juvenile court dispositions. Their preliminary analysis suggested that the seriousness of the most recent offense was the best predictor of disposition. However, nonlegal factors such as age, the number of codefendants, race, family stability, and sex also exerted an influence on the disposition. Controlling for these nonlegal variables, the researchers found that the seriousness of the offenses varied in explanatory power depending on interaction with other nonlegal variables. For example, it was found that the relative seriousness of the offense was greatest for a black male from a lower-class background, with a prior record. This finding suggests the significance of the stereotypes that social control agents impose on certain delinquents.

> These findings lead us to conclude that both legal and extralegal factors are being taken into consideration in the determination of whether to refer a given case for a formal hearing in the juvenile court. Indeed some social factors appear to provide an "insulation" which may inhibit such referrals.[141]

Their study affirmed the significance of the delinquent behavior itself, while demonstrating the relative importance of nonlegal variables in intake decisions.

Another valuable study on the impact of race and socioeconomic status in juvenile court decisions is Thornberry.[142] While controlling for both the "seriousness of the offense" and "recidivism," Thornberry found that the associations between race and socioeconomic status, and court decisions at both the intake and juvenile court level do not disappear. Thornberry draws the following conclusion:

> Finally, the present findings should be related to the assumption often found in the theoretical realms of criminology, namely, that blacks and members of low SES are treated more harshly than whites and high SES subjects in the juvenile justice system. Clearly, the findings of the present study are in agreement with that assumption.[143]

After reviewing previous research findings that conflict with his results, Thornberry concludes that while he is in disagreement with them, there are no overt methodological reasons to account for the discrepancies. The reader is reminded to be cautious in embracing the conclusions of any single study in this complex area of juvenile justice.

THE ROLE OF THE COURT

Although the number of youths affected by formal court proceedings is relatively small due to screening by police and intake staff, this stage of the juvenile justice process has grave consequences for the child. Labelling theorists view the role of the court as critical, since it can impose a stigma that will remain with the youth throughout adult life. Although the term delinquency was envisioned as a means of reducing the stigma of youthful crimes, it has come to be synonymous with adult crimes in the eyes of many. State and federal crime reporting agencies maintain complete files on all arrested youth, which crime control agencies routinely use in evaluating cases and selecting appropriate dispositions. Thus, a determination of delinquency is often redefined by other agencies to infer criminal behavior that a youth eluded only because of his age.

Unfortunately, there is little data available concerning the behavior of prosecutors, public defenders, referees, and juvenile judges to aid an analysis of these court personnel. The prestige, power, and status of the court have often inhibited social scientists from studying its decision making processes.

Apart from the inherent assumptions of *parens patriae*, benevolence, and paternalism, the court has a latent goal of expeditious processing of youth with minimal interagency conflict. Due to the burden of excessive caseloads, the court is forced to function as a coordinating unit in order to keep abreast of its statutory obligations. The emphasis is upon harmonious relationships, as was envisioned by early advocates of the public defender system:[144]

> The defense of the accused under a public defender law would require no more time nor effort than is now consumed. Indeed quite the contrary, for orderly arrangement of cases for trials would be far better effected between opposing offices than between a district attorney and a dozen lawyers with conflicting business.[145]

> The proper duty of the prosecuting attorney is not to secure a conviction, but to convict only after a fair and impartial trial. Upon the same principle it is not the duty of the public defender to secure aquittals of guilty persons, but to endeavor to ascertain the true facts and go to trial upon those facts, *the aim of both officials would be to go to work in harmony* to bring out a just administration of the law (emphasis added).[146]

A study of a public defender agency showed that all the actors in the court's adjudication and dispositional processes were highly dependent on each other's cooperation for the court to function in an orderly manner.[147] Juvenile defendants usually met with their assigned lawyers for a few minutes prior to the formal hearing, with the bulk of negotiation taking place outside the courtroom. The ability of the public defender and the prosecutor to play their roles and maintain the atmosphere of justice depended on their willingness to accept unreasonable decisions, with the assurance that in the long run such cooperation would ensure job stability and a more tolerable work atmosphere.

> [The public defender's] performance is judged by his superiors in a variety of ways. . . . He is expected to be properly prepared in court, not to ask for an unreasonable number of continuances, not to antagonize unnecessarily the state's witnesses, and not to offend the judges by requesting a change of venue on the grounds of prejudice. The public defender knows that assessments of his competence by judges will ultimately reach his boss.[148]

Similar pressures are imposed upon all members of the juvenile court, and the need for such compromises has increased with the expansion of juvenile procedural rights. The prosecutor and public defender are obliged to consult with one another prior to making appearances in court. This consultation extends to the intake unit, as the probation officer routinely consults with the district attorney's office prior to filing a petition.

> By law the district attorney is given no decision-making power in juvenile court. Only the probation officer can file a petition to bring a minor before the court. However, because of the almost routine presence of defense counsel in contested cases [in California] and the more rigorous demands on the type and sufficiency of evidence needed to sustain an allegation many probation departments consult regularly with the district attorney as to whether or not they have evidence to file a petition and, if so, what charges should be filed.[149]

The interlocking interests of defense and prosecution have not resulted in more equitable treatment for children. Some authors, such as Lemert, advance evidence to support the positive effect of attorneys in gaining favorable dispositions for young clients.[150] A closer analysis of Lemert's data reveals that lawyers have been most successful in negotiating dispositions, but have had negligible impact on avoiding the court's control over youth. Moreover, youth represented by counsel are more likely to be detained than those without attorney representation, since they are viewed as contesting the court and disrupting normal procedure.[151]

Although some have expressed fear that the presence of lawyers introduces an adversary character to juvenile court proceedings, there is little data to support this concern. While the court process may appear adversary in nature, attention is primarily focused on the efficient handling of children with minimal conflict and delay.

> Mutual cooperation by all court personnel makes possible the management of large caseloads. . . . The public defender must be careful not to obstruct the efficient processing of cases, for the other court functionaries are depending upon him to help finish or expedite the court call for the day. . . . Aside from the

role cooperation plays in facilitating the mechanics of the proceeding, it also makes the entire process more personally tolerable for everyone involved. Court interaction is intensely focused upon deciding the fate of other's lives and this responsibility is made impossible if conflict is the norm underlying the task at hand. The court functionaries see themselves as colleagues rather than adversaries, for "the probability of continued future relations and interaction must be preserved at all costs."[152]

This emphasis on the efficiency of the system is far removed from the ideal of the court acting on behalf of the child.*

COURT DISPOSITIONAL ALTERNATIVES

The court has two basic alternatives: either to find the child "not delinquent" and remove him from the jurisdiction of the court, or to find the child "delinquent" and make a dispositional judgment. Some states provide for special adjudication hearings, whose primary intent is to ascertain the legitimacy of the petition's allegations. In many instances, the judge is informally advised about a case by both prosecutor and public defender, so that the decision is made with involvement on the part of the youth. If the child is found delinquent, a separate dispositional hearing may be held at a later date, depending upon the policies of the court in a particular locale. Many states combine dispositional and adjudication hearings in the interest of saving time. California, among other states, strictly forbids introduction of presentence information in adjudication hearings.[153] Judges and referees have been known to base their findings on assessments of the child's social history made by probation officers, which may resemble hearsay evidence.

If the child is found delinquent, the court has a narrow range of dispositional alternatives available from which to select an appropriate treatment. These include probation, foster-home placement, incarceration for an indeterminate period, fine or restitution, and informal supervision. As previously noted, in our discussion of legal codes, the juvenile system is unique in that the period of court supervision is continuous through the age of maturity. Those youths placed on probation, in foster homes, or on informal probation, may have their disposition reviewed any time the court feels the child has violated the terms of the original disposition. This control is virtually unlimited, since a new hearing is not required to revoke prior decisions. Revocation is not necessarily predicated on subsequent delinquency, but may result from a youth's failure to

---

*Barak, *The Public Defender,* shows that the purpose of the public defender movement was not so much to help the poor by providing counsel. Rather the public defender idea was designed to make the court process more efficient, and to unburden lawyers from the financially unrewarding task of representing indigent defendants under the old assigned counsel system.

maintain regular contacts with probation officers, from family difficulties, or from school truancy. There is no requirement that facts
in a revocation request be verified, and often such cases receive informal disposition based on the probation officer's interpretation of
the case.

One of the primary factors believed to influence the court's
dispositions is the seriousness of the delinquent act. Even critics of
juvenile justice have assumed a positive correlation between the
seriousness of the offense and the disposition.

> In the case of minor first offenders, a warning and release are
> the usual disposition. Probation is more typically used for the
> second-time offenders or when the offense is more serious. . . .
> Institutional commitment, on the other hand, is described as
> reserved for the recidivists and hard-core offenders whose
> response to milder treatments is predictably unfavorable.[154]

However, a study of juvenile court dispositions in New York
during 1965 refutes assumptions about the relationship between the
seriousness of delinquency and disposition, and concludes:

1   PINS (persons in need of supervision, such as status of-
    fenders) are more likely to be detained than serious delin-
    quents (54 percent versus 31 percent).
2   Once detained, PINS are twice as likely to be detained for
    more than thirty days than serious delinquents (50 percent
    versus 25 percent).
3   The length of incarceration in juvenile prisons is two to
    twenty-eight months for the serious delinquents versus
    four to forty-eight months for PINS. The mean length of
    imprisonment is 10.7 months for serious delinquents versus
    16.3 months for PINS.
4   PINS are more likely to receive harsh dispositions and be
    sent to juvenile prisons than serious delinquents (26 per-
    cent versus 23 percent).
5   Nationally, Lerman estimates that 40 to 50 percent of the
    residents of juvenile institutions are status offenders or
    PINS, who are warehoused with the "more serious" of-
    fenders.[155]

If, as Lerman's data suggests, the seriousness of the delinquent
act is not the primary influence on the court's decision, it is necessary
to ascertain the main factors. Platt, Schectner, and Tiffany, in their
study of the public defender's office, suggest four criteria that are
employed by the defender's office to determine how a case will be
pled:

1   Does the juvenile claim to be innocent?
2   Is the alleged offense of a serious nature?
3   Does the juvenile have a criminal record?
4   Is the juvenile a "good kid" or a "bad kid?"[156]

The authors illustrate how these factors intertwine, and affect whether the public defender will plead the case guilty or innocent. They conclude that the public defender's decision is largely based on a subjective character judgment of the juvenile.

> The determination of whether a client is "good" or "bad" is, thus, crucial to the public defender's consideration of a case. How does he decide to apply these judgmental labels? To a great extent, he looks for criteria which positively indicate moral and social propriety.[157]

Here, once again, the notion of demeanor plays a crucial role in criminal justice decision making. These authors conclude that racial and economic discrimination does not result simply because most of the defendants are from the lower socioeconomic classes. Rather, judgments of character are derived from stereotypes prevalent in the dominant culture. Thus, the child treated most favorably by the court is the one who most successfully projects characteristics, such as charm and personality, which are viewed as positive traits in the white culture. Even the outward appearance of the client may be crucial in determining how a public defender responds to a given case.[158]

It is undeniable that because of discrimination based on race and class, there are a disproportionate number of Third World and poor people involved at the court adjudication stage. Although the impact in sheer numbers may not be as significant as at earlier stages, racial and class biases continue to operate at the court hearing. Thornberry's study lends empirical support to this position.[159] Examining dispositional institutionalization and probation placement, Thornberry sought the discriminating variables that explain variance in court dispositions. Using controls for both the seriousness of the delinquent act and prior record, Thornberry found that, at the court disposition stage, blacks are treated more severely than whites, and juveniles of low socioeconomic status are treated more harshly than those of high socioeconomic status. Though our analysis of the juvenile court is limited by a paucity of data, our suspicion is that the courts are similar to other juvenile control authorities in terms of racial, sexual, and socioeconomic biases.

CONCLUSION

We set two goals for this chapter. First, we intended to familiarize the reader with the juvenile justice system—its philosophy, the various state juvenile laws, and the practitioners who make the system work. Secondly, we offered a critical perspective on the juvenile justice system. Our analysis paints a dismal picture. Juvenile laws are vaguely worded and inconsistently applied, permitting extensive abuses in the handling of children by social control agencies whose discretion is largely unchecked. Instead of protecting children from injustices and unwarranted state intervention, the opposite effect has occurred. The practices and procedures of juvenile justice agents reflect class and racial prejudices that extend to the larger social order, and fall disproportionately on Third World and poor people.

These conclusions are not novel. Many students and practitioners within the juvenile court share this critical perspective. The vital question is "What is to be done?" Most critics of the juvenile court continue to offer narrow reform measures that do not confront the relationship between inequities in the juvenile justice system and inequities within society. Present innovations consist primarily of diversion, deterrence, decriminalization, and deinstitutionalization. Although these concepts embrace a critical perspective on the present justice system, they imply that through social planning strategies, the juvenile justice system can be transformed into a humane and equitable process. In short, they are merely calling for another era of child saving, using increased national planning and scientific management techniques.

Our analysis suggests that the injustices of this system of controlling youth can be remedied only through broad changes in society. These structural and economic forces that created such abuses of control will have to be confronted. The quest for juvenile justice is inextricably tied to the pursuit of social justice. Liberal reforms will continue to fail, as they have in the past, if they do not address the maldistribution of power and resources throughout society.

NOTES

1 U.S., Department of Health, Education, and Welfare, *Juvenile Court Statistics*, p. 1.

2 Edwin M. Lemert, *Instead of Court: Diversion in Juvenile Justice*, p. 1.

3 See Ivan F. Nye, James F. Short, Jr., and Virginia J. Olson, "Socioeconomic Status and Delinquent Behavior"; Edmund Vaz, *Middle-Class Juvenile Delinquency*; Martin Gold, *Delinquent Behavior in an American City*; James A. Gazel and G. Thomas Gitchoff, *Youth, Crime, and Society*; and Jay R. Williams and Martin Gold, "From Delinquent Behavior to Official Delinquency." Specifically, Williams and Gold, in their national study of self-report delinquency among 13-16 year-olds, found ". . . in no case is the relationship between social status and delinquent behavior strong" (p. 217).

4 See, for example, Anthony Platt, "The Triumph of Benevolence: The Origins of the Juvenile Justice System in the United States"; or Alexander Liazos, "Class Oppression and the Juvenile Justice System."

5 An excellent case study of the juvenile justice system is that of Ted Morgan, "They Think, 'I can kill because I'm 14'"; and Paul Lerman, "Child Convicts."

6 Eileen Younghusband, "Dilemma of the Juvenile Court."

106

7 See Barry Krisberg, *Crime and Privilege*; and Richard Quinney, *Critique of Legal Order.*

8 See Alexander Liazos, "The Poverty of the Sociology of Deviance: Nuts, Sluts and Preverts"; and Alex Thio, "Class Bias in the Sociology of Deviance."

9 See William Ryan, *Blaming the Victims*, for a good discussion of the limits of liberal reformism.

10 Edwin M. Lemert, *Social Action and Legal Change: Revolution Within the Juvenile Court.*

11 For excellent critiques of liberal conceptions of law, see Richard Quinney, *Critique of Legal Order* and Isaac Balbus, *The Dialectics of Legal Repression.*

12 Roscoe Pound, *An Introduction to the Philosophy of Law; Outline of Lectures on Jurisprudence; Social Control Through Law;* "The Rise of Socialized Criminal Justice"; and "A Survey of Social Interests."

13 Pound, "Social Interests," p. 39.

14 A review of the conflict perspective can be found in the works of Richard Quinney, *Crime and Justice in Society, The Social Reality of Crime, Criminology: Analysis and Critique of Crime in America*; Austin Turk, *Criminality and the Legal Order*, "Conflict and Criminality"; and George Vold, *Theoretical Criminology*. An excellent summary and critique of the conflict theorists is provided by Ian Taylor, Paul Walton, and Jock Young, *The New Criminology.*

15 See William Chambliss, "A Sociological Analysis of the Law of Vagrancy"; Troy Duster, *The Legislation of Morality*; Joseph Gusfield, *Symbolic Crusade: Status Politics and the American Temperance Movement.*

16 Lemert, *Revolution Within the Juvenile Court.*

17 John Wildeman, "The Crime Fighters."

18 Richard W. Kobetz and Betty B. Bosarge, *Juvenile Justice Administration*, p. iii.

19 Krisberg, *Crime and Privilege.*

20 For example, James Q. Wilson, *Thinking About Crime*; Ernest van den Haag, *Punishing Criminals: Concerning A Very Old and Painful Question*; Norval Morris, *The Future of Imprisonment*; or Ralph Schwitzgebel, *The Development and Legal Regulation of Coercive Behavior Modification Techniques with Offenders.*

21 Krisberg, *Crime and Privilege*, pp. 76-77.

22 135 F. Supp. 224 (C.C.C. 1955).

23 Elliot Currie, *Managing the Minds of Men: The Reformatory Movement 1865-1920.*

24 Greg Barak, "In Defense of the Rich: The Emergence of the Public Defender Movement."

25 Nicholas N. Kittrie, *The Right to be Different: Deviance and Enforced Therapy.*

26 Ibid., pp. 114-15.

27 California Department of Justice, *Crime and Delinquency in California, 1974*, p. 30.

28 Levin and Sarri, *Juvenile Delinquency*, pp. 11-12.

29 "Standard Juvenile Court Act—Text and Commentary," *National Probation and Parole Association*, p. 8.

30 Kobetz and Bosarge, *Juvenile Justice Administration*, p. 37.

31 Aaron Cicourel, *The Social Organization of Juvenile Justice*; Robert Emerson, *Judging Delinquents: Context and Process in Juvenile Court*; Irving Piliavin and Scott Briar, "Police Encounters with Juveniles"; Terence Thornberry, "Race, Socioeconomic Status, and Sentencing in the Juvenile System"; and Meda Chesney-Lind, "Judicial Paternalism and the Female Status Offender" are but a few of the numerous studies documenting such biases.

32 Frederick Sussman, *Law of Juvenile Delinquency*, p. 21.

33 James E. Starrs, "A Sense of Irony in Southern Juvenile Courts," p. 129.

34 U.S., Commission on Civil Rights, *Report*, p. 174.

35 Kittrie, *Deviance and Enforced Therapy*, pp. 120-21.

36 For example see Thornberry, "Sentencing in Juvenile Justice"; and Marvin Wolfgang and Bernard Cohen, *Race and Crime*.

37 Kent v. United States, 383 U.S. 541 (1966).

38 Jerome Skolnick, *Justice Without Trial: Law Enforcement in a Democratic Society*.

39 National Council on Crime and Delinquency, "Transfer of Cases between Juvenile and Criminal Courts—A Policy Statement."

40 Kittrie, *Deviance and Enforced Therapy*, pp. 167-68.

41 California, Governor's Special Study Commission on Juvenile Justice, *A Study of the Administration of Juvenile Justice in California*, part 1, p. 12.

42 State v. Mills (1959).

43 President's Commission on Law Enforcement and Administration of Justice, *The Challenge of Crime in a Free Society*, p. 234.

44 U.S. Department of Justice, Law Enforcement Assistance Administration, *Children in Custody: A Report on the Juvenile Detention and Correctional Facility Census of 1971*.

45 National Council on Crime and Delinquency, "Corrections in the United States."

46 California Department of Justice, *Juvenile Justice Administration in California, 1974*, p. 3.

47 Rosemary C. Sarri, *Under Lock and Key: Juveniles in Jails and Detention*, p. 4.

48 Wisconsin Division of Family Services, *Profile of Juveniles in Wisconsin: 1974*.

49 See Anthony Platt, Howard Schechter, and Phyllis Tiffany, "In Defense of Youth: A Case Study of the Public Defender in Juvenile Court"; Helen Sumner, "Locking Them Up"; and Sarri, *Juveniles in Jails and Detention*.

50 See Lerman, "Child Convicts"; and Sarri, *Juveniles in Jails and Detention*.

51 Sarri, *Juveniles in Jails and Detention*, p. 45.

52 Ibid.

53 Levin and Sarri, *Juvenile Delinquency*, p. 30.

54 U.S. Department of Justice, *National Jail Census, 1970: A Report on the Nation's Local Jails and Type of Inmates*.

55 Levin and Sarri, *Juvenile Delinquency*, p. 32.

56 Ibid.

57 Sarri, *Juveniles in Jails and Detention*, p. 64.

58 See Paul Lerman, *Community Treatment and Social Control: A Critical Analysis of Juvenile Correctional Policy*.

59 Levin and Sarri, *Juvenile Delinquency*, p. 38.

60   John Dineen, *Juvenile Court Organization and Status Offenses: A Statutory Profile*, p. 2.

61   Levin and Sarri, *Juvenile Delinquency*, pp. 43-44.

62   President's Commission, *Challenge of Crime*, p. 217.

63   Ibid., p. 216.

64   Levin and Sarri, *Juvenile Delinquency*, p. 46.

65   McKiever v. Pennsylvania, 403 U.S. 528 (1976).

66   Kobetz and Bosarge, *Juvenile Justice Administration*, p. 191.

67   National Council of Juvenile Court Judges, "Handbook for New Juvenile Court Judges."

68   In re Winship, 397 U.S. 358 (1970).

69   Levin and Sarri, *Juvenile Delinquency*, p. 53.

70   Many credit the labelling perspective for encouraging research on criminal justice practitioners. See, for example, Howard Becker, *Outsiders: Studies in the Sociology of Deviance*; Edwin Lemert, *Social Pathology*; and Richard Quinney, *The Social Reality of Crime*.

71   Anthony Platt's *The Child Savers* provides an excellent analysis of the narrow scope of delinquency research, as does David Matza, *Delinquency and Drift*.

72   See Quinney, *Critique of Legal Order*, pp. 60-75.

73   Kobetz and Bosarge, *Juvenile Justice Administration*, p. 111.

74   Ibid., p. 110.

75   Arthur Niederhoffer, *Behind the Shield: The Police in Urban Society*, p. 52.

76   Ibid., p. 227.

77   Cicourel, *The Social Organization of Juvenile Justice*, p. 62.

78   Ibid., p. 68.

79   Ibid., p. 69.

80   U.S. Department of Health, Education, and Welfare, Children's Bureau, *1964 Juvenile Court Statistics*, p. 10.

81   William H. Sheridan, "Juveniles who Commit Noncriminal Acts: Why Treat in a Correctional System?"

82   Dale Mann, *Intervening with Convicted Serious Juvenile Offenders* (Santa Monica, California: Rand Corporation, 1976).

83   Cicourel, *The Social Organization of Juvenile Justice*, p. 336.

84   David S. Bordua, "Recent Trends: Deviant Behavior and Social Control."

85   Ibid.

86   International Association of Chiefs of Police, *Survey of Police-Juvenile Operations*.

87   Herbert L. Packer, "Two Models of the Criminal Process."

88   Skolnick, *Justice Without Trial*, p. 183.

89   Ibid., p. 196.

90   Lemert, *Social Action and Legal Change*.

91   California Revised Juvenile Court Law, Section 626 W & I, 1961.

92   Chicago Police Department, *Manual of Procedure: Youth Division*, Sec. II, Part I.

93   Wichita Police Department, *Duty Manual*, Sec. 61.

94   Robert Carter and Joseph Lohman, *Middle-Class Delinquency: An Experiment In Community Control*.

95   Ibid., p. 20.

96 Cicourel, *The Social Organization of Juvenile Justice.*

97 Ibid., p. 243

98 Ibid., p. 331.

99 For example, Skolnick, *Justice Without Trial*; Cicourel, *The Social Organization of Juvenile Justice*; and Wilson, *Varieties of Police Behavior.*

100 Don C. Gibbons, *Delinquent Behavior*, p. 39.

101 Nathan Goldman, *The Differential Selection of Juvenile Offenders for Court Appearance*; Robert M. Terry, "Discrimination in the Handling of Juvenile Offenders by Social Control Agencies"; George E. Bodine, "Factors Related to Police Dispositions of Juvenile Offenders"; and A. W. McEachern and Riva Bauzer, "Factors Related to Disposition in Juvenile Police Contacts."

102 Cicourel, *The Social Organization of Juvenile Justice.*

103 Thornberry, "Sentencing in the Juvenile Justice System."

104 Wolfgang, Figlio, and Sellin, *Delinquency in a Birth Cohort.*

105 Thornberry, "Sentencing in the Juvenile Justice System," p. 97.

106 This study is in the tradition of self-report studies of delinquency, such as Nye, Short, and Olson, "Delinquent Behavior"; Lamar T. Empey and Maynard L. Erickson, "Hidden Delinquency and Social Status"; John P. Clark and Eugene P. Wenninger, "Socio-Economic Class and Area as Correlates of Illegal Behavior Among Juveniles"; and Albert J. Reiss, Jr., and Albert Lewis Rhodes, "The Distribution of Juvenile Delinquency in the Social Class Structure."

107 Edwin Schur, *Labeling Deviant Behavior: Its Sociological Implications.*

108 President's Commission, *Challenge of Crime*, p. 57.

109 Williams and Gold, "Delinquent Behavior," p. 226.

110 Irving Piliavin and Scott Briar, "Police Encounters with Juveniles."

111 Ibid., p. 212.

112 Ibid., p. 213.

113 William Kephart, *Racial Factors and Urban Law Enforcement*, pp. 94-95.

114 California Department of Justice, *Juvenile Justice, 1974*, p. 11.

115 Mann, *Juvenile Offenders*, pp. 8, 9.

116 Ernest A. Unwin, *California Correctional System Intake Study*, p. 26.

117 Ibid., p. 25.

118 Cicourel, *The Social Organization of Juvenile Justice*, p. 95.

119 Quinney, *The Social Reality of Crime*, p. 171.

120 Lloyd Ohlin, Herman Piven, and Donald Pappenfort, "Major Dilemmas of the Social Worker in Probation and Parole."

121 Unwin, *California Intake Study*, p. 46.

122 California Department of Justice, *Juvenile Justice, 1974*, p. 5.

123 Unwin, *California Intake Study*, p. 27.

124 Ibid., p. 31.

125 Ibid., p. 30.

126 Cicourel, *The Social Organization of Juvenile Justice.*

127 California Department of Justice, *Juvenile Justice, 1974*, p. 7.

128 Kobetz and Bosarge, *Juvenile Justice Administration*, p. 256.

129 William Sheridan, "Juvenile Court Intake," p. 58.

130 Elyce Ferster and Thomas Courtless, "Legislation: The Beginning of Juvenile Justice, Police Practices, and the Juvenile Offender."

131 Ibid., p. 131.

132 Kobetz and Bosarge, *Juvenile Justice Administration*, p. 319.

133 California Department of Justice, *Juvenile Justice, 1974*, p. 21.

134 President's Commission on Law Enforcement and Administration of Justice, *Task Force Report: Juvenile Delinquency and Youth Crime*, p. 21.

135 Virginia M. Burns and Leonard W. Stein, "The Prevention of Juvenile Delinquency," in President's Commission on Law Enforcement and the Administration of Justice, *The Challenge of Crime in a Free Society*, p. 396.

136 Gibbons, *Delinquent Behavior*, pp. 61-67; Edwin Lemert and Judy Rosberg, "The Administration of Justice to Minority Groups in Los Angeles County"; Lyle W. Shannon, "Types and Patterns of Delinquency Referral in a Middle-Sized City"; Robert Terry, "Discrimination in the Handling of Juvenile Offenders by Social Control Agencies"; Francesca Alexander, "A Preliminary Report on a Pilot Investigation of Some Social-Psychological Variables Influencing the Probation Officer"; Sidney Axelrad, "Negro and White Male Institutionalized Delinquents"; Yona Cohn, "Criteria for the Probation Officer's Recommendation to the Juvenile Court"; and Seymour Z. Cross, "The Prehearing Juvenile Report: Probation Officer's Conceptions."

137 Gibbons, *Delinquent Behavior*, p. 58.

138 Lawrence E. Cohen, *Delinquency Dispositions: An Empirical Analysis of Processing Decisions in Three Juvenile Courts*, pp. 53-54.

139 Cicourel *The Social Organization of Juvenile Justice*; and Carmi Harari and Jacob Chwast, "Class Bias in Psychodiagnosis of Delinquents."

140 Charles W. Thomas and Christopher M. Sieverdes, "Juvenile Court Intake: An Analysis of Discretionary Decision-Making."

141 Ibid., p. 425.

142 Thornberry, "Sentencing in the Juvenile Justice System."

143 Ibid., p. 98.

144 Barak, "Public Defender."

145 Clara Foltz, "Public Defenders."

146 Samuel Rubin, "Criminal Justice and the Poor."

147 Platt, Schechter, and Tiffany, "Public Defender in Juvenile Court," pp. 12-17.

148 Ibid., p. 14.

149 Unwin, *California Intake Study*, p. 42.

150 Lemert, *Revolution Within the Juvenile Court*, pp. 171-95.

151 Ibid., p. 148.

152 Platt, Schechter, and Tiffany, "Public Defender in Juvenile Court," pp. 15-17.

153 Unwin, *California Intake Study*, p. 52.

154 Kittrie, *Deviance and Enforced Therapy*, pp. 133-34.

155 Lerman, "Child Convicts," pp. 38-29.

156 Platt, Schechter, and Tiffany, "Public Defender in Juvenile Court," pp. 8-9.

157 Ibid., p. 10.

158 Ibid.

159 Thornberry, "Sentencing in the Juvenile Justice System."

BIBLIOGRAPHY

Alexander, Francesca. "A Preliminary Report on a Pilot Investigation of some Social-Psychological Variables Influencing the Probation Officer." Paper delivered at the Pacific Sociological Association meetings, 1964.

Axelrad, Sidney, "Negro and White Male Institutionalized Delinquents." *American Journal of Sociology*.

Balbas, Isaac. *The Dialectics of Legal Repression*. New York: Russell Sage Foundation, 1973.

Barak, Greg. "In Defense of the Rich: The Emergence of the Public Defender Movement." *Crime and Social Justice* 3 (1975): 2-14.

Becker, Howard S. *Outsiders: Studies in the Sociology of Deviance*. New York: The Free Press, 1963.

Blauner, Robert. *Racial Oppression in America*. New York: Russell Sage Foundation, 1972.

Bodine, George E. "Factors Related to Police Dispositions of Juvenile Offenders." Paper read at the American Sociological Association annual meeting, August 31, 1964, Montreal, Canada. Mimeographed.

Bordua, David J. "Recent Trends: Deviant Behavior and Social Control." *Annals of American Academy of Political and Social Science* 359 (1967): 149-63.

California Department of Justice, Bureau of Criminal Statistics. *Crime and Delinquency in California, 1974.* Sacramento, Calif., 1975.

———————— Division of Law Enforcement, Bureau of Criminal Statistics. *Juvenile Justice Administration in California, 1974.* Sacramento, Calif., 1976.

California, Governor's Special Study Commission on Juvenile Justice. *A Study of the Administration of Juvenile Justice.* Sacramento, Calif., 1960.

Carter, Robert M., and Lohman, Joseph D. *Middle-Class Delinquency: An Experiment in Community Control.* Berkeley: University of California, 1968.

Center for Research on Criminal Justice. *The Iron Fist and the Velvet Glove: An Analysis of the U.S. Police.* Berkeley, Calif., 1975.

Chambliss, William J. "A Sociological Analysis of the Law of Vagrancy." *Social Problems* 12 (1964): 67-77.

Chesney-Lind, Meda. "Judicial Paternalism and the Female Status Offender." *Crime and Delinquency* 23 (1977): 121-30.

Chicago Police Department. *Manual of Procedure: Youth Division.* Chicago: Chicago Police Department, 1971.

Cicourel, Aaron. *The Social Organization of Juvenile Justice.* New York: John Wiley and Sons, 1968.

Clark, John P., and Wenninger, Eugene P. "Socio-Economic Class and Area as Correlates of Illegal Behavior Among Juveniles." *American Sociological Review* 27 (1962): 826-34.

Cohen, Lawrence E. *Delinquency Dispositions: An Empirical Analysis of Processing Decisions in Three Juvenile Courts.* Analytic Report SD-AR-9. U.S. Department of Justice, Law Enforcement Assistance Administration, National Criminal Justice Information and Statistics Service, Washington D.C.: U.S. Government Printing Office, 1975.

Cohn, Yona. "Criteria for the Probation Officer's Recommendation to the Juvenile Court." *Crime and Delinquency* 9 (1963): 262-75.

Cross, Seymour Z. "The Prehearing Juvenile Report: Probation Officers' Conceptions." *Journal of Research in Crime and Delinquency* 4 (1967): 212-17.

112

Currie, Elliot. "Managing the Minds of Men: The Reformatory Movement, 1865-1920." Ph.D. dissertation, University of California, Berkeley, 1975.

Dineen, John. *Juvenile Court Organization and Status Offenses: A Statutory Profile.* Pittsburgh: National Center for Juvenile Justice, 1974.

Duster, Troy. *The Legislation of Morality: Laws, Drugs, and Moral Judgment.* New York: The Free Press, 1970.

Emerson, Robert M. *Judging Delinquents: Context and Process in Juvenile Court.* Chicago: Aldine Publishing Co., 1969.

Empey, La Mar T., and Erickson, Maynard L. "Hidden Delinquency and Social Status." *Social Forces* 44 (1966): 546-54.

Ferster, Elyce, and Courtless, Thomas. "Legislation: The Beginning of Juvenile Justice, Police Practices, and the Juvenile Offender." *Vanderbilt Law Review* 22 (1969): 567-608.

Foltz, Clara. "Public Defenders." *American Law Review* 31 (1897): 393-403.

Gazel, James A., and Gitchoff, G. Thomas, eds. *Youth, Crime, and Society.* Boston: Holbrook, 1973.

Gibbons, Don C. *Delinquent Behavior.* Englewood Cliffs, N.J.: Prentice-Hall, 1970.

Gold, Martin. *Delinquent Behavior in an American City.* Belmont, Calif.: Brooks/Cole, 1970.

Goldman, Nathan. "The Differential Selection of Juvenile Offenders for Court Appearance." National Research and Information Center, National Council on Crime and Delinquency, 1963.

Gusfield, Joseph. *Symbolic Crusade: Status Politics and the American Temperance Movement.* Urbana, Ill.: University of Illinois Press, 1968.

Harari, Carmi, and Chwast, Jacob. "Class Bias in Psychodiagnosis of Delinquents." *Crime and Delinquency* 10 (1964): 145-51.

International Association of Chiefs of Police. *Survey of Police-Juvenile Operations.* Gaithersburg, Md.: International Association of Chiefs of Police, Inc., 1971.

Kephart, William M. *Racial Factors and Urban Law Enforcement.* Philadelphia: University of Pennsylvania, 1957.

Kittrie, Nicholas N. *The Right to be Different: Deviance and Enforced Therapy.* Baltimore: Johns Hopkins Press, 1971.

Kobetz, Richard W., and Bosarge, Betty B. *Juvenile Justice Administration.* Gaithersburg, Md.: International Association of Chiefs of Police, Inc., 1973.

Krisberg, Barry. *Crime and Privilege: Toward A New Criminology.* Englewood Cliffs, N.J.: Prentice-Hall, 1975.

Lemert, Edwin M. *Instead of Court: Diversion in Juvenile Justice.* Rockville, Md.: National Institute of Mental Health, 1971.

————— *Social Action and Legal Change: Revolution Within the Juvenile Court.* Chicago: Aldine Publishing Co., 1970.

—————*Social Pathology.* New York: McGraw-Hill, 1951.

—————and Rosberg, Judy. "The Administration of Justice to Minority Groups in Los Angeles County." *University of California Publications in Culture and Society* 2 (1948): 1-28.

Lerman, Paul. "Child Convicts." *Trans-Action* 8 (1971): 35-44.

————— *Community Treatment and Social Control: A Critical Analysis of Juvenile Correctional Policy.* Chicago: University of Chicago Press, 1975.

Levin, Mark M., and Sarri, Rosemary C. *Juvenile Delinquency: A Comparative Analysis of Legal Codes in the United States.* Ann Arbor, Mich.: National Assessment of Juvenile Corrections, University of Michigan, 1974.

Liazos, Alexander. "Class Oppression: The Functions of Juvenile Justice." *Insurgent Sociologist* 1 (1974): 2-24.

————— "The Poverty of the Sociology of Deviance: Nuts, Sluts and Preverts." *Social Problems* 20 (1972): 103-120.

Matza, David. *Delinquency and Drift.* New York: John Wiley and Sons, 1964.

McEachern, A. W., and Bauzer, Riva. "Factors Related to Disposition in Juvenile Police Contacts." In *Juvenile Gangs in Context,* edited by Malcolm W. Klein. Englewood Cliffs, N.J.: Prentice-Hall, 1967.

Messinger, Sheldon L. "Confinement in the Community: A Selective Assessment of Paul Lerman's *Community Treatment and Social Control.*" *Journal of Research in Crime and Delinquency* 13 (1976): 82-92.

Morgan, Ted. "They Think, 'I can kill because I'm 14.'" *New York Times Magazine,* 1975, pp. 9-34.

Morris, Norval. *The Future of Imprisonment.* Chicago: University of Chicago Press, 1974.

National Council of Juvenile Court Judges. "Handbook for New Juvenile Court Judges." *Juvenile Court Judges Journal* 23 (1972): 1-31.

National Council on Crime and Delinquency. "Correction in the United States." *Crime and Delinquency* 13 (1967): 1-283.

————— "Transfer of Cases Between Juvenile and Criminal Courts—A Policy Statement." *Crime and Delinquency* 8 (1962): 3-11.

Niederhoffer, Arthur. *Behind the Shield: The Police in Urban Society.* Garden City, N.Y.: Doubleday and Company, 1969.

Nye, Ivan F.; Short, James F., Jr.; and Olson, Virgil. "Socioeconomic Status and Delinquent Behavior." *American Journal of Sociology* 63 (1958): 381-89.

Ohlin, Lloyd; Piven, Herman; and Pappenfort, Donald. "Major Dilemmas of the Social Worker in Probation and Parole." *National Probation and Parole Association* 2 (1956): 211-25.

Packer, Herbert L. "Two Models of the Criminal Process." *University of Pennsylvania Law Review* 118 (1964): 1-68.

Piliavin, Irving, and Briar, Scott. "Police Encounters with Juveniles." *American Journal of Sociology* 70 (1964): 206-14.

Platt, Anthony. *The Child Savers.* Chicago: University of Chicago Press, 1969.

————— "The Triumph of Benevolence: The Origins of the Juvenile Justice System in the United States." In *Criminal Justice in America: A Critical Understanding,* edited by Richard Quinney, pp. 356-89. Boston: Little, Brown and Co., 1964.

—————; Schechter, Howard; and Tiffany, Phyllis. "In Defense of Youth: A Case Study of the Public Defender in Juvenile Court." *Indiana Law Journal* 43 (1968): 1-28.

Pound, Roscoe. *An Introduction to the Philosophy of Law.* New Haven: Yale University Press, 1922.

————— "A Survey of Social Interests." *Harvard Law Review* 57 (1943): 1-39.

————— *Outline of Lectures on Jurisprudence.* Cambridge: Harvard University Press, 1928.

————— *Social Control Through Law.* New Haven: Yale University Press, 1942.

————— "The Rise of Socialized Criminal Justice." In *Roscoe Pound and Criminal Justice,* edited by Sheldon Glueck. Dobbs Ferry, N.Y.: Oceana, 1965.

President's Commission on Law Enforcement and Administration of Justice. *Task Force Report: Juvenile Delinquency and Youth Crime.* Washington, D.C.: U.S. Government Printing Office, 1967.

114

———— *The Challenge of Crime in a Free Society.* Washington, D.C.: U.S. Government Printing Office, 1967.

———— *The Challenge of Crime in a Free Society.* New York: Avon Books, 1968.

Quinney, Richard. *Crime and Justice in Society.* Boston: Little, Brown and Co., 1969.

———— *Criminology: Analysis and Critique of Crime in America.* Boston: Little, Brown and Co., 1975.

———— *Critique of Legal Order: Crime Control in Capitalist Society.* Boston: Little, Brown and Co., 1973.

———— *The Social Reality of Crime.* Boston: Little, Brown and Co., 1970.

Reiss, Albert J., Jr., and Rhodes, Albert Lewis. "The Distribution of Juvenile Delinquency in the Social Class Structure." *American Sociological Review* 26 (1961): 720-32.

Rubin, Samuel. "Criminal Justice and the Poor." *Journal of the American Institute of Criminal Law and Criminology* 22 (1931-32): 705-15.

Ryan, William. *Blaming the Victims.* New York: Random House, Vintage, 1971.

Sarri, Rosemary C. *Under Lock and Key: Juveniles in Jails and Detention.* Ann Arbor, Mich.: National Assessment of Juvenile Corrections, University of Michigan, 1974.

———— and Hasenfield, Yeheskel. *Brought to Justice? Juveniles, the Courts, and the Law.* Ann Arbor, Mich.: National Assessment of Juvenile Corrections, University of Michigan, 1976.

Schur, Edwin. *Labeling Deviant Behavior: Its Sociological Implications.* New York: Harper and Row, 1971.

Schwitzgebel, Ralph. *The Development and Legal Regulation of Coercive Behavior Modification Techniques with Offenders.* Washington, D.C.: National Institute of Mental Health Service Publication no. 2067, 1971.

Shannon, Lyle W. "Types and Patterns of Delinquency Referral in a Middle-Sized City." *British Journal of Criminology* 3 (1963): 24-36.

Sheridan, William. "Juvenile Court Intake." *Journal of Family Law* 2 (1962): 139-56.

———— "Juveniles Who Commit Noncriminal Acts: Why Treat in a Correctional System?" *Federal Probation* 31 (1967): 26-30.

Skolnick, Jerome. *Justice Without Trial: Law Enforcement in a Democratic Society.* New York: John Wiley and Sons, 1966.

"Standard Juvenile Court Act—Text and Commentary." *Journal of National Probation and Parole Association* 5 (1959): 324-91.

Starrs, James E. "A Sense of Irony in Southern Juvenile Courts." *Harvard Civil Liberties—Civil Rights Law Review* 1 (1966): 129-51.

Sumner, Helen. "Locking Them Up." *Crime and Delinquency* 17 (1971): 168-79.

Sussman, Frederick. *Law of Juvenile Delinquency.* Dobbs Ferry, N.Y.: Oceana, 1959.

Taylor, Ian; Watton, Paul; and Young, Jock. *The New Criminology: For a Social Theory of Deviance.* New York: Harper and Row, 1973.

Terry, Robert M. "Discrimination in the Handling of Juvenile Offenders by Social Control Agencies." *Journal of Research in Crime and Delinquency* 4 (1967): 218-30.

Thio, Alex. "Class Bias in the Sociology of Deviance." *The American Sociologist* 8 (1973): 1-12.

Thomas, Charles W., and Sieverdes, Christopher M. "Juvenile Court Intake: An Analysis of Discretionary Decision-Making." *Criminology* 12 (1975): 413-32.

Thornberry, Terence. "Race, Socioeconomic Status, and Sentencing in the Juvenile Justice System." *Journal of Criminal Law and Criminology* 64 (1973): 90-98.

Turk, Austin. "Conflict and Criminality." *American Sociological Review* 31 (1966): 338-52.

————— *Criminality and the Legal Order.* Chicago: Rand McNally and Co., 1969.

Unwin, Ernest A. *California Correctional System Intake Study.* Sunnyvale, Calif.: Public Systems, Inc., 1974.

U.S. Commission on Civil Rights. *Report.* Washington, D.C., 1965.

U.S. Department of Health, Education, and Welfare, Children's Bureau. *1964 Juvenile Court Statistics.* Washington, D.C., 1965.

U.S. Department of Health, Education, and Welfare. *Juvenile Court Statistics, 1973.* Washington, D.C., 1975.

U.S. Department of Justice, Law Enforcement Assistance Administration. *National Jail Census, 1970: A Report on the Nation's Local Jails and Type of Inmates.* Washington, D.C.: U.S. Government Printing Office, 1971.

van den Haag, Ernest. *Punishing Criminals: Concerning a Very Old and Painful Question.* New York: Basic Books, 1975.

Vaz, Edmund. *Middle-Class Juvenile Delinquency.* New York: Harper and Row, 1967.

Vold, George. *Theoretical Criminology.* New York: Oxford University Press, 1958.

Wichita Police Department. *Duty Manual.* Wichita, Kans.: Wichita Police Department, n.d.

Wildeman, John. "The Crime Fighters." Ph.D. dissertation, New York University, 1971.

Williams, Jay R., and Gold, Martin. "From Delinquent Behavior to Official Delinquency." *Social Problems* 20 (1972): 209-29.

Wilson, James Q. "The Police and the Delinquent in Two Cities." In *Controlling Delinquents,* edited by Stanton Wheeler, pp. 9-30. New York: John Wiley and Sons, 1968.

————— *Thinking About Crime.* New York: Basic Books, 1975.

————— *Varieties of Police Behavior.* Cambridge, Mass.: Harvard University Press, 1968.

Wisconsin Division of Family Services. *Profile of Juveniles in Wisconsin: 1974.* Madison, 1974.

Wolfgang, Marvin, and Cohen, Bernard. *Race and Crime.* New York: American Jewish Committee, Institute of Human Relations Press, 1970.

—————; Figlio, Robert; and Sellin, Thorsten. *Delinquency in a Birth Cohort.* Chicago: University of Chicago Press, 1972.

Younghusband, Eileen. "Dilemma of the Juvenile Court." *Social Service Review* 10 (1959).

Girls' Dormitory, New York House of Refuge

THEORIES OF
JUVENILE DELINQUENCY

CHAPTER 4

Academic speculation about the causes or explanation of juvenile delinquency has occupied a great many minds for several centuries. The theories that have emerged are products of their historical period, and have usually served as ideological defenses of the social order. Though they have revealed some new aspects to the nature of delinquency, theories of delinquency are most telling about the social attitudes of the times in which they were developed. The "professional ideology" of delinquency theorists reflects their positions as to the race, class, and privilege structure of society. In most instances, they have been middle-aged, white males with many years of formal education, with established professional careers in law, medicine, or university teaching. C. Wright Mills wrote the following about the professional ideology of the social pathologists:

> If members of an academic profession are recruited from similar social contexts and if their backgrounds and careers are similar, there is a tendency for them to be uniformly set for some common perspective. The common conditions of their profession often seem more important in this connection than similarity of extraction. Within such a homogeneous group there will tend to be fewer divergent points of view which would clash over the meaning of facts and thus give rise to interpretations on a more theoretical level.[1]

117

The racial, sexual, and class sameness of delinquency theorists has resulted in a narrow approach to the problem of delinquency, which is largely cast in a "correctional" perspective—that is, the analysts study a social phenomenon only to correct or eliminate it. There is virtually no evidence that delinquency theorists have attempted to *appreciate* the phenomenon by trying to truly understand the social meaning of the behavior that is labelled as delinquency. Rather, delinquency theorists have consciously or unwittingly pursued the construction of a stereotype of the delinquent.[2] This false image is designed to convince us that the delinquent is different from the "normal child"; that the delinquent is motivated by different social-psychological factors than the rest of us; and that the delinquent's behavior is fundamentally irrational.

During most of the nineteenth century, American scholars suggested that crime and delinquency were rooted in medical and biological problems.[3] Psychological theories of delinquency began to gain popularity in the first decades of the twentieth century, and have continued to play a dominant role in academic writing on the subject of delinquency. Recent research by Wolfgang, Figlio, and Thornberry has revealed that over three-quarters of the published material on the causes of crime between 1945 and 1972 consisted of psychiatric or psychological approaches to etiology. These re-searchers found that most of this work was of extremely poor quality if one applies standard criteria of research methodology and theory construction. A review of current treatment approaches for delin-quents reveals the dominance of psychological and psychiatric models.

Sociological approaches to delinquency appeared fairly late in America as compared with Europe. While there was a strong current of sociological criminology in Europe in the nineteenth century, there is scant evidence of an American sociological approach to crime until the social survey movement at the turn of the twentieth century, and the famous Chicago school, which followed. The major theoretical statements of the sociological approach to delinquency did not emerge until the late 1930s. While there was a vibrant socialist criminology in Europe, this perspective was largely repressed in the United States, and had only received veiled expression in the work of Sellin, Taft, and Vold, who were familiar with the European sources.

The sociological approach to delinquency received a boost of public support and attention during the decade of the sixties. Socio-logical theory was well suited to the governmental policies of the War on Poverty and the Great Society. Despite the acceptance of sociological perspectives within the academic community, however, juvenile justice practitioners still seem wedded to the psychiatric and psychological approaches of the past. This gap between academic theory and practice is especially visible in the case of labelling or conflict theory, which became stylish in academic circles in the sixties, and was responsible for a major shift in sociological ap-proaches of the time. But the labelling view has met with sharp

Theories of Juvenile Delinquency **119**

resistance from juvenile justice practitioners. Where this theory has been used to generate programs, the translation has made labelling theory appear to be but one more psychological explanation of delinquency.

Developments in the seventies have not sustained the growth of theory in the juvenile delinquency field. Governmental disaffection with the Great Society has led to support for more direct strategies for controlling the dangerous classes. The primary federal funding sources have turned an unsympathetic ear to most delinquency researchers wishing to continue work in sociological directions. The bulk of the money from the Law Enforcement Assistance Administration (LEAA) is directed toward research to improve the operations of the juvenile justice system. The limited funds that were made available to those interested in etiology were invested in a renaissance of biological and psychological approaches dressed up in new clothing of academic respectability.

Changes in delinquency theory, like changes in juvenile justice practice, are largely determined by changes in the social structure. Transformations in the political economy at large are reflected in the political economy of delinquency research, which generates ideas that reproduce the hegemony of the existing relations of property, race, and sexual privilege. Intellectuals who do not consciously reject the role become state servants who feed into the emerging social control technology. The social scientists who join the "societal therapy team" may do so to regain prestige, to build research empires, or because they truly believe in the ideas of those in positions of power. Those whose studies support attainment of social justice and social change face an uncertain professional future, and have grave difficulty getting the products of their research disseminated to public audiences.

It would be an important contribution to perform a thorough critique of delinquency theory, making connections between ideology and the maintenance of privilege. But this task would involve a great deal of basic research, and would require several years to complete. At present, a number of scholars are researching the necessary pieces of this story, and it is hoped that future editions of this text can be enriched by the products of that intellectual labor. At present we can only speculate about the outlines of that history of the development of criminological ideas.

The essential questions that must be asked of all delinquency theories go beyond the mere testing of formal hypotheses derived from theories, although even this has not been adequately done by traditional researchers in the delinquency field. We need to know something of the domain assumptions made about human nature, the nature of society, and the nature of law. There is a need to understand the ideological uses of the theory, which should be related to general features of the political economy. Theories must be exposed in terms of racial, sexual, and class biases, which falsify reality on behalf of the status quo. Finally, theories should be viewed as myths that can be used by oppressors to preserve the structure of domination.

> It is necessary for the oppressors to approach the people in order, via subjugation, to keep them passive. This approximation, however, does not involve being with the people, or require true communication. It is accomplished by the oppressor's depositing myths indispensable to the preservation of the status quo.[4]

It is hoped that applying a critical perspective to theories will reveal hidden ideologies that obscure the real nature of social phenomena, and limit our ability to develop more liberating alternatives to delinquency and other social problems.

BIOLOGICAL THEORIES

Many delinquency researchers have never given up the search for the biological bases of crime. The most prominent name in the biological field was the Italian army physician Cesare Lombroso, who became the founder of the positivist school of criminology at the end of the nineteenth century. Lombroso had a deep impact upon American writers, who sought a scientific basis for the study of crime. Although Lombroso's conceptions of the scientific method and of human biology were rather limited, his approach to the study of crime has had a lasting impact on the study of delinquency. Researchers today continue to search for "anomalies" that separate delinquents from nondelinquents in the hope that methods of natural science will yield answers to the problems of crime and delinquency.

It is unfair to characterize the Lombrosian position as simply biological, since he elaborated a systematic approach to crime that included psychological and social factors. Similarly, contemporary theorists who stress biological factors acknowledge that biological causes interact with social factors to produce delinquency. Biological researchers recognize the complex interaction between heredity and environment, which together explain human behavior.[5] But many modern researchers share with Lombroso the view that there is a residual category of biological deviant whose behavior can be best explained by bio-genetic factors. Not only are biological sources of crime often used to counter theories stressing social factors, but they also provide convenient explanations for the failures of other "sincere treatment approaches." Biological theorists paint an image of the criminal as a person who offends without free will, and cannot be cured by ordinary social or psychological means.

Biological causes of crime and delinquency can be grouped into eight main categories, which are debated in contemporary studies:

1   Tumors or lesions of the limbic system of the brain;
2   Certain side effects of epileptic seizures;

3   Endocrine or glandular disorders where heightened levels of male and female hormones or hypoglycemia are associated with certain types of behavioral disorders;

4   Prenatal or birth complications and mild forms of retardation or brain damage;

5   Minimal brain [disfunction] as measured by unusual Electroencephalograph patterns;

6   Genetic factors including the alleged inheritability of certain personality traits and psychopathic disorders;

7   Possible chromosomal disorders such as the XYY or Klinefelter's syndrome and anti-social behavior;

8   Recent studies of the association of physique, temperament and behavior.[6]

A fair number of pages have been written refuting the causal significance of each of these biological factors under the presumption that there might be some reliable scientific data that will demonstrate relations between these factors and criminal behavior. But there is a more devastating point to be made—*the scientific evidence does not support any one of these factors as causally related to delinquency or crime.* Instead, one finds an invariate pattern: early research shows optimistic findings, but later, more careful efforts fail to uphold the hypothesized relations. For example, until quite recently there was scientific support for the theory that tumors and lesions of the limbic system of the brain are related to certain unexplained violent or aggressive behavior. Recently, however, a review of the extant literature commissioned by the National Institute of Neurological Diseases and Stroke reported the following:

> There was a general consensus that so little is known concerning the morphophysiologic organization and functional properties of different components of the limbic-subcortical-mesencephalic continuum to make it impossible to predict unequivocally the consequences of lesions of this system in laboratory animals.[7]

The author of this report goes on to call for more careful research using better experimental procedures. In general, the search for biological causes of crime has been characterized by small samples, inadequate research designs, untested measurement instruments, and improper use of statistical techniques.

The persistence of the Lombrosian dream of isolating the biological foundation of delinquency has depended on factors other than scientific evidence. Some have explained the continued focus on biology by the alleged American fascination with miracle cures—that is, we want some simple technical solution such as psychosurgery, chemotherapy, or genetic engineering, which promises to solve our social problems without changing the social order. This tendency is most vividly illustrated by the recent trend in school districts to administer drugs to youngsters who are defined as hyperactive or suffering from minimal brain damage. In some districts, up to half the children are receiving some type of medication in school.

The ideological importance of biological factors should not be underestimated. In a nation which publicly espouses the principles of democracy and equal opportunity, it is difficult to rationalize the contradictions of large pools of individuals, who consistently remain on the bottom of the social structure. Biological or hereditary theories help to preserve the mythology of an open social structure, while at the same time explaining the failures of the "few." Even more dangerous has been the tendency of the biological school to support doctrines of eugenics, enforced sterilization, and preventive detention of those who are considered unfit.

It would be wrong to reject completely the assumption that bio-genetic factors influence human behavior. Better research in this area undoubtedly will present a clearer picture of the biological foundations of human behavior. But it is crucial to remember that crime and delinquency are forms of *social action*—behavior that is given meaning through human interpretation. Human interpretations of behavior are always circumscribed by class, cultural, and historical factors. Even if we acknowledge that people differ from one another, even in extreme ways, this does not necessarily indicate a social response that criminalizes or penalizes such differences. Definitions of normality and deviance are always related to the structure of privilege within the society and the ideas that support the edifice of privilege.

PSYCHODYNAMIC APPROACHES TO DELINQUENCY

The range of possible psychological explanations of delinquency is so broad that it defies simple classification. By far the majority of published studies of delinquency involve psychology, and the psychological model dominates treatment approaches. Early psychological explanations of delinquency were closely tied to biological theories.[8] Many efforts have been made to understand the interrelations between psychosis, mental defects, psychopathy, and criminality. Although there are some instances in which youthful offenders suffer from some mental disorder, research has failed to demonstrate consistent correlations between psychological disorders and delinquency. Nor is there convincing evidence to link delinquency to mental retardation, constitutional aspects of personality, or brain damage. While psychologists such as Hans Eysenck continue to search for static psychological traits that can be related to delinquency, one suspects that these theorists are motivated by the age-old premises of the biological theorists.

Far more important to contemporary treatment of juvenile delinquents are psychological approaches that stress dynamic relations within the individual. In chapter 2, we noted the influence of William Healy in placing the psychodynamic model at the center of the juvenile court practice. Healy's early work was augmented by the prestige of Freudian approaches to child development and delinquency. Indeed, the psychoanalytic approach has been the dominant model for studying the mental development of children in this country. The learning theory or symbolic interactionist approaches, which appeared later, had to struggle to obtain the professional respectability accorded to the followers of Freud and Healy. Until quite recently, the Freudian view that inner conflicts lead to deviant behavior has dominated social work practice, as well as most state intervention involving children.

The essence of the psychodynamic explanations of delinquency is that the problem derives from mental conflicts within the child. Conflicts may arise due to a lack of parental affection, too much affection, inconsistent expressions of parental love, unresolved oedipal feelings, or various other factors. Some psychodynamic theorists, such as Erikson, relate delinquency to social factors that create identity conflicts that are beyond the individual's ability to solve. Such approaches view delinquency and deviance as unconscious attempts to resolve inner conflicts. For some, the pressure to deviate is controlled by socialization or external controls that may not be present for the delinquent. Some delinquents have lost the social constraints that help them control inner conflicts because of cultural confusion produced by circumstances such as crises, or by their loyalties to deviant subcultures.

Often the psychodynamic theories explain delinquency by undersocialization, defective socialization, or interpersonal immaturity. These explanations of delinquency help justify psychologically oriented therapies, aimed at resocializing delinquents. These therapies include individual and group counseling, attack therapy, reality therapy, role playing, transactional analysis, transcendental meditation, guided-group interaction, and primal therapy, among others. Despite extensive testing of psychodynamically derived treatment approaches, there have not been consistently positive results with any approach.

Criticism of psychodynamic models has led some practitioners to favor applications of behavior modification strategies. Although behavior modification has been hailed as the new treatment panacea throughout the sixties and seventies, the results of such approaches have been inconclusive. Moreover, some observers challenge the ethics of researchers seeking to extend their abilities to manipulate human behavior. It is interesting to note that some researchers in this area attribute failures of their experiments to the inability of delinquents to learn from experience. In most cases, such attempts failed because they assumed an overly simplistic model of learning based on a single stimulus or response, often ignoring the context of the learning which usually took place within secure institutions and control procedures designed to enforce behavioral conformity among the delinquents. Managers of the institutions support behavior modification approaches, since they are respectable methods to insure the compliance of inmates under their custody.

Concern with the proper psychological classification of individual delinquents serves the ideological function of de-politicizing the subject of delinquency. Psychological approaches anchor the problem of delinquency at the level of personal problems, directing the focus away from issues of social structure. Such approaches deny the rationality and intentionality of delinquent behavior. Youths are confronted with powerful, but seemingly benevolent, practitioners who attempt to convince them that personal inadequacies can be cured through effort and self-discipline. Unless the child has strong self-confidence or the support of others, conflict with authorities will result in feelings of shame and guilt. Individual delinquents are confronted with culturally biased tests and psychological classifications that intensify feelings of self-doubt and insecurity. The tools of psychological warfare are potent and the world of the therapeutic is totalitarian in structure.[9]

There must be a valid psychology of crime and delinquency if we are to link personal experience with social problems. But the sources of the psychological approaches need to be closer to the phenomena themselves. Criminology once had a vibrant tradition of attempting to understand the ideas and feelings of delinquents. This approach was lost as criminologists sought to psychologically interpret the delinquents in order to cure them. The article by Barry Krisberg in chapter 5 attempts to return to that earlier position. In addition, there is a wealth of autobiographical material written by persons who were once delinquents, which can be used as basic data to formulate new psychological approaches.

There has been growth in a radical therapy, seeking to help individuals without losing sight of the forces in the larger political economy that exert selective pressures on individuals. New therapies, aimed at helping victims of oppression escape the "ghetto of the mind," are reflected in the writings of Ben Tong, Alvin Pousaint, Francis Wellsing Cress, and Paulo Freire. Perhaps a sensitive psychological study of delinquency will emerge from the intellectual traditions of these scholars and social activists.

SOCIOLOGICAL THEORIES

The concept of subculture, or the culture of an identifiable segment of society, has been a major component of sociological analyses of delinquency. The subculture contains norms and values that are different from those presumed to characterize the dominant or main culture. While sociologists have long considered ethnic groups to comprise unique subcultures, the term is also applied to adolescent peer associations, occupational groups, delinquent gangs, and social classes. Subcultural theorists are especially aware of the social norms and attitudes of members of the subculture. There is often a focus on distinctive uses of language, as well as specific customs or social rituals of members of the subculture. Subcultural theorists suggest that delinquency is the result of a commitment by the individual to subcultural values that either encourage delinquency or are antagonistic to the values of the dominant culture.

One of the earliest references to the subculture and its impact on delinquency is in Thorsten Sellin's *Culture Conflict and Crime*:

> We have noted that culture conflicts are the natural outgrowth of processes of social differentiation, which produce an infinity of social groupings, each with its own definitions of life situations, its own interpretations of social relationships, its own ignorance or misunderstanding of the social values of other groups. The transformation of a culture from a homogeneous and well-integrated type to a heterogeneous and disintegrated type is therefore accompanied by an increase in conflict situations.[10]

Sellin goes on to say that the conflict occurs when the behavior of one social group is defined as abnormal by another. In some cases, members of a subculture may experience mental conflict because there appears to be more than one rule governing correct social behavior in a given situation. Sellin proposes further study of the ways cultural conflicts induce delinquent behavior in individuals.

Criminologist Edwin Sutherland expanded the concept of subculture in his research on professional theft and his theory of differential association in the 1930s. Sutherland went beyond notions of mental conflicts and cultural clashes to demonstrate that criminals need a subculture of similar persons in order to conduct unlawful enterprises. A novice is encouraged to learn the techniques, values, and attitudes needed in a life of crime from professional thieves. Connections within the subculture provide financial or political support in case of arrest, as well as psychological support to dispel the fears and self-doubts of the thief.

Put simply, differential association theory states that crime is a learned form of human behavior. Although this message may not seem so shocking nowadays, Sutherland's insistence on a *social learning* theory of crime and delinquency contrasted sharply with the biological, constitutional, and static psychological theories of that day. The theory of differential association suggests that the nature, intensity, and frequency of contacts with persons and groups who hold definitions favorable or unfavorable to law violation would determine whether the individual would hold pro- or anti-legal attitudes. Sutherland assumed that attitudes favorable to law violation, together with a knowledge of specific skills, techniques, and motives, were the major factors in producing criminal or delinquent behavior. The theory of differential association emphasizes that learning principally takes place within intimate personal groups, and that criminal or delinquent values are assimilated through communication within such groups.

Subcultural theory was an important part of the perspective on social deviance developed by the Chicago school of the late 1920s and early 1930s. Under the intellectual leadership of Robert Park and Ernest Burgess, sociologists at the University of Chicago set out to chart the unique cultural characteristics of various social areas within the city of Chicago. These researches produced lively descriptions of many ethnic communities, as well as aspects of lower-class urban life. Clifford Shaw and Frederick Thrasher focused specifically upon juvenile delinquency and adolescent gangs. Sociologists of the Chicago school were fascinated by the distinctive cultures they found within different neighborhoods of the city. In each of their studies there is great attention to ethnographic detail in descriptions of diverse cultural groups. Part of the theory that emerged from these research efforts concerned the special cultures of specific areas. Clifford Shaw, for example, shows how young people are induced to take up criminal and delinquent careers by the values and roles they learn from people in their immediate social environment. Shaw used this idea to develop the Chicago Area Project, which was discussed in chapter 2. The main theoretical focus of the Chicago Area Project was the importance of influencing the immediate social relations of the child to instill law-abiding behavior.

Later formulations of subcultural theory by Albert Cohen, Cloward and Ohlin, and Walter Miller are largely based on concepts developed by these early writers. For most subcultural theorists, the behavior of individuals is influenced by the content of social learning within the immediate environment. While these authors identify different influences on delinquency, they concur that the delinquent values and orientations derive from a person's participation in a subculture. Albert Cohen extends the idea of conflict of cultures to social classes, which he believes are also distinctive cultures. Cohen views the delinquent subculture as a group solution to the problem of personal rejection faced by lower-class youngsters, who are negatively perceived according to middle-class standards. Walter Miller refers to lower-class culture as a "generating milieu of gang delinquency." But Miller views delinquent values as inherently lower class, rather than arising from the social response of lower-class individuals.

The theory of Cloward and Ohlin is similar to that of Albert Cohen in that both view delinquent subcultures as functional adaptations to the problems posed for the individual by the lack of legitimate and illegitimate opportunities within his social world. The delinquent group is a response to pressures to achieve material goods in a world where there is little real chance to accomplish this objective.

This chapter contains several classic selections based on a sociological perspective on crime, most of which fall within subcultural theory. Four of the papers are sociological explanations that either supplement the subcultural view, or provide alternative concepts. For example, the paper by Walter Reckless criticizes the subcultural school for not dealing with the forces inhibitting or encouraging an individual to join in delinquent activities. Robert Merton offers a potential linkage between the group-centered orientation of the subcultural school and contradictions in society that induce alienated persons to join deviant groups. Gresham Skyes and David Matza also focus on the contribution of the larger social structure to delinquency, but reject the significance of subcultures in influencing delinquency. For Skyes and Matza, delinquent values are inherent in the "vocabularies of motive" presented by the dominant culture— that is the dominant culture provides the values that justify breaking the rules. Howard Becker's paper on the labelling perspective briefly restates that theory, while responding to some of the criticisms that have been lodged against the labelling analysis of deviant behavior.

The papers presented here constitute the best theoretical works in the field of delinquency, according to many academic criminologists. But it should be made clear that we do not share this consensus. We have chosen to present the classics so that the reader may decide whether these theories shed any light on the subject of delinquency. At present there exists no fully developed statement of the alternative or critical theory of delinquency. Although the papers reprinted in chapter 5 begin to outline some of the essential concepts of that critical theory, there is no published material that synthesizes a critical view in a systematic manner. The work of Herman and Julia Schwendinger in chapter 5 emphasizes certain aspects of critical theory, but much work in this area still remains to be done.

Critical scholarship has not generally been given adequate funding or access to publication. The critical scholar must reexamine the history, empirical data, and concepts that his traditional colleagues have taken for granted. It seems necessary that alternative theories incorporate international perspectives that permit examination of delinquency in a variety of social structures and cultures. More importantly, critical theory must be sensitive to the actual conditions faced by persons labelled as delinquents.

NOTES

1   C. Wright Mills, *Power, Politics and People: The Collected Essays of C. Wright Mills*, p. 527.

2   See Dennis Chapman, *Sociology and the Stereotype of the Delinquent*.

3   Arthur Fink, *The Causes of Crime*.

4   Paulo Freire, *Pedagogy of the Oppressed*, p. 135.

5   See John Money, "Behavior Genetics: Principles, Methods and Examples from XO, XXY and XYY Syndromes"; or Saleem A. Shah, "Recent Developments in Human Genetics and Their Implications to Problems of Social Deviance."

6   List compiled by Robert Figlio, personal communication to authors, 1975.

7   Murray Goldstein, "Brain Research and Violent Behavior," p. 7.

8   Fink, *The Causes of Crime*, pp. 1-75, 211-39.

9   Philip Reiff, *The Triumph of the Therapeutic*.

10 Thorsten Sellin, *Culture Conflict and Crime*, p. 66.

BIBLIOGRAPHY

Chapman, Dennis. *Sociology and the Stereotype of the Delinquent.* London: Tavistock, 1968.

Fink, Arthur. *The Causes of Crime.* New York: A. S. Barnes and Co., 1962.

Freire, Paulo. *Pedagogy of the Oppressed.* New York: Herder and Herder, 1970.

Goldstein, Murray. "Brain Research and Violent Behavior." *Archives of Neurology* 30 (1974): 1-8.

Mills, C. Wright. In *Power, Politics and People: The Collected Essays of C. Wright Mills,* edited by Irving Louis Horowitz. New York: Oxford University Press, 1967.

Money, John. "Behavior Genetics: Principles, Methods and Examples from XO, XXY and XYY Syndromes." *Seminars in Psychiatry* 2 (1970): 22.

Reiff, Philip. *The Triumph of the Therapeutic.* New York: Harper and Row, 1966.

Sellin, Thorsten. *Culture Conflict and Crime.* New York: Social Science Research Council, 1938.

Shah, Saleem A. "Recent Developments in Human Genetics and Their Implications to Problems of Social Deviance." *National Foundation on Birth Defects* 8 (1972): 48-49.

Differential Association

EDWIN H. SUTHERLAND

From *Principles of Criminology, 4th edition,* by E. Sutherland. Reprinted by permission of the publisher, J. B. Lippincott Company. Copyright © 1947.

The scientific explanation of a phenomenon may be stated either in terms of the factors which are operating at the moment of the occurrence of a phenomenon or in terms of the processes operating in the earlier history of that phenomenon. In the first case the explanation is mechanistic, in the second historical or genetic; both are usable. The physical and biological scientists favor the first of these methods, and it would probably be superior as an explanation of criminal behavior. Efforts at explanations of the mechanistic type have been notably unsuccessful, perhaps largely because they have been concentrated on the attempt to isolate personal and social pathologies. Work from this point of view has, at least, resulted in the conclusion that the immediate factors in criminal behavior lie in the person-situation complex. Person and situation are not factors exclusive of each other, for the situation which is important is the situation as defined by the person who is involved. The tendencies and inhibitions at the moment of the criminal behavior are, to be sure, largely a product of the earlier history of the person, but the expression of these tendencies and inhibitions is a reaction to the immediate situation as defined by the person. The situation operates in many ways, of which perhaps the least important is the provision of an opportunity for a criminal act. A thief may steal from a fruit stand when the owner is not in sight but refrain when the owner is in sight; a bank burglar may attack a bank which is poorly protected but refrain from attacking a bank protected by watchmen and burglar alarms. A corporation which manufactures automobiles seldom or never violates the Pure Food and Drug Law, but a meat-packing corporation violates this law with great frequency.

The second type of explanation of criminal behavior is made in terms of the life experience of a person and is a historical or genetic explanation of criminal behavior. This, to be sure, assumes a situation to be defined by the person in terms of the inclinations and abilities which the person has acquired up to that date. The following paragraphs state such a genetic theory [i.e., the theory of differential association] of criminal behavior on the assumption that a criminal act occurs when a situation appropriate for it, as defined by a person, is present.

(1) *Criminal behavior is learned.* Negatively, this means that criminal behavior is not inherited, as such; also, the person who is not already trained in crime does not invent criminal behavior, just as a person does not make mechanical inventions unless he has had training in mechanics.

(2) *Criminal behavior is learned in interaction with other persons in a process of communication.* This communication is verbal in many respects but includes also "the communication of gestures."

(3) *The principal part of the learning of criminal behavior occurs within intimate personal groups.* Negatively, this means that the impersonal agencies of communication, such as picture shows and newspapers, play a relatively unimportant part in the genesis of criminal behavior.

(4) *When criminal behavior is learned, the learning includes (a) techniques of committing the crime, which are sometimes very simple; (b) the specific direction of motives, drives, rationalizations, and attitudes.*

(5) *The specific direction of motives and drives is learned from definitions of legal codes as favorable and unfavorable.* In some societies an individual is surrounded by persons who invariably define the legal codes as rules to be observed, whereas in others he is surrounded by persons whose definitions are favorable to the violation of the legal codes.

In our American society these definitions are almost always mixed, and consequently we have culture conflict in relation to the legal codes.

(6) *A person becomes delinquent because of an excess of definitions favorable to violation of law over definitions unfavorable to violation of law.* This is the principle of differential association. It refers to both criminal and anti-criminal associations and has to do with counteracting forces. When persons become criminals, they do so because of contacts with criminal patterns and also because of isolation from anti-criminal patterns. Any person inevitably assimilates the surrounding culture unless other patterns are in conflict; a Southerner does not pronounce "r" because other Southerners do not pronounce "r." Negatively, this proposition of differential association means that associations which are neutral so far as crime is concerned have little or no effect on the genesis of criminal behavior. Much of the experience of a person is neutral in this sense, e.g., learning to brush one's teeth. This behavior has no negative or positive effect on criminal behavior except as it may be related to associations which are concerned with the legal codes. This neutral behavior is important especially as an occupier of the time of a child so that he is not in contact with criminal behavior during the time he is engaged in neutral behavior.

(7) *Differential associations may vary in frequency, duration, priority, and intensity.* This means that associations with criminal behavior and also associations with anti-criminal behavior vary in those respects. "Frequency" and "duration" as modalities of associations are obvious and need no explanation. "Priority" is assumed to be important in the sense that lawful behavior developed in early childhood may persist throughout life, and also that delinquent behavior developed in early childhood may persist throughout life. This tendency, however, has not been adequately demonstrated, and priority seems to be important principally through its selective influence. "Intensity" is not precisely defined, but it has to do with such things as the prestige of the source of a criminal or anti-criminal pattern and with emotional reactions related to the associations. In a precise description of the criminal behavior of a person these modalities would be stated in quantitative form and a mathematical ratio would be reached. A formula in this sense has not been developed, and the development of such a formula would be extremely difficult.

(8) *The process of learning criminal behavior by association with criminal and anti-criminal patterns involves all of the mechanisms that are involved in any other learning.* Nega-

tively, this means that the learning of criminal behavior is not restricted to the process of imitation. A person who is seduced, for instance, learns criminal behavior by association, but this process would not ordinarily be described as imitation.

(9) *Though criminal behavior is an expression of general needs and values, it is not explained by those general needs and values since non-criminal behavior is an expression of the same needs and values.* Thieves generally steal in order to secure money, but likewise honest laborers work in order to secure money. The attempts by many scholars to explain criminal behavior by general drives and values, such as the happiness principle, striving for social status, the money motive, or frustration, have been and must continue to be futile since they explain lawful behavior as completely as they explain criminal behavior. They are similar to respiration, which is necessary for any behavior but which does not differentiate criminal from non-criminal behavior.

It is not necessary, on this level of discussion, to explain why a person has the associations which he has; this certainly involves a complex of many things. In an area where the delinquency rate is high a boy who is sociable, gregarious, active, and athletic is very likely to come in contact with the other boys in the neighborhood, learn delinquent behavior from them, and become a gangster; in the same neighborhood the psychopathic boy who is isolated, introverted, and inert may remain at home, not become acquainted with the other boys in the neighborhood, and not become delinquent. In another situation, the sociable, athletic, aggressive boy may become a member of a scout troop and not become involved in delinquent behavior. The person's associations are determined in a general context of social organization. A child is ordinarily reared in a family; the place of residence of the family is determined largely by family income; and the delinquency rate is in many respects related to the rental value of the houses. Many other factors enter into this social organization, including many personal group relationships.

The preceding explanation of criminal behavior was stated from the point of view of the person who engages in criminal behavior. It is also possible to state theories of criminal behavior from the point of view of the community, nation, or other group. The problem, when thus stated, is generally concerned with crime rates and involves a comparison of the crime rates of various groups or the crime rates of a particular group at different times. One of the best explanations of crime rates from this point of view is that a high crime rate is due to social disorganization. The term "social disorganization" is not entirely satisfactory, and it seems preferable to substitute for the term "differential social organization." The postulate on which this theory is based, regardless of the name, is that crime is rooted in the social organization and is an expression of that social organization. A group may be organized for criminal behavior or organized against criminal behavior. Most communities are organized both for criminal and anti-criminal behavior, and in that sense the crime rate is an expression of the differential group organization. Differential group organization as an explanation of a crime rate must be consistent with the explanation of the criminal behavior of the person, since the crime rate is a summary statement of the number of persons in the group who commit crimes and the frequency with which they commit crimes.

The Delinquent Subculture

ALBERT K. COHEN

Albert K. Cohen is a professor of sociology at the University of Connecticut.

Reprinted with permission of Macmillan Publishing Co., Inc. from *Delinquent Boys* by Albert K. Cohen, pp. 24-32. Copyright © 1955 by The Free Press, a Corporation.

The common expression, "juvenile crime," has unfortunate and misleading connotations. It suggests that we have two kinds of criminals, young and old, but only one kind of crime. It suggests that crime has its meanings and its motives which are much the same for young and old; that the young differ from the old as the apprentice and the master differ at the same trade; that we distinguish the young from the old only because the young are less "set in their ways," less "confirmed" in the same criminal habits, more amenable to treatment and more deserving, because of their tender age, of special consideration.

The problem of the relationship between juvenile delinquency and adult crime has many facets. To what extent are the offenses of children and adults distributed among the same legal categories, "burglary," "larceny," "vehicle-taking," and so forth? To what extent, even when the offenses are legally identical, do these acts have the same meaning for children and adults? To what extent are the careers of adult criminals continuations of careers of juvenile delinquency? We cannot solve these problems here, but we want to emphasize the danger of making facile and unproven assumptions. If we assume that "crime is crime," that child and adult criminals are practitioners of the same trade, and if our assumptions are false, then the road to error is wide and clear. Easily and unconsciously, we may impute a whole host of notions concerning the nature of crime and its causes, derived from our knowledge and fancies about adult crime, to a large realm of behavior to which these notions are irrelevant. It is better to make no such assumptions; it is better to look at juvenile delinquency with a fresh eye and try to explain what we see.

What we see when we look at the delinquent subculture (and we must not even assume that this describes *all juvenile* crime) is that it is *nonutilitarian, malicious* and *negativistic.*

We usually assume that when people steal things, they steal because they want them. They may want them because they can eat them, wear them or otherwise use them; or because they can sell them; or even—if we are given to a psychoanalytic turn of mind— because on some deep symbolic level they substitute or stand for something unconsciously desired but forbidden. All of these explanations have this in common, that they assume that the stealing is a means to an end, namely, the possession of some object of value, and that it is, in this sense, rational and "utilitarian." However, the fact cannot be blinked—and this fact is of crucial importance in defining our problem—that much gang stealing has no such motivation at all. Even where the value of the object stolen is itself a motivating consideration, the stolen sweets are often sweeter than those acquired by more legitimate and prosaic means. In homelier language, stealing "for the hell of it" and apart from considerations of gain and profit is a valued activity to which attaches glory, prowess and profound satisfaction. There is no accounting in rational and utilitarian terms for the effort expended and the danger run in stealing things which are often discarded, destroyed or casually given away. A group of boys enters a store where each takes a hat, a ball or a light bulb. They then move on to another store where these things are covertly exchanged for like articles. Then they move on to other stores to continue the game indefinitely. They steal a basket of peaches, desultorily munch on a few of them and leave the rest to spoil. They steal clothes they cannot wear and toys they will not use. Unquestionably, most delinquents are from the more "needy" and "underprivileged" classes, and unquestionably many things are stolen because they are intrinsically valued. However, a humane and compassionate regard for their economic disabilities should not blind us to the fact that stealing is not merely an alternative means to the acquisition of objects otherwise difficult of attainment.[1]

Can we then account for this stealing by simply describing it as another form of recreation, play or sport? Surely it is that, but why is this form of play so attractive to some and so unappealing to others? Mountain climbing, chess, pinball, number pools and bingo are also different kinds of recreation. Each of us, child or adult, can choose from a host of alternative means for satisfying our common "need" for recreation. But every choice expresses a preference, and every preference reflects something about the chooser or his circumstances that endows the object of his choice with some special quality or virtue. The choice is not self-explanatory nor is it arbitrary or random. Each form of recreation is distributed in a characteristic way among the age, sex and social class sectors of our population. The explanation of these distributions and of the way they change is often puzzling, sometimes fascinating and rarely platitudinous.

By the same logic, it is an imperfect answer to our problem to say: "Stealing is but another way of satisfying the universal desire for status." Nothing is more obvious from numberless case histories of subcultural delinquents that they steal to achieve recognition and to avoid isolation or opprobrium. This is an important insight and part of the foundation on which we shall build. But the question still haunts us: "Why is stealing a claim to status in one group and a degrading blot in another?"

If stealing itself is not motivated by rational, utilitarian considerations, still less are the manifold other activities which constitute the delinquent's repertoire. Throughout there is a kind of *malice* apparent, an enjoyment in the discomfiture of others, a delight in the defiance of taboos itself. Thrasher quotes one gang delinquent:

> We did all kinds of dirty tricks for fun. We'd see a sign, "Please keep the streets clean," but we'd tear it down and say, "We don't feel like keeping it clean." One day we put a can of glue in the engine of a man's car. We would always tear things down. That would make us laugh and feel good, to have so many jokes.[2]

The gang exhibits this gratuitous hostility toward nongang peers as well as adults. Apart from its more dramatic manifestations in the form of gang wars, there is keen delight in terrorizing "good" children, in driving them from playgrounds and gyms for which the gang itself may have little use, and in general in making themselves obnoxious to the virtuous. The same spirit is evident in playing hookey and in misbehavior in school. The teacher and her rules are not merely something onerous to be evaded. They are to be *flouted*. There is an element of active spite and malice, contempt and ridicule, challenge and defiance, exquisitely symbolized, in an incident described to the writer by Henry D. McKay, of defecating on the teacher's desk.[3]

All this suggests also the intention of our term "negativistic." The delinquent subculture is not only a set of rules, a design for living which is different from or indifferent to or even in conflict with the norms of the "respectable" adult society. It would appear at least plausible that it is defined by its "negative polarity" to those norms. That is, the delinquent subculture takes its norms from the larger culture but turns them upside down. The delinquent's conduct is right, by the standards of his subculture, precisely *because* it is wrong by the norms of the larger culture.[4] "Malicious" and "nega-tivistic" are foreign to the delinquent's vocabulary but he will often assure us, sometimes ruefully, sometimes with a touch of glee or even pride, that he is "just plain mean."

In describing what might be called the "spirit" of the delin-quent culture, we have suggested also its *versatility*. Of the "anti-social" activities of the delinquent gangs, stealing, of course, looms largest. Stealing itself can be, and for the gang usually is, a diversified occupation. It may steal milk bottles, candy, fruit, pencils, sports equipment and cars; it may steal from drunks, homes, stores, schools and filling stations. No gang runs the whole gamut but neither is it likely to "specialize" as do many adult criminal gangs and "solitary" delinquents. More to our point, however, is the fact that stealing tends to go hand-in-hand with "other property offenses," "malicious mischief," "vandalism," "trespass," and truancy. This quality of versatility and the fusion of versatility and malice are manifest in the following quotation:

> We would get some milk bottles in front of the grocery store and break them in somebody's hallway. Then we would break windows or get some garbage cans and throw them down some-one's front stairs. After doing all this dirty work and running through alleys and yards, we'd go over to a grocery store. There, some of the boys would hide in a hallway while I would get a basket of grapes. When the man came after me, why the boys would jump out of their places and each grab a basket of grapes.[5]

Dozens of young offenders, after relating to the writer this delin-quent episode and that, have summarized: "I guess we was just ornery." A generalized, diversified, protean "orneriness," not this or that specialized delinquent pursuit seems best to describe the voca-tion of the delinquent gang.[6]

Another characteristic of the subculture of the delinquent gang is *short-run hedonism*. There is little interest in long-run goals, in planning activities and budgeting time, or in activities involving knowledge and skills to be acquired only through practice, delibera-tion and study. The members of the gang typically congregate, with no specific activity in mind, at some street corner, candy store or other regular rendezvous. They "hang around," "roughhousing," "chewing the fat," and "waiting for something to turn up." They may respond impulsively to somebody's suggestion to play ball, go swimming, engage in some sort of mischief, or do something else that offers excitement. They do not take kindly to organized and super-vised recreation, which subjects them to a regime of schedules and impersonal rules. They are impatient, impetuous and out for "fun," with little heed to the remoter gains and costs. It is to be noted that this short-run hedonism is not inherently delinquent and indeed it would be a serious error to think of the delinquent gang as dedicated solely to the cultivation of juvenile crime. Even in the most seriously

136

delinquent gang only a small fraction of the "fun" is specifically and intrinsically delinquent. Furthermore, short-run hedonism is not characteristic of delinquent groups alone. On the contrary, it is common throughout the social class from which delinquents characteristically come. However, in the delinquent gang it reaches its finest flower. It is the fabric, as it were, of which delinquency is the most brilliant and spectacular thread.[7]

Another characteristic not peculiar to the delinquent gang but a conspicuous ingredient of its culture is an emphasis on *group autonomy*, or intolerance of restraint except from the informal pressures within the group itself. Relations with gang members tend to be intensely solidary and imperious. Relations with other groups tend to be indifferent, hostile or rebellious. Gang members are unusually resistant to the efforts of home, school and other agencies to regulate, not only their delinquent activities, but any activities carried on within the group, and to efforts to compete with the gang for the time and other resources of its members. It may be argued that the resistance of gang members to the authority of the home may not be a result of their membership in gangs but that membership in gangs on the contrary, is a result of ineffective family supervision, the breakdown of parental authority and the hostility of the child toward the parents; in short, that the delinquent gang recruits members who have already achieved autonomy. Certainly a previous breakdown in family controls facilitates recruitment into delinquent gangs. But we are not speaking of the autonomy, the emancipation of *individuals.* It is not the individual delinquent but the gang that is autonomous. For many of our subcultural delinquents the claims of the home are very real and very compelling. The point is that the gang is a separate, distinct and often irresistible focus of attraction, loyalty and solidarity. The claims of the home versus the claims of the gang may present a real dilemma, and in such cases the breakdown of family controls is as much a casualty as a cause of gang membership.[8]

NOTES

1   See H. M. Tiebout and M. E. Kirkpatrick, "Psychiatric Factors in Stealing," *American Journal of Orthopsychiatry*, II (April, 1932), 114-123, which discusses, in an exceptionally lucid manner, the distinction between motivating factors which center around the acquisition of the object and those which center around the commission of the act itself.

The non-utilitarian nature of juvenile delinquency has been noted by many students. ". . . while older offenders may have definitely crystallized beliefs about profitable returns from antisocial conduct, it is very clear that in childhood and in earlier youth delinquency is certainly not entered into as a paying proposition in any ordinary sense." William Healy and Augusta F. Bronner, *op. cit.*, p. 22. "The juvenile property offender's thefts, at least at the start, are usually 'for fun' and not for gain." Paul Tappan, *Juvenile Delinquency* (New York: McGraw Hill Book Company, (1949), p. 143. "Stealing, the leading predatory activity of the adolescent gang, is as much a result of the sport motive as of a desire for revenue."

Frederic M. Thrasher, *The Gang* (Chicago: University of Chicago Press, 1936), p. 143. "In its early stages, delinquency is clearly a form of play." Henry D. McKay, "The Neighborhood and Child Conduct," *Annals of the American Academy of Political and Social Science,* CCLXI (January, 1949), p. 37. See also Barbara Bellow, Milton L. Blum, Kenneth B. Clark, *et al.,* "Prejudice in Seaside," *Human Relations,* I (1947), 15-16 and Sophia M. Robison, Nathan Cohen and Murray Sachs, "An Unsolved Problem in Group Relations," *Journal of Educational Psychology,* XX (November, 1946), 154-162. The last cited paper is an excellent description of the nonutilitarian, malicious and negativistic quality of the delinquent subculture and is the clearest statement in the literature that a satisfactory theory of delinquency must make sense of these facts.

2   Frederick M. Thrasher, *The Gang* (Chicago: University of Chicago Press, 1936), pp. 94-95.

3   To justify the characterization of the delinquent subculture as "malicious" by multiplying citations from authorities would be empty pedantry. The malice is evident in any detailed description of juvenile gang life. We commend in particular, however, the cited works of Thrasher, Shaw and McKay and Robison *et al.* One aspect of this "gratuitous hostility" deserves special mention, however, for the benefit of those who see in the provision of facilities for "wholesome recreation" some magical therapeutic virtue. "On entering a playground or a gym the first activity of gang members is to disrupt and interrupt whatever activities are going on. Non-gang members flee, and when the coast is clear the gang plays desultorily on the apparatus or carries on horseplay." Sophia Robison *et. al., op. cit.,* p. 159. See, to the same effect, the excellent little book by Kenneth H. Rogers, *Street Gangs in Toronto* (Toronto: The Ryerson Press, 1945), pp. 18-19.

4   Shaw and McKay, in their *Social Factors in Juvenile Delinquency,* p. 241, come very close to making this point quite explicitly: "In fact the standards of these groups may represent a complete reversal of the standards and norms of conventional society. Types of conduct which result in personal degradation and dishonor in a conventional group, serve to enhance and elevate the personal prestige and status of a member of the delinquent group."

5   Clifford R. Shaw and Henry D. McKay, *Social Factors in Juvenile Delinquency,* Vol. II of National Commission on Law Observance and Enforcement, *Report on the Causes of Crime* (Washington: U.S. Government Printing Office, 1931), p. 18.

6   *Federal Probation,* XVIII (March, 1954), pp. 3-16 contains an extremely valuable symposium on vandalism, which highlights all of the characteristics we have imputed to the delinquent subculture. In the belief that no generalization can convey the flavor and scope of this subculture as well as a simple but massive enumeration, we quote at length from Joseph E. Murphy's contribution, pp. 8-9.

Studies of the complaints made by citizens and public officials reveal that hardly any property is safe from this form of aggression. Schools are often the object of attack by vandals. Windows are broken; records, books, desks, typewriters, supplies, and other equipment are stolen or destroyed. Public property of all types appears to offer peculiar allurement to children bent on destruction. Parks, playgrounds, highway signs, and markers are frequently defaced or destroyed. Trees, shrubs, flowers, benches, and other equipment suffer in like manner. Autoists are constantly reporting the slashing or releasing of air from tires, broken windows, stolen accessories. Golf clubs complain that benches, markers, flags, even expensive and difficult-to-replace putting greens are defaced broken or uprooted. Libraries report the theft and destruction of books and other equipment. Railroads complain of and demand protection from the destruction of freight car seals, theft of property, willful and deliberate throwing of stones at passenger car windows, tampering with rails and switches. Vacant houses are always the particular delight of children seeking outlets for destructive instincts; windows are broken, plumbing and hardware stolen, destroyed, or rendered unusable. Gasoline operators report pumps and other service equipment stolen, broken, or destroyed. Theatre managers, frequently in the "better" neighborhoods, complain of the slashing of seats, willful damaging of toilet facilities, even the burning of rugs, carpets, etc.

Recently the Newark *Evening News*, commenting editorially on the problem of vandalism in New York City housing projects, stated "housing authorities complain of the tearing out of steel banisters, incinerator openings, and mail boxes, damaging of elevators, defacing walls, smashing windows and light bulbs, stealing nozzles of fire hoses, destroying trees and benches on the project's grounds and occasionally plundering and setting fire to parked cars. Moreover, gangs have terrorized not only tenants but also the three hundred unarmed watchmen hired to protect the property."

This quotation places "stealing" in the context of a host of other manifestations of the protean "orneriness" of which we have spoken. The implication is strong that the fact that an object is "stolen" rather than destroyed or damaged is, from the standpoint of motivation, almost incidental. J. P. Shalloo, *ibid.*, pp. 6-7, states in a forceful way the problem which this creates for criminological theory: "Delinquency and crime are, and have been regarded as, purposeful behavior. But wanton and vicious destruction of property both public and private by teen-age hoodlums reveals no purpose, no rhyme, no reason. . . . These are not the actions of thoughtless youth. These are actions based upon a calculated contempt for the rights of others . . ."

It is widely believed that vandalism, on the scale we know it today, is a relatively recent phenomenon. Douglas H. MacNeil, *ibid.*, p. 16, observes that, although vandalism is a form of delinquency which has been neglected by social scientists, there is little reason to believe that it has increased spectacularly, if at all, in recent years. Apparently it is and it has been for many years part and parcel, indeed the very spirit, of the delinquent subculture.

In connection with the versatility of the delinquent subculture, it should be noted that truancy is also institutionalized in the delinquent gang. In Lester E. Hewitt and Richard L. Jenkins, *Fundamental Patterns of Maladjustment* (published by the State of Illinois, no date), p. 94, habitual truancy is found to have a tetrachoric coefficient of correlation of .10 with the "unsocialized aggressive" syndrome, $-.08$ with the "over-inhibited behavior" syndrome and .75 with the "socialized delinquent" syndrome. These findings are of special interest because the latter syndrome corresponds closely to what we have called the delinquent subculture. For summaries of studies on the relationship between truancy and other forms of delinquency see Norman Fenton, *The Delinquent Boy and the Correctional School* (Claremont, California: Claremont Colleges Guidance Center, 1935), pp. 66-69 and William Kvaraceus, *Juvenile Delinquency and the School* (Yonkers-on-Hudson: World Book Company, 1945), pp. 144-146.

7   See the splendid report on "Working with a Street Gang" in Sylvan S. Furman (ed.), *Reaching the Unreached* (New York: New York City Youth Board, 1952), pp. 112-121. On this quality of short-run hedonism we quote, p. 13:

"One boy once told me, 'Now, for example, you take an average day. What happens? We come down to the restaurant and we sit in the restaurant, and sit and sit. All right, say, er . . . after a couple of hours in the restaurant, maybe we'll go to a poolroom, shoot a little pool, that's if somebody's got the money. O.K., a little pool, come back. By this time the restaurant is closed. We go in the candy store, sit around the candy store for a while, and that's it, that's all we do, man.'"

See also Barbara Bellow *et al., op. cit.,* pp. 4-15, and Ruth Topping, "Treatment of the Pseudo-Social Boy," *American Journal of Orthopsychiatry,* XIII (April, 1943), p. 353.

8   The solidarity of the gang and the dependence of its members upon one another are especially well described in Barbara Bellow *et. al., op. cit.,* p. 16 and Sophia Robison *et al., op. cit.,* p. 158.

Lower Class Culture as a Generating Milieu of Gang Delinquency

WALTER B. MILLER

Walter B. Miller is a professor of sociology at Massachusetts Institute of Technology.

Reprinted from Walter B. Miller, "Lower Class Culture as a Generating Milieu of Gang Delinquency," *Journal of Social Issues* 14 (1958): 5-19.

The etiology of delinquency has long been a controversial issue, and is particularly so at present. As new frames of reference for explaining human behavior have been added to traditional theories, some authors have adopted the practice of citing the major postulates of each school of thought as they pertain to delinquency, and going on to state that causality must be conceived in terms of the dynamic interaction of a complex combination of variables on many levels. The major sets of etiological factors currently adduced to explain delinquency are, in simplified terms, the physiological (delinquency results from organic pathology), the psycho-dynamic (delinquency is a "behavioral disorder" resulting primarily from emotional disturbance generated by a defective mother-child relationship), and the environmental (delinquency is the producer of disruptive forces, "disorganization," in the actor's physical or social environment).

This paper selects one particular kind of "delinquency"[1]—law-violating acts committed by members of adolescent street corner groups in lower class communities—and attempts to show that the dominant component of motivation underlying these acts consists in directed attempt by the actor to adhere to forms of behavior, and to achieve standards of value as they are defined within that community. It takes as a premise that the motivation of behavior in this situation can be approached most productively by attempting to understand the nature of cultural forces impinging on the acting individual as they are perceived *by the actor himself*—although by no means only that segment of these forces of which the actor is consciously aware—rather than as they are perceived and evaluated from the reference position of another cultural system. In the case of "gang" delinquency, the cultural system which exerts the most direct influence on behavior is that of the lower class community itself—a long-established, distinctively patterned tradition with an integrity of its own—rather than a so-called "delinquent subculture" which has arisen through conflict with middle class culture and is oriented to the deliberate violation of middle class norms.

The bulk of the substantive data on which the following material is based was collected in connection with a service-research project in the control of gang delinquency. During the service aspect of the project, which lasted for three years, seven trained social workers maintained contact with twenty-one corner group units in a "slum" district of a large eastern city for periods of time ranging from ten to thirty months. Groups were Negro and white, male and female, and in early, middle, and late adolescence. Over eight thousand pages of direct observational data on behavior patterns of group members and other community residents were collected; almost daily contact was maintained for a total time period of about thirteen worker years. Data include workers' contact reports, participant observation reports by the writer—a cultural anthropologist—and direct tape recordings of group activities and discussions.[2]

FOCAL CONCERNS OF LOWER CLASS CULTURE

There is a substantial segment of present-day American society whose way of life, values, and characteristic patterns of behavior are the product of a distinctive cultural system which may be termed "lower class." Evidence indicates that this cultural system is becoming increasingly distinctive, and that the size of the group which shares this tradition is increasing.[3] The lower class way of life, in common with that of all distinctive cultural groups, is characterized by a set of focal concerns—areas or issues which command widespread and persistent attention and a high degree of emotional involvement. The specific concerns cited here, while by no means confined to the American lower classes, constitute a distinctive *patterning* of concerns which differs significantly, both in rank order and weighting from that of American middle class culture. Table 1 presents a highly schematic and simplified listing of six of the major concerns of lower class culture. Each is conceived as a "dimension" within which a fairly wide and varied range of alternative behavior patterns may be followed by different individuals under different situations. They are listed roughly in order of the degree of *explicit* attention accorded each, and, in this sense represent a weighted ranking of concerns. The "perceived alternatives" represent polar positions which define certain parameters within each dimension. As will be explained in more detail, it is necessary in relating the influence of these "concerns" to the motivation of delinquent behavior to specify *which* of its aspects is oriented to, whether orientation is *overt* or *covert*, *positive* (conforming to or seeking the aspect), or *negative* (rejecting or seeking to avoid the aspect).

The concept "focal concern" is used here in preference to the concept "value" for several interrelated reasons:

(1) It is more readily derivable from direct field observation.
(2) It is descriptively neutral—permitting independent consideration of positive and negative valences as varying under different conditions, whereas "value" carries a built-in positive valence.
(3) It makes possible more refined analysis of subcultural differences, since it reflects actual behavior, whereas "value" tends to wash out intracultural differences since it is colored by notions of the "official" ideal.

Table 1
Focal concerns of lower class culture

Area	Perceived Alternatives (state, quality, condition)	
1. *Trouble:*	law-abiding behavior	law-violating behavior
2. *Toughness:*	physical prowess, skill; "masculinity"; fearlessness, bravery, daring	weakness, ineptitude; effeminacy; timidity, cowardice, caution
3. *Smartness:*	ability to outsmart, dupe, "con"; gaining money by "wits"; shrewdness, adroitness in repartee	gullibility, "con-ability"; gaining money by hard work; slowness, dull-wittedness, verbal maladroitness
4. *Excitement:*	thrill; risk, danger; change, activity	boredom; "deadness," safeness; sameness, passivity
5. *Fate:*	favored by fortune, being "lucky"	ill-omened, being "unlucky"
6. *Autonomy:*	freedom from external constraint; freedom from superordinate authority; independence	presence of external constraint; presence of strong authority; dependency, being "cared for"

142

Trouble:

Concern over "trouble" is a dominant feature of lower class culture. The concept has various shades of meaning; "trouble" as one of its aspects represents a situation or a kind of behavior which results in unwelcome or complicating involvement with official authorities or agencies of middle class society. "Getting into trouble" and "staying out of trouble" represent major issues for male and female, adults and children. For men, "trouble" frequently involves fighting or sexual adventures while drinking; for women, sexual involvement with disadvantageous consequences. Expressed desire to avoid behavior which violates moral or legal norms is often based less on an explicit commitment to "official" moral or legal standards than on a desire to avoid "getting into trouble," e.g., the complicating consequences of the action.

The dominant concern over "trouble" involves a distinction of critical importance for the lower class community—that between "law-abiding" and "non-law-abiding" behavior. There is a high degree of sensitivity as to where each person stands in relation to these two classes of activity. Whereas in the middle class community a major dimension for evaluating a person's status is "achievement" and its external symbols, in the lower class, personal status is very frequently gauged along the law-abiding-non-law-abiding dimension. A mother will evaluate the suitability of her daughter's boyfriend less on the basis of his achievement potential than on the basis of his innate "trouble" potential. This sensitive awareness of the opposition of "trouble-producing" and "non-trouble-producing" behavior represents both a major basis for deriving status distinctions and an internalized conflict potential for the individual.

As in the case of other focal concerns, which of two perceived alternatives—"law-abiding" or "non-law-abiding"—is valued varies according to the individual and the circumstances; in many instances there is an overt commitment to the "law-abiding" alternative, but a covert commitment to the "non-law-abiding." In certain situations, "getting into trouble" is overtly recognized as prestige-conferring; for example, membership in certain adult and adolescent primary groupings ("gangs") is contingent on having demonstrated an explicit commitment to the law-violating alternative. It is most important to note that the choice between "law-abiding" and "non-law-abiding" behavior is still a choice *within* lower class culture; the distinction between the policeman and the criminal, the outlaw and the sheriff, involves primarily this one dimension; in other respects they have a high community of interests. Not infrequently brothers raised in an identical cultural milieu will become police and criminals respectively.

For a substantial segment of the lower class population "getting into trouble" is not in itself overtly defined as prestige-conferring, but is implicitly recognized as a means to other valued ends, e.g., the covertly valued desire to be "cared for" and subject to external constraint, or the overtly valued state of excitement or risk. Very frequently "getting into trouble" is multi-functional, and achieves several sets of valued ends.

Toughness

The concept of "toughness" in lower class culture represents a compound combination of qualities or states. Among its most important components are physical prowess, evidenced both by demonstrated possession of strength and endurance and athletic skill; "masculinity," symbolized by a distinctive complex of acts and avoidances (bodily tatooing; absence of sentimentality; non-concern with "art," "literature," conceptualization of women as conquest objects, etc.); and bravery in the face of physical threat. The model for the "tough guy" —hard, fearless, undemonstrative, skilled in physical combat—is represented by the movie gangster of the thirties, the "private eye," and the movie cowboy.

The genesis of the intense concern over "toughness" in lower class culture is probably related to the fact that a significant proportion of lower class males are reared in a predominantly female household, and lack a consistently present male figure with whom to identify and from whom to learn essential components of a "male" role. Since women serve as a primary object of identification during pre-adolescent years, the almost obsessive lower class concern with "masculinity" probably resembles a type of compulsive reaction-formation. A concern over homosexuality runs like a persistent thread through lower class culture. This is manifested by the institutionalized practice of baiting "queers," often accompanied by violent physical attacks, an expressed contempt for "softness" or frills, and the use of the local term for "homosexual" as a generalized pejorative epithet (e.g., higher class individuals or upwardly mobile peers are frequently characterized as "fags" or "queers"). The distinction between "overt" and "covert" orientation to aspects of an area of concern is especially important in regard to "toughness." A positive overt evaluation of behavior defined as "effeminate" would be out of the question for a lower class male; however, built into lower class culture is a range of devices which permit men to adopt behaviors and concerns which in other cultural milieux fall within the province of women, and at the same time to be defined as "tough" and manly. For example, lower class men can be professional short-order cooks in a diner and still be regarded as "tough." The highly intimate circumstances of the street corner gang involve the recurrent expression of strongly affectionate feelings towards other men. Such expressions, however, are disguised as their opposite, taking the form of ostensibly aggressive verbal and physical interaction (kidding, "ranking," roughhousing, etc.).

Smartness

"Smartness," as conceptualized in lower class culture, involves the capacity to outsmart, outfox, outwit, dupe, "take," "con" another or others, and the concomitant capacity to avoid being outwitted, "taken," or duped oneself. In its essence, smartness involves the capacity to achieve a valued entity—material goods, personal status—through a maximum use of mental agility and a minimum use of physical effort. This capacity has an extremely long tradition in lower class culture, and is highly valued. Lower class culture can be characterized as "non-intellectual" only if intellectualism is defined specifically in terms of control over a particular body of formally learned knowledge involving "culture" (art, literature, "good" music, etc.), a generalized perspective on the past and present conditions of our own and other societies, and other areas of knowledge imparted by formal educational institutions. This particular type of mental attainment is, in general, overtly disvalued and frequently associated with effeminacy; "smartness" in the lower class sense, however, is highly valued.

The lower class child learns and practices the use of this skill in the street corner situation. Individuals continually practice duping and outwitting one another through recurrent card games and other forms of gambling, mutual exchanges of insults, and "testing" for mutual "conability." Those who demonstrate competence in this skill are accorded considerable prestige. Leadership roles in the corner group are frequently allocated according to demonstrated capacity in the two areas of "smartness" and "toughness"; the ideal leader combines both, but the "smart" leader is often accorded more prestige than the "tough" one—reflecting a general lower class respect for "brain" in the "smartness" sense.[4]

The model of the "smart" person is represented in popular media by the card shark, the professional gambler, the "con" artist, the promoter. A conceptual distinction is made between two kinds of people: "suckers," easy marks, "lushes," dupes, who work for their money and are legitimate targets of exploitation; and sharp operators, the "brainy" ones, who live by their wits and "getting" from the suckers by mental adroitness.

Involved in the syndrome of capacities related to "smartness" is a dominant emphasis in lower class culture on ingenious aggressive repartee. This skill, learned and practiced in the context of the corner group, ranges in form from the widely prevalent semi-ritualized teasing, kidding, razzing "ranking," so characteristic of male peer group interaction, to the highly ritualized type of mutual insult interchange known as "the dirty dozens," "the dozens," "playing house," and other terms. This highly patterned cultural form is practiced on its most advanced level in adult male Negro society, but less polished variants are found throughout lower class culture—practiced, for example, by white children, male and female, as young as four or five. In essence, "doin' the dozens" involves two antagonists who vie with each other in the exchange of increasingly inflammatory insults, with incestuous and perverted sexual relations with the mother a dominant theme. In this form of insult interchange, as well as on other less ritualized occasions for joking, semi-serious, and serious mutual invective, a very high premium is placed on ingenuity, hair-trigger responsiveness, inventiveness, and the acute exercise of mental faculties.

Excitement

For many lower class individuals the rhythm of life fluctuates be- tween periods of relatively routine or repetitive activity and sought situations of great emotional stimulation. Many of the most char- acteristic features of lower class life are related to the search for excitement or "thrill." Involved here are the highly prevalent use of alcohol by both sexes and the widespread use of gambling of all kinds—playing the numbers, betting on horse races, dice, cards. The quest for excitement finds what is perhaps its most vivid expression in the highly patterned practice of the recurrent "night on the town." This practice, designated by various terms in different areas ("honky-tonkin'"; "goin' out on the town"; "bar hoppin'"), involves a patterned set of activities in which alcohol, music, and sexual ad- venturing are major components. A group or individual sets out to "make the rounds" of various bars or night clubs. Drinking continues progressively throughout the evening. Men seek to "pick up" women, and women play the risky game of entertaining sexual advances. Fights between men involving women, gambling, and claims of physical prowess, in various combinations, are frequent consequences of a night of making the rounds. The explosive potential of this type of adventuring with sex and aggression, frequently leading to "trouble," is semi-explicitly sought by the individual. Since there is always a good likelihood that being out on the town will eventuate in fights, etc., the practice involves elements of sought risk and desired danger.

Counterbalancing the "flirting with danger" aspect of the "excitement" concern is the prevalence in lower class culture of other well established patterns of activity which involve long periods of relative inaction, or passivity. The term "hanging out" in lower class culture refers to extended periods of standing around, often with peer mates, doing what is defined as "nothing," "shooting the breeze," etc. A definite periodicity exists in the pattern of activity relating to the two aspects of the "excitement" dimension. For many lower class individuals the venture into the high risk world of alcohol, sex, and fighting occurs regularly once a week, with interim periods devoted to accommodating to possible consequences of these periods, along with recurrent resolves not to become so involved again.

Fate

Related to the quest for excitement is the concern with fate, fortune, or luck. Here also a distinction is made between two states—being "lucky" or "in luck," and being unlucky or jinxed. Many lower class individuals feel that their lives are subject to a set of forces over which they have relatively little control. These are not directly equated with the supernatural forces of formally organized religion, but relate more to a concept of "destiny," or man as a pawn of magical powers. Not infrequently this often implicit world view is associated with a conception of the ultimate futility of directed effort towards a goal: if the cards are right, or the dice good to you, or if your lucky number comes up, things will go your way; if luck is against you, it's not worth trying. The concept of performing semimagical rituals so that one's "luck will change" is prevalent; one hopes that as a result he will move from the state of being "unlucky" to that of being "lucky." The element of fantasy plays an important part in this area. Related to and complementing the notion that "only suckers work" (Smartness) is the idea that once things start going your way, relatively independent of your own effort, all good things will come to you. Achieving great material rewards (big cars, big houses, a roll of cash to flash in a fancy night club), valued in lower class as well as in other parts of American culture, is a recurrent theme in lower class fantasy and folk lore; the cocaine dreams of Willie the Weeper or Minnie the Moocher present the components of this fantasy in vivid detail.

The prevalence in the lower class community of many forms of gambling, mentioned in connection with the "excitement" dimension, is also relevant here. Through cards and pool which involve skill, and thus both "toughness" and "smartness"; or through race horse betting, involving "smartness"; or through playing the numbers, involving predominantly "luck" one may make a big killing with a minimum of directed and persistent effort within conventional occupational channels. Gambling in its many forms illustrates the fact that many of the persistent features of lower class culture are multifunctional—serving a range of desired ends at the same time. Describing some of the incentives behind gambling has involved mention of all the focal concerns cited so far—Toughness, Smartness, and Excitement, in addition to Fate.

Autonomy

The extent and nature of control over the behavior of the individual —an important concern in most cultures—has a special significance and is distinctively patterned in lower class culture. The discrepancy between what is overtly valued and what is covertly sought is particularly striking in this area. On the overt level there is a strong and frequently expressed resentment of the idea of external controls, restrictions on behavior, and unjust or coercive authority. "No one's gonna push *me* around," or "I'm gonna tell him he can take the job and shove it. . . ." are commonly expressed sentiments. Similar explicit attitudes are maintained to systems of behavior-restricting rules, insofar as these are perceived as representing the injunctions, and bearing the sanctions of superordinate authority. In addition, in lower class culture a close conceptual connection is made between "authority" and "nurturance." To be restrictively or firmly controlled is to be cared for. Thus the overtly negative evaluation of superordinate authority frequently extends as well to nuturance, care, or protection. The desire for personal independence is often expressed in such terms as "I don't need *nobody* to take care of me. I can take care of myself!" Actual patterns of behavior, however, reveal a marked discrepancy between expressed sentiment and what is covertly valued. Many lower class people appear to seek out highly restrictive social environments wherein stringent external controls are maintained over their behavior. Such institutions as the armed forces, the mental hospital, the disciplinary school, the prison or correctional institution, provide environments which incorporate a strict and detailed set of rules defining and limiting behavior, and enforced by an authority system which controls and applies coercive sanctions for deviances from these rules. While under the jurisdiction of such systems, the lower class person generally expresses to his peers continual resentment of the coercive, unjust, and arbitrary exercise of authority. Having been released, or having escaped from these milieux, however, he will often act in such a way as to insure recommitment, or choose recommitment voluntarily after a temporary period of "freedom."

Lower class patients in mental hospitals will exercise considerable ingenuity to insure continued commitment while voicing the desire to get out; delinquent boys will frequently "run" from a correctional institution to activate efforts to return them; to be caught and returned means that one is cared for. Since "being controlled" is equated with "being cared for," attempts are frequently made to "test" the severity of strictness of superordinate authority to see if it remains firm. If intended or executed rebellion produces swift and firm punitive sanctions, the individual is reassured, at the same time that he is complaining bitterly at the injustice of being caught and punished. Some environmental milieux, having been tested in this fashion for the "firmness" of their coercive sanctions, are rejected, ostensibly for being too strict, actually for not being strict enough. This is frequently so in the case of "problematic" behavior by lower class youngsters in the public schools, which generally cannot command the coercive controls implicitly sought by the individual.

A similar discrepancy between what is overtly and covertly desired is found in the area of dependence-independence. The pose of tough rebellious independence often assumed by the lower class person frequently conceals powerful dependency cravings. These are manifested primarily by obliquely expressed resentment when "care" is not forthcoming rather than by expressed satisfaction when it is. The concern over autonomy-dependency is related both to "trouble" and "fate." Insofar as the lower class individual feels that his behavior is controlled by forces which often propel him into "trouble" in the face of an explicit determination to avoid it, there is an implied appeal to "save me from myself." A solution appears to lie in arranging things so that his behavior will be coercively restricted by an externally imposed set of controls strong enough to forcibly restrain his inexplicable inclination to get in trouble. The periodicity observed in connection with the "excitement" dimension is also relevant here; after involvement in trouble-producing behavior (assault, sexual adventure, a "drunk"), the individual will actively seek a locus of imposed control (his wife, prison, a restrictive job); after a given period of subjection to this control, resentment against it mounts, leading to a "break away" and a search for involvement in further "trouble."

FOCAL CONCERNS OF THE LOWER CLASS ADOLESCENT STREET CORNER GROUP

The one-sex peer group is a highly prevalent and significant structural form in the lower class community. There is a strong probability that the prevalence and stability of this type of unit is directly related to the prevalence of a stabilized type of lower class child-rearing unit—the "female-based" household. This is a nuclear kin unit in which a male parent is either absent from the household, present only sporadically, or, when present, only minimally or inconsistently involved in the support and rearing of children. This unit usually consists of one or more females of child-bearing age and their offspring. The females are frequently related to one another by blood or marriage ties, and the unit often includes two or more generations of women, e.g., the mother and/or aunt of the principal child-bearing female.

The nature of social groupings in the lower class community may be clarified if we make the assumption that it is the *one-sex peer unit* rather than the two-parent family unit which represents the most significant relational unit for both sexes in lower class communities. Lower class society may be pictured as comprising a set of age-graded one-sex groups which constitute the major psychic focus and reference group for those over twelve or thirteen. Men and women of mating age leave these groups periodically to form temporary marital alliances, but these lack stability, and after varying periods of "trying out" the two-sex family arrangement, gravitate back to the more "comfortable" one-sex grouping, whose members exert strong pressure on the individual *not* to disrupt the group by adopting a two-sex household pattern of life.[5] Membership in a stable and solidary peer unit is vital to the lower class individual precisely to the extent to which a range of essential functions—psychological, educational, and others, are not provided by the "family" unit.

The adolescent street corner group represents the adolescent variant of this lower class structural form. What has been called the "delinquent gang" is one subtype of this form, defined on the basis of frequency of participation in law-violating activity; this subtype should not be considered a legitimate unit of study per se, but rather as one particular variant of the adolescent street corner group. The "hanging" peer group is a unit of particular importance for the adolescent male. In many cases it is the most stable and solidary primary group he has ever belonged to; for boys reared in female-based households the corner group provides the first real opportunity to learn essential aspects of the male role in the context of peers facing similar problems of sex-role identification.

The form and functions of the adolescent corner group operate as a selective mechanism in recruiting members. The activity patterns of the group require a high level of intra-group solidarity; individual members must possess a good capacity for subordinating individual desires to general group interests as well as the capacity for intimate and persisting interaction. Thus highly "disturbed" individuals, or those who cannot tolerate consistently imposed sanctions on "deviant" behavior cannot remain accepted members; the group itself will extrude those whose behavior exceeds limits defined as "normal." This selective process produces a type of group whose members possess to an unusually high degree both the *capacity* and *motivation* to conform to perceived cultural norms, so that the nature of the system of norms and values oriented to is a particularly influential component of motivation.

Focal concerns of the male adolescent corner group are those of the general cultural milieu in which it functions. As would be expected, the relative weighting and importance of these concerns pattern somewhat differently for adolescents than for adults. The nature of this patterning centers around two additional "concerns" of particular importance to this group—concern with "belonging," and with "status." These may be conceptualized as being on a higher level of abstraction than concerns previously cited, since "status" and "belonging" are achieved *via* cited concern areas of Toughness, etc.

Belonging

Since the corner group fulfills essential functions for the individual, being a member in good standing of the group is of vital importance for its members. A continuing concern over who is "in" and who is not involves the citation and detailed discussion of highly refined criteria for "in-group" membership. The phrase "he hangs with us" means "he is accepted as a member in good standing by current consensus"; conversely, "he don't hang with us" means he is not so accepted. One achieves "belonging" primarily by demonstrating knowledge of and a determination to adhere to the system of standards and valued qualities defined by the group. One maintains membership by acting in conformity with valued aspects of Toughness, Smartness, Autonomy, etc. In those instances where conforming to norms of this reference group at the same time violates norms of other reference groups (e.g., middle class adults, institutional "officials"), immediate reference group norms are much more compelling since violation risks involving the group's most powerful sanction: exclusion.

Status

In common with most adolescents in American society, the lower class corner group manifests a dominant concern with status. What differentiates this type of group from others, however, is the particular set of criteria and weighting thereof by which "status" is defined. In general, status is achieved and maintained by demonstrated possession of the valued qualities of lower class culture—Toughness, Smartness, expressed resistance to authority, daring, etc. It is important to stress once more that the individual orients to these concerns *as they are defined within lower class society*; e.g., the status-conferring potential of "smartness" in the sense of scholastic achievement generally ranges from negligible to negative.

The concern with "status" is manifested in a variety of ways. Intragroup status is a continued concern, and is derived and tested constantly by means of a set of status-ranking activities; the intragroup "pecking order" is constantly at issue. One gains status within the group by demonstrated superiority in Toughness (physical prowess, bravery, skill in athletics and games such as pool and cards), Smartness (skill in repartee, capacity to "dupe" fellow group members), and the like. The term "ranking," used to refer to the pattern of intragroup aggressive repartee, indicates awareness of the fact that this is one device for establishing the intragroup status hierarchy.

The concern over status in the adolescent corner group involves in particular the component of "adultness," the intense desire to be seen as "grown up," and a corresponding aversion to "kid stuff." "Adult" status is defined less in terms of the assumption of "adult" responsibility than in terms of certain external symbols of adult status—a car, ready cash, and, in particular, a perceived "freedom" to drink, smoke, and gamble as one wishes and to come and go without restrictions. The desire to be seen as "adult" is often a more significant component of much involvement in illegal drinking, gambling, and automobile driving than the explicit enjoyment of the acts as such.

The intensity of the corner group member's desire to be seen as "adult" is sufficiently great that he feels called upon to demonstrate qualities associated with adultness (Toughness, Smartness, Autonomy) to a much greater degree than a lower class adult. This means that he will seek out and utilize those avenues to these qualities which he perceives as available with greater intensity than an adult and less regard for their "legitimacy." In this sense the adolescent variant of lower class culture represents a maximization of an intensified manifestation of many of its most characteristic features.

Concern over status is also manifested in reference to other street corner groups. The term "rep" used in this regard is especially significant, and has broad connotations. In its most frequent and explicit connotation, "rep" refers to the "toughness" of the corner group as a whole relative to that of other groups; a "pecking order" also exists among the several corner groups in a given interactional area, and there is a common perception that the safety or security of the group and all its members depends on maintaining a solid "rep" for toughness vis-à-vis other groups. This motive is most frequently advanced as a reason for involvement in gang fights: "We *can't* chicken out on this fight; our rep would be shot!"; this implies that the group would be relegated to the bottom of the status ladder and become a helpless and recurrent target of external attack.

On the other hand, there is implicit in the concept of "rep" the recognition that "rep" has or may have a dual basis—corresponding to the two aspects of the "trouble" dimension. It is recognized that group as well as individual status can be based on both "law-abiding" and "law-violating" behavior. The situational resolution of the persisting conflict between the "law-abiding" and "law-violating" bases of status comprises a vital set of dynamics in determining whether a "delinquent" mode of behavior will be adopted by a group, under what circumstances, and how persistently. The determinants of this choice are evidently highly complex and fluid, and rest on a range of factors including the presence and perceptual immediacy of different community reference-group loci (e.g., professional criminals, police, clergy, teachers, settlement house workers), the personality structures and "needs" of group members, the presence in the community of social work, recreation, or educational programs which can facilitate utilization of the "law-abiding" basis of status, and so on.

What remains constant is the critical importance of "status" both for the members of the group as individuals and for the group as a whole insofar as members perceive their individual destinies as linked to the destiny of the group, and the fact that action geared to attain status is much more acutely oriented to the fact of status itself than to the legality or illegality, morality or immorality of the means used to achieve it.

LOWER CLASS CULTURE AND THE MOTIVATION OF DELINQUENT BEHAVIOR

The customary set of activities of the adolescent street corner group includes activities which are in violation of laws and ordinances of the legal code. Most of these center around assault and theft of various types (the gang fight; auto theft; assault on an individual; petty pilfering and shoplifting; "mugging"; pocket-book theft). Members of street corner gangs are well aware of the law-violating nature of these acts; they are not psychopaths, nor physically or mentally "defective"; in fact, since the corner group supports and enforces a rigorous set of standards which demand a high degree of fitness and personal competence, it tends to recruit from the most "able" members of the community.

Why, then, is the commission of crimes a customary feature of gang activity? The most general answer is that the commission of crimes by members of adolescent street corner groups is motivated primarily by the attempt to achieve ends, states, or conditions, which are valued, and to avoid those that are disvalued within their most meaningful cultural milieu, through those culturally available avenues which appear as the most feasible means of attaining those ends.

The operation of these influences is well illustrated by the gang fight—a prevalent and characteristic type of corner group delinquency. This type of activity comprises a highly stylized and culturally patterned set of sequences. Although details vary under different circumstances, the following events are generally included. A member or several members of group A "trespass" on the claimed territory of group B. While there they commit an act or acts which group B defines as a violation of its rightful privileges, an affront to their honor, or a challenge to their "rep." Frequently this act involves advances to a girl associated with group B; it may occur at a dance or party; sometimes the mere act of "trespass" is seen as deliberate provocation. Members of group B then assault members of group A, if they are caught while still in B's territory. Assaulted members of group A return to their "home" territory and recount to members of their group details of the incident, stressing the insufficient nature of the provocation ("I just *looked* at her! Hardly even said anything!"), and the unfair circumstances of the assault ("About *twenty* guys jumped just the *two* of us!"). The highly colored account is acutely inflammatory; group A, perceiving its honor violated and its "rep" threatened, feels obligated to retaliate in force. Sessions of detailed planning now occur; allies are recruited if the size of group A and its potential allies appears to necessitate larger numbers; strategy is plotted, and messengers dispatched. Since the prospect of a gang fight is frightening to even the "toughest" group members, a constant rehearsal of the provocative incident or incidents and the essentially evil nature of the opponents accompanies the planning process to bolster possibly weakening motivation to fight. The excursion into "enemy" territory sometimes results in a full scale fight; more often group B cannot be found, or the police appear and stop the fight, "tipped off" by an anonymous informant. When this occurs, group members express disgust and disappointment; secretly there is much relief; their honor has been avenged without incurring injury; often the anonymous tipster is a member of the involved groups.

The basic elements of this type of delinquency are sufficiently stabilized and recurrent as to constitute an essentially ritualized pattern, resembling both in structure and expressed motives for action classic forms such as the European "duel," the American Indian tribal war, and the Celtic clan feud. Although the arousing and "acting out" of individual aggressive emotions are inevitably involved in the gang fight, neither its form nor motivational dynamics can be adequately handled within a predominantly personality-focused frame of reference.

It would be possible to develop in considerable detail the processes by which the commission of a range of illegal acts is either explicitly supported by, implicitly demanded by, or not materially inhibited by factors relating to the focal concerns of lower class culture. In place of such a development, the following three statements condense in general terms the operation of these processes:

1 Following cultural practices which comprise essential elements of the total life pattern of lower class culture automatically violates certain legal norms.
2 In instances where alternate avenues to similar objectives are available, the non-law-abiding avenue frequently provides a relatively greater and more immediate return for a relatively smaller investment of energy.
3 The "demanded" response to certain situations recurrently engendered within lower class culture involves the commission of illegal acts.

The primary thesis of this paper is that the dominant component of the motivation of "delinquent" behavior engaged in by members of lower class corner groups involves a positive effort to achieve states, conditions, or qualities valued within the actor's most significant cultural milieu. If "conformity to immediate reference group values" is the major component of motivation of "delinquent" behavior by gang members, why is such behavior frequently referred to as negativistic, malicious, or rebellious? Albert Cohen, for example, in *Delinquent Boys* (Glencoe: Free Press, 1955) describes behavior which violates school rules as comprising elements of "active spite and malice, contempt and ridicule, challenge and defiance." He ascribes to the gang "keen delight in terrorizing 'good' children, and in general making themselves obnoxious to the virtuous." A recent national conference on social work with "hard-to-reach" groups characterized lower class corner groups as "youth groups in conflict with the culture of their (*sic*) communities." Such characterizations are obviously the result of taking the middle class community and its institutions as an implicit point of reference.

A large body of systematically interrelated attitudes, practices, behaviors, and values characteristic of lower class culture are designed to support and maintain the basic features of the lower class way of life. In areas where these differ from features of middle class culture, action oriented to the achievement and maintenance of the lower class system may violate norms of middle class culture and be perceived as deliberately non-conforming or malicious by an observer strongly cathected to middle class norms. This does not mean, however, that violation of the middle class norm is the dominant component of motivation; it is a by-product of action primarily oriented to the lower class system. The standards of lower class culture cannot be seen merely as a reverse function of middle class culture—as middle class standards "turned upside down"; lower class culture is a distinctive tradition many centuries old with an integrity of its own.

From the viewpoint of the acting individual, functioning within a field of well-structured cultural forces, the relative impact of "conforming" and "rejective" elements in the motivation of gang delinquency is weighted preponderantly on the conforming side. Rejective or rebellious elements are inevitably involved, but their influence during the actual commission of delinquent acts is relatively small compared to the influence of pressures to achieve what is valued by the actor's most immediate reference groups. Expressed awareness by the actor of the element of rebellion often represents only that aspect of motivation of which he is explicitly conscious; the deepest and most compelling components of motivation—adherence to highly meaningful group standards of Toughness, Smartness, Excitement, etc.—are often unconsciously patterned. No cultural pattern as well-established as the practice of illegal acts by members of lower class corner groups could persist if buttressed primarily by negative, hostile, or rejective motives; its principal motivational support, as in the case of any persisting cultural tradition, derives from a positive effort to achieve what is valued within that tradition, and to conform to its explicit and implicit norms.

NOTES

1 The complex issues involved in deriving a definition of "delinquency" cannot be discussed here. The term "delinquent" is used in this paper to characterize behavior or acts committed by individuals within specified age limits which if known to official authorities could result in legal action. The concept of a "delinquent" individual has little or no utility in the approach used here; rather, specified types of *acts* which may be committed rarely or frequently by few or many individuals are characterized as "delinquent."

2 A three year research project is being financed under National Institutes of Health Grant M—1414, and administered through the Boston University School of Social Work. The primary research effort has subjected all collected material to a uniform data-coding process. All information bearing on some seventy areas of behavior (behavior in reference to school, police, theft, assault, sex, collective athletics, etc.) is extracted from the records, recorded on coded data cards, and filed under relevant categories. Analysis of these data aims to ascertain the actual nature of customary behavior in these areas, and the extent to which the social work effort was able to effect behavioral changes.

3 Between 40 and 60 percent of all Americans are directly influenced by lower class culture, with about 15 percent, or twenty-five million, com-

prising the "hard core" lower class group—defined primarily by its use of the "female-based" household as the basic form of child-rearing unit and of the "serial monogamy" mating pattern as the primary form of marriage. The term "lower class culture" as used here refers most specifically to the way of life of the "hard core" group; systematic research in this area would probably reveal at least four to six major subtypes of lower class culture, for some of which the "concerns" presented here would be differently weighted, especially for those subtypes in which "law-abiding" behavior has a high overt valuation. It is impossible within the compass of this short paper to make the finer intracultural distinctions which a more accurate presentation would require.

4 The "brains-brawn" set of capacities are often paired in lower class folk lore or accounts of lower class life, e.g., "Brer Fox" and "Brer Bear" in the Uncle Remus stories, or George and Lennie in "Of Mice and Men."

5 Further data on the female-based household unit (estimated as comprising about 15 per cent of all American "families") and the role of one-sex groupings in lower class culture are contained in Walter B. Miller, "Implications of Urban Lower Class Culture for Social Work." *Social Service Review*, 1959, 33, No. 3.

Social Structure and Anomie

ROBERT K. MERTON

Robert K. Merton is a professor of sociology at Columbia University.

Reprinted from Robert K. Merton, "Social Structure and Anomie," *American Sociological Review* (October 1938), 3:672-82.

There persists a notable tendency in sociological theory to attribute the malfunctioning of social structure primarily to those of man's imperious biological drives which are not adequately restrained by social control. In this view, the social order is solely a device for "impulse management" and the "social processing" of tensions. These impulses which break through social control, be it noted, are held to be biologically derived. Nonconformity is assumed to be rooted in original nature.[1] Conformity is by implication the result of an utilitarian calculus or unreasoned conditioning. This point of view, whatever its other deficiencies, clearly begs one question. It provides no basis for determining the nonbiological conditions which induce deviations from prescribed patterns of conduct. In this paper, it will be suggested that certain phases of social structure generate the circumstances in which infringement of social codes constitute a "normal" response.[2]

The conceptual scheme to be outlined is designed to provide a coherent, systematic approach to the study of socio-cultural sources of deviate behavior. Our primary aim lies in discovering how some social structures *exert a definite pressure* upon certain persons in the society to engage in nonconformist rather than conformist conduct. The many ramifications of the scheme cannot all be discussed; the problems mentioned outnumber those explicitly treated.

Among the elements of social and cultural structure, two are important for our purposes. These are analytically separable although they merge imperceptibly in concrete situations. The first consists of culturally defined goals, purposes, and interests. It comprises a frame of aspirational reference. These goals are more or less integrated and involve varying degrees of prestige and sentiment. They constitute a basic, but not the exclusive, component of what Linton aptly has called "designs for group living." Some of these cultural aspirations are related to the original drives of man, but they are not determined by them. The second phase of the social structure defines, regulates, and controls the acceptable modes of achieving these goals. Every social group invariably couples its scale of desired ends with moral or institutional regulation of permissible and required procedures for attaining these ends. These regulatory norms, and moral imperatives do not necessarily coincide with technical or efficiency norms. Many procedures which from the standpoint of *particular individuals* would be most efficient in securing desired values, e.g., illicit oil-stock schemes, theft, fraud, are ruled out of the institutional area of permitted conduct. The choice of expedients is limited by the institutional norms.

To say that these two elements, culture goals and institutional norms, operate jointly is not to say that the ranges of alternative behaviors and aims bear some constant relation to one another. The emphasis upon certain goals may vary independently of the degree of emphasis upon institutional means. There may develop a disproportionate, at times, a virtually exclusive, stress upon the value of specific goals, involving relatively slight concern with the institutionally appropriate modes of attaining these goals. The limiting case in this direction is reached when the range of alternative procedures is limited only by the technical rather than institutional considerations. Any and all devices which promise attainment of the all important goal would be permitted in this hypothetical polar case.[3] This constitutes one type of cultural malintegration. A second polar type is found in groups where activities originally conceived as instrumental are transmuted into ends in themselves. The original purposes are forgotten and ritualistic adherence to institutionally prescribed conduct becomes virtually obsessive.[4] Stability is largely ensured while change is flouted. The range of alternative behaviors is severely limited. There develops a tradition-bound, sacred society characterized by neophobia. The occupational psychosis of the bureaucrat may be cited as a case in point. Finally, there are the intermediate types of groups where a balance between culture goals and institutional means is maintained. These are the significantly integrated and relatively stable, though changing, groups.

An effective equilibrium between the two phases of the social structure is maintained as long as satisfactions accrue to individuals who conform to both constraints, viz., satisfactions from the achievement of the goals and satisfactions emerging directly from the institutionally canalized modes of striving to attain these ends. Success, in such equilibrated cases, is twofold. Success is reckoned in terms of the product and in terms of the process, in terms of the outcome and in terms of activities. Continuing satisfactions must derive from sheer *participation* in a competitive order as well as from eclipsing one's competitors if the order itself is to be sustained. The occasional sacrifices involved in institutionalized conduct must be compensated by socialized rewards. The distribution of statuses and roles through competition must be so organized that positive incentives for conformity to roles and adherence to status obligations are provided *for every position* within the distributive order. Aberrant conduct, therefore, may be viewed as a symptom of dissociation between culturally defined aspirations and socially structured means.

Of the types of groups which result from the independent variation of the two phases of the social structure, we shall be primarily concerned with the first, namely, that involving a disproportionate accent on goals. This statement must be recast in a proper perspective. In no group is there an absence of regulatory codes governing conduct, yet groups do vary in the degree to which these folkways, mores, and institutional controls are effectively integrated with the more diffuse goals which are part of the culture matrix. Emotional convictions may cluster about the complex of socially acclaimed ends, meanwhile shifting their support from the culturally defined implementation of these ends. As we shall see, certain aspects of the social structure may generate countermores and antisocial behavior precisely because of differential emphases on goals and regulations. In the extreme case, the latter may be so vitiated by the goal-emphasis that the range of behavior is limited only by considerations of technical expediency. The sole significant question then becomes, which available means is most efficient in netting the socially approved value?[5] The technically most feasible procedure, whether legitimate or not, is preferred to the institutionally prescribed conduct. As this process continues, the integration of the society becomes tenuous and anomie ensues.

Thus, in competitive athletics, when the aim of victory is shorn of its institutional trappings and success in contests becomes construed as "winning the game" rather than "winning through

158

circumscribed modes of activity," a premium is implicitly set upon the use of illegitimate but technically efficient means. The star of the opposing football team is surreptitiously slugged; the wrestler furtively incapacitates his opponent through ingenious but illicit techniques; university alumni covertly subsidize "students" whose talents are largely confined to the athletic field. The emphasis on the goal has so attenuated the satisfactions deriving from sheer participation in the competitive activity that these satisfactions are virtually confined to a successful outcome. Through the same process, tension generated by the desire to win in a poker game is relieved by successfully dealing oneself four aces, or when the cult of success has become completely dominant, by sagaciously shuffling the cards in a game of solitaire. The faint twinge of uneasiness in the last instance and the surreptitious nature of public delicts indicate clearly that the institutional rules of the game *are known* to those who evade them, but that the emotional supports of these rules are largely vitiated by cultural exaggeration of the success-goal.[6] They are microcosmic images of the social macrocosm.

Of course, this process is not restricted to the realm of sport. The process whereby exaltation of the end generates a *literal demoralization* i.e., a deinstitutionalization, of the means in one which characterizes many[7] groups in which the two phases of the social structure are not highly integrated. The extreme emphasis upon the accumulation of wealth as a symbol of success[8] in our own society militates against the completely effective control of institutionally regulated modes of acquiring a fortune.[9] Fraud, corruption, vice, crime, in short, the entire catalogue of proscribed behavior, becomes increasingly common when the emphasis on the *culturally induced* success-goal becomes divorced from a coordinated institutional emphasis. This observation is of crucial theoretical importance in examining the doctrine that antisocial behavior most frequently derives from biological drives breaking through the restraints imposed by society. The difference is one between a strictly utilitarian interpretation which conceives man's ends as random and an analysis which finds these ends deriving from the basic values of the culture.[10]

Our analysis can scarcely stop at this juncture. We must turn to other aspects of the social structure if we are to deal with the social genesis of the varying rates and types of deviate behavior characteristic of different societies. Thus far, we have sketched three ideal types of social orders constituted by distinctive patterns of relations between culture ends and means. Turning from these types of *culture patterning*, we find five logically possible, alternative modes of adjustment or adaptation *by individuals* within the culture-bearing society or group.[11] These are schematically presented in the following table, where (+) signifies "acceptance," (−) signifies "elimination" and (±) signifies "rejection and substitution of new goals and standards."

	Culture Goals	Institutionalized Means
I. Conformity	+	+
II. Innovation	+	−
III. Ritualism	−	+
IV. Retreatism	−	−
V. Rebellion[12]	±	±

Our discussion of the relation between these alternative responses and other phases of the social structure must be prefaced by the observation that persons may shift from one alternative to another as they engage in different social activities. These categories refer to role adjustments in specific situations, not to personality *in toto.* To treat the development of this process in various spheres of conduct would introduce a complexity unmanageable within the confines of this paper. For this reason, we shall be concerned primarily with economic activity in the broad sense, "the production, exchange, distribution and consumption of goods and services" in our competitive society, wherein wealth has taken on a highly symbolic cast. Our task is to search out some of the factors which exert pressure upon individuals to engage in certain of these logically possible alternative responses. This choice, as we shall see, is far from random.

In every society, Adaptation I (conformity to both culture goals and means) is the most common and widely diffused. Were this not so, the stability and continuity of the society could not be maintained. The mesh of expectancies which constitutes every social order is sustained by the modal behavior of its members falling within the first category. Conventional role behavior oriented toward the basic values of the group is the rule rather than the exception. It is this fact alone which permits us to speak of a human aggregate as comprising a group or society.

Conversely, Adaptation IV (rejection of goals and means) is the least common. Persons who "adjust" (or maladjust) in this fashion are, strictly speaking, *in* the society but not *of* it. Sociologically, these constitute the true "aliens." Not sharing the common frame of orientation, they can be included within the societal population merely in a functional sense. In this category are *some* of the activities of psychotics, psychoneurotics, chronic autists, pariahs, outcasts, vagrants, vagabonds, tramps, chronic drunkards and drug addicts.[13] These have relinquished, in certain spheres of activity, the culturally defined goals, involving complete aim-inhibition in the polar case, and their adjustments are not in accord with institutional norms. This is not to say that in some cases the source of their behavioral adjustments is not in part the very social structure which they have in effect repudiated nor that their very existence within a social area does not constitute a problem for the socialized population.

This mode of "adjustment" occurs, as far as structural sources are concerned, when both the culture goals and institutionalized procedures have been assimilated thoroughly by the individual and imbued with affect and high positive value, but where those institutionalized procedures which promise a measure of successful attainment of the goals are not available to the individual. In such instances, there results a twofold mental conflict insofar as the moral obligation for adopting institutional means conflict with the pressure to resort to illegitimate means (which may attain the goal) and inasmuch as the individual is shut off from means which are both legitimate *and* effective. The competitive order is maintained, but the frustrated and handicapped individual who cannot cope with this order drops out. Defeatism, quietism and resignation are manifested in escape mechanisms which ultimately lead the individual to "escape" from the requirements of the society. It is an expedient which arises from continued failure to attain the goal by legitimate measures and from an inability to adopt the illegitimate route because of internalized prohibitions and institutionalized compulsions, *during which process the supreme value of the success-goal has as yet not been renounced.* The conflict is resolved by eliminating both precipitating elements, the goals and means. The escape is complete, the conflict is eliminated and the individual is socialized.

Be it noted that where frustration derives from the inaccessibility of effective institutional means for attaining economic or any other type of highly valued "success," that Adaptations II, III and V (innovation, ritualism and rebellion) are also possible. The result will be determined by the particular personality, and thus, the *particular* cultural background, involved. Inadequate socialization will result in the innovation response whereby the conflict and frustration are eliminated by relinquishing the institutional means and retaining the success-aspiration; an extreme assimilation of institutional demands will lead to ritualism wherein the goal is dropped as beyond one's reach but conformity to the mores persists; and rebellion occurs when emancipation from the reigning standards, due to frustration or to marginalist perspectives, leads to the attempt to introduce a "new social order."

Our major concern is with the illegitimacy adjustment. This involves the use of coventionally proscribed but frequently effective means of attaining at least the simulacrum of culturally defined success—wealth, power, and the like. As we have seen, this adjustment occurs when the individual has assimilated the cultural emphasis on success without equally internalizing the morally prescribed norms governing means for its attainment. The question arises, Which phases of our social structure predispose toward this mode of adjustment? We may examine a concrete instance, effectively analyzed by Lohman,[14] which provides a clue to the answer. Lohman has shown that specialized areas of vice in the near north side of Chicago constitute a "normal" response to a situation where the cultural emphasis upon pecuniary success has been absorbed, but where there is little access to conventional and legitimate means for attaining such success. The conventional occupational opportunities of persons in this area are almost completely limited to manual labor. Given our cultural stigmatization of manual labor, and its correlate, the prestige of white collar work, it is clear that the result is a strain toward innovational practices. The limitation of opportunity to unskilled labor and the resultant low income can not compete *in terms of conventional standards of achievement* with the high income from organized vice.

For our purposes, this situation involves two important features. First, such antisocial behavior is in a sense "called forth" by certain conventional values of the culture *and* by the class structure involving differential access to the approved opportunities for legitimate, prestige-bearing pursuit of the culture goals. The lack of high integration between the means-and-end elements of the cultural pattern and the particular class structure combine to favor a heightened frequency of antisocial conduct in such groups. The second consideration is of equal significance. Recourse to the first of the alternative responses, legitimate effort, is limited by the fact that actual advance toward desired success-symbols through conventional channels is, despite our persisting open-class ideology,[15] relatively rare and difficult for those handicapped by little formal education and few economic resources. The dominant pressure of group standards of success is, therefore, on the gradual attenuation of legitimate, but by and large ineffective, strivings and the increasing use of illegitimate, but more or less effective, expedients of vice and crime. The cultural demands made on persons in this situation are incompatible. On the one hand, they are asked to orient their conduct toward the prospect of accumulating wealth and on the other, they are largely denied effective opportunities to do so institutionally. The consequences of such structural inconsistency are psychopathological personality, and/or antisocial conduct, and/or revolutionary activities. The equilibrium between culturally designated means and ends becomes highly unstable with the progressive emphasis on attaining the prestige-laden ends by any means whatsoever. Within this context, Capone represents the triumph of amoral intelligence over morally prescribed "failure," when the channels of vertical mobility are closed or narrowed[16] *in a society which places a high premium on economic affluence and social ascent for* all *its members.*[17]

This last qualification is of primary importance. It suggests that other phases of the social structure besides the extreme emphasis on pecuniary success, must be considered if we are to understand the social sources of antisocial behavior. A high frequency of deviate behavior is not generated simply by "lack of opportunity" or by this exaggerated pecuniary emphasis. A comparatively rigidified class structure, a feudalistic or caste order, may limit such opportunities far beyond the point which obtains in our society today. It is only when a system of cultural values extols, virtually above all else, certain *common* symbols of success *for the population at large* while its social structure rigorously restricts or completely eliminates access to approved modes of acquiring these symbols *for a considerable part of the same population*, that antisocial behavior ensues on a considerable scale. In other words, our egalitarian ideology denies by implication the existence of noncompeting groups and individuals in the pursuit of pecuniary success. The same body of success-symbols is held to be desirable for all. These goals are held to *transcend class lines*, not to be bounded by them, yet the actual social organization is such that there exist class differentials in the accessibility of these *common* success-symbols. Frustration and thwarted aspiration lead to the search for avenues of escape from a culturally induced intolerable situation; or unrelieved ambition may eventuate in illicit attempts to acquire the dominant values.[18] The American stress on pecuniary success and ambitiousness for all thus invites exaggerated anxieties, hostilities, neuroses and antisocial behavior.

This theoretical analysis may go far toward explaining the varying correlations between crime and poverty.[19] Poverty is not an isolated variable. It is one of a complex and interdependent on social and cultural variables. When viewed in such a context, it represents quite different states of affairs. Poverty as such, and consequent limitation of opportunity, are not sufficient to induce a conspicuously high rate of criminal behavior. Even the often mentioned "poverty in the midst of plenty" will not necessarily lead to this result. Only insofar as poverty and associated disadvantages in competition for the culture values approved for *all* members of the society is linked with the assimilation of a cultural emphasis on momentary accumulation as a symbol of success is antisocial conduct a "normal" outcome. Thus, poverty is less highly correlated with crime in southeastern Europe than in the United States. The possibilities of vertical mobility in these European areas would seem to be fewer than in this country, so that neither poverty *per se* nor its association with limited opportunity is sufficient to account for the varying correlations. It is only when the full configuration is considered, poverty, limited opportunity and a commonly shared system of success symbols, that we can explain the higher association between poverty and crime in our society than in others where rigidified class structure is coupled with *differential class symbols of achievement.*

In societies such as our own, then, the pressure of prestige-bearing success tends to eliminate the effective social constraint over means employed to this end. "The-end-justifies-the-means" doctrine becomes a guiding tenet for action when the cultural structure unduly exalts the end and the social organization unduly limits possible recourse to approved means. Otherwise put, this notion and associated behavior reflect a lack of cultural coordination. In international relations, the effects of this lack of integration are notoriously apparent. An emphasis upon national power is not readily coordinated with an inept organization of legitimate, i.e., internationally defined and accepted, means for attaining this goal. The result is a tendency toward the abrogation of international law, treaties become scraps of paper, "undeclared warfare" serves as a technical evasion, the bombing of civilian populations is rationalized,[20] just as the same societal situation induces the same sway of illegitimacy among individuals.

The social order we have described necessarily produces this "strain toward dissolution." The pressure of such an order is upon outdoing one's competitors. The choice of means within the ambit of institutional control will persist as long as the sentiments supporting a competitive system, i.e., deriving from the possibility of outranking competitors and hence enjoying the favorable response of others, are distributed throughout the entire system of activities and are not confined merely to the final result. A stable social structure demands a balanced distribution of affect among its various segments. When there occurs a shift of emphasis from the satisfactions deriving from competition itself to almost exclusive concern with successful competition, the resultant stress leads to the breakdown of the regulatory structure.[21] With the resulting attenuation of the institutional imperatives, there occurs an approximation of the situation erroneously held by utilitarians to be typical of society generally wherein calculations of advantage and fear of punishment are the sole regulating agencies. In such situations, as Hobbes observed, force and fraud come to constitute the sole virtues in view of their relative efficiency in attaining goals—which were for him, of course, not culturally derived.

It should be apparent that the foregoing discussion is not pitched on a moralistic plane. Whatever the sentiments of the writer or reader concerning the ethical desirability of coordinating the means-and-goals phases of the social structure, one must agree that lack of such coordination leads to anomie. Insofar as one of the most general functions of social organizations is to provide a basis for calculability and regularity of behavior, it is increasingly limited in effectiveness as these elements of the structure become dissociated. At the extreme, predictability virtually disappears and what may be properly termed cultural chaos or anomie intervenes.

This statement, being brief, is also incomplete. It has not included an exhaustive treatment of the various structural elements which predispose toward one rather than another of the alternative responses open to individuals; it has neglected, but not denied the relevance of, the factors determining the specific incidence of these responses; it has not enumerated the various concrete responses which are constituted by combinations of specific values of the analytical variables; it has omitted, or included only by implication, any consideration of the social functions performed by illicit responses; it has not tested the full explanatory power of the analytical scheme by examining a large number of group variations in the frequency of deviate and conformist behavior; it has not adequately dealt with rebellious conduct which seeks to refashion the social framework radically; it has not examined the relevance of cultural conflict for an analysis of culture-goal and institutional-means malintegration. It is suggested that these and related problems may be profitably analyzed by this scheme.

NOTES

1   E.g., Ernest Jones, *Social Aspects of Psychoanalysis*, 28, London, 1924. If the Freudian notion is a variety of the "original sin" dogma, then the interpretation advanced in this paper may be called the doctrine of "socially derived sin."

2   "Normal" in the sense of a culturally oriented, if not approved, response. The statement does not deny the relevance of biological and personality differences which may be significantly involved in the *incidence* of deviate conduct. Our focus of interest is the social and cultural matrix; hence we abstract from other factors. It is in this sense, I take it, that James S. Plant speaks the "normal reaction of normal people to abnormal conditions." See his *Personality and the Cultural Pattern*, 248, New York, 1937.

3   Contemporary American culture has been said to tend in this direction. See André Siegfried, *America Comes of Age*, 26-37, New York, 1927. The alleged extreme (?) emphasis on the goals of monetary success and material prosperity leads to dominant concern with technological and social instruments designed to produce the desired result, inasmuch as institutional controls become of secondary importance. In such a situation, innovation flourishes as the *range of means* employed is broadened. In a sense, then, there occurs the paradoxical emergence of "materialists" from an "idealistic" orientation. Cf. Durkheim's analysis of the cultural conditions which predispose toward crime and innovation, both of which are aimed toward efficiency, not moral norms. Durkheim was one of the first to see that "contrairement aux idées courantes le criminel n' apparait plus comme un être radicalement insociable, comme une sorte d'element parasitaire, de corps étranger et inassimilable, introduit au sein de la société; c'est un agent régulier de la vie sociale." See *Les Régles de la Méthode Sociologique*, 86-89, Paris, 1927.

4   Such ritualism may be associated with a mythology which rationalizes these actions so that they appear to retain their status as means, but the dominant pressure is in the direction of strict ritualistic conformity, irrespective of such rationalizations. In this sense, ritual has proceeded farthest when such rationalizations are not even called forth.

5   In this connection, one may see the relevance of Elton Mayo's paraphrase of the title of Tawney's well known book. "Actually the problem *is not that of the sickness of an acquisitive society; it is that of the acquisitiveness of a sick society.*" *Human Problems of an Industrial Civilization*, 153, New York, 1933. Mayo deals with the process through which wealth comes to be a symbol of social achievement. He sees this as arising from a state of anomie. We are considering the unintegrated monetary-success goals as an element in producing anomie. A complete analysis would involve both phases of this system of interdependent variables.

6   It is unlikely that interiorized norms are completely eliminated. Whatever residuum persists will induce personality tensions and conflict. The process involves a certain degree of ambivalence. A manifest rejection of the institutional norms is coupled with some latent retention of their emotional correlates. "Guilt feelings," "sense of sin," "pangs of conscience" are obvious manifestations of this unrelieved tension; symbolic adherence to the nominally repudiated values or rationalizations constitute a more subtle variety of tensional release.

7   "Many," and not all, unintegrated groups, for the reason already mentioned. In groups where the primary emphasis shifts to institutional means, i.e., when the range of alternatives is very limited, the outcome is a type of ritualism rather than anomie.

8   Money has several peculiarities which render it particularly apt to become a symbol of prestige divorced from institutional controls. As Simmel emphasized, money is highly abstract and impersonal. However acquired, through fraud or institutionally, it can be used to purchase the same goods and services. The anonymity of metropolitan culture, in conjunction with this peculiarity of money, permits wealth, the sources of which may be unknown to the community in which the plutocrat lives, to serve as a symbol of status.

9   The emphasis upon wealth as a success-symbol is possibly reflected in the use of the term "fortune" to refer to a stock of accumulated wealth. This meaning becomes common in the late sixteenth century (Spenser and Shakespeare). A similar usage of the Latin *fortuna* comes into prominence during the first century B.C. Both these periods were marked by the rise to prestige and power of the "bourgeoisie."

10   See Kingsley Davis, "Mental Hygiene and the Class Structure," *Psychiatry*, 1928, I, esp. 62-63; Talcott Parsons, *The Structure of Social Action*, 59-60, New York, 1937.

11   This is a level intermediate between the two planes distinguished by Edward Sapir; namely, culture patterns and personal habit systems. See his "Contribution of Psychiatry to an Understanding of Behavior in Society," *Amer. J. Sociol.*, 1937, 42: 862-70.

12   This fifth alternative is on a plane clearly different from that of the others. It represents a *transitional* response which seeks to *institutionalize* new procedures oriented toward revamped cultural goals shared by the members of the society. It thus involves efforts to *change* the existing structure rather than to perform accommodative actions *within* this structure, and introduces additional problems with which we are not at the moment concerned.

13   Obviously, this is an elliptical statement. These individuals may maintain some orientation to the values of their particular differentiated groupings within the larger society or, in part, of the conventional society itself. Insofar as they do so, their conduct cannot be classified in the "passive rejection" category (IV). Nels Anderson's description of the behavior and attitudes of the bum, for example, can readily be recast in terms of our analytical scheme. See *The Hobo*, 93-98, *et passim*, Chicago, 1923.

14   Joseph D. Lohman, "The Participant Observer in Community Studies," *Amer. Sociol. Rev.*, 1937, 2:890-98.

15   The shifting historical role of this ideology is a profitable subject for exploration. The "office-boy-to-president" stereotype was once in approximate accord with the facts. Such vertical mobility was probably more common then than now, when the class structure is more rigid. (See the following note.) The ideology largely persists, however, possibly because it still performs a useful function for maintaining the *status quo*. For

insofar as it is accepted by the "masses," it constitutes a useful sop for those who might rebel against the entire structure, were this consoling hope removed. This ideology now serves to lessen the probability of Adaptation V. In short, the role of this notion has changed from that of an approximately valid empirical theorem to that of an ideology, in Mannheim's sense.

16 There is a growing body of evidence, though none of it is clearly con- clusive, to the effect that our class structure is becoming rigidified and that vertical mobility is declining. Taussig and Joslyn found that American business leaders are being *increasingly* recruited from the upper ranks of our society. The Lynds have also found a "diminished chance to get ahead" for the working classes in Middletown. Manifestly, these objective changes are not alone significant; the individual's subjective evaluation of the situation is a major determinant of the response. The extent to which this change in opportunity for social mobility has been recognized by the least advantaged classes is still conjectural, although the Lynds present some suggestive materials. The writer suggests that a case in point is the increasing frequency of cartoons which observe in a tragi-comic vein that "my old man says everybody can't be President. He says if ya can get three days a week steady on W.P.A. work ya ain't doin' so bad either." See F. W. Taussig and C. S. Joslyn, *American Business Leaders*, New York, 1932; R. S. and H. M. Lynd, *Middletown in Transition*, 67 ff., chap. 12, New York, 1937.

17 The role of the Negro in this respect is of considerable theoretical interest. Certain elements of the Negro population have assimilated the dominant caste's values of pecuniary success and social advancement, but they also recognize that social ascent is at present restricted to their own caste almost exclusively. The pressures upon the Negro which would otherwise derive from the structural inconsistencies we have noticed are hence not identical with those upon lower class whites. See Kingsley Davis, *op. cit.*, 63; John Dollard, *Caste and Class in a Southern Town*, 66 ff., New Haven, 1936; Donald Young, *American Minority Peoples*, 581, New York, 1932.

18 The psychical coordinates of these processes have been partly established by the experimental evidence concerning *Anspruchsniveaus* and levels of performance. See Kurt Lewin, *Vorsatz, Wille and Bedurfnis*, Berlin, 1926; N. F. Hoppe, "Erfolg and Misserfolg," *Psychol. Forschung*, 1930, 14:1-63; Jerome D. Frank, "Individual Differences in Certain Aspects of the Level of Aspiration," *Amer. J. Psychol.*, 1935, 47:119-28.

19 Standard criminology texts summarize the data in this field. Our scheme of analysis may serve to resolve some of the theoretical contradictions which P. A. Sorokin indicates. For example, "not everywhere nor always do the poor show a greater proportion of crime . . . many poorer countries have had less crime than the richer countries . . . The [economic] improve- ment in the second half of the nineteenth century, and the beginning of the twentieth, has not been followed by a decrease of crime." See his *Contemporary Sociological Theories*, 560-61, New York, 1928. The crucial point is, however, that poverty has varying social significance in different social structures, as we shall see. Hence, one would not expect a linear correlation between crime and poverty.

20 See M. W. Royse, *Aerial Bombardment and the International Regulation of War*, New York, 1928.

21 Since our primary concern is with the socio-cultural aspects of this problem, the psychological correlates have been only implicitly considered. See Karen Horney, *The Neurotic Personality of Our Time*, New York, 1937, for a psychological discussion of this process.

Illegitimate Means, Differential Opportunity and Delinquent Subcultures

RICHARD CLOWARD and LLOYD E. OHLIN

Richard Cloward is a professor of social work at Columbia University. Lloyd E. Ohlin is a professor of law at Harvard University.

Reprinted with permission of Macmillan Publishing Co., Inc. from DELINQUENCY AND OPPORTUNITY by Richard Cloward and Lloyd Ohlin, pp. 145-59. © The Free Press, a Corporation, 1960.

THE AVAILABILITY OF ILLEGITIMATE MEANS

Social norms are two-sided. A prescription implies the existence of a prohibition, and vice versa. To advocate honesty is to demarcate and condemn a set of actions which are dishonest. In other words, norms that define legitimate practices also implicitly define illegitimate practices. One purpose of norms, in fact, is to delineate the boundary between legitimate and illegitimate practices. In setting this boundary, in segregating and classifying various types of behavior, they make us aware not only of behavior that is regarded as right and proper but also of behavior that is said to be wrong and improper. Thus the criminal who engages in theft or fraud does not invent a new way of life; the possibility of employing alternative means is acknowledged tacitly at least, by the norms of the culture.

This tendency for proscribed alternatives to be implicit in every prescription, and vice versa, although widely recognized, is nevertheless a reef upon which many a theory of delinquency has foundered. Much of the criminological literature assumes, for example, that one may explain a criminal act simply by accounting for the individual's readiness to employ illegal alternatives of which his culture, through its norms, has already made him generally aware. Such explanations are quite unsatisfactory, however, for they ignore a host of questions regarding the *relative availability* of illegal alternatives to various potential criminals. The aspiration to be a physician is hardly enough to explain the fact of becoming a physician; there is much that transpires between the aspiration and the achievement. This is no less true of the person who wants to be a successful criminal. Having decided that he "can't make it legitimately," he cannot simply choose among an array of illegitimate means, all equally available to him. It is assumed in the theory of anomie that access to conventional means is differentially distributed, that some individuals, because of their social class, enjoy certain advantages that are denied to those elsewhere in the class structure. For example, there are variations in the degree to which members of various classes are fully exposed to and thus acquire the values, knowledge, and skills that facilitate upward mobility. It should not be startling, therefore, to suggest that there are socially structured variations in the availability of illegitimate means as well. In connection with delinquent subcultures, we shall be concerned principally with differentials in access to illegitimate means within the lower class.

Many sociologists have alluded to differentials in access to illegitimate means without explicitly incorporating this variable into a theory of deviant behavior. This is particularly true of scholars in the "Chicago tradition" of criminology. Two closely related theoretical perspectives emerged from this school. The theory of "cultural transmission," advanced by Clifford R. Shaw and Henry D. McKay, focuses on the development in some urban neighborhoods of a criminal tradition that persists from one generation to another despite constant changes in population.[1] In the theory of "differential association," Edwin H. Sutherland described the processes by which criminal values are taken over by the individual.[2] He asserted that criminal behavior is learned, and that it is learned in interaction with others who have already incorporated criminal values. Thus the first theory stresses the value systems of different areas; the second, the systems of social relationships that facilitate or impede the acquisition of these values.

Scholars in the Chicago tradition, who emphasized the processes involved in learning to be criminal, were actually pointing to differentials in the availability of illegal means—although they did not explicitly recognize this variable in their analysis. This can perhaps best be seen by examining Sutherland's classic work, *The Professional Thief*. "An inclination to steal," according to Sutherland, "is not a sufficient explanation of the genesis of the professional thief."[3] The "self-made" thief, lacking knowledge of the ways of securing immunity from prosecution and similar techniques of defense, "would quickly land in prison . . . a person can be a professional thief only if he is recognized and received as such by other professional thieves." But recognition is not freely accorded: "Selection and tutelage are the two necessary elements in the process of acquiring recognition as a professional thief. . . . A person cannot acquire recognition as a professional thief until he has had tutelage in professional theft, *and tutelage is given only to a few persons selected from the total population.*" For one thing, "the person must be appreciated by the professional thieves. He must be appraised as having an adequate equipment of wits, front, talking-ability, honesty, reliability, nerve and determination." Furthermore, the aspirant is judged by high standards of performance, for only "a very small percentage of those who start on this process ever reach the stage of professional thief. . . ." Thus motivation and pressures toward deviance do not fully account for deviant behavior any more than motivation and pressures toward conformity account for conforming behavior. The individual must have access to a learning environment and, once having been trained, must be allowed to perform his role. Roles, whether conforming or deviant in content, are not necessarily freely available; access to them depends upon a variety of factors, such as one's socio-economic position, age, sex, ethnic affiliation, personality characteristics, and the like. The potential thief, like the potential physician, finds that access to his goal is governed by many criteria other than merit and motivation.

What we are asserting is that access to illegitimate roles is not freely available to all as is commonly assumed. Only those neighborhoods in which crime flourishes as a stable, indigenous institution are fertile criminal learning environments for the young. Because these environments afford integration of different age-levels of offender, selected young people are exposed to "differential association" through which tutelage is provided and criminal values and skills are acquired. To be prepared for the role may not, however, ensure that the individual will ever discharge it. One important limitation is that more youngsters are recruited into these patterns of differential associations than the adult criminal structure can possibly absorb. Since there is a surplus of contenders for these elite positions, criteria and mechanisms of selection must be evolved. Hence a certain proportion of those who aspire may not be permitted to engage in the behavior for which they have prepared themselves.

Thus we conclude that access to illegitimate roles, no less than access to legitimate roles, is limited by both social and psychological factors. We shall here be concerned primarily with socially structured differentials in illegitimate opportunities. Such differentials, we contend, have much to do with the type of delinquent subculture that develops.

LEARNING AND PERFORMANCE STRUCTURES

Our use of the term "opportunities," legitimate or illegitimate, implies access to both learning and performance structures. That is, the individual must have access to appropriate environments for the acquisition of the values and skills associated with the performance of a particular role, and he must be supported in the performance of the role once he has learned it.

Tannenbaum, several decades ago, vividly expressed the point that criminal role performance, no less than conventional role performance, presupposes a patterned set of relationships through which the requisite values and skills are transmitted by established practitioners to aspiring youth:

It takes a long time to make a good criminal, many years of specialized training and much preparation. But training is something that is given to people. People learn in a community where the materials and the knowledge are to be had. A craft needs an atmosphere saturated with purpose and promise. The community provides the attitudes, the point of view, the philosophy of life, the example, the motive, the contacts, the friendships, the incentives. No child brings those into the world. He finds them here and available for use and elaboration. The community gives the criminal his materials and habits, just as it gives the doctor, the lawyer, the teacher, and the candlestick-maker theirs.[4]

Sutherland systematized this general point of view, asserting that opportunity consists, at least in part, of learning structures. Thus "criminal behavior is learned" and, furthermore, it is learned "in interaction with other persons in a process of communication." However, he conceded that the differential-association theory does not constitute a full explanation of criminal behavior. In a paper circulated in 1944, he noted that "criminal behavior is partially a function of opportunities to commit [i.e., to perform] specific classes of crime, such as embezzlement, bank burglary, or illicit heterosexual intercourse." Therefore, "while opportunity may be partially a function of association with criminal patterns and of the specialized techniques thus acquired, it is not determined entirely in that manner, and consequently differential association is not the sufficient cause of criminal behavior."[5]

To Sutherland, then, illegitimate opportunity included conditions favorable to the performance of a criminal role as well as conditions favorable to learning of such a role (differential associations). These conditions, we suggest, depend upon certain features of the social structure of the community in which delinquency arises.

DIFFERENTIAL OPPORTUNITY: A HYPOTHESIS

We believe that each individual occupies a position in both legitimate and illegitimate opportunity structures. This is a new way of defining the situation. The theory of anomie views the individual primarily in terms of the legitimate opportunity structure. It poses questions regarding differentials in access to legitimate routes to success-goals; at the same time it assumes either that illegitimate avenues to success-goals are freely available or that differentials in their availability are of little significance. This tendency may be seen in the following statement by Merton:

Several researches have shown that specialized areas of vice and crime constitute a "normal" response to a situation where the cultural emphasis upon pecuniary success has been absorbed, but where there is little access to conventional and legitimate means for becoming successful. The occupational opportunities of people in these areas are largely confined to manual labor and the lesser white-collar jobs. Given the American stigmatization of manual labor *which has been found to hold rather uniformly for all social classes*, and the absence of realistic opportunities for advancement beyond this level, the result is a marked tendency toward deviant behavior. The status of unskilled labor and the consequent low income cannot readily compete *in terms of established standards of worth* with the promises of power and high income from organized vice, rackets and crime. . . . [Such a situation] leads toward the gradual attenuation of legitimate, but by and large ineffectual, strivings and the increasing use of illegitimate, but more or less effective, expedients.[6]

The cultural-transmission and differential-association tradition, on the other hand, assumes that access to illegitimate means is variable, but it does not recognize the significance of comparable differentials in access to legitimate means. Sutherland's "ninth proposition" in theory of differential association states:

Though criminal behavior is an expression of general needs and values, it is not explained by those general needs and values since non-criminal behavior is an expression of the same needs and values. Thieves generally steal in order to secure money, but likewise honest laborers work in order to secure money. The attempts by many scholars to explain criminal behavior by general drives and values, such as the happiness principle, striving for social status, the money motive, or frustration have been and must continue to be futile since they explain lawful behavior as completely as they explain criminal behavior.[7]

In this statement, Sutherland appears to assume that people have equal and free access to legitimate means regardless of their social position. At the very least, he does not treat access to legitimate means as variable. It is, of course, perfectly true that "striving for social status," "the money motive," and other socially approved drives do not fully account for either deviant or conforming behavior. But if goal-oriented behavior occurs under conditions in which there are socially structured obstacles to the satisfaction of these drives by legitimate means, the resulting pressures, we contend, might lead to devance.

The concept of differential opportunity structures permits us to unite the theory of anomie, which recognizes the concept of differentials in access to legitimate means, and the "Chicago tradition," in which the concept of differentials in access to illegitimate means is implicit. We can now look at the individual, not simply in relation to one or the other system of means, but in relation to both legitimate and illegitimate systems. This approach permits us to ask, for example, how the relative availability of illegitimate opportunities affects the resolution of adjustment problems leading to deviant behavior. We believe that the way in which these problems are resolved may depend upon the kind of support for one or another type of illegitimate activity that is given at different points in the social structure. If, in a given social location, illegal or criminal means are not readily available, then we should not expect a criminal subculture to develop among adolescents. By the same logic, we should expect the manipulation of violence to become a primary avenue to higher status only in areas where the means of violence are not denied to the young. To give a third example, drug addiction and participation in subcultures organized around the consumption of drugs presuppose that persons can secure access to drugs and knowledge about how to use them. In some parts of the social structure, this would be very difficult; in others, very easy. In short, there are marked differences from one part of the social structure to another in the types of illegitimate adaptation that are available to persons in search of solutions to problems of adjustment arising from the restricted availability of legitimate means.[8] In this sense, then, we can think of individuals as being located in two opportunity structures—one legitimate, the other illegitimate. Given limited access to success-goals by legitimate means, the nature of the delinquent response that may result will vary according to the availability of various illegitimate means.[9]

ILLEGITIMATE OPPORTUNITIES AND THE SOCIAL STRUCTURE OF THE SLUM

When we say that the form of delinquency that is adopted is conditioned by the presence or absence of appropriate illegitimate means, we are actually referring to crucial differences in the social organization of various slum areas, for our hypothesis implies that the local milieu affects the delinquent's choice of a solution to his problems of adjustment. One of the principal ways in which slum areas vary is in the extent to which they provide the young with alternative (albeit illegitimate) routes to higher status. Many of the works in the cultural-transmission and differential-association tradition are focused directly on the relationship between deviant behavior and lower-class social structure. By reconceptualizing aspects of that tradition, we hope to make our central hypothesis more explicit.

Integration of different age-levels of offender

In their ecological studies of the urban environment, Shaw and McKay found that delinquency tended to be confined to limited areas and to persist in these areas despite demographic changes. Hence they spoke of "criminal traditions" and of the "cultural transmission" of criminal values.[10] As a result of their observations of slum life, they concluded that particular importance must be assigned to the relationships between immature and sophisticated offenders—which we call the integration of different age-levels of offender. They suggested that many youngsters are recruited into criminal activities as a direct result of intimate associations with older and more experienced offenders:

> Stealing in the neighborhood was a common practice among the children and approved of by the parents. Whenever the boys got together they talked about robbing and made more plans for stealing. I hardly knew any boys who did not go robbing. The little fellows went in for petty stealing, breaking into freight cars, and stealing junk. The older guys did big jobs like stick-ups, burglary, and stealing autos. The little fellows admired the "big shots" and longed for the day when they could get into the big racket. Fellows who had "done time" were the big shots and looked up to and gave the little fellows tips on how to get by and pull off big jobs.[11]

Thus the "big shots"—conspicuous successes in the criminal world—become role-models for youth, much more important as such than successful figures in the conventional world, who are usually socially and geographically remote from the slum area. Through intimate and stable associations with these older criminals, the young acquire the values and skills required for participation in the criminal culture. Further, structural connections between delinquents, semimature criminals, and the adult criminal world, where they exist, provide opportunities for upward mobility; where such integrative arrangements do not exist, the young are cut off from this alternative pathway to higher status.

Integration of conventional and deviant values

Shaw and McKay were describing deviant learning structures—that is, alternative routes by which people seek access to the goals that society holds to be worthwhile. Their point was that access to criminal roles and advancement in the criminal hierarchy depend upon stable associations with older criminals from whom the necessary values and skills may be learned. Yet Shaw and McKay failed to give explicit recognition to the concept of illegitimate means and the socially structured conditions of access to them—probably because they tended to view slum areas as "disorganized." Although they consistently referred to illegitimate *activities* as "organized," they nevertheless tended to label high-rate delinquency *areas* "disorganized" because the values transmitted were criminal rather than conventional. Hence they sometimes made statements which we now perceive to be internally inconsistent, such as the following:

> This community situation was not only disorganized and thus ineffective as a unit of control, but it was characterized by a high rate of juvenile delinquency and adult crime, not to mention the widespread political corruption which had long existed in the area. Various forms of stealing and many organized delinquent and criminal gangs were prevalent in the area. These groups exercised a powerful influence and tended to create a community spirit which not only tolerated but actually fostered delinquent and criminal practices.[12]

Sutherland was among the first to perceive that the concept of social disorganization tends to obscure the stable patterns of interaction which exist among carriers of criminal values: "the organization of the delinquent group, which is often very complex, is social disorganization only from an ethical or some other particularistic point of view."[13] Like Shaw and McKay, he had observed that criminal activities in lower-class areas were organized in terms of a criminal value system, but he also observed that this alternative value *system was supported by a patterned system of social relations.* That is, he recognized the fact that crime, far from being a random, unorganized activity, is often an intricate and stable system of arrangements and relationships. He therefore rejected the "social disorganization" perspective: "At the suggestion of Albert K. Cohen, this concept has been changed to differential group organization, with organization for criminal activities on one side and organization against criminal activities on the other."[14]

William F. Whyte, in his classic study of an urban slum, carried the empirical description of the structure and organization of illegal means a step further. Like Sutherland, Whyte rejected the position of Shaw and McKay that the slum is *dis*organized simply because it is organized according to principles different from those in the conventional world:

> It is customary for the sociologist to study the slum district in terms of "social disorganization" and to neglect to see that an area such as Cornerville has a complex and well-established organization of its own. . . . I found that in every group there was a hierarchical structure of social relations binding the individuals to one another and that the groups were also related hierarchically to one another. Where the group was formally organized into a political club, this was immediately apparent, but for informal groups it was no less true.[15]

But Whyte's view of the slum differed somewhat from Sutherland's in that Whyte's emphasis was not on "differential group organization"—the idea that the slum is composed of two discrete systems, conventional and deviant. He stressed, rather, the way in which the occupants of various roles in these two systems become integrated in a single, stable structure which organizes and patterns the life of the community. Thus Whyte showed that individuals who participate in stable illicit enterprises do not constitute a separate or isolated segment of the community but are closely integrated with the occupants of conventional roles. He noted, for example, that "the rackets and political organizations extend from the bottom to the top of Cornerville society, mesh with one another, and integrate a large part of the life of the district. They provide a general framework for the understanding of the actions of both 'little guys' and 'big shots.'"[16]

In a recent article, Kobrin has clarified our understanding of slum areas by suggesting that they differ in the *degree* to which deviant and conventional value systems are integrated with each other. This difference, we argue, affects the relative accessibility of illegal means. Pointing the way to the development of a "typology of delinquent areas based on variations in the relationship between these two systems," Kobrin describes the "polar types" on such a continuum. The integrated area, he asserts, is characterized not only by structural integration between carriers of the two value systems but also by reciprocal participation by carriers of each in the value system of the other. Thus, he notes:

> Leaders of [illegal] enterprises frequently maintain membership in such conventional institutions of their local communities as churches, fraternal and mutual benefit societies and political parties. . . . Within this framework the influence of each of the two value systems is reciprocal, the leaders of illegal enterprise participating in the primary orientation of the conventional elements in the population, and the latter, through their participation in a local power structure sustained in large part by illicit activity, participating perforce in the alternate, criminal value system.[17]

The second polar type consists of areas in which the relationships between carriers of deviant and conventional values break down because of disorganizing forces such as "drastic change in the class, ethnic, or racial characteristics of [the] population." Kobrin suggests that in such slums "the bearers of the conventional culture and its value system are without the customary institutional machinery and therefore in effect partially demobilized with reference to the diffusion of their value system." At the same time, areas of this type are "characterized principally by the absence of systematic and organized adult activity in violation of the law, despite the fact that many adults in these areas commit violations." Thus both value systems remain implicit, but the fact that neither is "systematic and organized" precludes the possibility of effective integration.

How does the accessibility of illegal means vary with the relative integration of conventional and criminal values in a given area? Although Kobrin does not take up this problem explicitly, he does note that the integrated area apparently constitutes a "training ground" for the acquisition of criminal values and skills. Of his first polar type he says:

> The stable position of illicit enterprise in the adult society of the community is reflected in the character of delinquent conduct on the part of children. While delinquency in all high-rate areas is intrinsically disorderly in that it is unrelated to official programs for the education of the young, in the [integrated community] boys may more or less realistically recognize the potentialities for personal progress in local society through access to delinquency. In a general way, therefore, delinquent activity in these areas constitutes a training ground for the acquisition of skill in the use of violence, concealment of

offense, evasion of detection and arrest, and the purchase of immunity from punishment. Those who come to excel in these respects are frequently noted and valued by adult leaders in the rackets who are confronted, as are the leaders of all income-producing enterprises, with problems of the recruitment of competent personnel.[18]

Kobrin makes no mention of the extent to which learning structures and opportunities for criminal careers are available in the unintegrated area. Yet the fact that neither conventional nor criminal values are articulated in this type of area as he describes it suggests that the appropriate learning structures—principally integration of different age-levels of offenders—are not available. Furthermore, Kobrin's description of adult violative activity in such areas as "unorganized" suggests that illegal opportunities are severely limited. Even if youngsters were able to secure adequate preparation for criminal roles, the social structure of such neighborhoods would appear to provide few opportunities for stable criminal careers. Kobrin's analysis—as well as that of Whyte and others before him— supports our conclusion that *illegal opportunity structures tend to emerge only when there are stable patterns of accommodation between the adult carriers of conventional and of deviant values.* Where these two value systems are implicit, or where the carriers are in open conflict, opportunities for stable criminal-role perform- ance are limited. Where stable accommodative relationships exist between the adult carriers of criminal and conventional values, institutionalized criminal careers are available. The alienated adoles- cent need not rely on the vagaries of private entrepreneurship in crime, with the attendant dangers of detection and prosecution, imprisonment, fluctuations in income, and the like. Instead, he may aspire to rise in the organized criminal structure and to occupy a permanent position in some flourishing racket. Secure in such a position, he will be relatively immune from prosecution and imprison- ment, can expect a more or less stable income, and can look forward to acceptance by the local community—criminal and conventional.

Some urban neighborhoods, in short, provide relief from pressures arising from limitations on access to success-goals by legitimate means. Because alternative routes to higher status are made available to those who are ambitious, diligent, and meritorious, the frustrations of youth in these neighborhoods are drained off. Where such pathways do not exist, frustrations become all the greater.

NOTES

1   See esp. C. R. Shaw, *The Jack-Roller* (Chicago: University of Chicago Press, 1930); Shaw, *The Natural History of a Delinquent Career* (Chicago: Press, 1931); Shaw et al., *Delinquency Areas* (Chicago: University of Chicago Press, 1940); and Shaw and H. D. McKay, *Juvenile Delinquency and Urban Areas* (Chicago: University of Chicago Press, 1942).

2   E. H. Sutherland, ed., *The Professional Thief* (Chicago: University of Chicago Press, 1937); and Sutherland, *Principles of Criminology*, 4th Ed. (Philadelphia: Lippincott, 1947).

3   All quotations in this paragraph are from *The Professional Thief, op. cit.,* pp. 211-213. Emphasis added.

4   Frank Tannenbaum, "The Professional Criminal," *The Century*, Vol. 110 (May-Oct. 1925), p. 577.

5   See A. K. Cohen, Alfred Lindesmith, and Karl Schuessler, eds., *The Sutherland Papers* (Bloomington, Ind.: Indiana University Press, 1956), pp. 31-35.

6   R. K. Merton, *Social Theory and Social Structure*, Rev. and Enl. Ed. (Glencoe, Ill.: Free Press, 1957), pp. 145-146.

7   *Principles of Criminology, op. cit.,* pp. 7-8.

8   For an example of restrictions on access to illegitimate roles, note the impact of racial definitions in the following case: "I was greeted by two prisoners who were to be my cell buddies, Ernest was a first offender, charged with being a 'hold-up' man. Bill, the other buddy, was an old offender, going through the machinery of becoming a habitual criminal, in and out of jail. . . . The first thing they asked me was, 'What are you in for?' I said, 'Jack-rolling.' The hardened one (Bill) looked at me with a superior air and said, 'A hoodlum, eh? An ordinary sneak thief. Not willing to leave jack-rolling to the niggers, eh? That's all they're good for. Kid, jack-rolling's not a white man's job.' I could see that he was disgusted with me, and I was too scared to say anything" (Shaw, *The Jack-Roller, op. cit.,* p. 101).

9   For a discussion of the way in which the availability of illegitimate means influences the adaptations of inmates to prison life, see R. A. Cloward, "Social Control in the Prison," *Theoretical Studies of the Social Organization of the Prison,* Bulletin No. 15 (New York: Social Science Research Council, March 1960), pp. 20-48.

10 See esp. *Delinquency Areas, op. cit.,* Chap. 16.

11 Shaw, *The Jack-Roller, op. cit.,* p. 54.

12 Shaw, *The Natural History of a Delinquent Career, op. cit.,* p. 229.

13 Cohen, Lindesmith, and Schuessler, eds., *The Sutherland Papers, op. cit.,* p. 21.

14 *Ibid.*

15 W. F. Whyte, *Street Corner Society*, Enl. Ed. (Chicago: University of Chicago Press, 1955), p. viii.

16 *Ibid.*, p. xii.

17 Solomon Kobrin, "The Conflict of Values in Delinquency Areas," *American Sociological Review*, Vol. 16 (Oct. 1951), pp. 657-658.

18 *Ibid.*

Techniques of Neutralization:
A Theory of Delinquency

GRESHAM M. SYKES and DAVID MATZA

Gresham M. Sykes is a professor of sociology at the University
of Virginia. David Matza is a professor of sociology at the
University of California, Berkeley.

Reprinted from Gresham M. Sykes and David Matza,
"Techniques of Neutralization: A Theory of Delinquency,"
American Sociological Review (December, 1957), 22:664-670.

In attempting to uncover the roots of juvenile delinquency,
the social scientist has long since ceased to search for devils in the
mind or stigma of the body. It is now largely agreed that delinquent
behavior, like most social behavior, is learned in the process of social
interaction.

The classic statement of this position is found in Sutherland's
theory of differential association, which asserts that criminal or
delinquent behavior involves the learning of (a) techniques of committing crimes and (b) motives, drives, rationalizations, and attitudes
favorable to the violation of law.[1] Unfortunately, the specific content of what is learned—as opposed to the process by which it is
learned—has received relatively little attention in either theory or
research. Perhaps the single strongest school of thought on the
nature of this content has centered on the idea of a delinquent subculture. The basic characteristic of the delinquent sub-culture, it is
argued, is a system of values that represents an inversion of the
values held by respectable, law-abiding society. The world of the
delinquent is the world of the law-abiding turned upside down and
its norms constitute a countervailing force directed against the conforming social order. Cohen[2] sees the process of developing a delinquent sub-culture as a matter of building, maintaining, and reinforcing
a code for behavior which exists by opposition, which stands in
point by point contradiction to dominant values, particularly those
of the middle class. Cohen's portrayal of delinquency is executed
with a good deal of sophistication, and he carefully avoids overly
simple explanations such as those based on the principle of "follow
the leader" or easy generalizations about "emotional disturbances."
Furthermore, he does not accept the delinquent sub-culture as something given, but instead systematically examines the function of
delinquent values as a viable solution to the lower-class, male child's

problems in the area of social status. Yet in spite of its virtues, this image of juvenile delinquency as a form of behavior based on competing or countervailing values and norms appears to suffer from a number of serious defects. It is the nature of these defects and a possible alternative or modified explanation for a large portion of juvenile delinquency with which this paper is concerned.

The difficulties in viewing delinquent behavior as springing from a set of deviant values and norms—as arising, that is to say, from a situation in which the delinquent defines his delinquency as "right"— are both empirical and theoretical. In the first place, if there existed in fact a delinquent sub-culture such that the delinquent viewed his illegal behavior as morally correct, we could reasonably suppose that he would exhibit no feelings of guilt or shame at detection or confinement. Instead, the major reaction would tend in the direction of indignation or a sense of martyrdom.[3] It is true that some delinquents do react in the latter fashion, although the sense of martyrdom often seems to be based on the fact that others "get away with it" and indignation appears to be directed against the chance events or lack of skill that led to apprehension. More important, however, is the fact that there is a good deal of evidence suggesting that many delinquents *do* experience a sense of guilt or shame and its outward expression is not to be dismissed as a purely manipulative gesture to appease those in authority. Much of this evidence is, to be sure, of a clinical nature or in the form of impressionistic judgments of those who must deal first hand with the youthful offender. Assigning a weight to such evidence calls for caution, but it cannot be ignored if we are to avoid the gross stereotype of the juvenile delinquent as a hardened gangster in miniature.

In the second place, observers have noted that the juvenile delinquent frequently accords admiration and respect to law-abiding persons. The "really honest" person is often revered, and if the delinquent is sometimes overly keen to detect hypocrisy in those who conform, unquestioned probity is likely to win his approval. A fierce attachment to a humble, pious mother or a forgiving, upright priest (the former, according to many observers, is often encountered in both juvenile delinquents and adult criminals) might be dismissed as rank sentimentality, but at least it is clear that the delinquent does not necessarily regard those who abide by the legal rules as immoral. In similar vein, it can be noted that the juvenile delinquent may exhibit great resentment if illegal behavior is imputed to "significant others" in his immediate social environment or to heroes in the world of sport and entertainment. In other words, if the delinquent does hold to a set of values and norms that stand in complete opposition to those of respectable society, his norm-holding is of a peculiar sort. While supposedly thoroughly committed to the deviant system of the delinquent sub-culture, he would appear to recognize the moral validity of the dominant normative system in many instances.[4]

In the third place, there is much evidence that juvenile delinquents often draw a sharp line between those who can be victimized and those who cannot. Certain social groups are not to be viewed as "fair game" in the performance of supposedly approved delinquent acts while others warrant a variety of attacks. In general, the potentiality for victimization would seem to be a function of the social distance between the juvenile delinquent and others and thus we find implicit maxims in the world of the delinquent such as "don't steal from friends" or "don't commit vandalism against a church of your own faith."[5] This is all rather obvious, but the implications have not received sufficient attention. The fact that supposedly valued behavior tends to be directed against disvalued social groups hints that the "wrongfulness" of such delinquent behavior is more widely recognized by delinquents than the literature has indicated. When the pool of victims is limited by consideration of kinship, friendship, ethnic group, social class, age, sex, etc., we have reason to suspect that the virtue of delinquency is far from unquestioned.

In the fourth place, it is doubtful if many juvenile delinquents are totally immune from the demands for conformity made by the dominant social order. There is a strong likelihood that the family of the delinquent will agree with respectable society that delinquency is wrong, even though the family may be engaged in a variety of illegal activities. That is, the parental posture conducive to delinquency is not apt to be a positive prodding. Whatever may be the influence of parental example, what might be called the "Fagin" pattern of socialization into delinquency is probably rare. Furthermore, as Redl has indicated, the idea that certain neighborhoods are completely delinquent, offering the child a model for delinquent behavior without reservations, is simply not supported by the data.[6]

The fact that a child is punished by parents, school officials, and agencies of the legal system for his delinquency may, as a number of observers have cynically noted, suggest to the child that he should be more careful not to get caught. There is an equal or greater probability, however, that the child will internalize the demands for conformity. This is not to say that demands for conformity cannot be counteracted. In fact, as we shall see shortly, an understanding of how internal and external demands for conformity are neutralized may be crucial for understanding delinquent behavior. But it is to say that a complete denial of the validity of demands for conformity and the substitution of a new normative system is improbable, in light of the child's or adolescent's dependency on adults and enrichment by adults inherent in his status in the social structure. No matter how deeply enmeshed in patterns of delinquency he may be and no matter how much this involvement may outweigh his association with the law-abiding, he cannot escape the condemnation of his deviance. Somehow the demands for conformity must be met and answered; they cannot be ignored as part of an alien system of values and norms.

In short, the theoretical viewpoint that sees juvenile delinquency as a form of behavior based on the values and norms of a deviant subculture in precisely the same way as law-abiding behavior is based on the values and norms of the larger society is open to serious doubt. The fact that the world of the delinquent is embedded in the larger world of those who conform cannot be overlooked nor can the delinquent be equated with an adult thoroughly socialized into an alternative way of life. Instead, the juvenile delinquent would appear to be at least partially committed to the dominant social order in that he frequently exhibits guilt or shame when he violates its proscriptions, accords approval to certain conforming figures, and distinguishes between appropriate and inappropriate targets for his deviance. It is to an explanation for the apparently paradoxical fact of his delinquency that we now turn.

As Morris Cohen once said, one of the most fascinating problems about human behavior is why men violate the laws which they believe. This is the problem that confronts us when we attempt to explain why delinquency occurs despite a greater or lesser commitment to the usages of conformity. A basic clue is offered by the fact that social rules or norms calling for valued behavior seldom if ever take the form of categorical imperatives. Rather, values or norms appear as *qualified* guides for action, limited in their applicability in terms of time, place, persons, and social circumstances. The moral injunction against killing, for example, does not apply to the enemy during combat in time of war, although a captured enemy comes once again under the prohibition. Similarly, the taking and distributing of scarce goods in a time of acute social need is felt by many to be right, although under other circumstances private property is held inviolable. The normative system of a society, then, is marked by what Williams has termed *flexibility;* it does not consist of a body of rules held to be binding under all conditions.[7]

This flexibility is, in fact, an integral part of the criminal law in in that measures for "defenses to crimes" are provided in pleas such as non-age, necessity, insanity, drunkenness, compulsion, self-defense, and so on. The individual can avoid moral culpability for his criminal action—and thus avoid the negative sanctions of society—if he can prove that criminal intent was lacking. *It is our argument that much delinquency is based on what is essentially an unrecognized extension of defenses to crimes, in the form of justifications for deviance that are seen as valid by the delinquent but not by the legal system or society at large.*

These justifications are commonly described as rationalizations. They are viewed as following deviant behavior and as protecting the individual from self-blame and the blame of others after the act. But there is also reason to believe that they precede deviant behavior and make deviant behavior possible. It is this possibility that Sutherland mentioned only in passing and that other writers have failed to exploit from the viewpoint of sociological theory. Disapproval flowing

182

from internalized norms and conforming others in the social environment is neutralized, turned back, or deflected in advance. Social controls that serve to check or inhibit deviant motivational patterns are rendered inoperative, and the individual is freed to engage in delinquency without serious damage to his self image. In this sense, the delinquent both has his cake and eats it too, for he remains committed to the dominant normative system and yet so qualifies its imperatives that violations are "acceptable" if not "right." Thus the delinquent represents not a radical opposition to law-abiding society but something more like an apologetic failure, often more sinned against than sinning in his own eyes. We call these justifications of deviant behavior techniques of neutralization; and we believe these techniques make up a crucial component of Sutherland's "definitions favorable to the violation of law." It is by learning these techniques that the juvenile becomes delinquent, rather than by learning moral imperatives, values or attitudes standing in direct contradition to those of the dominant society. In analyzing these techniques, we have found it convenient to divide them into five major types.

THE DENIAL OF RESPONSIBILITY

Insofar as the delinquent can define himself as lacking responsibility for his deviant actions, the disapproval of self or others is sharply reduced in effectiveness as a restraining influence. As Justice Holmes has said, even a dog distinguishes between being stumbled over and being kicked, and modern society is no less careful to draw a line between injuries that are unintentional, i.e., where responsibility is lacking, and those that are intentional. As a technique of neutralization, however, the denial of responsibility extends much further than the claim that deviant acts are an "accident" or some similar negation of personal accountability. It may also be asserted that delinquent acts are due to forces outside of the individual and beyond his control such as unloving parents, bad companions, or a slum neighborhood. In effect, the delinquent approaches a "billiard ball" conception of himself in which he sees himself as helplessly propelled into new situations. From a psychodynamic viewpoint, this orientation toward one's own actions may represent a profound alienation from self, but it is important to stress the fact that interpretations of responsibility are cultural constructs and not merely idiosyncratic beliefs. The similarity between this mode of justifying illegal behavior assumed by the delinquent and the implications of a "sociological" frame of reference or a "humane" jurisprudence is readily apparent.[8] It is not the validity of this orientation that concerns us here, but its function of deflecting blame attached to violations of social norms and its relative independence of a particular personality structure.[9] By learning to view himself as more acted upon than acting, the delinquent prepares the way for deviance from the dominant normative system without the necessity of a formal assault on the norms themselves.

THE DENIAL OF INJURY

A second major technique of neutralization centers on the injury or harm involved in the delinquent act. The criminal law has long made a distinction between crimes which are *mala in se* and *male prohibita*—that is between acts that are wrong in themselves and acts that are illegal but not immoral—and the delinquent can make the same kind of distinction in evaluating the wrongfulness of his behavior. For the delinquent, however, wrongfulness may turn on the question of whether or not anyone has clearly been hurt by his deviance, and this matter is open to a variety of interpretations. Vandalism, for example, may be defined by the delinquent simply as "mischief"— after all, it may be claimed, the persons whose property has been destroyed can well afford it. Similarly, auto theft may be viewed as "borrowing," and gang fighting may be seen as a private quarrel, an agreed upon duel between two willing parties, and thus of no concern to the community at large. We are not suggesting that this technique of neutralization, labelled the denial of injury, involves an explicit dialectic. Rather, we are arguing that the delinquent frequently, and in a hazy fashion, feels that his behavior does not really cause any great harm despite the fact that it runs counter to law. Just as the link between the individual and his acts may be broken by the denial of responsibility, so may the link between acts and their consequences be broken by the denial of injury. Since society sometimes agrees with the delinquent, e.g., in matters such as truancy, "pranks," and so on, it merely reaffirms the idea that the delinquent's neutralization of social controls by means of qualifying the norms is an extension of common practice rather than a gesture of complete opposition.

THE DENIAL OF THE VICTIM

Even if the delinquent accepts the responsibility for his deviant actions and is willing to admit that his deviant actions involve an injury or hurt, the moral indignation of self and others may be neutralized by an insistence that the injury is not wrong in light of the circumstances. The injury, it may be claimed, is not really an injury; rather, it is a form of rightful retaliation or punishment. By a subtle alchemy the delinquent moves himself into the position of an avenger and the victim is transformed into a wrong-doer. Assaults on homosexuals or suspected homosexuals, attacks on members of minority groups who are said to have gotten "out of place," vandalism as revenge on an unfair teacher or school official, thefts from a "crooked" store owner—all may be hurts inflicted on a transgressor, in the eyes of the delinquent. As Orwell has pointed out, the type of criminal admired by the general public has probably changed over the course of years and Raffles no longer serves as a hero;[10] but Robin Hood, and his latter day derivatives such as the tough detective seeking justice outside the law, still capture the popular imagination, and the delinquent may view his acts as part of a similar role.

To deny the existence of the victim, then, by transforming him into a person deserving injury is an extreme form of a phenomenon we have mentioned before, namely, the delinquent's recognition of appropriate and inappropriate targets for his delinquent acts. In addition, however, the existence of the victim may be denied for the delinquent, in a somewhat different sense, by the circumstances of the delinquent act itself. Insofar as the victim is physically absent, unknown or a vague abstraction (as is often the case in delinquent acts committed against property), the awareness of the victim's existence is weakened. Internalized norms and anticipations of the reactions of others must somehow be activated, if they are to serve as guides for behavior; and it is possible that a diminished awareness of the victim plays an important part in determining whether or not this process is set in motion.

THE CONDEMNATION OF THE CONDEMNERS

A fourth technique of neutralization would appear to involve a condemnation of the condemners or, as McCorkle and Korn have phrased it, a rejection of the rejectors.[11] The delinquent shifts the focus of attention from his own deviant acts to the motives of his violations. His condemners, he may claim, are hypocrites, deviants in disguise, or impelled by personal spite. This orientation toward the conforming world may be of particular importance when it hardens into a bitter cynicism directed against those assigned the task of enforcing or expressing the norms of the dominant society. Police, it may be said, are corrupt, stupid, and brutal. Teachers always show favoritism and parents always "take it out" on their children. By a slight extension, the rewards of conformity—such as material success—become a matter of pull or luck, thus decreasing still further the stature of those who stand on the side of the law-abiding. The validity of this jaundiced viewpoint is not so important as its function in turning back or deflecting the negative sanctions attached to violations of the norms. The delinquent, in effect, has changed the subject of the conversation in the dialogue between his own deviant impulses and the reactions of others; and by attacking others, the wrongfulness of his own behavior is more easily repressed or lost to view.

THE APPEAL TO HIGHER LOYALTIES

Fifth, and last, internal and external social controls may be neutralized by sacrificing the demands of the larger society for the demands of the smaller social groups to which the delinquent belongs such as the sibling pair, the gang, or the friendship clique. It is important to note that the delinquent does not necessarily repudiate the imperatives of the dominant normative system, despite his failure to follow them. Rather, the delinquent may see himself as caught up in a dilemma that must be resolved, unfortunately, at the cost of violating the law. One aspect of this situation has been studied by Stouffer and Toby in their research on the conflict between particularistic and universalistic demands, between the claims of friendship and general social obligations, and their results suggest that "it is possible to classify people according to a predisposition to select one or the other horn of a dilemma in role conflict."[12] For our purposes, however, the most important point is that deviation from certain norms may occur not because the norms are rejected but because other norms, held to be more pressing or involving a higher loyalty, are accorded precedence. Indeed, it is the fact that both sets of norms are believed in that gives meaning to our concepts of dilemma and role conflict.

The conflict between the claims of friendship and the claims of law, or a similar dilemma, has of course long been recognized by the social scientist (and the novelist) as a common human problem. If the juvenile delinquent frequently resolves his dilemma by insisting that he must "always help a buddy" or "never squeal on a friend," even when it throws him into serious difficulties with the dominant social order, his choice remains familiar to the supposedly law-abiding. The delinquent is unusual, perhaps, in the extent to which he is able to see the fact that he acts in behalf of the smaller social groups to which he belongs as a justification for violations of society's norms, but it is a matter of degree rather than of kind.

"I didn't mean it." "I didn't really hurt anybody." "They had it coming to them." "Everybody's picking on me." "I didn't do it for myself." These slogans or their variants, we hypothesize, prepare the juvenile for delinquent acts. These "definitions of the situation" represent tangential or glancing blows at the dominant normative system rather than the creation of an opposing ideology; and they are extensions of patterns of thought prevalent in society rather than something created *de novo*.

Techniques of neutralization may not be powerful enough to fully shield the individual from the force of his own internalized values and the reactions of conforming others, for as we have pointed out, juvenile delinquents often appear to suffer from feelings of guilt and shame when called into account for their deviant behavior. And some delinquents may be so isolated from the world of conformity that techniques of neutralization need not be called into play. Nonetheless, we would argue that techniques of neutralization are critical in lessening the effectiveness of social controls and that they lie behind a large share of delinquent behavior. Empirical research in this area is scattered and fragmentary at the present time, but the work of Redl,[13] Cressey,[14] and others has supplied a body of significant data that has done much to clarify the theoretical issues and enlarge the fund of supporting evidence. Two lines of investigation seem to be critical at this stage. First, there is need for more knowledge concerning the differential distribution of techniques of neutralization, as operative patterns of thought, by age, sex, social class, ethnic group, etc. On *a priori* grounds it might be assumed that these justifications for deviance will be more readily seized by segments of society for whom a discrepancy between common social ideals and social practice is most apparent. It is also possible however, that the habit of "bending" the dominant normative system—if not "breaking" it—cuts across our cruder social categories and is to be traced primarily to patterns of social interaction within the familial circle. Second, there is a need for a greater understanding of the internal structure of techniques of neutralization, as a system of beliefs and attitudes, and its relationship to various types of delinquent behavior. Certain techniques of neutralization would appear to be better adapted to particular deviant acts than to others, as we have suggested, for example, in the case of offenses against property and the denial of the victim. But the issue remains far from clear and stands in need of more information.

In any case, techniques of neutralization appear to offer a promising line of research in enlarging and systematizing the theoretical grasp of juvenile delinquency. As more information is uncovered concerning techniques of neutralization, their origins, and their consequences, both juvenile delinquency in particular, and deviation from normative systems in general may be illuminated.

NOTES

1   E. H. Sutherland, *Principles of Criminology*, revised by D. R. Cressey, Chicago: Lippincott, 1955, pp. 77-80.

2   Albert K. Cohen, *Delinquent Boys*, Glencoe, Ill.: The Free Press, 1955.

3   This form of reaction among the adherents of a deviant subculture who fully believe in the "rightfulness" of their behavior and who are captured and punished by the agencies of the dominant social order can be illustrated, perhaps, by groups such as Jehovah's Witnesses, early Christian sects, nationalist movements in colonial areas, and conscientious objectors during World Wars I and II.

4   As Weber has pointed out, a thief may recognize the legitimacy of legal rules without accepting their moral validity. Cf. Max Weber, *The Theory of Social and Economic Organization* (translated by A. M. Henderson and Talcott Parsons), New York: Oxford University Press, 1947, p. 125. We are arguing here, however, that the juvenile delinquent frequently recognizes *both* the legitimacy of the dominant social order and its moral "rightness."

5   Thrasher's account of the "Itschkies"—a juvenile gang composed of Jewish boys—and the immunity from "rolling" enjoyed by Jewish drunkards is a good illustration. Cf. F. Thrasher, *The Gang*, Chicago: The University of Chicago Press, 1947, p. 315.

6   Cf. Solomon Kobrin, "The Conflict of Values in Delinquency Areas," *American Sociological Review*, 16 (October, 1951), pp. 653-661.

7   Cf. Robin Williams, Jr., *American Society*, New York: Knopf. 1951, p. 28.

8   A number of observers have wryly noted that many delinquents seem to show a surprising awareness of sociological and psychological explanations for their behavior and are quick to point out the causal role of their poor environment.

9   It is possible, of course, that certain personality structures can accept some techniques of neutralization more readily than others, but this question remains largely unexplored.

10   George Orwell, *Dickens, Dali, and Others*, New York: Reynal, 1946.

11   Lloyd W. McCorkle and Richard Korn, "Resocialization Within Walls," *The Annals of the American Academy of Political and Social Science*, 293 (May, 1954), pp. 88-98.

12   See Samuel A. Stouffer and Jackson Toby, "Role Conflict and Personality," in *Toward a General Theory of Action*, edited by Talcott Parsons and Edward A. Shils, Cambridge: Harvard University Press, 1951, p. 494.

13   See Fritz Redl and David Wineman, *Children Who Hate*, Glencoe: The Free Press, 1956.

14   See D. R. Cressey, *Other People's Money*, Glencoe: The Free Press, 1953.

Containment Theory

WALTER C. RECKLESS

Walter C. Reckless is an emeritus professor of sociology at Ohio State University.

Reprinted from Walter C. Reckless, "A Non-Causal Explanation: Containment Theory," *Excerpta Criminalogica* (March-April, 1962) 1:2:131-134.

Behavioral scientists, such as psychiatrists, psychologists, and sociologists, have had great difficulty in identifying the operation of various factors or conditions, assumed to be directly related to crime and delinquency. It has been almost impossible to isolate and measure the influence of conditions or factors on behavior of people generally.

The status of knowledge about the "etiology" of crime was so bad thirty years ago that it led two behavioral scientists to conclude: "The absurdity of any attempt to draw etiological conclusions from the findings of criminological research is so patent as not to warrant further discussion."[1] Progress has been made in criminological research and scholarship since that time but not enough to negate the above evaluation of Michael and Adler.

In 1940 the author suggested that criminologists should abandon the search for a general theory of crime causation and look for alternative approaches which are more realistic and appropriate.[2] Dissatisfaction with the application of the concept of causation to criminal behavior was expressed also by L. Radzinowicz at the Second United Nations Congress on the Prevention of Crime and Treatment of Offenders, London, August 1960.

It is quite likely that causation is not a valid concept to apply to human behavior such as crime and delinquency, and that a general theory of causation, which has validity for all or a large part of crime and delinquency, for various samples of offenders and non-offenders in various environments, is even more unrealistic, in spite of heroic efforts on the part of criminologists to search for a valid general theory.

The author proposes that criminologists formulate hypotheses about or explanations of delinquent and criminal behavior which do not require the concept of cause or a combination of causes. Containment theory is suggested as a substitute for causal theory. The following statement supplements three recently published statements of the theory.[3]

COMPONENTS OF EXTERNAL AND INTERNAL CONTAINMENT

The assumption is that there is a containing external social structure which holds individuals in line and that there is also an internal buffer which protects people against deviation from the social and legal norms. The two containments act as a defense against deviating from the legal and social norms, as an insulation against pressures and pulls, as a protection against demoralization and seduction. If there are "causes" which lead to deviant behavior, they are negated, neutralized, rendered impotent, or are paired by the two containing buffers.

In a mobile, industrialized, urban society such as exists in the United States and large parts of Northern and Western Europe, external containment will be found to reside principally in the family and other supportive groups in which individuals actively participate. In times past, the clan, the neighborhood, the village, the caste, the tribe, the sect have acted as supportive external buffers for the individual, in addition to the family. However, containment which exists for individuals within the family and other supportive groups of modern urban, industrialized society consists of one or more of the following components:

1 A role structure which provides scope for the individual.
2 A set of reasonable limits and responsibilities for members.
3 An opportunity for the individual to achieve a status.
4 Cohesion among members, including joint activity and togetherness.

5   Sense of belongingness (identification with the group).
6   Identification with one or more persons within the group.
7   Provision for supplying alternative ways and means of satisfaction (when one or more ways are closed).

Internal containment consists of "self" components—those having to do with the strength of the self as an operating person. It is composed of:

1   A favorable image of self in relation to other persons, groups, and institutions.
2   An awareness of being an inner directed, goal oriented person.
3   A high level of frustration tolerance.
4   Strongly internalized morals and ethics.
5   Well developed ego and super ego (in the sense of Fritz Redl,[4] as the control and management system of behavior).

A STATEMENT OF PROBABILITY

The components of the two containing systems are not causes. They are buffers or insulations against pressures, pulls, and pushes. They withstand the pressures, pulls, and pushes. When they are absent or weak, the person is likely to deviate from accepted social and legal norms, and is vulnerable for committing unofficial (unreported) and/or official (reported) delinquency or crime. When the two containing systems are strong, the individual will not deviate from the legal and social norms and will not be an unofficial or official offender.

Containment theory not only describes noncausal buffers against deviation but it also describes probability. What are the chances (probability) that official delinquency and crime (reported deviation of the legal norms) will occur or appear in an individual, with such and such assessment of his inner and outer containment. Obviously, individuals who can be classified as strong-strong (strong in external and strong in internal containment) will have a very low probability of committing crime or delinquency (becoming a legal deviant); whereas individuals who are classified as weak-weak (weak in external and weak in internal containment) will have a very high probability of committing crime and delinquency.

The writer is quite prepared to admit that of the two containing buffers against deviation, the inner containment is the more important in the mobile, industrialized settings of modern society. This is because individuals in such societies spend much of their time away from the family and other supportive groups which can contain them. As a result they must rely more on their own inner strength to function competently. It is also probable that the outer is operationally more important than the inner containing buffer in less industrialized societies where the clan, the caste, the tribe, the

Scheme 1
Probabilities of deviancy in mobile, industrialized,
urban societies

Inner Containment (put to a test in everyday living)		
External Containment	Strong	Weak
Strong	Very Low	Medium to Moderately High
Weak	Moderately Low	Very High

village retain their effectiveness or in the modern, intensively managed, communistic societies. In such societies the strength of the self, away from a circumscribed social structure, is not put to a test and we really do not know how strong it is or how well it can manage alone.

ASSESSMENT OF INDIVIDUALS

The assumption is that individuals of various samples can be assessed for the strength or weakness of their outer and inner containment by methods which are at least equal to, if not superior to, an ordinary physical examination or the schedule of information used by life insurance companies in computing the risk of an applicant. An evaluation or assessment of the external containment can be reliably made by a trained sociologist, psychologist, or social worker, working under an expert. And it should be possible for two or more investigators to obtain independently the same rating of the external containment of an individual, as a result of a field investigation. In the not too distant future, it should be possible for sociologists to develop a reliable and valid check list or a scale to measure the strength of external containment, which would help to standardize the assessments.

Likewise, an assessment of internal containment can be made reliably by competent psychiatrists, psychologists, or sociologists. Psychologists have already validated several personality scales and some of them could be used for measuring the strength of the self. It would be no large task for research psychologists, psychiatrists, or sociologists, familiar with measurement techniques, to validate a scale which tests several components of strength of self. Even without the aid of a measuring instrument, psychologists, psychiatrists, and sociologists could make a fairly reliable clinical evaluation of the inner containment, in terms of the components listed above, through an interview with the individual. And two or more equally trained

Scheme 2
Probabilities of deviancy in less advanced and in
highly managed societies

Inner Containment (probably not put to actual test)		
External Containment	Strong	Weak
Strong	Very Low	Moderately Low
Weak	Medium to Moderately High	Very High

experts could arrive at the same assessment of the self of an individual independently.

Known groups of juvenile and adult offenders can be assessed according to the two containing systems and comparisons can be made with the assessments of comparable groups (for age, sex, class, religion, etc.) of known nonoffenders. Preadolescent children can be assessed, say at 12 years of age, and records of official delinquency and adult crime could be cleared for this experimental sample until 21 years of age. Then inner and outer containment could be related to the absence of delinquency and crime, to the early onset and late onset (when they do occur), to continuation in delinquency and crime once having begun, etc.

ADVANTAGES IN USE OF CONTAINMENT THEORY

Apart from the research application of the theory, there are several distinct advantages and realistic aspects in the use of containment theory. In the first place, it applies equally well to modal conformity* to unofficial nonconformity (undetected and unreported deviation against social norms), to unofficial (unreported) and official (reported) deviation against the legal norms (crime and delinquency). Secondly, research methods can be developed to implement the theory and to make the assessments of both containing buffers. Thirdly, psychiatrists, psychologists, and sociologists have commonly shared interests in the various components of outer and inner containment. They could very readily join hands in research; could very readily form a research team with such a mutually shared orientation; they could very readily supplement and verify each other's work. Fourthly, containment theory is a good operational theory for treatment of offenders and the prevention of crime and delinquency.

---

*It is assumed that people are very infrequently saints and that most conforming people err sometimes; however, they are modally (prevalently) conformists.

Institutional programs and probation and aftercare service could seek to build up the strength of the self and reconstruct an outer containing buffer for holding individual offenders in line. Assessments of outer and inner containment in the preadolescent ages could provide the means of early case spotting of vulnerable children, so that parents, school, and welfare agencies might make special efforts to overcome the trend toward delinquency and crime. Special programs to reach vulnerable youth could focus upon implanting a stronger inner insulation against deviancy as well as developing supportive outer containments.

MIDDLE RANGE THEORY

Perhaps the most realistic aspect of the theory, from a scholarly and research point of view, is that it is a middle range theory. It does not apply to crime or delinquency at the extremes. It does not apply to crime or delinquency which is the result of overpowering internal pushes, such as compulsions, the illogical propensity for infantile gratification, manias, fugues, panics, hallucinations, paranoidal tendencies. The self as a controlling agent of the person, if it is strong enough, can cope with ordinary restlessness, ordinary disappointments, ordinary frustration, ordinary desires, but the self as specified in the inner containing buffer cannot contain abnormally strong internal pushes.

Likewise, containment theory does not apply to the other extreme, where begging, predatory activities, criminal pursuits are part of the prevailing way of life, such as the criminal tribes of India, the Gypsies of Europe, illegal whisky making in the Appalachian region of the United States, families who live by begging, etc. Persons inherit these criminal pursuits socially. Their prevalence is the natural order of events, since there are no alternate or competing modes of gaining a living. What needs to be explained in such instances is failure on the part of some members of these groups to follow the mode. Opium smoking among males in certain countries of Southeast Asia, gambling among Chinese migrants before World War I, abduction of marriageable females in the Punjab of former days, use of the machete for defense of personal honor in several Latin American countries, smuggling among coastal villagers or mountain villagers on a frontier, stealing of goats and sheep from neighboring flocks in the Near East have been prevalent enough to be considered in the same category of accepted pursuits or activities, which need no explanation in terms of deviancy. Some sociological criminologists have referred to such general pursuits and activities as "criminogenic patterns."

In between the extremes of abnormal pushes and criminogenic (widely practised) activities, is the large middle territory of delinquency and crime, which needs explanation, because it represents legal and social deviation. Consequently, a theory such as containment theory is needed to explain deviation from the legal and social norms as well as modal conformity to these norms.

One final reality aspect is also apparent in the use and application of containment theory. The microcosm reflects the macrocosm. The individual case mirrors the general formulation. In the actual research application of containment theory, each case in the various criminal or noncriminal samples must be assessed in terms of external and internal containment. It would be difficult to identify, uncover, or access the presence or absence of the components of Lombroso's, Feri's, Tarde's, Bonger's, von Hentig's, Exner's, or Sutherland's theories in individual case records of various samples of criminal and noncriminal populations. In these instances, and many others could be mentioned, one cannot get the microcosm to reflect the macrocosm.

NOTES

1   Jerome Michael and Mortimer J. Adler, *Crime, Law and Social Science*, New York, 1933, p. 169.

2   Walter C. Reckless, *Criminal Behavior*, New York, 1940, p. 255.

3   The first statement of "Containment Theory" is found in the third edition of the author's textbook on criminology, *The Crime Problem*, New York, 1961, Chapter 18; the second, in an article entitled "Halttheorie," which was published in *Monatschrift für Kriminologie und Strafrechtsreform*, Vol. 44, June 1961, pp. 1-14; the third, in *Federal Probation*, Vol. 25, No. 4, December 1961.

4   Fritz Redl and David Wineman, *Children who Hate*, Chicago, 1951, pp. 74-140.

Labelling Theory Reconsidered

HOWARD S. BECKER*

Howard S. Becker is a professor of sociology at Northwestern University.

Deviant phenomena have long provided one of the foci of sociological thought. Our theoretical interest in the nature of social order combines with practical interest in actions thought harmful to individuals and society to direct our attention to the broad arena of behavior variously called crime, vice, nonconformity, aberration, eccentricity, or madness. Whether we conceive it as a failure of socialization and sanctioning or simply as wrongdoing and misbehavior, we want to know why people act in disapproved ways.

In recent years, a naturalistic approach to these phenomena (Matza, 1969) has come to center on the interaction between those alleged to be engaged in wrongdoing and those making the allegations. A number of people—Frank Tannenbaum (1938), Edwin Lemert (1951), John Kitsuse (1962), Kai Erikson (1962) and myself (Becker, 1963), to name a few—contributed to the development of what has rather unfortunately been called "labelling theory." Since the initial statements, many people have criticized, extended, and argued over the original statements; others have contributed important research results.

I would like to look back on these developments and see where we stand (cf. Schur, 1969). What has been accomplished? What changes in our conceptions must we make? Three topics especially deserve discussion: the conception of deviance as collective action; the demystification of deviance; and the moral dilemmas of deviance theory. In each case, I intend the point I make to apply to sociological research and analysis generally, reaffirming the faith that the field of deviance is nothing special, just another kind of human activity to be studied and understood.

I might begin by disposing of some seemingly difficult points rather summarily, in a way which will make clear my dissatisfaction

*This paper was first presented at the meetings of the British Sociological Association, April, 1971, in London. A number of friends provided helpful comments on an earlier draft. I especially want to thank Eliot Freidson, Blanche Geer, Irving Louis Horowitz, and John I. Kitsuse.

with the expression "labelling theory." I never thought the original statements by myself and others warranted being called theories, at least not theories of the fully articulated kind they are now criticized for *not* being. A number of authors complained that labelling theory neither provides an etiological explanation of deviance (Gibbs, 1966; Bordua, 1967; Akers, 1968) nor tells how the people who commit deviant acts come to do that—and especially why *they* do it while others around them do not. Sometimes critics suggest that a theory was proposed, but that it was wrong. Thus, some thought the theory attempted to explain deviance by the responses others made to it. After one was labelled a deviant, according to this paraphrase, then one began to do deviant things, but not before. You can easily dispose of that theory by referring to facts of everyday experience.

The original proponents of the position, however, did not propose solutions to the etiological question. They had more modest aims. They wanted to enlarge the area taken into consideration in the study of deviant phenomena by including in it activities of others than the allegedly deviant actor. They supposed, of course, that when they did that, and as new sources of variance were included in the calculations, all the questions that students of deviance conventionally looked at would take on a different cast.

Further, the act of labelling, as carried out by moral entrepreneurs, while important, cannot possibly be conceived as the sole explanation of what alleged deviants actually do. It would be foolish to propose that stick-up men stick people up simply because someone has labelled them stick-up men, or that everything a homosexual does results from someone having called him homosexual. Nevertheless, one of the most important contributions of this approach has been to focus attention on the way labelling places the actor in circumstances which make it harder for him to continue the normal routines of everyday life and thus provoke him to "abnormal" actions (as when a prison record makes it harder to earn a living at a conventional occupation and so disposes its possessor to move into an illegal one). The degree to which labelling has such effects is, however, an empirical one, to be settled by research into specific cases rather than by theoretical fiat. (See Becker, 1963, pp. 34-35; Lemert, 1951, pp. 71-76; Ray, 1961; and Lemert, 1972.)

Finally, the theory, when it focuses attention on the undeniable actions of those officially in charge of defining deviance, does not make an empirical characterization of the results of particular social institutions. To suggest that defining someone as deviant may under certain circumstances dispose him to a particular line of action is not the same as saying that mental hospitals always drive people crazy or that jails always turn people into habitual criminals.

Labelling achieved its theoretical importance in quite another way. Classes of acts, and particular examples of them, may or may not be thought deviant by any of the various relevant audiences that view them. The difference in definition, in the label applied to the act, makes a difference in what everyone, audiences and actors alike, does subsequently. What the theory did, as Albert Cohen (1965; 1966; 1968) has pointed out, was to create a four-cell property space by combining two dichotomous variables, the commission or non-commission of a given act and the definition of that act as deviant or not. The theory is not a theory about one of the resulting four cells, but a theory about all four of them and their interrelations. In which of those cells we actually locate deviance proper is less important (merely a matter of definition though, like all such matters, not trivial) than understanding that we lose by looking at any one cell alone without seeing it in connection with the others.

My own original formulation created some confusion by referring to one of those variables as "obedient" (as opposed to "rule-breaking") behavior. The distinction implied the prior existence of a determination that rule-breaking had occurred, though, of course, it was just that that the theory proposed to make problematic. I think it better to describe that dimension as the commission or noncommission of a given act. Ordinarily, of course, we study those acts that others are likely to define as deviant; this maximizes our chances of seeing the complicated drama of accusation and definition that is the center of our field of study. Thus, we may be interested whether a person smokes marihuana, or engages in homosexual acts in public toilets, in part because these acts are likely to be defined as deviant when discovered. We also, of course, study them as phenomena which are interesting in other ways as well. Thus, by studying marihuana use, we can study the way people learn through social interaction to interpret their own physical experience (Becker, 1953). By studying homosexual encounters in public toilets, we can learn how people coordinate their activities through tacit communication (Humphreys, 1970). We can also ask how the high probability that the act will be defined as deviant affects learning the activity and continuing it. It is useful to have a term which indicates that others are likely to define such activities as deviant without making that a scientific judgment that the act is in fact deviant. I suggest we call such acts "potentially deviant."

Labelling theory, then, is neither a theory, with all the achievements and obligations that go with the title, nor focused so exclusively on the act of labelling as some have thought. It is, rather, a way of looking at a general area of human activity; a perspective whose value will appear, if at all, in increased understanding of things formerly obscure. (I will indulge my dislike of the conventional label for the theory by referring to it from now on as an interactionist theory of deviance.)

DEVIANCE AS COLLECTIVE ACTION

Sociologists agree that what they study is society, but the consensus persists only if we don't look into the nature of society too closely. I prefer to think of what we study as *collective action*. People act, as Mead (1934) and Blumer (1966; 1969) have made clearest, *together*. They do what they do with an eye on what others have done, are doing, and may do in the future. One tries to fit his own line of action into the actions of others, just as each of them likewise adjusts his own developing actions to what he sees and expects others to do. The result of all this adjusting and fitting in can be called a collective action, especially if it is kept in mind that the term covers more than just a conscious collective agreement to, let's say, go on strike, but also extends to participating in a school class, having a meal together, or crossing the street—each of these seen as something being done by a lot of people together.

I don't mean, in using terms like "adjustment" and "fitting in," to suggest an overly peaceful view of social life, or any necessity for people to succumb to social constraints. I mean only that people ordinarily take into account what is going on around them and what is likely to go on after they decide what they will do. The adjusting may consist of deciding that since the police will probably look *here*, I'll put the bomb *there*, as well as of deciding that since the police are going to look, I guess I won't make any bombs at all or even think about it any more.

Neither do I mean, in the foregoing discussion, to imply that social life consists only of face-to-face encounters between individuals. Individuals may engage in intense and persistent interaction though they never encounter one another face-to-face; the interaction of stamp collectors takes place largely through the mail. Further, the give-and-take of interaction, the fitting in and mutual adjustment of lines of activity, occur as well between groups and organizations. The political processes surrounding the drama of deviance have that character. Economic organizations, professional associations, trade unions, lobbyists, moral entrepreneurs, and legislators all interact to establish the conditions under which those who represent the state in enforcing laws, for example, interact with those alleged to have violated them.

If we can view any kind of human activity as collective, we can view deviance so. What results? One result is the general view I want to call "interactionist." In its simplest form, the theory insists that we look at all the people involved in any episode of alleged deviance. When we do, we discover that these activities require the overt or tacit cooperation of many people and groups to occur as they do. When workers collude to restrict industrial production (Roy, 1954), they do so with the help of inspectors, maintenance men, and the man in the tool crib. When members of industrial firms steal, they do so with the active cooperation of others above and below them in the firm's hierarchy (Dalton, 1959). Those observations alone cast doubt on theories that seek the origins of deviant acts in individual psychology, for we would have to posit a miraculous meeting of individual forms of pathology to account for the complicated forms of collective activity we observe. Because it is hard to cooperate with people whose reality-testing equipment is inadequate, people suffering from psychological difficulties don't fit well into criminal conspiracies.

When we see deviance as collective action, we immediately see that people act with an eye to the responses of others involved in that action. They take into account the way their fellows will evaluate what they do, and how that evaluation will affect their prestige and rank: The delinquents studied by Short and Strodtbeck (1965) did some of the things they got into trouble for because they wanted to maintain the positions of esteem they held in their gangs.

When we look at all the people and organizations involved in an episode of potentially deviant behavior, we discover too that the collective activity going on consists of more than acts of alleged wrongdoing. It is an involved drama in which making allegations of wrongdoing is a central feature. Indeed, Erikson (1966) and Douglas (1970), among others, have identified the study of deviance as essentially the study of the construction and reaffirmation of moral meanings in everyday social life. Some of the chief actors do not themselves engage in wrongdoing, but rather appear as enforcers of law or morality, as people who complain that other actors are doing wrong, take them into custody, bring them before legal authorities, or administer punishment themselves. If we look long enough and close enough, we discover that they do this sometimes, but not all the time; to some people but not others; in some places but not others. Those discrepancies cast doubt on simple notions about when something is, after all, wrong. We see that the actors themselves often disagree about what is deviant, and often doubt the deviant character of an act. The courts disagree; the police have reservations even when the law is clear; those engaged in the proscribed activity disagree with official definitions. We see, further, that some acts which, by commonly recognized standards, clearly ought to be defined as deviant are not defined that way by anyone. We see that enforcers of law and morality often temporize, allowing some acts to go undetected or unpunished because it would be too much trouble to pursue the matter, because they have limited resources and can't pursue everyone, because the wrongdoer has sufficient power to protect himself from their incursions, because they have been paid to look the other way.

If a sociologist looks for neat categories of crime and deviance and expects to be able to tell clearly when someone has committed one of these acts, so that he can look for its correlates, he finds all these anomalies troublesome. He may hope that they will be disposed of by improved techniques of data gathering and analysis. The long history of attempts to provide those devices ought to tell us the hope is misplaced: That area of human endeavor will not support a belief in the inevitability of progress.

The trouble is not technical. It is theoretical. We can construct workable definitions either of particular actions people might commit or of particular categories of deviance as the world (especially, but not only, the authorities) defines them. But we cannot make the two coincide completely, because they do not do so empirically. They belong to two distinct, though overlapping, systems of collective action. One consists of the people who cooperate to produce the act in question. The other consists of the people who cooperate in the drama of morality by which "wrongdoing" is discovered and dealt with, whether that procedure is formal and legal or quite informal.

Much of the heated discussion over interactionist theories comes from an equivocation in which the word "deviance" is made to stand for two distinct processes taking place in those two systems (a good example is Alvarez, 1968). On the one hand, some analysts want "deviance" to mean acts which, to any "reasonable" member of a society, or by some agreed-on definition (such as violation of an allegedly existent rule, statistical rarity, or psychological pathology), are wrong. They want to focus on the system of action in which those acts occur. The same analysts also want to apply the word to the people who are apprehended and treated as having committed that act. In this case, they want to focus on the system of action in which those judgments occur. This equivocation on the term causes no inaccuracy if and only if those who commit the act and those apprehended are the same. We know they are not. Therefore, if we take as our unit of study those who committed the act (assuming we can identify them), we necessarily include some who have not been apprehended and labelled; if we take as our unit those apprehended and labelled, we necessarily include some who never committed the act but were treated as if they had (Kitsuse and Cicourel, 1963).

Neither alternative pleases. What interactionist theorists have done is to treat the two systems as distinct, noting whatever overlap and interaction occurs between them but not assuming their occurrence. Thus, one can study the genesis of drug use, as Lindesmith (1968) and I did, and deal with etiological questions, never supposing, however, that what the people studied do has any necessary connection with a generalized quality of deviance. Or one can, as many recent studies have done (e.g., Gusfield, 1963), study the drama of moral rhetoric and action in which imputations of deviance are made, accepted, rejected, and fought over. The chief effect of interactionist theory has been to focus attention on that drama as an object of study, and especially to focus on some relatively unstudied participants in it—those sufficiently powerful to make their imputations of deviance stick: police, courts, physicians, school officials, and parents.

I intended my own original formulations to emphasize the logical independence of acts and the judgments people made of them. That formulation, however, contained ambiguities that bordered on self-contradiction, especially in connection with the notion of "secret deviance."[1] Examining those ambiguities and some possible resolutions of them shows us that fruitful development of the theory probably lies in a more detailed analysis than we have yet made of deviance as collective action.

If we begin by saying that an act is deviant when it is so defined, what can it mean to call an act an instance of secret deviance? Since no one has defined it as deviant it cannot, by definition, be deviant; but "secret" indicates that *we* know it is deviant, even if no one else does. Lorber partially resolved this paradox (1967) by suggesting that in an important class of cases the actor himself defined what he did as deviant, even though he managed to keep others from finding out about it, either believing that it really was deviant or recognizing that others would believe that.

But what if the actor failed to make that definition? What if, even more telling, there were no acts that scientists would recognize as capable of being so defined? (I have in mind here such offenses as witchcraft [Selby, unpublished]; we cannot imagine a case of a secret witch, since we "know" that no one can actually copulate with the Devil, or summon demons.) In neither case can we count on self-definition to resolve the paradox. But we can extend Lorber's idea by seeing that it implies a procedure which, were it applied by the appropriate people, would lead them to make such a judgment, given the "facts" of the particular case. People who believe in witches have ways of deciding when an act of witchcraft has been committed. We may know enough about the circumstances to know that, if those people use such methods, what they discover will lead them to conclude that witchcraft has occurred. In the case of less imaginary offenses, we may know, for instance, that a person has in his pocket materials which, should the police search him, would make him liable to a charge of possession of drugs.

In other words, secret deviance consists of being vulnerable to the commonly used procedures for discovering deviance of a particular kind, of being in a position where it will be easy to make the definition stick. What makes this distinctively collective is the collectively accepted character of the procedures of discovery and proof.

Even with this addition, however, difficulties remain. In another important class of cases—the construction of rules *ex post facto*—there can have been no secret deviance because the rule did not exist until after the act in question was alleged to have been committed (Katz, 1972). Case-finding procedures might elicit the facts that someone later uses to prove commission of a deviant act, but the person could not have been deviant, secretly or otherwise, because the rule did not exist. Yet he might well be defined as deviant, perhaps when what he might have done becomes public and someone decides that if there was no rule against it, there ought to be. Was he then secretly deviant before?

The paradox resolves itself when we recognize that, like all other forms of collective activity, the acts and definitions in the drama of deviance take place over time, and differ from one time to the next. Definitions of behavior occur sequentially, and an act may be defined as non-deviant at t_1 and deviant at t_2 without implying that it was both simultaneously. Making use of our previous result, we see that an act might *not* be secretly deviant at t_1 because no procedure then in use would produce evidence of an act which competent judges would take to be deviant. The same act *might* be secretly deviant at t_2 because, a new rule having been made in the interim, a procedure now existed which would allow that determination.

The last formulation reminds us of the important role that power plays in interactionist theories of deviance (Horowitz and Liebowitz, 1968). Under what circumstances do we make and enforce *ex post facto* rules? I think empirical investigation will show that it occurs when one party to a relationship is disproportionately powerful, so that he can enforce his will over others' objections but wishes to maintain an appearance of justice and rationality. This characteristically occurs in the relations of parents and children, and in such similarly paternalistic arrangements as welfare worker and client, or teacher and student.

By viewing deviance as a form of collective activity, to be investigated in all its facets like any other form of collective activity, we see that the object of our study is not an isolated act whose origin we are to discover. Rather, the act alleged to occur, when it has occurred, takes place in a complex network of acts involving others, and takes on some of that complexity because of the way various people and groups define it. The lesson applies to our studies of every other area of social life. Learning it will not free us from error fully, however, for our own theories and methods present persistent sources of trouble.

DEMYSTIFYING DEVIANCE

Sociologists have made trouble for themselves by their virtually unbreakable habit of making common events and experiences mysterious. I remember—one of my first experiences in graduate school—Ernest Burgess warning our class of novices against being led astray by common sense. At the same time, Everett Hughes enjoined us to pay close attention to what we could see and hear with our own eyes and ears. Some of us thought there might be a contradiction between the two imperatives, but suppressed our worry to save our sanity.

Both injunctions have a substantial kernel of truth. Common sense, in one of its meanings, can delude us. This common sense is the traditional wisdom of the tribe, the melange of "what everybody knows" that children learn as they grow up, the stereotypes of everyday life. It includes social-science generalizations about the nature of social phenomena, correlations between social categories (e.g., between race and crime, or class and intelligence), and the etiology of problematic social conditions like poverty and war. Common-sense generalizations resemble those of social science in formal structure; they differ largely in their immunity to contradictory observations. Social-science generalizations, in principle and often in fact, change when new observations show them incorrect. Common-sense generalizations don't. This kind of common sense, particularly because its errors are not random, favors established institutions.

Another meaning of common sense suggests that the common man, his head unencumbered by fancy theories and abstract professorial notions, can at least see what is right there in front of his nose. Philosophies as disparate as pragmatism and Zen enshrine a a respect for the common man's ability to see, with Sancho Panza, that a windmill is really a windmill. To think it a knight on horseback is, however you look at it, a real mistake.

Sociologists often ignore the injunctions of this version of common sense. We may not turn windmills into knights. But we often turn collective activity—people doing things together—into abstract nouns whose connection to people doing things together is tenuous. We then typically lose interest in the more mundane things people are actually doing. We ignore what we see because it is not abstract, and chase after the invisible "forces" and "conditions" we have learned to think sociology is all about.

Novice sociologists frequently have great trouble doing field research because they do not recognize sociology, as they have read it, in the human activity they see all around them. They spend eight hours observing a factory or a school, and return with two pages of notes and the explanation that "nothing much happened." They mean that they observed no instances of anomie or stratification or bureaucracy or any of the other conventional sociological topics. They don't see that we invented those terms to enable us to deal conveniently with a number of instances of people doing things together which we have decided are sufficiently alike in specific ways for us to treat them as the same for analytic purposes. Disdaining common sense, novices ignore what happens all around them. Failing to record the details of everyday life in their notes, they cannot use them to study such abstractions as anomie, or others they might themselves construct. An important methodological problem is to systematize the procedure by which we move from an appreciation of ethnographic detail to concepts useful in addressing problems we have come to our research with or have since become aware of.

Conversely, the people sociologists study often have trouble recognizing themselves and their activities in the sociological reports written about them. We ought to worry about that more than we do. We should not expect laymen to make our analyses for us. But neither should we ignore those matters laymen habitually take into account when we describe, or make assumptions about, how they carry on their activities. Many theories of deviance posit, implicitly or explicitly, that a particular set of attitudes underlies commission of some potentially rule-violating act, even though the theory bases itself on data (such as official records) which cannot speak to this point. Consider the descriptions of the actor's state of mind found in theorizing about anomie, from Durkheim through Merton to Cloward and Ohlin. If the people studied cannot recognize themselves in those descriptions without coaching, we should pay attention.

It is not only the descriptions of their own mental states that actors cannot recognize. They often cannot recognize the acts they are supposed to have engaged in, because the sociologist has not observed those acts closely, or paid any attention to their details when he has. The omission has serious results. It makes it impossible for us to put the real contingencies of action into our theories, to make them take account of the constraints and opportunities actually present. We may find ourselves theorizing about activities which never occur in the way we imagine.

If we look closely at what we observe we will very likely see the matters to which interactionist theory calls attention. We see that people who engage in acts conventionally thought deviant are not motivated by mysterious, unknowable forces. They do what they do for much the same reasons that justify more ordinary activities. We see that social rules, far from being fixed and immutable, are continually constructed anew in every situation, to suit the convenience, will, and power position of various participants. We see that activities thought deviant often require elaborate networks of cooperation such as could hardly be sustained by people suffering from disabling mental difficulties. Interactionist theory may be an almost inevitable consequence of submitting our theories of deviance to the editing of close observation of the things they purport to be about.

Insofar as both common sense and science enjoin us to look at things closely before we start theorizing about them, obedience to the injunction produces a complex theory that takes into account the actions and reactions of everyone involved in episodes of deviance. It leaves for empirical determination (instead of settling by assumption) such matters as whether the alleged acts actually occurred, and whether official reports are accurate and to what degree. In consequence (and this is a source of great difficulty to older styles of deviance research), great doubt arises as to the utility of the various statistical series and official records researchers have been accustomed to use. I will not rehearse the major criticisms of official records, the defenses that have been made of them, and the new uses suggested for them, but simply note that a closer look at people acting together has made us aware that records are also produced by people acting together, and must be understood in that context. (See Cicourel and Kitsuse, 1963; Garfinkel and Bittner, 1967; Cicourel, 1968; Biderman and Reiss, 1967; Douglas, 1967.)

The connection between an interactionist theory of deviance and a reliance on intensive field observation as a major method of data-gathering can hardly be accidental. On the other hand, I think it is not a necessary connection. Interactionist theory grows out of a frame of mind that takes the commonplace seriously and will not settle for mysterious invisible forces as explanatory mechanisms. That frame of mind undoubtedly flourishes when one continually confronts the details of the things he proposes to explain in all their complexity. It is easier to construct mythical wrongdoers, and give them whatever qualities go best with our hypothesized explanations, if we have only such fragments of fact as we might find in an official folder or in the answers to a questionnaire. As Galtung (1965) has suggested in another connection, mythical constructs cannot defend themselves against the onslaught of contrary fact produced by intimate acquaintance.

Some people have noted that too great an emphasis on first-hand observation may cause us unintentionally to limit ourselves to those groups and sites we can easily get access to, thus failing to study the powerful people and groups who can defend themselves against our incursions. In this way, preference for an observational technique could work against the theoretical recommendation to study all parties to the drama of deviance, and undo some of the advantages of an interactionist approach. We can guard against this danger both by varying our methods and by being more ingenious in our use of observational techniques. Mills (1956), among others, demonstrates the variety of methods that can be used to study the powerful, and especially the study of those documents that become public through inadvertence, by virtue of the workings of governmental agencies, or because the powerful sometimes fight among themselves and provide data for us when they do. Similarly, we can make use of techniques of unobtrusive entry and accidental access (Becker and Mack, 1971) to gather direct observational data. (Relevant problems of access and sampling are discussed in several papers in Habenstein, 1970.)

Sociologists have generally been reluctant to take the close look at what sits in front of their noses I have recommended here. That reluctance especially infected deviance studies. Overcoming it has produced the same gain in studies of deviance that similar moves produced in studies of industry, education, and communities. It also increased the moral complexity of our theories and research, and I turn to those problems now.

MORAL PROBLEMS

Moral problems arise in all sociological research but are especially provocatively posed by interactionist theories of deviance. Moral criticism has come from the political center and beyond; from the political Left, and from left field. Interactionist theories have been accused of giving aid and comfort to the enemy, be the enemy those who would upset the stability of the existing order or the Establishment. They have been accused of openly espousing unconventional norms, of refusing to support anti-Establishment positions, and (the left-field position) of appearing to support anti-Establishment causes while subtly favoring the *status quo*.

Interactionist theories as subversive

Many critics (not necessarily conservative, though some are) believe that interactionist theories of deviance openly or covertly attack conventional morality, willfully refusing to accept its definitions of what is and is not deviant, and calling into question the assumptions on which conventional organizations dealing with deviance operate. Lemert, for instance, says:

> On the surface deviance sociology seems to offer a relatively detached or scientific way of studying certain types of social problems. Yet its mood and tone and choice of research subjects disclose a strong fixed critical stance toward the ideology, values and methods of state dominated agencies of social control. In extreme statements deviance is portrayed as little more than the result of arbitrary, fortuitous, or biased decision-making, to be understood as a sociopsychological process by which groups seek to create conditions for perpetuating established values and ways of behaving or enhancing the power of special groups. One impression left is that agencies of social control are described and analyzed to expose their failures in what they try to do and their incidental encroachments on "inalienable rights" and "freedom." Thus seen, deviance sociology is more social criticism than science. It offers little to facilitate and foster the kinds of decisions and controls actually necessary to maintain the unique quality of our society—the freedom to choose. (Lemert, 1972, p. 24)

Such critics think that the principled determination to treat official and conventional viewpoints as things to be studied, instead of accepting them as fact or self-evident truth, is a mischievous assault on the social order (Bordua, 1967).

Consider again the criticism that "labelling theory" irremediably confuses what it proposed to explain with its explanation. If it treats deviance solely as a matter of definition by those who react to it, but simultaneously posits a deviant-something-to-which-they-react, then the deviance must somehow exist prior to the reaction. Some critics do not focus on the real logical difficulties I considered earlier, but rather insist that there must be some quality of an act that can be taken as deviant, independent of anyone's reaction. They usually find that quality in the act's violation of an agreed-on rule (e.g., Gibbs, 1966; Alvarez, 1968). They think theorists who will not admit that some acts are *really* deviant, at least in the sense of rule violation, perverse.

But interactionist theorists, not especially perverse, have emphasized the independence of act and reaction, creating a property space of four cells by combining the commission or noncommission of a potentially deviant act with a deviance-defining reaction or its absence. What seems to have bothered critics in this procedure is that the term "deviance" has then more often been applied to the pair of cells characterized by acts defined as deviant, whether the alleged acts occurred or not. The choice probably reflects analysts' unwillingness to seem to approve the derogatory classification of potentially deviant acts. The unwillingness arises out of their recognition of the intrinsically situational character of rules, which exist only in the perpetually renewed consensus of one situation after another rather than as persisting specific embodiments of basic value (see the concept of "negotiated order" in Strauss *et al.*, 1964).

In any event, had interactionists typically called deviant the commission of potentially deviant acts, whatever the reaction to them, fewer would have complained. Many of us used the term loosely to cover all three cases in which deviance might be implicated: commission of a potentially deviant act without deviance-defining; deviance-defining without commission; and their co-existence. That sloppiness deserves criticism, but the important point is that no one of these is itself the whole story of deviance. That lies in the interaction among all the parties involved.

To return to the larger point, the real attack on the social order is to insist that all parties involved are fit objects of study. The earlier definition of the field of deviance as the study of people alleged to have violated rules respected that order by exempting the creators and enforcers of those rules from study. To be exempted from study means that one's claims, theories, and statements of fact are not subjected to critical scrutiny (Becker, 1967).

The interactionist reluctance to accept conventional theories has led to a critical attitude toward the assertions of conventional authority and morality, and to a hostility toward interactionist analyses on the part of their spokesmen and defenders. Thus, police officials assert that most policemen are honest except for the few rotten apples found in every barrel. Sociological investigations showing that police misbehavior results from structural imperatives built into the organization of police work provoke "defenses" of the police against social scientists. Similarly, the assertion that mental illness is a matter of social definition (e.g., Scheff, 1966) provokes the reply that people in mental hospitals are really sick (Gove, 1970a, 1970b), an answer which misses the point of the definitional argument but hits at the implied moral one by suggesting that psychiatrists, after all, know what they're doing.

Interactionist theories as establishmentarian
For the reasons just suggested, interactionist theories look (and are) rather Left. Intentionally or otherwise, they are corrosive of con-

ventional modes of thought and established institutions. Neverthe-less, the Left has criticized those theories, and in a way that mirrors more middle-of-the-road objections.[2] Just as people who approve existing institutions dislike the way interactionist theories call their assumptions and legitimacy into question, people who think existing institutions rotten complain that interactionist theories fail to say that those institutions are rotten. Both complain of an ambiguous moral stance, locating the trouble in an unfortunate "value-free" ideology which pretends to neutrality while in fact espousing either a "radical" or "merely liberal" ideology, as the case may be (Mankoff, 1970; Liazos, 1972).

The trouble evidently comes from some equivocation over the notion of being value-free. I take it that all social scientists agree that, given a question and a method of reaching an answer, any scientist, whatever his political or other values, should arrive at much the same answer, an answer given by the world of recalcitrant fact that is "out there" whatever we think about it. Insofar as a left-wing sociologist proposes to base political action on his own or others' research findings, he had better strive for this and hope it can be done. Otherwise, his actions may fail because of what his values prevented him from seeing.

That simple formulation cannot be objectionable. But all social scientists miss that goal to some degree, and the missing may result in one way or another from the scientist's values. We may miscount black citizens in the census because we do not think it worth the extra trouble it may take, given their life style, to look for them. We may fail to investigate police corruption because we think it unlikely that it exists—or because it would be unseemly to call attention to it if it did. We may suggest that we can understand political protest by examining the personalities of protestors, thereby implying that the institutions they protest against play no part in the development of their acts of dissidence. We may do work which will be helpful to authorities in dealing with troublemakers, as would be the case were we to discover correlates of radicalism that school authorities, em-ployers, and police could use to weed out potential troublemakers.

The moral questions become more pressing as we move from the technical notion of value freedom to the choice of problems, ways of stating problems, and uses to which findings can be put. Some of these troubles follow from sociology's failure to take itself seriously, to follow the injunction that almost every version of our basic theory contains but which is perhaps clearest in interactionist theory (Blumer, 1967): to study all the parties to a situation, and their relationships. Following that injunction automatically leads us to police corruption where it exists and has anything to do with what we are studying. Following it, we would not study political protest as though it involved only the protestors. A value-free sociology which rigorously followed its own precepts would not trouble the Left this way.

The question of the use of the findings cannot be settled so easily, however. Nor can the question that has plagued many professional associations: whether professional sociologists have any right to a special opinion, by virtue of being sociologists, on moral and political questions. We can see that they might, where it is warranted, claim expertise with respect to the consequences of various policies. And we can see that they might be especially concerned about whose interests they were serving. But we find it harder to substantiate the assertion that the sociologist, by virtue of his science, has any special knowledge, or claim on our attention, with respect to moral questions. Why? Because science, we say, is value-free. We then go on to make tenuous distinctions, impossible to maintain in practice, between the sociologist as scientist and the sociologist as citizen. For we all agree that the citizen-sociologist not only may take moral positions, but cannot avoid doing so.

We cannot maintain these distinctions in practice because, as Edel[3] (1955) has so tellingly argued, ascertaining facts, constructing scientific theories, and arriving at ethical judgments cannot be so neatly separated. While you cannot logically deduce what *ought* to be done from premises about what *is*, responsible ethical judgments depend very much on our assessment of the way the world and its components are constructed, how they work, what they are capable of. Those assessments rest on good scientific work. They color our ethical decisions by making us see the full moral complexity of what we study; the particular way our general ethical commitments are embodied in a given situation; how our contingent ethical commitments to values like justice, health, mercy, or reason intersect, converge, and conflict.

Our work speaks continuously to ethical questions; it is continuously informed and directed by our ethical concerns. We don't want our values to interfere with our assessment of the validity of our propositions about social life, but we cannot help their influencing our choice of propositions to investigate, or the uses to which we put our findings. Nor should we mind that they do. Simultaneously, our ethical judgments cannot help being influenced by the increasing knowledge our scientific work confronts them with. Science and ethics interpenetrate.

Take marihuana use. Our judgment must change when we shift our view of it from a picture of unbridled indulgence in perverse pleasure to one of a merciless psychic compulsion to tranquilize inner conflict, as psychiatric theories and data proposed. Our judgment changes again when we view it as a relatively harmless recreation whose worst consequences, social and individual, seem to arise from how nonusers react to users. (See Kaplan, 1970; Goode, 1970.) Those of us concerned with maximizing human freedom will now concentrate on the question of the relative harm caused by the indulgence of pleasure as opposed to its repression. We might study the operation of enforcement systems, the development of vested interests among the bureaucrats and entrepreneurs who operate them, the forces that divert them from their intended aims, the irrelevance of their intended aims to the situations and consequences of uses—all this by way of pursuing the value of freedom. We would be prepared to discover that the premises on which our inquiries are based are incorrect (that, for example, enforcement systems do operate efficiently and honestly to deal with serious troubles for individuals and communities), and we would conduct our research so as to make such discovery possible.

Sociologists beginning from other ethical positions might investigate the pressures of peers, the mass media, and other sources of personal influence that lead to drug use and thus to the breakdown of social order via the mechanism of release from moral constraints. They might look into the subtle way those pressures force people to use drugs and thus limit freedom in the general way feared by earlier psychological theories, even though the mechanism involved differed. They too would be prepared to find their premises and hypotheses invalid. Sociologists who failed to look into the matter at all would thereby signify their belief that it was morally proper to ignore it.

Interactionist theories of deviance come under fire when critics find this complex picture of the relations between scientific research and ethical judgment overly subtle and insufficiently forthright. Just as centrist critics complain of interactionist theory's perverse unwillingness to acknowledge that rape, robbery, and murder are *really* deviant, so Left critics argue that it refuses to recognize that class oppression, racial discrimination, and imperialism are *really* deviant, or that poverty and injustice are *really* social problems, however people define them (Mankoff, 1968).[4] Both sides want to see their ethical preconceptions incorporated into scientific work in the form of uninspected factual assertions relying on the implicit use of ethical judgments about which there is a high degree of consensus.

Thus, if I say that rape is *really* deviant or imperialism *really* a social problem, I imply that those phenomena have certain empirical characteristics which, we would all agree, make them reprehensible. We might, by our studies, be able to establish just that; but we are very often asked to accept it by definition. Defining something as deviant or as a social problem makes empirical demonstration unnecessary and protects us from discovering that our preconception is incorrect (when the world isn't as we imagine it). When we protect our ethical judgments from empirical tests by enshrining them in definitions, we commit the error of sentimentalism.[5]

Scientists often wish to make it appear that some complicated combination of sociological theories, scientific evidence, and ethical judgments is really no more than a simple matter of definition. Scientists who have made strong value commitments (of whatever political or moral variety) seem especially likely to want that. Why do people want to disguise their morals as science? Most likely, they realize or intuit the contemporary rhetorical advantage of not having to admit that it is "only a moral judgment" one is making, and pretending instead that it is a scientific finding. All parties to any major social and moral controversy will attempt to gain that advantage and present their moral position as so axiomatic that it can be built into the presuppositions of their theory, research, and political dogma, without question. I suggest to the Left, whose sympathies I share, that we should attack injustice and oppression directly and openly, rather than pretend that the judgment that such things are evil is somehow deducible from sociological first principles, or warranted by empirical findings alone.

Our ethical dispositions and judgments, while they properly play a part in our scientific work, should play a different role in the various activities that constitute a sociologist's work. When we test our hypotheses and propositions against empirical evidence we try to minimize their influence, fearing that wishful thinking will color our conclusions. When we select problems for research, however, we take into account (along with such practical matters as our ability to gain access, and such theoretical concerns as the likelihood of achieving powerful general conclusions) the bearing of our potential findings on ethical problems we care about. We want to find out whether our initial judgments are correct, what possibilities of action are open to us and to other actors in the situation, what good might be accomplished with the knowledge we hope to gather. When we decide what actions to take on the basis of our findings, and when we decide whom to give advice to, our ethical commitments clearly dominate our choices—though we still want to be accurate in our assessment of the consequences of any such act. Finally, we sometimes begin with the actions we want to take and the people we want to help, as a basis for choosing problems and methods.

The criticism from left field

Some critics (e.g., Gouldner, 1968) have argued that interactionist theories of deviance, while appearing anti-Establishment, in fact support the Establishment by attacking lower-level functionaries of oppressive institutions, leaving the higher-ups responsible for the oppression unscathed and, indeed, assisting them by blowing the whistle on their unruly underlings.

In the present state of our knowledge, we can only deal with such questions speculatively. No evidence has been adduced to support the criticism, nor could one readily find evidence to refute it. The criticism speaks to the general moral thrust of interactionist theories, as well as to factual questions of the consequences of research and theorizing, and can be challenged on that ground.

Interactionist theories of deviance, like interactionist theories generally, pay attention to how social actors define each other and their environments. They pay particular attention to differentials in the power to define; in the way one group achieves and uses the power to define how other groups will be regarded, understood, and treated. Elites, ruling classes, bosses, adults, men, Caucasians—superordinate groups generally—maintain their power as much by controlling how people define the world, its components, and its possibilities, as by the use of more primitive forms of control. They may use more primitive means to establish hegemony. But control based on the manipulation of definitions and labels works more smoothly and costs less; superordinates prefer it. The attack on hierarchy begins with an attack on definitions, labels, and conventional conceptions of who's who and what's what.

History has moved us increasingly in the direction of disguised modes of control based on control of the definitions and labels applied to people. We exert control by accusing people of deviant acts of various kinds. In the United States, we indict political dissidents for using illegal drugs. Almost every modern state makes use of psychiatric diagnoses, facilities, and personnel to confine politically troublesome types as varied as Ezra Pound or Z. A. Medvedev (Szasz, 1965). When we study how moral entrepreneurs get rules made and how enforcers apply those rules in particular cases, we study the way superordinates of every description maintain their positions. To put it another way, we study some of the forms of oppression, and the means by which oppression achieves the status of being "normal," "everyday," and legitimate.

Most research on deviance in the interactionist mode has concentrated on the immediate participants in localized dramas of deviance: those who engage in various forms of crime and vice, and those enforcers they meet in their daily rounds. We have tended more to study policemen, mental-hospital attendants, prison guards, psychiatrists, and the like, and less their superiors or their superiors' superiors. (There are exceptions: Messinger's [1969] study of prison administration; Dalton's [1959] study of industrial managers; Skolnick's [1969] application of deviance theory to the politics of protest in the United States.)

But the focus on lower-level authorities not only is neither exclusive nor inevitable; its actual effect is to cast doubt on higher-level authorities who are responsible for the actions of their subordinates. They may explicitly order those actions, order them in Aesopian language so that they can deny having done it if necessary, or simply allow them to occur through incompetence or oversight. If the actions are reprehensible, then higher authorities, one way or another, share in the blame. Even if no general is ever brought to trial for the killings at My Lai, those events shook such faith as people had in the moral correctness of the military action in Vietnam and of those at the highest levels responsible for it. Similarly, when we understand how school psychiatrists operate as agents of school officials rather than of their patients (Szasz, 1967), we lose some of whatever faith we had in the institutions of conventional psychiatry. The rapidity with which official spokesmen at the highest levels move to counter analyses of even the lowest-level corruption, incompetence, or injustice should let us see at least as clearly as they do the degree to which those analyses attack institutions as well as their agents, and superiors as well as their subordinates. Such research has special moral sting to it when it allows us to inspect the practice of an institution in the light of its own professed aims and its own preferred descriptions of what it is about. Because of that, our work invariably has a critical thrust when it produces anything that can be construed as an evaluation of the operations of a society or any of its parts.

CONCLUSION

The interactionist approach to deviance has served not only to clarify the phenomena that have conventionally been studied under that rubric but also to complicate our moral view of them. The interactionist approach begins that double task of clarification and complication by making sociologists aware that a wider range of people and events needs to be included in our study of deviant phenomena, by sensitizing us to the importance of a wider range of fact. We study all the participants in these moral dramas, accusers as well as accused, offering a conventional exemption from our professional inquiries to no one, no matter how respectable or highly placed. We look carefully at the actual activities in question, attempting to understand the contingencies of action for everyone concerned. We accept no invocation of mysterious forces at work in the drama of deviance, respecting that version of common sense which focuses our attention on what we can see plainly as well as on those events and interests which require more subtle data-gathering and theoretical analysis.

At a second level, the interactionist approach shows sociologists that a major element in every aspect of the drama of deviance is the imposition of definitions—of situations, acts, and people—by those powerful enough or sufficiently legitimated to be able to do so. A full understanding requires the thorough study of those definitions and the processes by which they develop and attain legitimacy and taken-for-grantedness.

Both these levels of analysis give the interactionist approach, under present circumstances, a radical character. Interactionist analyses, by making moral entrepreneurs (as well as those they seek to control) objects of study, violate society's hierarchy of credibility. They question the monopoly on the truth and the "whole story" claimed by those in positions of power and authority. They suggest that we need to discover the truth about allegedly deviant phenomena for ourselves, instead of relying on the officially certified accounts which ought to be enough for any good citizen. They adopt a relativistic stance toward the accusations and definitions of deviance made by respectable people and constituted authority, treating them as the raw material of social science analysis rather than as statements of unquestioned moral truths.

Interactionist analyses of deviant phenomena become radical in a final sense by being treated as radical by conventional authorities. When authorities, political and otherwise, wield power in part by obfuscation and mystification, a science which makes things clearer inevitably attacks the bases of that power. The authorities whose institutions and jurisdictions become the object of interactionist analyses attack those analyses for their "biases," their failure to accept traditional wisdom and values, their destructive effect on public order.[6]

These consequences of interactionist analysis complicate our moral position as scientists by the very act of clarifying what is going on in such moral arenas as courts, hospitals, schools, and prisons. They make it impossible to ignore the moral implications of our work. Even if we want to do that, those authorities who feel themselves under attack destroy the illusion of a neutral science by insisting that we are responsible for those implications—as, of course, we are.

This discussion of recent developments in deviance theory makes a beginning on a consideration of the moral import of contemporary sociology. We can make further progress on that knotty problem by similar examinations in such other fields of sociology as the study of educational institutions, health services, the military, industry, and business—indeed, in *all* the other areas in which sociological study clarifies the activities of people and institutions, and thereby influences our moral evaluations of them.

NOTES

1   Jack Katz and John I. Kitsuse helped me greatly in the reanalysis of the problem of secret deviance.

2   Richard Berk has suggested to me that the chronic difficulty in deciding who is Left or "radical" leads to a situation in which the criticisms I am discussing, while they may come from people who so identify themselves and are so identified by some others, nevertheless do not flow out of a Marxist analysis of society which has perhaps a better claim to the label. He suggests further that such a line of criticism might focus on the degree to which it is possible to establish a continuity between the analysis of society-wide class groupings characteristic of that tradition and the more intensive study of smaller units characteristic of interactionist theories of deviance. I think the continuity exists, but am not in a position to argue the point analytically.

3   Irving Louis Horowitz prompted my belated acquaintance with the work of Abraham Edel.

4   The following statement embodies these themes neatly: "But is it not as much a *social fact*, even though few of us pay much attention to it, that the corporate economy kills and maims more, is more violent, than any violence committed by the poor (the usual subjects of studies of violence)? By what reasoning and necessity is the 'violence' of the poor in the ghettoes

more worthy of our attention than the military bootcamps which numb recruits from the horrors of killing the 'enemy' ('Oriental human beings,' as we learned during the Calley trial)? But because these acts are not labelled 'Deviant,' because they are covert, institutional, and normal, their 'deviant' qualities are overlooked and they do not become part of the province of the sociology of deviance. Despite their best liberal intentions, these sociologists seem to perpetuate the very notions they think they debunk, and others of which they are unaware." (Liazos, 1972, pp. 110-111)

5   At least one critic (Gouldner, 1968) has misread my criticism of sentimentalism as a fear of emotion. The definition given in the text of "Whose Side Are We On?" (Becker, 1967, p. 245) makes my actual meaning quite clear: "We are sentimental, especially, when our reason is that we would prefer not to know what is going on, if to know would be to violate some sympathy whose existence we may not even be aware of."

6   For a fuller discussion of the notion of radical sociology, see Becker and Horowitz, 1972.

REFERENCES

Akers, Ronald L. 1968. "Problems in the Sociology of Deviance: Social Definitions and Behavior." *Social Forces* 46 (June): 455-465.

Alvarez, Rodolfo. 1968. "Informal Reactions to Deviance in Simulated Work Organizations: A Laboratory Experiment." *American Sociological Review* 33 (December): 895-912.

Becker, Howard S. 1963. Outsiders: Studies in the Sociology of Deviance. New York: The Free Press of Glencoe.

Becker, Howard S. 1967. "Whose Side Are We On?" *Social Problems* 14 (Winter): 239-247.

Becker, Howard S. and Horowitz, Irving Louis. 1972. "Radical Politics and Sociological Research: Observations on Methodology and Ideology." *American Journal of Sociology* 78 (July): 48-66.

Becker, Howard S. and Mack, Raymond W. 1971. "Unobtrusive Entry and Accidental Access to Field Data." Unpublished paper presented at a conference on Methodological Problems in Comparative Sociological Research, Institute for Comparative Sociology, Indiana University.

Biderman, Albert D. and Reiss, Albert J., Jr. 1967. "On Exploring the Dark Figure." *The Annals* 374 (November): 1-15.

Bittner, Egon and Garfinkel, Harold. 1967. "'Good' Organizational Reasons for 'Bad' Clinic Records." In Harold Garfinkel, Studies in Ethnomethodology. Englewood Cliffs, New Jersey: Prentice-Hall.

Blumer, Herbert, 1966. "Sociological Implications of the Thought of George Herbert Mead." *American Journal of Sociology* 71 (March): 535-544.

Blumer, Herbert. 1967. "Threats from Agency-Determined Research: The Case of Camelot." In Irving Louis Horowitz, editor, The Rise and Fall of Project Camelot. Cambridge: M.I.T. Press. Pp. 153-174.

Blumer, Herbert. 1969. "The Methodological Position of Symbolic Interactionism." In his Symbolic Interactionism. Englewood Cliffs, New Jersey: Prentice-Hall. Pp. 1-60.

Bordua, David. 1967. "Recent Trends: Deviant Behavior and Social Control." *The Annals* 369 (January): 149-163.

Cicourel, Aaron. 1968. The Social Organization of Juvenile Justice. New York: John Wiley and Sons.

Cohen, Albert K. 1965. "The Sociology of the Deviant Act: Anomie Theory and Beyond." *American Sociological Review* 30 (February): 5-14.

Cohen, Albert K. 1966. Deviance and Control. Englewood Cliffs, New Jersey: Prentice-Hall.

Cohen, Albert K. 1968. "Deviant Behavior." In International Encyclopedia of the Social Sciences, Volume 4, pp. 148-155.

Cohen, Stanley, editor. 1971. Images of Deviance. Baltimore: Penguin Books.

Dalton, Melville, 1959. Men Who Manage. New York: John Wiley and Sons.

Douglas, Jack D. 1967. The Social Meanings of Suicide. Princeton: Princeton University Press.

Douglas, Jack D. 1970. "Deviance and Respectability: The Social Construction of Moral Meanings." In Jack D. Douglas, editor, Deviance and Respectability. New York: Basic Books, Inc.

Edel, Abraham. 1955. Ethical Judgment: The Uses of Science in Ethics. New York: The Free Press of Glencoe.

Erikson, Kai T. 1966. Wayward Puritans. New York: John Wiley and Sons.

Galtung, Johan. 1965. "Los Factores Socioculturales y el Desarrollo de la Sociologia en America Latina." *Revista Latino-americana de Sociologia* 1 (March).

Garfinkel, Harold. 1967. Studies in Ethnomethodology. Englewood Cliffs, New Jersey: Prentice-Hall.

Gibbs, Jack. 1966. "Conceptions of Deviant Behavior: The Old and the New." *Pacific Sociological Review* 9 (Spring): 9-14.

Goode, Erich. 1970. The Marihuana Smokers. New York: Basic Books, Inc.

Gouldner, Alvin W. 1968. "The Sociologist as Partisan: Sociology and the Welfare State." *The American Sociologist* 3 (May): 103-116.

Gove, Walter. 1970a. "Societal Reaction as an Explanation of Mental Illness: An Evaluation." *American Sociological Review* 35 (October): 873-884.

Gove, Walter. 1970b. "Who Is Hospitalized: A Critical Review of Some Sociological Studies of Mental Illness." *Journal of Health and Social Behavior* 11 (December): 294-303.

Gusfield, Joseph. 1963. Symbolic Crusade. Urbana: University of Illinois Press.

Habenstein, Robert W., editor. 1970. Pathways to Data: Field Methods for Studying Ongoing Social Organizations. Chicago: Aldine Publishing Co.

Horowitz, Irving Louis and Liebowitz, Martin. 1968. "Social Deviance and Political Marginality: Toward a Redefinition of the Relation Between Sociology and Politics." *Social Problems* 15 (Winter): 280-296.

Humphreys, Laud. 1970. Tearoom Trade. Chicago: Aldine Publishing Co.

Kaplan, John. 1970. Marihuana: The New Prohibition. New York: World Publishing Co.

Katz, Jack. 1972. "Deviance, Charisma and Rule-Defined Behavior." *Social Problems* 20 (Winter): 186-202.

Kitsuse, John I. 1962. "Societal Reaction to Deviant Behavior: Problems of Theory and Method." *Social Problems* 9 (Winter): 247-256.

Kitsuse, John I. and Cicourel, Aaron V. 1963. "A Note on the Uses of Official Statistics." *Social Problems* 11 (Fall): 131-139.

Lemert, Edwin M. 1951. Social Pathology. New York: McGraw-Hill Book Co.

Lemert, Edwin M. 1972. Human Deviance, Social Problems, and Social Control. 2nd edition. Englewood Cliffs, New Jersey: Prentice-Hall, Inc.

Liazos, Alexander. 1972. "The Poverty of the Sociology of Deviance: Nuts, Sluts, and Preverts." *Social Problems* 20 (Winter): 103-120.

216

Lindesmith, Alfred R. 1968. Addiction and Opiates. Chicago: Aldine Publishing Co.

Lorber, Judith. 1967. "Deviance and Performance: The Case of Illness." *Social Problems* 14 (Winter): 302-310.

Mankoff, Milton. 1970. "Power in Advanced Capitalist Society." *Social Problems* 17 (Winter): 418-430.

Mankoff, Milton. 1968. "On Alienation, Structural Strain, and Deviancy." *Social Problems* 16 (Summer): 114-116.

Matza, David. 1969. Becoming Deviant. Englewood Cliffs, New Jersey: Prentice-Hall, Inc.

Mead, George Herbert. 1934. Mind, Self and Society. Chicago: University of Chicago Press.

Messinger, Sheldon L. 1969. Strategies of Control. Unpublished Ph.D. dissertation, University of California at Los Angeles.

Mills, C. Wright. 1956. The Power Elite. New York: Oxford University Press.

Ray, Marsh. 1961. "The Cycle of Abstinence and Relapse among Heroin Addicts." *Social Problems* 9 (Fall): 132-140.

Roy, Donald. 1954. "Efficiency and the 'Fix': Informal Intergroup Relations in a Piecework Machine Shop." *American Journal of Sociology* 60 (November): 255-266.

Scheff, Thomas J. 1966. Being Mentally Ill. Chicago: Aldine Publishing Co.

Schur, Edwin M. 1969. "Reactions to Deviance: A Critical Assessment." *American Journal of Sociology* 75 (November): 309-322.

Selby, Henry. Not Every Man Is Humble. Unpublished manuscript.

Short, James F., Jr. and Strodtbeck, Fred L. 1965. Group Process and Gang Delinquency. Chicago: University of Chicago Press.

Skolnick, Jerome. 1969. The Politics of Protest. New York: Ballantine Books.

Strauss, Anselm L. *et al.* 1964. Psychiatric Ideologists and Institutions. New York: The Free Press of Glencoe.

Szasz, Thomas S. 1965. Psychiatric Justice. New York: MacMillan.

Szasz, Thomas S. 1967. "The Psychiatrist as Double Agent." *Trans-Action* 4 (October): 16-24.

Tannenbaum, Frank. 1938. Crime and the Community. New York: Ginn and Co.

Dining Hall, New York House of Refuge

DELINQUENCY AND SOCIAL STRUCTURE

CHAPTER 5

A major theme of our analysis is that one cannot understand juvenile delinquency and juvenile justice without analyzing the nature and structure of society. Theories of delinquency have limited applicability if the analysis is confined to investigation at the level of the individual and the immediate social environment. A fuller understanding of delinquency (and of other forms of social action) requires a discussion of how the political economy and social structure create conditions conducive to particular kinds of behavior.

On the other hand, exclusive concentration on social structure and its impact on the origins of delinquency may lead one to develop an overly deterministic view of human behavior: theories that are faithful to the naturalistic features of delinquency must include an analysis of individual choice and alternative responses to social circumstances. To focus on the plight of individuals does not imply the exclusion of such factors as race, sex, class, or age, all of which structure social relations between individuals. A critical perspective on juvenile delinquency should, in the words of C. Wright Mills, link the "personal problems of milieu" to the "public issues of social structure."

The articles in this section all attempt to correlate delinquent behavior with features of the social structure. Norwegian criminologist Nils Christie argues that the variable of age may be viewed as similar to the attributes of race and sex. He explains that highly industrialized societies must search for improved methods of controlling youth, who have become a surplus labor pool, no longer needed by the highly technological economy. Increases in juvenile delinquency parallel increases in youthful unemployment. Using official crime data from Norway, Christie discusses the changes that have taken place in the age-composition of offenders in his country over the last century. The strong link between the creation of a surplus pool of age-segregated youth and rising rates of youthful crime leads Christie to conclude that the only solution to delinquency is to stop using the category of age as a method of maintaining social privilege. Christie's implication is that delinquency will always exist where negative distinctions among people are based on personal characteristics such as age, race, class, or sex.

Richard Flacks, a prominent participant and observer of the youth movement of the 1960s, discusses the declining influence of the Protestant ethic as a socializing and control mechanism in American society. He argues that the economy has shifted from a focus on capital accumulation to a focus on large-scale bureaucratic management and monopoly capitalism. This economic transformation has not been accompanied by an adjustment of the cultural framework; thus, we are saddled with an outdated Protestant ethic, irrelevant to current political and economic realities. One casualty of the confusion in values has been the middle-class family, which was the cornerstone of industrial capitalism. Flacks views today's American family as ambivalent, and unsure of its value allegiances, since the culture is no longer appropriate to the material conditions. Youth grow up confused in such a society, and their exposure to glaring social contradictions severs ties to conventional values that would induce them to abide by laws and social norms. Although Flacks focuses his attention on the deviance of the middle classes, it is easy to see that such social confusion will also affect those lower in the social structure.

The remaining three selections illustrate how inequities in the social structure are linked to specific forms of delinquent behavior. Barry Krisberg discusses the theme of survival in his ethnographic study of gang youth in Philadelphia. The youthful street hustlers develop a psychology of survival as one means of coping with the harsh economic realities they have confronted throughout their lives. In their eyes, survival is dependent upon becoming successful entrepreneurs in the world of violent but petty crime, which they describe as their "hustles." While gang youth recognize that people who are successful in the straight world simply have "easier hustles," they see little opportunity to enter that world of upper-class hustling. Reviewing the ideologies they use to explain their world, Krisberg observes that the gang youth embrace the same ideologies as the privileged classes, who are ultimately responsible for the racial and economic oppression that fosters the hustling life-style.

British criminologist Stan Cohen examines the phenomenon of teenage vandalism and its relation to the social structure of Great Britain. Cohen analyzes pop culture to help understand the apparently meaningless behavior of youthful vandals. His paper focuses on youth who are not part of the middle-class youth culture. Cohen draws our attention to the youngsters at the bottom of the British social structure, who are forced to "grow up absurd," and accept the dead-end occupational and social roles provided by the dominant classes in society. Since even these meager social goals left to the children of the poor are becoming harder to attain, working-class youth resort to vandalism as a means of expressing their discontent and disillusionment with an "absurd and cruel" society. Cohen rejects the facile belief that vandalism reflects a misunderstanding or a generation gap. He concludes that while these youths clearly perceive their objective social conditions, it is the dominant society that chooses not to understand what these youths are communicating through their destructive and often violent behavior.

The final article, by Herman Schwendinger and Julia R. Schwendinger, provides a theoretical perspective on the process of marginalization within the youthful population. Youth in contemporary capitalist countries are treated as commodities, and receive unequal shares of the economy based on society's needs. Marginal populations, characteristic of capitalist countries, are replicated within the youthful population through major socializing institutions, such as the family and schools, which prepare youth for their eventual entry into the labor market. Delinquents and those in the lower classes are typically denied an equal share of society's socializing resources. According to the Schwendingers, short-term reform measures will predictably have a minimal impact on delinquency and marginalization unless social investments become more evenly distributed.

Youth as a Crime-Generating Phenomenon

NILS CHRISTIE[1]

Nils Christie is a professor of law at The University, Oslo, Norway.

Reprinted from Nils Christie, "Youth as a Crime-Generating Phenomena." *New Perspectives in Criminology*, 1975, pp. 1-10.

Summary: Age is discussed as a social category. Age belongs to the same class of ascribed attributes as sex and race, but is socially more useful, since it represents a continuous variable easily manipulated by the social system. Industrialized societies have difficulty integrating young people into the institution of work. The gradual extension of the period of youth can be seen as an answer to this problem. Youth can be regarded as a segregated group. Segregated groups are, however, particularly difficult to control. They do not have as much to lose, they tend to create cohesive subsystems, and they are handicapped in finding role-models outside their own categories. Together, these tendencies create a situation with greatly increased risk for conflicts with the formal system of control. Empirical data illustrate these conflicts.

AGE AS A SOCIAL CATEGORY

Age cannot be understood apart from the general social structure. The phenomenon has, of course, a biological base—as do sex, race, and sickness. But to society, and therefore also to the sociologist, the importance of age is related to its social consequences. Age is highly visible, and therefore highly useful as a classificatory category in social life.

Age—and, again, sex, race, and some forms of sickness—is unusually well-suited to creating order in social life. It now seems very clear that biological differences are actually of extremely limited value in explaining the varied attainment of position, power, and general functioning between races. Differences in pigmentation do, however, present nearly unlimited possibilities for differential treatment, and most societies appear to use such possibilities. Much the same situation probably exists concerning differences between the sexes. In addition to what might have been created by biological differences, sociology and anthropology contain many examples of how elaborate social arrangements are built upon the dichotomy between male and female.

The phenomenon of age is at least as important as that of sex in creating social arrangements. Sex has the social usefulness of being stable and also highly visible. But, here, as with age categorization, exceptions to the traditional male-female dichotomy are becoming increasingly frequent. Some individuals are crossing the sex-border. With some persons or groups we experience difficulty in recognizing their sex. The underplaying of sex-differences was one of the interesting features of the hippie culture.

Finally, race bears an even greater resemblance to age. Basically, race too concerns stable and highly visible attributes. In the extreme, differences are very clear between the very black and the very white— as clear as between the five-year-old and the fifty-year-old. But there are less extreme, and sociologically more interesting, cases. At the borders of dark or light pigmentation, both blacks and whites cross back and forth, pretending to have the pigment which happens to be the socially preferred one—just as people pretend to be the right age for buying liquor, for getting permission to work, or for gaining admission to ordinary sex-life.

Age, however, possesses two very important advantages to both sex and race. First, it is not a variable that forces the social system into dichotomous arrangements. On the contrary, it is a *continuous variable*. This is important, because it allows society to *decide on the cutting points*. Secondly, it is a *transitory category*. It is one that all human beings pass. All who live that long go through the stage of being fourteen; but, even as they *are* fourteen, they know—as does everyone—that it only lasts for a year and that there is a life after fourteen.

THE TEENAGER AS A SOCIAL INVENTION

With this background, it might be more easily seen that the phenomenon of youth in general and of teenagers in particular has to be discussed, not as a "natural biological phenomenon," but as a social invention. Old people never met a teenager. Maybe they met young people. Often they would only have discriminated between children and grown-ups in a dichotomy as tight as that between the sexes. Confirmation or bar-mitzvah in the Jewish culture most often represented the point of transfer from child to adult, and thus the entrance of the young people into the world of adults. Still further back in history, we can find some examples of a sort of total rejection of the whole concept of childhood. Children were portrayed as small adults. Most probably they were also treated as such.

In a cross-cultural perspective, we find the same thing. Looking around in the not-so-very united nations of the world, we will observe some striking regularities in the use of the age scale. If we classify societies according to their technological development or degree of industrialization, we will find that the use of the age scale increases as industrialization increases. We will, at a minimum, find that the dichotomy is converted into a trichotomy. To be a teenager is not a result of age, but rather of age within a particular social system. It also seems to be the case that the phenomenon of youth is extended into higher age-brackets as industrialization increases. Youngsters are becoming older.

Let me illustrate my point with the very simple and exaggerated Figure 1. The three boxes show the progression of age divisions from very limited use of age to the extensive use we make of it today. In Box A we find only the basic split between children and adults; by Box C it is illustrated how age is playing a greater role both in the beginning and in the end of the life.

Of course, the diagram cannot tell more than what we all know. What is happening?

Only the old story. Highly visible biological attributes are getting key functions in the distribution of privileges in society. Race and sex are still used as differentiating factors in the family of ascribed attributes, but, relatively speaking, age has gained importance. I could of course have formulated this in a more neutral way. Instead

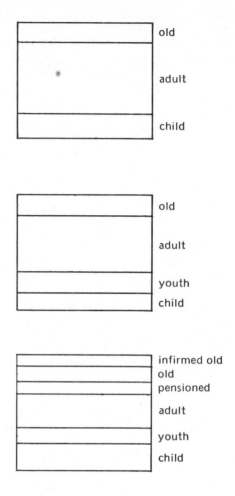

Figure 1
Developments in the use of age as a social category

of discussing the distribution of privilege, I could have used the more common terminology of youth as a role with obligations as well as rights. That would have been quite correct. But something would have been lost. I would have lost the perspective which I most want to convey; namely, that the choice in type of age structure has important consequences for the privilege structure within any society.

The use of the age scale, as found in most highly industrialized societies, can be seen—and understood—as an unusually successful case of apartheid. Measured from the bottom of the diagram, we can see an increasing number of age groups being placed outside of what large segments of the population define as core activities, namely *work*. And exactly the same thing takes place from the top of the diagram. The age for being pensioned is gradually being decreased within highly industrialized societies.

Initially, all these movements were regarded as privileges, while work was seen as the burden. Exemption from work was considered a blessing. In a stage where work meant manual work, and manual work meant suffering, this was natural. And of course, this situation still exists for many segments within many industrialized societies. But the case might also be viewed from the opposite angle—where participation is considered the privilege and where non-participation means suffering. Retired people will often perceive it that way. Women also.

In connection with long-term planning for the Norwegian government, a calculation of the demand for workers in the year 2000 has recently been made (2). Theoretically, we might be able to absorb the whole population into the labor force. That, however, would result in a fantastic increase in production. How could we ever absorb that production? And would it be right to use so much of our natural resources? As one premise in the calculation, it was therefore decided to keep production at 1970 levels.

But automation will still continue to increase productivity without any increase in effort. If we do not want to produce more in the year 2000 than we do in the year 1970, we will therefore *have* to reduce input in work. Three major alternatives are available: 1. We can reduce the age of retirement to 38. 2. We can reduce the number of work-days to about three per week. 3. We can increase the vacation time to 20 weeks every year. If women took a greater part in the work force than their very limited participation today, we would have to reduce male participation even further. From this perspective, we might be able to perceive *participation* as an outstanding privilege, which today may be more important than money or material gains. We might also be able to see how the status of youth could create certain special problems.

ON THE CONTROL OF SEGREGATED CATEGORIES

Outstanding persons, unusually creative ones, or leading personalities within any society are often rather lonely. This is probably partly a result of their status, and partly a reason for it. Loneliness means possibilities for unusual action. If the person has sufficient inner strength, she or he will, through this very same loneliness, have a sort of protection against common social demands. Being alone means that society has less of a grasp on a person. In an extreme case, no one can influence that individual. In this situation, unexpected behaviour cannot be met with the ultimate threat of losing other persons. There are none to lose.

A contrasting case occurs with the person perfectly integrated into the social system. Social integration cannot exist without links to other persons. An integrated person is therefore beautifully tied into a web of social relations. An unexpected move results in a magnitude of subtle counter-moves. Deviant behaviour is not necessarily seen as deviance or called deviance, but is kept under control through daily interaction with a number of other persons who are of great importance for the socially integrated person.

Segregated categories have some basic resemblances to outstanding persons. Segregation means lack of integration of the category. It means being isolated from the mainstream of society. The category is thereby less influenced by that society. And the potential for control is highly reduced.

In industrialized societies three major factors hamper possibilities for the control of young persons. First: Since young persons are not participants in the ordinary work force, they are outside the most easily applicable systems of rewards and punishments. They are not given money for their efforts, nor can they be punished for deviance through withholding of monetary rewards. Youth are in a similar position with regard to money as prisoners are to freedom. They both possess so little legitimate access to these commodities that it is difficult to employ even greater deprivation as an effective punishment. Pocket money might be withheld. But the term itself indicates the smallness of the negative sanction. Further, it is a sanction which runs the grave risk of destroying the only alternative form of control parents have in their possession: namely, their emotional ties to the youngsters. And this alternative is already highly strained by the reasons I will consider next.

Second: Members of segregated units could become difficult to control because they create a sub-system of equals. This means that as negative sanctions from the adults are given less consideration, such sanctions could even be converted into positive rewards. To a certain extent the ruling class might be able to "split and rule," and thereby to prevent the creation of sub-systems among the segregated class. The rulers might be able to define the situation as one where it was up to the segregated individual to work himself out of the segregated category "with empty hands from lower class to knighthood." But it is not that easy to sell the idea of working yourself out of an ascribed attribute such as age. And it is particularly difficult to do so when the rulers have created a system for the segregated ones in which they concentrate huge numbers together in the same buildings, most of the time under the surveillance of only a few adults.

Schools represent ingenious devices for keeping a substantial quota of the population out of circulation for a substantial proportion of their otherwise unwanted participation in the mainstream. I do not claim that schools are consciously intended for this purpose, but I do want to point out the convenience of schools for the rest of society as institutions where children and young persons are kept.

There may be some truth in the oft-repeated statements that schools are needed for transmitting the culture to the next generation. Personally I doubt it. But I am absolutely convinced that modern, industrialized society could not continue its recent existence if we did not have schools as institutions where children can be kept. For problems of control, some of the most interesting analogies can be found in the structural similarities between schools, prisons, and old people's homes. They play analogous roles in society, and the personnel within these institutions also face similar problems in controlling their clients (3).

A third major problem with regard to the control of youngsters is created by their clogging together and their great distance, in time and space, between themselves and grown-ups. This situation means decreased visibility both for adults in their control of the young, and for young persons in their attempts to know what it means to become an adult. The segregated position of youth leads to severe difficulty in perceiving a variety of adult role models. The alternative to adult models is often extensive nurturing of roles prescribed by the youth culture.

As a summary of some major points. one might say that youth is a segregated category and, therefore, one which creates special problems of control. Youths are outsiders. But—in contrast to both women and old people—they do know that, after a certain time, they will receive full access to what is defined as the most important areas of society. Left to each other during the years when their physical strength (and sex-drive) is at its zenith, they are forced into basic inactivity with regard to meaningful work. It is difficult to imagine a situation better designed for giving a group a greater risk of clashing with the formal agents of control in a society.

CRIME AMONG YOUTH IN AN INDUSTRIALIZED SOCIETY

Instead of words, I will present three major diagrams.

Figure 2 shows a picture of registered criminals in Norway, distributed according to age per 1000 persons within each age group. It looks like a Swiss mountain. And the impressive peak is reached at the not-so-very impressive age of 15. We had, in Norway, 30 males registered for crime for each thousand boys in that age, while for each thousand males among the thirty-year-olds, we had only six.

Figure 3 shows the contrasting pictures of 1860 and 1960. The old criminal was a mature man. The new is a youngster.

Figure 4 illustrates the development for the entire period from 1860 to 1960. Gradually, our *registered criminals* have *been converted* into very young persons. I do, however, want to stress that this diagram is based on all registered criminals. If, for instance, hidden tax evasions were included, the picture might have changed. Young people also represent an easily hit target.

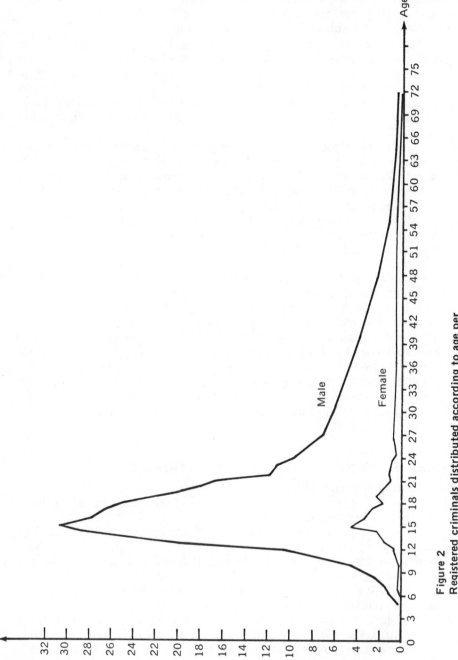

Figure 2
Registered criminals distributed according to age per
1000 persons within the age group

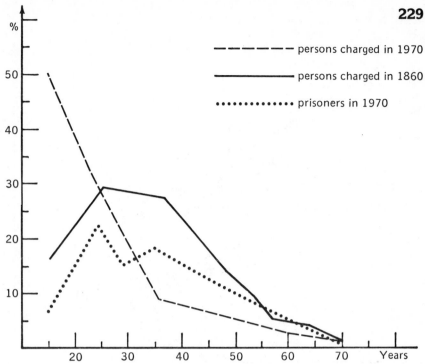

% — axis

- - - - - - - persons charged in 1970
———————— persons charged in 1860
•••••••••••• prisoners in 1970

50

40

30

20

10

20 30 40 50 60 70 Years

Figure 3
Persons charged in 1970; persons charged in 1860;
prisoners in 1970.

ON THE PREVENTION OF YOUTH CRIME

My time is up. Certain topics should also be left for discussion. Let me, therefore, simply end with a provocation which also happens to be my sincere opinion: We cannot expect to change the crime-generating tendencies among youth unless we change some of the basic structural arrangements in being young. In all simplicity, the solution to this problem is to abolish the social category defined as youth!

NOTE

1   An elaboration of these views can be found in (1).

BIBLIOGRAPHY

1) *Christie N.*: Hvor tett et samfunn? (Universitetsforlaget Oslo and Christian Ejlers forlag, Köbenhavn, 1975).

2) *Finansdepartementet*: Langtidsprogrammet 1974-1977. Spesialanalyse 5, Arbeid og fritid, Vedlegg 5 Stortingsmelding nr. 71 (1972/1973).

3) *Christie N.*: Hvis skolen ikke fantes (Universitetsforlaget, Oslo 1971). German translation: Wenn es die Schule nicht gäbe (Paul List, München 1974).

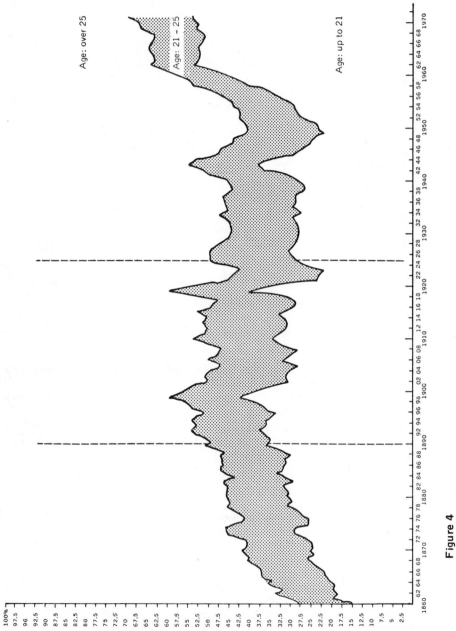

Figure 4
How the different age-categories are represented in the
total volume of registered ciminality, 1860–1970

Growing Up Confused: Cultural Crisis and Individual Character

RICHARD FLACKS

Richard Flacks is a professor of sociology at the University of California, Santa Barbara.

Richard Flacks, YOUTH AND SOCIAL CHANGE, © 1971 by Rand McNally College Publishing Company, Chicago, pp. 20-34.

It is not too great an oversimplification to say that the central, unifying theme of American culture has always been that cluster of values Max Weber called the "Protestant Ethic." In particular, Americans agreed that the meaning of life was given by one's work, that personal fulfillment and social responsibility required that males be fully engaged in a vocation, and that virtue was measured in terms of success in an occupation. The most valued work was entrepreneurial activity; the most valued model was the rational, thrifty, hard-working, self-denying, risk-taking entrepreneur.

Undoubtedly, the vitality of those values was important in the phenomenal growth of the American technological and economic system in the nineteenth century. In a period when accumulation and production were society's central problems, it was fortunate that the average man was highly motivated to produce, to work hard, and to save—in short, to resist temptations that might divert him from doing his part in building the country. It was also fortunate that aspirations for monetary success could be fulfilled by many, while many others could believe that their failure lay in themselves—in their own inability to achieve the cultural ideal—rather than in the ideal itself.

In the American ideal women were not regarded as virtuous if *they* sought independence and success in the world of work. Instead, they were valued if they supported their husbands' capacity to be single-mindedly devoted to work, if they themselves were skilled at producing a self-sufficient household, and if they raised their male children to be independent, self-reliant, self-denying, and achievement-oriented individuals.

Given the entrepreneurial opportunities, the open frontier, and the evident dynamism of American life, it is not surprising that most American young people who were socialized into this cultural framework accepted it with enthusiasm. Boys were eager to become men in the image of their fathers—although encouraged by their fathers and mothers, they were profoundly eager to surpass their fathers' achievements in work and status.

Observers agree that this cultural framework has been severely eroded or at least modified by what has happened in America in the twentieth century. What, in brief outline, happened?

1   An economic system organized around problems of capital accumulation and the need for saving, entrepreneurship, and self-reliance—a system of free market and individual competition—has been replaced by an economic system organized around problems of distribution and the need for spending, interdependence, bureaucratic management, planning, and large-scale organization.

2   As a consequence, work is now coordinated by massive private and public bureaucratic organizations, and work achievement is defined not in entrepreneurial terms, but in terms of successful fullfillment of a career within a bureaucratic or professional hierarchy.

3   These developments have permitted and been required by a tremendous technological leap. Consequently, a vast array of commodities for individual consumption is produced. On the one hand, this situation required that men consume; on the other hand, it obviated the sense of the need to save, postpone gratification, and be self-denying that had been justified by scarcity.

As a result of these massive changes—from individual entrepreneurship to large corporate organization, from free market competition to bureaucratic coordination and planning, from accumulation and scarcity to consumption and affluence—the vitality of the "Protestant Ethic" has declined. Throughout society during the past sixty years, more and more people have felt less committed to the entrepreneurial character and its virtues. Increasingly, self-worth and worth in the eyes of others is organized as much by one's style of life and one's consumption patterns as by one's occupational status as such. Furthermore, although instrumental and rational activity is still highly valued, all observers report that there has been a relaxation on prohibitions against expressiveness and hedonism. Indeed, a society in which the consumption of goods has become a fundamental problem requires that men cease to be ascetic and self-denying and abandon many of the guilts that they experience when they express their impulses.

By the middle of the twentieth century, the American society was qualitatively different from the society that had given birth to the cultural framework of capitalism. The family firm had been superseded by the giant corporation, the free market by the "welfare-warfare" state, and the entrepreneur by the manager and the bureaucrat. Technology had created a superabundant economy in which the traditional virtues of thrift, self-denial and living by the sweat of one's brow seemed not only absurd, but actually dangerous to prosperity. Technology seemed to promise not only an abundance of goods, but a world in which hard physical labor could be eliminated.

Yet, despite the need for new values and a new cultural framework, a cultural transformation was not occurring. Politicians, teachers, and preachers continued to give lip-service to the Protestant Ethic, while the mass media, without announcing the fact, purveyed an increasingly blatant hedonism. Many of the classic symptoms of "anomie" were widespread. Breakdown was widely evident, but new values were not.

I suppose that the best indication of the coherence of a culture is the degree to which parents can transmit a sense of it to their offspring with clarity and effectiveness. Cultural breakdown has reached the point of no return when the process of socialization no longer provides the new generation with coherent reasons to be enthusiastic about becoming adult members of the society. Perhaps the best way I can illustrate what I mean by cultural instability and breakdown is to discuss the American middle-class family as it seemed to most observers to be functioning by mid-twentieth century. An examination of family patterns and childrearing not only illuminates the cultural crisis, but also provides some clues to the sources of youthful discontent.

When you read what follows, remember that I am not criticizing American *parents* for faulty childrearing practices. On the contrary, the main point I am trying to make is that parental confusion is virtually inevitable in a society in which the culture is breaking down. Moreover, the outcomes of that confusion should not be labeled "pathological," in my opinion. On the contrary. When parents raise their children in a manner that causes them to have significant problems of "adjustment," if anything, this is a "healthy" circumstance I am arguing that the basic source of socially patterned maladjustment is a culture that no longer enables a person to find coherent meaning in his life. The maladjustment of youth offers one of the few hopes that new meanings can be found—that a new culture can be created.

The family, of course, is the primary institution for the inculcation of basic values and molding of culturally appropriate character structures. All observers agree that the American family, particularly the white, "middle class" family, has undergone a substantial transformation over the past several decades—a transformation that both reflects and contributes to the cultural crisis in the society at large.

A major structural change in the middle class family has been its "reduction"—that is, the erosion of close ties to relatives outside the nuclear family unit. Dissolution of extended family bonds is highly functional in a society based on technological development because it permits people to be relatively free of emotional and economic ties to "homes" and "relatives" and enables them to move freely in response to changing occupational requirements, and to take advantage of opportunities for career advancement wherever and whenever they become available. Since the nuclear family is expected to establish a self-contained household, it becomes a highly efficient mechanism for absorbing a vast array of consumer goods—each small family unit seeks to purchase the house, car, furnishings, appliances, and other commodities that will ensure its independence. (On the other hand, an extended family complex living contiguously probably would share many such goods, thereby reducing the need for each household in the network to buy its own.) Thus, in a structural sense the nuclear middle class family meshes nicely with the economy's demand for a mobile labor force and an actively consuming public.

In the typical middle class family, the father works away from home while the mother spends virtually all her time at home rearing the children. Authority—in principle—is shared by the parents (a marked change from the patriarchal structure of the past), but clearly, it is exercised far more intensively and continuously by the mother than by the father. Ideally, the mother (if she is modern) is less concerned with efforts to repress and restrict the expressive, impulsive behavior of her children than she was in the past, just as she is less likely to emphasize obedient, submissive behavior as desirable. Instead, she is expected to facilitate the child's desires to explore, to test the environment, and to encourage self-reliant and autonomous behavior. What is now "good" is not so much the obedient, quiet, clean, cautious child, but rather the child who acquires verbal and motor skills early, who is precocious in his understanding, who can do things for himself, and who relates well to strangers and to other children. Mother attempts to instill such qualities by use of so-called "psychological" techniques of discipline —giving and withdrawing her love. She tries to avoid the traditional, more "physical" forms of punishment, trying instead to convey a nondomineering attitude, nurturing nonauthoritarian style. Father, relatively a part of the background, strives for a generally warm, non-authoritarian and supportive approach.

This mode of childrearing has become ascendant in American culture in this century, especially in the last three decades. It relies, then, on a high degree of exclusive dependence on the mother coupled with strong demands on the child for cognitive mastery and a will to strive and achieve. Research suggests that this family situation is a superior one for generating precisely those character-istics that enable successful participation in a culture that stresses individual achievement, formal education, rationality, and flexibility. The culturally desired outcome of this family (and my emphasis here is on *male* character) is a child who achieves masculine identity and independence by fulfilling his mother's expectations that he will be independent and striving, whose guilt and anxiety is focused on achievement of internal standards of excellence, who enjoys testing and is capable of being tested, and who is able to handle sexual, aggressive, and other impulses and emotions by expressing them at the appropriate times and places while not letting them seriously interfere with his capacity for work, rational action, and self-reliance. Thus, impulses are not denied (as the traditional Protestant Ethic demanded) but managed. This process is greatly facilitated by the delicately balanced combination of demand and freedom, dependence and independence, and mothering and autonomy that ideally characterizes the suburban family.

How often such an "ideal" outcome actually results from this family situation is questionable. Although the mother-centered nuclear family meshes nicely with crucial *official values* embodied in the educational and occupational system, it appears to be highly vulnerable to a variety of severe contradictions that occur in the course of actual day-to-day life in the society. These contradictions are readily derivable from the general crisis of the culture I have been trying to sketch.

PARENTAL VALUE CONFLICT AND CONFUSION

Undoubtedly, parents experience a great deal of strain when they permit freedom and encourage autonomy on the part of their children. One source of such strain is the difference between the comparatively strict atmosphere in which most middle class parents were raised and the atmosphere they try to create in their own homes. Another is that many parents continue to be emotionally committed to the traditional virtues of cleanliness, obedience, emotional control, and the like. Undoubtedly, then, many mothers and fathers are quite inconsistent with respect to discipline and demands; sometimes they punish their children for infraction of their rules and at other times they do not; sometimes they insist on traditional "good habits" while sometimes they are more relaxed. Frequently such parental inconsistency may result in what has been called "absorption" of the child's personality. Rather than molding a flexible, striving, self-sufficient character, the result is a character who fears failure *and* success, experiences deep anxiety about his acceptance by others, finds it difficult to establish his own autonomy, and is, consequently, far more driven toward conformity and "security" than toward independence and personal achievement. Indeed, some social critics have argued that this "other-directed" character type is becoming ascendant and that the achievement-oriented, "inner-directed" type is fading. Whether or not this is true, it seems plain that parental confusion over the nature of discipline and virtue is widespread and seriously undermines cultural goals rooted in achievement motivation.

Many parents are clearly committed to providing opportunities for free expression and autonomy for their children. They favor a life of fulfillment, experiential richness, and less self-denial. They may desire such a life for *themselves*, but find it difficult to consistently and wholeheartedly treat their children in this manner. Clearly, parents in a small nuclear family revolving around the mother as the exclusive childcare specialist must expend a tremendous investment of patience and energy, especially if they exercise permissiveness. To permit children to wander, experiment, and test requires constant vigilance to protect their physical safety. To provide children intellectual stimulation and sensory variety requires intensive involvement in the quality of their activities. But if parents are to provide the quantities of time, energy, and patience required to achieve these goals they must limit their *own* recreation and pursuits and get enough sleep so that they will have sufficient energy and patience to allow their offspring to be the central focus of attention whenever the children are awake and around. Undoubtedly, this is a source of strain even for parents with articulate commitment to "liberated" values—perhaps especially for them, since they themselves want freedom, autonomy, and the like. This conflict between the demands of childrearing and the personal needs of the parents constitutes another source of parental inconsistency that undermines the "ideal" character of the modern middle class family.

A third source of parental confusion is the conflict between effort and indulgence. Typical middle class parents expect their offspring to strive and achieve and to understand the necessity for self-discipline and effort in attaining goals. Very often, however, such families have surplus incomes and try to provide their children with a sense of being well taken care of. Indeed, in many families parents indulge their children in order to demonstrate their love and care. Many fathers assuage the guilt they feel because of their absence from the home by showering their children with presents; many rationalize their own self-sacrifice by averring that anything that frees their kids from suffering is worthwhile. In any case, such parental indulgence (which is undoubtedly functional for the consumer goods sector of the economy) tends to weaken the offsprings' sense of necessity for self-discipline, sacrifice, and toil. Indeed, many children of affluence sense that as heirs of their parents' material property, they are likely to have some degree of permanent lifelong economic security. Under these circumstances, effort and achievement lose much of their motivational potency and moral meaning. This is especially so if fathers suggest to their sons (which they often do) that they can afford to enjoy life in ways that previous generations could not.

Thus, it seems plausible that incoherence and confusion are virtually inevitable features of the modern middle class family and the suburban style of life. As we shall see, the consequences for the general culture and for the youths who will inherit it contribute to the sense of crisis.

MATERNAL AMBIVALENCE

In addition to such value confusion, there are other sources of childrearing imbalance and parental inconsistency. One of the most significant is the ambivalence and discontent that many women experience as they try to play the new maternal roles dictated by the family structure and childraising ideology we have been depicting. These discontents revolve around the fact that the woman who becomes a mother is expected to be a full-time mother and housewife in a situation in which she is highly isolated from adult social relations and must perform tasks that are menial and meaningless. She is expected to accept this role even though her formal education before marriage and motherhood has made her qualified to perform other roles and despite her aspirations for independence and self-fulfillment. Understandably, such a woman finds it difficult to narrow her interests to the world of her three-year-old child and even more difficult not to feel guilty because she is discontent and hostile to her children and to her husband.

The ways in which women have adapted to this situation are diverse. Most adaptations that have been recorded, however, have been condemned as culturally dysfunctional and/or psychologically damaging to the child. For instance, there is the smothering, over-protective mother (whose protectiveness is said to be a screen for her unconscious hostility toward the child). The "seductive" mother (who becomes extremely close to her son as a displacement for her more general interpersonal and sexual frustrations); the mother who subtly, and often unconsciously, denigrates her husband to her children as an expression of her jealous resentment of his privilege and his abandonment of her; the mother who attempts to live vicariously through her children (hoping that they will achieve goals that she herself has been blocked from achieving); and the working mother (who, according to some childrearing experts, intensifies the child's fears of separation and abandonment).

All of these compensations are seen as damaging to the child's ability to manage and overcome his dependence on the mother, prolonging that dependency or forcing him to identify with her (instead of with the father) and weakening the male child's ability to accept culturally approved definitions of masculine identity. All of these patterns may weaken achievement motivation and damage the child's capacity for self-reliance.

Although many psychologists characterize such maternal behavior as "neurotic," a sociological perspective emphasizes the fact that such behavior is *socially determined—it is built into the maternal role* as it is now structured, especially considering the manner in which young women have been socialized and the increasing cultural support for the equality of women. More specifically, the discontent of middle class mothers is an inevitable consequence of the fact that they are forced into roles that do not match their aspirations and self-conceptions—aspirations and self-conceptions they have been taught are their right. Such a fundamental contradiction in women's roles is a further consequence and determinant of the general cultural crisis.

PATERNAL AMBIVALENCE

The paternal role contains its own built-in contradictions. This is so because fathers, as effective models of adult achievement, self-reliance, and rationality that they are expected to be, must be available for the psychological benefit of their children. At the same time, the middle class male who is striving or is already successful is likely to have a range of responsibilities and commitments outside the home. The highly career-oriented father may be available to his children hardly at all, partly from "necessity" and partly because he finds that life in the family is mundane when compared with life outside the home, where the responsibility and the power he can command are exciting.

Other fathers experience considerable regret and discontent with their work; they have ended up in positions that do not fulfill their earlier aspirations, they find their work unfulfilling or morally dubious, and they find work itself increasingly onerous. Many such fathers undoubtedly communicate their self-doubts and their skepticism to their sons. Still other men experience themselves as failures—as impotent and second rate in their work. The family, for them, becomes an arena for the exercise of power, aggression and self-importance which they cannot find elsewhere.

Like contradictions in the mothers' role, such paternal ambivalence is derived from fundamental cultural contradictions. These contradictions revolve around cultural demands for continuous striving and simultaneous demands for endless consumption—demands that men be dedicated careerists and, at the same time, good fathers, and that they compartmentalize the public and private worlds, reserving personal warmth, intimacy, and expressiveness for the latter.

A second source of strain for the middle class male is that the cultural measure of his worth (as well as his own sense of self-esteem) is based on his occupational success, but that success is a limitless goal on the one hand and is denied most men on the other. To the extent that the male accepts the cultural definition of his value, his self-esteem suffers. This inadequacy is communicated to his children; to the extent that he rejects the cultural standard, he communicates to his children a certain skepticism about the cultural framework.

As a result the developing child is exposed to another source of confusion. To the extent that the father embodies any of these contradictions, he is lacking in his effectiveness as a model, and since the typical suburban family is nuclear and isolated, the male child finds few alternatives to serve as effective models.

THE PACE OF SOCIAL CHANGE

A final source of parental confusion derives from the sense perhaps shared by most people in the culture—that the world in which children will be adults will be substantially different from the world in which they are children, in ways that are considerably obscure. Parents generally conceive of themselves—perhaps more than at any time in history—as inadequate models for their children because they are already obsolete. In this situation, the parental tone of voice lacks conviction, parental guidance has overtones of fatuousness, and parental authority is undermined by the parents' own lack of confidence. This particular source of cultural incoherence may not be directly related to the structure of the nuclear family itself, but it is a rather obvious consequence of a culture that values technological change and development as one of its central priorities. Presumably, a childrearing program that emphasizes independence, flexibility, and openmindedness meshes with a culture that values change. But as we have seen, such virtues are more easily espoused than instilled in a culture that places such heavy reliance on isolated and morally confused mothers and fathers to implement such a program.

It should not be hard to envision from our depiction of the built-in "strains" associated with the middle class nuclear family some idea of the consequences for young people. Briefly, such a family situation is likely to generate considerable confusion over values, goals, roles, and aspirations for the youth who experience it. More specifically, we can suggest that the "new" family is likely to impart a number of dispositions and personality "trends" in its offspring—traits or potentialities that predispose such youth to be restless with, skeptical of, or alienated from certain crucial aspects of conventional culture and, consequently, ready for certain kinds of cultural change.

A listing of some hypotheses concerning certain tendencies that the middle class family situation seems to generate in its offspring follows (I term them hypotheses, which await persuasive empirical tests, because for the most part, there is little direct evidence that these tendencies are clearly linked to childhood socialization):

1   Confusion and restlessness with conventional definitions of success. Such feelings would derive from the types of paternal ambivalence we have described, from the psychological distance of the father's work role from those of his sons', from the parental value confusions we have called attention to, and from the pattern of maternal domination. Even youths who have strong motivations to achieve and who may act these out in school would be likely to entertain doubts about whether material success, status-striving and careerism constitute appropriate avenues for expressing their desires to "do well." But neither conventional parents nor the conventional culture provide very many

clues about how one can achieve in ways other than the economic. The consequences of this combination of predispositions to question material success coupled with predispositions to achieve include profound indecisiveness about vocation (what Erik Erikson has called "role confusion"), vague yearnings for recognition and fame, and a restless search for alternative vocations and life styles.

2   Restlessness under conditions of imposed discipline. These derive from such features of the family as parental indulgence and permissiveness and are related to feelings of discontent with conventional definitions of vocation and achievement. Some consequences are discontent with classroom drill and learning situations requiring rote memorization; tendencies to feel bored and restless when concentration is required; avoidance of school subjects requiring discipline and attention to detail; and a generalized resistance to tasks that do not appear to be personally rewarding or are set without reference to goals determined by the self. These feelings are accompanied by intense desires for immediate pleasure and release and immediate experience, often coupled with guilt.

3   Restlessness with conditions of arbitrary or coercive authority. Such feelings might derive from expectations developed in the family for authority structures based on egalitarianism—expectations derived from parental fostering of participation, independence and autonomy and parental refusal to use physical punishment or coercion. Children raised in this way, we can speculate, may grow to expect that authority *outside* the family will be similarly responsive, democratic, nonpunitive and permissive. A consequence of such dispositions and expectations about authority is the tendency to be unusually trusting of teachers and other adults, but vociferously and unusually upset, angry and rebellious when such authority figures betray expectations that they will be egalitarian, democratic, and so forth. Or one might expect such children to be capable of more active expression of opposition and resistance to authority when it appears arbitrary, more skeptical of its claims in general, more likely to ask embarrassing questions, and more ready to systematically test the limits of its tolerance.

4   Discomfort with conventional sex-role definitions. Boys who have ambivalent fathers or who tend to identify with their mothers and have accepting, nonpunitive parents are likely to define masculinity in ways that are quite untraditional. They are likely to be less motivated for dominance, less physically aggressive and tough, less physically competitive, and more emotionally expressive and

aesthetically inclined. Presumably, many girls raised in these ways are likely to be less submissive, more assertive, and more self-assured and independent. Insofar as parents continue to expect conventional sex-role performance on the part of their children—and insofar as such performance is expected by the schools and by peers—confusion and feelings of inadequacy can be the result.

Speculation on the kinds of traits, dispositions, and feelings that might be expected to be patterned outcomes of the family structure and childrearing practices we have been discussing could go on indefinitely, but the main line of our argument should be clear: certain major changes in social structure and economy have had a direct impact on the structure of the family, especially in the "middle class." These changes have also had a profound impact on the values and practices of parents. The result is a mixed one: on the one hand, the "new" family appears eminently suitable as an instrument for technological society; on the other hand, inherent in the same family situation are tendencies to generate profound feelings of dislocation and discontent with established values, institutions and roles. Thus, the American family, especially the middle class, suburban American family with its confusions and ambivalences, reflects the general crisis of American culture. At the same time, it contributes to that crisis by generating in the next generation aspirations, expectations, and impulses that are not compatible with established norms and institutionalized patterns. It creates the psychic grounds for new identities in a society that provides no models, roles, or life styles around which such new identities can crystallize.

The middle class family is *necessary* in advanced industrial capitalism. Nevertheless, it *necessarily* creates many youths who have trouble accepting the society. When the key institutions of socialization inherently generate tendencies toward nonconformity, there surely is a cultural crisis. This seems to be the situation that has developed in the United States during the last three decades, as families have had to come to grips with a cultural framework that no longer fits social reality.

Meanwhile, a similar pattern of incoherence is played out in all the other institutions responsible for socialization and cultural indoctrination. In the schools, the media and the churches, such contradictory values as self-denial and self-expression, discipline and indulgence, and striving and being are preached, dramatized, fostered, and practiced all at once. On the one hand, television and magazines advocate hedonism, consumption, and living it up, while schools and churches continue, uneasily, to embody the Protestant Ethic. The economy demands discipline and self-control in order to *make* a living and spending and self-indulgence as a *way* of living. Political leaders tend to espouse the old virtues, while pop culture celebrities systematically flout them. Incentives to strive, compete,

242

and become disciplined are systematically undetermined by affluence, but all institutionalized means to be creative and productive (as in high-level professional work) continue to be linked with demands to be competitive, striving and self-denying. An incredible number and variety of means are provided for hedonistic pursuit and sensuality, yet all such experience is heavily laden with guilt, is often defined as illegal or immoral, is prohibited to minors, or is so highly commercialized as to lose its authentically expressive character.

The incoherence of the general culture thus interacts with the confusion of the individual family. It seems probable that virtually all American youth experience cultural incoherence and "anomie" as an integral feature of their growing up. The argument we are making, however, would lead us to predict that the youth who experience this situation most acutely are those for whom conventional values have been most weakened or irrelevant.

BIBLIOGRAPHICAL NOTES

1   The "decline" of the "Protestant Ethic" has been discussed in many ways by many people. Weber's classic definition of the culture of capitalism appears, of course, in his *The Protestant Ethic and the Spirit of Capitalism* (New York: Scribner's, 1958). Joseph Schumpeter prophesied the decline of entrepreneurial values in *Capitalism, Socialism and Democracy* (New York: Harper, 1942). An influential work describing changes in the American character was David Riesman's *The Lonely Crowd* (New York: Doubleday-Anchor, 1953). Seymour Martin Lipset and Leo Lowenthal, *Culture and Social Character* (Glencoe, Ill.: Free Press, 1961) contains important commentary on Reisman's work, especially an essay by Talcott Parsons and Winston White.

2   My discussion of the American middle class family is heavily indebted to the following: Kenneth Keniston, *The Uncommitted* (New York: Harcourt, Brace & World, 1962); Riesman, *The Lonely Crowd;* A. W. Green, "The Middle Class Male Child and Neurosis," *American Sociological Review* 11 (1946): 31-41; Talcott Parsons and Robert F. Bales, *Family, Socialization and Interaction Process* (Glencoe, Ill.: Free Press, 1955); Daniel Miller and Guy Swanson, *The Changing American Parent* (New York: Wiley, 1958); Betty Friedan, *The Feminine Mystique* (New York: Norton, 1963); David C. McClelland, *The Achieving Society* (Princeton, N.J.: Van Nostrand, 1961); and Philip Slater, *The Pursuit of Loneliness* (Boston: Beacon, 1970). In addition, I have relied on impressions gathered from my research on families of activist and nonactivist students and from my own experience as a parent.

Gang Youth and Hustling:
The Psychology of Survival

BARRY KRISBERG

Barry Krisberg was a professor of criminology at the University of California, Berkeley before joining the National Council on Crime and Delinquency.

Reprinted from Barry Krisberg, "Gang Youth Hustling: The Psychology of Survival." *Issues in Criminology*, Vol. 9 (Spring, 1974), 115-129.

I. INTRODUCTION

This paper will report the results of interviews and observations conducted among 22 youthful gang leaders in the city of Philadelphia. I first met the gang youth on the campus of the University of Pennsylvania. They were about to begin a training program which was jointly sponsored by the University and the Young Great Society, a Black community organization. The chief aim of the Urban Leadership Training Program was to train the young gang leaders for careers in community service. It was felt that the energies of gang youth could be channelled into positive neighborhood projects. My assignment was to provide an evaluation of the program, but during the research period, interest and concern extended to the subjects of gang delinquency, the effects of poverty, and other features of the community in which the gang leaders lived.

The participants of the Urban Leadership Training Program were leaders of five juvenile gangs in an area of West Philadelphia known as the Mantua area. Their ages ranged from 18 to 23 years. Each gang leader was a public school dropout. Their combined arrest records totalled more than 175 contacts with the law. Most of these arrests were for offenses involving violence, weapon use and assaultive behavior. Many in the group had served up to 36 months in state and local prisons. Their employment histories has been transitory and primarily unsuccessful. Planners of the Urban Leadership Training Program hoped to select program participants who had demonstrated leadership potential through their gang activities. Staff members of the Young Great Society contacted some of the more influential neighborhood gang leaders and discussed with them the purposes of the Urban Leadership Training Program. The gang leaders recruited members of their own groups to participate in the program.

During the process of researching the U.L.T. program, I had almost daily interactions with the gang leaders over an eight month period. A large proportion of time was spent in program sessions with the trainees, or accompanying them to and from various program events. Early in the program, I expressed a desire to become better acquainted with different aspects of gang life, but I waited for invitations by specific leaders before interviewing other members of their gangs. A reasonably good rapport was established with several of the gang leaders, and as a result, there were numerous invitations to join gang members at local bars, to participate in gang parties, and simply to "meet the fellows." The leaders typically introduced me as a friend who was writing a book about the Urban Leadership Training Program. The reception was warm and friendly, intermixed with some signs of suspicion, but in general, gang members responded to questions candidly and offered information generously. Introduction of the researcher by a well-respected gang member, together with my close ties with adult community leaders, facilitated discussions with gang members.

II. HUSTLING AND THE STRUGGLE TO SURVIVE

The theme of survival is an important one to the young men of the Urban Leadership Training Program. Few have experienced anything but severe economic deprivation throughout most of their lives. They were not accorded the comfort of material security during formative years, and they find themselves at the brink of adulthood without requisite education or training to compete successfully in the labor market. The harsh realities of ghetto existence have fostered in these young men a psychology of survival, as a functional adaptation to an uncompromising social environment.

> U.L.T.: Survival, man, it's survival of the fittest. You do unto others before they do unto you, and only do it to them first.[1]
>
> University
> Student: But you sound like we're in the wilderness, man.
> U.L.T.: But you got to do that to get what you need.

The need to "survive" felt deeply by these young men has led them into careers of illegal activities aimed at securing short-run material gain. Each man has his "hustle," some specialized illegal activity which helps him secure limited material wants.

> Like, I haven't worked in a hell of a long time, you know, on a job. I have no means of getting no money without that knowledge that I know in the streets. My game is hustling, period. See, I'm a good flim-flam man, you know. I know various things about various different arts that you all just heard about and read about.

A variety of activities form the core of hustles for the U.L.T. gang leaders. A few pursue persistent patterns of thefts and burglaries. One fellow's hustle involves robbing the participants of illegal dice games. His specialty, a dangerous one, always involves the carrying of a gun and often its use. His enemies are not only the police, but also those organized criminal interests in the neighborhood who share in the profits from illegal gambling. "The Mafia has a permanent contract out on me, man." Other gang leaders are petty loan sharks or continuous gamblers. Many of the U.L.T. group sell marijuana and other drugs in limited quantities. Three gang leaders are procurers for prostitutes. They are, for the most part, "small-time" operators in the sense that they are not connected with organized criminal interests, their "take" is relatively small, and they run afoul of law-enforcement officials regularly. The victims of their activities are almost always fellow residents of Mantua.

> Catch a man or woman coming down the street and they've been counting a little money, and I'd run up and take it from them, knock them down and go in their pocket and get all their money. You know, this kind of thing. And burglarize people's houses, you know, and it was a thing whereas, like, I mean, I had to survive and had to get to that money, and this is what I did to get to it.

There is a major contradiction in their tales of hustling activities. Often the listener is told that hustling is a great way for providing for wants, that one can hustle for all the money that one needs; most U.L.T. gang leaders enjoy bragging about their hustling skills. In contrast to this image, one often sensed that hustling was the mode of a desperate man, and that the rewards were small. Note the following explanation taken from an interview with James Bethal:

> Like, your stomach get to griping at one end, your ribs get to meeting your backbone, and every time you go to the bathroom you ain't doing nothing but shitting out water, Jack. Then it gets to the point whereas when you do go to the bathroom and that water won't come out, your butt's all hard and sore, man, and you get to saying I got to get me some money to get me something to eat. When you try to get this money, you try to get enough to hold you over, to keep you from doing this for a while. But it just don't happen that way, man, like, you take off something or somebody and you only wind up getting $20 out of the thing, and you got a half-assed room, the rent $20—you got to give the scratch right up. And you keep doing it. That's how these things go down. And when you want to dress, you want to see the fellows in a new pair of shoes or a nice suit or something, you want this for yourself, you rob people, break in their houses.

Bethal later told me that he would look for men in the neighborhood who would pay ten dollars to have somebody beat up. He described the way he used to get his victim when his objective was most vulnerable. Bethal felt little guilt about hurting this stranger. "See, as long as you get to that scratch, you ain't even worrying about it, man, and this is all there is to it."

Claude Brown, in his well-known autobiography, describes his career in hustling and particularly the impact of Reno, a twenty-one year old hustler who befriended Claude and promised to teach him all the tricks:

> So I just started hanging out with Reno. Reno had said he was going to show me all the hustling tricks. After a few months, I quit my first job and just dealt pot. I decided I was going to be a hustler. We were going to start from way back, from all the old hustling tricks and come up to the modern-day stuff (Brown, 1965:159).

Many of the gang leaders related a similar story about an older person, usually in his twenties, and often a former member of his gang, who befriended them and gave instructions in the hustling arts. The hustler is a much admired adult figure to gang youths. Abrahams (1970), in his study of Black folklore taken from the streets of Philadelphia, noted the folk figure of "Shine" or "Sam Shine" who closely approximated the hustling ideal in terms of coolness, natural intelligence, and the ability to manipulate others. The "hustler," like the "bad nigger," as portrayed in folklore, is always related to the total experience of Black people in America, particularly the need to attend to one's wants without evoking a repressive response from the "man." One relied upon "Mother wit" to meet the demands of every-day life. The hustler breaks the white man's laws, but does not flaunt them in the same manner as the "bad nigger." He is confident, self-assured, and demonstrates (at least at the level of the myth) that one need not accept the dull and menial low status jobs which the white society leaves open to the Black man. Firestone (1969:788-801) has described the hustler's role in his study of adolescent drug users.

> He achieved his goals by indirection, relying rather on persuasion and on a repertoire of manipulative techniques. . . . His idea was to get what he wanted through persuasion and ingratiation; to use the other fellow by deliberately outwitting him (Firestone, 1969:789).

Firestone suggests that the hustler sees himself as an "operator" who is completely skeptical of other persons' motives. Almost any relationship could be part of a "scheme" or lend itself to an angle. The "square" who is hard working, honest, and apparently virtuous, is ridiculed by the hustler, and yet the hustler suspects that "some squares were smarter than he, because they could enjoy all the forbidden pleasures which were his stock and trade, and maintain a reputation for respectability in the bargain" (*Ibid.*:790). A clear statement of this view can be seen in the following justification of one gang leader's continued hustling activities:

> Well, the reason why I continue to do this is because, like, the same game's being played. In other words, like, there are whites and Blacks out there that's doing the same thing I'm doing, only

they're doing it behind a desk. With a pen and a pencil, see? And this is what I'm coming to school for, to learn how to get at that top dollar. Right off the top, see, with a pen and a pencil.

The ideal of the hustler is perhaps best symbolized by the successful pimp. Firestone comments:

To be supported in idleness and luxury through the labors of one or more attractive "chicks" who shoplifted or engaged in prostitution or both, and dutifully handed over the proceeds, was one of his favorite fantasies (*Ibid.*).

The U.L.T. gang leaders referred to some women as "whores," and described how pleasant life would be if their women would give them money whenever they demanded it. "If a whore ain't gonna give you that scratch, man—what good is she?"[2]

Ned Polsky (1967) notes that the term "hustler" has been applied to persons who make their living by betting against opponents in different types of pool or billiard games. The use of the terms "hustler" and "hustling" in poolroom argot antedates the application to prostitutes. It might be added that the term is often used to describe salesmen in a variety of industries. Polsky's description of the work situation of the poolroom hustler illustrates several characteristics of the role. He observes the hustlers want "fast action"; that is, they don't care how much money is at stake in one game, but rather, they want cash to change hands quickly. Deception is central to pool hustling. "The hustler exploits the fact to deceive his opponent as to his [the hustler's] true level of skill" (*Ibid.*:54). However, the hustler must have "heart." He must play his best under pressure. Polsky is correct when he observes that the general role of the hustler applies to such diverse occupations as prostitution, pool playing, and *a number of legitimate activities in sales and service.* "As several parts of this study illustrate, hustling demands a continuous and complicated concern with how one is seen by others" (*Ibid.*:62).

The hustler can seldom produce or direct ideal scenes. He must depend upon being a continuously self-aware actor. He must manipulate how others evaluate him through his reactions to their evaluations and special behaviors designed to manipulate such evaluations. The "ideal cat," according to Firestone,

would always appear in public impeccably dressed, and would be able to sport a complete change of outfit several times a day. . . . Moreover, the "cat" feels himself to be any man's equal. He is convinced that he can go anywhere and mingle easily with anyone (Firestone, 1969:791).

The hustler cultivates his ability to generate appropriate images given relatively poor resources. Most important is the ability to converse, to convince the other with a deft use of language. Many of the U.L.T. gang leaders took pride in their "gift of gab" which was required for successful hustling activities. Even if "hustles" involve thefts, burglaries or the use of weapons, as opposed to "cons" or confidence schemes, the ghetto hustler needs to be able to talk his way out of difficult situations, particularly those involving the police. The U.L.T. gang leaders felt that they were usually able to outwit the police by appearing "clean" and not suspicious. Moreover, the skills of impression management are applied not only in illegal activities but are equally useful in interactions with one's peers. The definition of personal style projected to significant others in the social milieu becomes an important part of the hustler's self-conception, although it appears that at times these young men see through their own carefully constructed public faces. The pain of such insight partially explains the frequent resort to alcohol and drugs among ghetto hustlers. Malcolm X, recalling his hustling days, observed:

> For that matter, all the thousands of dollars I'd handled, and I had nothing. Just satisfying my cocaine habit alone cost me about twenty dollars a day. I guess another five dollars a day could have been added for reefers and plain tobacco, cigarettes that I smoked (Malcolm X, 1965:139).

III. HUSTLING, GANG CAREERS, AND WORLD VIEWS

By age eighteen, most of these gang leaders no longer considered themselves active members of their gangs. Participation in gang conflicts was no longer considered appropriate behavior for them. Many privately confessed fears that continued involvement would almost certainly result in arrests and return to prison. They were keenly aware that law enforcement agencies would treat them as adults and thus impose harsher penalties for gang-related behavior. Several saw the futility of fighting over turfs which really belonged to no group of adolescents. Gang warfare, as perceived by these young men, had become more violent in recent years, and they no longer viewed the risks of gang conflict as glamorous and justifiable. They made a clear distinction between what was appropriate for themselves in the past and what was now unacceptable behavior. Few openly criticized gang members for continued fighting or disavowed their past involvement. They had simply "put down gang warring" and felt no great desire to pick it up again. The gang leaders felt more mature now, and looked forward to more worthwhile activities. Some of the group were married and had children. Although few expressed pressures to provide material support for their families, they were concerned about what images their children might have of them as parents.

> I got a wife and two kids, man, you understand what I'm saying? I swear, I don't want my son growing up, Jack, and, like, I know my son won't grow up and it's going to be young cats say, "Yeah, I know your father—he robbed a bank. I know your father, Jack—he used to rumble."

Many of the group appeared eager to become involved in some positive activity in which they could take pride, and which might make others proud of them. Several of the gang leaders saw the training program as their last chance to accomplish something constructive with their lives.

Recognizing the nobility of these expressed intentions to benefit the community through the positive activities, it is important to assess the impact of the life histories of these young men upon their ability to make a meaningful new start. Kenneth Clark observed:

> It is now generally understood that chronic and remedial social injustice corrodes and damages the human personality, thereby robbing it of its effectiveness, of its creativity, if not its actual humanity. No matter how desperately one seeks to deny it, this simple fact persists and intrudes itself (Clark, 1965:63).

The gang leaders of the U.L.T. program have spent a significant portion of their young lives fighting against the reality of social deprivation, which constrains their existence. As ghetto hustlers, they have developed social-psychological mechanisms which seemed to them appropriate to the task of personal survival. We need to explore the implications of their modes of adaption in terms of their prospects for the future.

If the individual who emerges does not fit some ideal model of the community leader, or if he frightens us, the locus of criticism needs to be placed, not upon him, but at the origins of social inequities and injustices. These youthful gang leaders have not found the socially approved escape routes from poverty which are sparingly offered by the dominant white society.[3] They may remain an important source of indigenous leadership, but one must realistically look at who they are and what they may require before thrusting upon them missions and responsibilities for which they have not been properly prepared or motivated. It is as cruel to romanticize them now as it was to undervalue their abilities and potential in the past.

The gang leaders, not surprisingly, believe in strict determinism as an explanation of human behavior. Their life experiences teach that there is little area left open to the individual's ability to bring about personal change. "You get what your hand calls for," according to one gang leader. This is reminiscent of Miller's (1958) notion of fate as *a focal concern of lower class culture.*[4] Most often, the U.L.T. gang leaders used their deterministic view to explain away behavior of which they felt others might disapprove. Moreover, it seemed to constrain them from passing negative judgments about one another. If a fellow trainee missed classes, came to class "high" on drugs, or did not complete his assignments, this was excusable, or at least incapable of change. Matza and Skyes have also noted that "in effect, the delinquent approaches a 'billiard ball' conception of himself as helplessly propelled into new situations" (Matza and Sykes, 1970:290).

These young men understandably share a pragmatic and conservative view of the nature of humans. Theirs is a mirror image
world reflecting the larger society, turning around maxims; for
example, "Do unto others before they do unto you," is a first com-
mandment. This view limits, in their eyes, the amount of change which
they can expect to effect. Many of the trainees expressed an interest
in working with younger gang members. They would talk with youthful associates and relate their own experiences, but few felt that this
effort would have any effect. "They're going to do their thing, anyway, man. I never listened to nobody—why should they?"

One of the consequences of their deterministic model of human
behavior is a refusal to make plans for the future. Deacon, the most
eloquent spokesman of the group, saw the "Future as a distance,"
events that would happen without his control. Liebow has correctly
observed that this "present-time" orientation may be *a realistic appraisal of the future from the street corner man's perspective.*

> It is a future in which everything is uncertain except the
> ultimate destruction of his hopes and the eventual realization
> of his fears. The most he can reasonably look forward to is that
> these things do not come too soon (Liebow, 1967:66).

The street corner man, living on "the edge of both economic
and psychological subsistence," expends his resources in supporting
self-conceptions, from moment to moment. Planning—at least, the
open announcement of future goals—makes the person vulnerable to
possibilities of failures which are public and subject to the criticism
of others. The experience of having been labelled a failure by school
officials, employers, social control agents, and family members, conditions the individual against taking risks in terms of one's carefully
protected self-images. Thus, the individual does not invest too much
of his ego in any activity or aspiration. The U.L.T. gang leaders may
continue to dream, but they are reluctant to make personal expectations public knowledge.

The gang leaders of the U.L.T. program often expressed fears
that no matter how hopeful their prospects for success appeared,
something, either within themselves or from the hostile "system,"
would snatch the rewards from them in the final analysis. Dreams
and aspirations had "conned" them many times throughout their
young lives, but they were determined not to be hurt by disappointments in the future.

The hustling life-style with its emphasis upon an individualistic
orientation makes difficult the development of an awareness of the
outer worlds. For example, there was much talk about the problems of
racism and poverty, but the gang leaders evidenced little fundamental
understanding of the structural constraints placed upon their advancement by the white society. Acquaintance with the goals and programs
of well-known Black leaders appeared limited. Many confessed, for

example, that they knew the name Malcolm X, but didn't know anything about his philosophy. They seemed strangely detached from
militant Black organizations in their neighborhood. "I'm not too hip
about that Black Panther program." The use of the word "program"
did not reflect the sense of a political agenda, but rather a conception
of the Panther party as yet another short-run project started in
Mantua to reach the gang youths. It was a program like the Job
Corps or any number of other training projects. Some members had
"tried out that brother thing, wearing dashikis and all, but I didn't
dig it." Phrases borrowed from the Black Power movement were
often used by the trainees, but their usage was far more consistent
with a general reliance upon pat phrases in rhetorical style, rather
than an understanding of contemporary Black ideology.

Towards the close of the U.L.T. Program, the curriculum focused
on Black history and Black social movements. The gang leaders were
excited about this "new material," and pleaded with lecturers to tell
them more about their history. It is important to note that these gang
leaders had left school long before courses in Black Studies were offered in public schools. Likewise, their limited reading ability decreased the likelihood that they might have read the classics of the
Black social movement. What information they did possess was gained
mostly from the mass media. Some were exposed to ethnic thought
in prison, but their knowledge was limited and fragmentary. Middle-
class Blacks, those who had gone to college or who held relatively
important jobs, were treated with suspicion. "Did you grow up in the
ghetto?" or "Are you real?" were frequent questions put to Black
teachers. One fellow often used the word "colored folks" in class.
Other classmates criticized his use of "colored," and told him to use
the term "Black." He responded: "I know I should use 'Black,' but I
ain't used to it. I got to practice, man." In general the group did not
seem to have a high level of ethnic consciousness.

The gang leaders appeared not to have a well-defined sense of
class consciousness because, as previously mentioned, their orientation, in contrast to their behavior, is essentially middle-class. In
response to the question, "What is your idea of good architecture?,"
one leader described a suburban home with picture-windows and a
green lawn.

Q: What do you see for yourself? What do you want?
U.L.T.:   I just want to get everything I can and all I can.
           Really, when I finish, I want. . . . I expect, I expect a
           car here. I mean, I mean a big. . . . I want a big car,
           the biggest car I can get. Not going to own no
           Cadillac, though, because a Cadillac ain't nothing but
           a big, ugly mass. I don't want no Cadillac.
Q: Do you want some scratch [money]?
U.L.T.:   Yeah. I want to be comfortable. Yeah I want some
           scratch.

The group spent much time discussing clothes and new musical gadgetry. Many members of the class could be described as "conspicuous consumers," frequently flaunting new possessions to fellow trainees.

The gang leaders offered verbal support for middle-class values. Deacon explained that he made sure that his four children received proper health care. "I take them to the clinic myself, man." In countless other situations, the U.L.T. gang leaders professed allegiance to middle-class norms. This verbal behavior might prove a puzzle to most gang theorists; they delighted in debunking middle-class respectability and showed "the focal concerns of lower-class culture" (Miller, 1958), but at the same time they gave support to many aspects of the dominant value system.

We have noted a skepticism of middle-class conformists by the U.L.T. gang leaders, but not a rejection of socially approved means of attaining material rewards. The gang leaders suspected that "the men with clean shirts and nice ties" had a superior hustle; most wished they could participate in that system. One gang leader explained: "I want a job, J-O-B. The best hustlers got steady jobs. Anybody who don't want a job is a fool, man."

The street corner setting allows participants to espouse generally approved social values without the threat that others will point to the discrepancy between verbalizations and actions. Liebow's notion of a "shadow system of values" provides for him an understanding of the street corner world:

> Derivative, unsubstantial, and co-occurring with the parent system, it is as if the alternative value system is a shadow cast by the common value system in the distorting lower-class setting. Together, the two systems lie behind much that seems paradoxical and inconsistent, familiar and alien, to the middle-class observer from his one-system perspective (Liebow, 1967: 213).

David Matza explains this process through his concept of neutralization (Matza, 1964:60-62). Matza further asserts that the subculture of delinquents receives cultural support from the conventional traditions. From the dialectic between conventional values and subterranean traditions in American life emerges the justification for the deviant's life style. The romantic theme of the ghetto man-child committing thefts to support his economically deprived family, as well as the heroic portrayal of gang as protector of women and children which were offered in several interviews with the gang leaders, would be viewed as "appeals to higher loyalties" in Matza's terms.

> It is important to note that the delinquent does not necessarily repudiate the imperatives of the dominant normative system, despite his failure to follow them. Rather, the delinquent may see himself as caught up in a dilemma that must be resolved, unfortunately, at the cost of violating the law (Matza and Sykes, 1970:297).

This formulation is one way of interpreting the apparently large discrepancies between the words and deeds of the U.L.T. gang leaders. Their attack upon the dominant value system is viewed as subversion rather than open rebellion.

> Because, look at school now—I think school's a hip thing; I wish I could be back there. I wish I could get right back. I think school is really it, man. . . . I got left down twice. I never got left down for not learning. I got left down because I never came. But it was never because I was stupid or anything. I had one white teacher, but he just didn't know how to relate to me. He just didn't know how to come out, you know—*he wanted me to come to his level—he couldn't come down to mine—we couldn't meet each other half way* (emphasis added).

Middle-class values are not repudiated by the U.L.T. gang leader; rather, he carries a set of definitions about social reality which explains his deviance and which partially attenuates feelings of failure.

The individualistic orientation of the U.L.T. gang leaders is reflected in their views of socio-economic deprivation. One student explained:

> See, because like, positions and conditions and the way of life is, man, make you do these kinds of things. For a Black man, because it's really cold, man, out here, you know? It's cold, it's hard, but it's fair.

Most individuals in the gang leaders' world begin with limited resources. One succeeds over others by use of natural intelligence and learned skills, and each actor, in their view, is engaged in entrepreneurship, albeit of brute force in some instances. This orientation is further illustrated in the following exchange between a university student and a U.L.T. participant:

> Student: I know you have been deprived and are impatient with the power structure. . . .
>
> U.L.T.: Let me tell you something—I have never been denied cause I go out here and steal what I want, man, take what I want, man, and I get it, boy. Anything I want in life, I'm going to get. And I'm not going to let no fool tell me, well, look here, Jack, you can't do this here because it's against the law, and that kind of bullshit.

Another gang leader explained:

> I can't understand why anyone doesn't have enough food to eat or good clothes to wear. If they want these things, they can always hustle.

From these quotes, deprivation can be viewed as an individual's failing; but through enterprise, one can alleviate the pains of economic scarcity.

It seems appropriate to raise the question of whether the value orientations of these young men, as they entered the U.L.T. program, are desirable from the point of view of Mantua residents. The U.L.T. gang leaders, by their own admission, are not dreamers; rather, they take pride in their "realistic" appraisal of social reality. Often the students referred to their world as a jungle. The consequences of such a world-view are grave indeed. Malcolm X observed:

> As is the case in any jungle, the hustler's every waking hour is lived with both the practical and the subconscious knowledge that if he ever relaxes, if he ever slows down, the other hungry, restless foxes, ferrets, wolves and vultures out there with him won't hesitate to make him their prey (Malcolm X, 1965:109).

The psychology of survival, with its correlative conservative interpretation of social life, appears to be inconsistent with a theoretical focus upon qualitative social change or a humanistic approach towards interpersonal relations. The conversion of these young men to the mission of community leadership required that they become capable of "building more statelier missions," but the program proved to be yet another failure which only left the gang leaders alienated and cynical about community work in general.

The gang leaders often strike observers as free-spirited, blithe individuals. It appears that they have preserved a sense of independence despite encompassing pressures towards conformity in modern society. The gang leaders claim to be masters of their personal lives (although this is contrary to their deterministic conceptions of human actions), and they place a high priority on the maintenance of autonomy. This is illustrated by Deacon, who insisted that he would not get "hung up on belonging." The dark side of freedom is the profound lack of long-term and satisfying social attachments in one's life history.

> But overall, I mean, like, my life ain't been no playtoy. I mean, I had to really get out there and get it myself. Cause, like, I was travelling so fast like, it was a hell of a thing.

Most people derive pleasure from attachments of family, commitments to work-careers, or an abiding sense of community; but the majority of the U.L.T. gang leaders at this moment in life had not experienced these attachments.[5] Perhaps only their gang provided a feeling of meaning for a brief time in their lives. One does not sense in these Philadelphia gang leaders a profound sense of community, or a deeply-felt ethnic pride. Their Blackness meant "being a failure for 450 years," or "being disappointed." The hustling life-style and its consequent psychology of survival leaves little room for commitments. The process of attaching oneself to others will be necessarily difficult for the hustler who had developed a pervasive suspicion of others' claims for his loyalty. Malcolm X writes:

What I was learning was the hustling society's first rule: that you never trusted anyone outside of your own close-mouthed circle, and that you selected with time and care before you made any intimates even among these (Malcolm X, 1965:85).

The central point is that the resulting orientations we observe in the world of the U.L.T. gang leaders may be viewed as one possible adaptation to the experiences of Black men reared in conditions of poverty and racism. They have entered the career world of the ghetto hustler, and have developed appropriate ideologies, value orientations, and psychological defense mechanisms that fit perfectly with a superstructure essentially based upon race privilege and relations governing private property. Even the mask of autonomy and personal freedom is rooted in ideas taken from the ideology of oppression and domination.[6] Tragically, the gang youth have partially internalized the world view of those who are ultimately responsible for the conditions of racism and poverty which have constrained their lives.

IV. THE PROGRAM AND ITS CONSEQUENCES

The Urban Leadership Training Program ended like so many similar efforts without the realization of program goals. And as is all too frequent, it was the lack of jobs at the end of the training which caused the breakdown rather than the misdeeds of the participants, although the community leaders blamed the gang youth for "hustling on the program." In a fundamental sense, the program itself was "another hustle," revealing that the gang youth were still vulnerable to broken dreams and that the superstructural conditions had not changed. After the demise of the U.L.T. program, most of the gang leaders returned to the illegal activities which had sustained them before the start of the training. Some of the group experienced personal tailspins.

From its beginning, the U.L.T. program assumed a rather conventional nature. The slogan of the program was "Through Prosperity We Will Conquer," and the gang leaders were told to "play within the system." Political action was defined for them by the training staff as pressure upon political party committeemen; social action meant appeals to proper channels. All of this conventional approach to social participation was met with approval by the gang youth who were thinking about jobs, businesses and continued contact with "the big shots." None of these desired results was obtained. The gang youth were left bitter and disillusioned with the staff of the project.

Had program planners envisioned a more active role for the gang youth, the content of the training might have been different. The gang youth would have been asked to make personal sacrifices on behalf of fellow neighborhood residents. They might have been exposed to a broader range of social action. The content of the training would have openly attacked the conservative assumptions of their psychology of survival. Perhaps the gang youth might have been given a more accurate view of the etiology of conditions of internal colonization and racial oppression. We do not know for sure that this approach would have produced results much different from the U.L.T. program, but it is possible that the gang youth would have emerged better equipped to move towards democratic participation in the decisions affecting their lives.

NOTES

1   It is more than a little ironic that this key element of Spencerian sociology, long rejected by contemporary social scientists, finds expression in the context of the inner city ghetto. Moreover, the twist on the Biblical saying is fascinating.

2   Gordon (1972) points out that the "hustle" in its various forms contains the fundamental element of exploitation which is institutionalized in all social classes.

3   Many of these socially approved routes represent hustle with larger payoffs and different sets of costs. Consider the Robber Baron.

4   Given the emphasis in America upon individual competition and mobility, the concept of "fate" acts as a palliative as well as an explanation of the misery of the poor, but more importantly, it provides an explanation for the poor of why the rich became rich.

5   George Jackson wrote: "All my life I pretended with my folks, it was the thing in the street that was real" (Jackson, 1970:3).

6   See Maurice Boyd and Donald Worcester (1968).

REFERENCES

Abrahams, Roger D.
  1970   Deep Down in the Jungle. Chicago: Aldine.
Becker, Howard S.
  1963   Outsiders. New York: Free Press.
Boyd, Maurice and Donald Worcester
  1968   Contemporary America: Issues and Problems. New York: Allyn and Bacon.
Brown, Claude
  1965   Manchild in the Promised Land. New York: Signet Books.
Cohen, Albert K.
  1955   Delinquent Boys. New York: Free Press.
Clark, Kenneth
  1965   Dark Ghetto. New York: Harper
Cloward, Richard A. and Lloyd E. Ohlin
  1960   Delinquency and Opportunity. New York: Free Press.
Downes, David
  1965   The Delinquent Solution. New York: Free Press.
Firestone, Harold
  1969   "Cats, Kicks, and Color." Delinquency, Crime and Social Process. Edited by D. Cressey and D. Ward. New York: Harper and Row.
Gordon, David M.
  1971   "Class and the Economics of Crime." Union of Radical Political Economists 3:51.

The Social Context of Aspiration **257**

Grier, W. H. and P. M. Cobbs
    1968   Black Rage. New York: Bantam Books.
Jackson, George
    1970   Soledad Brother. New York: Coward-McCann.
Krisberg, Barry
    1971   Urban Leadership Training: An Ethnographic Study of 22 Gang Leaders. Doctoral dissertation, University of Pennsylvania, Philadelphia.
Liebow, Elliot
    1967   Tally's Corner. Boston: Little, Brown and Company.
Malcolm X
    1965   The Autobiography of Malcolm X. New York: Grove Press.
Matza David
    1964   Delinquency and Drift. New York: John Wiley and Sons.
Matza, David and Gresham Sykes
    1970   "Techniques of Delinquency." The Sociology of Crime and Delinquency. Edited by Marvin E. Wolfgang, Leonard Savitz, and Norman Johnston. Second edition. New York: John Wiley and Sons.
Miller, Walter B.
    1958   "Lower Class Culture as a Generating Milieu of Gang Delinquency." Journal of Social Issues 14:5-10.
Polsky, Ned
    1967   Hustlers, Beats and Others. Chicago: Aldine.

Breaking Out, Smashing Up and the Social Context of Aspiration

STAN COHEN

Stan Cohen is a professor of sociology at the University of Essex, England.

Reprinted from Stanley Cohen, "Breaking Out, Smashing Up and the Social Context of Aspiration," *Working Papers in Cultural Studies*, No. 5 (Spring 1974) pp. 37-63.

Wild ones terrorize a village: *Crowds of youngsters pour into a little fishing village each weekend. They come by bus, car, scooter and motor bike. With their guitars and haversacks they look as though they might be heading for a pop festival. But their arrival strikes a chord of fear in the hearts of the residents of Seahouses in North Northumberland. For among the newcomers are the wild ones— young thugs and their girlfriends whose only idea of fun is a weekend of wrecking and terror. Once again this summer, as the villagers open their souvenir shop and camping sites, they know*

> *that trouble lies ahead. They had their first real taste of it last year,*
> *when the sunshine brought weekends of vandalism and violence.*
> *The pattern has already been set for 1971. Last weekend, extra*
> *police with dogs had to be drafted into Seahouses to break up gangs*
> *who roamed the streets, fighting, jeering and stealing. The gangs—*
> *up to 30 strong—head for the picturesque resort mainly from the*
> *Newcastle upon Tyne area, more than 40 miles away. Youths and*
> *their girl friends sleep rough among sand dunes or in beach toilets*
> *. . . . "The feeling in Seahouses is one of bitterness," said local*
> *councillor Albert Brewer. "We try to provide reasonable and decent*
> *amenities for people to come here and enjoy themselves but these*
> *hooligans just come along and start breaking the place up. The*
> *stories we get of what goes on are disgusting. The summer simply*
> *brings us worry of what might happen. People begin to feel more*
> *and more apprehensive as the weekend draws near. I don't consider*
> *myself an unreasonable sort of person, but these thugs want*
> *birching."*
>
> (NEWS OF THE WORLD, *April 18, 1971*)

The adolescent who commits acts of violence or vandalism is the archetypal repository of the large fund of moral indignation which societies have in reserve. The constellation of action which is difficult to understand, let alone sympathize with, and actors who belong to a group of low power plus high visibility and vulnerability, ensures that the whole battery of fantasy and mythology will be invoked to comprehend this action and justify certain forms of social control against it.

The hooligan, the wild one, the vandal, the yob, the thug, the uncouth leather jacketed gang member: these are the images used to focus attention on a particular sort of person and to evoke a particular moral attitude. The picture is a composite one, made up of Hollywood movies (such as "The Wild One" from which our *News Of The World* report derives its headline), cartoons and folklore and—above all—years of tendentious, distorted and sensational reports in the mass media. Each generation supplies its images which make up the layers of the composite picture: spivs and cosh boys, Teddy Boys slashing cinema seats during rock and roll riots, Mods and Rockets brandishing deck chairs on the beaches of Brighton and Margate, vandals ripping out telephone kiosks, hooligans throwing bottles at football matches, skinheads putting the boot in.

There is a tendency to see these socially created folk devils as if they were distinct types of personalities. Situational and structural factors are ignored and the behaviour is explained simply by attributing it to a type of person. And these persons are always "others": football hooligans are not genuine supporters, but louts whose behaviour stigmatizes the well behaved majority; Mods were not decent fun loving holiday makers; kids who throw bottles around on council estates come from the rougher (or "multi-problem") families. Such images function to stress the discontinuity between deviants and others and heighten the sense of security to be derived from knowing that the deviant is not "one of us."

In addition, there is a tendency to attribute all variations of the disapproved-of action, to the same type of person. Thus, referring to trouble at football matches, the *Daily Sketch* (30.1.67) noted:

> ... the trouble makers are young hooligans who merely use football and excursion trains as an excuse for their stupid behaviour. The same brainless wonders spend their midweek ripping telephone boxes, slashing seats, defacing walls, pushing old ladies off the pavement and pinching fruit from barrows.

While the *Daily Mirror* (6.1.66) thought that telephone vandals ". . . are the same bird brained maniacs who slash railway carriage seats and throw bottles at the football referee and darts at the goal keeper."

But where do these brainless wonders and bird brained maniacs come from, the creatures who week after week evoke from thousands of Councillor Brewers the same bewilderment, bitterness and the eternal parental reproach "after all we've done for them . . ."? In this essay, I would like to examine one context in which this question could be answered: that of the aspirations generated for working class adolescents in this country during the last two decades or so. I will concentrate specifically on the leisure context, the one that the Councillor Brewers of our society are so bitter about: young people today are affluent, they've got plenty to do, we've given them so much, but they ". . . just come along and start breaking the place up." I will assume that such disapproved-of behaviour is not the reflex action of brainless wonders or bird brained maniacs, but is the solution—not necessarily a very satisfactory or attractive one—of problems which are differentially distributed in our society and whose approved of solutions are similarly accessible only to some. As I will make clear, the leisure context is where such problems are *felt*: their origins go further back, in the direction of the structure of education and work. If any prescriptions emerge from this essay they are directed towards these structures, particularly the educational one. But for a youth work audience the leisure context seems the more appropriate to focus on.

VANDALISM: AN INTRODUCTION

Before this, let me mention a few points which I've dealt with elsewhere in regard to adolescent violence as a whole and vandalism in particular. The first is that terms such as vandalism should not be reified to make them into actual and unambiguous behavioural syndromes. The illegal destruction or defacement of property belonging to someone else—a minimal behavioural definition of this form of rule breaking—does not invariably lead to its classification as the deviant act, vandalism. The behaviour can be institutionalized under at least the following conditions: *ritualism*: on certain ritual occasions, such as November 5th, New Year's Eve, property destruction is expected, condoned or even encouraged; *protection*: certain groups, particularly of high social status, such as students, are given some sort of collective licence to engage in property destruction; *play*: in certain areas, or among certain groups such as very small children, the rule breaking is not regarded as deviant or problematic because it is recognized as local tradition, part of a game, or the targets—say windows of derelict houses—are simply regarded as expendable. Part of the sociologist's task is to look at the conditions—ideological and political—under which differential labelling occurs and the consequences of the actions so labelled.

The second general point, is that contrary to the pervasive stereotype, even "ordinary" vandalism is not a homogeneous category. Most people will probably not find much difficulty in distinguishing between a ten year old boy throwing an old tyre onto a railway line, a group of football fans smashing shop windows on a Saturday afternoon and someone deliberately wrenching off the coin box of a public telephone. People tend to react, however *as if* they cannot make these distinctions, as if there is a vandal type responsible for the whole range of behaviour. Common sense (as well as research!) indicates that there is no such thing as a vandal type, even within the range of officially labelled and apprehended vandals. Thus, nearly two-thirds of telephone vandals are adults, while most railway vandalism (such as putting objects on the railway line) is carried out by young children between ten and twelve years old.

Finally, vandalism is not wanton, senseless or meaningless. It is patterned both in terms of the type of property that is damaged—more often public than private, more often derelict than well kept—and in the clusters of different meanings and motives attributed to it by the offender. Elsewhere, I have distinguished the following six subtypes:

1   Acquisitive vandalism. Damage done in order to acquire money or property: breaking open telephone coin boxes, electric or gas meters, slot machines, stripping lead and wire from buildings.
2   Tactical vandalism. The damage is a conscious tactic employed to advance some other end: breaking a window in order to be arrested and get a bed in prison, jamming a machine in a factory to ensure an enforced rest period, drawing attention to grievance.
3   Ideological vandalism. Similar to the last example of tactical vandalism, but carried out to further an explicit ideological cause or to deliver a message: breaking embassy windows during a demonstration, chalking slogans on walls.
4   Vindictive vandalism. The damage is done in order to gain

revenge: for example, windows of a youth club or school are broken to settle a grudge against the club leader or head teacher.

5 Play vandalism. The damage is done in the context of a game: who can break the most windows of a house, who can shoot out the most streat lamps?

6 Malicious vandalism. The damage is an expression of rage or frustration and is often directed at symbolic middle class property. It is this type that has the vicious and apparently senseless facade which people find so difficult to understand. Many types of juvenile vandalism have the elements of both play and malice: defecating in lifts (usually in council flats), urinating in public telephone receivers, cutting boats loose from their moorings, breaking lights in railway carriages.

The type of vandalism occurring during the episode quoted at the beginning of the essay may contain elements of vindictiveness, play and maliciousness. The analysis that follows is directed primarily towards vandalism which occurs (i) during late adolescence; (ii) in the context of large groups; and (iii) in public or semi-public settings. Although I fully realize the problematic nature of the boundary line between ideological and non-ideological, I am specifically excluding from consideration property damage or disturbances which are overtly connected with political, religious or racial conflict.

THE YOUTH SCENE

We must now turn to some generalizations about adolescence, primarily as it is manifested in a leisure oriented youth culture. I will then explore some of the links between this culture and "smashing up" and "breaking out" as types of fringe delinquency. In making these generalizations, I hope to achieve two incidental and quite modest objectives: the first is to remedy some of the more gross over-generalizations about the youth scene, particularly over the Sixties, and the second is to speak up on behalf of a section of young people whose voices don't get heard too often.

This second task may be looked upon as illegitimate for a sociologist to attempt and unnecessary for anyone to attempt. "Illegitimate" because sociologists are supposed to talk *about* people and not on their behalf. I can only say that this is a view of the subject I do not hold. "Unnecessary," because there are commonly supposed to be enough or too many channels for young people to be seen and heard. I doubt this is so, but in any event most of the group I will be discussing do not have access to such channels of communication. They do not appear on Late Night Line Up or N.U.S. press conferences, they are not photographed going in a minibus to Afghanistan or promenading along the King's Road; they are not seen under political banners in Trafalgar Square or going on charity walks for Shelter and Oxfam. They were not even to be seen in front of the cameras on Top of the Pops. The major distortion in talking about youth in Britain today—and the articulate defenders are as guilty as the articulate condemners—is not to understand that if there *is* a youth scene, there are many who are not on the stage and there are many more so insulated from where it's happening, that they are hardly even in the audience. It is these outsiders, who form the majority of the adolescent population, the 75 per cent or so who don't go on to higher education, who leave school at fifteen, whom I will be talking about.

The dominant sociological model of the youth culture goes something like this: in nonindustrial societies, young people were given tasks functionally related to the work of the adult world, they knew their place. In Western industrial society, there is discontinuity: neither any preparation for nor any smooth transition towards adult roles. The result is conflict and deviance. This gap is widened by the increasing differentiation of institutions: longer schooling and sharper segregation of young people helps the development of an autonomous youth culture, embodying values which insulate it from the problems of the age transition. Most sociological writing elaborates on this sort of theme; the picture both leaves something out and contains too much.

It leaves out the role of the rest of society in creating the teenage culture for its own needs and in so doing, neutralizes the conflict between the adolescent and society. The *relative* affluence and economic independence of the post-war adolescent in Britain means that he is now a new consumer, he can participate in the spectacle of commodities. This is his reward for mass production; any other participation is frowned upon. This is not a situation of one way "exploitation": the cynicism this term implies is present on both sides. It is insulting to think that young people, despite the education they've received, can be so easily conned.

As Frank Musgrove has eloquently noted, adults conveniently consign the young to a self-contained world of juvenile pre-occupations, they resist their entry into adult roles, they resent their pre-cociousness, their tendency to earlier marriage and higher earnings:

> Adolescents whose overt behaviour is suitably non-adult can be *made*. They can be excluded from responsible participation in affairs, rewarded for dependency, penalized for inconvenient display of initiative and so rendered sufficiently irresponsible to conform to the prevailing teenage stereotype. They can be made (via the teenage culture) into ineffectual outsiders.

They are not just ineffectual outsiders and powerless (except in spending terms) but outsiders onto whom are projected a set of stereotypes which—as Edgar Friedenberg often notes—are similar to the stereotyping of all minority groups. The teeanger is given the same characteristics as the Negro: exuberant, lazy and irresponsible with brutality just below the surface ready to break out in violence, childish and sexually aggressive.

This leads on to the unnecessary element in the sociological picture: the apparent identification of the teenage culture with delinquency, particularly of the aggressive, destructive sort. A few years ago, the Rolling Stones put out a record, on the sleeve of which (eventually withdrawn) was the following: "Cast into your pockets for loot to buy this disc. . . . If you don't have the bread, see that blind man, knock him on the head, steal his wallet and lo and behold, you have the loot. If you put in the boot, good. Another one sold."

One sociologist commented on this as follows: "One could hardly summarize the values of the delinquent youth culture more aptly or more adequately illustrate their convergence with contemporary entertainment values." This view, stressing the total discontinuity between the conformist adult culture and the deviant youth culture is misconceived for a number of important reasons.

The first is that a mainstream of teenage entertainment culture is—and has been since its creation in the Fifties—basically conformist in character. It is conspicuous for its passivity rather than its aggressiveness, its continuity with adult values rather than its encouragement of deviance. The first official representatives of the pop culture—those whom Ray Gosling called the "Dream Boys" of the Fifties embodied (at the same time as their music was being denounced) highly conservative aspirations. Let me quote Nicholas Walters' remarks about the beginning of this age of the Ordinary Kid:

> The Ordinary Kid was born in a working class home around the time of our Finest Hour, brought up in a council house, taught in a secondary modern school, thrown out into a causeless world of affluence and opportunity (for other people), and left to look for his own dream by himself. He drifted about in the eddies of pop music, until he found his man and became a Dream Boy. . . . Tommy Hicks, the merchant seaman from Bermondsey, found John Kennedy and Larry Parnes, and became Tommy Steele. Terry Williams, the record packer from Newington, found Hyman Zahl, and became Terry Dene. Reg Smith, the timber hunker from Greenwich, found Larry Parnes, and became Marty Wilde. Ron Wycherley, the deck hand from Birkenhead found Larry Parnes, and became Billy Fury. Terry Nelhams, the film boy from Acton, found John Barry and Evelyn Taylor, and became Adam Faith. Harry Webb, the factory clerk from Cheshunt, found George Ganjou and Norrie Paramor and Jack Good, and became Cliff Richard.

And it was Cliff Richard, the first real pop figure in this country, who, at the height of his fame, proclaimed that his Number One person in all the world was Prince Philip.

This strand continued into the Sixties (Brian Epstein's autobiography is a good record of this progress) not so much through the

Beatles (in some ways an exception) but such figures as Gerry and the Pacemakers, Freddy and the Dreamers, Cilla Black. At the end of the Sixties the lineal descendents of the Ordinary Kids were Tom Jones, Lulu, Englebert Humperdinck. The disc jockey and underground sage John Peel sadly remarked a couple of years ago that "young people in Britain have little to choose between Tariq Ali on the one hand and Englebert Humperdinck on the other." There should be little doubt about the choice of the statistically typical teenager: the working class female, either still at school or at a secretarial course, or more probably working in a shop or factory. She found Tariq Ali irrelevant (and anyway thought he should go back where he came from), looked at students with more contempt than jealousy, didn't listen to Zappa or Leonard Cohen and found the intellectualized rock scene boring although she might now dance to the music, say, of Led Zeppelin, Deep Purple or Black Sabbath. While she might not have approved of his personal reincarnations, she would probably have agreed with John Lennon's description of avant garde as "French for bullshit." The stream that strikes a receptive note is the safely insulated, boy meets girl world of those weekly magazines, which, despite recent excursions into the risqué by such products as *Jackie* and *19*—are not far removed from the old days of *Mirabelle* and *Marilyn*.

Of course, not all pop culture is Tom Jones singing about the "Green, Green Grass of Home." The Underground *has* opened up, and although it has been swallowed up by pop rather than transcending it, this has meant that thousands of kids have been exposed to influences richer and more diverse than the Dream Boys could ever have dreamt of. Over the Sixties, groups such as the Who and the Rolling Stones emerged in a more complicated way and with very different messages. Jeff Nuttall has described this background well. These were student drop-outs or hard working class kids with few illusions, who had come to pop by way of rhythm and blues and some identification with American Negro street culture. They had been through what he calls the "Sick Period": the emptiness following the decline of the anti-bomb movement, passivity, avoiding work, disengagement, the first wave of amphetamine usage when swallowing a handful of bennies was all one could do. Here for the first time, the separate traditions of pop, protest and art begin their uneasy mixture.

I'm sure that Nuttall and others are right in seeing the significance of this development and no student of youth culture can ignore what is happening on the pages of *IT*, *OZ*, *Friends* and the rest. (Although he might we well advised to remember Mick Jagger's reply to a query about his views in an article about the Rolling Stones in *New Left Review*: "What's New Left Review?") But at this point the sociologist must part company with the cultural critic and ask just what these exciting developments mean to five million or so adolescents in Great Britain. The heady mixture of rhetoric and overgeneralization which commentators on the youth scene employ must be translated into the day to day life of this group. This means looking at the considerable variations across educational, social class and regional lines in terms of the exposure to and meaning of the values which to the insider are core values. In a university town like Durham, the heads and the hairies might find a little common ground with the politicos, but all these groups are miles away from the rest of the university population with their college culture, their apathy, and their conservatism (nearly 50 per cent of a sample of third year students we surveyed wanted stricter control on immigration)—and light years away from the skins and greasers of the town (who were not allowed to the dances in the students' building).

In his current study of working class boys in secondary moderns in Sunderland, Paul Corrigan has found a vast and so far inexplicable diversity even within an apparently homogeneous environment. In one school, the choice of favourite pop figures was in line with the continuity theme: the favourites were the Beatles, Tom Jones, Cliff Richard, Elvis Presley and the Hollies. In another very similar school, in a similar area only a few miles away, the choices were unambiguously: Deep Purple, Led Zeppelin, Black Sabbath and Jimi Hendrix— all heavy, new sounds (Tom Jones only got two votes here compared with Deep Purple's 24 and his 13 votes in the first school).

Evidence for this heterogeneity is immediately apparent and much recent sociological research has deepened our picture of normative diversity and how institutions such as the school perpetuate this. David Hargreaves, for example, in his recent study of a Northern Secondary Modern, shows how rigid this diversity is even within a school. In the boys' Second Year, there is little evidence of normative or subcultural differentiation within the streams. By the Fourth Year, the lines have hardened: the C and D stream boys have not absorbed any of the aspirations and values of the school; they see themselves as deprived of status; they are disliked by the teachers (who see them as "worthless louts" with whom they cannot afford to "waste time") and this feeling is reciprocated; they are given the worst teachers, who ridicule them and unfavourably compare them to the other boys (and they are aware of this discrimination: 73 per cent of the D stream boys compared with only 10 per cent of the A streamers gave negative responses to the question "Teachers here think of me as . . ."); they dislike the A and B stream boys, some whom in turn don't even speak to them; they are more likely to spend their time in the billiard hall or beat club rather than in any "constructive" leisure settings; they prefer the long haired, more rebellious pop groups, their occupational aspirations are lower—and they are more likely to be delinquent.

I will come back later to the connections with delinquency. Let me repeat the point that to assess the meaning of subcultural values to the individual, it is not enough to point to superficial adaptations and changes, for example, in picking up certain expressions or changing clothing styles. Wearing beads does not mean that one is on the verge of a transcendental experience; displaying a badge with the slogan "Make Love, Not War" need be neither an affirmation of pacifism nor an invitation to promiscuity; saying "Yeah, man" does not altogether imply an identification with the Negroes of Harlem. And this is not to speak of the groups who have not even made such symbolic changes: the kids such as those on the streets during Durham Miners Gala or on the beaches of resorts in the North-East (such as Seahouses) or North-West who are wearing shoddy Rocker or Teddy Boy gear and paper hats saying "Kiss Me Quick."

This is not to say that symbolic changes are insignificant, but if we are talking about aspirations (and frustrations) these are changes which take time to percolate through and their significance must be understood in terms of how they are mediated by day to day experience. There were kids who grew up on the early Dylan, but did not know what revolution he was on about, kids who knew the words of "Mother's Little Helper" off by heart, but did not know what they sang was a cynical reference to drugs, kids today who dance to music with little awareness of its "message" or cultural history; this applies to Tamla and to Reggae as well as to heavy rock. This is not to put these kids down: why should they know? What "education" has equipped them for such understanding? We should not expect the relationship between symbol and action to be too close and we should not be surprised if the same young men who have heard one of the 1970 hits, Blue Mink's "What we need is a great big melting pot" a few hundred times, go out of the disco and kick a Pakistani on the head.

The connections between mass culture and active delinquency are there, but need a more complex teasing out than simply extrapolating from message to action.

AN ABSURD SOLUTION

I want to condense a number of complicated arguments in this section. The first is that growing up in industrial society is absurd in the same sense that Paul Goodman meant fifteen years ago in [*Grow-Up Absurd*,] which is still the best book on the subject: "If there is nothing worth while, it is hard to do anything at all." The second is that because of the structural and normative diversity in our society, this problem is felt in ways which lead to contrasting solutions. For some groups, the solution moves in the direction of drugs, dropping out, traditional Bohemian values or (and today these two sometimes coalesce) political rebellion, while for others—the group we are concerned with—it takes the form of fringe delinquency of the smashing up type. The third argument is that for this last group, it is in the realm of leisure that the problem is eventually most acutely experienced.

While my backdrop is essentially that depicted by Paul Goodman, the specific scenario is derived directly from the work on delinquency in this country by David Downes, and given empirical detail in studies by Peter Willmott (in the East End of London) and David Hargreaves. The process is described by Downes as the *dissociation* of the working class adolescent from school and conventional middle class values and his entry into a low ceilinged, dead end job market.

A whole stream of boys (not necessarily all) in working class areas go through the school system without showing any allegiance to its values or absorbing the aspirations it tries to inculcate. "The school," to quote from an essay written by one of Willmott's boys, "was always trying to turn you into something you were not. It was a waste of time." For a few, this perception is tied up with some sort of conscious revolt against the school, but most realize the pointlessness of lashing out here and retreat into a sullen resentment of the rules of the game. Thus—from preliminary findings by Paul Corrigan from his research in Sunderland—most of the boys think that long hair should be allowed, that school uniforms should not have to be worn, that smoking should be allowed. But half the group accepted that teachers should punish boys for smoking. Nearly all the group thought that teachers didn't understand them and agreed that teachers didn't really care what happened to them—they were just doing a job.

As Hargreaves makes clear, while the boy is still at school he is powerless. The teachers make and apply the rules and little open rebellion against them can be sustained. The odd rule is broken, one is invariably detected and one is punished. The occasional arena for more active flouting of the rules is provided, for example by a weak teacher. The low stream boys reject the good pupil role—not just as Hargreaves suggests, because it is one he cannot succeed in or (later) is antithetical to delinquent values—but because it seems so absurd. Too much attention is placed on why the pupil identity is rejected rather than understanding what sort of identity is offered. If we think seriously about what is happening when boys who have jeans or long hair are ridiculed, punished, refused help in finding jobs and excluded from the Leavers' Service in the local church because of the unfavourable impression they would create, then we begin to understand Jules Henry's comment that "school metamorphoses a child, giving it the kind of self the school can manage, and then proceeds to minister to the self it has made." We should not be surprised if such ministrations are rejected, and we must expect these rejections to show outside the school, somewhere which offers a possibility of winning, or at least making a gesture.

As soon as possible the boys leave their secondary moderns. They fairly accurately perceive the implications for their future lives of the education they've received. They are being realistic. The scope is small for non-apprentices and their aspirations reflect this low ceilinged job market. As Downes says, they are not inherently disillusioned about jobs any more than they are about education, the jobs are also dull and tedious. Money is therefore, and quite rightly, just about the most important occupational criterion. There's no point in ambition if you're driving a van, working on a building site or doing an unskilled factory job. Downes quotes the memorable words of Mandy Rice-Davis: "Nobody made a bomb by plodding along in a dull job." Theoretically, they might want the job to be interesting, but they know it really won't be. As Goodman says, nobody asks whether jobs are useful, worthy, dignified, honourable. People don't think that way, they grow up realising that "during my productive years I will spend eight hours a day doing what is no good."

These feelings obviously cross class and educational lines, and Goodman's diatribe against American society fifteen years ago is painfully obvious to many young people in Britain today:

> . . . young people grow up convinced that everything is done
> with mirrors, by "influence." Not even the personal influence
> of nepotism, but something more like the astrological influence
> of the planets. The sense of initiative, causality skill has been
> discouraged. Merit is a trait of "personality." Learning is the
> possession of a Diploma. Usefulness is a Union Card. Justification is Belonging.

Now however pervasive these feelings are—and I have little doubt that they will become increasingly apparent—the problem is more acute for the group we are interested in. If current trends in technology and the American experience are any guides, some of this group will simply be unemployable in a few decades. There are also differential modes of coping according to the person's position in the system and his chances in life. Students, for example—many of whom are more cynical (or sensitive?) than we give them credit for—see some of this, but murmur "what the hell" and immerse themselves in career aspirations, perhaps hoping to do something "useful" in their spare time. Others, who perceive accurately enough that they are being used and conned, draw some consolation from their future "prospects" and find plenty of momentary distraction— Charities Week, Rag, Rectorial Elections, politics on the level of getting another representative on the catering committee. Yet others rage a bit longer and take the Hippy trail, but with defeat already in their shoulder bags. Others take their politics and culture very seriously and join earnest left wing groups and/or hang up posters of Ché, Marx and Trotsky alongside those of Lennon, Brando and Raquel Welch.

And so on. In Goodman's paradigm, life seems an apparently closed room, in which there is a large rat race as the dominant centre of attention. Some will run the race; some will be disqualified from running, but hang around because there is nowhere else to go; some will run a race of their own, not on the official tracks; some will start, but break down and drop out; some will be more genuinely resigned and don't want to or don't have the heart to start; some will smash and track and shoot the starter; some will stand aside as spectators and comment cynically on the race. . . .

For working class kids in this country over the last fifteen years or so, not all these options have been open and one significant element—the mass teenage leisure culture—has pointed to new aspirations, but aspirations which are difficult to fulfill. Although the more traditional leisure preoccupations such as football and the more esoteric ones (such as the juvenile jazz bands of the North-East) are still strong they cannot on the whole compete with the glossy commercial image. The conventional youth service is equally unappealing and with few honourable and well-known (and mostly short-lived) exceptions it has never freed itself from its patronizing image or has simply not been what the kids want. Involvement in political or community work (V.S.O., Task Force and so on) has never been the option it has been to their middle class peers—even in a transitory or uncommitted way. Direct satisfaction through education or occupation is, as we've seen, precluded, and anyway not aspired to.

So only the town is left and here the group that asks the most gets the least. Opportunities for excitement, autonomy or, less ambitiously, a simple sense of *action*, are blocked. Either there is nothing there—in some housing estates, in towns round about the 50,000 population mark, in the less glamourous outer suburbs of large cities—or what is there, is drab and mediocre. What the young persons wants—or what the Message tells him he should want to want—cannot be reached. He doesn't have enough money to fully participate even vicariously, he doesn't have the talent, luck or contacts to really make it directly. The golden years of the Ordinary Kid are over and even those success stories look a bit jaded.

Faced by leisure goals he cannot reach, with little commitment or attachment to others and lacking a sense of any control over his future, his situation contains an edge of desperation. These are the feelings that David Matza identifies in his account of the drift into delinquency. This mood of fatalism, of seeing oneself as effect rather than cause, of being pushed around (in school, in work, at home) does not "determine" but is conducive to this drift. Rather than accept all this, rather than do nothing, one "manufactures excitement," one "makes things happen," one exploits situations. It is precisely this form which so much fringe delinquency in Britain over the last two decades has taken.

To anticipate an obvious criticism of this perspective, I don't think it reads into a situation things which the participants are unaware of, or endows them with an absent sophistication. The kids hanging around the street corners, Wimpies or amusement arcades who tell you that they want to do "nothing" should be taken at their face value. The Mods that we knew in the middle Nineteen Sixties were all too aware of the absurdity both of their problem and their solution. These were two responses on the Brighton beach:

> A journalist asked an Eltham boy whether he was enjoying himself. "Not really." Why did he come then, when this was all he knew he could find? "There's nothing to do in London." But what is there doing anywhere that you'd like to do? "Well, if you put it like that, there isn't."

> I asked a boy from Walthamstow why he'd come down. "Well, we're bored at home, so it's a change to come down here and be bored at Brighton."

These were sharp, stylish Mods, nearly as aware of themselves as their archetypal hero Pete Townshend (to my mind one of the few pop figures ever to have understood the values of the group they've symbolized). I do not want to suggest that the same awareness or process of drift will be found among, say, the skinheads of today or the greasers of the *News of the World* episode. But some variant of this constellation of dissociation and the subsequent quest for action and control in late adolescence, is there. It should be stressed that this stress is transitory: depending on opportunity, action by control agents and other contingencies, some might find their way into career crime, others—a handful—might develop some political consciousness. For the rest, as the Situationists express it, ". . . the lure of the product world proves too strong, and the hooligan decides to do his honest day's work: to this end a whole sector of production is devoted specifically to his recuperation. Clothes, discs, guitars, scooters, transistors, purple hearts to beckon him to the land of the consumer."

Two further dimensions might be added to this constellation. The first is Downes' argument that in addition to being originally aimed at the working class teenager, the leisure culture—or at least one important stream of it—represents working class culture transmuted to meet age-specific needs and styles. Each of what Walter Miller called the "focal concerns of working class culture" is mirrored in some leisure value. These include: (i) trouble: being on the look-out for trouble (aggro), how to steer clear of trouble with teachers and police, how to deal with it when it occurs. In the leisure culture this is reflected in concerns to stay cool, to avoid being bugged and in the drug version, the folklore about busts; (ii) *toughness*: in the traditional form, this was concerned with physical strength, compulsive masculinity and still takes this strong form in punitiveness towards queers, hippies, hairies, and other passive deviants. In the weak form, it is to be found in the pop culture's cynicism and stress on remaining uncommitted; (iii) *excitement*: this is obviously mirrored in adult phrases such as "doing it for kicks." In a weaker sense the leisure culture stresses the need to come alive, to be moved: to get stoned, smashed, turned on, high, all of which phrases have broader connotations than the strictly drug references; (iv) fate: the traditional stress on luck, lucky numbers coming up, things being in the stars is mirrored superficially in the romance oriented versions of the pop scene. More fundamentally, this sense of an "astrological influence of the planets" reflects the lack of personal control in one's destiny.

The point of Downes' argument here is not to stress the autonomous influence of symbolic communications, but to note the simultaneous dependence of the working class adolescent on the traditional culture and its teenage variants. To repeat: because he has low job aspirations and because he endorses traditional working class values, does not mean that the boy is content with his lot. He does not simply opt out of the work ethic, but has to insulate himself against what Downes calls the harsh implication of the creed which enjoins him either to "better himself" or "accept his station in life."

The deflection of aspirations into non-work, is of course not confined to the working class, to delinquents, or to adolescents. This leads on to a second dimension—particularly relevant in regard to vandalism and hooliganism as opposed to delinquency as a whole—the existence of what Matza and Sykes call subterranean values. Certain values and aspirations (the same ones ascribed by Veblen to the leisure classes) such as search for kicks, disdain of work and routine, the desire for the "big kill," the acceptance of toughness as a proof of masculinity, are hidden and insulated just below the surface of many conventional values. They are publicly denounced, but viewed in private with ambivalence and tolerated in stylized forms (the Hemingway hero, the gangster movie, the James Bond cult) or rise to the surface on ritual occasions. Acting out delinquency, in this view, is not so much an inversion of the middle class ethic as a caricature of it. Again though—as in our discussion of pop culture—we must note that the postulation of some general values only makes sense alongside the existence of differentiated opportunities and options.

BREAKING OUT AND SMASHING UP

Using the examples of the Teddy Boys and the Mods and Rockers, I have tried to show elsewhere how such folk devils are created by society. My interest here is less in how deviant actions become attached to particular social types, with ready-made labels such as hooligan, vandal and thug, but how a specific class of rule breaking—property destruction, rowdyism, breaking the place up—might be connected to the social trends so far depicted. In what senses are these rules the "right" ones to break?

This form of rule breaking is probably the most pervasive of all among children and adolescents. No property seems immune from destruction or defacement: trains and railway installations, buses, telephone kiosks, street lamps, bus shelters, cars, schools, parks, golf

courses, statues, dance halls, churches, cemeteries, public con-
veniences, sports grounds. Although the answers might seem obvious
enough, it is important to see why such damage is seen as problematic:
the societal response to deviance, and the perception or anticipation
by the deviant group of this response is built into the nexus which
affects the behaviour.

Societal interests and values are concerned with both the real
and symbolic value of the property. The real value is measured by
such indices as the cost of repairing the damage or replacing the
property and the cost of preventive measures. The symbolic value is
represented by the threat to the ethics, obligations and rights surrounding the possession of property. More specific problems are
posed in terms of inconvenience, annoyance, demoralization and
danger.

Vandalism presents further threats because of its stereotype of
being wanton and pointless. Even the mischievous play element in
some vandalism is threatening as it represents the fun morality (very
much a subterranean tradition) at its crudest. Vandalism is seen as an
inversion of the Puritan ethic which demands that action is carried
out for a recognizable utilitarian reason. The results of smashing
up—and when it takes place in public settings, the actions themselves—are physically visible, in the sense that, say, theft or fraud
are not. In a passage in *The Naked Lunch*, Burroughs catches perfectly a society's horrific vision of uncontrolled adolescent behaviour. Note how many acts of "perfectly" vicious and defiant
vandalism are included:

> Rock and Roll adolescent hoodlums storm the streets of all
> nations. They rush into the Louvre and throw acid in the Mona
> Lisa's face. They open zoos, insane asylums, prisons, burst
> water mains with air hammers, chop the floor out of passenger
> plane lavatories, shoot out light-houses, file elevator cables to
> one thin wire, turn sewers into the water supply, throw sharks
> and sting rays, electric eels and candiru into swimming pools.
> . . . in nautical costumes ram the "Queen Mary" full speed into
> New York Harbor, play chicken with passenger trains and buses,
> rush into hospitals in white coats carrying saws and axes and
> scalpels three feet long; throw paralytics out of iron lungs . . .
> administer injections with bicycle pumps, disconnect artificial
> kidneys, saw a woman in half with a two-man surgical saw,
> they drive herds of squealing pigs into the curb, they shit on
> the floor of the United Nations and wipe their ass with treaties,
> pacts, alliances. . . .

The "fusion of versatility and malice" (as sociologists have more
prosaically described delinquency) has always been taken as the
characteristic of vandalism. Thrasher's classic study of delinquency
in the Twenties contains the following example:

We did all kinds of dirty tricks for fun. We'd see a sign,
"Please keep the street clean," but we'd tear it down and say,
"We don't feel like keeping it clean." One day we put a can
of glue in the engine of a man's car. We would always tear
things down. That would make us laugh and feel good, to have
so many jokes.

Examples of this sort could be multiplied: pouring acid on car
roofs; pulling out all the flowers of floral clocks; strangling swans
in ornamental lakes; slashing the tyres of all the cars in a car park;
stripping the insulation round water mains; dumping the manhole
covers in a sewerage farm; putting matches in the tyre valves of
police cars (which causes the tyre to leak, and when it gets hot, the
match ignites); throwing life belts into the sea; placing sleepers on
railway lines; throwing stones at the drivers of passing trains; urinating
in public telephone receivers; defecating in the lifts of council flats;
pouring dye or acid into swimming baths; sabotaging the engines of
children's miniature trains; ripping out lavatory chains in public con-
veniences; placing bicycle chains on railway overhead wires to cause
short circuits. . . .

The edge of impotent rage rather than "fun" is shown in the
following example:

Using the hatchet from the emergency tool kit, four youths
smashed or tore off the following objects in fourteen parked
train coaches: 228 windows, 128 compartment mirrors and
picture glasses, 86 window blinds, 38 window straps, 190
electric light bulbs and 8 fire extinguishers.

In all such examples the motivation is diffuse and ambiguous
and we need to know more about each situation before consigning it
to a particular category. In some cases, the element of hostility is
more apparent and fun might be a secondary component, or, particularly in a large group situation, apparent to the actors well after the
action has been initiated. In other cases, the game element may be
primary. In some cases the act is intentionally designed to cause
serious damage or injury, in other cases, the actor might be hardly
aware of the consequences of what he has done. The difference is
often one of age. There are two peaks, the one at about 12 which
tends to be of the play type, while the next, among the 16-19 group
takes place in the more general context of rowdyism and is usually—
and quite rightly—seen to be more malicious and difficult to explain.
The recollections of this 15 year old boy in Willmott's East End
group, give some idea of this sequence:

When you're a little kid, you smash up the things people chuck
on the bomb sites, like old baths, old prams, old boxes and
that. And motor cars—there's always old motor vans on the
bomb sites that the kids smash up. At first they think that the
bits they pull off are going to be useful for something, but when

they get them off there's always something wrong with them, say some bracket won't come off, so they do some more smashing up. It goes in crazes. After that we used to smash up builder's boards and "House to Let" notices. We didn't do it very much, but I know for a time we was pulling up those "House to Let" boards, and we used to dump them in the canal or in the Victoria Park Lane. I don't know why we did it; it was for a giggle.

It is this latter type that I am interested in here. Phrases such as "doing it for a giggle" should be taken seriously, not just for the element of malice they contain but for their indication that behaviour which on the surface is meaningless and non-utilitarian, is responsive, directed and makes sense to the actor. At the most elementary level, the reason for vandalism being the chosen mode of attack is that it is simple and safe: no skills are required, there is seldom a personal victim at hand to retaliate, there is no property to dispose of, technological innovations as the aerosol spray and felt tipped pen have helped things, there is overall little chance of being detected.

Vandalism is not only easy, but it can also be particularly satisfactory. The oft-quoted lines about "the taste of the upper classes/for the sound of broken glasses" conveys something of this enjoyment, which is not altogether inconsistent with stressing the mood of desperation behind some vandalism. Consider the following examples from life in the merchant navy:

... we brushed bucketloads of rust under the bends in L-shaped girders, and in the furthermost corners we brushed nothing at all. It would all come out when the next cargo of petrol was delivered, and we sincerely hoped that it would give engine trouble to every motorist who used it in his car; if it ruined their engines altogether, that would be all the better.

When sailors are loading stores and accidentally let a sling load crash on to the wharf below, their action is usually one of suppressed glee rather than sorrow. Deck crews who are driven too hard can quite calmly paint over oil and water and take a malicious delight in doing so. All these private acts of hostility happen directly, without premeditation, without going through the formal process of making a complaint and getting no satisfaction: the seamen know the futility of making formal complaints and save themselves the time.

Such illustrations are perhaps too specific to be generalized. General theories of vandalism tend to vacillate between the poles of "wholly deliberate" or "wholly determined." The first type, perhaps more the layman's version, sees the behaviour arising out of a volitional perversity to destroy. Usually this desire is seen to be affected by a vague social malaise: breakdown in discipline, decline of national character, loss of respect for property and so on. The other view— more the social scientist's—sees the behaviour as wholly determined, particularly by psychological forces. The actor has no choice. The merchant navy illustrations, I think, make clear that neither view is particularly satisfactory: any account has to recognize the spontaneous and situational factors in vandalism, but also the setting in which it occurs and the social processes which are involved in the action.

The dominant context is the leisure one and we have already seen some of the structural reasons why this should be so. If one is looking for toughness, excitement, action then school and work (although as Laurie Taylor and Paul Walton have shown, this might be the setting for industrial sabotage generated by other important reasons), do not provide the right arenas. One deliberately enters into situations which provide real testing grounds, where the action is, where risks have to be taken. Here one plays what Goffman has called "character contests." These are ways of seeing who will have the honour and character to rise above the situation. James Dean, of course, was the classic player, the real pro. Action gets restructured around the familiar settings of street, sports ground, the weekend by the sea, railway stations. These are given new meanings by being made stages for these games. Vandalism is ideally suited for this: it is a perfect activity to raise the stakes, to make things more contrived. Thus one sprays acid on a whole street of parked cars, one waits for the last possible minute to do what could have been done easily.

If the stakes are raised in public, so much the better. This is a way not just of increasing risks of being observed and detected, but of deliberately provoking, of making a gesture. If the burglars of the town are outraged, this is just the point. I don't want to endow such gestures with a spurious meaning: the greasers descending on a dead coastal resort or hanging around a motorway cafe are not holy barbarians, White Negroes, hipsters making some existential gesture in the void. But they are only some distance from this. We must be wary of only allowing the more glamorous deviant an ideological interpretation and contemptuously dismissing the others through phrases which deny their actions any meaning.

Some of these public settings are more suitable than others. Indeed certain situations—cinemas showing a rock and roll film during the Fifties, beaches at Bank Holiday weekends during the middle Sixties, outdoor concerts, football matches—have either traditionally been defined as the escape valves through which subterranean values can be expressed (having a fling, letting your hair down) or become defined (particularly through the media) as places where violence is expected. Violence is somehow built into the situation. These crowd settings are particularly important for young people: adults find it difficult to understand that for a whole generation, just simply being in a crowd, is something, a form of action.

A final particular feature of smashing up is that it is very prone to unintentional elaboration. In a group context—particularly a large crowd, facing cameras, police and spectators—it is not difficult to go beyond one's original intention. This type of group contagion is not a mysterious or pathological process. In some cases it contains elements of what has been called group psychological intoxication: "the way people act when they go to a convention in somebody else's town." More generally one finds mutual suggestibility, the impression of "universality" (the perception that everyone else is doing it) and a high susceptibility because of the ambiguity of the situation, to rumours. These serve to focus on a particular target ("there's some skinheads moving into our pub") or validate a course of action ("they had it coming, you should have seen what they were doing").

SOME SORT OF CONCLUSION

I have so far talked about problems and solutions. Perhaps "escape" or "gesture" would be better than "solution." For smashing up, is a precarious, ugly and in the long run, not a particularly satisfying way out. But it is better than nothing. For a moment, it is a way of staking a claim to an identity other than that which you've been offered. It is not so much a release from commitment, because there is so little commitment there in the first place. It is self-defeating not just because as an alternative identity it is precarious, but because it just confirms what people think about you anyway: you are a thug and a hooligan who has rejected the opportunities that society has so munificently provided for you.

At the beginning of this essay, I noted the tendency to perceive not just violence and vandalism, not just adolescent violence and vandalism, but adolescence itself as a social problem. This problem is typically explained as if it had some autonomous existence. It is not understood that adolescence itself is a creation of industrial society and the attribution to it of problem status sometimes tells us more about the society than the problem. Further, the shape the problem takes is crucially affected by the way society reacts to particular manifestations of rule breaking.

These patterns have yet to be fully explained. Sociologists in their roles as observers—the cynical commentators standing on the touchline—direct their criticism correctly but incompletely at two sorts of responses. The first is the sheer punitive one ("I don't consider myself an unreasonable sort of man, but these thugs want birching") and this manning of the moral barricades is dismissed because of its failure to try to understand. This dismissal is incomplete because it too, fails to understand: what are the roots in terms of community and political conflict, power and ideology of such moral indignation and what is its effect?

The other criticism—incomplete because of our unawareness of when we do it ourselves—is directed towards the romantic attitudes. Wallowing in the youth culture, going native by adopting the poses and symbols as if they were one's own, is at best misleading and at worst ludicrous.

What is the sociologist's own response—not just to smashing up but to the whole range of drugs, hippies, political radicalism? Too often it is in terms of "identity crisis," "role confusion," "generation gap," "undersocialization," "failure of communication." But perhaps —as Paul Goodman says—there has not been a failure of communication. Perhaps the social message has been communicated all too clearly and has been found unacceptable. It is hard for adults to realize this, even when they are told it in articulate, literate and politically sophisticated terms; it is harder still if they are told in a muffled and ugly way.

AFTERWORD

This paper was originally prepared for a book on youth work and leisure and aimed primarily at an audience of youth workers. This accounts for the style: unacademic, somewhat polemical and more than a little thin conceptually. It was written at the beginning of 1971 and this—in a subject area such as youth culture—accounts for it being so touchingly out of date. The *Working Papers'* editors have convinced me that it is worth publishing completely unchanged (only the references have been up-dated) and to rescue it from the status of a quaint historical relic have allowed me to make these few observations. They are confined to problems other than those of simply incorporating developments in contemporary pop culture over the last three years, although this is no easy task in the light of phenomena as diverse as David Bowie, the Osmonds, Alice Cooper and the extraordinary difficulty now of finding any sort of identity in the current stagnation of pop culture.

1   The paper was far too pre-occupied with unravelling the connections between the mass leisure culture and a particular form of delinquency. Although these connections were located in the overall educational and class contexts, this location was not explicit enough. If writing on the subject again, I would want to take into account the more finely drawn research on the actual uses of pop culture in the school setting, especially the work of Graham Murdock and his colleagues[1] and—to be faithful to my concern expressed elsewhere[2]—to be much more careful in placing the interaction in specific local settings and traditions. On this latter point the work of Armstrong and Wilson in the Easterhouse estate of Glasgow,[3] *some* of the work of Patrick, also in Glasgow[4] and more recently Parker's fine research in the Roundhouse area of Liverpool[5] all reinforce the need to see delinquency in terms of total life styles and local traditions.

2   A related point—one of considerable theoretical density and not just a matter of "taking into account" further

research—is connected with the current work at the Centre for Contemporary Cultural Studies on the development of youth cultures in post-war Britain. My paper wholly glosses over the complex links between history and subjective experience or (more concretely in this case) the links on the one side between the history of youth subcultures and their articulation in the dominant culture and on the other, their intrusion into the individual's biography. It remains to be seen whether current work on skinheads, Teddy Boys, hippies and the like can do justice to both these forms of analysis.

3   One link between history and subjective experience implicit in the paper is that which can be made through the conceptual apparatus of accounts theory, derived from Mills' critical article on the sociology of motivation.[6] The work being currently carried out by Laurie Taylor and myself in this area has tried to be much more careful than my "Breaking Out" paper is in extricating the meaning of individual actors' statements of their own motivation. Although I would want to retain the emphasis on showing how society only allows what I called the "more glamorous deviant" an ideological meaning, we are somewhat more sceptical of our earlier attempts in this field which might have led to the spurious attribution of such qualities. The reverse problem is also apparent: in trying to normalize forms of deviance by rescuing them from the clutches of positivist criminology and the grosser stereotypes of the media and control agents, one might miss those cases— and certain forms of breaking out and smashing up are included—in which the rejection of everyday life is more noteworthy than the institutionalized, almost banal, features of the deviance on which I laid such great stress.

NOTES

1   See, for example, Graham Murdock and Guy Phelps, "Youth Culture and the School Revisited," *British Journal of* Sociology, Vol. XXIII, No. 4, December 1972, 478-482.

2   S. Cohen, "Directions for Research in Adolescent Group Violence and Vandalism," *British Journal of Criminology*, October 1971, 319-340.

3   Gail Armstrong and Mary Wilson, "City Politics and Deviancy Amplification" in I. Taylor and L. Taylor (eds.), *Politics and Deviance*, (Penguin, 1973).

4   James Patrick, *A Glasgow Gang Observed*, (Eyre Methuen, 1973).

5   Howard Parker, "The Catseye Kings: Some Notes on the Delinquent Careers of a Down Town Adolescent Network." Paper given at 14th National Deviancy Conference, September 1973 and *The View from the Boys*, (David and Charles, forthcoming).

6   C. Wright Mills, "Situated Actions and Vocabularies of Motive," *American Sociological Review*, Vol. 5, December 1940.

MAIN REFERENCES

Cohen, S. "Who Are the Vandals?" *New Society*, 12th December, 1968.

———*Folk Devils and Moral Panic: The Creation of the Mods and Rockers* (MacGibbon and Kee, 1972).

———"Property Destruction: Motives and Meanings" in Colin Ward (ed.), *Vandalism* (Architectural Press, 1973).

Downes, D. *The Delinquent Solution* (Routledge, 1966).

Friedenberg, E. Z. "The Image of the Adolescent Minority," *Dissent*, Spring 1973.

Goffman, E. *Where The Action Is* (Doubleday and Co., 1967).

Goodman, P. *Growing Up Absurd* (Random House, 1956).

Hargreaves, D. *Social Relations in a Secondary School* (Routledge, 1967).

———"The Delinquent Subculture and the School" in W. G. Carson and P. Wiles (eds.) *Crime and Delinquency in Britain* (Martin Robinson, 1971).

Henry, J. *Culture Against Man* (Tavistock, 1966).

Matza, D. and Sykes, G. "Delinquency and Subterranean Values," *American Sociological Review*, October 1961.

Matza, D. *Delinquency and Drift* (Wiley, 1964).

Musgrave, F. *Youth and the Social Order* (Routledge, 1964).

Nuttal, J. *Bomb Culture* (Paladin, 1968).

Rock, P. and Cohen, S. "The Teddy Boy" in V. Bogdanor and R. Skidelski (eds.) *The Age of Affluence: 1951-1964* (Macmillan, 1970).

Situationist International. "Of Student Poverty" (1968).

Taylor, L. and Walton, P. "Industrial Sabotage: Motives and Meanings" in S. Cohen (ed.) *Images of Deviance* (Penguin, 1971).

Walters, N. "The Young One," *Anarchy*, May 1963.

Willmott, P. *Adolescent Boys of East London* (Routledge, 1966).

Marginal Youth and Social Policy

HERMAN SCHWENDINGER and
JULIA R. SCHWENDINGER

Herman Schwendinger and Julia R. Schwendinger are professors of sociology at the University of Nevada, Las Vegas.

Reprinted from Herman Schwendinger and Julia R. Schwendinger, "Marginal Youth and Social Policy," *Social Problems*, Vol. 24, No. 2, pp. 184-191.

THE PROCESSES OF MARGINALIZATION

Whether it includes behavior inside or outside of school, the most sustained official reactions to delinquency usually involve a marginal population of youth, that has existed since the early centuries of capitalism. In those early centuries, however, many marginal youth were integrated within a larger population, composed of unemployed or subemployed laborers and debt-ridden artisans and farmers (Schwendinger and Schwendinger, 1976). Prior to the 19th century, marginals were originally produced and then "chastized for their enforced transformation into vagabonds and paupers," before manufacturing establishments could absorb their labor power (Marx, 1959:731-734). The process of marginalization subsequently annihilated urban artisanry and filled the debtors prisons with artisans bankrupted by the rise of pre-industrial manufactories and the domestic cottage industries. Afterward, the expansion of industrialism marginalized the toilers who had worked within the cottage industries. Simultaneously, this expansion absorbed millions of other marginals while it was producing a relative surplus population. With the rise of monopoly-capitalism, this population was generally restricted to the secondary labor market.

Long-term trends toward stagnation, also a characteristic of modern capitalist societies, inevitably occur and have only been overcome periodically. In colonial and semi-colonial capitalist societies, the effects of these trends on marginalization are particularly evident. Marginals in Venezuela, for instance, constitute almost one third of the population. The agrarian marginals live on subsistence payments or work without explicit wages. On the edges of the cities, rural migrants and urban marginals, who are underemployed, intermittently employed, and just plain unemployed, live in rat-infested slums. Some of these persons are employed in part-time or otherwise unproductive jobs, largely concentrated in the inflated tertiary sector (Hein and Stenzal, 1973). These persons are the menial "service workers" or the "penny capitalists," who desperately shift for themselves by scavenging, huckstering, working at odd jobs, and performing a variety of personal services for minimal payments.

The United States is also beset by long-term trends toward stagnation. The American economy no longer expands sufficiently to absorb most of its technologically displaced labor force—much less the new generations of workers. The rate of absorption has only surged for short periods during wartime or during a post-war boom. Generally the younger, the older, and the most oppressed workers have been excluded from the labor market. Millions have become marginal. From an economic standpoint, these persons at any given time are either absolutely or relatively superfluous.

Advanced capitalism prolongs the dependent status of youth. This prolongation elevates the theoretical importance of certain factors in the socialization agencies, which include the family, yet center on the modern school. These factors, as we shall see, uniquely recreate the process of marginalization *within* the socialization agencies themselves.

Analysis of the family and the school indicates that significant economic functions, which undoubtedly effect delinquent relations, are performed by these agencies. Most socialization agencies concentrate on youth who will generally become proletarians and who, therefore, require certain types of services for the production of their labor power. These services are largely provided by parents and by teachers, whose efforts are exerted in the family and the school. With regard to the reproduction of their labor power both socialization agencies seem to operate separately while, in fact, they are quite interdependent.

Various kinds of interdependent relations characterize these agencies: obviously, a child's success in school is dependent upon other family relations. Empirical studies also indicate that the family is a stronger determinant of the child's eventual "success" as a labor force participant. But *determination* of individual success cannot be equated with *domination* of the general standards which regulate successful striving. The family is forced to regulate its own productive relations according to the meritocratic and technical standards exerted by the school. For the long-term reproduction of labor power, therefore, the school is the dominating agency.

The reproductive relations in the school are in turn largely dominated by industrial relations. Social scientists have clearly demonstrated that educational standards "correspond" to the hierarchical and segmented organization of the labor force (Bowles and Gintis, 1973). The standards used to reward and punish a student's behavior within the school, therefore, are synchronized with the standards that are used by managers to control workers.

The reproductive relations within the family are also dominated by industry, but this form of domination is partly mediated by the school. As indicated, the school, in spite of appearances, essentially organizes its production relations around industrially related standards. By dominating production relations within the family, the school as well as industry imposes these standards upon parents and children.

At least two general consequences flow from these serial relations of domination. First, the reproductive relations within socialization agencies are synchronized with the alienated social relations that generally characterize commodity production. These synchronized relations are not confined to the youngsters who are in the process of acquiring the power to labor. They include both the parents and the teachers, who are involved in the long-term production of this commodity.

Second, these dominating relations are expressed in the same general laws of investment and profit maximization which culminate in the uneven development of various groups and nations (Bluestone, 1972). This means investments in the development of the labor force are allocated unevenly. Such investments concentrate on those groups of persons considered to have a greater potentiality for meeting the meritocratic criteria prevailing in educational institutions. Conversely, unless political struggles broaden educational policies, the investments of private or public resources—calculable in terms of money, equipment, facilities, faculties, and even in the teacher's time, attention, and expectations—will be minimal for the development of those groups of persons who do not appear to meet these criteria.

Consequently, the allocation of educational resources favors the youth who have already been the recipients of superior resources. They are recipients because of the advantages that are passed on to the members of certain ethnic, racial, or occupational strata, or because of the compensatory time and energy expended on them by self-sacrificing parents. During the elementary school period, a mutually reinforcing relationship is established between the activities of youth who show the productive signs of superior familial investments, and the patterns for selectively allocating resources within educational institutions. Throughout the child's formative period, educational capital continuously builds on the most favored students.

Simultaneously, the competitive position of the least favored students deteriorates and a process, analogous to marginalization within the economy, occurs in the context of the school and the family. This inherently contradictory trend results in anarchic behavior patterns, created by students who are not strongly motivated to achieve, and who do not make any disciplined effort to achieve. These are also the students who actually do not achieve the cognitive traits that generally favor sustained labor force participation in the future. Although their chances for future employment are somewhat independent of their status in socialization agencies, these children manifest early in life the adaptive characteristics that evolve in capitalism among numerous owners of the least valuable forms of labor power.

Thus, the relations that favor the uneven development of labor power early in life generate a youthful population of *prototypic* marginals, whose status is not actually determined directly by economic institutions. The members of this population are not usually counted among "the employed" or "the unemployed." Instead, they are usually regarded as students and, during most of their adolescent years, workaday life is very far from their minds.

Within communities across the United States, adolescents speak about these prototypic marginals. Such names as Greaser, Vato, Dude, Honcho, Hodad, and Hood appear whenever they are mentioned in conversations. These metaphors refer to individual marginals and, among other social regularities in their personal behavior, to their personal behavior, to their conduct, carriage, attitudes, gestures, grooming, argot, clothing, and delinquent acts.

The marginalization process under discussion is not directly determined by labor market relations. Here the term "marginal" simply refers to the "prototypic" rather than labor force marginal. The effects of this process will therefore be reflected in family and school relationships, but they are not classified by any official economic category.

It is taken for granted that certain types of family conflicts or "breakdowns" will definitely enhance the possibilities of marginalization. But these possibilities are also mediated by parental resources. Wealthy families can employ such "absorption mechanisms" as psychiatric counseling, boarding school, and the tutorial trip abroad to cushion the effects of family disturbance on the child. If these mechanisms are unsuccessful, then their wealth further provides children who are becoming marginalized with a second chance later in life. Some of these children, in fact, never have to concern themselves with labor market activity: they can be sustained by inherited property.

By contrast, working class families are exposed to greater hardships and difficulties. Absorption mechanisms are relatively unavailable and family problems directly influence the parents' and child's active contribution to the production of the child's labor power. They interact with the already disadvantaged competitive relations engendered by the school.

Consequently, traditional socio-economic attributes, such as the parents' income, education, and property, which represent the most widespread family characteristics, directly effect the likelihood of marginalization. Because of the long-term effects of the uneven development of capital, a greater proportion of marginal youth can be expected among lower status families. Alternatively, marginalization can certainly be expected among *higher* status families (or among "middle class" families), but to a lesser degree. This observation is important, because the literature on "middle class" delinquency has glossed over the differences between marginal "middle class" delinquents and *other* types of delinquents.

Let us now consider youth who, from the standpoint of the school, represent the most highly developed forms of labor power. As high academic achievers, they strikingly epitomize the division of labor among mental and manual workers in capitalist societies. They are usually very articulate, and some have broad interests in politics, culture, and science. Others, noted for their narrow academic and technical interests, symbolize how much young personalities have been influenced by the extreme labor force segmentation among mental workers. Their personal interests are "overspecialized," and they are organized largely by experiences based on the appropriation and dispensation of technical knowledge.

In this work, the term "prototypic intellectuals" will be used to characterize the youth mentioned above. The word "intellectual" classifies those persons who devote their occupational activities to the formulation of ideas, to the creation of artistic representations of ideas, or to the application of ideas, such as the application of scientific-technical knowledge to human affairs. The development of modern intellectuals can be traced back to the early capitalist period. But this development has been accelerated enormously by expansion of monopoly capitalism and the modern state (Schwendingers, 1974:

143-158, 360-361). Today the category of intellectuals includes writers, artists, librarians, social workers, city planners, teachers, and scientists.

The prototypic intellectual, on the other hand, refers to youth showing the personal interests and characteristics generated among adults by the developments mentioned above. Historically, educational institutions have played a very important role in regulating the formation of this particular population. Certain families, however, have contributed candidates disproportionately. Bourgeois families, including the small farmers as well as independent professions, have supplied the greatest proportions. In recent years, the established families of such "mental workers" as teachers, technicians, and scientists, also contribute relatively higher numbers of prototypic intellectuals.

On the other hand, because of bourgeois educational policies and the intergenerational effects of uneven investment, young women, youth of both sexes who belong to racially oppressed groups, and children of unskilled workers become candidates to a less degree. It has been chiefly the white families of higher socio-economic status that have established a mutually dependent relation with the school. The children of families that *have* more *get* more, because the public educational system converts human beings into potential commodities and builds upon *that* human material which already has considerable investment.

In communities across the United States, one finds that metaphors for this latter youth also appear in peer conversations. Included among these names are Intellectual, Brain, Pencil-Neck, Egg Head, Book Worm, and Walking Encyclopedia (See Schwendingers, forthcoming). For now, it should be noted that by contrast with many marginals, these youth are paragons of virtue. In fact, they are foremost members of the least delinquent population in a local society of youth.

SOCIAL POLICY

What social policies are required for the elimination of marginalization, uneven development and delinquency? Unfortunately, a theory of fundamental causes cannot provide either quick or direct answers to this question. Social policy formulation requires more than a causal theory. The level of the productive forces and hence the actual resources available in a given society must be considered. Conflicts over resources are also important. In fact, among the general determinants of social policies, class forces and political conflicts over control of these resources are most important.

In our opinion, an examination of both fundamental causes and social policy determinants lead to but one conclusion. The best possibilities for eliminating marginalization, uneven development, and delinquency exist in socialist societies. This conclusion, however, cannot be applied universally because socialist nations diverge in the course of their development, and the divergences have retrogressive as well as progressive consequences. Furthermore, some socialist nations, such as Yugoslavia, still retain anarchic market systems, which produce marginalization. Nevertheless, genuine socialist developments are numerous and they counter marginalization, uneven development, and delinquency.

As socialist societies overcome the anarchy of the market through economic planning, then marginalization and delinquency are curtailed sharply. The virtual elimination of unemployment and subemployment enormously decreases the numbers of adolescent marginals, and the size and stability of their delinquent group formations. (In capitalist societies, these groups are concentrated in slums and ghettos.) Walter O'Connor (1972:93), a liberal scholar, reports,

> Soviet delinquents tend to commit their offenses in groups . . . these groups, however, are generally rather small in number and fluid in composition, bearing little resemblance to the organized fighting gangs of large American cities in the 1950's. On the whole, it seems doubtful that we can speak of "gangs" at all in the Soviet case. The instances of Soviet delinquents acting in concert frequently seem to reflect a spontaneous and temporary coming together for the purpose of some relatively specific act.

China provides additional illustrations of the decrease in marginalization and delinquency. American journalists have been struck by the relative absence of crime in the People's Republic of China today. This absence cannot be due to cultural differences between the Eastern and the Western hemispheres, because the differences between "liberated China" and "nationalist China" were discerned long ago by American observors. William Hinton (1970:19), for instance, worked during the post war years in China as a representative of the United Nations Relief and Rehabilitation Administration. He observed that in 1947,

> The most striking thing about the [communist] towns was the absence of beggars . . . It was unbelievable but true. The same went for prostitutes: there did not seem to be any. I was never opportuned even though I wandered day and night in the main streets and back alleys of the biggest towns in the area. In Nationalist-held Peking, on the other hand, clerks and roomboys in the main hotels doubled as pimps, while little children touted for their sisters on the sidewalks.

Further illustrations can be obtained from Cuba and the German Democratic Republic. In the pre-revolutionary period, Havana was the center of organized crime in the Carribean. In addition, Cuba, like other Latin American countries, had an enormous population of marginals. Today, marginalization and organized crime, and their effects on children and adolescents, have disappeared from Cuba. Additional comparisons referring to unemployment that favor socialism can be made between the German Democratic Republic and the Federal Republic of Germany. With regard to crime, there has been a long-term decreasing trend in ordinary crime within the German Democratic Republic, but no comparable decline in West Germany. Again, since similar national groups are involved, such differences are due to their social orders.

The complete elimination of marginalization and delinquency depends upon advanced socialist changes. Socialism does not emerge full grown from the womb of class societies; it bears the imprint of thousands of years of class developments. Under socialism, school and family relations continue to reproduce the labor force, and some of these reproductive relations are not changed radically because certain bourgeois rights are maintained in industry. Such rights include equal pay for equal units of work; hence, they also include differentials in pay resulting from variations in individual skills, talents, and physical abilities. Consequently, since the products of labor are distributed during this transitional period "from each according to his or her ability; to each according to work performance," certain pre-existing socialization functions, social distinctions, and competitive relations are sustained. They are gradually eliminated, however, as their material basis is transformed, and the prevailing distributive principle becomes "... to each according to need." Consequently, as the state becomes a genuine expression of workers' power, and as the economy becomes regulated by "a settled plan," and as the creative powers of labor are devoted to social needs, then the social inequalities between town and country, between intellectual and manual workers, and between sexes, races, and nationalities will be eliminated. Marginalization, uneven development and delinquency will finally disappear.

Obviously, the formation of social policy planning in the United States is generally organized around different possibilities. The United States remains a capitalist society and, consequently, policy makers underwrite capital accumulation. They defend multinational interests through C.I.A. activity in Latin American countries and they enrich commercial interests through urban renewal programs in North American cities. By developing educational-industrial, police-industrial and other social-industrial complexes, they exploit domestic problems to maintain profits (O'Connor, 1974; McLaughan, 1975). Such developments undermine attempts to prevent marginalization, uneven development and delinquency.

Because of the domination by capital, social policy planning usually avoids conflict with essential structural relations, but this accommodation is self-defeating. Since they are subordinated to the very forces that cause these problems, social policy planners cannot deal with the problems successfully. Instead, they attack the problems piece-meal without regard to long-term strategies for structural changes. Although direct intervention into the immediate causes of marginalization, uneven development and delinquency is required even for the *amelioration* of these problems, such intervention is rarely attempted.

Take the numerous manpower training programs, which have concentrated on black marginals. The programs have failed to make any improvement in black communities, because they do not lower unemployment directly. Surveys report, therefore, that

> without a direct transformation and augmentation of the demand for their labor, significant improvement in the economic situation of ghetto dwellers is unlikely. Attempts to change the worker himself—whether to remedy his personal "defects" or to move him to a "better" environment—have not worked up until now, and the [several sources of data reported] in this study provide little if any evidence to support the belief that such attempts will be sufficient in the future (Harrison, 1975: 159-160).

Thus, without significant attempts to expand and stabilize the labor market directly through public works, the socialization of industries, and economic planning, the social investment in reducing marginalization through manpower training is irrational.

As indicated, such manpower programs are not integrated with policies that change structural relations in the economy; hence, their effects on marginalization are negligible. Similar relations apply to the school. Since compensatory education policies are also restricted by capital, they are not related to strategies that change structural relations in either the school or economy. Hence their effects on the equalization of school achievement are very limited.

While compensatory education has some positive effects on racial, ethnic, or economic groups that have higher proportions of prototypic marginal youth, the relative magnitude of these effects is questionable. Martin Carnoy's (1975:233-242) survey of studies about teacher performance indicates that compensatory programs have strikingly similar results.

> They generally show a positive relationship between so-called higher "quality" characteristics of teachers and exam scores. They also show significantly different teacher input-school output relationships for different ethnic groups and, in Puerto Rico, for different class groups. Finally, they show that even if increasing teacher quality results in higher achievement, average achievement scores will at best bring them only part of the way toward equality with presently high scoring groups . . . even if substantially higher-quality teaching is made available to the low-scoring than to the high-scoring students, the change would result in only a partial reduction of exam-score difference between the two. In the case of ethnic and racial minorities in the United States, the reduction may well be negligible.

Such findings are not surprising. Social investments do effect student development, but the combined effects of intergenerational and governmental investments, generally favoring groups with higher

288

statuses, far outweigh social investments into compensatory education. Consequently, the effects of that education are, of necessity, limited, and they cannot neutralize the tendencies toward uneven development. Furthermore, certain other limitations of compensatory education policies are not revealed by studies of isolated programs. The most severe test of these policies would be made if they were instituted everywhere. Under such conditions, various mechanisms (e.g., grading by the "thirds," or by other standardized scores) would maintain the same competitive and hierarchical school relationships, despite the fluctuations in average levels of individual productivity. Hence, marginal youth would still be produced, but with a higher achievement score than before.

With regard to the labor market, value-determining and price-making mechanisms accomplish similar ends. The distribution of educational investments has improved considerably over the last three decades. But, Carnoy (1975:369-370) points out,

> the payoff to schooling changes in a way that makes lower
> levels of schooling worth less over time relative to higher levels.
> Thus, the number of people who receive secondary schooling
> has increased markedly in the United States between 1939
> and 1959, but the payoff to that level actually fell. So just
> as the poor begin to get higher levels of schooling, the relative
> value to the labor market of those levels falls. Even when a
> society invests more in schooling for the poor, therefore, the
> labor market values that schooling less than before the poor
> were getting it.

The same dismal pattern characterizes delinquency policies. Numerous studies indicate that piece-meal and accommodative social policies have insignificant effects on delinquency. The failure of these policies, which involve counseling, job training, or diversion programs, simply reinforces the necessity for socialist strategies for change. To be successful, short-term programmatic solutions must be part of long-term strategies which support working-class movements that are primary agents of fundamental structural change. The linkage between short-term programs and these long-term strategies represents the central challenge to social policy analysts. There will be no magical solutions by professionals working to eliminate marginalization, uneven development, and delinquency, as long as structural relations in our society are disregarded.

REFERENCES

Bluestone, Barry
    1972   "Capitalism and poverty in America: A discussion." Monthly Review 2:64-71.
Bowles, Samuel and Herbert Ginitis
    1973   "I.Q. in the U.S. class structure." Social Policy 3:65-96.

Bremner, Robert H.
  1970   Children and Youth in America, A Documentary History, I. Cambridge, Massachusetts: Harvard University Press.

Carnoy, Martin
  1975   Schooling in a Corporate Society, the Political Economy of Education in America. Second Edition. New York: David McKay Company, Inc.

Carson, Robert B.
  1972   "Youthful labor surplus in disaccumulationist capitalism." Socialist Revolution 2:15-44.

The Editors
  1975   "Capitalism and unemployment." Monthly Review 27:1-13.

Harrison, Bennett
  1975   "Education and underemployment in the urban ghetto." Pp. 133-60 in Martin Carnoy (ed.), Schooling in a Corporate Society. New York: David McKay Company, Inc.

Hein, Wolfgang and Konrad Stenzal
  1973   "The capitalist state and underdevelopment in Latin America—the case of Venezuela." Kapitalistate 2:31-48.

Hinton, William
  1970   Iron Oxen. New York: Monthly Review Press.

Marx, Karl
  1959   Capital, I. Moscow: Foreign Languages Publishing House.

McLaughlan, Gregory
  1975   "LEAA: A case study in the development of the social industrial complex." Crime and Social Justice 4:15-23.

O'Connor, James
  1973   The Fiscal Crisis of the State. New York: St. Martin's Press.

O'Connor, Walter D.
  1972   Deviance in Soviet Society, Crime, Delinquency, and Alcoholism. New York: Columbia University Press.

Reich, Michael, David M. Gordon and Richard C. Edwards
  1973   "A theory of labor market segmentation," American Economic Review 63:359-365.

Schwendinger, Herman and Julia R. Schwendinger
  1974   The Sociologists of the Chair, A Radical Analysis of the Formative Years of North American Sociology (1883-1922). New York: Basic Books.

  1976   "The collective varieties of youth." Crime and Social Justice 5:7-25. Forthcoming The Collective Varieties of Youth Book.

A Child of Three Accused of Inaugurating a Reign of Terror

SOCIAL REACTION TO DELINQUENCY

CHAPTER 6

Traditional criminological research has focused almost exclusively on individual delinquents or criminals in an attempt to understand what types of persons violate laws. In contrast, the social reaction perspective focuses on police, probation officers, juvenile judges, and other regulators of wayward youth.[1] Social reaction studies show that "rate producing" social control agents play a significant role in the creation of delinquency, and that being processed by control agents can promote delinquent behavior among youth.[2] For example, Edwin Lemert's work on labelling has been used to support diversion programs, whereby children are diverted from the juvenile court, presumably to protect them from the stigmatizing effects of being labelled as delinquents.[3] Edwin Schur has used the research done by the social reaction school to advance his idea of radical nonintervention—a plea for all regulatory agencies to leave delinquent and marginally delinquent children alone whenever possible.[4]

The selections in this chapter can all be considered social reaction studies, in that they examine the role and consequences of official reactions to delinquent youth. In some instances, these selections repeat material presented in chapter 3. Specifically, the works of Thornberry and Platt, Schechter, and Tiffany are presented here in their entirety to allow the reader to examine more closely the methodology employed, as well as additional findings not presented earlier.

The first article by William Chambliss is an account of how two juvenile gangs, which differ only in the social class of their members, come to be defined as "good" or "bad" by the police, community, and school officials. In his study, Chambliss illustrates how delinquent activities of the Saints are tolerated by the community, whereas the Roughnecks are labelled as troublemakers, and become the focus of police control tactics. The differential treatment accorded the two gangs is linked to factors of visibility, demeanor, and the bias of police and school officials. Ultimately, the class structure of American society is isolated by the author to explain the discriminatory treatment, which often results in serious consequences for the persons involved.

The Williams and Gold study represents the best of several self-report studies now available. They draw a conceptual distinction between delinquent behavior and reported delinquent behavior. The former reflects the actual amount of delinquent behavior, while the latter mirrors the biases affecting police arrest decisions. Their data are based on a national survey of thirteen- to sixteen-year-olds, who disclose their actual delinquent involvement. These data are compared with the police records. The results document the biases of police arrest statistics.

Terence Thornberry's article goes beyond police action, and examines the processing of juveniles from the point of arrest to sentencing disposition in juvenile court. The data are based upon Wolfgang, Figlio, and Sellin's birth cohort study.[5] Thornberry, in a carefully controlled analysis, concludes that blacks and lower socio-economic juveniles are treated more harshly by social control agents than their white and upper-class counterparts.

Utilizing a participant-observation methodology, Anthony Platt, Howard Schechter, and Phyllis Tiffany studied the public defender in juvenile court. The authors assert that the public defender must alternately assume the conflicting roles of social worker, legal advocate, and court employee whose duty often consists of processing children as quickly and economically as possible. In order to accomplish these disparate objectives, the public defender often must base his defense tactics on highly subjective and superficial perceptions of his client, which are unrelated to the facts of the delinquency petition. The overriding conclusion of this study is that the legal representation afforded juveniles is less adequate than the minimal aid given indigent adults in criminal court.

One topic that is frequently ignored by juvenile court observers is the extent of sex discrimination within the juvenile justice system. It is widely accepted among male-dominated criminologists that females are treated more favorably than their male counterparts. This view is generally based on the arrest and court statistics of predominantly male delinquents. However, the final two articles by Jean

Strouse and Meda Chesney-Lind serve to demystify the relationship of sex to juvenile court practices.

Strouse cites existing sections of New York's Family Court Act that legitimate differential treatment of female status offenders. Specifically, she shows that the court maintains greater jurisdiction over females than male status offenders by extending the age limitations pertaining to females. Chesney-Lind shows that sexist attitudes are also evident in police and detention procedures that demean females and result in more severe handling of female offenders. Both authors conclude that while the court may receive a smaller proportion of female than male status offenders, those who reach the court hearing are treated more harshly than male delinquents. These oppressive practices are the result of the traditional perception of social control agencies that female offenders require more drastic treatment than male delinquents. By enforcing a separate, more rigid standard of sexual morality for females, the court's actions result not only in sexual discrimination but also in violation of civil rights. These articles debunk the popular myth that females are treated more leniently than males in the juvenile justice system.

Although the impact of factors such as sex, race, class, demeanor, complainant, and evidence, is not clearly defined, we must consider them if we are to gain a full understanding of the social reactions to delinquency. A major conclusion to be drawn from these studies is that social inequities that permeate society as a whole have a profound impact on juvenile justice practices. While it is important to study such biases, an analysis of delinquency based only on social reaction concepts would, however, be a mistake. Too much attention on the immediate agents of social control, such as police, probation, and the courts, may obscure the workings of power and privilege which affect the entire juvenile justice system. One should not expect to find an equitable justice system within an unequal social structure.

NOTES

1   See Richard Quinney, *The Social Reality of Crime.*
2   Anthony Platt, *The Childsavers: The Invention of Delinquency;* Aaron Cicourel, *The Social Organization of the Juvenile Court;* and Robert M. Emerson, *Judging Delinquents.*
3   Edwin Lemert, *Social Pathology.*
4   Edwin Schur, *Radical Non-Intervention.*
5   Marvin Wolfgang, Robert Figlio, and Thorsten Sellin, *Delinquency in a Birth Cohort.*

BIBLIOGRAPHY

Cicourel, Aaron. *The Social Organization of the Juvenile Court.* New York: John Wiley and Sons, Inc., 1968.
Emerson, Robert M. *Judging Delinquents.* Chicago: Aldine Publishing Co., 1969.
Lemert, Edwin. *Social Pathology.* New York: McGraw-Hill, 1951.

Platt, Anthony. *The Childsavers: The Invention of Delinquency.* Chicago: University of Chicago Press, 1968.

Quinney, Richard. *The Social Reality of Crime.* Boston: Little, Brown and Co., 1970.

Schur, Edwin. *Radical Non-Intervention.* Englewood Cliffs, N.J.: Prentice-Hall, Inc., 1973.

Wolfgang, Marvin; Figlio, Robert; and Sellin, Thorsten. *Delinquency in a Birth Cohort.* Chicago: University of Chicago Press, 1972.

The Saints and the Roughnecks

WILLIAM J. CHAMBLISS

William J. Chambliss is a professor of sociology at the University of Delaware.

Published by permission of Transaction, Inc., from SOCIETY, Volume 11, no. 1. Copyright ©1973, by Transaction, Inc.

Eight promising young men—children of good, stable, white upper-middle-class families, active in school affairs, good pre-college students—were some of the most delinquent boys at Hanibal High School. While community residents and parents knew that these boys occasionally sowed a few wild oats, they were totally unaware that sowing wild oats completely occupied the daily routine of these young men. The Saints were constantly occupied with truancy, drinking, wild driving, petty theft and vandalism. Yet not one was officially arrested for any misdeed during the two years I observed them.

This record was particularly surprising in light of my observations during the same two years of another gang of Hanibal High School students, six lower-class white boys known as the Roughnecks. The Roughnecks were constantly in trouble with police and community even though their rate of delinquency was about equal with that of the Saints. What was the cause of this disparity? the result? The following consideration of the activities, social class and community perceptions of both gangs may provide some answers.

THE SAINTS FROM MONDAY TO FRIDAY

The Saints' principal daily concern was with getting out of school as early as possible. The boys managed to get out of school with minimum danger that they would be accused of playing hookey through an elaborate procedure for obtaining "legitimate" release from class. The most common procedure was for one boy to obtain the release of another by fabricating a meeting of some committee, program or recognized club. Charles might raise his hand in his 9:00 chemistry class and ask to be excused—a euphemism for going to the bathroom. Charles would go to Ed's math class and inform the teacher that Ed was needed for a 9:30 rehearsal of the drama club play. The math teacher would recognize Ed and Charles as "good students" involved in numerous school activities and would permit Ed to leave at 9:30. Charles would return to his class, and Ed would go to Tom's English class to obtain his release. Tom would engineer Charles' escape. The strategy would continue until as many of the Saints as possible were freed. After a stealthy trip to the car (which had been parked in a strategic spot), the boys were off for a day of fun.

Over the two years I observed the Saints, this pattern was repeated nearly every day. There were variations on the theme, but in one form or another, the boys used this procedure for getting out of class and then off the school grounds. Rarely did all eight of the Saints manage to leave school at the same time. The average number avoiding school on the days I observed them was five.

Having escaped from the concrete corridors the boys usually went either to a pool hall on the other (lower-class) side of town or to a cafe in the suburbs. Both places were out of the way of people the boys were likely to know (family or school officials), and both provided a source of entertainment. The pool hall entertainment was the generally rough atmosphere, the occasional hustler, the sometimes drunk proprietor and, of course, the game of pool. The cafe's entertainment was provided by the owner. The boys would "accidentally" knock a glass on the floor or spill cola on the counter—not all the time, but enough to be sporting. They would also bend spoons, put salt in sugar bowls and generally tease whoever was working in the cafe. The owner had opened the cafe recently and was dependent on the boys' business which was, in fact, substantial since between the horsing around and the teasing they bought food and drinks.

THE SAINTS ON WEEKENDS

On weekends the automobile was even more critical than during the week, for on weekends the Saints went to Big Town—a large city with a population of over a million 25 miles from Hanibal. Every Friday and Saturday night most of the Saints would meet between 8:00 and 8:30 and would go into Big Town. Big Town activities included drinking heavily in taverns or nightclubs, driving drunkenly through the streets, and committing acts of vandalism and playing pranks.

By midnight on Fridays and Saturdays the Saints were usually thoroughly high, and one or two of them were often so drunk they had to be carried to the cars. Then the boys drove around town, calling obscenities to women and girls; occasionally trying (unsuccessfully so far as I could tell) to pick girls up; and driving recklessly through red lights and at high speeds with their lights out. Occasionally they played "chicken." One boy would climb out the back window of the car and across the roof to the driver's side of the car while the car was moving at high speed (between 40 and 50 miles an hour); then the driver would move over and the boy who had just crawled across the car roof would take the driver's seat.

Searching for "fair game" for a prank was the boys' principal activity after they left the tavern. The boys would drive alongside a foot patrolman and ask directions to some street. If the policeman leaned on the car in the course of answering the question, the driver would speed away, causing him to lose his balance. The Saints were careful to play this prank only in an area where they were not going to spend much time and where they could quickly disappear around a corner to avoid having their license plate number taken.

Construction sites and road repair areas were the special province of the Saints' mischief. A soon-to-be-repaired hole in the road inevitably invited the Saints to remove lanterns and wooden barricades and put them in the car, leaving the hole unprotected. The boys would find a safe vantage point and wait for an unsuspecting motorist to drive into the hole. Often, though not always, the boys would go up to the motorist and commiserate with him about the dreadful way the city protected its citizenry.

Leaving the scene of the open hole and the motorist, the boys would then go searching for an appropriate place to erect the stolen barricade. An "appropriate place" was often a spot on a highway near a curve in the road where the barricade would not be seen by an oncoming motorist. The boys would wait to watch an unsuspecting motorist attempt to stop and (usually) crash into the wooden barricade. With saintly bearing the boys might offer help and understanding.

A stolen lantern might well find its way onto the back of a police car or hang from a street lamp. Once a lantern served as a prop for a reenactment of the "midnight ride of Paul Revere" until the "play," which was taking place at 2:00 AM in the center of a main street of Big Town, was interrupted by a police car several blocks away. The boys ran, leaving the lanterns on the street, and managed to avoid being apprehended.

Abandoned houses, especially if they were located in out-of-the-way places, were fair game for destruction and spontaneous vandalism. The boys would break windows, remove furniture to the yard and tear it apart, urinate on the walls and scrawl obscenities inside.

Through all the pranks, drinking and reckless driving, the boys managed miraculously to avoid being stopped by police. Only twice in two years was I aware that they had been stopped by a Big City policeman. Once was for speeding (which they did every time they drove whether they were drunk or sober), and the driver managed to convince the policeman that it was simply an error. The second time they were stopped they had just left a nightclub and were walking through an alley. Aaron stopped to urinate and the boys began making obscene remarks. A foot patrolman came into the alley, lectured the boys and sent them home. Before the boys got to the car one began talking in a loud voice again. The policeman, who had followed them down the alley, arrested this boy for disturbing the peace and took him to the police station where the other Saints gathered. After paying a $5.00 fine, and with the assurance that there would be no permanent record of the arrest, the boy was released.

The boys had a spirit of frivolity and fun about their escapades. They did not view what they were engaged in as "delinquency," though it surely was by any reasonable definition of that word. They simply viewed themselves as having a little fun and who, they would ask, was really hurt by it? The answer had to be no one, although this fact remains one of the most difficult things to explain about the gang's behavior. Unlikely though it seems, in two years of drinking, driving, carousing and vandalism no one was seriously injured as a result of the Saints' activities.

THE SAINTS IN SCHOOL

The Saints were highly successful in school. The average grade for the group was "B," with two of the boys having close to a straight "A" average. Almost all of the boys were popular and many of them held offices in the school. One of the boys was vice-president of the student body one year. Six of the boys played on athletic teams.

At the end of their senior year, the student body selected ten seniors for special recognition as the "school wheels"; four of the ten were Saints. Teachers and school officials saw no problem with any of these boys and anticipated that they would all "make something of themselves."

How the boys managed to maintain this impression is surprising in view of their actual behavior while in school. Their technique for covering truancy was so successful that teachers did not even realize that the boys were absent from school much of the time. Occasionally, of course, the system would backfire and then the boy was on his own. A boy who was caught would be most contrite, would plead guilty and ask for mercy. He inevitably got the mercy he sought.

Cheating on examinations was rampant, even to the point of orally communicating answers to exams as well as looking at one another's papers. Since none of the group studied, and since they were primarily dependent on one another for help, it is surprising that grades were so high. Teachers contributed to the deception in their admitted inclination to give these boys (and presumably others like them) the benefit of the doubt. When asked how the boys did in school, and when pressed on specific examinations, teachers might admit that they were disappointed in John's performance, but would quickly add that they "knew that he was capable of doing better," so John was given a higher grade than he had actually earned. How often this happened is impossible to know. During the time that I observed the group, I never saw any of the boys take homework home. Teachers may have been "understanding" very regularly.

One exception to the gang's generally good performance was Jerry, who had a "C" average in his junior year, experienced disaster the next year and failed to graduate. Jerry had always been a little more nonchalant than the others about the liberties he took in school. Rather than wait for someone to come get him from class, he would offer his own excuse and leave. Although he probably did not miss any more classes than most of the others in the group, he did not take the requisite pains to cover his absences. Jerry was the only Saint whom I ever heard talk back to a teacher. Although teachers often called him a "cut up" or a "smart kid," they never referred to him as a troublemaker or as a kid headed for trouble. It seems likely, then, that Jerry's failure his senior year and his mediocre performance his junior year were consequences of his not playing the game the proper way (possibly because he was disturbed by his parents' divorce). His teachers regarded him as "immature" and not quite ready to get out of high school.

THE POLICE AND THE SAINTS

The local police saw the Saints as good boys who were among the leaders of the youth in the community. Rarely, the boys might be stopped in town for speeding or for running a stop sign. When this happened the boys were always polite, contrite and pled for mercy. As in school, they received the mercy they asked for. None ever received a ticket or was taken into the precinct by the local police.

The situation in Big City, where the boys engaged in most of their delinquency, was only slightly different. The police there did not know the boys at all, although occasionally the boys were stopped by a patrolman. Once they were caught taking a lantern from a construction site. Another time they were stopped for running a stop sign, and on several occasions they were stopped for speeding. Their behavior was as before: contrite, polite and penitent. The urban police, like the local police, accepted their demeanor as sincere. More important, the urban police were convinced that these were good boys just out for a lark.

THE ROUGHNECKS

Hanibal townspeople never perceived the Saints' high level of delinquency. The Saints were good boys who just went in for an occasional prank. After all, they were well dressed, well mannered and had nice cars. The Roughnecks were a different story. Although the two gangs of boys were the same age, and both groups engaged in an equal amount of wild-oat sowing, everyone agreed that the not-so-well-dressed, not-so-well-mannered, not-so-rich boys were heading for trouble. Townspeople would say, "You can see the gang members at the drugstore, night after night, leaning against the storefront (sometimes drunk) or slouching around inside buying cokes, reading magazines, and probably stealing old Mr. Wall blind. When they are outside and girls walk by, even respectable girls, these boys make suggestive remarks. Sometimes their remarks are downright lewd."

From the community's viewpoint, the real indication that these kids were in for trouble was that they were constantly involved with the police. Some of them had been picked up for stealing, mostly small stuff, of course, "but still it's stealing small stuff that leads to big time crimes." "Too bad," people said. "Too bad that these boys couldn't behave like the other kids in town; stay out of trouble, be polite to adults, and look to their future."

The community's impression of the degree to which this group of six boys (ranging in age from 16 to 19) engaged in delinquency was somewhat distorted. In some ways the gang was more delinquent than the community thought; in other ways they were less.

The fighting activities of the group were fairly readily and accurately perceived by almost everyone. At least once a month, the boys would get into some sort of fight, although most fights were scraps between members of the group or involved only one member of the group and some peripheral hanger-on. Only three times in the period of observation did the group fight together: once against a gang from across town, once against two blacks and once against a group of boys from another school. For the first two fights the group went out "looking for trouble"—and they found it both times. The third fight followed a football game and began spontaneously with an argument on the football field between one of the Roughnecks and a member of the opposition's football team.

Jack had a particular propensity for fighting and was involved in most of the brawls. He was a prime mover of the escalation of arguments into fights.

More serious than fighting, had the community been aware of it, was theft. Although almost everyone was aware that the boys occasionally stole things, they did not realize the extent of the activity. Petty stealing was a frequent event for the Roughnecks. Sometimes they stole as a group and coordinated their efforts; other times they stole in pairs. Rarely did they steal alone.

The thefts ranged from very small things like paperback books, comics and ballpoint pens to expensive items like watches. The nature of the thefts varied from time to time. The gang would go through a period of systematically shoplifting items from automobiles or school lockers. Types of thievery varied with the whim of the gang. Some forms of thievery were more profitable than others, but all thefts were for profit, not just thrills.

Roughnecks siphoned gasoline from cars as often as they had access to an automobile, which was not very often. Unlike the Saints, who owned their own cars, the Roughnecks would have to borrow their parents' cars, an event which occurred only eight or nine times a year. The boys claimed to have stolen cars for joy rides from time to time.

Ron committed the most serious of the group's offenses. With an unidentified associate the boy attempted to burglarize a gasoline station. Although this station had been robbed twice previously in the same month, Ron denied any involvement in either of the other thefts. When Ron and his accomplice approached the station, the owner was hiding in the bushes beside the station. He fired both barrels of a double-barreled shotgun at the boys. Ron was severely injured; the other boy ran away and was never caught. Though he remained in critical condition for several months, Ron finally recovered and served six months of the following year in reform school. Upon release from reform school, Ron was put back a grade in school, and began running around with a different gang of boys. The Roughnecks considered the new gang less delinquent than themselves, and during the following year Ron had no more trouble with the police.

The Roughnecks, then, engaged mainly in three types of delinquency: theft, drinking and fighting. Although community members perceived that this gang of kids was delinquent, they mistakenly believed that their illegal activities were primarily drinking, fighting and being a nuisance to passersby. Drinking was limited among the gang members, although it did occur, and theft was much more prevalent than anyone realized.

Drinking would doubtless have been more prevalent had the boys had ready access to liquor. Since they rarely had automobiles at their disposal, they could not travel very far, and the bars in town would not serve them. Most of the boys had little money, and this, too, inhibited their purchase of alcohol. Their major source of liquor was a local drunk who would buy them a fifth if they would give him enough extra to buy himself a pint of whiskey or a bottle of wine.

The community's perception of drinking as prevalent stemmed from the fact that it was the most obvious delinquency the boys engaged in. When one of the boys had been drinking, even a casual observer seeing him on the corner would suspect that he was high.

There was a high level of mutual distrust and dislike between the Roughnecks and the police. The boys felt very strongly that the police were unfair and corrupt. Some evidence existed that the boys were correct in their perception.

The main source of the boys' dislike for the police undoubtedly stemmed from the fact that the police would sporadically harass the group. From the standpoint of the boys, these acts of occasional enforcement of the law were whimsical and uncalled for. It made no sense to them, for example, that the police would come to the corner occasionally and threaten them with arrest for loitering when the night before the boys had been out siphoning gasoline from cars and the police had been nowhere in sight. To the boys, the police were stupid on the one hand, for not being where they should have been and catching the boys in a serious offense, and unfair on the other hand, for trumping up "loitering" charges against them.

From the viewpoint of the police, the situation was quite different. They knew, with all the confidence necessary to be a policeman, that these boys were engaged in criminal activities. They knew this partly from occasionally catching them, mostly from circumstantial evidence ("the boys were around when those tires were slashed"), and partly because the police shared the view of the community in general that this was a bad bunch of boys. The best the police could hope to do was to be sensitive to the fact that these boys were engaged in illegal acts and arrest them whenever there was some evidence that they had been involved. Whether or not the boys had in fact committed a particular act in a particular way was not especially important. The police had a broader view: their job was to stamp out these kids' crimes; the tactics were not as important as the end result.

Over the period that the group was under observation, each member was arrested at least once. Several of the boys were arrested a number of times and spent at least one night in jail. While most were never taken to court, two of the boys were sentenced to six months' incarceration in boys' schools.

THE ROUGHNECKS IN SCHOOL

The Roughnecks' behavior in school was not particularly disruptive. During school hours they did not all hang around together, but tended instead to spend most of their time with one or two other members of the gang who were their special buddies. Although every member of the gang attempted to avoid school as much as possible, they were not particularly successful and most of them attended school with surprising regularity. They considered school a burden—something to be gotten through with a minimum of conflict. If they were "bugged" by a particular teacher, it could lead to trouble. One of the boys, Al, once threatened to beat up a teacher and, according to the other boys, the teacher hid under a desk to escape him.

Teachers saw the boys the way the general community did, as heading for trouble, as being uninterested in making something of themselves. Some were also seen as being incapable of meeting the academic standards of the school. Most of the teachers expressed concern for this group of boys and were willing to pass them despite

poor performance, in the belief that failing them would only aggra-
vate the problem.

The group of boys had a grade point average just slightly above
"C." No one in the group failed either grade, and no one had better
than a "C" average. They were very consistent in their achievement
or, at least, the teachers were consistent in their perception of the
boys' achievement.

Two of the boys were good football players. Herb was acknowledged to be the best player in the school and Jack was almost as
good. Both boys were criticized for their failure to abide by training
rules, for refusing to come to practice as often as they should, and
for not playing their best during practice. What they lacked in sports-
manship they made up for in skill, apparently, and played every game
no matter how poorly they had performed in practice or how many
practice sessions they had missed.

TWO QUESTIONS

Why did the community, the school and the police react to the Saints
as though they were good, upstanding, nondelinquent youths with
bright futures but to the Roughnecks as though they were tough,
young criminals who were headed for trouble? Why did the Roughnecks and the Saints in fact have quite different careers after high
school—careers which, by and large, lived up to the expectations of
the community?

The most obvious explanation for the differences in the community's and law enforcement agencies' reactions to the two gangs
is that one group of boys was "more delinquent" than the other.
Which group *was* more delinquent? The answer to this question will
determine in part how we explain the differential responses to these
groups by the members of the community and, particularly, by law
enforcement and school officials.

In sheer number of illegal acts, the Saints were the more delinquent. They were truant from school for at least part of the day
almost every day of the week. In addition, their drinking and vandalism occurred with surprising regularity. The Roughnecks, in contrast,
engaged sporadically in delinquent episodes. While these episodes
were frequent, they certainly did not occur on a daily or even a
weekly basis.

The difference in frequency of offenses was probably caused by
the Roughnecks' inability to obtain liquor and to manipulate legitimate excuses from school. Since the Roughnecks had less money
than the Saints, and teachers carefully supervised their school activities, the Roughnecks' hearts may have been as black as the Saints',
but their misdeeds were not nearly as frequent.

There are really no clear-cut criteria by which to measure qualitative differences in antisocial behavior. The most important dimen-

sion of the difference is generally referred to as the "seriousness" of the offenses.

If seriousness encompasses the relative economic costs of delinquent acts, then some assessment can be made. The Roughnecks probably stole an average of about $5.00 worth of goods a week. Some weeks the figure was considerably higher, but these times must be balanced against long periods when almost nothing was stolen.

The Saints were more continuously engaged in delinquency but their acts were not for the most part costly to property. Only their vandalism and occasional theft of gasoline would so qualify. Perhaps once or twice a month they would siphon a tankful of gas. The other costly items were street signs, construction lanterns and the like. All of these acts combined probably did not quite average $5.00 a week, partly because much of the stolen equipment was abandoned and presumably could be recovered. The difference in cost of stolen property between the two groups was trivial, but the Roughnecks probably had a slightly more expensive set of activities than did the Saints.

Another meaning of seriousness is the potential threat of physical harm to members of the community and to the boys themselves. The Roughnecks were more prone to physical violence; they not only welcomed an opportunity to fight; they went seeking it. In addition, they fought among themselves frequently. Although the fighting never included deadly weapons, it was still a menace, however minor, to the physical safety of those involved.

The Saints never fought. They avoided physical conflict both inside and outside the group. At the same time, though, the Saints frequently endangered their own and other people's lives. They did so almost every time they drove a car, especially if they had been drinking. Sober, their driving was risky; under the influence of alcohol it was horrendous. In addition, the Saints endangered the lives of others with their pranks. Street excavations left unmarked were a very serious hazard.

Evaluating the relative seriousness of the two gangs' activities is difficult. The community reacted as though the behavior of the Roughnecks was a problem, and they reacted as though the behavior of the Saints was not. But the members of the community were ignorant of the array of delinquent acts that characterized the Saints' behavior. Although concerned citizens were unaware of much of the Roughnecks' behavior as well, they were much better informed about the Roughnecks' involvement in delinquency than they were about the Saints'.

VISIBILITY

Differential treatment of the two gangs resulted in part because one gang was infinitely more visible than the other. This differential visi-

304

bility was a direct function of the economic standing of the families. The Saints had access to automobiles and were able to remove themselves from the sight of the community. In as routine a decision as to where to go to have a milkshake after school, the Saints stayed away from the mainstream of community life. Lacking transportation, the Roughnecks could not make it to the edge of town. The center of town was the only practical place for them to meet since their homes were scattered throughout the town and any noncentral meeting place put an undue hardship on some members. Through necessity the Roughnecks congregated in a crowded area where everyone in the community passed frequently, including teachers and law enforcement officers. They could easily see the Roughnecks hanging around the drugstore.

The Roughnecks, of course, made themselves even more visible by making remarks to passersby and by occasionally getting into fights on the corner. Meanwhile, just as regularly, the Saints were either at the cafe on one edge of town or in the pool hall at the other edge of town. Without any particular realization that they were making themselves inconspicuous, the Saints were able to hide their time-wasting. Not only were they removed from the mainstream of traffic, but they were almost always inside a building.

On their escapades the Saints were also relatively invisible, since they left Hanibal and travelled to Big City. Here, too, they were mobile, roaming the city, rarely going to the same area twice.

DEMEANOR

To the notion of visibility must be added the differences in the responses of group members to outside intervention with their activities. If one of the Saints was confronted with an accusing policeman, even if he felt he was truly innocent of a wrongdoing, his demeanor was apologetic and penitent. A Roughneck's attitude was almost the polar opposite. When confronted with a threatening adult authority, even one who tried to be pleasant, the Roughneck's hostility and disdain were clearly observable. Sometimes he might attempt to put up a veneer of respect, but it was thin and was not accepted as sincere by the authority.

School was no different from the community at large. The Saints could manipulate the system by feigning compliance with the school norms. The availability of cars at school meant that once free from the immediate sight of the teacher, the boys could disappear rapidly. And this escape was well enough planned that no administrator or teacher was nearby when the boys left. A Roughneck who wished to escape for a few hours was in a bind. If it were possible to get free from class, downtown was still a mile away, and even if he arrived there, he was still very visible. Truancy for the Roughnecks meant almost certain detection, while the Saints enjoyed almost complete immunity from sanctions.

BIAS

Community members were not aware of the transgressions of the Saints. Even if the Saints had been less discreet, their favorite delinquencies would have been perceived as less serious than those of the Roughnecks.

In the eyes of the police and school officials, a boy who drinks in an alley and stands intoxicated on the street corner is committing a more serious offense than is a boy who drinks to inebriation in a nightclub or a tavern and drives around afterwards in a car. Similarly, a boy who steals a wallet from a store will be viewed as having committed a more serious offense than a boy who steals a lantern from a construction site.

Perceptual bias also operates with respect to the demeanor of the boys in the two groups when they are confronted by adults. It is not simply that adults dislike the posture affected by boys of the Roughneck ilk; more important is the conviction that the posture adopted by the Roughnecks is an indication of their devotion and commitment to deviance as a way of life. The posture becomes a cue, just as the type of the offense is a cue, to the degree to which the known transgressions are indicators of the youths' potential for other problems.

Visibility, demeanor and bias are surface variables which explain the day-to-day operations of the police. Why do these surface variables operate as they do? Why did the police choose to disregard the Saints' delinquencies while breathing down the backs of the Roughnecks?

The answer lies in the class structure of American society and the control of legal institutions by those at the top of the class structure. Obviously, no representative of the upper class drew up the operational chart for the police which led them to look in the ghettoes and on streetcorners—which led them to see the demeanor of lower-class youth as troublesome and that of upper-middle-class youth as tolerable. Rather, the procedures simply developed from experience—experience with irate and influential upper-middle-class parents insisting that their son's vandalism was simply a prank and his drunkenness only a momentary "sowing of wild oats"—experience with cooperative or indifferent, powerless, lower-class parents who acquiesced to the laws' definition of their son's behavior.

ADULT CAREERS OF THE SAINTS
AND THE ROUGHNECKS

The community's confidence in the potential of the Saints and the Roughnecks apparently was justified. If anything, the community members underestimated the degree to which these youngsters would turn out "good" or "bad."

Seven of the eight members of the Saints went on to college immediately after high school. Five of the boys graduated from college in four years. The sixth one finished college after two years in the army, and the seventh spent four years in the air force before returning to college and receiving a B.A. degree. Of these seven college graduates, three went on for advanced degrees. One finished law school and is now active in state politics, one finished medical school and is practicing near Hanibal, and one boy is now working for a Ph.D. The other four college graduates entered submanagerial, managerial or executive training positions with larger firms.

The only Saint who did not complete college was Jerry. Jerry had failed to graduate from high school with the other Saints. During his second senior year, after the other Saints had gone on to college, Jerry began to hang around with what several teachers described as a "rough crowd"—the gang that was heir apparent to the Roughnecks. At the end of his second senior year, when he did graduate from high school, Jerry took a job as a used-car salesman, got married and quickly had a child. Although he made several abortive attempts to go to college by attending night school, when I last saw him (ten years after high school) Jerry was unemployed and had been living on unemployment for almost a year. His wife worked as a waitress.

Some of the Roughnecks have lived up to community expectations. A number of them were headed for trouble. A few were not.

Jack and Herb were the athletes among the Roughnecks and their athletic prowess paid off handsomely. Both boys received unsolicited athletic scholarships to college. After Herb received his scholarship (near the end of his senior year), he apparently did an about-face. His demeanor became very similar to that of the Saints. Although he remained a member in good standing of the Roughnecks, he stopped participating in most activities and did not hang out on the corner as often.

Jack did not change. If anything, he became more prone to fighting. He even made excuses for accepting the scholarship. He told the other gang members that the school had guaranteed him a "C" average if he would come to play football—an idea that seems far-fetched even in this day of highly competitive recruiting.

During the summer after graduation from high school, Jack attempted suicide by jumping from a tall building. The jump would certainly have killed most people trying it, but Jack survived. He entered college in the fall and played four years of football. He and Herb graduated in four years, and both are teaching and coaching in high schools. They are married and have stable families. If anything, Jack appears to have a more prestigious position in the community than does Herb, though both are well respected and secure in their positions.

Two of the boys never finished high school. Tommy left at the end of his junior year and went to another state. That summer he was arrested and placed on probation on a manslaughter charge. Three years later he was arrested for murder; he pleaded guilty to second degree murder and is serving a 30-year sentence in the state penitentiary.

Al, the other boy who did not finish high school, also left the state in his senior year. He is serving a life sentence in a state penitentiary for first degree murder.

Wes is a small-time gambler. He finished high school and "bummed around." After several years he made contact with a bookmaker who employed him as a runner. Later he acquired his own area and has been working it ever since. His position among the bookmakers is almost identical to the position he had in the gang; he is always around but no one is really aware of him. He makes no trouble and he does not get into any. Steady, reliable, capable of keeping his mouth closed, he plays the game by the rules, even though the game is an illegal one.

That leaves only Ron. Some of his former friends reported that they had heard he was "driving a truck up north," but no one could provide any concrete information.

REINFORCEMENT

The community responded to the Roughnecks as boys in trouble, and the boys agreed with that perception. Their pattern of deviancy was reinforced, and breaking away from it became increasingly unlikely. Once the boys acquired an image of themselves as deviants, they selected new friends who affirmed that self-image. As that self-conception became more firmly entrenched, they also became willing to try new and more extreme deviances. With their growing alienation came freer expression of disrespect and hostility for representatives of the legitimate society. This disrespect increased the community's negativism, perpetuating the entire process of commitment to deviance. Lack of a commitment to deviance works the same way. In either case, the process will perpetuate itself unless some event (like a scholarship to college or a sudden failure) external to the established relationship intervenes. For two of the Roughnecks (Herb and Jack), receiving college athletic scholarships created new relations and culminated in a break with the established pattern of deviance. In the case of one of the Saints (Jerry), his parents' divorce and his failing to graduate from high school changed some of his other relations. Being held back in school for a year and losing his place among the Saints had sufficient impact on Jerry to alter his self-image and virtually to assure that he would not go on to college as his peers did. Although the experiments of life can rarely be reversed, it seems likely in view of the behavior of the other boys who did not enjoy this special treatment by the school that Jerry, too, would have "become something" had he graduated as anticipated. For Herb and Jack outside intervention worked to their advantage; for Jerry it was his undoing.

Selective perception and labelling—finding, processing and punishing some kinds of criminality and not others—means that visible,
poor, nonmobile, outspoken, undiplomatic "tough" kids will be
noticed, whether their actions are seriously delinquent or not. Other
kids, who have established a reputation for being bright (even though
underachieving), disciplined and involved in respectable activities,
who are mobile and monied, will be invisible when they deviate from
sanctioned activities. They'll sow their wild oats—perhaps even wider
and thicker than their lower-class cohorts—but they won't be noticed.
When it's time to leave adolescence most will follow the expected
path, settling into the ways of the middle class, remembering fondly
the delinquent but unnoticed fling of their youth. The Roughnecks
and others like them may turn around, too. It is more likely that
their noticeable deviance will have been so reinforced by police and
community that their lives will be effectively channelled into careers
consistent with their adolescent background.

From Delinquent Behavior to
Official Delinquency

JAY R. WILLIAMS[1] and MARTIN GOLD*

Jay R. Williams is an associate with the Research Triangle Institute. Martin Gold is a professor of sociology at the University
of Michigan.

Reprinted from Jay R. Williams and Martin Gold, "From
Delinquent Behavior to Official Delinquency," *Social
Problems*, 20:2 (Fall, 1972), 209-229.

In order to better understand the dynamics of deviant
behavior it is vital to draw a distinction between delinquent behavior
and official delinquency. Delinquent behavior is norm violating behavior of a juvenile which, if detected by an appropriate authority,

*We are grateful to the International Association of Chiefs of Police and the
National Council of Juvenile Court Judges, and to many law enforcement officers, judges, and court workers who helped us with the collection of the data
reported here. We also want to acknowledge the helpful comments on the manuscript made by Dr. Jack J. Preiss of Duke University, Dr. Saleem Shah of NIMH,
and Rebecca F. Williams of Eastern Michigan University. The study was funded
by Grants MH15837, MH02311, and MH14797 from the U.S. Public Health
Service.

would expose the actor to legally prescribed sanctions. Official delinquency is the identification of and response to delinquent behavior by the police and courts.

Both definitions of delinquent behavior and of official delinquency assume the existence of formal community norms or laws. We are not concerned here with whether the offender regards his behavior as right or wrong. While such a focus is a legitimate concern for those interested in deviant behavior, it is not considered here.

Official delinquency is a complex, multi-level concept. For example, a youngster may run a red light on his bicycle and be seen (detected) by a policeman. If the policeman chooses to ignore the violation (no response to the behavior), delinquent behavior has occurred but official delinquency has not. Any sanctioning on the part of the policeman such as warning, scolding, and arrest, possibly leading to juvenile court and ultimately a juvenile detention facility, would constitute official delinquency. Official delinquency is defined by official response to alleged delinquent behavior.

The major reason for stressing the distinction between these two terms is that, in the past, studies of official delinquency have done a disservice to the understanding of delinquent behavior. Typically, samples of apprehended youths (such as reformatory populations) have been used to analyze and categorize "delinquent behavior" (which really meant the behavior of official delinquents). Not only does this violate our definition, but it ignores the vast amount of delinquent behavior which never becomes official delinquency.

Considering official delinquency to be representative of delinquent behavior naturally leads the investigator away from the selection process involved in official delinquency. Whether the policeman in our example chose to ignore or not to ignore the delinquent behavior may have been contingent on such factors as the juvenile's sex, age, race, social status (as perceived by the policeman), and citizen complaint (which limits the policeman's options). The policeman's response to the detected delinquent behavior is only the first stage in a lengthy filtering process from informal notice through formal arrest to court referral to incarceration in a reformatory.

The often cited finding of official delinquency as a lower-class phenomenon is a product of the above mentioned filtering process. This finding, which is by our definition quite valid, now takes on new meaning: official identification of and response to delinquent behavior shows a strong relationship to lower-status juveniles. However, it does not necessarily mean that lower-status youths are involved in more delinquent behavior than any other social status group.

In sum, almost all of what we believed we knew about delinquent behavior—its official actors, its nature, and its causes—we inferred until the late 1950's from the records of official delinquency and from observing identified delinquents. Although this is less true today and becoming increasingly less true, the two concepts are still about as frequently confused in the literature as not.

But the recent empirical literature on delinquent behavior should leave no doubt about the major differences between the two. Clearly they differ not only in the frequency of their occurrence—the earliest difference between the two that was generally acknowledged—but also in their distribution in the juvenile population, in their major causes, and in their functions for individuals and for the society. One need only cite the marked difference regularly found between the two in their distribution among social statuses to underscore the important theoretical and social implications of the distinction between them (e.g., Nye, 1958; Voss, 1966; Gold, 1970).

We shall attempt to emphasize and to clarify the distinction between delinquent behavior and official delinquency by reporting parallel studies of both among the same representative population of American teenagers. Presented here are the distributions of each by some theoretically important and empirically ubiquitous social categories—sex, age, race, and social status. In addition, consideration is given to the part these variables play in the conversion of delinquent behavior into official delinquency; other variables, such as the nature of the offensive behavior, are also considered in this context.

Finally, on the basis of the data presented, we conclude with a strongly cautionary summary describing the distorted images one may get of delinquent behavior and official delinquency by confusing them.

METHODOLOGY

The National Survey of Youth

Data were drawn from interviews and records of the 847 13- to 16-year old boys and girls who comprised the probability sample of the 1967 National Survey of Youth. The 1967 Survey is the first of a proposed series of surveys which will, among other interests, gauge periodically whether the frequency and seriousness of delinquent behavior in the United States is changing.

The teenage respondents were selected through the clustered probability sampling frame of the Institute for Social Research. The household compositions of recent surveys taken by the Survey Research Center were searched to identify those dwelling units which at the time of their original contact included individuals who would be 13- through 16-years old in the spring and summer of 1967. One thousand three hundred and sixty-seven dwellings were so identified and contacted; 959 (70 percent) were found still to house an eligible respondent. Of these, 810 (85 percent) yielded an interview, with only one eligible respondent interviewed in each dwelling. An additional 37 black youths were chosen by random supplementary sampling. Eligible respondents then absent from home were interviewed wherever possible, including reformatories.

Various tests of the sample against population figures and against some known characteristics of the sampling frame indicated that the sample of 847 is adequately representative of the population of 13- through 16-year olds residing in the 48 contiguous states at the time.

The sample was particularly checked for two potential distortions. First, tests were run to determine if corrections were necessitated by the undersampling of teenagers from large families, which resulted from taking just one interview from each household; no adjustment was deemed necessary.

Second, checks were made to discover if undersampling of teenagers whose families had high geographical mobility distorted the findings; for choosing dwelling units from previous surveys had resulted in missing 28 percent of the teenagers who had once resided there. But the geographic mobility of those who fell in the sample was found to be unrelated to any of the variables under study.

Interviewing   Interviewers were University of Michigan graduate students, married couples trained for this specific survey. Men interviewed boys; women, girls.

With few exceptions, interviews were conducted outside the youngsters' homes: in community centers, churches, libraries, and other sites out of ear-shot of the respondents' parents. Interviews lasted from 45 minutes to several hours, with an average of about 105 minutes.

Measures of delinquent behavior   Indices of delinquent behavior were constructed from the reports of the teenagers. Toward the end of an interview which covered a wide range of topics relevant to adolescent life—family, school, dating, aspirations for the future, and so on—each respondent was told that he would next be asked about behavior that "would get teenagers into trouble if they were caught." Assurances of confidentiality were reinforced along with a repetition of a request for frankness on the respondent's part. Then each respondent was given a pack of 16 pre-punched and pre-printed Hollerith cards, with the instructions:

> Here is a set of things other kids have told us they have done. Which of them have you done in the past three years, whether you were caught or not. . . . Sort them into these three piles— you have *never* done it . . . you have done it *just once* in the past three years . . . you've done it *more than once.* . . .

When the respondent had completed the card sort, he was then questioned on some of the details of each admitted offense—where it had happened, when, if he had been caught, by whom, and so on. No more than the three most recent of each of the 16 types of offenses were subjected to this probing.[2]

In this analysis we consider two of the indices built from teenagers' reports.[3] One measures the *frequency* of delinquent behavior; it is simply the sum of the number of offenses confessed and subjected to probing, after some confessions of non-delinquent acts were screened out. The other includes a weighting procedure for the *seriousness* of the delinquent behavior, the weight for each probed offense assigned according to the system devised by Sellin and Wolfgang (1963, 1964). These two measures are of course correlated since they are derived from the same information. But their correlation is only moderate ($r = .61$), and they will later be shown to yield somewhat different findings.

Measures of official delinquency   Indices of official delinquency were built from the reports of the teenagers and from those records of the teenage sample found in the files of law enforcement agencies in their areas of residence. Two years after the interviews had been taken, court and police files were searched. Since the confessions of teenagers revealed that 84 percent of their delinquent behavior had been committed within five miles of their homes, we restricted the search for official and quasi-official records to the sampled teenagers' counties of residence and all contiguous counties.

It is likely that some records of the older respondents in our sample had been expunged in the two years between interviewing and searching the files, for some jurisdictions discard juvenile records when a youngster becomes a potential adult criminal. However, we doubt that we lost more than a few records in this way.

Teenagers' reports and records found in files generated three measures of official delinquency: (1) the number of *police contacts*, i.e., the number of times each respondent said that he had been apprehended by a policeman for some delinquent act; (2) the number of *police records*, i.e., the number of instances of delinquent activity for which each respondent was recorded in some official or quasi-official file of a law enforcement agency; and (3) the number of *court records*, i.e., the number of times each respondent was referred to a court for delinquent activity.

DELINQUENT BEHAVIOR

Eighty-eight percent of the teenagers in the sample confessed to committing at least one chargeable offense in the three years prior to their interview. The distribution of their delinquent behavior, in terms of frequency and seriousness, is described by the curves in Figure 1. It is clear that, if the authorities were omniscient and technically zealous, a large majority of American 13- to 16-year olds would be labelled "juvenile delinquents"; but it is also clear that the numbers of adolescents decrease sharply as the measures indicate more frequent and serious delinquent behavior.

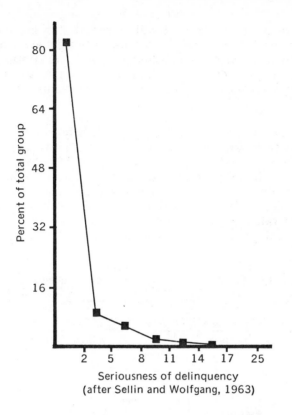

Seriousness of delinquency
(after Sellin and Wolfgang, 1963)

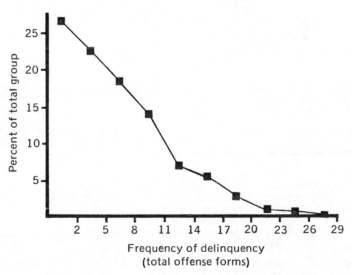

Frequency of delinquency
(total offense forms)

Figure 1
Frequency and seriousness of delinquency for total
group (N= 847)

Furthermore, anticipating what will be reported in more detail below, less than three percent of the offenses were detected by the police; only 22 percent of the youngsters ever had any contact with the police, only nine percent in the three years prior to the survey; and less than two percent of the sample had ever been under judicial consideration.

Sex differences   American girls behave delinquently less frequently and less seriously than American boys (see Figure 2). For ease of presentation, we have divided the curve of delinquent behavior at the median. Obviously, the proportion of boys exceeds the proportion of girls above the median for both frequency and seriousness of delinquent behavior. The difference between the sexes for both measures is highly reliable (Mann-Whitney U-test: $p < .00006$; all statistical tests reported in this paper are two-tailed unless specified otherwise).

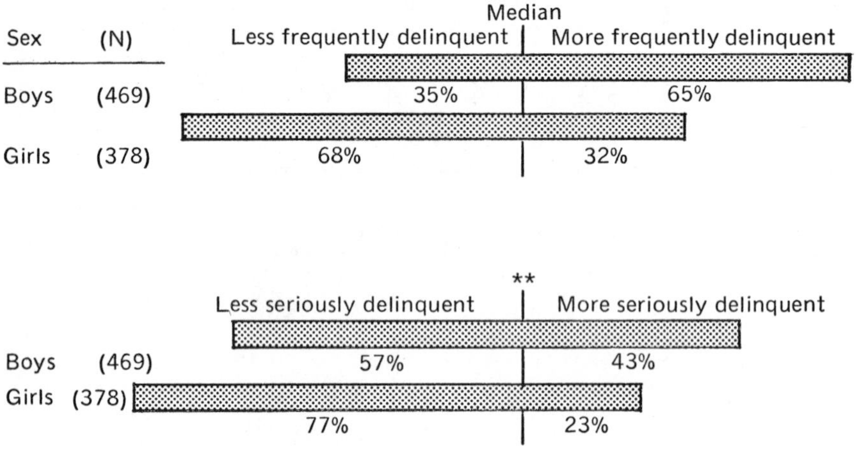

		Median
Sex	(N)	Less frequently delinquent ǀ More frequently delinquent

| Boys | (469) | 35% ǀ 65% |
| Girls | (378) | 68% ǀ 32% |

		**
		Less seriously delinquent ǀ More seriously delinquent
Boys	(469)	57% ǀ 43%
Girls	(378)	77% ǀ 23%

*Those persons falling below the median on frequency of delinquent behavior for the total group were placed in the category "less frequently delinquent" while those above were categorized as "more frequently delinquent."

**Since 60 percent of the total group had a zero score on seriousness of delinquent behavior, they were assigned to the "less seriously delinquent" category. The remaining group was assigned to the "more seriously delinquent" category.

Figure 2
Frequency and seriousness of delinquent behavior by sex*

Age differences   The relationship between age and delinquent behavior is reliable but rather slight. Figure 3 demonstrates that older teenagers are more frequently and seriously delinquent than younger ones. The relationship of age to frequency of delinquent behavior is stronger than its relationship to seriousness (Tau C $= .13, p < .0001$,

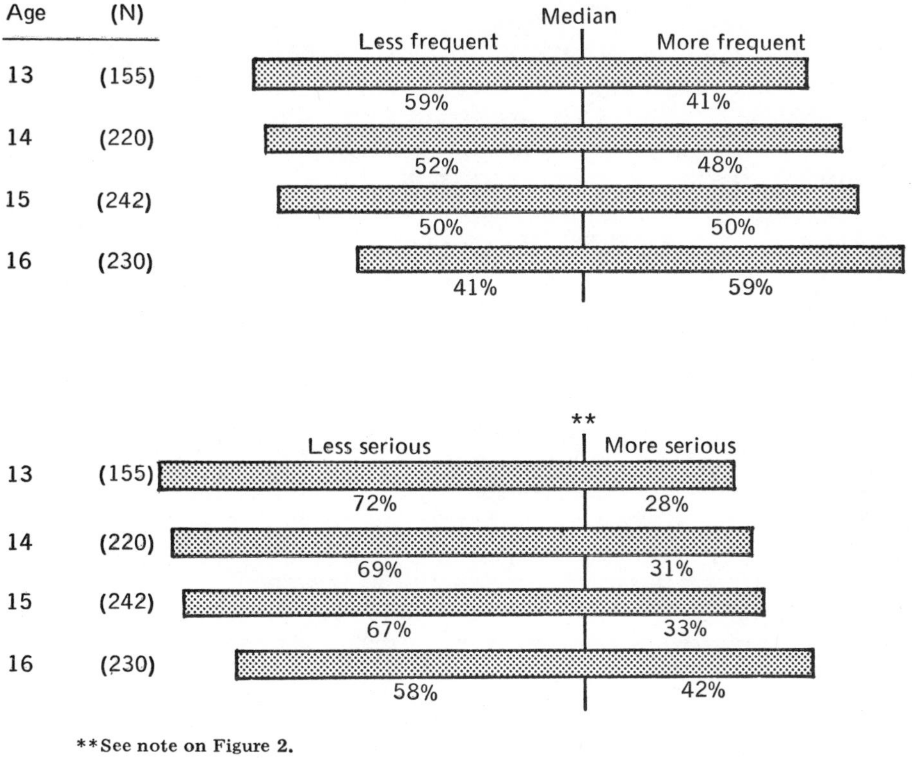

Age	(N)	
13	(155)	
14	(220)	
15	(242)	
16	(230)	

Median

Less frequent | More frequent

13 (155) — 59% / 41%
14 (220) — 52% / 48%
15 (242) — 50% / 50%
16 (230) — 41% / 59%

**

Less serious | More serious

13 (155) — 72% / 28%
14 (220) — 69% / 31%
15 (242) — 67% / 33%
16 (230) — 58% / 42%

**See note on Figure 2.

Figure 3
Frequency and seriousness of delinquent behavior by age

compared to Tau C = .09, p < .0002). This is at least partly due to less serious offenses like drinking accelerating more rapidly with age than more serious offenses like theft.

Racial differences   This analysis of racial differences includes only the 736 whites and 101 blacks in the sample, for the ten in the other racial categories are too few to permit comparisons. Furthermore, we found it necessary to make racial comparisons separately for boys and girls. For white girls are no more nor less frequently or seriously delinquent than black girls; and white boys, no more nor less *frequently* delinquent than black boys; but white boys are *less seriously* delinquent than black boys (see Figure 4). Mann-Whitney U-tests of differences between white and black girls yield p-levels of .64 and .49 for frequency and seriousness respectively; and, between white and black boys, p-levels of .75 and .06.

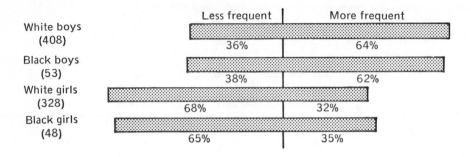

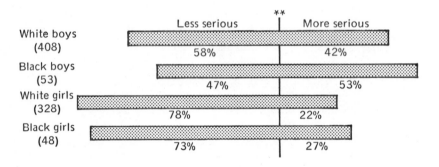

**See note on Figure 2.

Figure 4
Frequency and seriousness of delinquent behavior by race and sex

What are black boys doing to appear more seriously delinquent? An analysis of the components of the index of seriousness reveals that three offenses in combination account for most of the serious delinquency among both white and black boys: property damage, theft, and personal injury to another (assault and aggravated assault).

White boys damage relatively less property less seriously than black boys. While black boys steal less often than white boys, they steal more expensive items when they do steal. The stealing referred to here is only larceny and does not include burglary, which includes breaking into or entering the premises as well as stealing. Proportionately more of the blacks burgle. Finally, while black boys are involved in relatively fewer assaults than their white peers, they tend to inflict more serious injury. Assaults, burglary, theft, and property damage—in that order—account for the greater seriousness of the delinquent behavior of black compared to white boys.

We must at this point turn to the issue of differences in delinquent behavior among social statuses. Since, of course, the blacks in our representative sample are disproportionately clustered in the lower statuses (two-thirds of them are found among the 30 percent in the sample who are lowest in social status), it may be argued that the racial differences in the seriousness of male delinquency which have just been reported are actually attributable to social status differences. However, the relationship between the social status of white boys and their delinquent behavior fails to support this explanation.

Table 1
Social status and delinquent behavior

Sex and Race	Frequency		Seriousness	
	Gamma	p-Level	Gamma	p-Level
Boys				
Whites only	.05	.38	.12	.03
(N = 408)				
Whites and Blacks	.05	.31	.06	.20
(N = 461)				
Girls				
Whites only	.03	.74	.02	.84
(N = 328)				
Whites and Blacks	.05	.51	.03	.70
(N = 376)				

Differences among social statuses Our measure of social status is taken from teenagers' reports of the occupations of the chief breadwinners in their families. When youngsters could not describe those occupations precisely enough for coding, the question was pursued further with a parent when the respondent was returned to his home. Occupations have been ranked for social status according to the index described by Reiss *et al.* (1961).

This procedure, however, truncates social differences among blacks in America so as to lose meaningful distinctions. Measures of social status appropriate for whites are not directly applicable to blacks; when they are applied, they distort and compress the status of blacks downward. Thus, any relationship between variables such as delinquent behavior and social status *within the black community* is lost to a lumping effect which white-standardized social status measures impose on black stratification patterns. (For a discussion of this point, see Williams, 1968.) In order not to confuse racial differences with differences among social statuses, we present the relationships between delinquent behavior and social status first for whites only. It is also necessary to consider boys and girls separately.

In no case is the relationship between social status and delinquent behavior strong.[4] Indeed, the only statistically reliable relationship in Table 1 is that between the social status of white boys and the seriousness of their delinquent behavior (Gamma = .12, p. = .03). Figure 5 demonstrates that the higher status white boys are the more seriously delinquent. (See Voss [1966] for a similar finding, with which Gold [1967] quarreled at the time.) When the sample of black boys is included in the figures in Table 1, the relationship between social status and delinquent behavior becomes negligible.

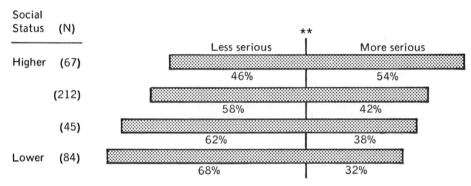

**See note on Figure 2.

Figure 5
Social status and seriousness of delinquent behavior
among white boys

The greater seriousness of the higher status boys' delinquent behavior stems from their committing proportionally more thefts, driving away more cars without the permission of the owners, and assaulting more people than their lower status peers. Differences among social statuses in the commission of vandalism are negligible. Table 2 indicates the per capita number of offenses reported by white boys in four levels of social status; the offenses are those included on Sellin and Wolfgang's index of seriousness.

It is notable that these findings contradict evidence of greater lower status delinquency in official records. These data cast into doubt a major assumption upon which most of the theory about delinquency (delinquent behavior) has been erected and from which most of the programs to prevent delinquency (delinquent behavior) have been launched. We begin now to trace how these figures on delinquent behavior are converted into quite different figures on official delinquency.

Table 2
Per capita serious offenses by social status (White boys)

Offense	Social Status			
	Higher (N = 67)	(N = 212)	(N = 45)	Lower (N = 84)
Theft	.72	.64	.55	.34
Joy-riding	.13	.08	.04	.06
Assault	.51	.34	.33	.34
Vandalism	.36	.37	.33	.33

CAUGHT BY POLICE

Nine percent of the sample reported detection by the police in some delinquent act in the three years prior to the survey. The acts in which they were caught comprise less than three percent of their total chargeable acts of delinquency.

What are some of the determinants of getting caught? That is, by what factors are some youngsters initially selected to be processed into official delinquents?

The frequency of teenagers' delinquent behavior is positively associated with their getting caught (Tau C = .11, p < .00001). To a lesser degree, so is the seriousness of their behavior (Tau C = .09, p < .0001). If seriousness is partialed out, the relationship of frequency to apprehension is Tau C = .09; if frequency is partialed out, the relationship of seriousness to apprehension is Tau C = .06. So the frequency of delinquent behavior is more predictive of getting caught by the police than the seriousness of that behavior. This is largely due to the fact that most (88 percent) of the offenses detected were discovered by police or someone else who happened by while the offenses were being committed. Thus, getting caught is to a great extent a chance occurrence. That the seriousness of an offense contributes at all to the likelihood of its resulting in contact with the police is due to two factors: (1) offenses directly against victims, like assault, are on the one hand considered more serious and, by the same token, include someone who may summon the police and identify the offender; and (2) the police are more likely to investigate a more serious offense (police investigations accounted for only 10 percent of all the apprehensions in our sample, but for 17 percent of the more serious offenses).

Sex differences Thirteen percent of the boys and three percent of the girls reported being apprehended by the police for some delinquent act in the three-year period. The relationships of the frequency

and seriousness of their delinquent behavior to their being caught are
the same for both sexes. And since, as we have seen, boys are more
frequently and seriously delinquent than girls, boys are more vulnerable to apprehension. However, since getting caught is to some degree
a function of compound probabilities based on frequency of delinquent behavior, the ratio of boys to girls caught exaggerates somewhat the difference in their delinquent behavior. While boys account
for 70 percent of all offenses reported, they show a larger percentage
(85 percent) of the total police contacts recorded.

Age differences   As is to be expected from the foregoing, older teenagers reported more contacts with the police than younger ones did
(see Figure 6).

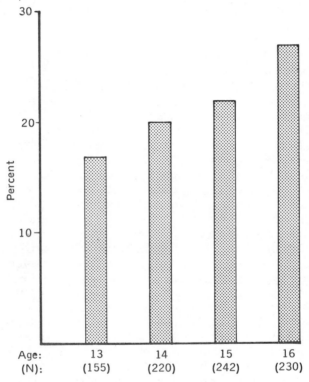

Figure 6
Percent caught by age

Racial differences   About the same proportions of white and black
teenagers reported some contact with the police (22 percent and 21
percent respectively).

   We pause here briefly to consider the implications of this finding for what is to come. So far we have presented small and in a sense
counterbalancing differences in the delinquent behavior of white and
black teenagers. And their general similarity seems to yield equal

contact with the police. Still, we are well aware that official records of delinquency include higher proportions of blacks and that the populations of reformatories are characteristically disproportionately black.[5] The discrepancy between the racial distribution of delinquent behavior and official delinquency is apparently not generated by differential apprehension rates. Presumably, it results from postapprehension dispositions. We will look at that phenomenon below.[6]

Differences among social statuses

Figure 7 demonstrates that almost twice the percentage of higher-status white boys report some contact with the police compared to their lower-status white peers. But the relationship between social status and police contacts is negligible (Gamma = .07, p < .45). This distribution follows the same direction as the reliably greater seriousness of the higher-status white boys' confessed delinquent behavior, but the present result is not so statistically reliable as the earlier one.

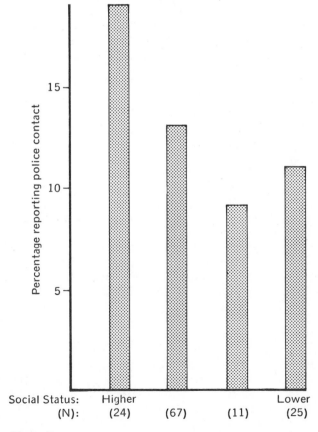

Social Status:	Higher			Lower
(N):	(24)	(67)	(11)	(25)

Figure 7
Social status and police contacts for white boys

As the inclusion of black boys into the analysis of the relationship between social status and delinquent behavior essentially washed out any reliable relationship, so also their inclusion in this analysis pertaining to police contacts diminishes the relationship with police contacts (Gamma = .04).

There is no reliable relationship between social status and police contacts among girls (Gamma = $-$ .11).

POLICE RECORDS

Not every teenager in our sample who reported contact with the police was recorded in some official or quasi-official file. When these files were searched two years after interviewing, we found the names of only four percent of the total sample. Less than one percent of the chargeable offenses committed in the three years prior to the interviews were recorded as official delinquency. A major reason for this is, of course, that many offenses go altogether undetected by any authority. And when offenses do come to the attention of police, they often result in warnings, "station adjustments," and a host of other possible police actions that fall short of delinquency records for teenagers. Given the above factors indicating a general reluctance of officials to give youths juvenile records, these data are understandable. (For other studies of police decisions, see Terry, 1967; Cicourel, 1968; Black, 1970; and Black and Reiss, 1970.)

The seriousness of teenagers' delinquent behavior is related to their having a police record and accounts for about nine percent of the variance; the frequency of their delinquent behavior accounts for a negligible proportion of the variation in having acquired records. Since police were for the most part unaware of most of the delinquent behavior of the youngsters they apprehended, the finding that they more often made records on those generally more seriously delinquent is probably due to the small relationship between the seriousness of the apprehended offense and the overall seriousness of an offender's delinquent behavior.

The important point to note here is that having a police record is only slightly related to the seriousness of teenagers' delinquent behavior, is not related at all to its frequency, and is less indicative of both the frequency and seriousness of delinquent behavior than having a number of contacts with police.[7]

Sex differences

Evidently, police put equal proportions of apprehended boys and girls on record (19 percent and 17 percent respectively). So six percent of the boys in our sample and two percent of the girls were identified in some official or quasi-official police file, a ratio which parallels their ratio of getting caught.

Age differences

More older teenagers were found to have police records than younger ones (see Figure 8). This is not due solely to the greater frequency and seriousness of the older teenagers' delinquent behavior. Police make a record on a higher proportion of those older teenagers whom they apprehend. The differential decision to make a record amplifies the relationship of age to delinquency. We have already noted that the relationship between age and delinquent behavior is slight. But police records make it appear that age is highly correlated with delinquency: 16-year olds appear eight times more delinquent than 13-year olds, as a proportion of their age group who have police records; and 16-year olds account for 17+ times more of the police records than 13-year olds do.

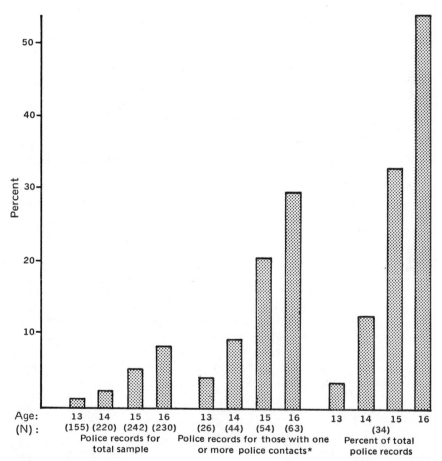

*The number of police contacts in this figure is larger than in previous figures because it includes youngsters who reported police contact at any time prior to being interviewed rather than just those having contact with the police only in the previous three years. The former figure is preferable here because it matches the longer time span covered by the police records.

Figure 8
Age and police records

Several factors seem to lead police to put older offenders on record more often. The greater frequency of their delinquent behavior in a given period of time and their longer life-span both result in more of them being caught more than once. (Since, as we have pointed out, getting caught is partly a matter of compounded probabilities, some of the amplification occurs right here.) Repeaters are more often put on record. Another factor is the greater seriousness of the delinquent behavior the older ones are caught at. Factors we have not measured probably have some effect—police believing that older adolescents "should know better," or are not so frightened as younger ones by a mere warning, or are no longer so easily corrected by their parents, and so on. It appears that official delinquency is more closely related to age than is delinquent behavior.

Racial differences

Four percent of the whites and five percent of the blacks in our sample were found in police records. Blacks comprised 15 percent of the 34 teenagers with records, a chance difference from the 12 percent in the total sample. Police did not seem to discriminate along racial lines in dealing with apprehended offenders: they put 17 percent of the apprehended whites and 24 percent of the apprehended blacks on record, not a statistically reliable difference in dispositions.[8]

Still, we are aware that court records contain a disproportionate number of blacks and reformatories an even greater disproportion. Apparently, decisions made by the police are not significant sources of these disproportions. Police records reflect the similarity between whites' and blacks' delinquent behavior.

Social status

The relationship of social status to police records is negligible among white boys (Gamma $= -.02$) but moderately high and statistically reliable among white girls (Gamma $= -.41$, $p < .03$, two-tailed). Lower-status white girls more often acquired police records, eight percent in the lowest status category having at least one, only two percent of those in the highest. Since we have found no reliable relationship between social status and delinquent behavior among girls, nor between social status and police contacts, we must attribute this last finding to the decisions police made about which girls to put on record. Girls' social status is somehow implicated in those decisions.

That such determinations are largely independent of the nature of frequency of the girls' delinquent behavior is likely, but one feature of our study makes us uncertain. We suspect that sexual offenses, or behavior which may lead to or involve sexual offenses, such as running away from home, are more likely to result in a girl's acquiring a record than are other offenses. For example, an earlier study (Gold, 1970) revealed that girls' official records contained a higher proportion of sexual offenses than was reflected in their detected and undetected delinquent behavior. But we are unable to consider to what extent sexual offenses are responsible for the social status differences in girls' police records because for reasons beyond our control, we could not in this survey ask teenagers about their sexual delinquency.

The absence of social status differences in boys' police records has something of the same significance as the absence of racial differences; for court records of delinquency characteristically yield reliable differences among social statuses. Here again, the relationship of official delinquency to social status apparently is introduced into the processing of offenders after police decisions are made about records.

Court records

Not every teenager who has a record of delinquency in some official or quasi-official file has been formally declared a juvenile delinquent by a court. The records we have been discussing exist not only in the files of juvenile courts but also in the files of juvenile bureaus of larger police departments, in sheriffs' files, some in the informal files of small-town constables, and elsewhere. The maintenance of such files is in some states technically illegal, but they serve nevertheless as the memories for law enforcement agencies. So while 34 teenagers in our sample were found to have police records, only 16 of these had ever been referred to a juvenile court, 11 declared delinquent.

We are, at this point, obviously beyond the limits of our data. With only 16 individuals—less than two percent of the total sample—having court records, we cannot hope to discover much about how they were selected for that condition from among the rest of the sample. But we offer a few observations based on our perusal of the data. (For data focused on aspects of selection of juvenile offenders for appearance in court, see Cohn, 1963; Erickson and Empey, 1963; Ferdinand and Luchterhand, 1970, especially concerning racial factors; and Piliavin and Briar, 1964, and Black and Reiss, 1970, on juveniles' demeanor.)

The data suggest that blacks were referred to juvenile court relatively more often, and that differential disposition of offenses committed by whites and blacks is almost completely restricted to the disposition made of the *repeated* offenses recorded: blacks with more than one recorded offense were referred to court more often than whites with more than one recorded offense. We may have here the beginnings of the process which results in the overrepresentation of black youth in juvenile court records and in reformatories. While court records and reformatory populations may by definition accurately reflect racial differences in *official delinquency* they do not accurately reflect racial differences in *delinquent behavior*.[9]

SUMMARY AND CONCLUSION

It will come as no surprise to students of delinquency that official measures of delinquency do not accurately reflect delinquent behavior. It is clear that when measurements are taken only a step or two along in the process—at police contact or in police files—a great deal of discrepancy has already been introduced. So the distribution of official delinquency among categories of sex, age, race, and social status does not parallel the distribution of delinquent behavior.

The character of the discrepancies differs from category to category. Age and sex differences in official delinquency are amplifications of differences in delinquent behavior. Because younger teenagers and girls commit fewer and less serious offenses, they are less often caught than older ones and boys, and when caught, their crimes are less often recorded.

The racial difference in official delinquency is also an amplification of the difference in delinquent behavior. (Indeed, whatever difference is inferred from the former to the latter among *girls* seems to be a fabrication rather than an amplification.) Our data indicate that the discrepancy regarding race is introduced at a different point in the process than the discrepancies involving sex and age. The blacks in our sample probably began to receive differential treatment when juvenile court referrals were being considered rather than earlier in the process, at the points of police contact or police record. Their differential treatment at that point cannot be attributed to the greater seriousness of their offenses compared to whites'; for the seriousness of offenses seems to matter little in the determination of court referrals. We speculate that it is more likely that the backgrounds of black youngsters are more often judged to require the intervention of the court. Or perhaps it is officers' perception of the black youngsters' demeanor.

Social status differences characteristically found in official records of juvenile delinquency contradict the evidence regarding the delinquent behavior reported here. That is, the only difference in these data identified the *higher* status white boys as more seriously delinquent than lower status white boys. However, this difference is small, albeit statistically reliable, and it almost completely disappears upon contact with the police; it is gone at the point that police records are made. In its place is a statistically reliable difference in police records on girls, identifying the lower-status girls, with race controlled, as more delinquent. Then a social status difference among boys, which marks the lower-status boys as more delinquent, may be introduced at the level of court referral through the differential treatment of black offenders, who are almost exclusively lower status. It is probable that lower-status black boys become more officially delinquent than higher-status white boys during the judicial process, but our data do not adequately extend to that stage.

It is important then for researchers in this area to be clear about what they intend to study. Both delinquent behavior and official delinquency are important phenomena deserving attention, but they are not by any means the same thing. Measures of one, we have seen, are far from isomorphic with measures of the other. Social scientists interested in social psychological determinants and functions of individual deviance should focus their attention on delinquent behavior; those concerned with formal social organizational determinants and functions of deviance should properly study official delinquency.

Insofar as research in this field may help shape social policy, then it is crucial that we be clear about the distinction that has been so heavily stressed here. For what we tell those whose job it is to treat individuals for their delinquent behavior will derive little of use to themselves from data on official delinquency. The seeming failure of almost all attempts to treat delinquency from the point of view of an individual's behavior may be attributed in large part to misleading data.

Most misleading has been the interpretation that whatever differentiates official delinquents from "non-delinquents" is a clue to the causes of delinquent behavior; when in fact the differentials pertain to the causes of the behavior of a social system which includes at least juveniles and police officers, often judges, and less directly, other roles in the community and society. The delinquent behavior of the juvenile is but one element in the behavior of that whole social system which generates official delinquency. So, for example, those concerned with official delinquency are well-advised to give much attention to variables like social status and race. But those interested in delinquent behavior may attend less to these variables according to the data reported here.

Some consequences of the confusion between delinquent behavior and official delinquency are apparent for social practice. Treatment and prevention programs are aimed primarily at populations which are not uniquely delinquent, like the poor and the black, thus falsely stereotyping these populations while missing other youngsters in need of help. Furthermore, the techniques of social practice are shaped to deal with largely extraneous forces, so that their effectiveness is ironically deflected: teenagers who are caught, and become formally or informally identified as juvenile delinquents and are more or less subjected to these techniques, tend to commit more offenses afterward than control offenders who are not caught (Gold and Williams, 1969; Gold, 1970).

NOTES

1 Now at Research Triangle Institute, Center for Study of Social Behavior, Research Triangle Park, North Carolina 27709.

2 For a report on the validity of this measure of delinquent behavior, see Gold (1970), which describes its use in an earlier study.

3 We are aware that some students of delinquency hold that global measures are not as useful as the identification of more specific types of delinquent behavior. However, our experience with data from a previous study (Gold, 1970:32-34) and from this study indicates that typologies of offenses are not empirically justified. Powerful clustering techniques such as cluster analysis, factor analysis, smallest space analysis, and others continue producing global dimensions of frequency and seriousness and do not generate reliable typologies.

4   The notion that delinquent behavior is a lower-class phenomenon is widely held at present. In a recent book, Schur (1969:95-115) documents the theoretical and empirical rise in sociology of this notion. In his excellent review, Schur is careful to indicate that while this represents current "major sociological perspectives," not all sociologists agree.

      In a recent summary report, The President's Commission on Law Enforcement and Administration of Justice endorses the notion that delinquency is a lower-class phenomenon. Despite a brief reference to "recent self-report studies," the report concludes: "But there is still no reason to doubt that delinquency, and especially the most serious delinquency, is committed disproportionately by slum and lower-class youth" (The President's Commission on Law Enforcement and Administration of Justice, 1967:57).

      A primary barrier to exploring the relationship between delinquent behavior and social class has been the failure to distinguish between delinquent behavior and official delinquency (for an extensive discussion of this point, see Gold, 1966:27-46). However, among those researchers making the distinction, most concur with the findings reported here (see for example, Nye *et al.*, 1958; Empey and Erickson, 1966; Empey, 1967; for mixed findings, see Clark and Wenninger, 1962; and for findings contrary to those reported here, see Reiss and Rhodes, 1961).

5   Thirty-three percent of the inmates of public institutions for delinquents in 1956 were non-white (Rowland, 1958). No more recent data are available because the U.S. Children's Bureau stopped reporting the racial composition of the inmate population after the 1958 publication.

6   Piliavin and Briar (1964) suggest that police tend to stop and interrogate black boys relatively more often than white because of common racial stereotypes. But if this is in fact the case, it would not necessarily result in relatively more frequent police contacts *for delinquent acts*, which we are reporting here. Piliavin and Briar observe that the result of this practice is that a larger proportion of black boys are immediately dismissed on the street or at the station for lack of evidence.

7   Kobrin (1951) has suggested that, of the records of official delinquency available, recorded contacts with the police are the most indicative of the degree of actual delinquent behavior. These data indicate that, while these records may be the most closely related to delinquent behavior of all the records, there is a great deal of distortion already introduced at this early stage of the process.

8   Black and Reiss (1970) report that police in Boston, Chicago, and Washington D.C. more often arrested black youth than whites because black complainants against black offenders urged investigating policemen to be more severe than did white complainants against white youth. Black and Reiss consider transporting the juvenile to the station as an "arrest"; juveniles arrested in this sense do not necessarily acquire records. It is possible that, with the complainant out of the way, the police generally make decisions to record names independent of racial characteristics. See also Black (1970). On the other hand, Piliavin and Briar (1964) report that the police in another metropolis did record relatively more offenses by blacks than by whites.

9   McEachern and Bauzer (1964) present data which demonstrate that police in Los Angeles County did not differentially refer blacks or Mexicans to juvenile court, compared to whites. The contradiction between their finding and ours suggests that there is diversity in the criteria used by different police departments—even different policemen—to determine which juvenile offenders should be referred. Other data presented by McEachern and Bauzer reveal such diversity within one county. For example, Goldman (1963) found that police in the four cities he studied did refer proportionately more black juveniles to court than white, as did the police observed by Ferdinand and Luchterhand (1970).

REFERENCES

Black, D. J.
1970   "Production of crime rates." American Sociological Review 35 (August): 733-748.

Black, D. J. and A. J. Reiss, Jr.
1970   "Control of Juveniles." American Sociological Review 35 (February): 63-77.

Cicourel, A. V.
1968   Juvenile Justice. New York: Wiley.

Clark, J. P. and E. P. Wenninger
1962   "Socio-economic class and area as correlates of illegal behavior among juveniles." American Sociological Review 27 (December): 826-834.

Cohn, Y.
1963   "Criteria for the probation officer's recommendations to the juvenile court judge." Crime and Delinquency 9 (July): 262-275.

Empey, L. T.
1967   "Delinquency theory and recent research." The Journal of Research in Crime and Delinquency 4 (January): 28-42.

Empey, L. T. and M. L. Erickson
1966   "Hidden delinquency and social status." Social Forces 44 (June): 546-554.

Erickson, M. L. and L. T. Empey
1963   "Court records, undetected delinquency and decision-making." The Journal of Criminal Law, Criminology and Police Science 54 (December): 456-469.

Ferdinand, T. N. and E. G. Luchterhand
1970   "Inner-city youth, the police, the juvenile court, and justice." Social Problems 17 (Spring): 510-527.

Gold, M.
1966   "Undetected delinquent behavior." The Journal of Research in Crime and Delinquency 3 (January): 27-46.

1967   "On social status and delinquency." Social Problems 15 (Summer): 114-116.

1970   Delinquent Behavior in an American City. Belmont, Cal.: Brooks/Cole.

Gold, M. and J. R. Williams
1969   "The effect of getting caught: Apprehension of the juvenile offender as a cause of subsequent delinquencies." Prospectus 3 (December): 1-12.

Goldman, N.
1963   The Differential Selection of Juvenile Offenders for Court Appearance. New York: National Council on Crime and Delinquency.

Kobrin, S.
1951   "The conflict of values in delinquency areas." American Sociological Review 16 (October): 653-661.

McEachern, A. W. and R. Bauzer
1964   "Factors related to disposition in juvenile police contacts," pp. 192-210 in M. W. Klein and B. G. Myeroff (eds.), Juvenile Gangs in Context. Los Angeles: University of Southern California, Youth Studies Center.

Nye, F. I.
1958   Family Relationships and Delinquent Behavior. New York: Wiley.

Nye, F. I., J. F. Short, Jr., and V. J. Olson
1958   "Socioeconomic status and delinquent behavior." The American Journal of Sociology 63 (January): 381-389.

Piliavin, I. and S. Briar
  1964   "Police encounters with juveniles." American Journal of Sociology
           70 (September): 206-214.
The President's Commission on Law Enforcement and Administration of Justice
  1967   The Challenge of Crime in a Free Society. Washington, D.C.: U.S.
           Government Printing Office.
Reiss, A. J., Jr., O. D. Duncan, P. K. Hatt, and C. C. North
  1961   Occupations and Social Status. New York: Free Press.
Reiss, A. J., Jr. and A. L. Rhodes
  1961   "The distribution of juvenile delinquency in the social class struc-
           ture." American Sociological Review 26 (October): 720-732.
Rowland, R.
  1958   Statistics on Public Institutions for Delinquent Children. Washington,
           D.C.: Children's Bureau.
Schur, E. M.
  1969   Our Criminal Society. Englewood Cliffs, N.J.: Prentice-Hall.
Sellin, T. and M. E. Wolfgang
  1963   Constructing an Index of Delinquency: A Manual. Philadelphia: Uni-
           versity of Pennsylvania Center of Criminal Research.
  1964   The Measurement of Delinquency. New York: Wiley.
Terry, R. M.
  1967   "The screening of juvenile offenders." Journal of Criminal Law,
           Criminology, and Police Science 58 (June): 173-181.
U.S. Department of Commerce, Bureau of the Census
  1968   Current Population Reports. P-25, #385. Washington, D.C.: U.S.
           Government Printing Office.
Voss, H. L.
  1966   "Socio-economic status and reported delinquent behavior." Social
           Problems 13 (Winter): 314-324.
Williams, J. R.
  1968   Social Stratification and the Negro American: An Exploration of
           Some Problems in Social Class Measurement. Unpublished Ph.D. dis-
           sertation, Department of Sociology, Duke University.

Race, Socioeconomic Status and Sentencing in the Juvenile Justice System

TERENCE P. THORNBERRY*

Terence P. Thornberry is assistant director of the Center for
Studies in Criminology and Criminal Law, University of
Pennsylvania.

Reprinted from Terence P. Thornberry, "Race, Socioeconomic
Status and Sentencing in the Juvenile Justice System," *Journal
of Criminal Law and Criminology* 64 (1973): 90-98.

Racial and social class discrimination in the administration
of justice has long been of theoretical and empirical interest to criminologists. Although many theoretical works assume that such discrimination exists, Terry has pointed out that this assumption has
been made ". . . even though empirical research dealing with these
issues is relatively sparse and poorly conceived."[1] For example,
Lemert states that "Members of minority groups, migrants, and persons with limited economic means are often the . . . scapegoats of the
frustrated police in our local communities."[2] Clinard makes a similar
assumption: "It is a generally established fact that the Negroes, as
well as Spanish speaking peoples, on the whole, are arrested, tried,
convicted, and returned to prison more often than others who commit comparable offenses."[3] Sutherland and Cressey, without data,
assert:

> (a) Negroes are more liable to arrest than whites . . . (c) Negroes
> have a higher conviction rate than whites. (d) Negroes are often
> punished more severely than whites, but this is not true for all
> crimes. (e) Whites are most likely to receive probation and sus-
> pended sentences. (f) Negroes receive pardons less often than
> do whites.[4]

The purpose of the present study is to examine empirically the
validity of this assumption using data from the juvenile justice system
in Philadelphia. The basic question to be answered is: Do blacks and
members of a low socioeconomic strata (SES) receive more severe
dispositions than whites and members of a high SES?

*The author would like to express his thanks to Drs. Marvin E. Wolfgang, Frank
J. Cannavale and Robert A. Silverman for their critical reading of earlier drafts
of this article.

The answer is not simple for there are legal variables to be considered. The principles of Anglo-Saxon justice should not permit nonlegal variables like race and social class to affect the severity of dispositions. Legal variables, however, such as the seriousness of the offenses committed by the defendant, may be expected to have a decisive effect on the disposition.

The fact that blacks and lower SES subjects are more likely to be recidivists and to commit serious offenses[5] suggests that these legal variables should be controlled in any attempt to examine the effect of race and socioeconomic status. Otherwise, to find that blacks and lower SES subjects receive more severe dispositions may only reflect the fact that they are indeed more serious offenders. Conclusions about the relationship between social characteristics and dispositions should only be made when these legal variables are held constant.

PREVIOUS WORK[6]

Terry conducted a study based on a sample of all the cases of delinquent behavior that occurred between 1958 and 1962 in a midwestern community with a population of 100,000.[7] Terry ranked the dispositions according to the severity that the police, the probation department and the juvenile court could give an individual, and then correlated them with a number of independent variables. Although the dispositions in the jurisdiction that Terry studied are slightly different from the dispositions used in Philadelphia, their rank order in terms of severity are quite similar to the scheme employed here.

The most important finding in Terry's study concerns the nonlegal variables of race and SES. In zero-order relationships race and SES were consistently, but not very strongly, related to the severity of the dispositions; but after the number of previous offenses and the seriousness of the offense were controlled, the weak relationships that did exist vanished. "The evidence indicates that the severity of the disposition is not a function of the degree of minority status of the juvenile offender or his socioeconomic status."[8] Age, however, was significantly and positively related to the severity of dispositions, and when the legal variables were controlled, this relationship remained.

The legal variables, on the other hand, were strongly related to the severity of dispositions.

> Only one of the major hypotheses is completely and consistently supported at the three stages of the legal-judicial system. . . . The severity of the societal reaction is a function, at least in part, of the amount of deviance [previous offenses] engaged in by the offender. Also relevant, but less clearly so, [is] the degree of deviation [the seriousness of the offense] . . .[9]

None of the other legal or nonlegal variables that Terry studied were significantly or consistently related to the dependent variable of dispositions, with the sole exception of the number of adult offenders involved in a given offense. ". . . [I]t seems to be a safe conclusion that legalistic variables play a significant role in the process at all of the stages considered."[10] The same cannot be said for the nonlegal variables, however. With the exception of age, they were not strongly related to dispositions, and with the introduction of the legal variables as controls the relationship vanished.

A number of other studies have arrived at similar conclusions. McEachern and Bauzer examined patterns of police referrals to the juvenile court in Santa Monica, California.[11] No relationship between race and disposition was found. "The proportions of petitions requested for the three ethnic categories used in this analysis are .28 for Negroes, .27 for Mexican-Americans, and .26 for Angloes."[12] Thus, even when the legal variables were ignored, ethnic group membership did not affect the referral practices of the police. As in Terry's study, McEachern and Bauzer found the legal variables to be most strongly related to dispositions. Delinquents who committed serious offenses, who had a greater number of previous offenses, and who were on probation when arrested were far more likely to be referred to the juvenile court than their counterparts.

An earlier study conducted by Goldman closely parallels the work of McEachern and Bauzer, for it is also concerned with the manner in which the police referred cases to the juvenile court.[13] In general, black children were more likely than white children to be referred to the juvenile court. For example, 6.1 per cent of all the cases involved black delinquents but the blacks ". . . constituted 11.4 per cent of those referred to the juvenile court."[14] Although the black children were more likely to be referred to juvenile court, they were also more likely to commit more serious offenses and to have had a greater amount of previous contact with the police. Although the legal variables were not held constant, the author suggests that they tend to explain the relationship. "It must be noted that all of the Negro children who were referred to court were involved in instances of serious offenses . . ."[15]

Shannon used an ecological approach to investigate the referral behavior of the police in three communities of Madison, Wisconsin.[16] One area was predominantly lower class, another predominantly middle class but with some working class sections, and the third was a mixture of middle and "high class" sections. As would be expected, the lower class had a disproportionately high referral rate to the juvenile court, while the higher class area had a disproportionately low rate. The referral rate in the middle class area was about the same as the expected rate. When Shannon controlled for the seriousness of the offense committed, the relationship between social class and dispositions was eliminated. Delinquents from the lower class area committed more serious offenses than delinquents from the other areas. "This means that . . . juveniles engaging in comparable types of delinquent behavior receive pretty much the same treatment from the Madison police."[17]

Hohenstein examined the referral practices of the police in Philadelphia, basing his analysis on 504 delinquent events committed in 1960.[18] These 504 events constitute a ten per cent sample of all the index offenses committed in 1960, as defined by Sellin and Wolfgang.[19] Using predictive attribute analysis to examine the data, Hohenstein found that "three important factors were involved in determining the disposition decision: (1) the attitude of the victim, (2) the previous record of the offender, and (3) the seriousness of the present event."[20] The most striking finding was that the attitude of the victim was the most important variable involved. Regardless of the amount of recidivism or the seriousness of the event, when the victim did not favor prosecution, the offender was almost always given the least serious disposition available. However, when the victim was in favor of prosecution, the offender was usually arrested. Relative to nonlegal variables, Hohenstein found race to be virtually unrelated to dispositions and the age of the offender was totally unrelated.[21] The legal variables of seriousness, recidivism, and the attitude of the victim, however, were found to relate to dispositions.

In general, the preceding research shows that when legal variables such as the seriousness of the offense and the number of previous offenses committed are held constant, the nonlegal variables of race and SES have been found not to affect disposition decisions. Terry's concluding remarks can be used to summarize this body of literature:

> While our research has focused on only some of the many variables that may be relevant in [disposing of juvenile offenders], it seems to be a safe conclusion that legalistic variables play a significant role in the process at all of the stages considered.[22]

Clearly, the findings of these previous studies do not support the assumptions of Lemert, Clinard and others. Given the findings of the research reported to date, blacks and low SES subjects are not more likely than their counterparts to be treated more severely in the juvenile justice system when recidivism and the seriousness of the offense are held constant.

The studies discussed serve two functions: first, to limit the number of variables to be examined; and second, to form hypotheses. The present research deals only with the variables that were previously found to be most significantly related to dispositions: race, SES, number of previous offenses, and the seriousness of the offense. Other analyzed variables were generally found to be unrelated to dispositions. For example, Terry found that variables such as the number of individuals involved in the offense, the delinquency rate of the area of residence, the degree of involvement with offenders of the opposite sex did not affect the severity of dispositions given by legal agencies. The hypotheses which may be formed are:

1   Blacks and delinquents from the low SES receive more severe dispositions than their counterparts.
2   Juveniles who commit serious offenses and have many previous offenses also receive more severe dispositions.
3   When legal variables are held constant, nonlegal variables are unrelated to disposition decisions.

METHODOLOGY

To test these hypotheses data collected by Wolfgang, Figlio and Sellin were used.[23] This study gathered information on all males who were born in 1945 and who lived in Philadelphia at least from the ages of ten through seventeen years. By using the records of a variety of agencies, primarily the schools of Philadelphia, the cohort study delimited a population of 9,945 boys. Of this cohort, 3,475 boys were found to have committed at least one delinquent act, and it is this group of delinquents who were analyzed in the present study. After delimiting the cohort population, a search was made by Wolfgang *et al.* through the files of the Philadelphia Police Department for all *officially* recorded delinquent acts committed by the cohort subjects. There were 10,214 delinquent events, with final dispositions recorded for 9,601 cases.[24]

Measurement of the dependent variable, the severity of legal dispositions, is relatively clear-cut because it is a legal variable already defined by the penal code of Pennsylvania. According to police records, the dispositions that can be given to a juvenile in Philadelphia are the following:

1   *Remedial arrest:* handled entirely by the police. In this case, the juvenile is almost always taken to the police station and detained for an hour or so. His case is not forwarded to any other legal agency (e.g., the courts), but his parents or legal guardians are notified and the case is often referred to the city's Department of Welfare. The offense, however, is listed in his police file. (6515)[25]
2   *Discharged:* cases referred by the police but dismissed at the first juvenile court hearing or after a court continuance, unaccompanied by probation. (590)
3   *Adjusted:* cases dismissed at the juvenile court, either by a juvenile court judge or a member of the court staff after the case is adjusted, but without the use of probation. (748)
4   *Fine and/or restitution:* cases in which the juvenile pays a fine, makes restitution to the victim, or both. (20)
5   *Probation:* cases in which the juvenile court sentences the individual to a certain period of time on probation. (1074)
6   *Institutionalization:* cases in which the juvenile court sentences the individual to spend a certain period of time in a correctional institution. (654)

Because of the similarity of some categories and the small frequencies in others, these six dispositions have been collapsed into the following four:

Remedial arrest	6,515	67.9%
Adjusted (Adjusted and Discharged)	1,338	13.9%
Probation (Probation and Fine and/ or Restitution)	1,094	11.4%
Institutionalization	654	6.8%
Total	9,601	100.0%

Data are presented so as to allow examination of differential disposition at each of the major stages of the juvenile justice system: the police, intake hearings by the juvenile court's probation department, and hearings by the juvenile court itself. The major decision for the police is whether to treat a juvenile leniently by giving him a remedial arrest, or to treat him more severely by referring him to the juvenile court. We shall compare the percentage of cases given remedial arrests with the percentage of cases referred to the court. At the level of the intake hearing the major decision is whether to adjust the case, the more lenient option, or to refer the case for a formal juvenile court hearing. The comparison is between the adjusted category and the referred category—the sum of the cases given a sentence of probation or institutionalization. Finally, the major decision for the juvenile court judge concerns probation which is the lenient alternative, or institutionalization, the severe alternative. These two dispositions will be compared. In sum, the following comparisons are made: (1) for the police—remedial vs. referral; (2) for the intake process—adjusted vs. referral; (3) for the juvenile court—probation vs. institutionalization.

RACE AND DISPOSITION

As can be seen in Table 1, black offenders are more likely than white offenders to receive a more severe disposition at each of the three stages. The police, for example, give a remedial disposition to 78.8 per cent of the white juveniles, but to only 59.2 per cent of the blacks. At the intake hearing the racial differences are not as great, but are still in the same direction. Blacks are less likely (41.8%) than whites (47.1%) to have their cases adjusted, but are more likely (58.2%) than whites (52.9%) to be referred for a court hearing. At the stage of the court hearing the differences are of the same magnitude as the differences observed at the police level. For example, 42.3 per cent of the blacks are sent to correctional institutions, but only 24.4 per cent of whites are handled in this fashion.

Table 1
Disposition by race

Disposition	Race		Total
	Black	White	
Remedial %	59.2	78.8	67.9
Referral %	40.8	21.2	32.1
	(5362)*	(4239)	(9601)
Adjusted %	41.8	47.1	43.4
Referral %	58.2	52.9	56.6
	(2186)	(900)	(3086)
Probation %	57.7	75.6	62.6
Institution %	42.3	24.4	37.4
	(1272)	(476)	(1748)

*In this and all subsequent tables the numbers upon which the percentages are based are presented in parentheses.

The race of the juvenile makes a difference in the way he is handled by the juvenile justice system. However, this difference may be explained by such legal variables as the seriousness of the offense and the subject's previous record. Before controlling for these variables, their relationship to the dependent variable must be determined. Table 2 presents the relationship between the seriousness of the offense and the severity of disposition. At all three stages the more serious the offense, the more severe the disposition. The differences between seriousness of offense and type of disposition are greatest at the police level and least at the juvenile court level.

When the amount of recidivism is used as the independent variable, as in Table 3, similar differences are observed. The expected relationship is present at all three stages and the differences are strong at all stages. At the police level, for example, remedial disposition for first offenders occurs in 79.6 per cent of the cases, while offenders with three or more previous offenses are given remedial dispositions in only 54.2 per cent of the cases. At the juvenile court level first offenders are sent to an institution in 14.0 per cent of the cases, but 50.0 per cent of the juveniles with three or more previous offenses are institutionalized. These two legal variables are strongly associated with disposition decisions as would be expected from previous studies. The task now is to see if they explain the relationship between race and disposition.

Table 2
Disposition by seriousness

Disposition	Seriousness*		Total
	Low	High	
Remedial %	88.0	37.3	67.9
Referral %	12.0	62.7	32.1
	(5782)	(3819)	(9601)
Adjusted %	65.4	37.0	43.4
Referral %	34.6	63.0	56.6
	(691)	(2395)	(3086)
Probation %	66.5	62.0	62.6
Institution %	33.5	38.0	37.4
	(239)	(1509)	(1748)

*Seriousness is measured by the Sellin-Wolfgang index. See footnote 19. A low seriousness score is less than 1 and a high score is 1 or more.

Table 3
Disposition by number of previous offenses

Disposition	Number of Previous Offenses			Total
	None	1 or 2	3+	
Remedial %	79.6	69.6	54.2	67.9
Referral %	20.4	30.4	45.8	32.1
	(3404)	(2912)	(3285)	(9601)
Adjusted %	57.0	47.0	34.9	43.4
Referral %	43.0	53.0	65.1	56.6
	(696)	(886)	(1504)	(3086)
Probation %	86.0	73.8	50.0	62.6
Institution %	14.0	26.2	50.0	37.4
	(299)	(470)	(979)	(1748)

In Table 4 the racial differences are presented, holding constant the seriousness of the offense. The striking finding is that racial differences are still quite apparent even when the influence of the seriousness of the offense is controlled. In only one of the six com-

Table 4
Disposition by seriousness and race

Disposition	Seriousness			
	Low		High	
	Black	White	Black	White
Remedial %	83.9	92.3	30.0	50.4
Referral %	16.1	7.7	70.0	49.6
	(2909)	(2873)	(2453)	(1366)
Adjusted %	61.4	73.9	36.5	38.4
Referral %	38.6	26.1	63.5	61.6
	(469)	(222)	(1717)	(678)
Probation %	60.8	84.5	57.2	74.4
Institution %	39.2	15.5	42.8	25.6
	(181)	(58)	(1091)	(418)

parisons, the intake stage for high seriousness offenses, does the difference come close to disappearing, and even here blacks are less likely than whites (36.5% vs. 38.4%) to have their cases adjusted. In the other five comparisons the differences are relatively large. Taking the juvenile court stage as one example, we see that for offenses with a low seriousness score, 39.2 per cent of blacks are institutionalized compared to only 15.2 per cent of whites. For the more serious offenses, 42.8 per cent of blacks are institutionalized, but only 25.6 per cent of whites are so treated. Racial differences observed in the zero-order relationship are not explained by the seriousness of the offense.

If the first and third columns and the second and fourth columns in Table 4 are compared, we observe the relationship between seriousness and dispositions when race is held constant. From these comparisons it is clear that the seriousness of the offense plays a major role in determining the severity of the disposition. Both black and white subjects are more likely to receive a severe disposition when they commit serious offenses. This fact is true at all three stages of the juvenile justice system. Race and seriousness tend to interact in relation to dispositions. Thus, for all three stages, white subjects who committed offenses of low seriousness are most likely to receive a lenient disposition while black subjects who committed a high seriousness offense are least likely to receive a lenient disposition.

This finding should not obscure the major result of Table 4. Even when the seriousness of the offense is held constant, blacks are more likely than whites to receive a more severe disposition at all three stages of the juvenile justice system. This finding refutes the

Table 5
Disposition by number of previous offenses and race

| Disposition | Number of Previous Offenses | | | | | |
| | None | | 1 or 2 | | 3+ | |
	Black	White	Black	White	Black	White
Remedial %	70.6	86.0	62.7	77.6	50.2	64.8
Referral %	29.4	14.0	37.3	22.4	49.8	35.2
	(1426)	(1978)	(1564)	(1347)	(2371)	(914)
Adjusted %	56.9	57.2	46.6	47.7	34.1	37.9
Referral %	43.1	42.8	53.4	52.3	65.9	62.1
	(420)	(276)	(584)	(302)	(1182)	(322)
Probation %	84.5	88.1	71.2	79.1	46.1	65.5
Institution %	15.5	11.9	28.8	20.9	53.9	34.5
	(181)	(118)	(312)	(158)	(779)	(200)

hypothesis based on the results of previous studies. Unlike the other studies, the seriousness of the offense does not explain the relationship between race and disposition.

This finding is essentially the same when the number of previous offenses is held constant as in Table 5. At the police level, blacks are considerably less likely than whites to receive a remedial disposition, regardless of their previous record. At the intake hearing, however, the situation is somewhat different. For the three categories of the control variable, the rates are approximately equal, but in all three cases the small differences that do exist are in the same direction as the differences found when the seriousness of the offense was held constant. At the juvenile court level, blacks are again more likely than whites to be treated severely, especially as the number of previous offenses increases. Although the difference is not great for first offenders (15.5% vs. 11.9% institutionalized), it is sizeable (53.9% vs. 34.5% institutionalized) for those who committed three or more previous offenses. In general, the number of previous offenses does not explain differential dispositions by race.

Finally, racial differences can be examined while both major legal variables are simultaneously controlled as in Table 6. When this is done, racial differences are still clearly observable. At the police level the differences are sizeable, and in all six comparisons blacks are less likely than whites to receive a remedial disposition. The situation for the juvenile court is quite similar. Again the differences are relatively large and all in the same direction. In all six comparisons blacks are more likely to be institutionalized and less likely to be put on probation than are whites. At the intake hearing the results are not as consistent. When dealing with offenses that have a low seriousness

Table 6
Disposition by seriousness, number of previous offenses and race

	Seriousness of Offense											
	Low						High					
	None		1 or 2		3+		None		1 or 2		3+	
Disposition	Black	White	Black	White	Black	White	Black	White	Black	White	Black	White
Remedial %	90.7	94.9	86.6	92.2	77.6	86.1	44.1	65.2	34.4	47.0	19.5	28.8
Referral %	9.3	5.1	13.4	7.8	22.4	13.9	55.9	34.7	65.6	53.0	80.5	76.2
	(809)	(1388)	(849)	(911)	(1251)	(574)	(617)	(590)	(716)	(436)	(1120)	(340)
Adjusted %	73.3	81.7	67.5	73.2	55.7	67.5	53.3	48.8	41.5	39.4	27.4	28.1
Referral %	22.7	18.3	32.5	26.8	44.3	32.5	46.7	51.2	58.5	60.6	72.6	71.9
	(75)	(71)	(114)	(71)	(280)	(80)	(345)	(205)	(470)	(231)	(902)	(242)
Probation %	80.0	84.6	75.7	89.5	53.2	80.8	85.1	88.6	70.5	78.2	44.7	63.2
Institution %	20.0	15.4	24.3	10.5	46.8	19.2	14.9	11.4	29.5	22.3	55.3	36.8
	(20)	(13)	(37)	(19)	(124)	(26)	(161)	(105)	(275)	(139)	(655)	(174)

Table 7
Disposition by SES

Disposition	SES*		
	Low	High	Total
Remedial %	63.2	78.5	67.9
Referral %	36.9	21.5	32.1
	(6657)	(2944)	(9601)
Adjusted %	42.2	47.6	43.4
Referral %	57.7	52.4	56.6
	(2452)	(634)	(3086)
Probation %	60.5	71.4	62.6
Institution %	39.5	28.6	37.4
	(1416)	(332)	(1748)

*The measurement of this variable is based upon the median income of the census tract of residence for each subject. For a detailed discussion of the measurement of this variable see the work of Wolfgang, Figlio & Sellin cited in footnote 23.

score the results are consistent with the findings concerning the police and juvenile court levels. Regardless of the number of previous offenses, blacks are more likely than whites to receive a severe disposition, i.e., to be referred to the juvenile court. On the other hand, when dealing with offenses with a high seriousness score, there are very small differences between the races, and in two of the three comparisons whites are treated more severely than blacks. For example, for first offenders who committed serious offenses, blacks receive an adjusted disposition in 53.3 per cent of the cases, whereas whites do so in 48.8 per cent of the cases.

In conclusion, the data reveal that blacks are treated more severely than whites throughout the juvenile justice system. At the levels of the police and juvenile court there are no deviations from this finding, even when the seriousness of the offense and the number of previous offenses are simultaneously held constant. At the level of the intake hearing this conclusion is generally supported.

SOCIOECONOMIC STATUS AND DISPOSITION

The relationship between SES and the severity of the disposition is quite similar to that observed when race was the independent variable. As can be seen in Table 7, members of the low SES are more likely than members of the high SES to receive a severe disposition at each of the three stages of the juvenile justice system. As was true with race, differences in disposition by SES are greater at the levels

Table 8
Disposition by seriousness, number of previous offenses and SES

Disposition	Seriousness of Offense											
	Low						High					
	None		1 or 2		3+		None		1 or 2		3+	
	Lower SES	Higher SES	Lower SES	Higher SES	Lower SES	Higher SES	Lower SES	Higher SES	Lower SES	Higher SES	Lower SES	Higher SES
Remedial %	91.0	96.2	88.3	91.8	79.8	81.8	49.0	65.3	36.2	47.4	20.5	28.2
Referral %	9.0	3.8	11.7	8.2	20.2	18.2	51.0	34.7	63.8	52.6	79.5	71.8
	(1208)	(989)	(1151)	(609)	(1423)	(402)	(804)	(403)	(860)	(289)	(1211)	(252)
Adjusted %	76.8	78.9	68.1	74.0	54.7	72.6	52.4	49.3	41.9	37.5	26.9	30.9
Referral %	23.1	21.0	31.8	26.0	45.3	27.4	47.6	50.7	58.1	62.5	73.1	69.1
	(108)	(38)	(135)	(50)	(287)	(73)	(410)	(140)	(549)	(152)	(963)	(181)
Probation %	80.0	87.5	79.1	84.6	56.2	70.0	85.6	88.8	74.0	69.5	46.4	60.8
Institution %	20.0	12.5	20.9	15.4	43.8	30.0	14.4	11.2	26.0	30.5	53.6	39.2
	(25)	(8)	(43)	(13)	(130)	(20)	(195)	(71)	(319)	(95)	(704)	(125)

of the police and the juvenile court than at the intake hearing level; but at all three levels they are clearly observable. The question now becomes: Do these differences remain when the legal variables are held constant?

Because the analysis of SES is similar to that of race, tables in which the seriousness of the offense and the number of previous offenses are controlled separately are not presented here.[26] The patterns are almost identical to those in Tables 4 and 5.

When these two variables are controlled simultaneously, as in Table 8, SES differences are still present. Dealing first with the level of the police, we see that in all six comparisons the low SES subjects are less likely than the high SES subjects to be given a remedial disposition. These differences are greatest when the offense committed had a high seriousness score, but even for offenses with a low seriousness score the differences conform to the same pattern.

The findings for the intake hearing level, however, are not as consistent. In two of the six comparisons, those involving high seriousness offenses with no previous offenses or with one or two previous offenses, the pattern of the previous results is reversed. In these two cases the low SES subjects are more likely than the high SES subjects to be treated leniently. On the other hand, in the other four comparisons the reverse is true, since the low SES subjects are less likely to be treated leniently.

At the court level, the data are consistent with the previous results of this study. In five of the six comparisons, low SES subjects are less likely to be put on probation and more likely to be institutionalized than high SES subjects.

The findings with respect to SES are remarkably similar to those concerning race. At the levels of the police and the juvenile court the low SES subjects are treated consistently more severely than their counterparts, even when both legal variables are simultaneously controlled. At the level of the intake hearing the results are similar, but not as pronounced. When both legal variables are controlled simultaneously, and when the offense had a high seriousness score, the low SES subjects are not more likely to be treated more severely than the high SES subjects. However, this is the only deviation from the general pattern of the results. Thus, the third hypothesis—that the legal variables can explain the relationship between SES and dispositions—should be rejected.

DISCUSSION

We have noted that a number of earlier studies found that racial and social class disparities in dispositions could generally be explained by legal variables such as the seriousness of the offense and the number of previous offenses committed. That is, when the seriousness of the offense or the degree of recidivism were held constant, blacks did not receive more severe dispositions than whites, and low SES subjects did not receive more severe dispositions than high SES subjects.

An analysis of comparable data for the Philadelphia birth cohort, however, yields findings that are quite different. With the earlier studies, we found that both the legal and nonlegal variables are related to dispositions. But unlike the previous studies, the present study shows that when the two legal variables were held constant, the racial and SES differences did not disappear. Blacks and low SES subjects were more likely than whites and high SES subjects to receive severe dispositions. Although these differences were more noticeable at the levels of the police and the juvenile court than at the level of the intake hearing, they are generally observable at all three levels.

Furthermore, both sets of variables are related to the severity of dispositions and neither set "explains away" the other. When race and SES were held constant, serious offenders and recidivists still received more severe dispositions than minor offenders and first offenders. However, as we have noted, the effect of the nonlegal variables did not disappear when the legal variables were held constant. The two sets of variables tended to interact in relation to dispositions. Using race and seriousness to illustrate this interaction, we see that the most lenient dispositions were associated with white, minor offenders, and the most severe dispositions were associated with black, serious offenders.

The most important finding, however, in relation to the previous research done in this area, is that the nonlegal variables are still related to the severity of the dispositions received, even when the legal variables are held constant. Why this happens in the birth cohort data and not in the previous studies is not readily apparent. The different nature of the surveys, cross-sectional vs. cohort, should not explain it because the cohort data have been treated in a cross-sectional fashion in this paper. Nor can other plausible factors explain this disparity. all the studies were conducted in urban areas; data were collected during similar time periods (the late 1950's and early 1960's); they used comparable measures of the major variables; and they employed a valid sample of the juvenile delinquency cases occurring in the cities in which the studies were conducted.

One other possible reason should be discussed. Only two legal variables were controlled in the present study—seriousness and recidivism. Perhaps if other variables such as the demeanor of the youth, the "quality" of the juvenile's home, and the attitude of the victim were controlled, racial and SES differences would be eliminated. These items were not tested in this study. However, the other studies controlled only for seriousness and recidivism and concluded that race and SES were not related to dispositions. Thus, although the absence of these other variables limits the scope of these findings, it does not explain the discrepancy between this study and the previous ones.

Finally, the present findings should be related to the assumption often found in the theoretical realms of criminology, namely, that blacks and members of the low SES are treated more harshly than whites and high SES subjects in the juvenile justice system. Clearly, the findings of the present study are in agreement with that assumption. But to conclude that this study confirms the assumption would perhaps be to make a generalization beyond the scope of the data. This study should, however, be used as another piece of evidence in the more general process of confirming or disconfirming that assumption.

NOTES

1   Terry, "Discrimination in the Handling of Juvenile Offenders by Social Control Agencies," 1967. *J. Research in Crime and Delinquency* 218, 219.

2   E. Lemert, *Social Pathology: A Systematic Approach to the Theory of Sociopathic Behavior* 311 (1951).

3   M. Clinard, *The Sociology of Deviant Behavior* 550-51 (1963).

4   E. Sutherland & D. Cressey, *Principles of Criminology* 286 (1960). These passages are meant to be illustrative of the more general acceptance of this assumption and certainly do not exhaust the case. Further examples and references concerning this question can be found in Terry, *supra* note 1, at 219-20.

5   *See* M. Wolfgang, R. Figlio & T. Sellin, *Delinquency in a Birth Cohort* Ch. 5-6 (1972).

6   Because of the differences between the adult and juvenile court systems, only studies dealing with the latter will be reviewed. Since the present study is based on official police records, only studies based on similar data are considered. Observational studies, like Piliavin and Briar's, will not be treated because of methodological differences. *See* Piliavin, Irving & Briar, "Police Encounters with Juveniles," 70 *Am. J. Soc.* 206 (1964).

7   Terry, *supra* note 1, and "The Screening of Juvenile Offenders," 58 *J. Crim. L.C. & P.S.* 173 (1967) [hereinafter cited as "Screening"]. The same study is the basis of two articles.

8   Terry, *supra* note 1, at 228.

9   "Screening," *supra* note 7, at 179.

10   *Id.* at 181.

11   McEachern & Bauzer, "Factors Related to Disposition in Juvenile Police Contacts" in *Juvenile Gangs in Context* 148 (M. Klein & B. Myerhoff eds. 1964).

12   *Id.* at 150.

13   N. Goldman, "Police Reporting of Offenders to Juvenile Court 11" (mimeographed paper on file with author).

14   *Id.* at 2.

15   *Id.* at 3.

16   Shannon, "Types and Patterns of Delinquency Referral in a Middle-Sized City," 4 *Brit. J. Delinquency* 24 (1963).

17   *Id.* at 33.

18   Hohenstein, "Factors Influencing the Police Disposition of Juvenile Offenders," in *Delinquency: Selected Essays* 138 (T. Sellin & M. Wolfgang eds. 1969).

19   T. Sellin & M. Wolfgang, *The Measurement of Delinquency* (1964).

20   Hohenstein, *supra* note 18, at 146.

21 This study did not contain information on SES.

22 "Screening," *supra* note 7, at 181.

23 M. Wolfgang, R. Figlio, & T. Sellin, *supra* note 5. The writer wishes to express his deep appreciation to these authors for their generous cooperation in the present research.

24 For a variety of reasons, information on the dispositions of the other 613 offenses was missing or incomplete.

25 The number following each definition refers to the number of cohort offenses that received such disposition.

26 These tables may, however, be requested from the author.

In Defense of Youth: A Case Study of the Public Defender in Juvenile Court

ANTHONY PLATT, HOWARD SCHECHTER, and PHYLLIS TIFFANY*

Reprinted from Anthony Platt, Howard Schechter, and Phyllis Tiffany, "In Defense of Youth: A Case Study of the Public Defender in Juvenile Court." *Indiana Law Journal* 43 (1968): 619-640.

The purpose of this paper is to analyze one major consequence in *In re Gault*[1] in which the United States Supreme Court held, *inter alia*, that juveniles are entitled to: (1) timely notice of the specific charges against them, (2) notification of the right to be represented by counsel in proceedings which "may result in commitment to an institution in which the juvenile's freedom is curtailed,"[2] (3) the right to confront and cross-examine complainants and other witnesses, and (4) adequate warning of the privilege against self-incrimination and the right to remain silent. The right to counsel was a fundamental issue in the *Gault* case because it encompassed procedural regularity and the implementation of related principles:

> (a) proceeding where the issue is whether the child will be found to be "delinquent" and subjected to the loss of his liberty for years is comparable in seriousness to a felony prosecution. The juvenile needs the assistance of counsel to cope with problems of law, to make skilled inquiry into the facts, to insist upon regularity of the proceedings, and to ascertain whether he has a defense and to prepare and submit it.[3]

*This paper was in every sense a shared enterprise. The research was supported by the Center for Studies in Criminal Justice, Univ. of Chicago. We are grateful to our colleagues in the Center—especially Sharon Dunkle, Ruth Friedman, Gordon Hawkins and Jerome Skolnick—for their critical comments on an earlier draft of this paper.

The *Gault* decision came shortly after the President's Commission on Law Enforcement and Administration of Justice had made even stronger recommendations concerning the right to counsel:

> [C]ounsel must be appointed where it can be shown that failure to do so would prejudice the right of the person involved. . . . Nor does reason appear for the argument that counsel should be provided in some situations but not in others; in delinquency proceedings, for example, but not in neglect. *Wherever coercive action is a possibility, the presence of counsel is imperative. . . .* [W]hat is urgent and imperative is that counsel be provided in the juvenile courts at once and as a regular matter for all who cannot afford to retain their own. . . . *Counsel should be appointed . . . without requiring any affirmative choice by child or parent.*[4]

Not much is yet known about how the new "legalized" juvenile courts are working but some information is available concerning the role of the lawyer in juvenile court. It is worthwhile discussing the impact of this "major institutional change" because much of the constitutional argument relies on the effectiveness of legal representation.[5] Before the enactment of the New York Family Court Act in 1962,[6] a study by Schinitsky revealed that ninety-two percent of juvenile respondents in New York were not represented by counsel.[7] A similar inquiry in California found that "in most counties attorneys are present in 1% or less of juvenile court cases."[8] Another study, based on a national survey of juvenile court judges in 1964, found that "in most courts lawyers represent children in less than 5% of the cases which go to hearing."[9]

Lemert recently studied the effects of the 1961 California Juvenile Court Act and found that the percentage of cases in which counsel appeared more than trebled in four years, rising from a median of three to ten percent.[10] "The evidence is impressive," writes Lemert, "that representation by counsel more often secures a favorable outcome of the case than where there is no counsel. Proportionally, dismissals were ordered nearly three times as frequently in attorney as in non-attorney cases."[11] Close analysis of the data, however, shows that attorneys were mostly successful in neglect cases and had almost no impact on delinquency cases. In fact, juveniles without attorneys were less likely to be detained while awaiting trial in one county studied.[12]

The appropriate role of the lawyer in juvenile court has been given considerable attention in the literature. Isaacs, in a recent study of the New York Family Court, proposes that the juvenile court lawyer performs the functions of advocate, guardian, and officer of the court. As advocate, he "must stand as the ardent defender of his client's constitutional and legal rights"; as guardian, he is required to have regard for the "general welfare of the minor"; and as officer of the court, he "must assume the duty of interpreting the court and its objectives to both child and parent, of preventing misrepresentation and perjury in the presentation of facts, [and] of disclosing to the court all facts in his possession which bear upon a proper disposition of the matter. . . ."[13] But Isaacs' tripartite definition represents an ideal rather than a statement of current realities. Lemert, in an empirical study of California Juvenile Courts, found that adversary tactics are marginal in relation to the attorney's function as a negotiator and interpreter between judge and family.[14] And the public defender is more likely than a private attorney to be "co-opted into the organization of the court, even becoming its superficial appendage. Factors encouraging this are the low priority public defenders give to juvenile work and the growth of inter-departmental or informal reciprocity with probation officers."[15]

There is strong pressure from legislatures, judges, and legal commentators to formally constrain the defense lawyer in juvenile court. In the "law guardians" system in New York, "the concept of 'guardianship,' " according to one of its sponsors, "would seem to require that not only the legal rights but the general welfare of the minor be thrown on the scale in the weighing by counsel of his course of action."[16] Similarly, the Florida legislature has interpreted *Gault* by providing both prosecution and representation through the State Division of Youth Services.[17] This provision reinforces the juvenile court's traditional policy of assuming that state officials are always likely to act in the best interests of young persons charged with crimes. Most juvenile judges "see the lawyer's chief value as lying in the areas of interpretation of the court's approach and securing cooperation in the court's disposition rather than more traditional roles of fact elicitation and preservation of legal rights."[18] Welch, writing from the perspective of the constitutionalist, also perceives the attorney as interpreter rather than advocate because

> he is better situated than anyone to explain the nature and objectives of the juvenile courts. He should explain that the juvenile is not being tried as a criminal, the court is not going to punish him, and criminal court tactics of resistance are not appropriate in juvenile court. . . . Above all, the attorney in a delinquency hearing should discard any personal interest in winning cases. Where punishment has truly been eliminated, real "victory" is realized when a delinquent has been rehabilitated. The real "defeat" lies in obstructing the legitimate operation of the rehabilitation mechanism.[19]

The success of *Gault* will ultimately depend on the availability and quality of defense lawyers.[20] This task will fall to legal aid and public defender organizations because, as we recently reported, private lawyers make only sporadic and hazardous appearances in juvenile court.[21] In this paper, we will analyze the role played by the public defender representing juveniles in a large midwestern city which we shall call Metro. Metro's juvenile court handles nearly 17,000 referrals annually and requires the daily presence of six judges and a presiding judge.

The data for this paper were collected in a variety of ways. The paper is essentially based upon four months of participant observation;[22] approximately twenty hours a week were spent with a public defender as he performed his daily functions. We also analyzed the files of a public defender's caseload during a twelve-month period.[23] Information concerning court personnel and lawyers is the result of over a year's observations in Metro's juvenile court.

PROFILE OF A PUBLIC DEFENDER'S CLIENTELE[24]

The *Gault* decision encouraged legal aid and public defender offices to send lawyers into juvenile court. Many such organizations anticipated the Supreme Court's ruling and established special services for juveniles in 1966.[25] Legal agencies around the country reported the following juvenile caseload for 1967: Newark–500, Oakland–1324, Cincinnati–526, Houston–114, Cleveland–400, Los Angeles–2951, and San Francisco–324. Even in a small town like Rockford, Illinois, the public defender handled as many as 250 cases during 1967.[26]

Metro's juvenile court is subject to a relatively new state statute. Although proceedings under the act are "not intended to be adversary in character," Metro's juvenile court in effect operates like a minor criminal court. The state is represented by the State's Attorney's Office and, correspondingly, juveniles have the right to be represented by either private or court-appointed counsel. In April 1966, the County Public Defender assigned one full-time attorney to Metro's juvenile court and, in the same year, the Legal Aid Bureau established a special office to handle juvenile cases.[27]

Metro's juvenile court processes juveniles on petitions for delinquency, minors in need of supervision, dependency and neglect. We shall restrict our remarks in this paper to delinquency which is properly within the jurisdiction of the public defender. In 1966, Metro's juvenile court handled a total of 11,636 delinquency cases, of which almost twenty-five percent were "adjusted" by administrative officers in the complaint department and were not referred to the courts due to a lack of evidence or seriousness. During the last seven years [1960–67], Metro's court has never processed less than 10,000 juveniles annually. The statistical trend from 1960 to 1967 was disrupted by a new juvenile court statute but 1966 appears to be a typical example of future trends.[28]

In a twelve-month period, the public defender handled 345 (four percent) delinquency cases out of a total juvenile court caseload of 8,920 cases. His clients were generally representative of all defendants in juvenile court. The public defender's clients are selected for him by the court and analysis by offenses shows that the public defender is more likely to be appointed in cases considered "serious" by judges, such as injury to person or property, burglary, and sex offenses.[29]

The public defender's 345 delinquency cases account for eighty-seven percent of his total caseload during the year.[30] His clients are on the average fourteen and one-half years old, predominantly Negro, and male.[31] Analysis of individual cases shows that the public defender (1) rarely appeared at detention hearings,[32] (2) made oral rather than written motions (in eighty-three percent of his cases he made no motions at all), (3) had no continuances in one-third of his cases, (4) held only one client conference prior to the court hearing in almost one-half of his cases, (5) had no witnesses in over one-half of his cases, and (6) on the basis of the above criteria, investigated minimally in sixty-seven percent and moderately in twenty-five percent of his cases.

The lack of investigation does not reflect upon the personal competence of the public defender but rather upon his heavy caseload, lack of assistance and systematic pressures to expedite his cases. Comparing defendants with and without the services of the public defender suggests that the public defender's clients stand a better chance of having their case dismissed or receiving probation. On the other hand, the public defender's clients are more apt to be committed to a penal institution. But it should be remembered that juveniles with records and charged with serious offenses are more likely to be assigned to the public defender.[33]

PUBLIC DEFENDER AS A SOCIAL WORKER

The public defender in Metro's juvenile court maintains two seemingly conflicting roles. As an "officer of the court," whose prevailing ethic is "child saving,"[34] the public defender sees himself as a social worker. At the same time, however, he is a defense attorney who takes pride in the craft of advocacy. As a social worker, the public defender is an integral part of the court's rehabilitative machinery and committed to helping children in trouble.[35]

While playing the social worker's role, the public defender must acknowledge that juveniles are naturally dependent and require supervision by mature adults.[36] He is required to listen sympathetically to family problems, to comfort juveniles before or after a court appearance, to interpret judicial mysteries for the child, and to point out the beneficial value of court decisions. His personal involvement in cases is motivated by a desire to determine exactly what is "best for a kid." Unlike his colleagues in the criminal courts, the public defender does not merely see himself as a bargaining agent who tries to win cases or negotiate a short sentence, i.e., "in criminal court I would just do everything I could to get my client off. But here I won't." How then does he determine what is best and how does this influence his handling of a case? We shall answer this question by first attempting to systematize the four criteria which the public defender employs in constructing his strategy:

1)   does the juvenile claim to be innocent or guilty?
2)   is the alleged offense of a "serious" nature?
3)   does the juvenile have a criminal record?
4)   is the juvenile a "good kid" or a "bad kid"?

If a client in his first encounter with the public defender declares his innocence and shows no glaring inconsistencies in his story, the public defender will assume his client's statement to be truthful, plead him not guilty, and attempt to secure a dismissal or the most lenient sentence possible. This is a clear-cut situation which makes up about one-half of the public defender's caseload. The rest of the caseload, consisting of clients who declare themselves guilty, is more problematic and involves a variety of determining factors.[37] If the public defender considers his client a "good kid" with little or no criminal record, he will plead him guilty on the grounds that he will receive only a lecture, or supervision,[38] or probation. The public defender believes that a minimal sanction is often what a client needs; the idea is that "these kids need a good scare. They should learn that they can't get away with anything. A lot of them need extra supervision."

In situations where his client is a "good kid" but has a more substantial record, the public defender will do something quite different. He will plead the youth not guilty, force the state to prove its case and attempt to secure a dismissal or a lenient sentence. He follows the same procedure when the youth involved is a "good kid" who is charged with a "serious" offense. In both instances he knows that a finding of guilty may well mean automatic commitment to a reformatory. The public defender does not subscribe to the notion that reformatories are rehabilitative institutions capable of remedying his clients' problems. Metro's institutional resources are publicly recognized as inadequate, overcrowded, and ineffectual instruments of either reform or deterrence.[39]

"Bad kids" invite an attitude of despair. The public defender assumes, along with all juvenile court functionaries, that little can be done to "help" these clients. He pleads them guilty and cooperates in processing them into reformatories. They have long records, they admit the offense, no "responsible" adults are willing to be their spokesmen, and they are likely to antagonize judges with their poor school record. The public defender does not waste his time on "bad kids." A serious effort on behalf of these clients would only jeopardize his chances with more "worthy" defendants.

The determination of whether a client is "good" or "bad" is, thus, crucial to the public defender's consideration of a case. How does he decide to apply these judgmental labels? To a great extent, he looks for criteria which positively indicate moral and social propriety. "Badness" is a residual category[40] applied to clients who do not meet these wholesome criteria. His decision primarily is based upon the demeanor of his client and secondarily upon the demeanor of his client's parents.[41] Race, class, and economic status play a minimal role in this decision because most of his clients are poor and non-white. He is concerned, however, with how his client speaks, the amount of respect he is shown, the way the client dresses, and with such highly subjective factors as "charm," "personality," and how "cute," "pretty," or "handsome" the client might be. If the client is a "clean kid," said a former juvenile court public defender, "you go out of your way to help him." Whether the client is in school or has a job, as opposed to being a "drop-out" or unemployed, are meaningful indices of worthiness. Parents who are employed and show "proper" concern for their child are considered by the public defender to be positive assets. The previous arrest record is also of great importance in making this "determination." It is quite possible for a boy with a substantial record to be seen as "good" if he scores high, so to speak, on the above criteria. However, it is a negative factor in the overall determination. Conversely, any client who has no previous record at all is automatically defined as "good."

The public defender first contacts the child and his parents in his office. If the boy is in custody, he will see him in the "bullpen" before the arraignment. This initial encounter is of crucial importance, for it is here that the public defender sizes up his client on the basis of the above criteria and makes his determination. The public defender is more likely to be enthusiastic about a case if a client presents an image of forthrightness and sincerity. One client, for example, denied his complicity in a theft. "It looks like you're getting railroaded," said the public defender, "but I'm quite sure they won't be able to prove it. . . . You give the impression of being very sincere about this. Some boys come up here and I know they're lying through their teeth."

The public defender has two other important sources of raw materials for labelling clients who have had previous contact with the court. These are the diagnostic reports of the court and of probation officers. The public defender relies heavily on the formal and informal judgments of probation officers; he often consults a probation officer for his personal recommendation about a client and the conversation is usually simple and brief: "what kind of kid is this Smith boy?" is typically answered by, "he's a good kid, doing well in school, hasn't been in serious trouble before." The public defender may also ask to see the court's psychological report. He attaches great importance to this document when evaluating a client and determining his best interests.[42]

PUBLIC DEFENDER AS AN ADVOCATE

As has been pointed out, the public defender sees himself as a defense attorney and advocate for the accused. He takes pride in performing this craft with competence and style; he is well trained in both procedural and substantive law, and he gets great satisfaction from a well executed trial. If a case "goes to trial," the state's attorney needs a properly prepared, coherent presentation if he wants to obtain a guilty verdict against a client of the public defender.

During a trial, the public defender's professionalism and competence are quite apparent. He plays the role of a disinterested advocate, making his moves with the skill and dexterity of a craftsman. This professionalism is not necessarily suspended at the end of a trial; for example, it is quite common for the public defender, state's attorney, and the judge to hold an amicable conference after a case. The attorneys review the trial, pointing out where one or another might have taken an advantage. It resembles the interaction of chess players discussing the strategies of a completed game.

The public defender places a great deal of emphasis on making the system appear legal and just. It is very important to him that it appear that there has been a fair hearing, even if the case concludes with a punitive sentence. As the public defender has commented, "the appearance of justice is all important."

Although the public defender enjoys the contest of a trial, advocacy is nevertheless a limited commodity in Metro's juvenile court. Appeals are rare, jury trials are prohibited, police testimony is hard to repudiate, and witnesses often prove unreliable when faced with cross-examination. The public defender does not rehearse a client who, according to his demeanor and story, is probably innocent. If he is telling the truth, the public defender believes that his testimony should be natural and spontaneous. Most lawyers, however, feel that juvenile clients have "poor memories," "don't remember," "don't have the social and intellectual maturity of an adult," are likely to blurt out and convict themselves," and "easily spill the beans."[43]

The public defender is, however, something more than a personal social worker or lawyer for individual clients. He is also an "officer of the court" and an employee of a system in which he must operate from day to day. As Blumberg has observed, "accused persons come and go in the court system scheme, but the structure and its occupational incumbents remain to carry on their respective career, occupational and organizational enterprise. . . ."[44] The public defender is "in the system" in a number of ways. First, he is a member of a political community. His job, however, is much less politically significant than those of judges and state's attorneys who, in return for sponsorship, are expected to remain faithful to their political party and may even be required to perform political tasks, such as supporting election campaigns or contributing technical expertise. Secondly, the public defender is a county employee and is paid from the same budget that supports all court personnel. Finally, the public defender is a court employee and, like his counterparts in the state's attorney's office, is subject to the authority and discretionary powers of individual judges.

His performance is judged by his superiors in a variety of ways.

Thus, he is concerned with his "batting average," i.e., the percentage of cases won and lost, and "doing a good job." He is expected to be properly prepared in court, not to ask for an unreasonable number of continuances, not to antagonize unnecessarily the state's witnesses, and not to offend the judges by requesting a change of venue on the grounds of prejudice. The public defender knows that assessments of his competence by judges will ultimately reach his boss.

The public defender has informal, friendly relationships with judges, prosecutors, and bailiffs in juvenile court. A former public defender said that he was "on a first name basis with everybody in court." One prosecutor was a personal friend of his and it was not uncommon for the public defender to go out to lunch with a group of judges and prosecutors. Being "in the system" provides the public defender with tactical advantages because he quickly learns the personal idiosyncrasies of judges and prosecutors. For example, "I know Judge D is prosecution-minded, but I've had a lot of good dismissals from him." Also, the public defender is attuned to politically sensitive issues and wants to avoid confrontations which will discredit his membership in the court community. "The judges don't like to hear about police brutality," said a former juvenile court public defender. "I'd rather not handle this type of case because I get a lot of police officers to testify for me. I've won cases that way. They wouldn't want to do that for a guy who was trying to cut their throats at every opportunity on police brutality."

Although the public defender accepts the "child saving" ethic which pervades the juvenile court, he is also faced with the problem of handling huge caseloads in a manner which is expedient[45] and, hopefully, just. Like almost all situations where people work together, informal ties affect the performance of the objective task at hand.[46] This is no less true in the "halls of justice" than it is in a factory, store, or other work location. The public defender often sits in a judge's chambers, not discussing the next case but the next vacation, not pondering the problems of gang behavior but the relative merits of the city's night clubs. It is not unreasonable then that we find the state's attorney on occasion dropping a charge for no other reason than it is a favor of convenience for his friend, the public defender. It is not unreasonable also that a judge can say to a public defender: "I wouldn't have dismissed this case unless you were handling it." The converse situation is true. The public defender will take a particular course of action as a gesture of friendship to other court personnel. According to Blumberg, "the accused's lawyer has far greater professional, economic, intellectual and other ties to the various elements of the court system than he does to his own client. In short, the court is a closed community."[47]

Mutual cooperation by all court personnel makes possible the management of large caseloads. The bailiffs of each courtroom give preference to the public defender cases, getting him in and out of the courtroom with as little waiting time as possible. Private lawyers are denied this fringe benefit.[48] In return, the public defender must be careful not to obstruct the efficient processing of cases, for the other court functionaries are depending on him to help finish or expedite the court call for the day. Due to his large caseload, some of the formal rules which apply to private attorneys are waived for the public defender. For example, written motions are seldom necessary and special arrangements to circumvent particular formalities are not difficult to obtain at any given time.

The large caseload also creates problems of preparation and presentation. Quite often the state's attorney will be briefed on the details of a case by the public defender so that he may be prepared to deal with it. He will do a similar service for a judge who is confused about the status of a case. It is a reciprocal arrangement and the public defender is often informed by the state's attorney on matters crucial to his presentation of a defense. "The state's attorney will usually tell me ahead of time what kind of tactics he'll use and how hard he's going to hit. He'll say, '[w]e've got this case up today,' he gives you the arrest report, 'I'm bringing in so-and-so as a witness, the police officer will say thus-and-so. . . .'" This information is never questioned as biased data but immediately accepted as true, as if it had come from a disinterested source.

Aside from the role cooperation plays in facilitating the mechanics of the proceeding, it also makes the entire process more personally tolerable for everyone involved. Court interaction is intensely focused upon deciding the fate of others' lives and this responsibility is made impossible if conflict is the norm underlying the task at hand.[49] The court functionaries see themselves as colleagues rather than adversaries, for "the probability of continued future relations and interaction must be preserved at all costs."[50]

PLEA BARGAINING

Given this added notion of the public defender's being "in the court system," how must we modify our earlier presentation of the manner in which the public defender defends his clients? The requisite modification consists in adding the concept of plea bargaining to describe more accurately the "routine grounds"[51] of the public defender's behavior.[52] The American system of criminal justice, as Skolnick has pointed out, is predominantly pre-trial in character and full-scale trials reflect a breakdown of negotiations between the defense and prosecuting attorneys.[53] Approximately ninety percent of all convictions in lower criminal courts are the result of a negotiated plea or "deal."[54] Rules of evidence are routinely ignored or bypassed and advocacy is subordinate to, what Blumberg has called, "bureaucratically ordained and controlled 'work crimes,' short cuts, deviations, and outright rule violations."[55] "The 'trial' becomes a perfunctory reiteration and validation of the pretrial interrogation and investigation."[56]

There are limited opportunities for plea bargaining in Metro's juvenile court because a defendant can only be found guilty of "delinquency" no matter what criminal charge is proved. Nothing is gained by reducing "aggravated battery" to "assault" if the outcome is the same in either case. The state's attorneys cannot make deals about reduced "time" in exchange for a guilty plea because they do not have the power to fix sentences.[57] The state youth commission operates under a policy of indeterminate sentencing and only the commission and its staff have the power to release juveniles from reformatories.

Some plea bargaining, however, is possible and necessary for efficient, cooperative work relations. A guilty plea can be offered in exchange for a warning, supervision, probation, or even some "short time" in the court's detention facility. The basic capital with which the public defender can bargain is time. A plea of guilty saves a tremendous amount of time, effort and labor for the state's attorneys, judges, and other court functionaries. In the return for a guilty plea, the judge and state's attorney willingly make concessions as to the fate of the public defender's client. An effective public defender, therefore, must be an accomplished entrepreneur with an affable demeanor and sociable personality.

How does plea bargaining affect the public defender's handling of cases? First, there are a significant number of cases in which the public defender would prefer to enter a guilty plea; these he does not need to negotiate and they facilitate the job of the state's attorney and judge. These cases consist of the "good kids" with little or no previous records who are charged with minor offenses. Further, it includes all the clients in the "bad kid" category. It is with the remaining cases that he has an opportunity to negotiate and thus contribute to the court's efficiency. These cases are instances in which the public defender would like to plead not guilty and achieve dismissals or light sentences. If he is fairly certain that he can prove his client not guilty, he will neither encourage nor be receptive to a negotiated plea. He makes this determination by examining his client's story, the availability of witnesses, his client's demeanor and any other factors which might be relevant to the expectations and idiosyncrasies of a particular judge.

If the public defender, in assessing these factors, feels he has a good chance of winning the case, he will enter a plea of not guilty and attempt to secure a dismissal. If, on the other hand, the case does not look promising, he will seek a negotiated settlement. The judge is always informally aware that a "deal" has been made and it is an unwritten rule that he accepts the state's attorney's recommendation. Mindful of this cooperation, the judge will not only be agreeing to a reduced sentence but also implicitly encouraging future negotiated guilty pleas. George, commenting on the likely implications of the

Gault case, observes that any lawyer in juvenile court will be required to

> adapt the lesson that he has learned elsewhere, that overzealous advocacy, or even advocacy that is standard and proper from the standpoint of the legal profession, is not in the long run to the advantage of the client who continues to be affected detrimentally by administrative actions that for the time being are beyond the reach of the courts to remedy.[58]

THE PUBLIC DEFENDER AND CLIENTS

The clients' perception of the public defender is difficult to ascertain because they say very little in court which is indicative of their feelings.[59] We will discuss, therefore, some of the structural properties of the public defender's behavior which are likely to influence clients. Many of the following comments will necessarily have a speculative quality.

It is quite apparent that in some ways the public defender goes out of his way to initiate a genuine, client-lawyer relationship. In the first meeting with a defendant, he immediately makes it clear that the juvenile is "his" client. The public defender shows that he expects his client to trust in his expertise. He listens respectfully to his client's comments and deals with him as an individual. In fact, he communicates unusually well with a group of people who differ from him significantly in terms of social, economic, and educational background.

It appears, however, that these few courtesies cannot overcome the overwhelming number of factors which might serve to alienate the youth from the public defender. The structural demands under which the public defender operates make it apparent to his clients that he is not "their" advocate—dedicated to the best defense possible. The client is usually directed to the public defender, he brings no fee, and makes demands upon the public defender's time and expertise. Structurally, the relationship is one of passivity and dependence.[60] It is not surprising, therefore, that among juveniles the public defender is characterized as a person of dubious loyalty to his clients:

> [y]ou always got to have a lawyer. I would never take one of those public defenders because they work for the city. . . .
> They sit down with the judge and they got this piece of paper and they talk it over and decide what this nigger's gonna get, whether he's gonna get six months or less. The cat don't talk to you till you come in. They bring you in from the bullpen and you're standing in front of the judge and he kind of puts his hand up over his mouth and whispers sideways to you, "What happened? How do you plead?" And you tell him in three minutes and then he goes on and you get busted. So I would never take no public defender, because those ofays down there in court just want to put you away.[61]

Clients usually must wait a long time outside the public defender's office which is located between the police and the clerks' offices. After a few hours of waiting, they may get a chance to see the public defender, but, more likely, they see one of his student assistants. Often the public defender will be in a hurry or trying to get a few minutes rest in between cases. The interview is short and typically there is little time for more than "name, rank, and serial number" and a sketchy outline of the client's story. Many times the public defender receives calls or visits from probation officers, clerks, and state's attorneys. The close relationship of the public defender and prosecutor is likely to make clients question the allegiance of "their" attorney. One former public defender said that his clients did not really think of him as an attorney. "They think of me as functioning as their representative in court, as somebody who might get them off." There are no credentials or diplomas on the wall to identify the public defender as a lawyer. "They say, '[t]he judge sent us over here to get a lawyer. We need an attorney on this case. . . .' After they ask me if I'm the public defender, they say '[w]ell, I think we need an *attorney*.' I say, 'I'm an attorney' and they say, 'Oh yeah?'."

The public defender's cooperation with parties who are seemingly non-supportive of his clients' position is very visible. The public defender has no inhibitions about discussing other cases with a prosecutor in the presence of clients and he may even talk openly about "deals." These relationships are so non-secret that the public defender was able to say in court, "[i]n light of my previous cooperation with the prosecuting attorney in securing admissions from clients, I am sure that he won't object to my motion. . . ." After a judge has decided a case, it becomes quite apparent that the public defender is involved in matters beyond defense work. For example, he has never been heard to criticize the juvenile court system in the presence of a client. Often it is clear that he is trying to justify a harsh decision to a client, despite his own personal reservations.

The public defender, however, is not the only party who makes it apparent that the "appearance of justice" is really a sham. The whole court experience tends to reduce a juvenile to a "non-person."[62] This ceremonial degradation of juveniles can take many forms. A minor issue, perhaps, is court etiquette. For example, defendants are ordered where to stand, how to stand (hands out of pockets and on the bar), and are continually policed by bailiffs. On the other hand, it is not uncommon to see prosecutors leaning against the bar, or a clerk chewing gum or other functionaries wandering in and out of the courtroom. Similarly, the swearing-in process is handled with disarming speed and it is never made sufficiently clear who is supposed to raise his right hand. The rule of privacy in hearings is rigidly enforced, but it is a routine matter to see juveniles in handcuffs being led through the corridors. It is unlikely that these inconsistencies between theory and reality go unnoticed.

The "halls" of Metro's juvenile court are overcrowded waiting rooms where, again, people are forced to wait hours for a hearing that often lasts only minutes. Perhaps the most degrading of all aspects of the court process is the general lack of credibility invested in the juvenile by the court. He is seldom spoken to and when he is addressed, it is usually in the form of a moralistic lecture or verbal disciplining. Most judges assess a wide variety of adolescent behavior in terms of mental or moral impairments. Truancy, glue-sniffing, fighting, sex, and running away, for example, are rarely viewed as "normal," socially learned behavior, but rather as symptoms of underlying pathology.[63] The concept of cultural relativism is apparently unknown to most juvenile court judges who appear to feel compelled to lecture and moralize even if a youth is found not guilty. Take, for example, the following case involving a Negro boy charged with "deviate sexual assault." The case was dismissed after the judge said, "you're a pig, and you [the girl] are no better. Why doesn't the state file a petition against this girl? You're both animals! No decent girl would go to someone's apartment with another boy. . . . You're both a total discredit to society. A case like this sets your race back a hundred years."

CONCLUSIONS

In this paper, we have analyzed the probable impact of one consequence of the *Gault* decision. It seems likely that the public defender model of representation will become widely operative in urban juvenile courts, and that court-appointed lawyers will be charged with the task of implementing reforms suggested by the Supreme Court. Private lawyers still find juvenile court to be occupationally and economically unprofitable. Fortunately, county boards and legal aid organizations around the country have recognized the importance of providing funds and lawyers for juveniles charged with delinquency.

The pattern of the public defender's performance in juvenile court differs considerably from the work of public defenders in Metro's other courts.[64] Relatively few of his cases (three and one-half percent) are dismissed on the motion of the state's attorneys. Prosecutors are apparently unwilling to release juvenile defendants, even though concrete evidence for a conviction may be lacking. The public defender in juvenile court is formally discouraged from plea bargaining and he pleads fewer clients guilty (twenty-five percent) than do his counterparts in criminal courts. Moreover, the public defender loses more cases which go to trial (thirty-one percent), because the rule of "reasonable doubt" does not apply and prosecutors win cases with minimal evidence. The public defender in juvenile court is not, however, as it has been suggested of his counterparts in criminal courts, merely an instrumentality for processing guilty clients.[65] He does not assume the guilt of his clients but, rather, after informing them of the functional importance of "telling it like it is,"

Table 1
Number and disposition of delinquency cases
in Metro's juvenile court, 1960–1967

	Delinquency Referrals	Delinquency Petitions Filed	Case Dismissed	Probation	Penal Institution
1960	10,407	5,984	2,541	837	1,389
1961	10,118	5,529	2,644	1,015	1,450
1962	11,758	6,649	3,014	2,536	1,199
1963	10,148	Not Available	Not Available	Not Available	Not Available
1964	13,075	8,307	2,096	3,579	1,478
1965	13,078	8,979	2,341	3,410	1,657
1966[70]	11,636	8,388	4,414	2,966	1,339
1967	11,452	8,356	3,398	2,770	1,293

he "believes everything [his] kids tell [him]. [He] couldn't operate any other way."

The findings of this paper indicate that delinquency, aside from its psychological and "subcultural" motivation, is the product of social judgment and "procedural definition" by officials.[66] The public defender, as a member of the juvenile court community, is in an important position to create and influence official judgments. The perspective employed by the public defender in organizing and defining his job suggests that juvenile court advocacy differs in many ways from criminal court advocacy. Juvenile clients do not get the same standard of representation that is accorded to adult defendants.

Finally, it is worth noting that we do not mean to imply that the public defender has been "co-opted"[67] into a juvenile court superstructure. On the contrary, our research supports Skolnick's assertion that the public defender can often be more effective than a private lawyer in obtaining dismissals or light sentences.[68] It is inaccurate to regard the public defender as a "fallen" lawyer who sells out his client in return for emotional well-being or bureaucratic expediency. Rather, the public defender brings to his job common-sense notions about adolescence and "troublesome" behavior. His views on youth and delinquency are really no different from other

Table 2
Percentage of juvenile court and public defender caseload by sex, race, and offense in Metro's juvenile court, 1966

	Sex		Race		Offense							
	Male	Female	Negro	White	Injury to Person	Burglary	Sex Offenses	Injury to Property	Robbery	Theft	Auto Theft	Other Delinquency Offenses[71]
Juvenile Court N=8,920	89	11	60	33	21.7	18.2	4.9	7	9.4	10.8	21.7	6.3
Public Defender N=345	85	15	70	24	30.9	17	11.7	8.5	7.8	5.2	9.6	9.3

adult officials (teachers, social workers, youth officers, etc.) who are charged with regulating youthful behavior. Juveniles get the same kind of treatment in juvenile courts that they get in school or at home and the public defender accepts this as one of the inevitable and appropriate consequences of adolescence.[69]

Table 3
Percentage distributions of disposition of cases with and without the public defender in Metro's Juvenile Court, 1966

Disposition	With Public Defender N=345	Without Public Defender[72] N=8,575	Total N=8,920
Dismissed[73]	41.1	21.6	22.3
Probation	37.3	33.1	33.2
Institution[74]	18.8	14.9	15.1
Other[75]	2.8	30.4	29.4

NOTES

1   387 U.S. 1 (1967).
2   *Id.* at 41.
3   *Id.* at 36.
4   *President's Commission on Law Enforcement and Administration of Justice, Task Force Report, Juvenile Delinquency and Youth Crime* 31, 33, 35 (1967) (emphasis added); *President's Commission on Law Enforcement and Administration of Justice, The Challenge of Crime in a Free Society* 87 (1967).
5   Skoler and Tenney, "Attorney Representation in Juvenile Court," 4 *J. Family L.* 97 (1964).
6   *N.Y. Family Ct. Act.* (McKinney 1963).
7   Schinitsky, "The Role of the Lawyer in Children's Court," 17 *Record of N.Y.C.B.A.* 10-26 (1962).
8   *Task Force Reports Juvenile Delinquency, supra* note 4, at 32.
9   Skoler and Tenney, *supra* note 5, 77-96.
10   Lemert, "Legislating Change in the Juvenile Court," 1967 *Wis. L. Rev.* 421-48.
11   *Id.* at 442.
12   *Id.* at 443.
13   Isaacs, "The Role of the Lawyer in Representing Minors in the New York Family Court," 12 *Buff. L. Rev.* 501, 506-7 (1963).
14   Lemert, "Juvenile Justice—Quest and Reality," 4 *Trans-Action* 40 (1967).

Table 4
Process of evaluation and subsequent representation (including plea bargaining) of juveniles by the public defender

Record	Seems Guilty to Public Defender				Seems Not Guilty to Public Defender
	"Good Kids"		"Bad Kids"		
	Not Serious	Serious	Not Serious	Serious	
Little or no previous record	Pleas of *Guilty* 1. "Scare" 2. Lecture 3. Supervision	Pleas of *Not Guilty* 1. Make State prove case 2. Wants dismissal or minimum sentence 3. Plea Bargaining	Open Cell (No bad kids without previous record)		Plea of *Not Guilty* 1. Make State prove case 2. Wants dismissal or minimum sentence 3. Plea Bargaining
Substantial previous record	Pleas of *Guilty* 1. Make State prove case 2. Wants dismissal or minimum sentence 3. Plea Bargaining	Pleas of *Not Guilty* 1. Make State prove case 2. Wants dismissal or minimum sentence 3. Plea Bargaining	Pleas *Guilty* 1. Expects conviction	Pleas *Guilty* 1. Expects conviction	

15 Lemert, *supra* note 10, at 431. See also Sudnow, "Normal Crimes: Socio-logical Features of the Penal Code in a Public Defender Office," 12 *Social Problems* 255-76 (1965).

16 Isaacs, *supra* note 13, at 507.

17 Fla. Legislature, S. 1506 (June 2, 1967).

18 Skoler and Tenney, *supra* note 5, at 97.

19 Welch, "Delinquency Proceedings—Fundamental Fairness for the Accused in a Quasi-Criminal Forum," 50 *Minn. L. Rev.* 681-82 (1966).

20 B. George, *Gault and the Juvenile Court Revolution* 52-54 (1968). Ac-cording to two recent commentators, the *Gault* decision "highlights the urgency of adequate provision by the states for representation by counsel competent to appear in juvenile proceedings." Dorsen and Rezneck, "In Re Gault and the Future of Juvenile Law," 1 *Family L. Q.* 18 (Dec. 1967).

21 Platt and Friedman, "The Limits of Advocacy: Occupational Hazards in Juvenile Court," *passim*, to be published in *U. Pa. L. Rev.* (1968).

22 The methodology of participant observation is fully discussed in the fol-lowing literature: Becker and Geer, "Participant Observation: The Analy-sis of Qualitative Field Data," in *Human Organization Research* 267-89 (Adams and Preiss ed. 1966); S. Bruyn, *The Human Perspective in Sociol-ogy* (1966); Lohman, "The Participant Observer in Community Studies," 2 *Am. Sociological Rev.* 890-97 (1937).

23 We would like to thank Metro County's Public Defender and the Assistant Public Defenders in juvenile court for their cooperation in this study.

24 The statistical data were obtained from the juvenile court's statistician and the Public Defender's files. Some twenty-five items of information were abstracted from the public defender's case files for a twelve-month period. All data were checked for accuracy by cross-reference to police files. The Assistant Public Defender who was responsible for the files also validated our analysis.

25 The *Gault* decision was rendered on May 15, 1967.

26 Personal correspondence with Legal Aid and Public Defender organizations in these cities.

27 In February, 1968, Metro County's Public Defender assigned another three full-time attorneys to juvenile court.

28 See Table 1, *infra.*

29 See Table 2, *infra.*

30 The remainder of his caseload is delinquency and neglect cases.

31 The average of all defendants in juvenile court is fifteen years. The public defender represented thirty-six girls on delinquency charges. Although he proportionally represented more girls than the total juvenile court case-load, he underrepresented Negro girls (public defender—fifty-five percent, juvenile court—sixty-eight percent).

32 "Unless sooner released, a minor taken into temporary custody must be brought before a judicial officer within 48 hours for a detention hearing to determine whether he shall be further detained" pending the adjudi-cation hearing. (State juvenile court act.)

33 Our following observations do not refer to the public defender who was discussed in the introductory sections. The public defender referred to hereafter is the supervising public defender in Metro's Juvenile Court.

34 A. Platt, *The Child Savers: The Invention of Delinquency* (University of Chicago Press, 1969).

35 The basic philosophy of the juvenile court was considered antithetical to narrow, restrictively specific jurisdictional requisites, which were discarded in favor of all-encompassing formulations intended to bring within the

court's jurisdiction virtually every child in need of help, for whatever the reason and however the need was manifested. . . . The rationale for this comprehensive array of jurisdictional pegs generally emphasized the growth of social as opposed to legalistic justice and the new efforts to bring the law out of isolation and into partnership with the ascending social and behavioral sciences. It was strengthened by precepts of optimism and paternalism. Children, assumed to be malleable, seem eminently salvageable; as the rehabilitative theme crept into the criminal law, it naturally appeared most applicable to children. Thus the juvenile court was to arrest the development of full-fledged criminals by catching them early and uncovering and ameliorating the causes of their disaffection. Symptoms take many shapes, some of them only indirectly related to the disease. The "child savers" saw in youthful cursing and carousing the beginnings of a life of crime, and they feared that the conditions of the neglected were all too likely to breed the behavior of the delinquent. *Task Force Report: Juvenile Delinquency, supra* note 4, at 22-23.

36   Juvenile court personnel subscribe to the notion that children are naturally dependent and that it is, therefore, their task to punish premature independence. This point is documented by A. Platt, *supra* note 34. See also D. Matza, *Delinquency and Drift* 101-151 (1964).

37   See Table 4, *infra.*

38   "Supervision" means a lengthy continuance during which time the client is expected to keep out of trouble. If he is judged to have kept out of trouble until the trial date, the case is dismissed. This procedure is similar to the "sitting out period" used in criminal courts, except in that case the defendant serves "dead time" under the misconception that he is avoiding a record.

39   See F. Allen, *The Borderland of Criminal Justice* (1964).; *Task Force Report: Juvenile Delinquency, supra* note 4, at 107-13.

40   The idea of "residual category" is taken from Bittner, "Police Discretion in Emergency Apprehension of Mentally Ill Persons," 14 *Social Problems* 278-92 (1967).

41   For an analogous account of the importance of demeanor in the interaction of juveniles with police, see Piliavin and Briar, "Police Encounters with Juveniles," 70 *Am. J. of Sociology* 206-14 (1964).

42   For a discussion of the importance of the psychiatric and psychological perspective in the juvenile court, see Hakeem, "A Critique of the Psychiatric Approach to the Prevention of Juvenile Delinquency," 5 *Social Problems* 194-205 (1957).

43   Platt and Friedman, *supra* note 21.

44   Blumberg, "The Practice of Law as a Confidence Game: Organizational Cooptation of a Profession," 1 *L. & Society Rev.* 20 (June, 1967).

45   On expediency and efficiency in processing court cases, see Skolnick, "Social Control in the Adversary System," 11 *J. Conflict Resolution* 52-70 (1967).

46   For discussions of the crucial role the "informal" organization plays in shaping the goals of the formal structure, see P. Blau, *Bureaucracy in Modern Society* 45-67 (1956); Selznick, "An Approach to a Theory of Bureaucracy," 8 *Am. Sociological Rev.* 47-54 (1943). For empirical work which has validated this process, see P. Blau, *The Dynamics of Bureaucracy* (1955); A. Gouldner, *Patterns of Industrial Bureaucracy* (1955); P. Selznick, *T.V.A. and the Grass Roots* (1949); Roth, "Hired Hand Research," 1 *Am. Sociologist* 190-96 (1966).

47   Blumberg, *supra* note 44, at 21.

48   Platt & Friedman, *supra* note 21.

49 "Closely knit groups in which there exists a high frequency of interaction and high personality involvement of the members have a tendency to suppress conflict." L. Coser, *The Functions of Social Conflict* 151 (1956).

50 Blumberg, *supra* note 44, at 20.

51 H. Garfinkel, *Studies in Ethnomethodology* 35-75 (1967).

52 See Table 4, *infra*.

53 Skolnick, *supra* note 45.

54 Blumberg, *supra* note 44, at 22. See also, D. Newman, *Conviction: The Determination of Guilt or Innocence Without Trial* (1966).

55 Blumberg, *supra* note 44, at 22.

56 *Id.* at 19.

57 It should be noted that the state's attorney has no power to fix sentences in adult criminal cases, but that the effect of prosecuting under a reduced charge is a lesser sentence. It should also be noted that agreements to a reduced plea must have judicial approval in adult cases.

58 B. George, *supra* note 20, at 121-22.

59 Formal interviews of juveniles, particularly of black youth by white adults, tell us very little about the subjective experience of being represented by a public defender.

60 Korn, "The Private Citizen, the Social Expert, and the Social Problem: An Excursion through an Unacknowledged Utopia," in *Mass Society in Crisis* 576-93 (Rosenberg, Gerver, and Howton ed. 1964).

61 Interview with sixteen-year-old Negro Youth a few days after his trial in juvenile court. This interview is part of a larger, related study of juvenile justice.

62 E. Goffman, *Presentation of Self in Everyday Life* 151-53 (1959).

63 See D. Matza, *supra* note 36.

64 Although the following comparative data from municipal courts are not especially reliable they nevertheless give a crude indication of the different patterns of representation:

Percentage comparison of public defenders' dispositions in Metro's municipal and juvenile courts

Public defender	Acquitted by motion of state	Plea of guilty	Found guilty at trial	Total guilty	Found not guilty at trial	Total not guilty
Juvenile court N=345	3.5	25.0	31.1	56.1	37.6	41.1
Municipal court N=2104	15.8	30.5	9.4	39.9	44.3	60.1

65 See Blumberg, *supra* note 44; Lemert, *supra* note 10; Sudnow, *supra* note 15. The point is most forcefully expressed by Blumberg, *supra* note 44, at 23: "The defense attorneys . . . ultimately are concerned with strategies which tend to lead to a plea." Less emphatic is Sudnow, *supra* note 15, at 262: "Both P.D. and D.A. are concerned to obtain a guilty plea wherever possible and thereby avoid a trial."

66 The notion of "procedural definition" is developed by D. Sudnow, *Passing On: The Social Organization of Dying, passim* (1967). See also Kitsuse and Cicourel, "A Note on the Uses of Official Statistics," 11 *Social Problems* 131-39 (1963).

67 This term is especially used *passim* by Blumberg, *supra* note 44; Lemert, *supra* note 10.

68 Skolnick, *supra* note 45.

69 This idea is explored more fully in F. Musgrove, *Youth and the Social Order* (1964).

70 New juvenile court act in effect.

71 Includes disorderly behavior, mob action, etc.

72 Includes representation by private lawyers and legal aid organizations (approximately 770).

73 Includes dismissals on motion of state's attorneys and "supervision."

74 Includes commitment to private institutions and state hospitals.

75 Includes continuances, transferred cases, etc.

To Be Minor and Female: The Legal Rights of Women Under 21

JEAN STROUSE

Jean Strouse is an editor at Pantheon Books.

Reprinted from Jean Strouse, "To Be Minor and Female," *Ms Magazine*, August 1972, pp. 70-75.

To be minor and female is to be doubly vulnerable—not only in New York, where these cases were found, but under similar laws in other states across the country. Under the guise of "protection" from the harsh sanctions applicable to adult criminal behavior, minors in trouble with the law have been treated to an Alice-in-Wonderland version of justice to which few constitutional standards of fairness and due process apply. "Punishment" is called "rehabilitation" ("When *I* use a word," Humpty-Dumpty said, "it means just what I choose it to mean"). Authority is often as arbitrary and irascible as Carroll's Queen of Hearts. And under the guise of "protection" from a long list of evils including criminal sanctions, sexuality, and moral depravity, girls can be "treated" for longer than boys for acts that would not be considered criminal at all if committed by adults.

1   Ellen S., a 17-year-old runaway from Scarsdale, is picked up by the police in New York's East Village, and returned to her parents.

2   Mark S., a 17-year-old runaway from Scarsdale, is picked up by the police in the East Village, and released as soon as his age has been established as over 16.

3   Jane M., 16½, is brought to court by her parents because she stays out too late at night, hangs around with a boy her parents have forbidden her to see, and has contracted a venereal disease. She is, claim the parents, "incorrigible, ungovernable, and habitually disobedient." She is declared by the court to be a "Person in Need of Supervision," and sent to a state training school for "rehabilitation."

4   John M., 16½, is brought to court by his family because he stays out too late at night, hangs around with a "wild" group, and has contracted a venereal disease. He is, claim his parents, "incorrigible, ungovernable, and habitually disobedient." "Boys will be boys," the judge admonishes, as he informs John's parents that John is past the age (16) for non-criminal treatment of boys in Family Court. As long as he has not committed a crime, no court action may be taken against him.

5   Cheryl P. and David B., both 15, have run away from home to live together in a friend's loft. Neither has been to school for six months. They are found by a truant officer and taken to Family Court, where the judge finds them both to be "Persons in Need of Supervision." He sends David to the Warwick School for Boys, and Cheryl to the Brookwood Center for Girls. Both have problems in training school, and each time their respective commitments come up for review, they are renewed and extended. David remains at Warwick for three years, until he is 18 and must be released because he is no longer under the jurisdiction of the Family Court. Cheryl stays at Brookwood for five years, until she is 20, at which age girls are no longer under the jurisdiction of the Family Court.

There are, for example, three laws in New York's Family Court Act that made possible the discriminatory treatment of Ellen S., Jane M., and Cheryl P.

Section 718 (a)

providing that:

A peace officer may return to his parent or other person legally responsible for his care any male under the age of 16 or female under the age of 18 who has run away from home without just cause or who, in the reasonable opinion of the peace officer, appears to have run away from home without just cause. . . .

Section 712 (b)

providing that:

"Person in need of supervision" means a male less than 16 years of age and a female less than 18 years of age who does not attend school . . . or who is incorrigible, ungovernable, or habitually disobedient and beyond the lawful control of parent or other lawful authority. . . .

Section 756 (c)

providing that:

Successive extensions (of the original placement) may be granted, but no placement may be made or continued under this section beyond the child's eighteenth birthday, if male, or twentieth birthday, if female, without his or her consent and in no event past his or her twenty-first birthday. . . .

"Person in Need of Supervision" (PINS) is the awkward appellation given to a New York minor who is in some trouble with the law, but hasn't actually committed a crime. (A minor who has committed a crime is called a "juvenile delinquent" until age 16. A boy or girl who does something *that would be criminal if an adult did it*, as distinct from being "incorrigible" or truant, may be subject to criminal prosecution.) The PINS statute was designed to provide an alternative to criminal prosecution, and that alternative is available to girls for two years longer than it is available to boys.

If in fact the PINS statute were applied to girls between the ages of 16 and 18 who committed crimes—if it were protective in granting them immunity from criminal prosecution—an argument could be made that boys 16 to 18 are being denied equal protection under the law because they have no PINS option after 16. In March, 1972, for instance, the U.S. Court of Appeals for the 10th Circuit held that an Oklahoma statute defining "juvenile" as a male under 16 and a female under 18 is unconstitutional in that it denies *to boys* the equal protection guaranteed by the Fourteenth Amendment. In that case, Odie Lee Ree, 17 years old, tried as an adult for a felony crime of burglary, argued that he should have been treated as a juvenile instead, since females are granted the benefits of juvenile court proceedings until the age of 18. The Court held:

> We have not been presented with a logical constitutional justification for the discrimination inherent in [the statute defining delinquency]. The state, in its brief and oral argument, has simply relied upon the unexplained "demonstrated facts of life." Because the purpose of the disparity in the age classification between 16- and 18-year-old males and 16- to 18-year-old females has not been demonstrated, we hold that [the statute] is violative of the Equal Protection Clause.
>
> Reed v. Page, 40 US LW 2631
> (10th Cir 3/11/72)

But no such argument has been made in New York because, according to lawyers and judges who work with PINS-age girls, the law there is not in fact protective. Girls between 16 and 18 who commit crimes are treated exactly like boys who commit crimes, but girls have the additional burden of being brought to court and deprived of liberty for *noncriminal* conduct. Women's rights groups in New York have begun to work on challenging the PINS statute on grounds of equal protection.

Ironically, laws governing the age at which a minor may marry discriminate in the opposite direction. Girls in most states may marry at 16 with the consent of their parents, and at 18 without it, while boys can't marry until 18 with parental consent and 21 without. Although these laws appear to favor women, they in fact strengthen the traditional view that the goal of womanhood is marriage, and that women should be encouraged to marry early and have children—to jump from one "custodial" situation into another—while men are expected to stay free, and prepare themselves for larger social roles.

That the law views and treats girls and young women differently from boys and young men is clear. Not so clear are the justifications for this differential treatment—the contemporary relevance of "protectionism" as applied to women and children, and the actual differences between male and female adolescence, male and female criminal or quasi-criminal behavior, male and female responses to incarceration and to treatment.

Are there, for instance, enough real differences in the numbers and kinds of offenses committed by boys and girls to justify the legal discrimination between the two groups?

Since female offenders have rarely been taken seriously enough to be the subjects of studies, there is not a great deal of information available about girls in trouble with the law. But certain general trends are apparent. Boys, for example, have a substantially higher delinquency rate than girls. According to the 1965 Juvenile Court statistics compiled by the Children's Bureau of the Department of Health, Education and Welfare: "Delinquency remains primarily a boys' problem. They are referred to court four times as often as girls." (Recent statistics, however, show female juvenile delinquency to be rising twice as fast as male: a Government crime report quoted in *The New York Times* on April 12, 1972, found that the boy-to-girl ratio of court referrals narrowed from four to one in the mid-sixties to three to one in 1970.)

The kinds of offenses committed by boys and girls also differ. The President's Commission on Law Enforcement and Administration of Justice stated in a 1967 report, "The Challenge of Crime in a Free Society," that:

> . . . Children's Bureau statistics based on large city court reports reveal that more than half of the girls referred to juvenile court in 1965 were referred for conduct that would not be criminal if committed by adults; only one-fifth of the boys were referred for such conduct. Boys were primarily referred for larceny, burglary, and motor-vehicle theft, in order of frequency. Girls for running away, ungovernable behavior, larceny, and sex offenses.

And Edward Eldefonso, in *Law Enforcement and the Youthful Offender*, reported a California study of sex differences in juvenile arrests in 1964 which found that *fifteen times* as many boys were arrested for major law violations as girls. Even in delinquent girl-gangs associated with gangs of boys, according to New York City lawyer Sarah Gold, the girls' activities were found in a recent study to be relatively innocuous (i.e., noncriminal): the girls are sexually intimate with boy members, work as prostitutes to obtain money for the boys, and serve as courier and errand girls.

In general, it appears that the less violent values of the women's culture are reflected in the kinds of crimes females do and don't commit.

Yet, in spite of the fact that girls' offenses are less serious than boys', girls are neither sentenced to shorter reformatory terms nor given probation more readily. Statistics for the nation as a whole set the boy-girl sex ratio in institutions at about 3 to 1. Thus there are apparently more girls in institutions than the *number* of their offenses warrants, even disregarding the fact that the *kinds* of offenses they commit are minor in comparison to boys.

> Future: That 27 percent of unmarried girls 15 to 19 years old have had sexual relations; that 95 percent of all girls 15 to 19 know about the Pill; that teenagers accounted for about one quarter of the abortions performed under the New York abortion law during its first year; that pregnancy is the number one cause of school dropout among females in the United States; that teenage mothers have a suicide attempt rate 10 times that of the general population—in spite of this overwhelming evidence of considerable sexual activity among young unmarried girls, there are insufficient programs for making contraceptive advice and services available to young women, and doctors are reluctant to treat minors for venereal disease, contraception, or abortion without the parents' knowledge and permission.

It is abundantly clear from the above examples, from the comparison of the kinds of offenses committed by boys and girls, and from a review of the literature on women and crime, that the definition of social misconduct in women is primarily sexual. "An unstated fear or dislike of sexual promiscuity and illegitimate births by young women and girls" is behind the unequal treatment implicit in the New York Family Court Act, says Sarah Gold, author of an excellent article on "Equal Protection for Juvenile Girls in Need of Supervision in New York State" (from the *New York Law Forum*, Volume XVII, Number 2, 1971).

A probation officer interviewed by Gold says that truancy, ungovernability, incorrigibility, etc., are simply "buffer charges" for "promiscuity" in girls. And the FBI Uniform Crime Report for 1964 claims that, "Promiscuity among girls was quite prevalent. . . . Girls accounted for 4 percent of sexual offenses other than forcible rape as compared to 1.5 percent of the boys arrested."

Maybe girls actually commit more sexual offenses than boys. But maybe the above facts are true because parents, judges, police, teachers, and probation officers are more uptight about female sexual activity than about male. The argument is frequently made that females, being physically smaller, weaker, and less aggressive than males, are more likely to "act out" their impulses in self-destructive sexual behavior than in violent, other-directed crimes. "Acting out"

—a complex psychoanalytic concept that has to do with behavior expressing an unconscious impulse or fantasy—has become a jargon-ized term for any behavior of which a judge or social worker or correction officer disapproves; i.e., a girl is "acting out" if she is re-bellious, or angry, or noisy, or self-destructive—precisely *what* she is acting out, or why, never gets asked. In any case, since the *conse-quences* of sexual activity are visible in females, they are punishable, as explained by Albert J. Reiss in an article in *Law and Contempo-rary Problems* (Volume 25):

> While heterosexual intercourse is permitted if it is a private act between an adolescent boy and girl, society clearly does not tolerate the behavior if it becomes public and thereby flouts the mores. Nowhere is this more apparent than in the public reaction to the illegitimate child of the single adoles-cent girl. The boy is not treated as problematic in this case, but rather it is the girl who is the offender. It has been sug-gested that the reason for this is that pregnancy by its social visibility challenges the mores. The challenge must, perforce, be met with negative sanctions.

New York Family Court Judge Justine Wise Polier described to Sarah Gold the double standard that is applied to behavior which qualifies as "ungovernable," attributing the differences mainly to the fact that boys don't get pregnant.

The vagueness of such quasi-legal definitions leaves plenty of room for biases and double standards to enter the judicial process: Reiss cites 1,500 cases decided by a metropolitan juvenile court judge, in which the judge

> refused to treat any form of sexual behavior on the part of boys, even the most bizarre forms, as warranting more than probationary status. The judge, however, regarded girls as the "cause" of sexual deviation of boys in all cases of coition involving an adolescent couple and refused to hear the com-plaints of the girl and her family. The girl was regarded as a prostitute.

Attempts to "protect" young females from sexuality—often their own—reflect society's profound confusion and ambivalence about both females and their sexuality. Side by side with the judge who regards girls as the "cause" of sexual deviation in boys—and laws which punish prostitutes but not their customers, and the sexual-political assumption that anybody who gets raped wants to— is all the rhetoric about protection of females and children, and crimes such as "seduction" and "statutory rape." Seduction exists as a crime, according to Gerhard Mueller (in *Legal Regulation of Sexual Conduct*) in order to protect

> a weakness which the legislator assumes to exist, especially in young . . . or unmarried female persons. While an act of intercourse with such a person . . . alone may be nothing

worse than fornication, in seduction the surrender of the body (in some states: the surrender of chastity) must be achieved by artifice, strategem, trickery, and deceit, or a promise of marriage and in some states solely by the latter.

Needless to say, a man who marries a woman he has "seduced" will not be prosecuted. Statutory rape is defined as sexual intercourse with a female who is under a certain age, regardless of consent, and has nothing at all to do with forcible rape. The age of consent is usually 16, although Delaware has for some reason established it at 7. That the "victims" of seduction and statutory rape are always female reflects society's judgment that girls under a certain age are not capable of making responsible decisions to engage in sexual intercourse; it makes no similar judgment about boys.

If judgments based on age or sex have to be made at all in the interests of a complex and ostensibly rational social order, they must be, in fact, rational. That is, they must be related to contemporary reality, informed about the actual lives they regulate, nondiscriminatory, and relatively free of personal bias or social prejudice. Present laws which in the name of protection treat girls to longer and different punishments than boys, simply because they are girls and able to bear children, are irrational, discriminatory, and rooted in obsolete social stereotypes. No factual differences between teen-age boys and girls have been shown to justify greater supervisory intervention in girls' lives. On the contrary, adolescent girls are generally assumed to mature faster than boys, both physically and emotionally. No differences between male and female delinquency have been shown to justify longer incarcerations of females—quite the opposite, in fact— or looser applications of constitutional fairness doctrines.

The proposed Equal Rights Amendment provides, two years after ratification, for the states to review sex-based legislation and eliminate distinctions which deny equal protection on the basis of sex. That seems a little like hoping all the king's horses and all the king's men will patch up Humpty-Dumpty—and it raises several large questions about the patch-up job. What is equality anyway—as distinct from equal rights, or equal protection? What are the relationships among people to be based on? How does the law influence human relationships?

Those are among the real questions to be asked about the tangle of protective and punitive laws that surround minors who are also females. It is, of course, confusing to be told that it is up to you to say no because girls are more mature than boys, that you are ready for marriage sooner than boys—while you are being supervised much more closely than boys at home, or school, and in court. Laws which perpetuate that confusion only increase social ignorance about the nature of adolescence, and about what it means to be male or female. In order to understand the rising rate of female delinquency, for instance, one would have to begin with a definition of delinquency that applied equally to both sexes. Only then would the biases in reporting and the actual differences in male-female behavior become clear—and only then could one ask if girls are in fact becoming more aggressive; if "liberation" means only the freedom to act like boys; or if female delinquency is primarily a function of social fear about young girls in "danger of falling into habits of vice."

Protection as a legal principle does cut both ways, and laws which favor females—like the Oklahoma delinquency statute—as well as those like New York's PINS statutes which discriminates against them should fall under the new Amendment. The contradictions in contemporary attitudes about women and protection are most blatant with regard to females who are also minors. If there is to be any change in laws affecting women, the Gordian knot around the condition of being a girl is the place to begin.

Judicial Paternalism and the Female Status Offender: Training Women to Know Their Place

MEDA CHESNEY-LIND

Meda Chesney-Lind is an instructor in the Department of Sociology, Honolulu Community College.

Reprinted with permission of the National Council on Crime and Delinquency from *Crime and Delinquency*, April 1977, pp. 121-30.

Criticism of the juvenile court's jurisdiction over the status offender consistently neglects one important aspect of the issue. As a product of the court's history of extralegal paternalism, status offenses have involved the system in the maintenance of traditional family norms, which require greater obedience and chastity from females than from males.

The enforcement of status offenses has created a *de facto* double standard of juvenile justice in America. Like "good parents," police and court personnel tend to select for punishment girls whose behavior threatens parental authority and boys whose behavior is beyond that which can be excused as "boys will be boys." This pattern explains both the overrepresentation of girls charged with status offenses in court populations and the relatively harsh official response to this behavior. Evidence is presented to show that, at every level in the system, girls charged with status offenses are treated more harshly than girls charged with crimes. Further, the noncriminal activity of girls is frequently seen as requiring more drastic intervention than the criminal behavior of boys.

The controversy surrounding the juvenile court system's jurisdiction over youth charged with noncriminal or status offenses has taken on the character of a national debate, and yet one important aspect of this issue seems consistently neglected. Although females constitute only about a quarter of the juvenile court populations across the country, they may be a majority of those charged with noncriminal offenses.[1] Young women, it seems, are far more likely than their male counterparts to be arrested and referred to court for offenses which apply only to youth: "running away from home," "incorrigibility," "waywardness," "curfew violation," or being a "person in need of supervision." One recent national study found, for example, that 75 per cent of the females in the juvenile justice system were there for status offenses rather than criminal behavior.[2] Simply stated, girls account for an inordinate proportion of persons brought into the juvenile justice system for status offenses.

Why are women, who generally constitute a very small proportion of those in the criminal justice system, so frequently charged with status offenses? The answer to this question supplies both a major explanation of the court's relatively harsh response to youth labeled as status offenders and an important argument for the removal of these cases from court jurisdiction.

ENFORCEMENT OF PATRIARCHAL AUTHORITY

A brief look at the history of the juvenile court provides a partial explanation for the preponderance of women charged with status offenses in the court populations across the country. Contrary to the popular myth that juvenile courts were established to prevent juveniles from being tried and sentenced as adults, the actual history of the institution reveals quite different motives. In 1899, the first juvenile court was established in Chicago, culminating a long campaign to create a separate judicial system for youthful offenders. While using rhetoric about protecting children from the horrors of the adult system, the court's founders were actually interested in a system which would shore up "traditional" American institutions like the family. Imagining these to be threatened by foreign immigration and urbanization, the largely middle-class, Anglo-Saxon conservatives set up a court to reinforce their definition of appropriate adolescent deportment.[3]

Consequently, they were not interested in children accused of the classic crimes against property, nor were they opposed to the imprisonment of youth. Instead, says sociologist Anthony Platt, they were concerned with insuring the normative behavior of youth by instilling proper attitudes toward authority, family relationships, and personal morality. Assuming the natural dependence of children, they created a special court to prevent "premature" independence and to monitor and enforce traditional family authority.

This mission, which originally supplied the logic for the arrest, detention, and incarceration of youth for "incorrigibility," "ungovernability," or "running away from home," is not simply of historical interest. The court's continuing commitment to the enforcement of family authority is clearly reflected in recent statistics that show a steady increase in the proportion of these cases in the court populations.[4] But more to the point, the institution's undiminished willingness to involve itself in the enforcement of traditional family values is particularly ominous for young women.

The traditional family has always exerted greater control over the behavior of its daughters in order to protect their virginity or virginal reputation. A "good girl" is obedient to parental demands and, while sexy, is never sexual. Sons, on the other hand, are encouraged by their parents to "sow wild oats," and their independent behavior is, if not encouraged, then at least tolerated.

Like good parents, police and court personnel respond differently to the indiscretions of young men and women. Routine procedures encourage officials to ignore all but the most extreme misbehavior of boys while looking very closely at all girls' delinquency. The juvenile justice system is concerned that girls allowed to run wild might be tempted to experiment sexually and thus endanger their marriageability.

The court involves itself in the enforcement of adolescent morality and parental authority through the vehicle of status offenses. The use of these offense categories, it will be shown, creates a *de facto* double standard of juvenile justice in America, one for men and another for women, and results in the preponderance of young women facing such charges before the court.

POLICE DISCRETION

Much attention has been given recently to the startling increases in the "female crime rate," and there seems to be some basis for this concern. The number of female arrests is increasing, and this is especially true for adolescent women. Between 1960 and 1974, arrests of adult women were up 76.5 per cent; during the same period, arrests of women under eighteen were up 235.1 per cent.[5] The meaning of this dramatic increase is less clear, however; and facile characterizations of adolescent women enthusiastically breaking into formerly male bastions of criminal activity obscure more than they explain.

Self-report studies measuring the actual volume and character of juvenile misconduct have shown that official statistics consistently underestimate girls' criminal activity and overestimate status offenses.[6] One of these studies, for example, showed that status offenses comprised "only 8 per cent of girls' delinquent acts and not much less of boys', 6 per cent."[7] The overemphasis of girls charged with status offenses has been explained, in part, by the routine police practice of ignoring (or releasing without arrest) girls accused of criminal activity and arresting those suspected of juvenile offenses.[8]

Recent arrest statistics published by the Federal Bureau of Investigation indicate a possible change in police behavior and an increase in the number of juvenile women arrested for criminal behavior (particularly larceny and drug offenses). These changes in enforcement patterns, while producing dramatic percentage increases in certain offense categories, do not signal a basic change in female delinquency or the official response to it. Nearly one-third (28.6 per cent) of the young women arrested in 1974 were taken into custody for either running away from home or curfew violations, and these women, along with others arrested for uniquely juvenile offenses, are far more likely to remain in the juvenile justice system than are their counterparts charged with crimes.

Decisions after arrest, which determine whether a youth will be "counseled and released" or "referred to court," reveal a consistent pattern of police paternalism that penalizes women. In 1965, the last year for which national data are available, girls charged with juvenile offenses made up about a third of those arrested but about half of those referred to juvenile courts. Only about 20 per cent of the boys were referred to court for these offenses. Boys were more likely to find their way to court for criminal offenses: burglary, larceny, and car theft.[9]

More recent statistics from Honolulu indicate that the situation has not changed.[10] In 1972, girls charged with noncriminal offenses were far more likely than girls charged with crimes to be referred to juvenile court. Only 6.1 per cent of the girls arrested for the most serious adult offenses and 12.7 per cent of the girls arrested for less serious adult offenses were referred to court, compared with 33.7 per cent of those arrested for juvenile offenses. The police were also a good deal more likely to refer a girl than a boy arrested for a juvenile offense to court (33.6 per cent and 22.7 per cent, respectively).

This harsh police response to the noncriminal activity of young girls is, in some respects, the result of parental attitudes. Boys and girls who are brought to the attention of the police for criminal offenses have natural advocates in their parents; but three out of every four youths charged with status offenses are, according to one study, brought to the attention of the police by their parents.[11]

The parental role in the initiation of police action also explains why girls make up so preponderant a part of persons charged with these noncriminal offenses. Parents have different standards of behavior for their sons and daughters; and they tend to demand greater obedience and chastity from their daughters. For example, they would seldom ask police to arrest a son who fails to come home from a date at the expected time, but this is a common reason for seeking a daughter's arrest. Since the statutes simply require adolescents to obey their parents, the police often find themselves unwittingly involved in the unequal application of the law.

DISCRIMINATION IN DETENTION

After arrest, this double standard victimizes females who enter the juvenile justice system in yet another fashion. Not only are girls charged with violations of their sexual role more likely than boys to be referred to court, but they are more likely than boys to be held in jails or juvenile detention facilities across the nation.

In 1971, girls constituted only 22.3 per cent of all juvenile arrests but 33 per cent of those held in juvenile detention centers. Further, 75 per cent of the detained girls but only between 20 and 30 per cent of the detained boys are charged with noncriminal offenses. Girls may also stay longer in detention since youths detained for juvenile offenses stayed longer in these facilities than did youths charged with crimes.[12] Data collected by Paul Lerman in New York indicated that adolescents charged with juvenile offenses were twice as likely as youths charged with crimes to be detained for more than thirty days. Since girls are overwhelmingly charged with these offenses, it seems likely that they spend more time in detention than their male counterparts.

These statistics are startling and indicate that girls who have not violated the law are punished more severely after arrest than either boys or girls charged with crimes. Like good parents, the family court officials feel the need to "protect" their "daughters"—usually from sexual experimentation.

Further evidence of this paternalistic interest in girls' sexuality is found in the widespread use of pelvic examinations in detention centers across the nation. Elizabeth Gold reports that all girls brought before the family court in New York are given vaginal smears, even girls brought before the court for nonsexual offenses.[13] Similarly, in Philadelphia, each girl who enters the Youth Study Center, regardless of age, must submit to an internal examination. Some may argue that, given the problem of venereal disease among teen-agers, such examination is medically justified. However, it must be remembered that the exam takes place in an institutional setting and in concert with other entry rituals and, thus, is both degrading and depersonalizing.

For example, one detention center surveyed by the National Council of Jewish Women required all girls to undergo a pelvic exam "to determine if they are pregnant" and at the same time subjected them "in a group" to the Cuprex Delouse test, in which their bodies are sprayed with a "burning substance."[14] The director of the Philadelphia Youth Study Center was a little more specific about the administration of the pelvic exam required of all women who entered his institution:

"We do put a girl on the table in the stirrups and we do have a smear. . . . We do have a swab. You go in and get a smear." When asked whether a girl who refused to undergo this pelvic exam would be placed in "medical lock-up"—a polite term for solitary confinement—he responded, "Yes, we may have to."[15]

Aside from being a degrading experience for a young girl and probably a violation of her right to privacy, the routine administration of pelvic exams demonstrates the court's assumption that girls who come to the attention of the police and the courts are quite probably engaging in "promiscuous" sexual activity; in short, the court tends to equate female delinquency with sexuality. Like adult women, girls are more likely to be labeled as "carriers" of venereal disease and at fault if they are pregnant and unwed. Such labels as "runaway" and "incorrigible" are buffer charges for suspected sexuality, providing legal categories to cover the court's real interest in the girls' obedience to sexual norms. It is for this reason that girls charged with these offenses are so often incarcerated and subjected to pelvic exams.

This perspective also explains why the court sees no problem with the lengthy incarceration of girls who are not charged with crimes. Court personnel argue that the girls "have no place to go." In fact, court officials demand that the girl choose between continued incarceration and some form of court-arranged and court-approved living situation. Like the girl's parents, they feel that the girl must be controlled and "protected" from the temptations of the street. Only rarely does the court manifest the same concern for the protection of boys in its jurisdiction.

JUDICIAL PATERNALISM

It is within the court system proper that the paternalistic nature of the juvenile justice becomes explicit. While girls are about one-quarter of the total juvenile court population, they are apparently the majority of those charged with juvenile offenses.

What happens to girls charged with these juvenile offenses once they enter the system? Since they have committed no crime, they would be expected to disappear from the system rapidly. Yet, while some girls do indeed receive lenient treatment, all evidence seems to suggest that they are the ones referred for law violations.

At intake, probation officers determine which of the cases are the most serious, and those are generally referred to a formal hearing before a juvenile court judge. One would assume that the serious categories of offenses would have higher rates of referral. But such is not the case. Astonishingly, many "PINS" or noncriminal cases are referred by the intake officer to a hearing rather than to informal procedure.

The New York researchers found that, to intake officers, parental objection to a daughter's boy friend (64 per cent of the referred cases) was more serious than a charge of larceny (57 per cent of the cases referred). Referral rates are higher for verbal abuse than for assault; a refusal to obey and coming home late will get you before a judge more quickly than arson or illegal entry.[16] Data from Honolulu during 1967–72 are less specific but show that girls were six times more likely than boys to appear before a juvenile court judge on their first offense.

This treatment is often the result of pressure from parents. In the New York study, for example, Andrews and Cohn reported that parents come to probation interviews armed with a long list of offenses that the child has allegedly committed. These charges may range from running away from home or being truant to having a boy friend the parents do not approve of, staying out late at night, "having an abortion against parental wishes, sleeping all day, . . . banging a door in reaction to a parental command, wanting to get married, . . . and being an 'invertebrate [sic] liar.' "[17]

Juvenile court judges also seem to participate enthusiastically, though perhaps unconsciously, in the judicial enforcement of the female role. Part of their behavior, while discriminatory, is understandable. Their legal background provides them with clear guidelines when confronting youths charged with crimes. Standards of evidence are clear, elements of the crime are laid down by statute, and the youth's civil rights are, at least to some extent, protected by law.

But in the case of a boy or a girl charged with incorrigibility or ungovernability, the court is without legal guidelines. Many of these judges find themselves in a legal never-never land; and, in this void, fall back on the role of benevolent but harsh parent which is built into the juvenile justice system.

Andrews and Cohn's review of the handling of cases of ungovernability in New York concluded with the comment that judges were acting "upon personal feelings and predilections in making decisions" and gave as evidence for this statement several courtroom lectures they recorded during the course of their study. For example: "She thinks she's a pretty hot number; I'd be worried about leaving my kid with her in a room alone. She needs to get her mind off boys."[18]

Similar attitudes expressing concern about premature female sexuality and the proper parental response are evident throughout the comments. One judge remarked that at age fourteen some girls "get some crazy ideas. They want to fool around with *men*, and that's sure as hell trouble." Another judge admonished a girl:

> I want you to promise me to obey your mother, to have
> perfect school attendance and not miss a day of school, to
> give up these people who are trying to lead you to do wrong,

not to hang out in candy stores or tobacco shops or street
corners where these people are, and to be in when your
mother says. . . . I don't want to see you on the streets of
this city except with your parents or with your clergyman or
to get a doctor. Do you understand?[19]

The judges are not apologetic about the consequences of their
double standard of justice. Comments made in June 1975 by Hunter
Hurst, director of the Juvenile Justice Division of the National Council of Juvenile Court Judges, are very revealing in this regard:

The issue is that status offenses are offenses against our values.
Girls are seemingly over-represented as status offenders
because we have a strong heritage of being protective toward
females in this country. It offends our sensibility and our
values to have a fourteen year old girl engage in sexually promiscuous activity. It's not the way we like to think about
females in this country. As long as it offends our values, be
sure that police, or the church or vigilante groups, or somebody is going to do something about it. For me, I would
rather that something occur in the court where the rights of
the parties can be protected.[20]

Hurst's enthusiasm about the quality of the court's commitment to
the rights of women should be tempered by the legal controversy
presently surrounding the issue of the rights of minors charged with
juvenile status offenses. He should also be somewhat troubled by an
argument that lumps the juvenile justice system with vigilante groups
in the enforcement of community prejudices against women. The
fact that these sexist community norms exist is no justification for
involving agencies of the law in their enforcement.

TRAINING WOMEN

"For her own protection. . . ." These words take on a very special
meaning in the juvenile justice system. The logical extension of
judicial paternalism, they mask the fact that the young woman is
being sentenced to a juvenile prison.

The most recent census of these institutions indicated that, at
any one time, over eight thousand young women are held in training
schools across America.[21] Young women account for over 20 per
cent of those held in training schools—in marked contrast to adult
women, who were only 3.2 per cent of those held in state and federal
prisons in 1971. Looking at these figures in another way, we see that
girls, while only 40 per cent of all arrests of all females, constituted
60 per cent of all females in prisons, because after arrest a girl is
almost seven times more likely than her adult counterpart to end up
in prison.[22]

Girls tend to be placed in training schools "for their own protection," which actually means protection from "temptation" and

their own sexuality. Thus, 70 per cent of the girls committed to training schools across the nation are there for juvenile offenses.[23]

A detailed review of one training school in Connecticut reveals the true meaning of the court's protection. In her study of Long Lane, Kristine Rogers reports that the staff express a great deal of interest in the girl's sexual history and habits:

> A girl is subjected to several interrogations upon entrance to Long Lane about her past sexual relations, her menses, any vaginal discharges, etc. Pregnancy is seen as "getting what she deserves," and the staff hope that if girls are made to live through one in such a punitive surrounding perhaps it won't happen again.[24]

The evidence seems to indicate that the girls at Long Lane get the message about the evils of sexuality. Rogers reported that the girls referred to their own pregnancies as "unmentionable situations," a variation on the school's "UM" designation for their "unmarried" status.

The school's twin remedies for sexual precosity are clear: training in the womanly arts and lengthy incarceration. Emphasis in this institution is on "religious" training coupled with sewing, cooking, and "beauty culture" to prepare the girls for their eventual role as "homemakers." No other vocational training occurs at the school and, while boys in Connecticut were paid for their work in the institution, girls were not.

This archaic regime was complemented in Connecticut by incarcerating the girls for longer periods of time; girls spent an average of seven months in the institution, compared with five months for boys. This pattern is not unique to Long Lane. In 1965, the nation-wide median stay for girls was two months longer than for boys; and more recently, girls in New York averaged twelve-month stays while boys averaged nine months.[25]

As to the reasons for this policy, the court officials in Connecticut are quite candid:

> Why, most of the girls I commit are for status offenses. I figure if a girl is about to get pregnant, we'll keep her until she's sixteen and then ADC [Aid to Dependent Children] will pick her up![26]

The pervasive concern about potential sexual misconduct at this school in Connecticut is not atypical. An ambitious survey of fifty training schools across the nation concluded with this comment: "The fact is that many girls wind up in institutions for sexual offenses."[27] In essence, these "training schools" are the logical culmination of a pattern of paternalistic justice that characterizes all stages in the juvenile system. At a time when sex roles are clearly changing, the wisdom of involving official agencies of the government in the enforcement of a nineteenth-century view of womanhood is, to say the least, questionable.

CONCLUSION

This paper has reviewed evidence that the juvenile court's historic commitment to traditional morality and obedience to parental authority results in a *de facto* double standard of juvenile justice. Routine police and court procedures seem to select out girls whose offenses threaten parental authority and boys whose offenses cannot be explained away as "boys will be boys." The court does this because both its history and its structure encourage extra-legal paternalism as well as law enforcement.

The evidence is clear that girls charged with status offenses receive harsher treatment than girls suspected of crimes at the level of referral to court, pretrial detention, and incarceration. It is also apparent that girls are far more likely than boys to be brought into the court system as status offenders despite evidence that boys commit as much of this type of behavior as girls.

Putting this another way, status offenses have allowed the construction of a double standard of juvenile justice. These vague offense categories coupled with the court's commitment to operate *in loco parentis* encourage the court to involve itself in the maintenance of traditional sex roles which require women to be obedient and chaste while encouraging young men to "sow wild oats."

The court is clearly applying the law in an unequal manner. But more importantly, the court is punishing the noncriminal behavior of girls as harshly as the criminal behavior of boys. Incarceration, whitewashed by such phrases as "for her own protection," is incarceration nonetheless. Most of the girls incarcerated in American training schools and detention centers have not violated any law or committed any crime. They are there because they cannot get along with their parents and the court will not allow them to be free. These abuses of judicial discretion make it imperative that the court's authority over the status offender be limited and other sorts of responses to youth in trouble be sought. Fortunately, encouraging movement in this direction is under way.

While efforts to extend due process rights to the status offender have been disappointing,[28] challenges that status offenses are unconstitutionally vague have been more successful. Two recent federal court decisions have held that statutes which permitted officials to take children into custody because they were "in danger of leading an idle, dissolute, lewd or immoral life" (*Gonzalez v. Maillard*)[29] or because they were "in danger of becoming morally depraved" (*Gesicki v. Oswald*)[30] were impermissibly vague. In May 1972 the United States Supreme Court affirmed the *Gesicki* decision without opinion.[31]

Pressure for legislative reform of the court's broad authority over status offenders is also building. The Juvenile Justice and Delinquency Prevention Act of 1974, which provides resources for states and communities to set up new programs for juvenile offenders, requires that states receiving funds must develop and implement plans to treat the status offender without recourse to juvenile detention or correctional facilities.[32]

While neither of these reforms removes the status offender from court jurisdiction, they do begin to place limits on the court's power to intervene in the lives of adolescents who have not committed crimes. Clearly, these efforts must be supported and other community resources must be created to deal with family problems. Runaway shelters and halfway houses for young people in conflict with their parents already exist in many communities, and their success should encourage others to explore these options.

While these reforms can be, and have been, supported for a wide variety of humanitarian reasons, this paper has suggested that one of the most compelling is that status offenses have encouraged the uncritical enforcement of a restrictive female role. This in turn may mean that the juvenile justice system has engaged in the violation of the civil rights of most of the females who have come into its jurisdiction.

NOTES

1 National data on this are unavailable. However, recent statistics cited for the New York area in R. Hale Andrews and Andrew H. Cohn, "Ungovernability: the Unjustifiable Jurisdiction," *Yale Law Journal*, June 1974, pp. 1383-1409, indicate that 62 per cent of those charged with "ungovernability" are girls. My research in Hawaii indicates that girls are roughly 60 per cent of all status offenders.

2 Rosemary C. Sarri and Robert D. Vinter, "Juvenile Justice and Injustice," *Resolution*, Winter 1975, p. 47.

3 Anthony M. Platt, *The Childsavers: The Invention of Delinquency* (Chicago: University of Chicago Press, 1969).

4 Nora Klapmuts, "Children's Rights," *Crime and Delinquency Literature*, September 1972.

5 Federal Bureau of Investigation, *Uniform Crime Reports* (U.S. Department of Justice: Washington, D.C., 1975), p. 184.

6 For a more complete summary of these self-report studies see Meda Chesney-Lind, "Judicial Enforcement of the Female Sex-Role: The Family Court and the Female Delinquent," *Issues in Criminology*, Fall 1973, p. 55.

7 Martin Gold, *Delinquent Behavior in an American City* (Belmont, Calif.: Brooks/Cole, 1970), pp. 63-64.

8 Thomas P. Monahan, "Police Dispositions of Juvenile Offenders," *Phylon*, Summer 1970.

9 Children's Bureau, Department of Health, Education and Welfare, "Statistics on Public Institutions for Delinquent Children, 1965," Washington, D.C., 1967.

10 Meda Chesney-Lind, "Juvenile Delinquency: The Sexualization of Female Crime," *Psychology Today*, July 1974, pp. 43-46.

11 Kathryn W. Burkhart, "The Child and the Law: Helping the Status Offender," Public Affairs Pamphlet No. 530, 1975, p. 4.

12 Rosemary Sarri, *Under Lock and Key: Juveniles in Jail and Detention* (Ann Arbor: University of Michigan, 1974).

13 Jean Strouse, "To Be Minor and Female: The Legal Rights of Women under 21," *Ms.*, August 1972, p. 74.

14 Edward Wakin, *Children without Justice: A Report by the National Council of Jewish Women* (New York: National Council of Jewish Women, 1975), p. 45.

15 Loretta Schwartz, "The Kids Nobody Wants." Paper distributed by the Philadelphia Program for Women and Girl Offenders.

16 Andrews and Cohn, *supra* note 1, p. 1388.

17 *Id.*, note 33, p. 1388.

18 *Id.*, note 124, p. 1403.

19 *Id.*, notes 126, 129, p. 1404.

20 Hunter Hurst, "Juvenile Status Offenders," a speech given to the New Mexico Council on Crime and Delinquency, June 20, 1975.

21 U.S. Department of Justice, "Children in Custody: A Report on Juvenile Detention Facility Census" (Washington, D.C.: U.S. Govt. Printing Office, 1973), p. 7.

22 These figures were compiled by comparing statistics on juvenile and adult female offenders contained in the U.S. Department of Justice's *Sourcebook on Criminal Justice Statistics*, 1973.

23 U.S. Justice Dept., *supra* note 21, p. 9.

24 Kristine Rogers, " 'For Her Own Protection . . .': Conditions of Incarceration for Female Juvenile Offenders in the State of Connecticut," *Law and Society Review*, Winter 1972, p. 235.

25 Linda Singer, "Women and the Correction Process," *American Criminal Law Review*, Winter 1973, p. 299.

26 Rogers, *supra* note 24, p. 227.

27 Wakin, *op. cit. supra* note 14, p. 79.

28 See Linda Riback, "Juvenile Delinquency Laws: Juvenile Women and the Double Standard of Morality," *UCLA Law Review*, 1971, p. 313; and "The Dilemma of the 'Uniquely Juvenile Offender,' " *William and Mary Law Review*, Winter 1972.

29 Civil No. 50424 (N.D. Cal. 1972).

30 336 F. Supp 371 (S.D.N.Y. 1971).

31 523 F. Supp 781 (1971).

32 Public Law 93-415, 93rd Congress, S. 821, Sept. 7, 1974.

Whipping Boys at the House of Refuge

EVALUATING TREATMENT APPROACHES TO DELINQUENCY

CHAPTER 7

The juvenile justice system mobilizes rehabilitative and treatment resources in an attempt to "cure" delinquent children. The assumption is that a specialized juvenile system can successfully treat youths, thereby reducing the likelihood of more serious delinquent acts. The selections that follow examine the ability of the system to prevent and treat delinquency.

The recent influx of massive federal funds to local governments to combat rising delinquency rates has resulted in studies that evaluate prevention and correctional projects. Government policies now require that each experimental program be evaluated to determine if the goals and objectives of the program are achieved. In the past, little research was done in this area due to insufficient funds, as well as the low prestige of applied research among social scientists. However, the funds now available have produced a growing body of literature analyzing the effectiveness of traditional treatment approaches in curbing delinquency and recidivism. The articles presented here unanimously conclude that the system is failing in its treatment efforts.

Sheldon Messinger outlines the development of a new penal institution for delinquent youth in California, and explores the processes that undermine such well-intentioned treatment efforts. His description of "The Dumping Ground" poses serious questions about implementing any sort of rehabilitative program within a prison setting. Messinger shows how the various goals of administrators, treatment personnel, and other correctional staff workers are often in conflict with one another, producing undesirable consequences for all concerned.

Barry Krisberg examines an Urban Leadership Training program designed to provide jobs in community work to older gang youths. Analyzing the project's demise, he argues that its failure was due to conflicts between the goals and expectations of the project staff and planners, and the youths who were supposed to benefit from the program. The staff on the project improved their personal employment prospects by furthering the professional commitment to reducing juvenile delinquency. The community organization, which sponsored the project, was primarily concerned with curbing the gang violence that was disrupting business and community growth. The university supporting the program used the effort to promote positive public relations within the adjoining community to facilitate their plans to expand campus facilities into that area. But the participating gang leaders gained little beyond temporarily escaping from their violent social milieu. The short-run benefits quickly disappeared, since a realistic and genuine follow-up program was not created.

In contrast to Krisberg's and Messinger's analyses of single programs, the article by Marc Riedel and Terence P. Thornberry provides a comprehensive review of large bodies of evaluation studies made over the past thirty years. The authors attempt to uncover trends and patterns in treatment approaches that succeeded in treating delinquency and crime. Although some of the data are from adult institutional, parole, or probation settings, such findings also apply to juvenile situations since treatment techniques such as reduced caseloads, intensive group and individual counseling, and vocational training typically originated in the juvenile system. Riedel and Thornberry examine the impact of programs ranging from educational and vocational training, individual and group counseling, altering the institutional environment, better medical treatment, differential lengths of sentencing, community-based projects, psychotherapy in the community, and probation or parole in lieu of incarceration. They conclude that rehabilitation efforts have not been successful, partly due to poor research designs.

Institutional officials have recently become more receptive to the use of behavior modification techniques based on principles of operant conditioning, in attempts to quiet disruptive and violent juvenile inmates. William S. Davidson and Edward Seidman review reports and evaluations of behavior modification programs used within and outside institutional settings to ascertain the overall impact of such treatment efforts. The studies are subdivided according to whether classroom or delinquent behavior is to be altered. Though the authors find that behavior modification techniques initially achieve limited success in reducing nonconforming behavior in institutional and program settings, it remains unanswered whether such modifications will persist. Furthermore, a closer critique of the evaluation designs on which these findings are based reveals several alternative hypotheses, minimizing the alleged success of behavior modification. Davidson and Seidman's study constitutes a plea for additional and more rigorous evaluation strategies. As a postscript, Davidson and Seidman suggest that the helping profession should question the moral consequences of using social science principles to justify forcing nonconforming youth to fit into an "unfit" society.

The next article considers the significance of the ethics of project evaluators who do the business of research, but who do not share the risks of their conclusions and recommendations. Barry Krisberg and Paul Takagi suggest that recommendations of project evaluators can have tragic consequences for both the project staff and participants. The authors describe a project in a major city, designed to curb gang violence, which was affecting the tourist trade. The evaluators sensed that the project would not reduce street violence, but it was not until a tragedy occurred that their uneasiness was confirmed. Krisberg and Takagi assert that criminologists and other social scientists have become involved in the development of delinquency prevention and treatment programs of dubious value. Such programs are imposed on poor communities, often with disastrous results. Krisberg and Takagi end with a plea to the academic community to weigh the moral and political significance of their participation in delinquency prevention efforts.

It has become fashionable to call for a return to the punitive practices of the past, citing the inadequacies of the rehabilitation model. Many assume that treatment approaches have been adequately tried and evaluated. In many instances, the adoption of a treatment model by correctional agencies has involved little more than the semantic transformation of prisons into "correctional institutions." Guards have become "correctional officers," inmates are called "clients" or "residents," and solitary confinement facilities have been redefined as "adjustment centers." Any claims that prevention and treatment approaches have failed implies that adequate efforts have been made to implement these goals, beyond mere verbal changes.

In the final article, Clarence Schrag critically reviews three recent works that propose a return to punishment and deterrence in criminal justice. Using national data, Schrag persuasively argues that policies based on "just desserts" will have no significant impact on criminal behavior. Such policies would produce an escalation of state intervention and control over powerless social groups, increase toleration of political and white-collar crimes, and increase costs. Calls for "simple justice" or deterrence, in effect, help justify further punishment and control of those who are victims of the existing social arrangement.

The Dumping Ground: Notes on the Evolution of a Prison

SHELDON L. MESSINGER

Sheldon L. Messinger is a professor of law at the University of California, Berkeley.

The California Vocational Institution, later known as Deuel Vocational Institution or "DVI," received its first inmates in 1946. By the early 1960s it was a complex of social and physical arrangements housing some 1,700 male offenders, and had become widely known as a "dumping ground" for the most troublesome juveniles and youths in California correctional institutions. How it earned this reputation is the subject of this paper.[1]

THE CORRECTION OF YOUTH OFFENDERS

The history of DVI can be traced to 1941, when the California legislature passed a "Youth Authority Act." This act aimed to "protect society more effectively by substituting for retributive punishment methods of training and treatment directed toward the correction and rehabilitation of young persons found guilty of public offenses."[2]

Plans for youth offenders

The act proposed a three-man board with state-wide authority to prescribe and pursue a unified plan for the correction of youth offenders. With certain exceptions, all youths convicted of crimes were to be committed to this "Youth Authority." In turn, the Youth Authority was to be responsible primarily for youths, not other offenders. The act defined a "youth" as a person less than twenty-three years old at the time of apprehension, who was not brought before the juvenile court to be heard as a juvenile offender. Because the juvenile court heard the cases of few offenders eighteen or over, persons eighteen to twenty-three years of age were the most likely to be so classified.

Upon commitment to the Authority, each youth was to be examined in order to develop an individualized correctional program meeting his needs. The Authority was to have broad discretion to specify the nature and duration of each youth's program. This discretion was created by modifying the sentences the criminal court could give to convicted persons under twenty-three years of age.

Thus, prior to the act, an offender under twenty-three years of age convicted of burglary in the second degree could be placed on probation, fined, sentenced to up to a year in county jail, or committed to state prison. If the court chose to commit the offender to state prison, he was subject to not less than one nor more than fifteen years imprisonment—his exact term to be set by a state parole board. Upon release, his civil rights were severely restricted. After passage of the act, however, if the criminal court did not wish to place a burglar under twenty-three on probation, to fine him, or to sentence him to county jail for a maximum of ninety days, it was obligated to treat him as a youth offender and commit him to the Youth Authority. If the Authority agreed to accept the commitment, the Authority was given complete discretion over the offender's minimum sentence. His maximum sentence could not ordinarily extend beyond his twenty-third birthday or until two years after commitment, whichever was later. Finally, under the act there was no formal loss of civil rights.

Persons convicted of major crimes who were under twenty-three years of age (except those sentenced by law to life imprisonment or death) were also to be placed in youth offender status and committed to the Authority. Thus, prior to the act, a person under twenty-three years of age convicted of a felony such as robbery in the first degree was subject to at least five years imprisonment. After passage of the act, such a person had to be committed to the Youth Authority as a youth offender. As a youth offender he could be paroled or discharged at any time, since his conviction carried no minimum term. Unless the Youth Authority petitioned the committing court to extend the sentence to the maximum term prescribed by law for the particular offense, his commitment terminated when the youth offender reached his twenty-fifth birthday or two years after commitment, whichever was later.

The juvenile court as well as the criminal court was empowered to commit persons to the new Authority. The act was permissive in this respect, however, rather than mandatory, suggesting that the juvenile court was expected to use this power only in exceptional circumstances. And even if the juvenile court committed offenders to the new Authority, they would remain "juvenile offenders" rather than become "youth offenders." But the juvenile court could continue to commit offenders directly to private, county, and state correctional facilities as it had been doing, rather than to the Authority, where they would remain the responsibility of the juvenile court and those who administered the juvenile correctional system.

The Youth Authority Act contained provisions permitting the new agency to gradually assume its responsibilities. Although the criminal court was required to commit most convicted offenders under twenty-three years of age to the Youth Authority, the Authority could accept or reject jurisdiction over these offenders. If the Authority rejected jurisdiction, holding that the offender would not be "materially benefited" by its program or that "proper and adequate facilities" did not exist for his care, the offender was to be returned to the criminal court for further disposition. This would presumably result in commitment to state prison as an adult offender. But it is important to stress that this arrangement was conceived as a temporary device to permit the Authority "to lay the foundations of an appropriate program in anticipation of the time when it would carry a full case load."[3]

In order to accomplish its purpose, the Authority was empowered to establish diagnostic and classification centers. At the start, the Authority could use existing correctional facilities, although it was not given control over or responsibility for the operation of these facilities. In time, with sufficient experience and funds, the Authority was expected to build facilities of its own specially suited to the needs of youth offenders.

Enter juvenile offenders

Even as it organized, an event took place that profoundly affected the character of the Youth Authority and the provisions it would make for the correction of youth offenders. The new board was appointed in December 1941 and held its first meeting during January 1942. During April 1942, allegations that the correctional institutions for juveniles were badly run moved the Governor to ask the Youth Authority to take over their management. This was formalized by legislation passed the next year. Thus ended plans for an agency primarily responsible for youth offenders.

Other changes served to narrow the Authority's responsibility for youth offenders. During 1943, in recognition of its enlarged task, the time limit for acceptance by the Youth Authority of criminal court commitments was extended from January 1, 1944, to January 1, 1946. Although the Authority would presumably have to accept all youth offenders after the beginning of 1946, the change permitted the agency to continue to shift responsibility for such offenders to the adult correctional system until that time. During this period, the Youth Authority rejected a large proportion of commitments from the criminal court.

In 1944, the upper age limit for criminal court commitments to the Youth Authority was reduced from twenty-three to twenty-one years. This, too, reflected recognition of the enlarged task faced by the agency. It also reflected the Authority's emergent character as an agency primarily responsible for offenders under eighteen years of age. Moreover, the change was made in conjunction with a reorganization of the adult correctional system, which was designed to centralize management and to encourage the use of rehabilitative principles in the handling of adult offenders. A "Department of Corrections" was established, headed by a "Director"; an "Adult Authority" was created with powers over adult offenders similar to those the Youth Authority had relative to juveniles and youths. With the reorganization, it doubtless seemed less imperative to compel commitment of youths over twenty to the Youth Authority. The age change redefined "youth" as persons *under twenty-one years of age* not processed as juvenile offenders. The act continued to require that the criminal court commit most such persons convicted of crimes to the Youth Authority.

Finally, in 1945, the criminal court was granted the power to decide whether persons under twenty-one years should be committed to the Youth Authority or to the Department of Corrections; commitment of this group to the Youth Authority was made optional rather than mandatory. This redefined "youth" as persons under twenty-one years of age, not processed as juvenile offenders, *who were committed to the Youth Authority*. The revised definition of youths implied that the court had the power and responsibility to determine which young criminals deserved treatment as youth offenders and which did not. The former would be committed to the Youth Authority, becoming, thus, "youth offenders"; the latter to the Department of Corrections, where they would remain "adult offenders," subject to more severe penalties. Although the Youth Authority remained able to reject criminal court commitments for the time being, after 1945 such rejections ran contrary to the considered judgment of the court. Thus reason was created for the Authority to be more sparing of such actions. And as we shall see, by 1945 the Youth Authority made other plans, permitting it to accept a greater proportion of commitments from the criminal court.

ESTABLISHMENT OF DVI

Until 1946, the Youth Authority made liberal use of its power to reject criminal court commitments by redefining them as adult offenders and transferring responsibility for their custody and care to the adult correctional system. Some of the criminal court commitments that were accepted were housed at the Preston School of Industry, the state correctional institution for older juvenile offenders. Others were placed in two wartime work camps, also part of the juvenile correctional system. By administrative agreement, the Authority arranged to transfer a small number of youth offenders proving recalcitrant in juvenile correctional facilities to San Quentin. It also experimented by assigning a small number directly to the Institution for Men at Chino, another state prison.

None of these arrangements promised a long-run solution to the Authority's impending problem of managing all youth offenders committed by the criminal court. Rejecting commitments was obviously no solution. Housing youth offenders in juvenile correctional institutions or in existing adult institutions threatened to present serious disciplinary problems and recreated an important part of the situation that the Youth Authority had been designed to rectify. And, as both the juvenile and adult correctional institutions became increasingly overcrowded with "juveniles" and "adults," "youths"

were stranded in county jails awaiting delivery to the Youth Authority, bringing complaints from county officials and others.

An institution for "young" offenders
A new institution was proposed in 1944 to solve these problems:

> A new institution for youthful offenders between the ages of
> 18 and 24 would assist in solving the most critical problem
> which confronts the Department of Corrections and the Cali-
> fornia Youth Authority. [It would provide for the] inter-
> mediate age group, many of whom, in their late teens and
> early twenties, create a difficult problem at San Quentin
> because of lack of facilities to segregate them from older and
> more hardened offenders. It would also provide for the older
> group of boys at the Preston School of Industry . . . who
> create a problem because of lack of facilities to segregate them
> from the younger boys.[4]

The statement went on to suggest that seven hundred San Quentin
inmates "should be in such an institution," as well as three hundred
Youth Authority inmates immediately, followed by a larger number
after World War II.

In 1945, legislative authorization was received to establish an
institution within the Department of Corrections to:

> provide custody, care, industrial, vocational, and other train-
> ing, guidance, and reformatory help for young men, too
> mature to be benefited by the programs of correctional
> schools for juveniles and too immature in crime for confine-
> ment in prisons.[5]

Temporary quarters were secured in southern California in an abandoned flight school. In view of the limited capacity of these quarters
and the existing pressure to house older Youth Authority commitments, it was decided to confine the inmate population to Youth
Authority inmates, "YAs,"* except for a small work crew of adult
inmates. Lingering doubt about public acceptance of joint housing of
juvenile, youth, and adult offenders also contributed to this decision.

Provisions for "security risks"
The new institution, planned for youth offenders and other similar
offenders, was established within the Department of Corrections. To
understand this decision, it is helpful to review the situation of the

---

*We shall henceforward frequently refer to inmates under the jurisdiction of the
Youth Authority as *YAs*. The term is intended to include both juvenile offenders
and youth offenders. We shall frequently refer to inmates under the jurisdiction
of the Department of Corrections as *A#s*. This shorthand derives from the correctional system practice of assigning identification numbers to inmates that
began with YA and A, depending on the department to which an inmate was
officially committed. It was institutional practice, as well, to speak of *YA-s* and
A-numbers.

Youth Authority in 1944. Created to design and administer a correctional program for *youth* offenders, the Authority had been placed in charge of the *juvenile* corrections system. As a result, the attention of the Youth Authority shifted from an exclusive concern with youth offenders to a heavy concern with juveniles. During the first two years of its existence, the Authority focused almost entirely on building a proper program for the latter group, stressing the relative importance of probation and parole services and the necessity of having "training schools" rather than "prisons."[6] Youth offenders remained a somewhat unknown grouping to the Authority. Many were rejected and reclassified as adults, while others were accepted and later transferred to adult correctional institutions when they proved to be troublesome.

On the basis of these experiences, administrators of the Youth Authority and the Department of Corrections made two assumptions that affected their conception of a proper facility for youth offenders. They assumed (1) that a large proportion of offenders committed by the criminal court to the Youth Authority posed "security risks" and required armed detention and (2) that such inmates should not be housed in Authority-administered institutions.[7] The second assumption reflected the emerging conception of the Youth Authority as an agency principally concerned with juvenile offenders:

> A certain reluctance to assume full responsibility for [youth offenders] was apparent in the Youth Authority administration. The departmental leadership was drawn largely from the "juvenile" corrections field and there was some question of the desirability of the administrative assignment of this young adult group to the juvenile agency. The state's precedent had been to treat them as adults and there were no "youth corrections" models to be followed.[8]

Proceeding on these assumptions, it was decided to house most youth offenders in an institution within the Department of Corrections:

> With little objective data on which to predicate a logical division, an operating agreement was reached between the departmental Directors. The Youth Authority would plan to handle approximately one-third of the institutionalized population at any one time and the other two-thirds would be accommodated in Department of Corrections institutions. This, in effect, assumed that two-thirds of the group posed such security risks as to require the armed guard.[9]

Accordingly, the new institution was to receive those criminal court commitments to the Youth Authority posing the greatest "security risks." It was also apparent that the Youth Authority could transfer older juveniles who posed "security risks" at training schools to DVI, if space were available. By definition, DVI was to receive the "worst" of the older Youth Authority commitments. Later, when more spacious quarters were built, DVI was expected to receive young adult offenders, who created a problem in other Department of Corrections institutions "because of lack of facilities to segregate them from older and more hardened offenders."[10]

A program of training

A fence patrolled by officers carrying guns would help insure that the inmate population remained in the new institution. Administrators also emphasized the advantages of having an educational program, especially training for various trades. Prior to the arrival of the first inmate, it was announced that the typical schedule for inmates would consist of a half day in an academic classroom and a half day in a vocational shop.

A statement prepared by DVI's staff in late 1946 describes in more detail the institution's plans for a "program of treatment." First, the institution would focus on formal education as "treatment":

> Diploma courses shall include any courses designed to improve the man in the fundamental subjects even though not specifically related to a particular trade training course. This would include classes to provide credit toward the granting of an elementary or high school diploma.
> Courses leading to a certificate of literacy to be provided by the Director of Corrections and the institutional Supervisor of Education after an illiterate has achieved by test the minimum of a sixth grade education.
> A certificate in any of the approved vocational schools of the Department of Corrections such as the school of airplane mechanics to be established at [Deuel] Vocational Institution or the school of barbering under consideration for San Quentin. The program for these schools will consist of trade training, prescribed academic education, and on the job experience. . . .*

Inmates who did not qualify for formal education would be provided:

> General training and treatment . . . This will involve routine work directed primarily toward the development and improvement in acceptable work habits.

The "program of treatment" would also provide:

> Physical hygiene: medical care and treatment in health habits.
> Preparation for wholesome pursuits during leisure time. Recreational reading, avocational studies, hobbies, music, art, games, and athletics.
> Religious counseling and training.
> Social guidance in family and community responsibility.

---

*This and later quotations without specific source citations are taken from unpublished memoranda and letters written by DVI personnel.

Finally, inmates would receive:

> Mental hygiene: psychiatric treatment, psychological and vocational counseling, and guidance in personal problems of adjustment.

THE EMERGENCE OF A CUSTODIAL IMAGE: 1946–52

DVI occupied temporary quarters until 1953, housing an average daily inmate population of about five hundred, mostly YAs. It housed most of the youth offenders in state correctional facilities. A few A#s, though seldom more than a dozen, were also housed at DVI as members of the institution's work crew.

Given the agreement between the Youth Authority and the Department of Corrections, and because the Youth Authority operated institutions and camps primarily intended for juveniles, it is reasonable to suppose that DVI never received those youth offenders who were believed easiest to manage. To balance this factor, DVI staff attempted to transfer some cases posing special "security" problems to other Department of Corrections institutions, usually San Quentin. This was sometimes accomplished, but the Youth Authority was reluctant to approve such transfers, a matter which it controlled.

Nor did DVI's inmate population only tend to contain the more difficult *youth* offenders. Some 13 to 20 percent of the YAs at DVI during this period were *juvenile* offenders, mainly recently returned parole violators. In addition, some juvenile offenders were transferred to DVI from Youth Authority facilities on the grounds that they required housing in an institution providing greater "security" than those operated by the Authority itself. In a memorandum written during 1961, a high DVI official noted about such transfers from Youth Authority institutions: "The mere fact of sending a Juvenile Court case to Deuel Vocational Institution tags him as a behavior problem—else he would have been kept at Preston." Interviews suggest it was no different from 1946 through 1952, the period being discussed. We shall later also see that DVI's administrators had no higher estimate of the docility of juvenile parole violators.

The training program

The institution's training program developed rapidly. By 1948, YAs at DVI were offered many vocational courses by state-credentialed instructors. On the job training was being given in auto servicing, clerical and commercial work, food handling, hospital orderly services, librarianship, meat-cutting, photography, and warehousing. Other classes included arts and crafts and physical education. Academic instruction was offered in grades one through twelve, including a special class designed to meet the needs of illiterates.

Another part of the program, identified separately in official reports, was "care and treatment," which was said to include the classification of inmates for various institution programs and jobs, the preparation of reports for the use of the parole board, and, especially, individual counseling. The counseling program "began operations during the month of November [1946]. Every inmate leaving [reception status] is assigned to a counselor. Approximately 50 counselors have been designated and no one individual [staff member] will have more than 10 counselees."[11] By 1948, it was held that:

> A comprehensive counseling program for the individual inmate
> has been established and is operating successfully. The purpose
> is to redirect the inmate's thinking in a way that will lead him
> into socially acceptable lines of action in the institution and
> after release. This phase of the care-treatment program comes
> under the direction of the senior sociologist who is organizing
> personnel doing this work on a voluntary basis. It has been
> necessary to slowly organize and direct these counselors
> along the lines of case-work thinking.[12]

By 1949, the individual counseling program reportedly involved 92 voluntary counselors who conducted more than 300 interviews with 292 inmates during August.[13]

Development of "security" measures

DVI's administrators also gave early emphasis to the necessity of having adequate means of coping with "security risks." The assumption that the institution's inmate population would pose such risks was apparently substantiated from the outset. Within the first several months of DVI's existence, there was a rash of escapes, fourteen in one month alone. One escapee forced a local couple to drive him to Los Angeles, doing little to encourage a sanguine view of DVI's inmate population. After the first several months of operation, the escape problem was reduced, doubtless due in large part to the "construction of a 4,000 foot fence around the security area, the construction of five guard towers and the [installation of] necessary fence lights."[14] In addition, the development of training, counseling, and recreation programs within the institution helped "hold" inmates, according to the superintendent.

But the security needs of the institution in another and ultimately more important sense showed few signs of being reduced. DVI's inmate population displayed a high propensity for creating violent disorder *within* the institution; and DVI's staff soon began to develop characteristic modes of response to this propensity. One of the superintendent's first acts was to speed completion of an "isolation unit" to "serve as a lock-up for inmates who must be disciplined."[15] This concrete block building, ready October 1946, contained ten rooms, and replaced chain link fence cells that had been erected inside an abandoned airplane hangar in institution property. These precautions were not to prove sufficient, however, and by 1948 further steps were taken. These included a fence built across one of the dormitories to provide "protective custody" for "homosexuals and informers,"[16] and the acquisition of an old navy brig with eighteen rooms to segregate "behavior problem cases" and "incorrigibles" for indefinite periods. These facilities embodied in embryo the predominant mode of discipline still practiced during the early 1960s.

Another major control mechanism developed early. Inmate housing consisted of four 100-man dormitories and twelve cottages, each capable of holding twelve men. DVI was quickly pressed to use this housing to the full, and the twelve-man cottages proved difficult to supervise without an inordinate expenditure of custodial resources. The solution to this problem, devised by DVI staff, was a "system" whereby inmates with three months "clean time" (with no recorded major rule infraction) and "good grades" from supervisory staff, were "promoted" from the dormitories to the cottages. The chief reward was less supervision. This mode of control came to be known as the "honor system." In addition, as is partially explicit in the superintendent's view that training and treatment programs helped "hold" inmates, top staff members began to appreciate the "security" possibilities of programs like the individual counseling program, and to attempt to use them for that purpose.

When DVI moved to its permanent quarters in 1953, these tools of control moved with it. In addition, DVI had developed an image. Its inmates were considered to be among the most unruly and potentially violent, and its staff members to be among the firmest disciplinarians, in the correctional system.

THE FASHIONING OF A ROLE: 1953-62

In 1953, a new, larger, and "permanent" Deuel Vocational Institution was completed seventy miles east of San Francisco, at Tracy, California. This was to be *the* facility for "young" offenders, containing *both* Youth Authority commitments and offenders of similar ages committed to the Department of Corrections. Its planned capacity was 1,200 inmates. And it was designed to reduce the security problems of the temporary facility, both by providing more secure quarters at the perimeter and internally, and by providing more space for educational, particularly vocational, training.

The new plant was built with an eye to containing trouble. A double fence, dotted with barbed wire and gun towers, surrounded it. It was constructed of steel and concrete, with plans originally calling for individual rooms throughout, each fitted with a steel door. Movement from one part of the institution to another could be controlled by locked doors and steel grilles electrically operated from a central control room that scanned the corridors. The institution contained a "maximum security" unit, fitted with "inside" rooms to les-

402

sen the possibility of escape by sawing through window grilles. Two floors of another unit were designed as an "adjustment center" for control of persistently troublesome inmates. In addition to these security provisions, a variety of training facilities was provided. Of special importance in the eyes of management were shops for trade training. Academic, recreational, and some industrial facilities were also provided.

Selection of inmates: A#s

It will be recalled that in 1944 it was believed that DVI could house a substantial portion of those A#s under twenty-five years of age, as well as most YAs from the criminal court. By the end of 1952, however, the number of A#s in the correctional system had grown to 13,619, about 15 percent (or over two thousand) of whom were less than twenty-five years of age.[17] Since DVI was designed for only 1,200 inmates, it became imperative to specify how many and which young A#s it would house.

The question of how many A#s would be housed at DVI was more or less tacitly resolved by the earlier agreement between the Youth Authority and the Department of Corrections that about two-thirds of the youth offenders would be housed in Department of Corrections institutions, principally DVI. Given the population of youth offenders in correctional institutions at the time, this meant that less than one-half of DVI's inmates would be A#s.

The proportion of A#s residing at DVI was a matter of more than passing concern, however. It was the urgent conviction of the superintendent, shared by his staff, that henceforth a substantial, if unknown, proportion of DVI's inmates *should* be A#s. These should not be just any A#s, moreover, but offenders selected for their capacity and motivation to participate in the institution's education program, and for their tractability. It was felt further that DVI should be able to transfer A#s proving troublesome to other Department of Corrections institutions with a minimum of difficulty.

These concerns were embodied in formal orders governing the selection and transfer of young A#s to DVI:

> An extensive program of academic and vocational education is available, and priority should be given to the transfer of those youthful inmates who are best able to profit from intensive educational activities. . . . Inmates under the age of 25 who are clearly qualified and motivated for [this program] should be transferred to the Deuel Vocational Institution as the institution of choice.
> Because the Youth Authority must confine a considerable number of very youthful wards, including some committed by juvenile courts at this institution, it is of great importance that the transfer of adult homosexual inmates to the Deuel Vocational Institution should be avoided. . . . Transfer of [adult] inmates to the Deuel Vocational Institution for con-

finement in the Adjustment Center will be resorted to only under exceptional circumstances.*

It is recognized that unsuccessful placements of [adult] inmates at this institution may from time to time occur. These situations may arise from unsuccessful trials of inmates in special vocational training programs or on work crew assignments. They may also arise as a result of unforeseen behavior problems which cannot be contained in an institution with this type of program. Because of the highly developed program, it is essential that inmates who cannot participate in it be transferred as soon as their limitations are established. Therefore, the Superintendent shall provide for regular review . . . of [adult] inmates whose response to the program is negative, looking toward transfer to institutions more suited to their needs.[18]

In the view of DVI's administrators, A#s would help compensate for the unruliness of YAs, as well as the difficulties of stabilizing the institution's education program with an inmate population composed largely of YAs. The administrative view of YAs as unruly is reflected in a memorandum written by a high DVI official in 1955:†

I think that the DVI employees and inmates alike deserve adequate protection from the inmates who are assaultive or dangerous. Nearly 10 years of experience in DVI has shown us that many Youth Authority wards have this nature. Of course, most A–number inmates are well controlled. Also, many of the worst assaultive inmates are from the juvenile courts.

And the administrative assessment of the possibility of operating a meaningful education program with YAs, especially a program emphasizing trade training, is suggested by a DVI staff member's reflections on the results of a study done in early 1956.

A random sampling of 200 Youth Authority inmates enrolled in vocational education since our move to Tracy . . . [shows] that only slightly more than one-third . . . are staying in the training program for more than six months. This is not long enough for them to learn the trade and certainly will not turn out enough skilled workmen to get the best production out of our extensive vocational training program. We need a good percentage of A-numbers in our vocational classes in order to give continuity of training.

––––––––––

*As noted above, the "Adjustment Center" was a special housing unit to segregate and provide a program for inmates proving persistently troublesome.

†The memorandum was addressed to the issue of whether inmates committed by the juvenile court should be subject to the same laws as inmates committed by the criminal court, such as Cal. Pen. Code (1955) § 4502, which made it a felony for an inmate to possess a "dirk or dagger or sharp instrument," as well as other weapons. Perhaps needless to say, the DVI official believed that juveniles should have no special prerogatives.

The assignment of A#s to DVI was a conscious attempt to improve the situation, while leaving DVI responsible for the management and training of many Youth Authority inmates held unsuitable for housing in Youth Authority institutions. As noted by Ohmart and Taron:

> In an effort to compensate for the deteriorated quality of the
> Youth Authority portion of [DVI's] population, the Department of Corrections reception centers have assigned to that
> institution a substantial number of the most tractable and
> the best motivated from those youthful commitments to the
> Department of Corrections. . . . It is logical and understandable
> that [these inmates] are . . . placed in the choice training
> assignments, whereas the control needs and minimal abilities
> of the Youth Authority group finds them in the menial assignments of the institution.[19]

It is worth adding that commitment to an inmate population at DVI composed of one-third A#s would have other consequences as well. It would inevitably mean that when the number of youth offenders increased to the point where DVI could no longer house two-thirds, some further principles of selection of youth offenders for DVI would have to be developed. This situation was not long in coming.

Selection of inmates: YAs

In its new quarters, DVI continued to house most of the criminal court commitments to the Youth Authority. Indeed, from 1953 through 1957 it housed a greater proportion than ever before. To accommodate the steadily increasing number of such cases, some inmate rooms at DVI were "double-bunked" in the mid-fifties, increasing capacity to about fifteen hundred inmates. In the meantime, plans were laid for other institutions for older Youth Authority commitments, within both the Department of Corrections and the Youth Authority.

During 1958, the California Training Facility-North ("North Facility") was opened by the Department of Corrections to house twelve hundred inmates similar to DVI's: roughly one-half YAs committed by the criminal court and one-half young A#s. Two questions naturally arise in connection with the planned use of North Facility. First, why was another Department of Corrections institution to be used for housing Youth Authority inmates; why not build a new Youth Authority institution? This seems to have been due mainly to the continued belief that two-thirds of Youth Authority criminal court commitments were appropriately handled by the Department of Corrections. Second, why were neither DVI nor North Facility set aside entirely for housing YAs? The answer is that, as noted above, DVI administrators believed that an institution with an inmate population composed principally of those youth offenders held unsuitable for Youth Authority institutions would prove extremely difficult to operate. If older juvenile offenders were added to this population—as had occurred—difficulties would be exacerbated. A#s were needed to compensate for such problems. The decision to house a roughly equal proportion of YAs and young, trainable, tractable A#s at North Facility reflects acceptance of this premise within the correctional system. One consequence of this policy for DVI was that it would no longer receive the bulk of YAs from the criminal court but rather an even more selected portion of them. This trend was further reinforced in 1960 when the Youth Training School (YTS) was opened by the Youth Authority to house YAs, including criminal court commitments. At least one-third of its expected twelve hundred inmates were to be criminal court commitments.

Most offenders newly committed by the courts, as well as parole violators, were initially sent to reception centers. They were then routed to particular facilities. Between 1960 and 1962, DVI received most of its YAs directly from reception centers. Youth Authority policy, both written and unwritten, limited the placement options open to center personnel. Most criminal court offenders were to be sent to DVI or North Facility. A few could be selected for YTS and for camps, or paroled directly from the center.

When reception center personnel were deciding among DVI, North Facility, and YTS, the main destinations of criminal court YAs, what criteria did they use? Formal criteria for the selection of YAs for DVI never existed. This is understandable when it is recalled that DVI was to receive substantially all criminal court YAs. From the pool of available criminal court YAs, reception center personnel have selected those fitting selection criteria of *other* institutions.

Although North Facility was supposed to receive YAs similar to those sent to DVI, there is reason to believe that reception center personnel selected a higher proportion of YAs believed to be tractable for North Facility. Ohmart and Taron make this observation:

Because [North Facility] ... was a newly organized institution and because they were experimenting with new program ideas, they requested and were assigned the more tractable youths from both the Youth Authority and Department of Corrections populations. The lesser security provided by the single fence [as against DVI's double fence] and the absence of their own adjustment center further supported the logic of their receiving the more manageable of the population.[20]

Formal criteria for selection and transfer of YAs to North Facility set forth during 1958 emphasize these matters:

Youth Authority wards shall be eligible for medium custody. The security at Soledad North Facility is limited to a single fence covered by armed towers. Wards with histories of escape or attempted escape from institutions with armed walls or fences shall not be recommended for the North Facility.

Wards with severe psychiatric problems or who are in need of psychiatric services will not be recommended for the North Facility.

Wards who present serious behavioral and management problems will not be recommended for the Soledad North Facility. If adjustment center placement is necessary, they should be recommended ordinarily for the DVI adjustment center.

The Soledad North Facility will have a program of group counseling in which all wards will be encouraged to participate.[21]

The criteria used to select YAs for Youth Training School, developed late in 1959, made it even more likely that "better" criminal court commitments would not be sent to DVI. The selection of inmates for YTS was based on vocational aptitudes and a capacity for training. Inmates with an average grade placement level of at least 6.8 and an intelligence quotient of 80 or better were sought.

The Youth Training School became the "bright star" in the Youth Authority firmament. Accordingly, the departmental administration and Board asked . . . for the assignment of the more trainable, better motivated Youth Authority ward [to YTS].[22]

All of this has resulted in the feeling of DVI staff members that, always assigned a difficult group of YAs, by the early 1960s they were receiving the "bottom of the barrel." A memorandum written by a high DVI official in 1960 phrased it this way:

The present criteria for transfer of YA wards leaves us with largely the hoodlum type of inmate with which to try to carry on a program. Figuratively speaking, only Eagle Scouts are to go to Ontario [YTS]; 1st, 2nd and 3rd class Scouts to Soledad [North Facility] and Camps; and we keep what is left. This policy is resulting in the concentration at DVI of a highly explosive and dangerous type of inmate. . . . We recognize that we must keep more than our share of this type of inmate, but concentrating the cast-offs of more than 2500 YA wards in this one institution is likely to cause a bad explosion.

On top of this, DVI received about one-fifth of its YAs through transfers from Youth Authority institutions and camps.* Most YAs were transferred to DVI as a security or disciplinary measure. By 1961, the implications of this situation had become a matter for open discussion among DVI staff members.

---

*For comparative purposes, it should be noted that during 1962 North Facility received about 7 percent of its YAs via transfer rather than from a reception center. DVI received about 25 percent of its YAs through transfer during the same period. Data from the California Youth Authority Research Division.

DVI population has changed during the past seven months by
having to keep disciplinary [cases] and troublemakers and
sending "Eagle Scouts" elsewhere. Because of the continued
"skimming off" of all potential management problems for
retention at DVI, the quality of our YA population has become
increasingly lower. [Further] under present criteria, aggressive
or acting out behavior or other management problems not
screened out [for retention at DVI in the first place] are
returned to DVI as soon as they give any trouble at Soledad-
North [North Facility], YTS or Camp. Because of this consistent lowering of quality, YA wards who would ordinarily
conform in a better, more acceptable manner are now conforming to the more delinquent, unacceptable behavior
patterns, due to the constant pressure from the concentrated
lower quality delinquent group.

As some staff members bitterly noted, DVI had fully assumed the
role of "dumping ground for the Youth Authority."

CONCLUSION

Putting this administrative insight less colorfully, DVI had come to
perform a control function for the correctional system itself, particularly for that segment mainly concerned with juveniles. Inmates who
were thought likely to disrupt the routines and programs of Youth
Authority training schools were tagged and shipped to DVI. If mis-
takes were made in initial classifications, DVI stood as a potential
and actual transfer destination, providing both a threat and a reality
for those who later proved troublesome. And it could always be
hoped that DVI would develop means for encouraging such inmates
to conform.

The pressures brought to bear on DVI to accept and retain
troublesome inmates were particularly clearcut, but they are in no
way unusual. Prison officials, seeking to establish and maintain the
character of their own institutions, attempt to have "tractable" inmates housed in them and "intractable" inmates sent elsewhere in
the system. This possibility is inherent in a state correctional system
with more than one prison. Thus operating officials will attempt to
influence the initial distribution of inmates among the prisons. Although DVI's staff found the initial distribution of YAs almost impossible to affect, as shown they were far more successful in their
effort to have substantial numbers of A#s assigned to the institution,
and the "best" A#s at that.

Nor is the initial distribution of inmates all that is at issue: prison
administrators are concerned to rid their institutions of troublemakers, whenever the latter are identified, by transferring them to
other prisons. DVI, as noted, could not do so easily with YAs. But
DVI administrators, while generally accepting the policy that their
institution was the "end-of-the-line" for troublesome YAs, were quite

408

alive to the possibility that this situation might be modified and, on occasion, circumvented. Thus one conclusion drawn by DVI administrators in 1960 was:

> It would appear . . . that the criteria for transfer of YA wards should be examined and re-evaluated immediately. Two suggestions: send older juvenile court cases to Soledad (North Facility) which I believe is permissible under new legislation and send a limited number of "won't work" and agitating types to San Quentin.*

And, of course, DVI officials remained interested in insuring not only that "better" A#s were housed at DVI, but that any A#s proving troublesome could be shipped out immediately.

As for circumventing their mandate to house recalcitrant YAs, the main possibility during the early 1960s appeared to be a diagnosis of a YA as in need of psychiatric care, and thus a candidate for transfer to the California Medical Facility, the main psychiatric facility within the Department of Corrections. The Youth Authority permitted a certain number of such transfers. As the matter was sometimes put: "Someone has defined this YA as our kind of nut; now our problem is to define him as the Facility's kind of nut." It is not clear how successful DVI was in this enterprise, but at best it involved a small number of inmates.

In the circumstances, there was little DVI officials could do about the role of the prison they administered. Which is part of the point: prisons like other institutions are powerfully influenced by environing forces, including the other organizations with which they interact. This is a matter deserving considerable study.†

NOTES

1   To save space, documentation has been reduced to a minimum. Fuller documentation may be found in Sheldon L. Messinger, *Strategies of Control* (Ph.D. diss., University of California, Los Angeles, 1969), esp. pp. 80-137. Also see Elliot Studt, Sheldon L. Messinger, and Thomas P. Wilson, *C-Unit: Search for Community in Prison* (New York: Russell Sage Foundation Press, 1968), which also deals with DVI.

2   California Statutes 1941, Chapter 937. Originally called the "Youth Correction Authority Act," the term "correction" was deleted by California Statutes 1943, Chapter 690.

3   In re Herrerra, 23 Cal. 2d 206, 143 P. 2d 345 (1943).

---

*The other main conclusion was that docile A#s in sufficient number should be housed at DVI.

†This article was written in the mid-1970s. At this writing, DVI still exists as part of the Department of Corrections, but has long since ceased to house a substantial number of youth offenders, most of whom are housed in institutions administered by the Youth Authority. But this is another story.

4   California State Department of Corrections, *Report for Governor's Council September 25, 1944*, n.p.

5   California Statutes 1945, Chapter 1454.

6   See Robert L. Smith, "Youth and Corrections: An Institutional Analysis of the California Youth Authority" (Master's thesis, University of California, Berkeley, 1955).

7   Howard Ohmart and Ernst Taron, *The Youthful Offender in California* (Sacramento, California: California Youth and Adult Corrections Agency, 1963), p. 24.

8   Lawrence Bennett and Howard Ohmart, "The Youth Authority Ward in the Department of Corrections," mimeographed. (Sacramento, California: California Youth and Adult Corrections Agency, 1964), p. 30.

9   Ohmart and Taron, *The Youthful Offender in California*, p. 24.

10   California State Department of Corrections, *Report for Governor's Council September 25, 1944*.

11   California State Department of Corrections, *Report for Governor's Council December 30, 1946*, n.p.

12   California State Department of Corrections, *Bi-Annual Report for the Period Ending December 1, 1948*, n.p.

13   California State Department of Corrections, *Report for Governor's Council September 19, 1949*, n.p.

14   California State Department of Corrections, *Bi-Annual Report 1946*, n.p.

15   California State Department of Corrections, *Report for Governor's Council May 27, 1946*, n.p.

16   California State Department of Corrections, *Bi-Annual Report for the Period Ending December 1, 1948*, n.p.

17   See [California State] Department of Corrections, *California Prisoners 1960* (Sacramento, California), pp. 6, 38. On December 31, 1945, there were 5,710 A#s in the Department of Corrections and about 10 percent were under twenty-five years of age.

18   California State Department of Corrections, *Inmate Classification Manual*, n.p., n.d., Chapter XI. In addition, provisions were made for selection of an institution work crew, composed of A#s of any age who were not known to be homosexuals, not believed to be violence-prone, not committed for notorious offenses, nor having a record of "current or recent disciplinary infractions requiring punitive action by isolation."

19   Ohmart and Taron, *The Youthful Offender in California*, p. 28.

20   *Ibid.*, p. 12.

21   California State Department of Corrections, *Administrative Bulletin No. 58/61*, December 10, 1958.

22   Ohmart and Taron, *The Youthful Offender in California*, p. 12.

The Politics of Delinquency Prevention:
The Urban Leadership Training Program
BARRY KRISBERG

Reprinted from Barry Krisberg, "The Politics of Delinquency
Prevention: The Urban Leadership Training Program." *Social
Policy*, Vol. 5 (July/August, 1974), 53-56.

The demise of the Urban Leadership Training Program, which was designed to reach hard-core delinquents, exemplifies the fact that programs which best serve institutional or political ends often poorly serve the needs of the participants in whose interests they were originally conceived. Here I will deal with the uses of an experimental program for delinquents to the institutions that planned, supported, and executed it.

THE URBAN LEADERSHIP TRAINING PROGRAM

The chief aim of the program was to train 22 youthful Black gang leaders, aged 18 to 23, to be effective community leaders. It was a joint undertaking involving a major eastern university and a Black community organization which functions in an economically depressed neighborhood adjoining the university campus. The program was proposed by the leaders of the community organization to several members of the university staff. Members of a University Management Research Unit helped draft a proposal and persuaded university officials to donate classroom space for the experiment. The director of a Criminology Research Center agreed to supervise the evaluative research on the project. Several other members of the university staff volunteered their services as instructors or technical assistants to the program. Limited funding was provided by a number of small grants from local civic organizations.

The students were leaders of five juvenile gangs in the target area. Each gang leader was a public school dropout. Their combined arrest records totaled more than 175 contacts with the law. Most had served up to 36 months in state and local prisons. Their employment histories had been transitory and primarily unsuccessful. Program planners hoped to select students who had demonstrated leadership potential through their gang activities. Staff members of the community organization contacted some of the more influential neighborhood gang leaders and discussed with them the purposes of the Urban Leadership Training Program. The gang leaders recruited members from their own groups to participate in the program.

The training program consisted of a 21-week, full-time course which mixed formal classroom instruction on the university campus with field work in the adjoining community. Courses included economics, sociology, communications, criminology, law, community health, political science, and Black studies. Part of the instruction was provided by members of the university faculty and part by staff of the community organization who had worked for some time at solving neighborhood problems. Students received regular salaries of $80 per week during the program. Moreover, the group was to receive a share of the profits made from a 60-minute documentary film made about the entire project. The costs of the filming were provided through a grant from a local business firm. The community organization promised to find jobs in community service for each program graduate at the conclusion of the training period.

A central premise of the Urban Leadership Training Program was that the abilities and energies of hard-core delinquents could be redirected into positive and socially desirable projects. The gang delinquent could be "cured" by providing an opportunity for him to benefit his community and thus to be reintegrated with socially meaningful groups. Reiff observes:

> From Plato and Aristotle, through Burke and de Tocqueville,
> the therapeutic implication of social theory is remarkably
> consistent; an individual can exercise his gifts and powers
> fully only by participating in the common life. This is the
> classical ideal. The healthy man is, in fact, the good citizen.[1]

If the community itself is disordered then social theories are constructed to reorder social life so that personal salvation can be obtained through participation in attempts to found a more perfect social order.

The educational content of the ULT program was aimed at convincing the delinquent of the desirability and necessity of his commitment to his fellow neighborhood residents. Further, the specific courses suggested a number of ways in which trainees could become directly involved in efforts to improve the community.

THE PROGRAM'S DEMISE

The Urban Leadership Training Program had style. Its 22 main actors were filmed daily, tape-recorded, and proudly displayed to business leaders, city officials, and congressmen. The gang leaders sported attractive summer jackets which announced their affiliation with the program and carried portable tape recorders given to them by the research staff to help "facilitate data collection for the evaluation" but which were more often used to record popular music. After nearly four months of a reasonably successful educational program,[2] the participants and project staff celebrated their apparent accomplishments with a seven-day, all-expense-paid trip to Puerto Rico, financed by a major beer company and by funds made available through the Criminology Research Center. There was an elaborate prom with over 200 invited guests and a cap-and-gown graduation ceremony complete with diplomas.

Ceremonies marking the end of a training program are happy occasions for participants and staff members but far more important to the ultimate success of the project are the events which take place after the formal training sessions have been concluded. The ULT trainees often expressed the fear that "this would be just another training program," meaning that they would not receive the promised employment opportunities and would be compelled to return to former activities. Tragically, their fears were well founded despite apparently sincere efforts to avoid repeating the errors of other training programs.

After the close of the training period, participants worked at their community projects full-time for approximately six weeks before a financial crisis within the community organization limited the amount of money that they could be paid for their services. Program trainees were extremely upset with the decline in their income. The program graduates, who had never really experienced the rewards of community work that regular organization staff had enjoyed, could not accept the cuts in salary which were more easily borne by permanent staff members. Many of the ULT graduates felt betrayed by the community leaders who had promised but not obtained full-time employment for them. Several returned to the illegal activities which had partially supported them prior to their program involvement and began to neglect their assigned community projects. Leaders of the community organization accused the ULT graduates of "hustling on the program," placing on them the full responsibility for the apparent program failure. The only remaining potential source of funds for the participants was their share of the profits from the film being made about the program, but this support seemed extremely uncertain because the documentary remained unfinished and the film makers reported that the film had little chance of ever making a profit.

To conclude that the ULT graduates were angry and disillusioned hardly seems an adequate expression of the harsh frustration and bitter disappointment experienced by the young men who had completed the program. Several program participants experienced personal tailspins after the abrupt end of the program. Two graduates became heavy narcotics users during that summer. The demise of the program represented the destruction of the hopes of these youthful leaders who have been too familiar with deprivation and feelings of failure throughout their young lives.

For the community organization, the postprogram events meant a severe, perhaps unrecoupable, setback in plans to enrich the lives of neighborhood residents. The program did not produce a corps of leaders which would reach those neighborhood youths engaged in destructive gang violence and which would provide meaningful resources for the future expansion of community redevelopment.

IN SEARCH OF ANSWERS

In an attempt to explain why the program suddenly collapsed, I strained to approximate detached analysis, searching for general forces that account for the failure of many well-intentioned experiments. These forces include the chronic budget problems of community organizations, the difficulties of obtaining continued program funding from governmental agencies, the insufficient efforts by community leaders and university personnel to plan for the postprogram placement of graduates, and the failure of the project staff to better prepare the young men to face the sacrifices entailed in community service.

But these "answers" remain uncomfortably inadequate. A number of unresolved questions persist. How was it possible that talented community leaders, experienced project staff members, and skilled university faculty were unable to anticipate and respond to the problems of providing a meaningful program followup? What accounted for the high level of shared optimism about the program which caused practical people to fail to grasp the harsh realities of the postprogram situation? Finally, why did community organization leaders place the entire burden of guilt for the program's demise upon the participants?

To provide a more satisfying and less sociologically naïve response to these questions is to state an obvious but oft-unspoken observation—that the interests or ends of program participants differ from the interests and goals of program planners and staff. Institutions and organizations which sponsor delinquency-prevention and resocialization programs receive substantial benefits from such enterprises which are not necessarily related to successful program outcomes for the delinquents who participate in them. Indeed planners, supporters, and staff members accumulate many more rewards *during* a training process and greater costs at the *conclusion* of such efforts. While project personnel are reaping immediate gratifications, the participants must defer gratification pending possible, but usually uncertain, payoffs at the end of the training period.

Let us examine the nature of program rewards available to various organizations and individuals which supported the effort. These include the payoffs which the university, or more specifically, some segments of the university community, received from its participation in the project, the positive consequences of the training program for the community organization, and the rewards that project staff members obtained through their involvement.

The university

The university's involvement in the affairs of the adjoining Black community began approximately three years before the start of the ULT program. Like many private eastern schools, the university did not possess a reputation for a high degree of social conscience with respect to the poor or to minority-group members in its immediate environment. Typically, the issue of institutional expansion was central to the first serious confrontation between the academic enclave and the community. A massive University City Science Center, heavily financed by the university, required annexation of substantial portions of land in the adjoining community. Project plans involved redeveloping land which had been primarily used for low-income housing and thus displacing many poor families. Initial resistance from the community was present although not to the degree observed in other localities, such as the dispute between Columbia University and the Morningside Heights community. In 1968, university students seized the administration building and demanded numerous educational and social reforms. Student leaders' dissent crystalized over the issue of the University City Science Center project and the perceived usurpation of the neighboring Black community. Peaceful protests resulted in a compromise between students and university administrators including the formation of a commission composed of students, college administrators, faculty, and community people which would attempt to build a more positive relationship between the school and the community. University plans to complete the science center project continued without major objections by student or community leaders.

Limited arrangements were begun to include community leaders in some areas of university planning, and some faculty offered their consulting services to an emerging community organization. Most of these efforts were located with the Management Science Unit of the School of Business Administration with apparently mutually beneficial results.[3] The university's involvement in the ULT program was a result of these preliminary collaborative efforts. The program represented the first project in which neighborhood youth were invited to use university facilities in an extensive manner.

There were several suggestions that university officials perceived the project as a high-risk venture. Classroom space was originally planned for two weeks after the project began. A number of university administration staff were assigned to coordinate and oversee the project. The program participants were forewarned by the project staff that they would be under constant scrutiny by the university community. Their behavior while on campus had to be exemplary so that opportunities for future programs would not be lost. Throughout the early part of the training, the project coordinator received many reports of alleged ULT trainee misbehavior on campus which attested to a fair degree of campuswide paranoia about the project. Generally speaking, the trainees responded admirably to this surveillance, resolving to prove to others that they could be trusted, although their special status evoked some resentment among them toward the university personnel.

Against this background the major reward for the university can be seen. The program represented a symbolic display of the school's sincerity in dealing with the neighboring community. Thus it could be viewed as an attempt to insure peaceful relations with members of that community as well as an attempt to placate university students' demands for increased social participation by the school. An additional reward was the public relations benefits which might accrue through publicizing such an effort. Staff of the University Information Service produced numerous press releases celebrating the new program. A brief film about the ULT project was shown during halftime of a televised college football game. This same film was given to all local television news shows. There was a story about the project in the student newspaper.

Many of the faculty who participated in the training program discussed plans for future collaboration in the areas of health, social service, urban planning, and communications. ULT participants were asked to serve as consultants to some ongoing research efforts and were asked to reflect attitudes of people in their neighborhood on a variety of issues. Thus university faculty and students could study their responses in the protected environment of the campus and not have to venture out into the neighborhood.

The community organization

For several years the community organization had met with a good deal of success in its efforts to serve people in the neighborhood. The group began its work with delinquent youth in the community and expanded into a wide spectrum of planning, educational, and social service programs. The organization has an annual budget of approximately $500,000 and enjoys a good deal of support from the business and political leaders of the city. (Part of this success might be attributed to its stable relationship with the university.) Despite its expansion in community services, the organization's strength remains heavily rooted in its ability to control gang warfare among neighborhood youth.[4] Community leaders recognized that to continue to have influence on the street corners required a cadre of younger men who were closer to the gang youth. The graduates of the program were to serve this function of maintaining youth involvement in community projects. Moreover, it seemed clear that other, more militant voices were appealing to the gang constituency. The community organization wanted to counteract these newer messages and solidify its program.

A second political end served by the ULT program was to extend the influence of the community organization to more people in
the neighborhood. Before the program began the community organization had concentrated its efforts in the eastern portion of the
area. The desire to extend services (and political control) to the western half of the community is reflected in the composition of the gang
youths selected for the program. Almost two-thirds of the training
group were members of gangs in the western half of the neighborhood. Through the incorporation of these young men into community projects, the organization hoped to encourage other residents of
the community to participate in its program.

The program participants served another very important function for the community leaders. Former gang leaders whose behavior
could be predicted were introduced to business and government
officials in efforts to obtain new sources of funding for neighborhood
projects. Project staff presented four or five of the "best" trainees to
executives who seemed to delight in tales of past gang violence and
seemed so willing to reach out to the people of the ghetto. Members
of the ULT group were key participants in discussions involving such
business ventures as a community-owned movie theater, an automobile service station, and a coin-operated laundry service. Most of these
enterprises were too large to be handled by the participants themselves, and after initial encounters with money sources, the organization staff continued the negotiation and planning process. The
ULT group soon learned the appropriate rhetoric that would appeal
to influential people. They were militant, dedicated, and believable
to the extent necessary to "hustle bread from the bigshots."[5]

Project staff

Small-scale delinquency prevention programs provide valuable learning experiences for their usually youthful staff. The dedication and
energy of staff members often compensate for lack of specific training in the required program skills. In the ULT project, the coordinator, many of the teachers from the community organization, and
the researcher (myself) were all new to such endeavors. The ongoing
demands of the program forced staff people to increase their expertise and skills in relevant areas. While this situation often produces
desirable consequences, the potential benefits of such participation
are greater for the novice professionals than for the program participants.

Benefits to the staff of prevention projects are often directly
related to labor market demands for expertise in specific areas. Thus
the ULT program added several pertinent items to the professional
résumés of its staff members. The irony of this fact is that the manifest purpose of a training effort is to improve the "employment
prospects" for the delinquent, but it is often the staff members who
benefit more directly in terms of future job security, and this is virtually independent of the program payoffs for the trainees. Nascent

careers are often helped by involvement in "sincere but unproductive" programs.

The moral dilemmas are particularly acute for the researcher, who may or may not continue his commitment to the people whom he observes and writes about. In the case of the ULT program, my participation resulted in a lively topic for a doctoral dissertation and partially helped my successful entry into the academic labor force. How does one relate these enormous personal rewards with the plight of the program participants who returned to a former way of life, tantalized by, but not delivered, the rewards which were promised by the ULT program?

The pattern I have described is not uncommon in human service work; indeed, by the end of the 1960s professional servers and their research colleagues were regarded with extreme distrust in the various communities they entered to do their work. This case study is written in the hope that on the basis of a clear confrontation with that history it will be possible to judge program termination with respect to the particular parties concerned, rather than simply to throw out the idea of providing services to people in an involved-community model.[6]

NOTES

1   Philip Reiff, *The Triumph of the Therapeutic* (New York: Harper & Row, 1966), p. 68.

2   See Barry Krisberg, "Urban Leadership Training: An Ethnographic Study of 22 Gang Leaders" (Ph.D. Dissertation, University of Pennsylvania, Philadelphia, 1971).

3   See Russell Ackoff, "A Black Ghetto's Research on a University," *Operations Research* 18 (1970), p. 176.

4   On this problem see Irving A. Spergel, "Politics, Policies, and the Gang Problem," in Paul Lerman, ed., *Delinquency and Social Policy* (New York: Praeger, 1970).

5   This practice is described by Tom Wolfe in *Mau Mauing the Flack Catchers* (New York: Bantam, 1970).

6   For other detailed studies of involved-community models see George A. Brager and Frances P. Purcell, eds., *Community Action Against Poverty* (New Haven: College and University Press, 1967); Harold Weissman, ed., *Community Development in the Mobilization for Youth* (New York: Association Press, 1969); Solomon Kobrin, "The Chicago Area Project: A 30 Year Appraisal," in Norman Johnson et al., eds., *The Sociology of Punishment and Correction* (New York: John Wiley, 1970); Dale Sechrest, "The Community Approach to Juvenile Delinquency," (mimeo, School of Criminology, University of California, Berkeley, 1970); and Anatole Shaffer, "The Cincinnati Social Unit Experiment," *Social Service Review* 45 (1971), pp. 159-171.

The Effectiveness of Correctional Programs: An Assessment of the Field

MARC RIEDEL and TERENCE P. THORNBERRY[*]

Marc Riedel is a research associate at the Center for Studies in Criminology and Criminal Law, University of Pennsylvania. Terence P. Thornberry is assistant director of the Center for Studies in Criminology and Criminal Law, University of Pennsylvania.

INTRODUCTION

The effectiveness of various treatment approaches with criminals is being questioned with increasing frequency. The ideal of rehabilitation, the cornerstone of the American correctional field, is being challenged, not only by researchers and practitioners, but by administrators, politicians, and the public as well. We can no longer assume that treatment is beneficial to offenders, and that in time we will discover the most efficient form of treatment. On the contrary, recent research indicates that contemporary treatment approaches have not been successful, and some of them may actually be detrimental to offenders. The purpose of this paper is to summarize such research, and to synthesize findings concerning the effectiveness of various treatment approaches.

This paper is based not on original research papers, but rather on studies that summarize evaluation research. The added distance from actual empirical studies allows for a broader and more diversified scope. Before presenting the reviews of evaluation research, however, a major methodological issue must first be addressed.

A FRAME OF REFERENCE

The most important consideration in evaluating the success of treatment programs is to understand what is meant by success. While a large segment of the population is in agreement that the purpose of the criminal justice system is to reduce crime, there is little agreement as to how this goal can be reached. For example, there is considerable controversy whether criminal justice should emphasize the traditional goal of deterrence. Deterrence refers both to compliance

[*] An earlier version of this paper appeared as part of a report the authors wrote for the Educational Development Center of Wilkes College, entitled "Measurement and the Effectiveness of Correctional Programs" (1975).

with the law by actual offenders (specific deterrence), as well as that of potential offenders (general deterrence). According to deterrence theory, it is unimportant why offenders choose to obey the law, but only that criminal sanctions are sufficient to produce compliance.

Not only does deterrence assume that the offender has a choice in the matter, but criminal law posits a model of free will and individual responsibility. On the other hand, social science assumes that individual choices are not free, and are to an extent predetermined. Criminal behavior is learned and the quality of the person's environment plays an influential role in that process. If the offender has not learned to make appropriate responses, then the task of criminal justice is to institute programs to alter those responses, and thus rehabilitate him. Whether rehabilitation involves insight into one's problems, better social adjustment, or improved job skills, the aim of these programs is to change offender's response patterns, by viewing criminal behavior as symptomatic of some malfunction.*

It is tenuous indeed, however, whether such programs result in crime reduction. While a better understanding of the psychological and social causes of crime may produce better adjusted individuals, this does not necessarily lead to more law-abiding behavior. Although these programs may help criminals to become better adjusted, they are criminals nevertheless. As a result, we take a skeptical view of this approach. The theories that correlate crime with inappropriate learning are not sufficiently well defined to be used in mapping policies. Since evaluations of treatment programs rarely meet minimum research criteria, policy decisions are premised on tenuous grounds.

There is a further question whether the millions of dollars committed to action or treatment programs can be justified if the programs do not result in crime reduction. As we have noted, offenders may be rehabilitated in the sense of gaining insight into their problems, and becoming better adjusted, and yet continue to commit offenses. Although the adjustment of potential criminals may be important, there are higher priorities for appropriations for treatment or action programs. While individuals or groups may be secondarily affected by treatment or action programs, the primary purpose of such programs must be the reduction of crime. Where crime has not been significantly reduced, programs designed to reduce crime must be seriously questioned. Even if the secondary purposes are realized, such programs cannot be viewed as successful unless they

---

*Another view suggests that a person's environment is more responsible for inappropriate behavior than the learning process. Rather than expecting offenders to adapt to a bad environment, it is acknowledged that some reorganization is necessary. Since the latter view challenges powerful economic and political interests with a stake in the present social arrangement, most current treatment programs focus on changing individual learning processes. As a result our review will focus on that perspective as well.

lead to a reduction in crime. The necessity for crime reduction does not preclude research on many of the secondary purposes of action programs. It means only that programs designed to meet the secondary purposes should not be supported by agencies whose primary task is to reduce crime.

It follows from the preceding discussion that the most significant variables in a review of evaluation studies are those that measure crime reduction, either through statistics of repeated contact with criminal justice agencies (recidivism), or through self-report of victimization statistics. In research terminology, crime reduction is the dependent variable, while those associated with secondary purposes are intervening variables. If the action program results in a reduction in criminal behavior or if variations in the measure of intervening variables are successful responses, this is viewed as positive. While a program may be able to produce positive changes in the intervening variables, reduced criminality is the most important consideration in determining overall success. The same is true of negative responses to intervening variables. Only a reduction in crime is evidence of a successful program.

ASSESSING THE EFFECTIVENESS OF ACTION PROGRAMS

In collecting relevant literature for this paper, a search was made for studies on criminal justice evaluation, methods of evaluation, critiques and analyses of outcome measures, and measures used in criminal justice evaluation. The following sources were consulted: *Educational Abstracts, Psychological Abstracts, Sociological Abstracts, Crime and Delinquency Abstracts, Criminological Abstracts, The Seventh Mental Measurements Yearbook*, and two computer-based information retrieval systems, Educational Resources Information Center (ERIC) and the National Criminal Justice Reference Service. The material used in this report is representative of current reference material, and includes available reviews of evaluations. Where the review was published as an agency report, attempts were made to obtain it, although in two cases the specific reviews could not be obtained and secondary sources were used. The reviews of evaluations will be presented in an author-by-author fashion rather than by topic. Not only do different authors interpret the same evidence differently, but such a presentation permits us to examine the types of interpretative and methodological assumptions used in reaching conclusions. While all the reviews focus on the question of correctional effectiveness, the later articles examine the quality of the research in greater depth.

Robison and Smith (1971)

Robison and Smith reviewed literature relating to the effectiveness of correctional programs in California. They evaluate literature in five critical areas of criminal processing: (1) imprisonment or probation, (2) length of stay in prison, (3) treatment programs in prison, (4) intensity of parole or probation supervision, and (5) outright discharge from prison or release on parole.

1 Imprisonment or probation Robison and Smith indicate that a comparison of recidivism rates between prison and probation does not demonstrate different rates of success, since courts place their best risks on probation, resulting in an inherent bias toward those on probation. One can control for case differences by making a random assignment of cases to either probation or prison, as was done in the California Youth Authority's Community Treatment Project (CTP).* This project, which has been in operation since 1961, has been widely acclaimed for its promise. After random assignment to experimental and control groups, an evaluation was conducted after fifteen months. The results indicated that only 30 percent of the male experimental subjects had violated parole or been unfavorably discharged, while 51 percent of the male control subjects had violated parole or been unfavorably discharged. By the twenty-four month follow-up, 63 percent of the control group failed, as compared with only forty-three percent of the experimental group, confirming the efficacy of probation.

However, Robison and Smith found that most of the differences between the experimental and control groups could be explained by the decision making authority: "In the CTP study the recidivism rates were managed to make the experimentals appear favorable."[1] An analysis indicated that juveniles in the control and experimental groups were handled similarly only when offenses were of a serious nature. Where the offenses were less serious, control subjects were more likely than experimental subjects to have their probationary status revoked. On the basis of this and another study comparing professional casework to a jail or prison term, Robison and Smith conclude that there is no evidence that community supervision is more effective than institutional confinement.

2 Length of stay in prison Robison and Smith review the research of Jarman, who studied the effect of length of sentence on recidivism. Studies of robbery offenders at six, twelve, and twenty-four month periods indicated that the longer offenders were kept in prison, the more likely they were to recidivate. To counter the argument that poorer risks were kept longer, Jarman introduced extensive statistical controls, and found that length of stay was the relevant variable affecting the probability of recidivism. Robison and Smith suggest that administrative needs may be more significant in determining length of stay than the characteristics of the inmates.

---

*Citations to specific studies in cited reviews are given in the review. Unless otherwise indicated by citation, all references to authors in this paper are cited in detail in the evaluation report under discussion.

3 Treatment programs in prison Group counseling has been one of the most widely used prison treatment techniques. In reviewing a careful study of group counseling, Robison and Smith agree with Ward, Kassenbaum, and Wilner, who conducted the study. These authors found no significant differences between experimental and control groups, and concluded that improvements in offender behavior were not sufficient to warrant continued use of group counseling. Robison and Smith conclude: "Despite the continuing popularization of various treatment programs and the increased attention devoted to more rigorous designs for their evaluation, *there are still no treatment techniques which have unequivocally demonstrated themselves capable of reducing recidivism.* "[2]

4 Intensity of parole or probation supervision Numerous demonstration projects have decreased the size of the caseload in the belief that a smaller caseload would mean more intensive supervision and a lower rate of recidivism. Review of the Special Intensive Parole Unit (SIPU) program, initiated in California in 1953, indicated that a fifteen-man caseload did not differ from a thirty-man caseload in terms of parole outcome.

Robison and Smith also look at the results of the 1964 Work Unit program, in which the size of the caseload was determined in large part by the seriousness of the offense. The Work Unit caseload averaged about thirty-five people, compared to conventional caseloads of seventy people. The small difference of 3.2 percent in favor of the Work Unit becomes insignificant when controls for parolee risk level are introduced. The Work Unit's parolees, in other words, were a better risk. Robison and Smith found that reducing the caseload size was not effective in reducing recidivism.

5 Outright discharge from prison or release on parole Robison and Smith also compare differences in recidivism rates for men officially discharged from prison and those released on parole. Reviewing a study by Mueller, the authors found that during the first two years after release from prison, the discharged offenders are less likely to commit another crime than those paroled. However, after three years there was no difference between the two groups in postinstitutional disposition.

Robison and Smith conclude, after reviewing California studies with recidivism as the dependent variable:

> Analysis of findings in a review of the major California correctional programs that permit relatively rigorous evaluation strongly suggests the following conclusion: *There is no evidence to support any program's claim of superior rehabilitive [sic] efficacy.*
>> The single answer, then, to each of the five questions originally posed—"Will the clients act differently if we lock

them up, or keep them locked up longer, or do something with them inside, or watch them more closely afterward, or cut them loose officially—is: *"Probably not."*[3]

We find only minor shortcomings in the Robison and Smith review. Although they claim only to review programs with rigorous evaluations, the authors do not indicate what they mean by "rigorous." While their research judgments are sound, verification is difficult, since many of the studies on which their judgments are based are not in readily accessible published sources. Even with these limitations and given that the coverage of studies is limited to California, their results contribute to the conclusion that no program has demonstrated effectiveness in reducing recidivism.

Adams (1967)

From his review of twenty-two California studies on the effects of reduced caseload, Adams concludes that thirteen of these programs show either significant reduction in recidivism or a benefit/cost ratio higher than unity. This general conclusion contrasts sharply with the findings of Robison and Smith concerning correctional caseloads. A comparison between the two studies may determine why the authors differed in their conclusions, since in several instances they reviewed the same studies.

The Special Intensive Parole Unit (SIPU) program and related research is divided into five phases. According to Adams, two of the researched phases show negative results, while the latter three display positive results. The fifth and final phase, which is the basis of the Robison and Smith results, was the most elaborate, reflecting knowledge about the research design and program accumulated from previous phases.

After reviewing the major findings of this program, Adams concludes:

> The only variable that made a real difference in parole outcome was the amount of time the parole agent had to devote to supervision. Interaction between agent and parolee characteristics did not appear related to outcome in this phase. Furthermore, the 15-man caseloads performed no better than 30-man caseloads.[4]

These conclusions, which do not differ substantively from those of Robison and Smith, apparently led Adams to classify SIPU as a successful program. But the grounds for his conclusion are unclear.

Adams also reviewed the Work Unit program evaluated by Robison and Smith. Adams concludes that there were significant reductions in returns to prisons for the experimental group. However, Adams did not consider the effect of the parolee risk level. As Robison and Smith indicate, when parolee risk level is introduced as a control, the significant differences disappear.

It is often difficult to assess Adams's claims for the success of programs because he does not clearly delineate what measures of success are used. In some instances, Adams defines success as a reduction in recidivism, while in other cases, he measures success by changes in intervening variables. Frequently success is claimed where there is no difference between experimental and control groups, when the former is less expensive. For example, Adams reports on an evaluation of the Willowbrook-Harbor Intensive Supervision Project, which utilized sixteen-boy community treatment caseloads as the experimental condition and forestry camp placements as a control condition. There was no difference in the success rates, but the average monthly costs for the experimental group was $115, while that for the control group was $326. The argument that although one treatment is no better than another, one is cheaper has frequently been used to bolster conclusions that a particular program is successful. It seems to the authors that when success turns on financial advantages rather than either reduction of crime or rehabilitation, such rationales are an admission of defeat. Such efforts do not support claims of success any more than positive variations in scores on personality inventories. From an analysis of Adams's review we do not find compelling evidence to reject Robison and Smith's conclusion.

Adams (1976)

The review of corrections research by Adams parallels our own efforts, in that he also reviews the results of other evaluations. We and Adams both review evaluations by Bailey;[5] Adams;[6] Robison and Smith;[7] Kassenbaum, Ward, and Wilner;[8] and Martinson.[9] Two reviews examined by Adams—Speer and Berkowitz—were unavailable to us. Adams summarizes the results of these studies as follows:

> D. C. Speer (1972) examined twenty-one controlled experimental studies of psychotherapy in corrections and identified eleven that included follow-up data on community performance after treatment. Of the eleven studies, six (55 percent) indicated a reduction in subsequent arrests and time spent in jail. The most definitive finding was that out of eight studies of juvenile treatment, six showed significant improvement; of the three involving adults, none showed significant improvement.

> F. Berkowitz (1973) reviewed thirty-eight evaluative studies that were generally representative of 400 LEAA-funded projects under the California Council of Criminal Justice. Specified within the thirty-eight projects were 154 measurable objectives. Of these, sixty (or about 40 percent) were judged to have been achieved. The reviewer also identified seventy-three methodological deficiencies in the thirty-eight projects. Goal attainment was highest and deficiency rate lowest in the five experimental projects among the thirty-eight studies.[10]

Since we were unable to examine the unpublished reviews, comments about their conclusions must necessarily be tentative. However, we do believe that Speer's conclusion is not supported by other reviewers. It is difficult to evaluate Berkowitz's claims since he provides no clear definition of what he meant by "goal attainment" for each of these projects.

What is significant is Adams's conclusion after reviewing these studies: ". . . there is one sense in which all seven observers agree. Some are much more skeptical than others, but all see research with practical payoff as being a small percentage of the total."

Kirby (1954)

Kirby reviews research prior to 1954 in four treatment areas: (1) probation and parole; (2) correctional institutions; (3) psychotherapy, counseling and other noninstitutional treatment; and (4) capital punishment as a deterrent. The criteria used to arrive at judgments were not introduced. The nature of the coverages was described as an examination of "the leading journals in sociology, social work and penology . . . as well as a number of criminology textbooks, proceedings of various annual meetings and conferences, and periodical indexes."[11]

The studies mentioned by Kirby suffer from such basic methodological limitations that a review of specifics does not lend new insights to the discussion. Also, his examination of studies at least twenty years old has only limited value. But while Kirby's research is old, his conclusion is contemporary: "It is quite clear from this survey that most treatment programs are based on hope and perhaps informed speculation rather than on verified information."[12] Although we have progressed since 1954 in the number and methodological sophistication of programs, there has not been progress in the generation and implementation of effective programs.

Bailey (1966)

The relative effectiveness of action programs is dependent on the quality of the research methodology used to evaluate it. Bailey reviewed 100 evaluation reports published between 1940 and 1960, all of which were empirical studies. The selection of reports was guided by three principles: (1) the report must be based on empirical data; (2) the treatment evaluated must depend on the manipulation of some form of interpersonal relations as the independent or causal variable; and (3) the behavior to be corrected must be potentially or actually subject to legal sanctions.

1   Frequency of types of reports   Of the 100 correctional reports only 22 percent were classified as using experimental designs; 26 percent used control procedures with no control group; and 52 percent were empirical studies with no control procedures. In other words, the more rigorous the research, the less frequently it is done.

2 Frequency of types of treatment   As might be expected, group treatment was the most frequently used treatment (58 percent of the reports), while individual forms constituted 42 percent of the reports. The types of research designs were about equally represented in the evaluation reports of group treatment.

3 Frequency of type of settings   A slight majority (54 percent) of the evaluations were carried out in correctional settings, in contrast to noncorrectional settings. Only reports using experimental designs or control procedures were used in this comparison.

4 Professional identification of researchers   Focusing only on the reports using experimental designs, ten of the twenty-one reports were authored by psychologists, while sociologists authored six of the reports. Psychiatrists, educators, and social workers contributed one study each, and two could not be classified.

5 Theories used in correctional outcome studies   Under the assumption that treatment theory helps to guide treatment, Bailey classified behavioral theories used in the 100 correctional reports into two basic categories. The first, based on "the sick premise," suggests that deviant behavior is symptomatic of underlying psychopathology. The second type, "the group relations premise" assumes that behavior, including deviant behavior, is primarily a function of group relations. Of course, both types of theories may apply to a particular treatment program. Of the 100 reports, 47 percent employed the sick premise approach. A substantial majority (67 percent) employed both types of theories. Interestingly, despite the finding that over 50 percent of the reports evaluate group treatment, only 9 percent of the reports used the group relations premise as a theoretical justification for intervention.

6 Effectiveness of treatment   Of the total sample of reports, 10 percent described the treatments as having either harmful or no effects; 38 percent of the studies reported some improvement;* 37 percent reported statistically significant improvement; and 5 percent could not be classified. "Thus, roughly one-half of the outcome reports" concluded that there was considerable improvement.† Of course, it should be noted that Bailey's conclusion does not control for the method used to gauge success.

Bailey reported that as the rigor of the design increases, there is only a slight increase in the number of reported successes. This led

---

*Some improvement means that the experimental group had better scores than the comparison group, but that the difference was not statistically significant.

†The percentages, which are presented here as they are given in the original, do not sum to 100. We are relying on Bailey's statement that roughly one-half of the projects were successful.

him to conclude that the rigor of the research design exerts little influence on the frequency of reported successes. Although approximately one-half of the 100 reports concluded that treatment programs were successful, it is difficult to interpret these findings. Bailey indicates, however, that reports of success are based on the conclusions of the original reports, and that a critical evaluation of the actual research designs would decrease the number of successful outcomes. On the basis of his research, Bailey concludes that "evidence supporting the efficacy of correctional treatment is slight, inconsistent, and of questionable reliability."[13]

Logan (1972)

More recently, Logan presented a more sophisticated evaluation of 100 studies made since 1940 that used techniques of corrective or preventive treatment. Logan proposed ten criteria for evaluation of the reports:

1 The program of technique should be adequately defined so that it can be placed in operation and tested.
2 The technique must be capable of being routinized. It must also be possible to implement all its components at various times by different administrators using diverse subjects.
3 There must be provision for a control group.
4 Subjects for experimental and control groups should be randomly selected.
5 Where it is appropriate, the control group should be selected using a matching technique.
6 There must be evidence that the treatment group receives treatment, while the control group does not.
7 Measurements of the behavioral change must be made before and after, with both experimental and control groups.
8 The definition of success must be sufficiently operational that it provides a valid and reliable measurement for determining outcome.
9 Definition of success must be compatible with normal notions of success, and should refer to correction or prevention of criminal behavior rather than personal adjustment or mental health.
10 There must be some follow-up measurement in the community for both treatment and control groups.

If we regard the ten criteria as minimal methodological requirements, Logan concludes, none of the studies can be described as completely adequate, since none meet all ten criteria. Only forty-two of the programs attempt to use a control group, only nine use well-defined techniques, and only one study uses a measurable definition of success.

The studies claimed various degrees of success as follows: sixteen claimed high amounts of success; four claimed good to high success; twenty-four studies claimed good success; eleven claimed fair to good success; fifteen claimed fair success; sixteen admitted failure; and fourteen could not be classified. On this basis one might conclude that treatment projects are relatively successful, but Logan's conclusion is somewhat more tempered.

> Thus, there is a strong current of optimism in these studies, with only a small minority (16%) admitting to failure. Perhaps most striking in view of the universal inadequacy of research design is the fact that so few studies insisted on suspending judgment altogether. . . . "Education" programs, as a group, made the highest claims of success while fulfilling the fewest methodological criteria required to support such claims.[14]

Lipton, Martinson, and Wilks (1975)

The last review analyzed here is not only the most recent, but certainly the most comprehensive one yet done. Like Bailey and Logan, the work by Lipton et al. employed research criteria to select the evaluation reports. In order to be selected for review the study had to:

1 Be an evaluation of a treatment method.
2 Include empirical data resulting from a comparison of experimental and control groups.
3 Employ an independent measure of the improvement resulting from the treatment.

Studies were excluded for methodological reasons such as the following:

1 Reports had insufficient data, or were preliminary or summary reports.
2 Results were confused by the inclusion of extraneous factors.
3 Evaluators used unreliable measures.
4 Descriptions of treatment could not be clearly understood.
5 Evaluators drew spurious conclusions from their data.
6 Samples were either too small or not adequately described.
7 Inappropriate statistical tests were used and insufficient information was presented to recompute the data.

Using the preceding standards, Lipton et al. reviewed every available report published in English that measured attempts at rehabilitation made from 1945 through 1967. From this process, they chose 231 studies that met the criteria proposed for inclusion. These studies were then divided according to the type of treatment used, and the success variable that was measured. The treatment categories include: probation, imprisonment, parole, casework and individual counseling, skill development, individual psychotherapy, group therapy methods, milieu therapy, partial physical custody, medical methods, and leisure-time activities. The success variables are: recidivism, institutional achievement, drug and alcohol readdiction, personality and attitude change, and community adjustment. Since our concern is with recidivism our discussion will focus on that variable, although the overall conclusions are fundamentally the same for any of the measures.

The major conclusion of the study is that "while some treatment programs have had modest successes, it still must be concluded that the field of corrections has not as yet found satisfactory ways to reduce recidivism by significant amounts."[15] The same conclusion could be made about the success of any of the ten types of treatments in reducing recidivism. Within each of the ten treatment categories, specific types of success can be seen. For instance, a treatment might be more successful for males than females, for a particular age group, or when administered by a certain type of therapist. Results relating to individual psychotherapy provide an example of this type of finding:

> Individual psychotherapy is more likely to be more effective when it is enthusiastically administered to youthful (16 to 20) amenable offenders by interested and concerned therapists with a pragmatic orientation. It is likely to be unsuccessful, and perhaps even harmful, if it is administered to nonamenable or younger offenders by unenthusiastic therapists with a psychoanalytic orientation.[16]

While individual psychotherapy can have positive results in certain situations, for most offenders it has not significantly reduced recidivism rates. The same is also true of the other nine types of treatment strategies surveyed. Though all demonstrate modest success in specific situations, they cannot by and large be considered successful strategies for reducing recidivism.

Moreover, the same conclusion holds for the other outcome measures surveyed by Lipton et al. There is no clearly demonstrated way to improve institutional adjustment, vocational adjustment, educational achievement, the tendency toward drug and alcohol readdiction, personality and attitude change, or community adjustment. In an earlier article one of Lipton's coauthors reached the following conclusion: *"With few and isolated exceptions, the rehabilitative efforts that have been reported so far have had no appreciable effect on recidivism."*[17] We see no reason to dispute Martinson's conclusion.

CONCLUSION

After reviewing seven reports, which evaluate hundreds of treatment or action programs, our major conclusion is that there is no systematic evidence that rehabilitation efforts have had a significant impact on recidivism. While a few rehabilitation programs have produced changes in intervening variables and recidivism, these isolated examples do not demonstrate the overall effectiveness of such programs.

Given this pessimistic conclusion, there are two basic options open to us—to abandon the rehabilitative ideal and turn to other models for dealing with offenders, or to work with the rehabilitative ideal to salvage what is worthwhile within it. At another level, however, it is clear that the two positions are not mutually exclusive, and certain contexts can be combined.

We do not agree with critics of the rehabilitative ideal who argue that individualized treatment programs such as those discussed in this paper should be eliminated in favor of mandatory, incapacitative, and deterrent punishments. Such an approach is a straightforward but erroneous extension of the research reported in this paper. Although this research suggests that the evaluated projects were failures, that conclusion does not lead ineluctably to the disavowal of the rehabilitative ideal. For one thing, this conclusion is based on a finite number of studies. Indeed, given the flexible criteria and the scope of the literature search in the study by Lipton et al., it is surprising that they uncovered only 231 studies to evaluate—an average of only 11.5 studies per year for their study period.[18] Moreover, many of these studies as well as ones reviewed by Logan, Bailey, and others are methodologically flawed, resulting in a small number of conclusive studies. To repudiate the rehabilitative ideal on such scant evidence would merely throw the criminal justice system into a fruitless search for a solution to the crime problem.

Rather, we suggest shifting from implementation of particular treatment approaches to a strategy of search, in which a scientific and experimental ethos dominates the search for effective responses to criminal behavior.[19] We are interested, for instance, in broad implementation of a group therapy program only after its effectiveness has been demonstrated. If it is not effective, the strategy of search will lead us to other possible approaches.[20] In this way, we can proceed without grossly disrupting the operations of the correctional system, while at the same time gaining a better understanding of the rehabilitative ideal.

But this is not to say that we should ignore the results of the evaluation studies summarized here. Those evaluations demonstrate that certain types of treatments are more successful with certain types of offenders than with others. Moreover, these studies show that such systemic variables as amenability to treatment and the concern of the therapist are of paramount importance in initiating new treatment strategies.

But since the conclusions of these evaluations are negative, we must question the wisdom of continuing to use the rehabilitative ideal as the keystone of our correctional policy. The strategy of search should clearly include other perspectives such as deterrence and mandatory sentencing. Specifically, proposals such as those put forth by Norval Morris, in which incarceration, treatment, and release are dealt with separately rather than intermingled, should be tried and tested.[21] Similarly, the consequences of increased and decreased length of sentence should also be examined for their affect on recidivism. But all of these should be viewed as elements of a strategy of search rather than as new solutions to the crime problem. They are hypotheses and no more than that. If we abandon the rehabilitative ideal tomorrow, substituting a system of mandatory sentencing, and ignoring the relation between the individual and the treatment, we will not have progressed an inch. But if a strategy of search is implemented, which includes the rehabilitative ideal as well as other models, the prospect for logical advances is enhanced.

NOTES

1 James Robison and Gerald Smith, "The Effectiveness of Correctional Programs," p. 69.
2 *Ibid.*, p. 74.
3 *Ibid.*, p. 80.
4 Stuart Adams, "Evaluative Research in Corrections: Status and Prospects," p. 49.
5 Walter C. Bailey, "Correctional Outcomes: An Evaluation of 100 Reports."
6 Stuart Adams, "Some Findings from Correctional Caseload Research."
7 Robison and Smith, "The Effectiveness of Correctional Programs."
8 Gene Kassenbaum, David Ward, and Daniel Wilner, *Prison Treatment and Parole Survival: An Empirical Assessment.*
9 Robert Martinson, "What Works?—Questions and Answers About Prison Reform."
10 Adams, "Correctional Caseload Research," pp. 10-11.
11 Bernard C. Kirby, "Measuring Effects of Treatment of Criminals and Delinquents," p. 368.
12 *Ibid.*, p. 373.
13 Bailey, "Correctional Outcomes," p. 157.
14 Charles H. Logan, "Evaluation Research in Crime and Delinquency: A Reappraisal," p. 381.
15 Douglas Lipton, Robert Martinson, and Judith Wilks, *The Effectiveness of Correctional Treatment: A Survey of Treatment Evaluation Studies*, p. 627.
16 *Ibid.*, p. 525.
17 Martinson, "What Works?", p. 25.
18 Lipton et al., *Effectiveness of Correctional Treatment.*
19 Paul Lerman, *Community Treatment and Social Control: A Critical Analysis of Juvenile Correctional Policy.*
20 Terence P. Thornberry, "The Once and Future Promise of the Rehabilitative Ideal: A Review of *Community Treatment and Social Control* and *The Effectiveness of Correctional Treatment.*"
21 Norval Morris, *The Future of Imprisonment.*

432

BIBLIOGRAPHY

Adams, Stuart. "Evaluative Research in Corrections: Status and Prospects." In *Issues in Criminal Justice: Planning and Evaluation*, edited by M. Riedel and D. Chapell. New York: Praeger Publishers, 1976.

Adams, Stuart. "Some Findings from Correctional Caseload Research." *Federal Probation* 31 (1967): 48-57.

Bailey, Walter C. "Correctional Outcomes: An Evaluation of 100 Reports." *Journal of Criminal Law, Criminology and Police Science* 57 (1966): 153-60.

Kassenbaum, Gene; Ward, David; and Wilner, Daniel. *Prison Treatment and Parole Survival: An Empirical Assessment.* New York: Wiley, 1971.

Kirby, Bernard C. "Measuring Effects of Treatment of Criminals and Delinquents." *Sociology and Social Research* 38 (1954): 368-74.

Lerman, Paul. *Community Treatment and Social Control: A Critical Analysis of Juvenile Correctional Policy.* Chicago: University of Chicago Press, 1975.

Lipton, Douglas; Martinson, Robert; and Wilks, Judith. *The Effectiveness of Correctional Treatment: A Survey of Treatment Evaluation Studies.* New York: Praeger Publishers, 1975.

Logan, Charles H. "Evaluation Research in Crime and Delinquency: A Reappraisal." *Journal of Criminal Law, Criminology, and Police Science* 63 (1972): 378-87.

Martinson, Robert. "What Works?—Questions and Answers About Prison Reform." *Public Interest*, June 1974, 22-55.

Morris, Norval. *The Future of Imprisonment.* Chicago: University of Chicago Press, 1974.

Riedel, Marc, and Thornberry, Terence P. *Measurement and The Effectiveness of Correctional Programs.* Educational Development Center, Wilkes College, 1975.

Robison, James, and Smith, Gerald. "The Effectiveness of Correctional Programs." *Crime and Delinquency* 17 (1971): 67-80.

Thornberry, Terence P. "The Once and Future Promise of the Rehabilitative Ideal: A Review of *Community Treatment and Social Control* and *The Effectiveness of Correctional Treatment*." *Journal of Criminal Law and Criminology* 77 (1976): 117-22.

Studies of Behavior Modification and Juvenile Delinquency: A Review, Methodological Critique, and Social Perspective

WILLIAM S. DAVIDSON II and EDWARD SEIDMAN[1]

Reprinted from William S. Davidson and Edward Seidman,
"Studies of Behavior Modification and Juvenile Delinquency.
Psychological Bulletin, Vol. 81 (1974), 998-1011.

An increasing concern of contemporary society is the prevention, treatment, and control of juvenile delinquency. This concern is found in the mass media, heard in political rhetoric, and demonstrated by increased federal funding for law enforcement agencies. At the same time, social scientists have been asked to provide explanations and solutions for the problems posed by juvenile delinquency. Their work has been concerned, among other things, with the identification of demographic, physical, and personality correlates of delinquency (Glueck & Glueck, 1970); examination of social structure as it affects the availability of legitimate goals (Merton, 1957); suggestion of genetic predeterminants of delinquent behavior (Court Brown, 1968); exploration of the crucial role of criminal associations (Sutherland & Cressey, 1960); explanation of criminality as a result of intrapsychic conflict (Freud, 1960, originally published 1923; Munroe, 1955); and consideration of retarded cognitive development as an important variable in the prediction of delinquent activity (Kidder, 1971). Each of the above has had an impact on correctional practices.

It is only within the last decade that the methods of applied behavior analysis, based on the principles of operant conditioning, have been used in the modification and prevention of juvenile delinquency. Two previous reviews have concluded that preliminary findings were promising, but that methodological weaknesses limit the confidence that can be placed in reported successes (Stumphauser, 1970; Zimberoff, 1968).

This article reviews the published literature, from 1960 through June 1973, investigating methods of behavior analysis applied to the modification of delinquent behavior.[2] The review is organized according to the type of behavior to be modified: educational behavior, program behavior, or delinquent behavior per se. Each of the latter categories is further segmented according to the research design employed: case studies, single-group studies, control group studies, and

A–B–A studies. Rather than scrutinize each study separately, the next section presents an overall methodological evaluation and critique of the research designs used in the studies reviewed. A final section is concerned with social implications of the review.

REVIEW

Educational behavior

This section includes research concerned with attempts to change classroom or school-related performance, such as academic achievement, of youths labeled delinquent.

Case studies   Early research aimed at modifying the academic performance of delinquents was primarily in the form of case studies. For example, in focusing on the reading problems of a 14-year-old institutionalized delinquent, Staats and Butterfield (1965) instituted contingency management procedures and made use of programmed reading material. With successful completion of the prescribed reading units as the criterion, a high rate of attending and performance was produced by the token system during 40 hours of instruction over a 4½-month period. There was not only a gradual reduction in errors on the programmed reading material, but also a 2½-year gain in reading achievement. Lastly, there was a reduction in general school misbehavior as rated by the teacher.

Tyler (1967) focused on report card grades. With a 16-year-old delinquent in a state training school, token reinforcement was provided on the basis of daily grades from each class. The tokens were exchangeable for a mattress to sleep on, civilian clothes, or canteen items. Results indicated a slight improvement in report card grades over a 30-week span.

Control group designs   Tyler and Brown (1968) examined the effects of contingent versus noncontingent reinforcement. Fifteen institutionalized males were randomly assigned to one of two groups. Each group was the recipient of the same two treatments in reverse order. The treatments were reinforcement contingent upon correct answers to daily news quizzes and noncontingent reinforcement. Group 1 received contingent reinforcement for 17 days followed by 12 days of noncontingent reinforcement. Group 2 received 17 days of noncontingent reinforcement followed by 12 days of contingent reinforcement. Results indicated a significant main effect for both the order of conditions and contingent versus noncontingent factors. More specific examination of the findings demonstrates that contingent reinforcement produced higher rates of correct answers and that the group receiving the contingent reinforcement first showed less of a decrement in the noncontingent condition.

Meichenbaum, Bowers, and Ross (1968) found that appropriate classroom behavior levels of 10 institutionalized females (half the rate of same-age nondelinquent peers at baseline) could be raised to normal levels (80% appropriate behavior) through contingency management. The criterion constituted a dichotomous (appropriate-inappropriate) observation schedule based on 10-second intervals. Appropriate behavior was defined as any behavior that was consistent with the tasks set forth by the teacher; inappropriate behavior was behavior that was not task specific. The phases of the intervention were: (a) baseline; (b) earning up to $2.00 only in the afternoon classroom for the percentage of appropriate behavior exhibited; (c) earning up to $3.50 in the morning and afternoon classroom and the provision of feedback in terms of dollars and cents rather than percentage of appropriate behavior; and (d) the addition of fines (response cost) for inappropriate behavior and a reduction of reinforcement available to $1.50. The conditions lasted for five days, seven days, three days, and three days, respectively. The results indicated that the contingency conditions successfully raised appropriate behavior to normal levels, although the authors concluded that the study was too short to assess the relative efficacy of the various experimental conditions.

One of the first studies to use multiple outcome measures and a pretest-posttest control group design was reported by Bednar, Zelhart, Greathouse, and Weinberg (1970). Thirty-two institutionalized delinquents were randomly divided into either a reinforced or nonreinforced group. Both groups attended 18 weekly evening study sessions in which programmed reading materials were used. The reinforced group, during the first two evening sessions, earned 10¢ for every five minutes they were "attending, cooperating, and persisting." During the balance of the research period, the reinforced group continued to earn money on a graduated scale for their performance on proficiency tests. On the SRA (Science Research Associates) Achievement tests, both groups showed significant increases in reading, but the experimental group demonstrated significantly more improvement than the control group on the word comprehension subscale. On the Gaites-MacGinitie Achievement Test the experimental group showed significant improvement over the control group for both reading and word comprehension. Neither group exhibited any change in scores on the San Diego Inventory of Reading Attitudes. A teacher rating scale showed significantly more improvement for the experimental subjects in persistence, attention, liking school, sociability, and cooperation.

Clements and McKee (1968) compared the influence of self-managed contingencies and experimenter-determined performance criteria with regard to the amount and accuracy of school work completed. Following a baseline condition during which the 16 institutionalized male offenders serving as subjects attended programmed instruction sessions with no contingencies in effect, a reinforcer menu consisting of various recreational activities, such as reading magazines or playing pool, was offered and made contingent on completion of specified criterion performance levels on the instructional material. During the experimenter management condition, the investigator set the performance criterion at 20% over baseline. During the self-management condition, each subject set his own reward criterion with the stipulation that it not be less than baseline. Under both conditions the amount and accuracy of work was significantly increased over baseline rates.

A-B-A designs A series of three studies (Bailey, Wolf, & Phillips, 1970) demonstrated the efficacy of home-based reinforcement contingent on school performance with five delinquents in a community setting. The criteria for contingent reward were whether the student had studied during an entire class period and had obeyed class rules. Privileges in the home were contingent on daily report-card ratings completed by the teacher. Significant improvement in teacher ratings was demonstrated when privileges were earned for "yes" ratings and lost for "no" ratings on the criterion behavior. The report cards and reinforcement contingencies could be gradually faded with no apparent decrement in performance.

A study by Miller (1971) contrasted the effects of token rewards only and tokens with backup reinforcers. In both groups, receipt of reinforcement was contingent on the amount and accuracy of school work completed. The tokens-only condition produced high rates of performance initially, but the performance returned to baseline quickly after the reversal condition was instituted. Token reinforcement with monetary backup maintained relatively high performance levels through the reversal phase.

In describing the initiation of a variety of contingency management procedures in a juvenile correctional facility, Jesness and DeRisi (1973) reported a study of the effects of immediate versus delayed rewards on classroom behavior. An average of 15 male delinquents were in the classroom for the duration of the study. During baseline (39 days) and reversal conditions (30 days), points earned for completion of academic assignments in the classroom were exchangeable only in the institutionwide token economy. The experimental manipulation (62 days) was the implementation of a separate contingency system within the classroom. Classroom money could be exchanged immediately for work materials (e.g., desk, pencils), beverages, smoke breaks, and free time. Inappropriate behavior was fined. The results demonstrated that the number of classroom points lost during the experimental sessions was about half of those lost during baseline and reversal sessions, indicating a general improvement in classroom behavior.

Summary   Interventions using improved educational performance as the criterion produce positive outcome in a variety of settings. However, more careful examination is needed of the generalizability of the changes produced and the robustness of the techniques employed.

Program behaviors

One approach to developing an indirect strategy for dealing with delinquency is to focus on increasing the frequency of behaviors thought to be desirable within a specific treatment or correctional program (e.g., promptness for meals). Whether such programs are institutional or noninstitutional, it is assumed that generalization to other domains of behavior, both inside and outside the program, will occur. These approaches are examined in this sections.

Single group designs   A six-month exploratory study of contingent rewards was instituted by Fineman (1968) in a juvenile detention facility. A system in which points were earned for staff-defined desirable behaviors was implemented, with inmates competing for reinforcement such that only the top point earners received the payoffs. Staff interviews at the end of the six months indicated a generally positive rating of the effectiveness of the procedures. A parallel program, with similar results and measures, is presented in discussion of a token program in a state training school (Rice, 1970).

Burchard and Barrera (1972) examined the use of varying timeout and response-cost procedures in reducing the occurrence of swearing, fighting, destroying property, and disobedience. Eleven institutionalized male delinquents were alternately exposed to the loss of 5 tokens, 5 minutes of isolation, the loss of 30 tokens, and 30 minutes of isolation contingent on the undesired behavior. Each of the four conditions was in effect for 12 days. Only the two more severe conditions (30 tokens and 30 minutes) reduced the undesirable behaviors below baseline levels.

Control group designs   A study by Pavlott (1971) focused on rule compliance in a juvenile correctional institution. Sixty females were randomly placed in either a token economy program or the regular institutional routine. The token system targeted various self-care and social behaviors. After three months the token economy group showed significantly greater improvement than the control group on the staff-rated problem behavior checklist.

A study by Krueger (1971) examined the effect of different sources and schedules of reinforcement on positive comments made in group sessions. Eighteen institutionalized male offenders were randomly assigned to attend one of three group sessions. In the first, the reinforcement was presented by peers contingent on positive comments about self or others. In the second, adult staff served as the dispensers. The third group received reinforcement randomly from staff. In general, the peer reinforcement group showed a significantly higher rate of positive comment, the improved rates were more resistant to extinction, and the changes showed more generalization to other institutional settings.

A-B-A designs   Twelve institutionalized retarded delinquents served as subjects for a study of a token economy aimed at improving school and workshop performances (Burchard, 1967). Comparing contingent and noncontingent reward and penalty conditions, both workshop and school performances were brought to desired levels by means of the token economy with contingent rewards and penalties.

Tyler and Brown (1967) examined the use of brief isolation for the purpose of reducing rule violations while playing pool. Initially (6 weeks), rule violations resulted in immediate placement in isolation for 15 minutes. The second phase (14 weeks) involved only the use of usual staff verbal disapproval for rule violation. The third phase (20 weeks) reinstituted the isolation procedure. Results indicated the efficacy of isolation in suppressing the rule violations of 15 institutionalized male delinquents.

The next three studies are only a sample of the research that has been produced by the Achievement Place Program. Were it to be presented in its entirety, a separate paper could be devoted to an adequate review.[3] Thus, the three studies reviewed here have been selected as representative of the behaviors targeted for change, methodology employed, and results reported.

An initial study in the series (Phillips, 1968) was designed to evaluate the effectiveness of a contingent reward system in a home-style residential treatment program for adjudicated boys. Three residents participated in five A-B-A design experiments, each focusing on different behaviors. The first sought to eliminate aggressive statements. Conditions included observation of naturally occurring rates, verbal correction, penalties within the token economy, and the threat of penalties. The penalty conditions were the most successful, but only the higher penalty condition completely eliminated the aggressive statements. The second sought to enhance room-cleaning behaviors. The conditions included baseline, auctioning among students to manage contingencies, fining the entire group, appointing a student contingency manager, and group election of a manager. The appointed and elected manager conditions were found to be most effective in producing near perfect performance. The third experiment found fines to be most effective in eliminating being late to school, returning from errands on time, and being in bed on time. The fourth sought to increase accurate completion of homework. Conditions included baseline, monetary reinforcement contingent on performance, weekly time out of the house, daily time out, and points within the general contingency system. The earning-of-points condition was found to be the most effective. The last experiment focused on the elimination of "ain't" from student conversation. The conditions were baseline, verbal correction, and verbal correction plus penalties. The correction-plus-penalties condition was successful in eliminating "ain't" and a postcheck indicated the elimination of the performance had been maintained without further intervention.

The second report of Achievement Place research included four experiments with an average of four subjects each. The first was concerned with promptness for meals and found the loss of points to be more effective than threats. The second experiment was concerned with room cleaning and it was found that the positive and negative contingency condition was more effective than demands, threats, feedback, or instructions. In addition, the contingencies were faded with no decrease in rate of performance. In the third study it was found that the students could be induced to place a portion of their monetary earnings in a savings account by proportionately matching their savings with point earnings. Three reversals produced complete return to baseline rates of no savings. The fourth type of behavior analyzed was that of correct answers to daily news quizzes. It was found that a system including contingent points for correct answers and point loss for errors was effective in producing both high rates of news watching and correct answers on quizzes (Phillips, Phillips, Fixsen, & Wolf, 1971).

A recent study examined the notion of training Achievement Place residents to reliably report their own and peer performances. In general, it was found that reinforcement contingent on accurate (compared with staff) reporting was effective when combined with specific instructions and staff observation. However, the accurate reporting did not generalize to reports of performances not under close staff supervision or performances after close supervision had been terminated (Fixsen, Phillips, & Wolf, 1972).

Summary   Again, the effectiveness of behavioral principles has been demonstrated, yet the question of the lasting nature of effects is largely unanswered.

Delinquent behaviors
It might be said that the investigations reviewed in the previous two sections approached the problem of delinquent behavior indirectly by using educational or program performances as success criteria. Another approach is to examine the effect of interventions on illegal or delinquent behavior per se.

Case studies   A case study of a 9-year-old institutionalized male focused on controlling aggressive behavior. The intervention consisted of using a "matter-of-fact" time-out procedure and initiating a token economy to reduce disruptive behavior. The disruptions gradually declined until they became nonexistent (Burchard & Tyler, 1965). An additional case study was concerned with stealing behavior in a

10-year-old institutionalized male. Home visits were made contingent on the cessation of stealing, which resulted in its elimination over three months and its continued absence in a one-month follow-up study (Wetzel, 1966).

In another case, Brown and Tyler (1968) examined the effect of a brief isolation procedure in reducing the intimidating-aggressive behavior of a 16-year-old institutionalized delinquent. During the 10-month duration of the study, the staff records indicated that his behavior improved and that the incidence of intimidation had decreased.

Stuart (1971) presented a case study of a 16-year-old female who had a history of incorrigibility, alleged sexual offenses, and school-related difficulty. Behavioral contracting was employed consisting of explicitly stating, in writing, the privileges and responsibilities of each party in an interpersonal situation according to the principles of reciprocity. In this case the two parties involved were the girl and her parents. Such behaviors as curfew, household chores, and school work were under contract. Presentation of performance probabilities in a Markov chain format indicated a high rate of contract compliance. In addition, court wardship was terminated and further delinquent activities were absent. The author does not indicate the length of intervention.

Single-group designs   The Behavioral Research Project provided consultation to various community "mediators" (e.g., parents, teachers) on behalf of 89 delinquents (Tharp & Wetzel, 1969). This innovative intervention consisted of instructing the mediators in the utilization of contingency management for specific problem performance areas. A number of individual cases are presented as representative of typical increases in desired performances (e.g., attending school). Three posttermination assessments of up to 18 months indicate declines in delinquent offenses, increases in grade point averages, and improvements in behavioral ratings from the mediators. In a similar program, using a detached caseworker model in a large Midwestern urban area, Rose, Sundel, DeLange, Corwin, and Palumbo (1970) provided delinquents and their families behavioral counseling and community resource coordination. Successful case reports provided a positive outcome evaluation.

A related strategy is presented by Alvord (1971), who provided 28 families of incorrigible children with two hours of discussion training in the operation of contingency management systems in the home. The rules for contracting between parents and children were based on the principles of reciprocity. The only data presented were that 24 of the 28 families considered the intervention a success.

Further efforts to remove undesired actions are reported by Fodor (1972). Group discussion sessions, with eight girls in a state training school, consisted of negative verbal feedback by staff when the girls talked of running away. Although no statistical analyses are presented, a pretest-posttest comparison showed a decrease in runaway behavior in the target group.

A-B-A designs   Horton (1970) investigated the generalization of aggressive statements in delinquent boys. Aggressive behavior toward peers was observed in two settings. In the first setting, pairs of subjects played cards (war) and were exposed to five conditions. During the baseline and two reversal conditions they earned money according to the number of cards won. During the two experimental conditions the six male subjects were reinforced for aggressive responses (hitting the opponent). In the second setting, two teams of three members played a second game (steal the bacon). No experimenter-manipulated contingencies were in effect in the second situation. The results indicated that aggressive responses increased during the experimental sessions and that they generalized to the second situation.

Control group designs   One of the first behavioral treatment interventions reported in this area involved interviews with delinquents in a street corner project. The investigators (Schwitzgebel, 1964; Schwitzgebel & Kolb, 1964) hired delinquent males to tell their stories into tape recorders. The subjects were recruited from local pool halls, clubs, etc., and were offered the job if they were able to produce verification of a criminal record. Twenty male delinquents averaging 17 years of age and eight previous arrests were used as experimental subjects. They were matched with 20 control subjects on demographic variables and previous criminal histories. The experimental intervention consisted of shaping interview attendance and content using a variable schedule of monetary, food, and other reinforcement. It was demonstrated over the course of one year that both prompt attendance and interview content improved. In addition, in follow-up studies at one-, two-, and three-year intervals the experimental group showed significantly fewer arrests and significantly less time in correctional institutions. Further replication of this methodology not only has produced similar results but has successfully altered other behaviors, that is, an increase in positive comments about self or others and a decrease in hostile comments (Schwitzgebel, 1967, 1969). It should be noted that this is one of the few community-based (or noninstitutional) intervention studies. Anthony, Buell, Sharratt, and Althoff (1972) found that for mental patients the particular type of institutional treatment is unrelated to durability in terms of recidivism and/or employment. What appeared to be most critical was the amount of community follow-up provided. Similarly, positive change in institutionally based delinquency studies may have little relevance for the durability of change outside institutions.

The CASE Project of the National Training School for Boys has been carefully described in a recent book by Cohen and Filipczak (1971). The data presented show desirable results in the use of the token economy program. High rates of academic and social performances were observed in studies within the program. The 41 students in the CASE Project were compared with a similar group of students from the standard training school program. Follow-up data on recidivism was gathered at one-, two-, and three-year intervals. At both one- and two-year follow-ups, the CASE subjects showed considerably less recidivism. However, by the third year of follow-up, the recidivism rates for the two groups were essentially equal. Additional comparisons of a group of students paroled directly from CASE and a group of students transferred to other institutions from CASE prior to parole indicated that the direct release group recidivated significantly less.

Alexander and Parsons (1973) reported a comparative study of short-term behavioral intervention, client-centered groups, psychodynamic groups, and no intervention with delinquent families. Forty-six families were randomly assigned to the behavioral intervention, which consisted of five to six weeks of individual family sessions focusing on the negotiation of behavioral contracts (Stuart, 1971), systematic verbal feedback from the therapist about family communication patterns, reading of family training manuals, and home-based token economies. Nineteen families were assigned to client-centered groups, focusing on attitudes and feelings about family relationships. Eleven families were assigned to a church-sponsored family group, and an additional 10 were released from court with no additional contact. A test situation was designed to have each family discuss changes other family members desired and responses to problem situations. Observations of the discussion indicated that families receiving the behavioral intervention were significantly more balanced in the amount of discussion by each family member, talked significantly more during the designated 20 minutes, and interrupted each other for clarification significantly more often. In addition, such interactions appeared to be predictive of nonrecidivism. Within 6–18 months the families receiving the behavioral intervention showed significantly less recidivism in terms of referral to juvenile court but those referred did not have significantly fewer alleged criminal offenses.

Summary   The studies of interventions focusing on delinquent performances as criteria have also shown positive results. Varying degrees of generalization have been selected for examination. Most studies have focused only on the behaviors targeted, while the community-based interventions of Schwitzgebel (1964, 1967, 1969) have demonstrated durable and generalized positive results; the institutional interventions of Cohen and Filipczak (1971) have manifested some deteriorations in generalization after three years.

METHODOLOGICAL EVALUATION AND CRITIQUE

The results of the research reviewed here present a positive pattern with some generality. However, in observing the use of consistently similar research designs, a number of concerns and suggestions need elaboration. While many of the comments may appear to be criticisms of the single subject methodology (Sidman, 1960) and a request for switching exclusively to group designs (Underwood, 1957), such is not the intention. Rather, a significant number of questions remain unanswered, particularly in the outcome domain, which require careful examination if recommendations about efficacious strategies for the juvenile justice system are to be put forth.

The crucial question to which we address ourselves is, How methodologically sound are our grounds for belief in the efficacy of behavior modification techniques with delinquent populations? In other words, have the important questions related to interventions with juvenile delinquents been adequately answered and to what extent have alternative explanations for our findings been considered or ruled out?

An initial concern is whether the observed changes would have occurred without the experimental manipulations under investigation. This is a particularly important issue when adolescent delinquents are under study. They are often at a point in their lives when maturation, social role change, etc., produce behavioral changes. In the literature reviewed here, 82% of the studies did not include equivalent no-treatment control groups. This is a similar figure to that reported by Stumphauser (1970) in his review. On the other hand, a considerable portion of the studies proposed demonstration of behavior control and functional relationships through reversals and selection of highly specific performances. Yet, only 36% of the investigations reported reversal data, generally considered necessary for demonstration of functional relationships.

A second issue, that of baseline measurement (or premeasurement), involves two concerns. First, a major portion of the literature used the A–B–A paradigm in order to demonstrate functional relationships. A central concept of the Sidman (1960) paradigm of research is that of stable states of behavior. The establishment of a stable state or baseline is generally considered a necessary condition for initiating various manipulations. It is also essential for adequate reversal conditions. The question of establishing stable state criteria has been of some concern, particularly with highly variable performances. When infrequent performances (e.g., occurring daily) are targeted, the concerns for establishing stable state criteria are amplified. Short of the criteria of the "interocular t test," adequate judgments about stable states are difficult. It might be proposed that statistical procedures be used in examining the effect of time passage and concomitant rate variability during baseline, manipulation, and reversal conditions (Gentile, Roden, & Klein, 1972; Gottman, 1973).

An additional concern with regard to baseline measurement has to do with more general assessment issues. Our definition of baseline has included the use of premeasures. For example, the effects of observation should be ruled out by sufficient recording prior to the initiation of an experimental condition. Similarly, when performance tasks or standardized tests are used as measures, practice and regression effects become viable alternative explanations of observed changes. This is particularly true when the performance levels are at the extremes of the distribution. Although 59% (Table 1) of the studies gathered premeasurement or baseline data, few exhibited unquestionably stable states. Of those that reported only one pre-observation, essentially all are open to the criticism of practice and/ or regression effects. Additional research endeavors must include methodological safeguards against such alternative explanations. An additional concern is with the interaction of the experimental manip-ulations and the measures used (Lana, 1969). Often it is quite clear to experimental subjects what changes are desired during experi-mental conditions on the basis of baseline observation or measure-ment. Again, further research must examine this issue and its potency.

A third methodological problem, systematic variation of treat-ment, is concerned with separation of the various mechanisms responsible for the observed change. For example, in attempting to cull out the source of efficacy it is important to separate the instruc-tions from the varying amounts of contingent reinforcement (Kazdin, 1973). Such questions may be examined by the use of factorial or multiple baseline designs. They are central to maximum standardiza-tion of strategies, pointing out the important elements in various settings, and eliminating superstitious components. Of the studies reviewed here, 62% included no such manipulation. Further, while the various components of the treatment manipulations are described, rarely, if ever, are the operative processes systematically monitored.

The fourth methodological issue concerns the use of multiple measures for the assessment of both the outcome and process of be-havior change procedures. No single measurement operation, behav-ioral observation included, is inherently valid. This issue has been extensively examined in the course of traditional psychological measurement (Campbell & Fiske, 1959). However, the same concerns are applicable to examining the efficacy of treatment strategies. Given the complexity of the phenomena labeled delinquency, it seems that multiple measures of experimental effects and their degree of agreement are necessary. For adequate assessment of effects the evaluation of parents, police, teachers, etc., must all be considered in addition to that of the experimenter, observers, and the tests em-ployed. Potentially, the multitrait multimethod paradigm, although proposed for quite different use, is applicable as a beginning. Even though 35% of the research reviewed included multiple measures, and the data portrayed general agreement within groups across measures, the next necessary step is to examine the extent to which separate measures covary across individuals both within and between targeted variables. In short, concern over the convergent and discriminant validity for methods of measurement of target behaviors has been significantly lacking.

The fifth issue, unbiased data collectors, has to do with many of the issues outlined by Rosenthal and Rosnow (1969). More specifi-cally, to what extent do the experimenter's expectations affect the

Table 1
Overview of studies on behavior modification
and juvenile delinquency

Author	N	Setting	Target Behavior	Specific Research Issue						
				Control Group	Baseline	Reversal	Systematic Variation of Treatment	Multiple Measures	Unbiased Data Collector	Follow-up
			Criteria of Study: Educational Behaviors							
Staats & Butterfield, 1965	1	Institution	Programmed instruction	No	Yes	No	No	Yes	No	No
Tyler, 1967	1	Institution	Grades	No	No	No	No	Yes	No	No
Tyler & Brown, 1968	15	Institution	Answers to news quiz	No	No	–	Yes	No	No	No
Meichenbaum, Bowers, & Ross, 1968	10	Institution	Appropriate class behavior	No	Yes	No	No	No	Yes	No
Bednar, Zelhart, Greathouse, & Weinberg, 1970	32	Institution	Academic achievement	No	Yes	–	No	Yes	No	No
Clements & McKee, 1968	16	Institution	Programmed instruction	No	Yes	No	Yes	Yes	No	No
Bailey, Wolf, & Phillips, 1970	5	Community	Daily teacher ratings	No	Yes	Yes	Yes	No	No	No
Miller, 1971	40	School	English classwork	No	Yes	Yes	Yes	Yes	?	No
Jesness & DeRisi, 1973	15	Institution	Classroom behavior	No	Yes	Yes	No	No	No	No
Percentage of studies including each specific issue				0%	78%	43%	55%	55%	13%	0%

Table 1   (Continued)

Author	N	Setting	Target Behavior	Criteria of Study: Program Behavior						
				Control Group	Baseline	Reversal	Systematic Variation of Treatment	Multiple Measures	Unbiased Data Collector	Follow-up
Tyler & Brown, 1967	15	Institution	Rule violation	No	No	Yes	No	Yes	No	No
Burchard, 1967	12	Institution	Sitting in seat	No	No	Yes	No	No	No	No
Fineman, 1968	20	Institution	Rule compliance	No	No	No	No	No	No	No
Phillips, 1968	3	Community	Aggressive statements	No	Yes	Yes	Yes	No	No	No
Rice, 1970	10	Institution	Rule compliance	No	No	No	No	No	No	No
Phillips, Phillips, Fixsen, & Wolf, 1971	4	Community	Promptness	No	Yes	Yes	Yes	No	No	No
Pavlot, 1971	60	Institution	Self-care	Yes	No	–	No	No	No	No
Krueger, 1971	18	Institution	Positive comments	No	No	No	Yes	No	No	No
Burchard & Barrera, 1972	11	Institution	Aggressive behavior	No	Yes	No	Yes	No	No	No
Fixsen, Phillips, & Wolf, 1972	68	Community	Accurate observation	No	Yes	Yes	Yes	No	No	No
Percentage of studies including each specific research issue				10%	40%	55%	50%	10%	0%	0%

Criteria of Study: Delinquent Behavior

Study	N	Setting	Criteria							
Schwitzgebel, 1964	20	Community	Recidivism	Yes	Yes	—	No	Yes	No	Yes
Schwitzgebel & Kolb, 1964	20	Community	Interview attendance	Yes	Yes	—	No	Yes	No	Yes
Burchard & Tyler, 1965	1	Institution	Disruptive behavior	No	No	No	No	No	No	No
Wetzel, 1966	1	Institution	Stealing	No	No	No	No	No	No	Yes
Schwitzgebel, 1967	48	Community	Interview content	Yes	Yes	—	Yes	Yes	No	No
Brown & Tyler, 1968	1	Institution	Intimidation	No	No	No	No	No	No	No
Schwitzgebel, 1969	18	Community	Interview attendance	No	Yes	—	Yes	No	No	No
Tharp & Wetzel, 1969	89	Community	Desired performances	No	Yes	No	No	Yes	No	Yes
Rose, Sundel, Delange, Corwin, & Palumbo, 1970	?	Community	Desired performances	No	No	No	No	No	No	No
Horton, 1970	6	Institution	Aggressive behavior	No	Yes	Yes	No	No	No	No
Alvord, 1971	28	Community	Child management	No	No	No	No	No	No	No
Cohen & Filipczak, 1971	41	Institution	Academic achievement	Yes	Yes	—	No	Yes	No	Yes
Stuart, 1971	1	Community	Curfew, chores	No	Yes	No	No	No	No	No
Fodor, 1972	8	Institution	Runaway	No	Yes	No	No	No	No	No
Alexander & Parsons, 1973	86	Community	Family interactions	Yes	No	—	Yes	Yes	No	Yes
Percentage of studies including each specific research issue				33%	60%	11%	20%	40%	0%	40%
Overall percentage of studies including each specific research issue				18%	59%	36%	38%	35%	3%	18%

448

collection and analysis of data and even the actions of the subjects? Given that only one of the studies used naive observers, that many took place in applied settings with a high premium on successful outcomes, and that contemporary publication practices demand successful results, a note of caution must be added to the generality of reported success. Empirical demonstration of the extent of influence of the experimenter expectancy phenomena with these techniques, settings, and populations needs investigation.

A final methodological problem, follow-up measures, is based on the proposition that therapeutic changes should continue once experimental manipulations have been discontinued. However, if the desired performances are functionally related to the therapeutic interventions, then they should be expected to reverse once the intervention is terminated. Although this concern is not as vital for strictly research efforts, if the changes induced are desirable or presented under the guise of required or court-ordered treatment, the responsibility to insure and assess carry-over seems paramount. In addition, if correctional systems are to implement new strategies, the long-term effectiveness of interventions must be of primary importance. The fact that only 18% of the studies (Table 1) report follow-up data or present any description of their attempts at enhancing treatment generalization is less than desirable.

An overriding concern must be with the generalizability of the results reported. Seldom are the selection procedures for subjects outlined. The representativeness of the behaviors studied is another question requiring examination (Winett & Winkler, 1972). For example, to what extent is there a consensus that improvement on a given achievement test or time spent on a task represents general improvement in school behavior or produces desirable educational settings? Similar questions can be raised about the specifics of the techniques used.

The issues raised concerning generalizability of the behavioral improvements reported in this body of literature are indicative of more pervasive theoretical concerns. Several of these concerns are highlighted by the recent work of Wahler (1969) with two disruptive elementary school children. This research has demonstrated the situational specificity of behavioral interventions in home and school settings. By implication from this study, as well as the body of literature reviewed, it seems premature to assume generalization of specific treatment effects. Second, given the high degree of situational specificity in Wahler's study it seems similarly premature to argue that generalization could be expected if operant techniques such as fading or noncontinuous schedules of reinforcement were instituted at multiple points in the process of reintegrating a juvenile delinquent back into his or her natural environment. Thus, to fail to include examinations of generalization effects in subsequent investigations seems naive, at best.

From a broader perspective, the literature reviewed renders theoretical interpretation difficult. This body of research cannot be classified as confirmatory in nature due to limitations of the research designs used and the concomitant failure to rule out alternative explanations as detailed above. In addition, this area of research suffers from ideologically based inattention to multiple methods of measurement and omission of such potentially important variables as the role of change agent, subject, and contextual characteristics. On the other hand, this research cannot be construed as exploratory in any real sense. The important variables have been selected a priori and any others systematically left out of investigative efforts. There is no real sense of an effort toward discovery, rather only the application of a conceptually closed paradigm to a new content area.

Overall, the behavioral interventions with delinquents have, to date, provided promising results. The above comments are not intended to discount the findings but rather to outline some of the areas of concern involved in appropriate interpretation of the body of knowledge and for further research planning. It appears that research workers in this area have chosen consistently similar paths at each decision point in the research process. This fact somewhat restricts available conclusions and definitive recommendations. Research of better quality is sorely needed.

SOCIETAL PERSPECTIVE

Additional comments are necessary regarding the relevance of the literature reviewed for social policy decisions and its impact on the various social systems that affect the lives of the youth who become labeled delinquent. Investigators and program administrators in the field must become acutely aware of how their results and studies affect decisions regarding the future treatment of juvenile offenders (Caplan & Nelson, 1973). It is highly possible that a new technology will merely be used to attain old ends more effectively (i.e., control) and a generally damaging juvenile justice system will continue unaffected (Gold & Williams, 1969; James, 1969). We need not pursue a path of shaping all adjudicated youth in the direction of passive attention to programmed materials, coming to the evening meal on time, or serving their sentences more appropriately (Winett & Winkler, 1972). Ours has never claimed to be a monolithic society, but all too often the helping professions have been guilty of guiding clients toward conformity and blaming those who do not respond to their efforts (Ryan, 1971). The issue of toward what ends our innovative efforts are leading needs to be forced by those working in the field. The current body of literature on the subject of behavioral interventions with delinquents provides no direct information relevant to these concerns. Open discussion of valued change and ultimate goals is needed.

There is also the need for further investigation of effective behavioral approaches for systems-level changes and the inclusion of data related to the impact of interventions on the systems of which they are a part (Kelly, 1971). If our concerns in working with delinquents are truly preventive, then direct modification of law enforcement systems, schools, neighborhoods, etc., may provide a much more efficient entry point for enhancing the lives of youth in general. Although this will necessitate some political entanglements, Ring[4] has recently argued that politics and science need not be mutually exclusive. Our primary responsibility must be to the youth we work with, as consumers or clients. Their position should not be compromised. The study of delinquency intervention not only should focus on the repair of adjudicated offenders but should begin active attempts at modifying social conditions leading to the adjudication.

NOTES

1 Preparation of this manuscript was aided by Grant MH 22336 from the National Institute of Mental Health. The authors wish to express their appreciation to William H. Redd and Julian Rappaport for their helpful comments.

2 The study of juvenile delinquency is replete with definitional problems (Schur, 1973). Depending on whether delinquency is defined by self-perceptions, official records, or any other means, different populations of delinquents result. This review is concerned with only those studies that dealt with adjudicated, and therefore legally defined, delinquents.

3 For additional information the reader is referred to Bailey, Timbers, Phillips, and Wolf (1971), Fixsen, Phillips, and Wolf (1973), Wolf, Phillips, and Fixsen (1972), Wolf and Risley (1971) and to the following unpublished references:

C. J. Braukmann, D. M. Maloney, D. L. Fixsen, E. L. Phillips, and M. M. Wolf. An Analysis of the Effects of Training on Interview Skills. Paper presented at the 79th Annual Convention of American Psychological Association, Washington, D.C., September 1971.

K. A. Kirigin, E. L. Phillips, D. L. Fixsen, and M. M. Wolf. Modification of the Homework Behavior and Academic Performance of Predelinquents with Home-Based Reinforcement. Paper presented at the Symposium on Behavior Analysis in Education, Lawrence, Kansas, May 1971.

E. L. Phillips, E. A. Phillips, G. D. Timbers, D. L. Fixsen, and M. M. Wolf. Achievement Place: Alternative to Institutionalization for Predelinquent Youths. Paper presented at the 79th Convention of the American Psychological Association, Washington, D.C., September 1971.

G. D. Timbers, E. L. Phillips, D. L. Fixsen, and M. M. Wolf. Modification of the Verbal Interaction Behavior of a Predelinquent Youth. Paper presented at the 79th Annual Convention of the American Psychological Association, Washington, D.C., September 1971.

4 K. Ring. Let's Get Started: An Appeal to What's Left in Psychology. University of Connecticut, 1972. (Mimeo)

REFERENCES

Alexander, J. F., & Parsons, B. V. Short-term behavioral intervention with delinquent families: Impact on family process and recidivism. *Journal of Abnormal Psychology*, 1973, 81, 219-225.

Alvord, J. R. The home token economy: A motivational system for the home. *Corrective Psychiatry and Journal of Social Therapy*, 1971, 17, 6-13.

Anthony, W. A., Buell, G. J., Sharratt, S., & Althoff, M. E. Efficacy of psychiatric rehabilitation. *Psychological Bulletin*, 1972, 78, 447-456.

Bailey, J. S., Timbers, G. D., Phillips, E. L., & Wolf, M. M. Modification of articulation errors of predelinquents by their peers. *Journal of Applied Behavior Analysis*, 1971, 4, 265-281.

Bailey, J. S., Wolf, M. M., & Phillips, E. L. Home-based reinforcement and the modification of predelinquents' classroom behavior. *Journal of Applied Behavior Analysis*, 1970, 3, 223-233.

Bednar, R. I., Zelhart, P. F., Greathouse, L., & Weinberg, S. Operant conditioning principles in the treatment of learning and behavior problems with delinquent boys. *Journal of Counseling Psychology*, 1970, 17, 492-497.

Brown, G. D., & Tyler, V. O. Time out from reinforcement: A technique for dethroning the "duke" of an institutionalized delinquent group. *Journal of Child Psychology and Psychiatry*, 1968, 9, 203-211.

Burchard, J. D. Systematic socialization: A programmed environment for the habilitation of antisocial retardates. *Psychological Record*, 1967, 17, 461-476.

Burchard, J. D., & Barrera, F. An analysis of time out and response cost in a programmed environment. *Journal of Applied Behavior Analysis*, 1972, 5, 271-282.

Burchard, J. D., & Tyler, V. The modification of delinquent behavior through operant conditioning. *Behavior Research and Therapy*, 1965, 2, 245-250.

Campbell, D. T., & Fiske, D. W. Convergent and discriminant validation by the multitrait multimethod matrix. *Psychological Bulletin*, 1959, 56, 81-105.

Caplan, N., & Nelson, S. D. On being useful: The nature and consequences of psychological research on social problems. *American Psychologist*, 1973, 28, 199-211.

Clements, C. B., & McKee, J. M. Programmed instruction for institutionalized offenders: Contingency management and performance contracts. *Psychological Report*, 1968, 22, 957-964.

Cohen, H. L., & Filipczak, J. *A new learning environment.* San Francisco, Calif.: Jossey-Bass, 1971.

Court Brown, W. M. Males with an XYY sex chromosome complement. *Journal of Medical Genetics*, 1968, 5, 325-327.

Fineman, K. R. An operant conditioning program in a juvenile detention facility. *Psychological Reports*, 1968, 22, 1119-1120.

Fixsen, D. L., Phillips, E. L., & Wolf, M. M. Achievement place: The reliability of self-reporting and peer reporting and their effects on behavior. *Journal of Applied Behavior Analysis*, 1972, 5, 19-30.

Fixsen, D. L., Phillips, E. L., & Wolf, M. M. Achievement place: Experiments in self-government with predelinquents. *Journal of Applied Behavior Analysis*, 1973, 6, 31-47.

Fodor, I. E. The use of behavior modification techniques with female delinquents. *Child Welfare*, 1972, 51, 93-101.

Freud, S. (1923). *The ego and the id.* (Edit. by J. Stachey) New York: Norton, 1960.

452

Gentile, J. R., Roden, A. H., & Klein, R. D. An analysis-of-variance model for the intrasubject replication design. *Journal of Applied Behavior Analysis*, 1972, 5, 193-198.

Glueck, S., & Glueck, E. *Toward a typology of juvenile offenders.* New York: Grune and Stratton, 1970.

Gold, M., & Williams, J. R. The effect of getting caught: Apprehension of the juvenile offenders as a cause of subsequent delinquencies. *Prospectus: A Journal of Law Reform*, 1969, 3, 1-12.

Gottman, J. M. N-of-one and N-of-two research in psychotherapy. *Psychological Bulletin*, 1973, 80, 93-105.

Horton, L. E. Generalization of aggressive behavior in adolescent delinquent boys. *Journal of Applied Behavior Analysis*, 1970, 3, 205-211.

James, H. *Children in trouble: A national scandal.* New York: Christian Science Monitor Publishers, 1969.

Jesness, C. F., & DeRisi, W. J. Some variations in techniques of contingency management in a school for delinquents. In J. Stumphauser (Ed.), *Behavior therapy with delinquents.* Springfield, Ill.: Charles C. Thomas, 1973.

Kazdin, A. E. Methodological and assessment considerations in evaluating reinforcement programs in applied settings. *Journal of Applied Behavior Analysis*, 1973, 6, 517-531.

Kelly, J. G. The quest for valid preventive interventions. In, *Issues in community psychology and preventive mental health.* New York: Behavioral Publications, 1971.

Kidder, D. A. Identifying habitual criminals by means of the Kahn test of symbol arrangement. *Journal of Consulting and Clinical Psychology*, 1971, 37, 148-150.

Krueger, D. E. Operant group therapy with delinquent boys using therapist's versus peer's reinforcement. Unpublished doctoral dissertation, University of Miami, 1971.

Lana, R. E. Pretest sensitization. In R. Rosenthal & R. L. Rosnow (Eds.), *Artifact in behavioral research.* New York: Academic Press, 1969.

Meichenbaum, D. H., Bowers, K. S., & Ross, R. R. Modification of classroom behavior of institutionalized female adolescent offenders. *Behavior Research and Therapy*, 1968, 6, 343-353.

Merton, R. K. *Social theory and social structure.* New York: Glencoe Press, 1957.

Miller, L. J. Effects of tokens and tokens with backup reinforcers on the academic performance of juvenile delinquents. Unpublished doctoral dissertation, University of Kansas, 1971.

Munroe, R. L. *Schools of psychoanalytic thought.* New York: Dryden, 1955.

Pavlott, J. Effects of reinforcement procedures on negative behaviors in delinquent girls. Unpublished doctoral dissertation, University of Pittsburgh, 1971.

Phillips, E. L. Achievement place: Token reinforcement procedures in a home style rehabilitation setting for pre-delinquent boys. *Journal of Applied Behavior Analysis*, 1968, 1, 213-223.

Phillips, E. L., Phillips, E. A., Fixsen, D. L., & Wolf, M. M. Achievement place: Modification of the behavior of pre-delinquent boys within a token economy. *Journal of Applied Behavior Analysis*, 1971, 4, 45-59.

Rice, P. R. Educo-therapy: A new approach to delinquent behavior. *Journal of Learning Disabilities*, 1970, 3, 16-23.

Rose, S. D., Sundel, M., DeLange, J., Corwin, L., & Palumbo, A. The Hartwig project: A behavioral approach to the treatment of juvenile offenders. In R. Ulrich, R. Stachnik, & J. Mabry (Eds.), *Control of human behavior.* Vol. 2. New York: Scott, Foreman, 1970.

Rosenthal, R., & Rosnow, R. *Artifact in behavioral research.* New York: Academic Press, 1969.

Ryan, W. *Blaming the victim.* New York: Random House, 1971.

Schur, E. M. *Radical non-intervention: Rethinking the delinquency problem.* Englewood Cliffs, N.J.: Prentice-Hall, 1973.

Schwitzgebel, R. *Streetcorner research.* Cambridge: Harvard Press, 1964.

Schwitzgebel, R. L. Short-term operant conditioning of adolescent offenders on socially relevant variables. *Journal of Abnormal Psychology,* 1967, 72, 134-142.

Schwitzgebel, R. L. Preliminary socialization for psychotherapy of behavior-disordered adolescents. *Journal of Consulting and Clinical Psychology,* 1969, 33, 71-77.

Schwitzgebel, R., & Kolb, D. A. Inducing behavior change in adolescent delinquents. *Behavior Research and Therapy,* 1964, 1, 297-304.

Sidman, M. *Tactics of scientific research.* New York: Basic Books, 1960.

Staats, A. W., & Butterfield, W. H. Treatment of non-reading in a culturally deprived delinquent: An application of reinforcement principles. *Child Development,* 1965, 36, 925-942.

Stuart, R. B. Behavioral contracting within the families of delinquents. *Journal of Behavior Therapy and Experimental Psychiatry,* 1971, 2, 1-11.

Stumphauser, J. S. Behavior modification with juvenile delinquents: A critical review. *Federal Correctional Institution Technical and Treatment Notes,* 1970, 1, 1-22.

Sutherland, E. H., & Cressy, D. R. *Principles of criminology.* Philadelphia: Lippincott, 1960.

Tharp, R. G., & Wetzel, R. J. *Behavior modification in the natural environment.* New York: Academic Press, 1969.

Tyler, V. O. Application of operant token reinforcement to academic performance of an institutionalized delinquent. *Psychological Reports,* 1967, 21, 249-260.

Tyler, V. O., & Brown, G. D. The use of swift, brief isolation as a group control device for institutionalized delinquents. *Behavior Research and Therapy,* 1967, 5, 1-9.

Tyler, V. O., & Brown, G. D. Token reinforcement of academic performance with institutionalized delinquent boys. *Journal of Educational Psychology,* 1968, 59, 164-168.

Underwood, B. J. *Psychological research.* New York: Appleton-Century-Crofts, 1957.

Wahler, R. G. Setting generality: Some specific and general effects of child behavior therapy. *Journal of Applied Behavior Analysis,* 1969, 2, 239-246.

Wetzel, R. Use of behavioral techniques in a case of compulsive stealing. *Journal of Consulting Psychology,* 1966, 30, 367-374.

Winett, R. A., & Winkler, R. C. Current behavior modification in the classroom: Be still, be quiet, be docile. *Journal of Applied Behavior Analysis,* 1972, 5, 499-504.

Wolf, M. M., Phillips, E. L., & Fixsen, D. L. The teaching family: A new model for the treatment of deviant child behavior in the community. In S. W. Bijou & L. Ribies-Inesta (Eds.), *First symposium on behavior modification in Mexico.* New York: Academic Press, 1972.

Wolf, M. M., & Risley, T. R. Reinforcement: Applied research. In R. Glaser (Ed.), *The nature of reinforcement.* Columbus, Ohio: Merrill, 1971.

Zimberoff, S. J. Behavior and modification with delinquents. *Correctional Psychologist,* 1968, 3, 11-25.

454

Ethical Issues in Evaluating Criminal Justice Demonstration Projects

BARRY KRISBERG and PAUL TAKAGI*

Barry Krisberg was a professor of criminology at the University
of California, Berkeley before joining the National Council on
Crime and Delinquency. Paul Takagi is a professor of criminology at the University of California, Berkeley.

INTRODUCTION

With the increase in Law Enforcement Assistance Administration (LEAA) funding, academic criminologists have seen an increasing number of Requests for Proposals (RFPs) come across their
desks. Most of these involve either planning or evaluation research,
which is fairly easy to conceptualize and design, as well as to suggest
sampling and measurement procedures. Although some RFPs allow
the contractor up to three weeks to prepare a proposal, most are due
in a matter of days. As a result, proposals are usually prepared with
great haste and later clarified in discussions with high level officials
in Washington, D.C., or those on state or regional criminal justice
planning boards. In this process, it is rare that the people who work
for the programs under study or the clients of the projects themselves
are consulted about research design or objectives. Often the research
procedures employed violate ethical standards with respect to the
use of human subjects, especially the question of informed consent.
Ethical standards have not yet been clearly defined by the government or by the academic organizations that conduct the bulk of this
research. But of equal concern is the fact that most of these proposals are prepared in a social and political vacuum in which the
researcher often knows nothing about the community where the
demonstration project is embedded. This sociopolitical ignorance can
have catastrophic consequences, since evaluations of criminal justice
programs call for assessments as well as recommendations, requiring
the investigator to be more than just technically competent. Put
bluntly, program evaluations can have life or death consequences for
the community and its members.

---

*Prepared for the Annual Meetings of the American Criminology Society, New
York City, November 1973.

It is the purpose of this paper to describe in narrative form the humbling experiences we encountered in an evaluative study of San Francisco's Chinatown Youth Services and Coordinating Center, an LEAA-funded delinquency prevention project.[1] Our experiences were deeply affected by the ethical and political issues that emerged during the course of our research. Our aim is to illustrate the moral dilemmas that may be inherent in an evaluative study.

THE CHINATOWN YOUTH SERVICE CENTER

The Chinatown Youth Service Center was a relatively simple diversion model, supplemented with community-based services, such as individual counselling, group therapy, street work with gangs, and a twenty-four-hour residential treatment center for girls. The project director contacted the dean of the School of Criminology at the University of California, Berkeley, and asked if there was anyone on the faculty who might like to evaluate the project. One of us called the director, and we met to discuss the details. There was approximately $22,000 available to do the evaluation, and the project staff needed to recommend the appropriate researchers. We were told that an agency in the Department of Health, Education, and Welfare had a "good deal of ego wrapped up in the idea of Youth Service Bureaus," and "the head of the agency has a special fondness for the China-town-North Beach Area."

We met with project staff and community people, and agreed to do the interim evaluation required by LEAA grant guidelines. We had ten days to do the field work and seven days to write the final report. The Board of Managers of the project awarded the one-year evaluation grant to a private research organization that had one year to study the project; we had one month.*

CRIME AND DELINQUENCY IN CHINATOWN

The Chinatown Youth Service Center was founded in the summer of 1970 in response to a sudden and enormous increase in police arrests and citations of Chinese youngsters. There were 85 juvenile arrests and citations in 1964, but this figure rose to 442 arrests and citations in 1970, an increase of over 600 percent in seven years. Informed residents of the San Francisco Chinese community viewed these statistics as merely the tip of the iceberg. Many told us that "there is much unreported crime in Chinatown. The problem is much larger than police or court figures show."[2] The community was concerned

---

*At the time of our discussions with the Youth Service Center staff we were unwilling to commit ourselves to do a large-scale study on a project that appeared too simple to warrant a $22,000 one-year study.

not only about the rising youth crime, but even more with the increase in juvenile gang killings.

During the mid-sixties arrests by the police drew attention to a group called "The Bugs," a gang of young Chinese burglars who dressed completely in black, with high-heeled boots and an upswept hairstyle. The Bugs had burglarized forty-eight Chinatown businesses, and had extended their activities to the neighboring Russian Hill area, a posh white community. In 1965, the gang phenomenon again came to public attention, but in the form of stylized violence reminiscent of organized gangland slayings. This form of gang violence continues to the present, and has claimed eighteen lives as of August 1973. The victims in almost every case were shot in the head several times, sometimes in broad daylight before one hundred fifty to two hundred witnesses. Police have been largely unable to bring suspects to trial. In fact, some community residents feel that the police are harassing large numbers of Chinese youth out of frustration over unproductive investigations. It appears that the crime-free description of the Chinese community is largely fictional, and we have been misled by a mythology constructed out of benign neglect, racism, and poor research observations. One of our graduate students uncovered California prison commitment statistics dating just prior to the twentieth century revealing that the Chinese in the 1890s had a prison commitment rate of 38 per 10,000 population as compared to the white rate of 10 per 10,000. The Chinese population declined after the turn of the century, largely due to restrictive legislation directed against the Chinese. Increases in departures accelerated considerably when Chinese women were discouraged from entering the United States. As late as the 1930s, the Chinese-American community had a sex ratio of eleven men to one woman.

Today, San Francisco's Chinatown consists of forty thousand people compressed into an area of forty-two blocks. The density rate is 885 people per acre, ten times the city's average. A recent social survey revealed that the average family monthly income was $311. As of 1969, 63 percent of Chinatown's families had an annual income under $3,600.[3] The unemployment rate as of 1973 was 13 percent. The Chinese in San Francisco have a suicide rate three times the national average, as well as the nation's highest tuberculosis rate. Two-thirds of the adults have less than a seventh grade education. The rate of substandard housing is 67 percent, as compared with a figure of 19 percent for the rest of San Francisco.[4] Chinatown has a labor force of eight thousand; of these, thirty-five hundred, mostly women, work in the garment industry at piecework wages averaging 67 cents an hour. These statistics reveal the grim social conditions behind the facade of "a mysterious and exotic Chinatown" displayed in travel folders assembled by the San Francisco Chamber of Commerce. The bitter irony of Chinatown is captured by the statement of a community worker who observed, "This is the only ghetto in the United States with a Grey Line bus tour."

THE EVALUATION RESEARCH

We quickly learned from our field work that the Chinatown Youth Service Center was not an ordinary delinquency prevention project in a typical poverty-stricken ghetto community. Although the project had been initiated by community people, we learned that it was of low priority in the distribution of LEAA funds by the state planning board. Although not highly regarded by state-wide criminal justice planners, the Chinatown project appeared to be of high priority to political and civic leaders in San Francisco. During an interview with a well-known and politically influential criminologist, we learned that it was he who had written the original proposal for the project, and had influenced people in Sacramento to get the project funded and then refunded for the second year. We believe that the criminologist was motivated by his sympathy and interest for the people of China-town, but subsequent events in our research, which we will discuss shortly, *suggest that the Chinatown project achieved political support because it appeared as a way to clear the streets of gang violence, and thus keep Chinatown open and safe as a tourist attraction for the city.*

During the brief research period, we spent a large portion of our time interviewing community leaders and knowledgeable informants, subjecting them to intensive examination in order to determine criteria to measure the success or failure of the project. This task was not easy, since there was considerable dissensus among those interviewed about the goals and objectives of the project. Even among the Board of Managers, which served as the executive body for the project, the scope of disagreement over the desired goals of the project was enormous.

The original proposal called for the establishment of a Youth Service Bureau with a youth advocacy unit, which would attempt to divert Chinese youngsters from juvenile court referrals. But many of the people with whom we talked had something more in mind when they thought of the project. Everyone we talked to had uppermost in their minds the gang problem. Some criticized the Youth Service Center for using a diversion model, which they felt was inappropriate for the gang delinquency problem in Chinatown.

The director of the center, a former probation officer and a graduate of the Berkeley School of Criminology, had put together a series of fairly traditional approaches to delinquency prevention, including counselling, group sessions, and crisis intervention in the schools. The youth of the community requested that the center develop a coffeehouse, drop-in center in response to an offer by the center that, "We have so much money, and such and such a place. What would *you* like to see happen to it and what will best serve you and your friends?"[5] The director of the project was attempting to implement some of the principles of the Chicago Area Project, in which "the philosophy of youth involvement (it is to be emphasized) in every aspect of the program . . . from planning, to hiring (personnel), to implementation, and to the kinds of programs."[6] The director was successful in obtaining from the Board of Managers a promise "not to sabotage any plans the youth come up with," and to facilitate their ideas in the most helpful fashion.

The coffeehouse was to include an arts and crafts center, a twenty-four-hour counselling service, and English classes for newly arrived immigrants—all programs requested by the street youth. The director and a staff member did nightly street-corner work to solicit interest and maintain enthusiasm for the drop-in center.

One of the key members of the project, a former state parole agent and a member of the bar, advised us that he felt the Chinatown project should focus on younger children, and stay away from the gangs. We later learned that this individual had received a beating, presumably from gang youth, which was interpreted by community leaders as a message by the gang youth to "lay off." Other community informants told us that the center should be organized to offer direct services when these are requested by an individual or his family. Several community leaders cautioned us that a "professionally designed" program strategy would not solve the delinquency problem in Chinatown.[7] Although everyone in the community was concerned about the gang killings, most were guarded in their discussions about the subject. The only persons who felt that the project should do more street work with gangs included the well-known criminologist, mentioned earlier, and the two law enforcement officials, a police juvenile bureau chief and the chief of juvenile probation, both members of the Board of Managers.

Our field work clearly showed the disagreements over the purpose of the Chinatown Youth Service Center. One of us had spent over a year researching a project with violent gangs in an eastern city, which led to the conclusion that without major changes in the political economy, gang violence would probably continue unaffected by conventional approaches. As we continued our field work and mulled over possible interpretations, we became increasingly apprehensive about efforts by the director to reach the gangs of Chinatown. This is what we wrote in our report:

> It is clear that the recent series of shootings and killings were important in terms of many individuals' definitions of Chinatown's "Youth Problem." It is important to note that both project staff and outside observers expressed doubts that doing conventional street work with gangs would be effective in reducing the apparently high level of intergroup violence. Many interviewees theorized that juvenile gangs in Chinatown are manifestations of the complex internal structure of the Chinese community in San Francisco and that these gangs more nearly approximated organized crime than delinquency. From what little we understand about the social structure of Chinatown we would tentatively agree with the view

expressed by some Center staff that their scarce resources should be directed towards working with the younger siblings of gang members and others to deflect them from becoming gang members. It appears to us that until such time as indigenous leaders decide to control the gang problem and agree to actively work towards that end, the street shootings and killings are likely to continue.[8]

In our recommendations we included a section about the project directorship, which reflected our feelings on an obviously dangerous situation. We recommended the following:

The director of the Center cannot alone make decisions that affect the staff, the clients, and ultimately relations within and outside of Chinatown. This is too much to ask of a director as a responsibility, and more importantly, the consequences can be enormous. We believe that the director of the Center by virtue of his position is not only a professional but a political decision-maker as well. In view of this, we recommend the establishment of an executive decision-making committee. . . .[9]

Our evaluation report was turned over to the center on May 2, 1973.

On June 26, 1973, at 11:10 P.M., the director of the center, Barry Fong-Torres, was chatting with a friend in his apartment, when someone rang the doorbell. Moments after he opened the door, five shots were fired, with bullets striking him in the head, eye, mouth, and chest. He died almost instantly. A few days later in a press conference, a high elected official in San Francisco, although expressing dismay over the killings, attempted to minimize them by reassuring white people that they would be safe in Chinatown, since all of the murder victims had been Chinese.

CRIMINOLOGY, PROGRAM RESEARCH, AND PROFESSIONAL MORALITY

We were deeply shaken by the death of Barry Fong-Torres, whom we had known to be a deeply committed and humane individual. We re-reviewed our report, field notes, taped interviews, and other data to determine if our evaluation activities had in any way precipitated the tragedy, or if there were any clues that the director's life was in danger. The only thing we could pinpoint was the vague and uneasy feeling that the situation was dangerous, as we had indicated in our report.

In reflecting on our experiences in Chinatown, we have come to realize that what we witnessed there was but another example of the sheer arrogance of criminologists, who for the most part represent the establishment, to impose upon communities delinquency control measures of questionable value. This is what our interviewees were telling us when they said that direct services should be provided when requested. Rationally designed programs created in a sociopolitical vacuum and *assumed* to benefit the community are simply pretensions of charity, masking the dynamics of internal colonization.

We do not suggest that criminologists are the only culpable ones in the countless tragedies resulting from social programs. But all too often the academic and professional community, which cooks up new project ideas, sells these packages to politicians and funding agencies, or, more subtly, remains silent about their worthless or even harmful effects. Rather than suggesting that criminologists pack their bags, we urge our colleagues to *practice their knowledge* when dealing with communities concerned about delinquency and crime problems. We are aware that the history of delinquency prevention has been grossly disappointing. From the Glueck's 1926 study of Judge Baker's Child Guidance Clinic to the highly sophisticated and elaborate study by Empey and Lubeck in the 1971 *Silverlake Experiment*, not one single delinquency project has demonstrated the achievement of programmatic goals. Published "success" stories often turn out to be little more than program huckstering through the use of pseudo-scientific research designs. This clearly means that delinquency prevention, including diversion projects, are not viable enterprises, or that our research methodology is not yet capable of yielding fruitful results. In short, the state of the art is that criminologists cannot yet predict with any degree of certainty which delinquency programs will succeed. If this is true, is it not a big lie to impose programs that we suspect will not work upon communities?

THEORY AND COMMUNITY PRACTICE

An out-of-print, but often cited publication is Helen Witmer and Edith Tufts's classic paper summarizing the evaluation of delinquency prevention programs.[10] Witmer and Tufts make the distinction between "programs for improving the environment," and "educational and therapeutic programs," which make fundamentally different assumptions about the nature of delinquency. The best known examples of the former model are the Chicago Area Project and the Mobilization for Youth, which had a strong community control component. The Cincinnati Social Unit Experiment, while less well known, was perhaps even more successful.[11] In these three programs designed to "improve the environment," either the funds were cut off, or control of the program was taken over by the state. In two of the projects. local political officials aroused fears of Communism to subvert the program by direct political interference. Thus, to date we do not know the potential for delinquency prevention and control in programs of this nature.

Most of the delinquency prevention programs consist of individually oriented approaches to education and treatment, which are basically variations on those introduced by William Healy and August Aichhorn at the turn of the twentieth century. Such programs assume that the delinquent is sick, unsocialized, or inadequate, and that by state intervention, the delinquent may be redeemed. Such efforts continue to be designed and funded, despite criticism by both clients and communities, who do not view themselves as pathological or inferior. Programs of this sort are attractive because they deflect attention away from problems of the social structure.

Indeed, criminologists familiar with the history of delinquency prevention in the United States know that few granting agencies or universities have sponsored projects that openly seek to correct conditions of poverty, racism, and internal colonization that foster and maintain Chinatowns and similar communities throughout America. "The recent demise of extra-murally funded projects in ghetto communities from East Oakland on the West Coast to Bedford Stuyvesant on the East Coast makes very clear the distinction between projects designed to control the 'dangerous classes' and those that are abruptly terminated because they threaten existing political and economic relations."[12]

Lacking the firm knowledge that would allow us to make constructive recommendations, we can only rely upon our experiences and our biases. We, through rather different professional and life experiences, have reached a consensus that our bias lies with community-controlled approaches to delinquency prevention. This conclusion is based partly on our knowledge about the failure of more conventional approaches to delinquency prevention, but more persuasive, is the accumulated research findings that more than any other variables poverty and racism contribute to the victimization we label delinquency. Because of our bias we recommended in our evaluation of the Chinatown Youth Center that they explore the feasibility of establishing a community-controlled effort.

A number of community-controlled efforts are being attempted in communities throughout America. These include free medical health examinations, mini-schools, escort services for the elderly in ghetto communities, and drug abuse control centers. It may come as a surprise to some, but groups such as the Black Panther party, La Raza Unidas, RAP in San Francisco and Washington, D.C., and the Community Concern 13 in Philadelphia are actively seeking to reduce delinquency and crime through such programs. Criminologists have not studied the efforts of these groups for a variety of reasons. First, since these groups are not generally funded by extramural grants, there is no money available for evaluation studies. Second, these groups would probably reject the attempt of criminologists from outside the community to study neighborhood residents without some concrete reward for their people. Finally, government agencies and law enforcement officials are often openly hostile to these groups, and would prefer that these groups not be positively portrayed.

Students of delinquency, despite the problems mentioned above, need to move out into the communities to understand the relationship between crime, social injustice, and racism. We need to study the effects of systems of internal colonization that may have stripped some of our minority communities of the ability to handle local problems. We need to understand how selective processes within the superstructure force members of the community to adapt to the techno-economic environment in deviant and socially harmful ways. Finally, we believe that criminologists have a professional and moral responsibility to aid criminal justice workers in seeing the vacuousness of conventional approaches to delinquency prevention and control. We should be aware that it is no accident that poor and Third World people are the principal clients of the criminal justice system, and the principal victims of its injustices. We ask you to join us in nailing the coffin-lid on the ideas of August Aichhorn and William Healy, which have inappropriately dominated correctional philosophy for the last sixty years.

NOTES

1   Barry Krisberg and Paul Takagi, "Evaluation of the Chinatown Youth Services and Coordinating Center."
2   Barry Fong-Torres, "Narrative Description."
3   San Francisco Department of Social Services.
4   Dean Lan, "The Chinatown Sweatshops: Oppression and An Alternative."
5   Barry Fong-Torres, in a letter to Mr. Robert Foster, Youth Development and Delinquency Prevention Administration.
6   *Ibid.*
7   L. Ling-Chi Wang, "An Interview with L. Ling-Chi Wang."
8   Krisberg and Takagi, "Chinatown Center," pp. 6-7.
9   *Ibid.*, p. 20.
10   Helen Witmer and Edith Tufts, "The Effectiveness of Delinquency Prevention Programs."
11   Anatole Shaffer, "The Cincinnati Social Unit Experiment."
12   Barry Krisberg, "The Gang and the Community," p. 128.

BIBLIOGRAPHY

Fong-Torres, Barry. "Narrative Description." Unpublished paper, San Francisco: Chinatown Youth Services and Coordinating Center, 1971.

Fong-Torres, Barry. Letter to Mr. Robert Foster, Youth Development and Delinquency Prevention Administration, Department of Health, Education, and Welfare, Washington, D.C., January 5, 1972.

Krisberg, Barry. "The Gang and the Community. Unpublished paper, Berkeley: School of Criminology, University of California, December 1972.

Krisberg, Barry, and Takagi, Paul. "Evaluation of the Chinatown Youth Services and Coordinating Center." Unpublished paper, Berkeley: School of Criminology, University of California, May 2, 1972.

Lan, Dean. "The Chinatown Sweatshops: Oppression and An Alternative." *Amerasia Journal*, 1:(1971), pp. 40-57.

Report of the San Francisco Chinese Community Citizen's Survey and Fact Finding Committee, San Francisco: H. J. Carle and Sons, 1969.

Shaffer, Anatole. "The Cincinnati Social Unit Experiment." *Social Service Review*, 45:(1971), pp. 159-71.

Wang, L. Ling-Chi. "An Interview with L. Ling-Chi Wang." In *Roots: An Asian American Reader,* edited by Amy Tachiki et al., Berkeley: Asian American Study Center, University of California, 1971.

Warren, Marguerite. "Correctional Treatment in Community Settings, A Report of Current Research." Washington, D.C.: National Institute of Mental Health, U.S. Government Printing Office, 1972.

Witmer, Helen, and Tufts, Edith. "The Effectiveness of Delinquency Prevention Programs." Washington, D.C.: U.S. Children's Bureau, Department of Health, Education and Welfare, U.S. Government Printing Office, 1954.

Rediscovering Punitive Justice

CLARENCE SCHRAG

Clarence Schrag is a professor of sociology at the University of Washington, Seattle.

Reprinted from Clarence Schrag, *Criminology,* Vol. 14, No. 4 (February 1977), pp. 569-573.

These are among a rapidly growing number of works advocating greater use of punitive methods in crime control.* Although the authors fail to agree on some details, they seem united in their views concerning concepts such as just deserts, judicial discretion, incapacitation, and indeterminate sentences. Their basic argument, stripped of much rhetoric and numerous disclaimers, can perhaps be outlined in the following terms. Crime prevention through programs of social reform is not within the purview of criminal justice. Criminal courts should not be organized around the "largely mythic task of determining guilt" (Wilson, p. 179). Their main business is sentencing convicted offenders. Moreover, since the treatment of offenders is regarded as having little effect on either recidivism or the amount of crime, the purpose of corrections should be "to isolate and to punish" (Wilson, p. 172). What remains as the justice system's essential function, then, is the administration of punishment.

---

*Based on a book review of:

Thinking About Crime. By James Q. Wilson. New York: Basic Books, 1975. 231p.

Punishing Criminals: Concerning a Very Old and Painful Question. By Ernest van den Haag. New York: Basic Books, 1975. 283p.

We Are the Living Proof: The Justice Model for Corrections. By David Fogel. Cincinnati: W. H. Anderson Company, 1975. 328p.

Offenders accordingly have the right to accept or reject treatment. Avoidance of punishment, however, is a miscarriage of justice—"even if nobody needs to be deterred . . . punishment must be inflicted for the sake of justice because it is deserved" (van den Haag, p. 183; also Fogel, pp. 183–185). For this reason practices such as plea bargaining, diversion, judicial discretion, and even probation and parole, for example, are viewed with suspicion. Wilson and van den Haag aver that our courts and corrections, rather than the police or the public, are responsible for the failure of most offenders to be punished.

Punishment is justified, the authors say, on grounds of both utility (deterrence) and fundamental fairness (just deserts). Deterrence and incapacitation demand certainty of punishment. "We know that confining criminals prevents them from harming society, and we have grounds for suspecting that some would-be criminals can be deterred by the confinement of others" (Wilson, p. 208). Fairness calls for graded punishments, with severity fitted to the offense committed. Various kinds of punishment are recommended by van der Haag, including restitution, day fines, banishment, and "non-penal confinement" (chs. 19–22); but imprisonment has the advantage because it is the most stigmatizing and incapacitating (van den Haag, pp. 241–250). Fogel's "justice model" aims at bringing fairness to prison management through inmate self-government, voluntary treatment, conflict resolution, legal aid, ombudsman services, and flat-time sentences (pp. 204–236, 245–260). Wilson sees the possibility that "the rate of serious crime would be only one-third what it is today if every person convicted of a serious offense were imprisoned for three years" (p. 201), arguing that a sizable reduction in crime would still ensue even if the estimate were overly optimistic by a factor of two.

Apparently, such appeals and promises are taken seriously by more and more citizens. But there is more to the story. What does "just deserts" mean, for example, when none of the authors pays any attention to white-collar crime or to crimes of government, business, and labor? Wilson's comment in this regard is revealing: "I am rather tolerant of some forms of civic corruption (if a good mayor can stay in office and govern effectively only by making deals with highway contractors and insurance agents, I do not get overly alarmed), but I am rather intolerant of those forms of corruption that debase the law enforcement process, discredit its agents, or lead people to believe that equal justice is available only for a price" (p. xviii). Perhaps it is not irrational for people to believe that "justice" has its price when Richard Nixon, accused of common crimes, retires on a federal pension of $60,000 per year plus a cost-of-living increase, when Spiro Agnew has charges against him dismissed following a plea of *nolo contendere*, when Robert Vesco is protected against extradition after allegedly defrauding the public of $300 million, or when incidents of this kind are reported almost daily in the press. Such offenses, by all accounts, cost the people far more than street crime.

Or consider the contention that judicial discretion is the reason why common criminals are not punished. Recent victimization surveys suggest that approximately 40% of the crimes committed are reported to the police. Of those reported, about 20% are cleared by arrest, according to Uniform Crime Reports. This means that around 90% of our offenses are destined to escape referral to the courts. They escape because the people, including victims, or the police, or both, are unwilling or unable to take effective action. Under these circumstances, it hardly seems prudent to blame courts and corrections for the failure of punishment.

Moreover, there are some indications that saturated surveillance by the police may increase the costs and reduce the rewards for many kinds of law violations. Unfortunately, surveillance comes at a high price, one the public is not always willing to pay. Thus, in the New York subway system, where the number of robberies was lessened by increasing the size of the police force, the expenditure of funds needed to prevent a single robbery was estimated at $35,000. The cure in this case was considered more costly than the crime.

Is incapacitation in prison any more effective or less costly? Uniform Parole Reports give some very crude estimates of the amount of crime that might be prevented if the number of paroles were greatly decreased for a period of one year. Assume that the current number of parole releases, about 75,000, were reduced to 50,000. This would keep 25,000 prospective parolees in confinement instead of being released to prey on the public. Assume also zero crimes during the year in prison for the cohort of 25,000 who normally would have been paroled. This is admittedly a harsh assumption to make, since it disregards any crimes committed against prisoners or correctional personnel at a time when murder rates, for example, in many of our large prisons are greater than in the free community by a factor of about 50, i.e., around 500 prison murders versus 10 murders per 100,000 population.

The amount of crime prevented in the free community by incapacitation of 25,000 prisoners depends on the number of crimes these offenders would have committed had they been released. Records show that about 20% of our parolees violate parole and return to prison by the end of a year. Less than 5% return on new convictions. Another 5% or so are accused of new offenses but not tried in court. Some 10% return for technical reasons involving no crimes. One of the prisoners killed in the Attica riot, for instance, reportedly was returned for driving without a license.

In sum, we can assume that, had our prospective parolees been released from prison, about 10% would be accused or convicted of new offenses, major or minor, within a year. For the cohort of 25,000, this amounts to some 2,500 crimes that might be prevented by detaining the offenders in prison. Hardly a dent in the 8 or 10 million offenses reported to the police annually.

What cost? Prison operating expenses vary from around $10 to more than $30 per inmate per day. At $10, then, it costs $91,250,000 to confine 25,000 prisoners for one year. Not all of this can be charged to incapacitation, however, since 10% of the cohort could be expected to return to prison if released. Assuming that the average stay outside of prison is six months in these cases, the cost of reconfinement for the rest of the year is slightly more than $4.5 million. Subtracting this from the previous total leaves $86,687,500 as the amount presumably required to prevent 2,500 crimes. That is $34,675 for each offense prevented, about the same as in the New York transport system. And this cost-benefit ratio is inclined to get worse after the first year, inasmuch as parole violation rates tend to get lower with the passage of time.

Incapacitation might have other counterproductive side effects. Delay of parole rarely means permanent imprisonment. Ordinarily, prisoners are discharged, regardless of risk, at the expiration of their sentences (van den Haag recommends "post-punishment incapacitation" for recidivists and dangerous offenders, pp. 250-251). Whether crime is prevented therefore depends, in the long run, on the relationship between recidivism and time served. If recidivism increases with lengthier sentences, as most studies seem to suggest, crimes may merely be deferred instead of prevented by continued confinement.

Delayed release also contributes to the growing prisoner population. Although the United States has long maintained the highest rate of incarceration in the Western world, the number of prisoners is increasing by more than 10% per year. It has now reached 250,000 —the highest in our history. Even before incapacitation came into vogue, blueprints for many new prisons were on the drawing board, their projected cost running into billions of dollars. Secure facilities are built for around $50,000 per cell, not counting the cost of amortizing public bonds, and housing for 25,000 prisons would run to about one and a quarter billion dollars. Even when prorated over 20 or 40 years, including maintenance and operations, this may more than double the price of imprisonment, whether it affects crime rates or not.

It seems fair to question whether incapacitation by imprisonment has any advantage over other alternatives in protecting citizens against crime. Prisons generally cost more and probably achieve less in the long run. Their effects on offenders are mainly social and economic, often making pariahs out of ordinary street criminals, while wealthy and powerful criminals go free.

Incapacitation has a certain attraction for persons in positions of power and authority. By equating justice with the administration of punishment, it helps preserve the government's monopoly over legal force and coercion. By directing the people's attention to street crimes, it tends to make things a little safer for those who profit from corruption in high places. By justifying the isolation of offenders on moral grounds, it shelters the justice system from public criticism and empirical investigation. In the end, just deserts and incapacitation provide little more than an apologia for prolonged imprisonment of common criminals—certainly one of the oldest, best tested, and most thoroughly discredited of all forms of crime control.

Boys' Washing Room, New York House of Refuge

JUVENILE JUSTICE, DELINQUENCY PREVENTION, AND SOCIAL POLICY

CHAPTER 8

Criticism of the nation's methods of handling wayward youth continues to grow in the wake of recent changes in court practice and ideology. The *parens patriae* doctrine and belief in the rehabilitative ideal are being challenged by critics on the left and the right. The articles in this chapter are intended to bring the reader up-to-date with current policy issues in juvenile justice. It is hoped that the information and analyses provided in earlier chapters will help to advance a critical perspective on questions of public policy.

Policies are always shaped by understandings of social structure, such that proponents of concrete social action tend to offer proposals consistent with their overall views of society. For example, some liberals respond to the current crisis of confidence in juvenile justice by reaffirming their faith that reform lies in reducing the ability of the state to intervene in the lives of children. This view, which is consistent with classical liberal theory, offers policy recommendations such as diversion, de-institutionalization, decriminalization of status offenses, and the expansion of due process rights to juveniles. In contrast, conservatives generally call for a return to the more traditional and punitive methods of the past, arguing that the present court is too permissive. The failure of treatment is understandable to them, since they do not believe that social welfare approaches will positively motivate the poor. Conservatives stress policies based on the theory of deterrence, and call for more severe penalties, longer periods of incarceration, and reform of the present system to make it more efficient and less costly.

Radicals argue that reform of the present system is only possible within the context of broader reform of the entire society. Generally, they support short-term reforms to encourage redistribution of power to community groups and the poor. They support programs designed and overseen by community groups, and programs that offer alternatives to the existing system.

The direction of reform is of crucial significance to those who work in the juvenile justice system, and to those who have traditionally borne the brunt of the system's inequities. The following selections represent a range of opinions in support of various policy positions.

The first piece, by Jerris Leonard and Thomas Madden, is an analysis of the role of the federal government in funding juvenile delinquency prevention programs. The authors claim that while the Law Enforcement Assistance Administration (LEAA) "was established for the purpose of dealing with the root causes of crime," the problems of unemployment and educational deprivation are too distantly related to the problem of crime to receive federal funds. Leonard and Madden express the official LEAA position that the main purpose of the funding is to assist existing justice agencies in building their operational capacities. Ironically, their rationale for ignoring programs designed to prevent delinquency is that prevention strategies have not been effective, while traditional practices such as probation and incarceration have been. The net result of this LEAA position is to keep funding in the hands of the same persons who currently control the juvenile justice system.

In contrast, the selection from the White House Conference on Children held in 1970 expresses a need for an expansive federal role in the area of youth development and delinquency prevention. The authors of this selection feel that government should be responsible for the development of healthy identities among the young. Children are seen as powerless social actors, whose needs are often ignored or sacrificed to the goals of those in power. The White House Conference on Children recommends that the nationwide neglect of children be remedied through the development of a base of power for children at all levels of government.

The next article, by Andrew Rutherford, reports on the dramatic efforts in 1970 in Massachusetts to close down all of the juvenile training schools. By effective mass media appeals, the director of Youth Services, Jerome Miller, was able to mobilize sufficient political strength to gain support for his "Children's Crusade." Miller believes that the best way to reform the juvenile justice system is to destroy the most repressive elements of the system, and thus force other components of the process to adjust their practices to the new social arrangements. There was a rapid and virulent campaign to denounce and discredit the Massachusetts experiment by many of the vested interests of the juvenile justice system, especially judges and training school administrators. In his article, Rutherford provides careful answers to each of these criticisms. Despite the apparent successes of Miller in Massachusetts, there does not appear to be a huge constituency supporting similar efforts in other jurisdictions. Indeed, Miller has found grave difficulties in his efforts to replicate the "Children's Crusade" in Illinois and Pennsylvania.

A number of community-based alternatives to the present juvenile justice system are currently being tried. San Francisco journalist Dexter Waugh reports on the development and history of such programs in the San Francisco Bay Area. This article provides an excellent description of the philosophies and styles of these alternative programs, and details the difficult relationships that develop between these groups and court officials. Waugh analyzes the forces contributing to the co-optation of community efforts by the justice system. In addition, he discusses the central issues inherent in bringing about meaningful alternatives to established methods of processing youth.

The final piece, by Sheldon Messinger, reviews the research of Paul Lerman on community-based corrections programs in California. Lerman's research is at the center of controversy concerning the merits of de-institutionalization programs. Messinger provides a useful summary of the Lerman research, as well as a fine description of the methodological limits of Lerman's approach. More importantly, Messinger expands the focus of Lerman's research in the area of public policy by elaborating on the issues involved in de-institutionalization strategies. Messinger points out that such community-based strategies may actually expand the network of control over children.

One can only speculate about the future course of reform efforts in the juvenile justice area. The point of this chapter is to promote a critical understanding of the various reforms and changes occurring today. If we can understand the present system, and continue to search for alternative answers to long-standing contradictions in the juvenile justice process, we will move a step toward improving social justice for the Children of Ishmael.

Federal Anticrime Funds for Juvenile Delinquency Prevention

JERRIS LEONARD and THOMAS J. MADDEN*

Jerris Leonard is associated with the Law Enforcement Assistance Administration. Thomas J. Madden is associated with the
Law Enforcement Assistance Administration.

Reprinted from the National Advisory Committee Task Force
on Community Crime Prevention, Washington, D.C.: U.S.
Government Printing Office.

HEADNOTE

The sharply rising desire of States and communities to reduce crime through the prevention of juvenile delinquency has generated new calls for Federal funds to support those efforts. Fundamental questions have arisen about the use of funds from the Law Enforcement Assistance Administration (LEAA) to support programs which only remotely touch the juvenile justice system.

These programs may be meritorious, but does LEAA have the authority to support them? What was the intent of Congress in this regard? What interpretation should LEAA place on the basic statutes? What is the proper role of other Federal agencies in this area? How can Federal resources best be focused on the prevention of juvenile delinquency—which may prove to be one of the Nation's most important attacks on crime at all levels.

INTRODUCTION

Assume that a public school superintendent wants to establish an alternate remedial education program for high school dropouts who may, he thinks, tend to become juvenile delinquents.

Is that program eligible for funding from the Law Enforcement Assistance Administration (LEAA)? From some other Federal agency?

Is the situation any different if the dropouts have in fact been adjudicated as delinquent or are on probation?

Assume that a mayor wants to establish a program of professional counseling for any youths who seek it at community guidance centers.

*The authors wish to acknowledge the invaluable research assistance of Patricia Trumbull of the Georgetown University School of Law.

This paper has been submitted to the *Kansas University Law Review* for publication.

Is that program eligible for LEAA funds? Is the situation any different if the counseling is directed at youths showing an early tendency to use drugs?

These are examples of typical program ideas that abound in the United States. All States and most communities are developing innovative approaches to the prevention of juvenile delinquency.

A central issue concerns the legal authority of LEAA to support such programs. Analysis of this issue depends upon an understanding of the intent of Congress in establishing LEAA, of the funding machinery operated by LEAA, of the statutory scheme Congress has enacted involving other Federal agencies, and of what is meant by "prevention" in the first place.

A precise differentiation among the many Federal agencies involved in juvenile delinquency clearly is desirable. Without a neat assignment of certain roles of certain agencies, there will be duplication of effort, wasted funds, and probably a number of missed opportunities in terms of support for worthy programs.

The stakes in this area are high. States and communities generally lack the financial resources to do an adequate job, and are looking to the Federal Government for financial assistance—if not for policy guidance and technical and expert advice.

Federal assistance is available in large measures. In fiscal year 1971, the Federal Government financed general youth development programs with funds totaling about $10.5 billion. Almost $1 billion was spent specifically on juvenile delinquency programs, including such programs as education and counseling services, community activities, juvenile correctional centers and rehabilitation efforts, and research and training.

LEAA alone spent about $100 million on juvenile delinquency programs in fiscal year 1972 and anticipates continuing to spend a large proportion of its funds in this area. The LEAA budget for fiscal 1973 is $850 million.

LEAA has been criticized from both ends of the spectrum of juvenile delinquency prevention programming. Some critics say that it has been too restrictive in its interpretations of the law and in its policies, and that it could broaden its definition of juvenile delinquency. Other critics contend that LEAA has gone too far in allowing its funds to be used for programs not specifically related to juvenile offenders.

This paper explores the efforts of LEAA to meet this issue, it describes how the issue developed, and it proposes guidelines for eventual adoption by LEAA.

LEAA DEFINITION OF THE PROBLEM

LEAA has tried to devise a plan or set of standards that would delineate its funding authority in delinquency prevention. First, an attempt was made to define the problem and categorize the types of programs which were involved.

A study was made of the kinds of programs that conceivably could be employed in delinquency prevention. LEAA examined these program types to determine how involved the agency already was in each, and whether such involvement was tenable given the legislative mandate and goals. At this point, thought was being given to using program typologies to guide funding.

As a result of this study, delinquency prevention programs were divided into four categories or levels: Level I, programs within the juvenile justice system; Level II, programs targeted solely for juvenile delinquents and/or potential delinquents; Level III, programs which service referrals from the juvenile justice system among others; and Level IV, programs which seek to prevent delinquency by attacking the known characteristics of juvenile delinquents. These levels represented the entire spectrum of delinquency programming in which LEAA might be involved or could envision itself being involved under Title I authority.

The order of the levels indicated the order of program types from the least controversial and most clearly fundable under Title I, to the most controversial and least clearly fundable.

Level I encompassed all those programs employed in conjunction with any aspect of law enforcement and the juvenile justice system, as long as the program was exclusively devoted to youths within the juvenile justice system. Level I would include all those programs, community-based or otherwise, to which a juvenile and/or his family is referred after official police contact, after contact with any youth division section of the police, or other intake officer, or any program, service, or facility employed by intake officers, social service officers, probation officers, courts, parole, and so forth.[1]

These programs are the most closely related to law enforcement and the criminal justice system, which are the prime areas of LEAA focus. Although greatly needed, however, these programs are not purely preventive in nature because they seek to service youth who are already within the juvenile justice system. They are, however, unquestionably fundable with LEAA money.

Level II encompassed a broader scope of programs. This level includes those programs directed toward youths who had given the community some reason to believe they were potential delinquents. In order to develop such programs, it was necessary to develop means of identification. It was thought that this identification could be done on either a case-by-case basis[2] or on an area basis.[3]

Level III programs were viewed as an alternative to Level II. Level III programs encompassed any program that serviced juveniles who were referrals from the juvenile justice system. With a determination of a certain percentage of such referrals, LEAA funds justifiably might be used to totally fund the program.

The final level, Level IV, encompassed all other programs that sought to stop delinquency before its occurrence by addressing characteristics of known juveniles.[4] This program area tended to be highly speculative without much empirical evidence in support. This is also the area on which other Federal agencies are focusing; therefore, LEAA involvement here has met with a great deal of criticism.[5] This is precisely the area around which the controversy over the scope of LEAA's prevention effort has revolved.

After delineating these categories,[6] a limited effort was made to see how delinquency prevention programs already funded in 1971 fitted into these four levels.

An intra-agency study based on a sampling (one State) of the 10 LEAA Regions,[7] indicated that out of approximately 110 juvenile programs, only 29 programs were not limited to Level I. Of the 110, only about seven did not involve youths determined by the respective States to be high risk or potential delinquents. Only five of the 110 did not include among their clientele youths referred from the juvenile justice system, even though the rest of the recipients were not even always high risk youth. This is a small sampling but it shows how cautious States have been in delinquency prevention. This is not to say that such caution is desirable, but it does illustrate an apparent lack of abuse.

This caution probably can be attributed to the unwritten policy that LEAA funds were to be used exclusively for activities within the criminal justice system. Prevention was viewed as recidivism prevention rather than delinquency prevention. Once a youth was in the juvenile justice system, LEAA money could be used without doubt for any program, service, facility, or equipment necessary. The few States that ventured into programs somewhat or completely outside the criminal justice system, although justifying their adventure as necessary to combat delinquency in their circumstances, did so at their own risk. Since in-house policy and legislative intent were and still are somewhat vague, these States might or might not be questioned about the propriety of using LEAA funds to support their programs.

THE BLOCK GRANT APPROACH

LEAA's basic fund disbursement machinery, the block grant,[8] is premised upon a concept of regionalization and localization of government.

In 1967 the President's Commission on Law Enforcement and Administration of Justice indicated that much of the responsibility for effective crime reduction measures and criminal justice system improvements must be borne by State and local governments with Federal aid.[9]

Partly in response to this report and partly in response to the overwhelming national need for an improved law enforcement and criminal justice system, Title I of the Omnibus Crime Control and

Safe Streets Act [hereinafter Title I] was enacted.[10] This act created LEAA and a fund disbursement program which emphasized law enforcement improvement at the State and local level.[11]

Pursuant to this regional concept, Title I established a matching grant-in-aid program under which LEAA makes annual block planning and action grants to the States.[12] The grants are called block grants because the funds are required by Title I to be allocated in lump sums among the States, on the basis of population. It was intended that funds distribution and expenditure be by the States and cities according to criteria and priorities determined by them.[13] Although 85 percent of action funds must be disbursed in the block grant programs, LEAA also makes discretionary grants which may be directly distributed by LEAA to the States for categorical purposes.[14]

Block planning grants are utilized by the States to establish and maintain State Planning Agencies [hereinafter SPA's] which are appointed by and are under the jurisdiction of the chief executive of the State.[15] Each SPA determines its needs and priorities for the improvement of law enforcement throughout the State. It also defines, develops, and correlates programs—including juvenile delinquency prevention programs—to improve and strengthen law enforcement for its State and all the units of local government within it.

The accumulated information is then incorporated into a comprehensive statewide plan for the improvement of law enforcement and the reduction of crime in that State and the plan is submitted to LEAA for review and approval.[16]

When a State plan has been reviewed and approved, the State is eligible to receive its allocated block action grant for that fiscal year. It should be noted that LEAA is required by statute to make block action grants if the SPA has an approved comprehensive plan which conforms with the purposes and requirements of the Safe Streets Act,[17] and with rules, regulations and procedures established by LEAA consistent with the Safe Streets Act.[18]

None of the conditions or guidelines imposed by LEAA is in conflict with the basic principles of the block grant concept.

Given the block grant approach, with its virtual "hands off" character, LEAA's involvement in the implementation of juvenile delinquency prevention programs can be no more than vicarious. It is clear that LEAA cannot under this funding system dictate the program areas that must or should be pursued by the States. This funding method is a real, although desirable, limitation on this Federal agency's influence on the character of prevention programming.

With certain minimal limitations, the States are the sole determiners as to their program needs. They are to establish the extent of their delinquency problem and how best to combat the problem. Due to the degree of self-determination involved under this funding approach, LEAA has incurred an interesting problem unparalleled in any other area of criminal justice planning.

Prevention may encompass projects not immediately related to the occurrence of crime. Can such projects deemed worthy by the SPA's be funded with LEAA money? Does LEAA have the authority to limit the breadth of their prevention involvement? Assuming that it does, does LEAA want to limit the breadth of delinquency prevention programming?

Possible answers to these and other questions require an inquiry into the background of Title I for legislative guidance.

PREVENTION FUNDING AUTHORITY UNDER TITLE I

This discussion focuses on those provisions concerning crime prevention generally, as well as provisions concerning juvenile delinquency prevention and control. This is done to give the reader a better idea of the role prevention plays in LEAA's mandate to reduce crime and delinquency.

Legislative language

The language of Title I suggests that Congress envisioned the use of LEAA funds in some crime prevention activities. Examples of this language are contained in the following provisions: the Congressional Findings section, where Congress speaks of the need of coordinated and intensified efforts at all levels of government in order to prevent crime and assure the people's safety;[19] section 301(b)(1) authorizes the use of action grants for the implementation of methods and devices to improve law enforcement and reduce crime;[20] section 301 (b)(3) addresses public education relating to crime prevention among other things;[21] section 301(b)(9) directly concerns the development and operation of community-based delinquency prevention programs;[22] and section 601(a) defines law enforcement as used throughout the Title, as any activity pertaining to crime prevention.[23]

These examples say nothing of the specific references to other prevention efforts relating to organized crime, civil disturbances, and community service officer directed neighborhood programs.[24]

There seems to be little doubt that Title I authorized the funding of crime and delinquency prevention programs. The basic question, however, is what is prevention as envisioned by Congress? How encompassing was crime prevention intended to be? This is especially relevant since prevention can be and has been interpreted by experts in the field as crossing through all segments of human life.[25]

Given the potential breadth of prevention, it is necessary to explore whether the prevention effort enunciated by Congress in this act was intended to allow the funding of activities remotely or indirectly related to actual crime and the system which deals with criminal law violators.

Legislative history

The language of Congressional Findings section and sections 301(b) (1) and (3) concern the objectives of the 1968 act, which are further explained by way of delineation of specific program areas and include crime prevention. These objectives changed little during the act's historical development, as evidenced by the similarity of the language of section 301 in both the House and Senate bills.[26] Thus, it can be assumed that from the beginning, crime prevention was intended by Congress to be a key aim of the act. During hearings in the House, the Attorney General testified that the proposed grant program would include, among other things, crime prevention programs in schools, colleges, welfare agencies, and other institutions.[27]

Further evidence of the intent that prevention programs be funded can be seen in the supplemental comments by Representatives William McCullock and Charles McC. Mathias, Jr., in the House report indicating that they supported Title I because they envisioned it as a moderate, progressive approach combining improvements in law enforcement and criminal justice along with advances in rehabilitation and prevention. This they felt was a desirable alternative to an approach that focused on social ills or an approach which fostered a "police state" system.[28]

These comments give weight to the idea that although LEAA is to be involved in crime and delinquency prevention, it was not intended that it become involved in the sociological aspects of prevention which are not somehow related to the criminal justice system.

The Senate Report (1968) indicates that the act's purpose was:

1   to encourage States and local governments to adopt comprehensive plans to increase the effectiveness of their law enforcement (which includes prevention);
2   to authorize grants to States and local governments to improve and strengthen their law enforcement;
3   to encourage research and development toward strengthening law enforcement, and the development of new prevention methods;
4   to control and eradicate organized crime; and
5   to control and prevent riots.[29]

As explicit as this enumeration of purpose is, it still fails to shed light on what was intended or even anticipated when prevention funding was authorized.

In the 1971 amendments to Title I, the House proposed to change the definition of law enforcement as follows:

> . . . all activities pertaining to the administration of criminal justice, including, but not limited to, police efforts to prevent crime and to apprehend criminals, activities of the criminal courts and related agencies, and activities of corrections, probation, and parole.[30]

The Senate rejected this definition because it was not broad enough. It was then revised in the Senate Judiciary Committee:

... to make sure that the term would remain as broad in coverage as it is under the present Act.

The language finally agreed upon covers "... all activities pertaining to crime prevention or reduction and enforcement of the criminal law."[31]

The Senate's rejection and the final agreement on the present definition as amended indicate that the intended concept of prevention was broader than just police efforts to prevent crime. It is thus reasonable to assume that LEAA's prevention mandate is broader than the criminal justice system, and LEAA's funding authority in regard to juvenile delinquency prevention, though not explained, also is not so limited by legislative language or history.

The legislative history of section 301(b)(9), added by the 1971 amendments, indicates that it was intended to act as an incentive for the States to initiate community-based prevention and rehabilitation facilities for juveniles, although such facilities had always been fundable under the act.[32] It appears that Congress was mainly concerned with the community-based rehabilitation aspect and it once again left the prevention aspect unexplained—and unlimited.

Subsequent to the enactment of Title I and its amendments, the use of LEAA funds in prevention activities became the subject of congressional criticism.[33] In a House Committee on Government Operations' report, LEAA funded programs that were outside the criminal justice system, but were theoretically related to the grantee's delinquency prevention needs as determined by them, were considered by the Committee as misallocation of funds for activities outside the funding purview of Title I.

This criticism, whether accurate or not, resulted in a chain reaction cry from the SPA's for more direction as to what is eligible for delinquency prevention projects. This, of course, put pressure on LEAA to interpret a broad prevention mandate with little or no relevant history in an area that has no definable parameters of its own, and in such a way so as not to impinge on the "hands-off" nature of the block grant.

LEAA was specifically criticized for allowing the use of its funds for a learning disability workshop for preschoolers and an employment project.[34] Regardless of whether these projects are fundable under Title I, the Committee legitimately pinpointed a problem that is inherent in prevention program funding: What is prevention? As shall be seen, this is not easily answered and Congress never attempted to answer it in either Title I or the legislative history of the act. If prevention does include such things as education and employment, should LEAA fund these activities, especially when other agencies are purposely authorized and funded to concentrate on these activities?

JUVENILE DELINQUENCY PREVENTION ACT

In 1968 Congress passed the Juvenile Delinquency Prevention and Control Act. The purpose of this act was to enable the Department of Health, Education, and Welfare (HEW) to assist and coordinate the efforts of public and private agencies engaged in combating juvenile delinquency.[35]

Unlike Title I, this act was a categorical grant program. Its thrust, however, was similar to that of LEAA's prevention mandate. The Juvenile Delinquency Act was intended to cover a whole spectrum of activities which LEAA, under its general mandate, also could fund. This seeming duplication became more pronounced after enactment of the 1971 amendments to Title I, when community-based juvenile delinquency prevention programming was specifically included as an action grant area.

Yet Congress evidently did not intend that the two programs work at odds with each other, or even duplicate the same efforts. Congress saw the Juvenile Delinquency Act as only a part of a larger, comprehensive effort to solve the problems of delinquency. As described by the Senate Report, this legislation:

> . . . will achieve its maximum potential only if administered as a part of an enlightened network of antipoverty, antislum, and youth programs. It should not just be another categorical program that is administered in relative isolation from much larger efforts such as Community Action Program, Model Cities, and the Manpower Development and Training Act. Moreover, the committee amendment requires effective coordination with Justice Department programs in the delinquency area.[36]

Although Congress may not have intended duplication, potential duplication was created. This potential was recognized and criticized at the time the legislation was drafted. Senator Javits pointed out that the overlapping and duplication of Federal programs was what he considered the major problem with the Juvenile Delinquency Prevention and Control Act.[37] He said, "The key to controlling crime in this country is to prevent juvenile crime and to provide effective rehabilitation of juvenile offenders."[38] Given this need and LEAA's goal-oriented mandate to reduce crime, it is clear that regardless of HEW's authority to invest in delinquency prevention, LEAA must also be involved in fulfilling this need to some extent.

After 1968, there was at least a rhetorical rivalry between HEW and LEAA as to their roles in juvenile delinquency prevention programming. An effort to delineate the roles of these two agencies was made in an exchange of letters between the Attorney General and the Secretary of HEW in 1971. It was agreed that the agencies must work in concert. It was also acknowledged that, as a practical matter, HEW would concentrate on prevention while LEAA concentrated on rehabilitation.[39]

More importantly, however, these letters gave official agency recognition to the need for coordination. This exchange also resulted in an agreement to combine State planning efforts so that the requirements of both agencies were fulfilled with one plan.

Because LEAA has been more adequately funded than the Youth Development and Delinquency Prevention Administration (YDDPA) of HEW, LEAA has become more dominant in this area, which has not tended to reduce the confusion about the agencies' roles.[40] This funding reality, coupled with LEAA's authority and willingness to become involved in delinquency prevention, have contributed to State and local reliance on LEAA funds for these efforts.

In 1971, the Juvenile Delinquency Prevention and Control Act of 1968 was amended and extended.[41] The amendments established an Interdepartmental Council to Coordinate All Federal Juvenile Delinquency Programs. The Attorney General is chairman of the Council, but he delegated that function to the Administrator of LEAA. This council is currently involved in four major areas. First, it is developing program, evaluation, and management data. Second, it is sponsoring a joint effort by the member agencies to coordinate their programs. Third, it is developing coordinating mechanisms at the Federal, State, and local levels. Finally, it is preparing for public hearings in which it will seek recommendations from private and public interest groups on implementing coordination goals.[42]

On August 14, 1972, Congress renewed and amended the Juvenile Delinquency Act.[43] The purpose and emphasis of this act was changed to reflect a division of responsibility between HEW and LEAA. The focus of the new act is the prevention of delinquency in youths by assisting States and local education agencies and other public and nonprofit private agencies to establish and operate community-based programs, including school programs.[44] One of the discernible differences, however, is that the emphasis in the act is on school-related programs. Although LEAA conceivably can, and has funded prevention programs concerning the schools, it is fair to say that the school has not and probably should not be the focal point for LEAA prevention efforts.

The 1972 amendments to the Juvenile Delinquency Act constituted an attempt to define the roles of HEW and LEAA in delinquency programming by specifically delineating HEW's role.[45] Some members of Congress saw LEAA as involved only in those areas of prevention encompassed by the criminal justice system, while they saw HEW as covering presystem programs, especially those operating in concert with the schools.

There is little doubt that the congressional framers of the Juvenile Delinquency Act and the congressional critics of LEAA have in mind a definite division in functions between the two agencies. Even so, the limitation on LEAA's authority that would result from this division is not warranted either by the language or legislative history of Title I.

Yet, considering all of these difficulties, good management and planning dictate that duplication in effort without increased dividends is not desirable. Duplication alone, however, may not be undesirable if the expected return is valuable, and if any one agency cannot sufficiently impact the area to produce the return. Basically, what is needed is not a division of labor or a jurisdictional stand-off, but a cooperative effort to achieve the specified goals. If one agency can more effectively treat an area than another agency, then it benefits all for the first agency to apply its expertise to that area. If, however, there are occasions for overlap, because such overlap has been deemed necessary to achieve a common desired goal, like the prevention of delinquency, then such overlap, if based on sound planning, may not be so abhorrent.

With such a broad legislative mandate, LEAA must be and is in the process of designing guidelines, standards, and planning mechanisms which hopefully will impact delinquency without engaging itself or encouraging its grantees to engage in wasteful duplication, while still being able to fund whatever the State and local authorities find necessary to improve their system and reduce crime.

PREVENTION: THE STATE OF THE ART

Much confusion about the kinds of delinquency prevention programs LEAA can and should fund stems from the fact that the state of the art of prevention is underdeveloped.

Legally, juvenile delinquency can consist of two things. It can be the violation of a criminal statute for which adults are also prosecuted.[46] Uniquely, however, it can also be the violation of certain behavioral prescriptions which apply only to children—that is, the status offenses.[47]

There are arguments for questioning the soundness of status offense legislation.[48] Some of these arguments are legally based and have constitutional implications.[49] Some are practical and sociologically based.[50] As far as LEAA is concerned, however, the status offenses are simply offenses for which children are adjudicated and detained as delinquents. All of these youths enter the system much as a criminal law violator does; unfortunately, they probably leave the system much as a criminal law violator does, as well.

LEAA's legislative goal is to reduce crime, and status offenders are not often thought to be engaged in crime, or at least not the type of crime that " . . . threatens the peace, security, and general welfare of the Nation and its citizens."[51] It might be said, therefore, that LEAA funds should not be expended in the prevention of youth deviancy culminating in status offenses such as truancy, waywardness, or failing to obey the reasonable commands of a parent.

To take such a position, however, denies reality. Whether criminal or not, these youthful offenders are treated as criminals and their respective jurisdictions have designated them as law violators. It seems reasonable that jurisdictions should be able to dedicate money and efforts toward diverting all youthful offenders. Any success in diverting these juveniles from the criminal justice system can be viewed as crime prevention; experience has proven that a large percentage of correctional system service recipients will return.[52] These juveniles would be better serviced by some other community agency without exposing them to the stigma and harshness of the criminal justice system.

If it is legitimate to use LEAA funds for juvenile delinquency prevention programs at all, therefore, it should be sound policy to extend such programs to include youths caught up in status offense violations.

With juvenile delinquency thus defined, it is appropriate to discuss the state of the art of juvenile delinquency prevention.

Crime prevention is a socially attractive goal, yet little is known about what it entails. There is still debate on whether crime can even be prevented.[53] As Peter Lejins points out, society is dealing here with something moralistically desirable, politically ripe, and scientifically undeveloped.[54]

There is a diversity of opinion among the social scientists about what direction prevention must take to be successful. One position, supported by the President's Commission on Law Enforcement and Administration of Justice in 1967, is that juvenile delinquency and youth crime are symptoms of a community's failure to provide services for itself.[55] The recommended response to this problem is to engage in comprehensive programming tending to upgrade the community services in hopes that the delinquency problem would also be solved.[56] The Commission recommended that three areas be considered: employment, education, and community services. The Commission advocated an " . . . opportunity to develop the necessary abilities and skills to participate meaningfully in society, and thereby to gain a sense of personal dignity and competence."[57]

Other theories stress the importance of addressing specifically identifiable areas of youth crime and delinquency, such as auto theft and burglary.[58] Supporters of these theories are skeptical that comprehensive programming can be implemented successfully in "the face of high mobility and social change in the inner city area."[59] They are concerned that the target population will be missed completely or that other variables will intercede and preclude successful prevention.[60]

One analysis of the varied concepts of prevention is provided by Peter Lejins in The Field of Prevention.[61] He identifies three kinds of prevention: punitive, corrective, and mechanical.

The theory behind punitive prevention is deterrence; forestalling delinquency by threatening punishment. This can be broken down into special and general prevention. Special prevention seeks to deter further criminal conduct by punishing the offender for past conduct. General prevention relies on vicarious punishment; it seeks to deter the individual by assuring the punishment of others who commit crime.[62]

The second type of prevention is corrective prevention. "Here prevention is based on the assumption that criminal behavior, just as any other human behavior, has its causes, is influenced by certain factors and is the result of a certain motivation . . . "[63] These prevention efforts concentrate on attacking causes, factors, or motivations before delinquency occurs.[64] This is the type of prevention most commonly advocated today even though its successful implementation is still primitive.

The third type of prevention is mechanical. This involves placing obstacles so that delinquent activity cannot be successfully performed. There is no attempt to affect personalities, motivations, or community deficiencies. The emphasis is on such things as increased police protection and better security devices. Crime is prevented by making criminal conduct more difficult.[65]

The two types of prevention most often funded by the States with LEAA funds are the latter two. Punitive prevention is legislative in nature and not of the type generally envisioned by Title I. Corrective prevention is perhaps the more popular. Mechanical prevention is an area in which LEAA funds are employed enthusiastically. Improved crime detection, police surveillance, high intensity lighting, and public security systems are apt subjects of LEAA funding.

The majority of delinquency prevention work is being done in the areas of symptom detection and treatment and of servicing high crime areas. The potentials for involvement are vast. Assuming that it is possible to identify characteristics common to delinquents by determining the common characteristics of youths who have already come into contact with the criminal justice system, it must still be decided if there is a reasonable correlation between these characteristics and antisocial behavior and what can be done to correct negative characteristics so that juveniles not yet within the system can be kept out of it. It must also be determined whether the program has achieved a reduction in delinquency.

The Task Force report on Youth Crime and Delinquency reinforces the pervasiveness of prevention with its recommendations for improvements in such institutions as the family, the community, the school, and the job,[66] especially in the inner city areas where the crime rate is high. This is Lejins' idea of corrective prevention at work. Most of the States with which LEAA works share this idea of prevention. Thus, LEAA as a matter of practical policy must establish how involved it can or should become in education, employment, family, and community services.

LEAA recognizes the elusive nature of prevention, especially corrective prevention, and the necessity for investment in this area. The goal is the reduction of crime. It is not the improvement of the Nation's education system, employment opportunities, or standard of living. If involvement in these areas can impact directly on crime and delinquency, then LEAA can allow its grantees to invest in this type of program. The key is the impact on delinquency either hypothetical—if previously untested—or real.[67]

DEVELOPING NEW LEAA GUIDELINES

Regardless of the evident reluctance to fund prevention programs outside the system, an increasing number of States have requested authority to fund what they consider legitimate delinquency prevention programs which focus on youth and youth problems prior to any contact with the system. This coupled with congressional criticism has led to the drafting of what LEAA considers minimum standards on the eligibility of juvenile delinquency prevention programs for LEAA funding.

After breaking the area down into the levels already discussed, the agency decided that any type of program typology—that is, listing fundable programs, programs that might be obviously ineligible for funding, and programs that would fall in the middle depending upon the circumstances—was an undesirable strategy given LEAA's "special revenue sharing" nature. It also was an undesirable method because due to the state of the art, it could be unnecessarily inhibiting; locking the States into programming which could become quickly outmoded. Rather than a list of "do's" and "don'ts," what was really needed was a process approach.

LEAA is now developing and trying to implement a planning process whereby the SPA's will learn to be able to identify their crime problem with greater accuracy, therefore enabling them to develop law enforcement and crime prevention projects which are specifically calculated to impact on the crime problem as it exists in their state.

This process is known as crime-specific planning. Its basic premise is that a planner should know the nature of his crime problem. Such things as the type of crime (burglary, rape, etc.), the victim (stranger to stranger, etc.), the frequency of occurrence, the time of occurrence, the criminal justice system response to the crime, the geographic area in which the crime is committed, and the characteristics of the offender must be documented before a criminal justice planner can adequately plan programs and projects of access needs and improvements in law enforcement and prevention.

Given this information, the planner can then make intelligent decisions as to the strategies required to combat crime. He can justify his decisions based upon his data and he can maximize his impact on the crime problem because he will know exactly what he is attacking and why, with some expectations as to the specific impact.

Since this process is aimed only at improving criminal justice planning and not at dictating specific program strategies, the "hands-off" character of LEAA's block grant approach is not jeopardized or undermined by Federal (LEAA) interference in State and local government programming decisions.

The appeal of this process approach as opposed to a program typology approach in the delinquency prevention area is obvious. As we have seen, juvenile delinquency is a multi-dimensional problem. There are many theories as to how to go about preventing delinquency, even though some of the theories are as of yet unproved. There are many agencies working in the general area of youth problems; therefore without definable parameters there is a great deal of potential overlap without a corresponding impact on crime. There is an obvious danger in locking the States into only certain approaches, not to mention the fact that such a static approach violates the spirit if not the letter of the block grant methodology. Therefore, the crime-specific planning approach is aptly suited to the needs of the SPA's in the area of juvenile delinquency prevention programming.

By implementing this planning process LEAA has drawn up tentative minimum standards for all LEAA grantees to help them in deciding whether their prevention programs and strategies are eligible for LEAA funding. The implementation of this process also assures LEAA and Congress that LEAA money is only being used for those prevention projects which are calculated to impact on delinquency. The key is the objective "[t]o prevent crime and to insure the greater safety of the people . . ."[68]

If prevention programs are reasonably premised upon preventing delinquency, based upon tangible data, and cost effectiveness analyses, then the program can hardly be questioned as being outside the purview of Title I. Such a process approach also allows the programming to progress with the progress in the state of the art of prevention.

It also allows States to progress with LEAA funding at a rate commensurate with their sophistication. It takes LEAA out of the position of overseeing the type of project or program proposed. If there are any doubts LEAA need only ask why, and if crime-specific planning has been implemented the SPA should have no problem showing LEAA why.

The standards as proposed are as follows:

1   Juvenile delinquency prevention programs exclusively within the criminal justice system.

        The following types of programs or projects are generally not considered problematical when funded by Part C action funds. It should be noted, however, that these programs are not always desirable in and of themselves, because all programs should be the result of careful goal-oriented planning. Thus, any program which is implemented without addressing a need, or which is not able to meet or achieve the envisioned prevention goals, is not desirable from a practical planning standpoint, and it does not work to achieve the overall goal of LEAA to reduce crime.

Programs which are devised and operated to service youths who have already come into the system through arrest or complaint (these contacts are considered to be prior to petitioning or prior to the decision to hold over for judicial action) are obviously fundable under Part C or Part E in whole or in part depending upon the character of the recipient population. Therefore, it is considered that community services or institutional services to which juveniles are referred by the police (this may even encompass those referral services employed by individual policemen in jurisdictions where they have the discretion to dispose of a juvenile prior to formal police action), by youth service divisions of police, by other intake officers, social service officers within the system, probation officers, courts, parole, corrections and etc. This could include both mandatory and voluntary programs.

These programs are all considered programs well within the juvenile justice system and as long as they are reasonably designed to reduce delinquency or the recurrence of delinquency and/or to improve the criminal justice system, they are of the type of program envisioned by Congress as eligible for action grants.

2 Delinquency prevention programs outside the criminal justice system.*

For programs which are intended to deal with the prevention of delinquency as opposed to the treatment of juveniles already considered delinquent, the following crime-oriented planning methodology must be employed. This approach is particularly appropriate for determining the eligibility of programs geared toward servicing what are commonly considered high risk youth, or youth who, although not yet involved in the system, are for some well reasoned, researched and documented reason considered on the verge of entering the system.

Necessary elements for planning an eligible program outside the criminal justice system.

    a. Crime or delinquency analysis—A State or local government must know how its delinquency problem manifests itself. It should know all characteristics of the problem it seeks to solve.

    b. Quantified objectives—Ideally, program or project objectives should be stated in terms of the

---

*Part C funds only may be used for these programs. Part E funds are bound by the additional requirement of use only within the criminal justice system.

anticipated impact on crime during a specified period of time and by a measurable amount. If, during crime analysis, the case can be made to establish more immediate quantified objectives that are not stated in crime impact terms, such objectives are acceptable if they meet the following criteria:

    (1) The sequential relationship between attaining the short-range objective and crime reduction is established.

    (2) The significance—when compared to other possible causative factors—of the behavioral or procedural circumstances to be impacted upon must be documented (e.g., truancy or narcotics use or court delay).

c.   Adequate data—Determining the adequacy of data will always be subjective, but the following list of questions will suggest the range and volume of data necessary for good program development:

    (1) Have you documented the juvenile crime problem in your jurisdiction by type of crime?

    (2) For each priority offense, what can you say about the event, the target or victim, the offender, and the criminal justice response to the event?

    (3) Does the data support the program alternative when compared against other programs that have different short-range objectives as well as programs that have similar objectives?

    (4) Is the program cost effective?

    (5) Can the program be effectively evaluated?

d.   Maintenance of supporting data—Supporting documentation should be on file at the SPA for LEAA monitoring or audit.

As a rule, if current data is inadequate or unavailable, the program should include a component that is designed to supply relevant usable data.

The key to this planning approach is two-fold. At all times the planner should be goal or objective oriented. These questions must always be asked and answered: Will this program impact on our delinquency problem? Why do we believe it will achieve this goal? In order to answer these questions the planner must know his problem and the reason for his chosen solution.

Since much confusion currently exists concerning the eligibility or appropriateness of LEAA funding juvenile delinquency prevention efforts that are ordinarily undertaken by agencies which lie outside of the criminal justice system, it is important that the cited crime-specific planning approach be faithfully implemented. The field of delinquency prevention is still new and sometimes still experimental, therefore any programming or funding decision which is based on less information than outlined above comes perilously close to an unauthorized diffusion of LEAA funds without any significant return in terms of improving law enforcement or reducing crime and delinquency, which is the goal for which LEAA money is appropriated.

Another factor which is not to be slighted is the need for coordination. Delinquency prevention is not an effort which can be successfully implemented with the money of any one agency or State. The delinquency prevention effort is broad and by necessity is the subject of many Federal and State agency funded programs. LEAA money alone cannot sufficiently solve the problem of delinquency, therefore all criminal justice planners should be cognizant of other funding and expertise potentials. LEAA grantees should make a concerted effort to seek funds from those other agencies whose normal scope of activities encompasses areas which may be the focus of delinquency prevention programs.

In this way the delinquency prevention effort benefits from the increased source of funds, the wide variety of experts, and the comprehensive impact. The most obvious example of this cooperative need is in the area of education. The potentialities for delinquency prevention programs in the schools are vast. HEW is the Federal expert in education, and HEW also has its own delinquency prevention authority, therefore programming involving education must be coordinated with HEW. Absence of such coordination jeopardizes additional fund sources and expert insights unique to other agencies.

3   Innovative delinquency prevention programming.*

This final category is intended to recognize the need for new untried approaches to delinquency prevention. Since the whole area of crime and delinquency causation and prevention is still developing there are necessarily programs and approaches designed by sophisticated criminal justice planners which may be so novel as to be dubiously

---

*Part C funds only may be used for these programs. Part F funds are bound by the additional requirement of use only within the criminal justice system.

eligible for funding by LEAA because of their apparent remoteness to the actual incidents of crime.

So as not to completely preclude the innovative initiation and implementation of programs which seek to reduce delinquency through treating symptoms of delinquency or characteristics of delinquents in youth who are not yet even considered high risk youth, such programs can be conceivably funded with LEAA money provided the following criteria are met:

a. All of the planning and data requirements of section 2 must be met.

b. The reduction of delinquency must be the goal and there must be a reasonable basis supported by documented data for the cause and effect relationship between the goal and the program.

c. There must be an extensive evaluation of the alternative programs along with a justification for the one chosen.

d. The program must be coordinated with other funding agencies which might also have cognizance of the program area.

e. There must be a cost effectiveness analysis.

f. The funding request should be approved by an affirmative vote of a majority of the SPA supervisory-board, so that the individual States have the responsibility of determining whether the program complies with the criteria envisioned in crime-specific planning.

g. The supporting justifications must be maintained on file with the SPA for monitoring or audit by LEAA.

CONCLUSION

Through crime-specific planning LEAA can effectively assure that those delinquency prevention programs which are funded under Title I will indeed impact the rate of youth crime. Even though there is some possibility that activities outside the juvenile justice system can be funded under this planning process, the goal of LEAA, fighting crime, will still be realized.

The minimum standards outlined by this agency stress that the problem of youth crime is not one which any one agency, State, or locality can combat alone. A comprehensive effort is necessary, therefore, LEAA grantees are compelled to seek out assistance, both monetary and technical from other agencies which are experts in the fields of employment, education, housing, recreation, and so forth.

LEAA must work to prevent juvenile delinquency within the parameters of the block grant concept and Title I. But that is not to say that this agency will be blind to the changing state of the art. Fighting crime is LEAA's mandate, therefore:

> LEAA's job is to impact immediately on crime itself. LEAA is not in the business, it is not charged with by Congress, and it wasn't established for the purpose of dealing with root causes.
> That does not mean that we're not concerned about them because we, in the criminal justice system, like everybody else, recognize that the criminal justice system deals with somebody else's failures. So we are interested in what the educational community and the welfare community, the entire social spectrum, are doing in the root cause area.[69]

NOTES

1   Parole and correction programs and services are also eligible for funding, independent of the prevention mandate in Title I, under Part F. Grants for Correctional Institutions and Facilities, Title I, *supra* § 451 et. seq.

2   Some credence is given to this approach by Virginia Burns and Leonard Stern in "The Prevention of Juvenile Delinquency," Task Force, *supra* at 353. They state that:

> ". . . we know enough about which danger signals require our attention. Some studies indicate that school failure—academic and behavior— is a reliable early warning sign, regardless of class and geography. Certain types of encounter with the police lead more frequently than others to continued and intensified delinquent acts. Older youths who are out of school and unemployed have a greater potential for delinquent involvement than others. Young people who have been through some part of the correctional system and have returned to the free society with the record and association of institutionalization have a significant rate of recidivism. And certain signs of disengagement and alienation may be precursors to delinquency."

3   "In many census tracts of inner city slum areas, huge proportions—up to 70 percent or more—of all youth find themselves in trouble with the law at some point in their adolescence. Given this fact, we can assume that, in such areas, all youth are vulnerable, and prevention efforts based on such probabilities should provide services and opportunities across the board to all youth." *Id.* at 362.

4   The theory of Level IV is that certain characteristics as education, employment, status, use of narcotics can be determined from present prison populations and that some cause and effect decisions may be deducible from this information. Note that any reference to programs which seek to alleviate the causes of crime is purposely avoided because the determination of crime or delinquency causes is considered even more tenuous than either prevention itself or a causal relationship between verifiable characteristics of offenders and the occurrence of the offense.

5   H. R. Rep. No. 92-1072, *supra* (note 50).

6   These categories were not intended necessarily to be sociologically acceptable but were intended only as illustration tools within LEAA. By way of this categorizing process, it was hoped that the problem LEAA was addressing could be more clearly delineated so that the agency could develop a position on prevention that would neither inhibit effective prevention techniques that might still be in the infant stage of development while at the same time would not allow rampant diffusion of LEAA money into areas addressed by other agencies and remotely connected with crime.

7   The 10 States which were sampled were Massachusetts, New Jersey, Pennsylvania, Georgia, Kansas, California, Illinois, Texas, Washington, and Colorado. These States were picked only because they each represent one of the 10 regions into which the country is divided. The analysis of their programs came from their 1971 comprehensive State plans. All program analyses are based upon proposed programming under Part C and Part E of Title I. Discretionary grants were not considered.

8   Block grant is the disbursement of a lump sum amount of money based upon a legislative formula which will be more specifically disbursed by the State.

9   President's Commission on Law Enforcement and Administration of Justice, *The Challenge of Crime in a Free Society*, xi (1967).

10   Act of June 19, 1968, P. L. 90-351, Title I, 82 Stat. 197 et seq.; amended by P. L. 91-644, Title I, January 2, 1971, 84 Stat. 1881 [hereinafter Title I].

11   Title I, *supra*, § 100, Congressional Findings: "Congress finds further that crime is essentially a local problem that must be dealt with by State and local governments if it is to be controlled effectively.

     "It is therefore the declared policy of the Congress to assist State and local governments in strengthening and improving law enforcement at every level by national assistance. It is the purpose of this chapter to (1) encourage States and units of general local government to prepare and adopt comprehensive plans based upon their evaluation of State and local problems of law enforcement; (2) authorize grants to States and units of local government in order to improve and strengthen law enforcement; and (3) encourage research and development directed toward the improvement of law enforcement and the development of new methods for the prevention and reduction of crime and the detection and apprehension of criminals."

12   Title I, *supra*, § 201-205.

13   Title I, *supra*, § 202.

14   Title I, *supra*, § 306.

15   Title I, *supra*, § 202, 203.

16   Title I, *supra*, § 302.

17   Title I, *supra*, § 201.

18   Title I, *supra*, § 205.

19   Title I, *supra*, Congressional Findings:

     "Congress finds that the high incidence of crime in the United States threatens the peace, security, and general welfare of the Nation and its citizens. To *prevent crime* and to insure the greater safety of the people, law enforcement efforts must be better coordinated, intensified, and made more effective at all levels of government. (Emphasis added.)

20   Title I, *supra*, § 301(b)(1):

     "The Administration is authorized to make grants to States having comprehensive State plans approved by it under this subchapter for—(1) Public protection, including the development, demonstration, evaluation, implementation, and purchase of *methods, devices, facilities*, and *equipment* designed to improve and strengthen *law enforcement* (see § 601(a), and *reduce crime* in public and private places." (Emphasis added.)

21   Title I, *supra*, § 301(b)(3):

     "(3) Public education relating to *crime prevention* and encouraging respect for law and order, including education programs in schools and programs to improve public understanding of and cooperation with law enforcement agencies." (Emphasis added.)

22   Title I, *supra*, § 301(b)(9):
      "(9) The development and operation of community based *delinquent prevention* and correctional programs, emphasizing halfway houses and other community based rehabilitation centers for initial preconviction or postconviction referral of offenders; expanded probationary programs, including paraprofessional and volunteer participation; and community service centers for the guidance and supervision of potential repeat youthful offenders." (Emphasis added.)

23   Title I, *supra*, § 601(a):
      " 'Law Enforcement' means any *activity* pertaining to *crime prevention*, control, or reduction or the enforcement of the criminal law, including, but not limited to, police efforts to prevent, control, or reduce crime or to apprehend criminals, activities of courts having criminal jurisdiction and related agencies, activities of corrections, probation, or parole authorities and programs relating to *prevention*, control, reduction of *juvenile delinquency* or narcotic addiction." (Emphasis added.)

24   Title I, *supra*, § 301(b)(5)-(7).

25   "For 'crime' is not a single simple phenomenon that can be examined, analyzed, and described in one piece. It occurs in every part of the country and in every stratum of society. Its practitioners and its victims are people of all ages, incomes, and backgrounds. Its trends are difficult to ascertain. Its causes are legion. Its cures are speculative and controversial. An examination of any single kind of crime, let alone of 'crime in America,' raises a myriad of issues of the utmost complexity." President's Commission on Crime Report, *supra*, at 1.

26   The language of § 301(b)(1), (3), and (7) is very similar and in the case of § 301(b)(1) is identical to the language of H.R. 5037, *supra*, and S. 917, *supra*, the original bills. Neither the House Judiciary Committee nor House amendments changed the objectives of H.R. 5037. Though the Senate Judiciary Committee made slight changes in S. 917's objectives, the subsequent Amendment No. 715, *supra*, did not alter them. See Remarks of Senator Hruska, 114 Cong. Rec. S5349 (daily ed., May 10, 1968). This means that all stages of the legislative history regarding the objectives can be given greater credibility.

27   H. Rep. No. 488, 90th Cong., 1st Sess. 10 (1967).

28   Supplemental Comments of Congressman William McCullock and Charles McC. Mathias, Jr., H. Rep. No. 488, *supra*, at 24.

29   S. Rep. No. 1097, 90th Cong., 2d Sess. 30 (1968).

30   H.R. 17825, § 8(1)(a), 91st Cong., 2d Sess., June 30, 1970.

31   S. Rep. No. 1270, 91st Cong., 2d Sess., 37 (1970).

32   S. Rep. No. 91-1253, 91st Cong., 2d Sess. 30, 31 (1970).

33   House Committee on Government Operations, Block Grant Programs of the Law Enforcement Assistance Administration, H.R. Rep. No. 92-1072, 92nd Cong., 2d Sess. (1972).

34   H. R. Rep. No. 92-1072, *supra*, at 62.

35   "It is therefore the purpose of this act to help State and local communities strengthen their juvenile justice and juvenile aid systems, including courts, correctional systems, police agencies, and law enforcement and other agencies which deal with juveniles, and to assist communities in providing diagnosis, treatment, rehabilitative, and preventive services to youths who are delinquent or in danger of becoming delinquent." Juvenile Delinquency Prevention and Control Act of 1968, P.L. 90-445; 82 Stat. 462, Findings and Purpose [hereinafter J.D. Act].

36   S. Rep. No. 1332, 90th Cong., 2d. 2832 (1968).

37 Supplemental Comments by Senator Jacob K. Javits, S. Rep. No. 1332, *supra*, at 2, U. S. Code Cong. & Ad. News 2851 (1968).

38 S. Rep. No. 1332, *supra*, at 2, U. S. Code Cong. & Ad. News 2833 (1968).

39 Letter from the Secretary of Health, Education, and Welfare to the Attorney General and letter from the Attorney General to the Secretary of Health, Education, and Welfare in response, May 25, 1971.

40 Senate Committee on the Judiciary, The Juvenile Delinquency Prevention and Control Act Amendments of 1972, S. Rep. No. 92-867, 92d Cong., 2d Sess., 6 (1972).

41 Juvenile Delinquency Prevention and Control Act Amendments of 1971, P. L. 92-31.

42 Jerris Leonard and Thomas Madden, *The Role of the Federal Government in the Development of Juvenile Delinquency Policy*, ALA L. R. (1972).

43 Juvenile Delinquency Prevention Act, P. L. 92-381; 86 Stat. 532 (August 14, 1972).

44 P. L. 92-381, *supra*, § 101, Statement of Purpose.

45 "The bill also attempts to sort out the typical administrative mess of such programs by limiting the use of funds to projects outside the traditional court system, leaving that area to the Justice Department, which administers the Omnibus Crime Control and Safe Streets Act." 118 Cong. Rec. H6546 (daily ed., July 17, 1972), Remarks by Congressman Harrington.

46 See D. C. Code, § 16-2301(6), (7):
    "(6) The term 'delinquent child' means a child who has committed a delinquent act and is in need of care or rehabilitation.
    (7) The term 'delinquent act' means an act designated as an offense under the law of the District of Columbia, or of a State if the act occurred in a State, or under Federal law. Traffic offenses shall not be deemed delinquent acts unless committed by an individual who is under the age of sixteen."
    See also California Welfare and Institutions Code, § 602.
    See also The President's Commission on Law Enforcement and Administration of Justice, *Task Force Report: Juvenile Delinquency and Youth Crime*, 25-26 (1967) [hereinafter Task Force].

47 See D. C. Code, § 16-2301(8) (1971):
    "(8) The term 'child in need of supervision' means a child who—
        (A) (i) is subject to compulsory school attendance and habitually is truant from school without justification;
            (ii) has committed an offense committable only by children; or
            (iii) is habitually disobedient of the reasonable and lawful commands of his parent, guardian, or other custodian and is ungovernable; and
        (B) is in need of care or rehabilitation."
    See also, Task Force, *supra*, at 23, and California Welfare and Institutions Code, § 601.

48 See Edwin M. Lemert, *The Juvenile Court—Quest and Realities*, Task Force Report, *supra*, at 99 and 100 where Mr. Lemert points out that status offenders statutes risk the making of juvenile delinquents through the labelling process. These statutes also invite the use of the court to resolve conflicts that are not ordinarily handled in the criminal justice system. Also see Edwin M. Lemert, *Instead of Court, Diversion in Juvenile Justice*, National Clearinghouse 91 (1971), where Mr. Lemert calls for the annihilation of special classes of children's offenses.

49 See *E.S.G. v. State*, 447 S. W. 2d 225 (Tex. App. 1969); and *Smith v. State*, 444 S. W. 2d 941 (Tex. App. 1969).

50 Stigma is always a problem when anyone enters the criminal justice system but is an unjustified problem when children by legislative definition are stigmatized without even having engaged in criminal conduct.

51 Title I, *supra*, Congressional Findings section.

52 See generally McKay, Report on the Criminal Careers of Male Delinquents in Chicago, Task Force Report, *supra*, at 107. In recognition of the recidivism problem the Congress placed special emphasis on upgrading the correctional system when it passed the 1971 amendments, P. L. 91-644, *supra*.

Congressman Nedzi, in support of these amendments, stated, "The youth offender constitutes the largest and most virulent portion of the danger on the streets of our cities. His recidivism rates are enormously high.

"We simply must get them off the streets, then do a better job of saving them once they are off the streets." Cong. Rec. H6207 (daily ed., June 30, 1970).

53 Harlow, Prevention of Crime and Delinquency, A Review of the Literature, citing Durkheim, The Rules of the Sociological Method (1938), in 1 National Council on Crime and Delinquency, *Information Review on Crime and Delinquency* 2 (1969).

54 The field of prevention is by far the least developed area of criminology: Current popular views are naive, vague, mostly erroneous, and for the most part devoid of any awareness of research findings; there is a demand for action on the basis of general moralistic beliefs, discarded criminological theories of bygone days, and other equally invalid opinions and reasons. In scientific and professional circles the subject of prevention has received remarkably little serious attention. There has been very little theory-building, and attempted research under such circumstances has failed to produce any significant result." Lejins, The Field of Prevention, *supra* at 1-2.

55 Wheeler, Cottrell, and Romasco, Juvenile Delinquency—Its Prevention and Control in Delinquency and Social Policy 428 (Peter Lejins ed. 1970).

56 *Id.*

57 *Id.* at 429.

58 *Id.* at 430.

59 *Id.* at 431.

60 *Id.*

61 Lejins, The Field of Prevention, *supra*.

62 *Id.* at 3.

63 *Id.* at 4.

64 *Id.*

65 *Id.* at 5.

66 Task Force, *supra*, 41-56.

67 Congressman Smith aptly summed up the problem and articulated the need in his dialogue with Jerris Leonard in the 1973 House Appropriations Hearings: "It seems to me that this is where the weakness in the whole program is. We need money for law enforcement, but it's going to turn people off if you don't use it in a way that will do the most good." Hearings on 1973 Appropriations Before the Subcommittee on Department of State, Justice, and Commerce, The Judiciary, and Related Agencies of the House Committee on Appropriations. 92d Cong., 2d Sess., pt. 1, at 1126.

68 Title I, *supra*, Congressional Findings section.

69 Jerris Leonard at a press conference in Portland, Oreg., June 19, 1972.

Emergence of Identity

From the WHITE HOUSE CONFERENCE ON CHILDREN (FORUM 2)

"Emergence of Identity." From *Report to the President: White House Conference on Children* (Washington, D.C.: U.S. Government Printing Office, 1970).

To discuss the problems of emergence of identity, some common understandings about the meaning of "identity" are important. In the behavioral science literature, having a sense of identity has come to mean being able to answer satisfactorily the questions, "Who am I?" and "Where am I going?" Some would add, "Where did I come from?" The "Who am I?" includes knowing what I can do, what I am unable to do, what kind of person I am, and what is my best way of doing things. The "Where am I going?" includes an understanding of such things as what I can become, what I can learn to do, what I cannot learn to do, and what I want to become.

A strong sense of identity, however, is not enough. What is needed is a healthy sense of identity—one both favorable and realistic. The following characteristics have been attributed to the person with a healthy sense of identity:

- A feeling of being in one piece, with an integrated rather than confused or diffused self-concept
- Certainty about one's place in the world and about how to behave
- Autonomy as a person and confidence in self, ability to establish and maintain independent judgments without reference to external sources
- Insistence upon being oneself rather than playing at being oneself
- High capacity for empathy and for respecting the identity of others

There are many types of identity—ethnic and cultural, religious, political, economic, physical, sexual, and intellectual. Identity involves all aspects of a person's being. Research during the past few decades has firmly established the validity of the concept of the uniqueness of each individual. And more recent evidence strongly indicates that the foundation for this individual unique identity is established in the early years.

To fully realize one's human potential, each person must have a strong, healthy identity and must recognize, acknowledge, and respect the identity of others in the same terms. Today we fall short on both counts, often because broad discrepancies exist between common social practices and knowledge about individuality. Many children develop both unfavorable and unrealistic identities; many lack virtually any identity.

Several workshops tried to formulate new and more satisfying definitions of identity. Some of the more interesting ones are listed below.

- My identity depends upon my knowing who I am, where I came from, who I may become and how I relate to others. Therefore, when I am young and helpless, people must give me what I must have to be aware, alert, healthy, and secure. I have a good identity if I know people like me, if people respect me, if I can do most of the things that are important to me—then, when I am old enough to know what I want to do with my life, I hope to live my life. I hope to live in and help shape a society that will give me that chance.

- Identity is a uniquely human characteristic which is a natural by-product of human experience. From birth (and before) a baby has a mind and experiences a private consciousness. The infant must relate as a separate being to things in the universe. The essence of human identity does not rest in ethnicity, language, sex, religion, or material surroundings. These are only variables of identity which can and do change—sometimes quite rapidly. The essence of identity is a person's capacity to think and to feel—to be a conscious being.

- Identity is the totality of one's thoughts and feelings about the universe—one's self, one's surroundings, others, and the unknown. As a child develops, he or she will become aware of and relate to more and more of a personal universe. The child will develop a positive, healthy identity only if capacities to think and feel are guided toward knowledge and love. Knowing and loving must expand with awareness, and a child must come to know and to love self and others. Only if these capacities continue to expand will the child be able to fulfill his or her human potential and become his or her true self. If this expansion of knowledge or love is frustrated or blocked, the child will remain unhappy, unsatisfied, even disturbed.

- If a child is to be equipped to continue to grow and develop a strong, healthy identity, he or she will have a positive attitude toward those things that he or she does not know A child must learn to love the unknown and must be comfortable with infinity. He or she must become attracted to this unknown in himself or herself, in others, and in the universe itself.

- We believe that every human being has a right to optimally develop his potentialities. Every person is unique and each has his own potentialities, goals, precepts, liabilities, and assets. Society's task, then, is to help each child, without force or pressure, to grow in relationship to his uniqueness and to become a productive member of society.

Perhaps the dominating concern of the 1970 White House Conference on Children was to reaffirm the value of children. This concern has arisen because in America many adults have become separated, almost imperceptibly but surely, from the everyday lives of children. The worlds of childhood and adulthood must be more effectively meshed so children may both learn about, and try on, a variety of grown-up experiences; and so adults may share their children's dreams, thoughts, joys, disappointments, and, indeed, their playfulness. Understanding a child's developmental tasks is fundamental to drawing together adults and children. Such understanding can also reform and refocus both old and new programs designed for children and their families.

This report considers factors which enhance or impede the development of a child's sense of identity and suggests ways of ensuring that each child has the maximum opportunity for developing his own functional, healthy sense of identity—whatever his cultural, ethnic, or social background.

The phrase "emergence of identity" emphasizes the creative, self-acting nature of human beings and implies that in the early years a child's sense of identity comes about unaided, and, in a sense, this is just what happens. Yet many things can happen to prevent a child from developing a sense of identity or to cause him to develop an unfavorable and unrealistic sense of identity.

Initially, the infant has no conscious sense of self and cannot differentiate between "me" and "not me." The beginnings of a sense of self originate in the infant's body through countless experiments involving touch, sight, hearing, smell, and movement. Gradually the notion dawns that things exist outside oneself.

Another aspect of identity emerges with a change in the infant's attachment to the predominant person or persons in his or her life from one based on need and need gratification (during the first six months) to one of love, largely independent of need gratification (second six months). The infant's sense of identity continues to emerge as he learns that certain actions elicit response from his environment.

Attaining the physical skill of creeping firmly establishes the infant's sense of separateness. Creeping enables him to discover and rediscover objects and learn that objects exist independently of his subjective experience. He begins to understand that people and things follow their own laws and not his, although he also begins increasing his repertoire of skills for controlling both people and things. He begins naming things and asking the names of new things encountered, a sign that he is aware of himself as one object among other objects.

By the time he is two and one-half years a child knows "I" and "you." He has learned that he is a person. He is now ready for the task of learning his sex identity. During his third, fourth, and fifth years, he begins to learn his family, ethnic, religious, economic, physical and athletic, and intellectual identity. This learning becomes increasingly complex depending upon the nature of the child's individuality and the way the environment treats it. The average three-year-old, for example, may learn little about his intellectual identity. Yet the intellectually gifted three- or four-year-old who begins reading without instruction may learn a great deal about it. Even if his parents try to prevent others from knowing that he reads, the child will learn that his accomplishment is unusual from his peers or adults who witness his verbal skills. If a child successfully accomplishes these multiple and demanding developmental tasks, he will have a firm beginning sense of identity by the age of six.

The work of Forum 2 cannot be fully understood without knowing something of how its recommendations have emerged. Before the task force met, the Chairman prepared a background paper delineating the issues and summarizing research information about them. In its first series of meetings, task force members listed problems regarding identity emergence during the early years, formulated ideas about how various persons might facilitate emergence of healthy identities, and proffered some ideas about how these persons might be educated to perform these roles. These problems were discussed from multiple viewpoints since the task force members, coming from immensely diverse backgrounds, included an Indian public health physician, a social worker, a child psychologist, a cartoonist, a religious educator, and a designer of child environments, to name but a few.

The task force identified the following major obstacles to the emergence of strong healthy identities;

- Deprivation (economic, psychological, social, cultural)
- Sex discrimination and overemphasis on socially determined sex differences unrelated to sexuality
- Ethnic, racial, and religious prejudice and discrimination
- Taboos against acceptance of biological identity
- Taboos against acceptance and expression of affection
- Failure to learn skills of mastery and competence
- Overemphasis on conformity and uniformity with a resultant discrepancy between a healthy identity and a functional identity

The task force generally agreed that parents are the most important mediators of these influences, but that even brief contacts with the following persons may also strongly influence emergence of identity in the early years:

- Workers in day care centers
- Workers in church nurseries and other religious organizations that work with children
- Pediatricians and pediatric nurses
- Child psychologists and child psychiatrists
- Welfare workers
- Writers of children's books, comic strips, television shows, films, etc.

Ideas for action by each of these groups were produced by Forum members.

- Workers in community agencies
- Architects, toy designers, environmental designers
- Lawyers, judges, etc.
- Trainers of personnel for nurseries, day care centers, kindergartens, and child development centers

In the second series of Forum meetings, the task force recognized that the emergence of identity in the early years is largely influenced by certain harmful cultural assumptions widespread in the United States. These cultural assumptions must be changed to reflect existing knowledge about the nature of man and human development. Some existing assumptions and their more valid alternatives are listed below.

Current cultural assumptions	*Alternative cultural assumptions*
• Man is innately evil.	• Man is born neither good nor bad but with dignity and innate potential for largely determining his "human" development.
• Giving attention to "inadequate" behavior motivates "adequate" behavior.	• Attending "adequate" behavior motivates "adequate" behavior.
• The good child is a modest child.	• Recognition and acceptance of positive characteristics are necessary for self-realization.
• Suffering produces character and prevents spoiling.	• Coping positively and constructively with developmental and emergency problems is healthy.

Current cultural assumptions	*Alternative cultural assumptions*
• Independent behavior is the behavior necessary to achieve personal and cultural competence.	• Interdependent behavior is the road to cultural competence and interpersonal satisfaction. Dependence is natural and healthy; it will diminish with increasing maturity.
• Competition is a behavior innate to the nature of man. (The only way one man can rise is to best someone else.)	• Each individual is unique and has particular strengths which must be valued.
• There is a superior race and/or set of cultural characteristics to be emulated. (Too much difference weakens the American way of life.)	• There is no superior race, sex, or set of cultural characteristics. Accept qualitative human differences without judging superiority or inferiority.
• Parenthood is essential to male and female actualization.	• Parenthood is only one socially acceptable alternative life style.
• Expression of feelings demonstrates weakness.	• Expression of feelings is essential to mental health.
• Genetics is the factor that determines what one is and what one can become.	• Genetics provides the basis for behavior, interacting with the internal and external environment.

It is not suggested that these assumptions and their alternatives exist as sharp dichotomies. Rather they should be thought of as part of a continuum.

This list is tentative and was not unanimously accepted by the Forum, although the delegates agreed that we need to reappraise our cultural assumptions and search for more valid ones.

When Forum task force members and delegates met during the Conference, an attempt was made to create an atmosphere that would stimulate creative problem solving. To facilitate this process, a group of process experts and content experts worked together to enable the total Forum, as well as workshop groups, to communicate and make decisions without using formal, parliamentary procedure. Such positive, communicative informality gave all delegates a chance to express their views in a way which would not have been possible under more formal procedures.

To stimulate delegates' thinking in terms of what the child experiences as he forms his identity so that recommendations would be relevant and implementable at the Federal, state, local, and personal levels, a series of pre-discussion activities was devised. These included experiences dealing with the emergence of identity through movement; a trip through a "Tree House" environment, designed to aid delegates in intimately experiencing the world of the infant, the world of stress and strain of the young child, and the world of young children's play and worship; and a video laboratory in which eight television screens simultaneously displayed the behavior of eight different children of different ages ranging from three months to three and one-half years.

These "opening up" experiences also enabled delegates to freely express their feelings. Many Forum members had feelings of frustration, doubt, anger, and fear, particularly fear that no government action would be taken on recommendations. To deal with these frustrations, one group took positive action in the form of a march for children to the White House, and another group recommended that no Conference recommendations be government processed until an independent office of child advocacy was established. As communication continued, however, the Forum delegates decided against refusing to submit a formal report, but to follow the previously described structure and submit recommendations. The total Conference experiences brought delegates new insights about themselves, about ways of working creatively and productively in small and large groups, and working both with and outside "the established system." Such insight may be a truly important serendipitous outcome of the Forum's emergence of identity.

In developing their report and formulating their final recommendations, the delegates considered such topics as infant individuality, family influences, the effect of failure, motility, the development of intelligence, and identity emergence in disadvantaged children.

The report of the 1950 White House Conference on Children and Youth pointed out that children of all ages manifest a high degree of individuality. Even newborn infants differ not only in physical characteristics such as weight and height, but also in their reactions to environmental stimuli. The report recognized, however, the acute scarcity of empirically tested knowledge concerning individual differences among children.

Although empirically established information about the individuality and emergence of identity among children below age six is still scarce, significant data have been collected since 1950. Thomas, Birch, Chess, Hertzig, and Korn demonstrated that children can be identified by styles of functioning at very early ages. Their study also implies that all infants will not respond in the same fashion to the same environmental influence and that child-rearing practices have different behavioral results depending upon the child's nature. The study questions attempts to apply the same rules to all children and stresses that each child's primary reaction pattern should be understood and respected.

The more important social forces affecting the child's development and emergence of identity include the family, the family constellation, the peer group, and other significant people. The family represents an ethnic background, a religion, and a social status. The child is even affected by the father's occupation, since it tends to place him in a certain cultural context. The child's experiences within the family develop his sense of acceptance or rejection.

The availability of parental identity figures also seems critical in the emergence of identity. Clinicians often observe that young people and adults with serious identity problems lacked appropriate identity figures during childhood. Early identity patterns acquired through imitation, incorporation, and identification with parental figures, however, may impose powerful inhibitions upon subsequent activity and structural differentiation in other areas. For example, potential talent may be blocked from extensive development by such deep-laid self-concepts.

To facilitate the emergence of strong, healthy identities and foster creative potentialities, family interaction should have the following characteristics:

- Families should create conditions that encourage curiosity, exploration, experimentation, fantasy, questioning and testing the limits, and development of creative talents.
- They should provide opportunities for developing the skills of creative expression, creative problem solving, and constructive response to stress and change.
- They should prepare family members for new experiences and help them develop creative ways of coping with them.
- They should find ways of transforming destructive energy into constructive, productive behavior rather than relying upon punitive methods of control.
- They should find creative ways of resolving conflicts between the needs of any two family members.
- Every family member should be given individual attention and respect and the opportunities to make significant, creative contributions to the welfare of the family as a whole.
- Families should imaginatively use community resources as well as supplement the community's efforts.
- Family interaction should provide purpose, commitment, and courage.

There is consensus that the emergence of a healthy sense of identity is damaged by continuous failure and by situations in which the child senses that he is "less than others." A growing body of evidence favors emphasizing a child's strengths instead of stressing his weaknesses and insisting that he overcome them. Discouragement and a feeling of hopelessness seem especially debilitating and may stem from a lack of confidence in one's capacity to cope with problems.

Movement can be a prime motivating force for young children and can offer opportunities for exploration and achievement. White's study on "The Concept of Competence" establishes that motility is a drive in its own right and feelings of competence are dependent, in part, on opportunities for movement exploration.

Rowen believes that it is natural for children to use movement in the first years of life for creative expression. She believes further that, since movement is an early expression of children's creativity, it can be used to cultivate and keep alive their creative impulses so they can be carried into adult life with heightened power.

Since the last White House Conference, much evidence has been accumulated concerning the impact of the child's first years of life on his later functioning. From several studies, J. McV. Hunt has assembled evidence to discredit the following concepts about the nature and measurement of intelligence:

- A belief in fixed intelligence
- A belief in predetermined development
- A belief in the fixed and static, telephone-switchboard nature of brain function
- A belief that experience during the early years, and particularly before the development of speech, is unimportant
- A belief that whatever experience does affect later development is a matter of emotional reactions based on instinctual needs
- A belief that learning must be motivated by homeostatic need, by painful stimulation, or by acquired drives based on one of these

Early care exerts very powerful influences on a child. Existing studies indicate that, when deprived of early care, a child's development is almost always retarded—physically, intellectually, and socially.

The first years of life were investigated by Skeels in his "Iowa Studies" of the 1930's. Almost by chance Skeels discovered that two orphaned infants who had been personally cared for by mentally retarded adolescent girls showed unexpected spurts in development. Skeels and Dye then arranged a study in which retarded adolescent girls cared for 13 infants who were failing to thrive in an orphanage environment. At the time of transfer, the babies were about 19 months old and had a mean IQ of 64. A comparison group of 12 infants was found, averaging 16.6 months of age and having a mean IQ of 86.7. After an experimental period of 19 months, the children receiving personal attention from retarded adolescent girls showed an average IQ gain of 28.5 points, while the comparison group in the orphanage, after an average interval of 30.7 months, lost 26.2 IQ points. Skeels' work has been reinforced by Benjamin Bloom, who also stressed the importance of the first years of life for intellectual development.

Our society, with its emphasis on power and wealth, has neglected its most valuable resource, children. Strangely, however, we have failed to count the cost of this neglect. In the Skeels study described above, the institutionalized children having primarily custodial care continued to cost society throughout their lives, while the similar children who experienced human affection during their early years lived outside institutions and became contributing members of society. In terms of 1963 money values, Skeels estimated that one case placed in the institution had cost the state $100,000. If we multiply this figure by the current number of delinquent, mentally ill, and unemployable children, the cost of neglect to society becomes staggering.

Another aspect of research in the 1960's focused on the child who grows up in severe economic, cultural, and educational deprivation. This research has generally emphasized the intellectual deficits of disadvantaged children, and corrective programs have been compensatory in nature.

It is generally agreed that race and minority group awareness emerge in very early childhood and powerfully affects the emergence of a healthy identity. One of the most remarkable developments of the past decade has been moves by black, red, and brown groups in the United States to create more healthy identities based on this early race awareness. The more positive leaders of these movements stress the positive aspects of their racial identities and the contributions of members of their races. Most of these leaders deplore the sameness implied in equality and call for either recognition of those aspects of their own cultures they regard as superior—or at least the right to retain these features.

Woodward has presented a provocative and persuasive rationale for "Black Power" and "Achievement Motivation." He believes that Black Power is a useful conceptual framework for understanding the high achievement of those Afro-Americans who have overcome seemingly impossible odds to lead highly productive lives. Such reflections of the Black Power concept as James Brown's popular song, "Say it loud, I'm Black and I am proud!" have done much to foster a new kind of identity among Blacks.

Sensitive observers and young Indian leaders indicate that Indians want to conserve all that is best in their own heritage as summed up in the slogan "Integrity, Not Integration." They say their tribal traditions give them a sense of identity, and in some tribes interest in teaching young children tribal dances and other traditions has reawakened. Indians say that in their own community setting identity is no problem. Problems arise when the Indian comes in contact with the "mainstream." Here the Indian has either no identity or a negative one.

Some observers believe that the expression "Chicano is Beautiful" is serving much the same purpose as "Black is Beautiful." Unlike Blacks, however, Mexican-Americans have fairly structured images of their past and have retained important elements of their heritage, including the language.

One manifestation of these minority group movements has been recent objections by the Blacks and Mexican-Americans that their children do not find themselves in the books produced in the United States. Until recently, authors of children's books, history books, comic strips, and television programs treated the black, brown, and red groups as though they did not exist, and when they appeared at all, only negative stereotypes were presented. Children have received practically no information about the culture, true nature, and contributions of these groups.

Within the past two or three years, however, tremendous changes have been occurring in all media. Many basal readers, such as Ginn's Reading 360 Program, now emphasize the plurality of United States culture. Trade books for children increasingly show black, brown, and red children and their families. Heroes and heroines of these groups are also appearing in children's books in increasing numbers. Some publishers now employ ethnic consultants to review manuscripts for inaccuracies and omissions of minority group contributions. In comic strips and cartoons, the Black child from the inner city can find himself portrayed with ethnic authenticity through *Luther* and *Wee Pals.* He can also see himself in TV productions such as *"Sesame Street." Luther* and *"Sesame Street"* are examples of mass media that deliberately try to help young Blacks in their search for healthy identities. It remains for social scientists, educators, writers for children, toy makers, and others to support the idea of racial pride with their creative productions and research.

Although some headway has been made in presenting minority groups in the media, the picture remains bleak. Minorities are economically, religiously, and academically exploited. Much profit is realized annually by maintaining ghettos and exploiting American Indians on reservations. Religious groups pressure minorities to join their failing churches. Underclothed, underfed, poverty-stricken children often see themselves stereotyped as worthless. Here there is little opportunity for developing healthy identities. Although much money is spent each year to study poverty and minority culture, being studied immediately places one in an inferior position, at least as studies are usually conducted. While studies are profitable for some, they have become another means of cruel exploitation.

Even when the Federal Government grants money to ameliorate the effects of such abuses, further abuses occur and funds are often diverted from their intended purpose. As this report is being written, newspapers are recounting such abuses in Head Start programs in Harlem, in predominantly Indian schools, and in programs for Mexican-American children. One reader of the "confidential" report of the Harvard Center for Law and Education on the use of Federal funds intended for deprived Indian children writes that "every page of the document bristles with abuses." Funds intended for school lunches for Indians were often subverted, leaving Indian children with empty stomachs. Navajo parents were known to have sold their sheep and pawned their few possessions to pay the lunch bills sent home by school authorities. Transportation funds seemed to vanish as did funds to improve school buildings so inadequate as to constitute health hazards.

Paralleling the movements for more healthy racial and ethnic identities are movements designed to bring about more favorable and realistic identities for women. A major focus of these movements has been to create new identities for women with accompanying changes in the treatment of females from infancy through employment, career development, and old age. Like Blacks, the militant women's organizations are bringing about change in the history books, writing children's books that change the female stereotype, and writing books about the heroines of history.

For the emergence of strong, healthy identities, all children must interact with a healthy emotional and physical environment. Many children have healthy emotional environments in the early months of life when their universe is limited to their family. However, most children encounter hostile emotional, behavioral, and physical environments once their universe extends beyond the family unit or immediate neighborhood. Either they are not exposed to other cultures and races, a subtle form of racism, or they experience early destructive effects of overt racism.

In addition, community planning and design often serves the needs of industry, neglecting its most important citizens, children. Childhood has been regarded simply as a transitional period to adulthood, yet we always have children with us. Houses, public buildings, furniture, and recreational areas have been constructed (except for a token swing) for adult living, as if no children are expected to live "there."

With the current rates of urbanization, automation, pollution, and social and technological change, it is increasingly urgent to make the environment more favorable to the emergence of healthy identity among young children.

The fundamental goal of Forum 2 is to enable all children to develop healthy, strong identities during their early years, so they may have a chance to fully realize their potentialities. This goal can be attained only if the child's environment responds to his or her individuality (even before birth). The child should be taught from birth about his individuality, and the environment should recognize, acknowledge, and respect the child's individuality.

Since the child's identity and the environment's response to this identity serve as powerful guides to a child's behavior, failure to attain this goal will prevent children from reaching their full potential.

The results will be increased rates of delinquency and crime, increasing rates of emotional disturbance and mental illness, debased talent, violence and destruction, and general lack of involvement in life and work. Conditions inimical to the emergence of strong, healthy identities among young children have reached a danger point which threaten to destroy our society.

The new agencies and measures proposed in the following section were those judged most promising for solving problems of sound identity emergence and achieving our goal.

Children, who are powerless and need a strong voice to represent them as a minority group, are now without political clout in this country. Therefore, *we recommend that top priority be given to quickly establishing a child advocacy agency financed by the Federal Government and other sources with full ethnic, cultural, racial, and sexual representation.* This agency would be highly autonomous and be charged with fostering, coordinating, and implementing all programs related to the emergence and development of healthy identity among children. The agency would be especially concerned with programs to strengthen family life in all its forms, including: education for parenting, which emphasizes and values the uniqueness of every child; establishing a national commission to strengthen and enhance cultural pluralism, developing community-based comprehensive resource centers for families; and establishing child-oriented environmental commissions at national, state, and local levels.

In view of our past neglect of children, Forum 2 believes that such an agency is necessary before other recommendations can be effectively implemented.

The following guidelines are suggested for implementing this recommendation:

- The system shall include a Child Advocate who is a member of the Cabinet of the President of the United States; an interdepartmental office directly under the President's office, headed by the Child Advocate, which coordinates all Federal agencies in matters related to children; a Child Advocate at the state level in every state who reports directly to the governor; a Child Advocate on every governing body of cities, towns, and villages.
- Funding at the national level shall be similar to that of the American Red Cross, which receives funds not only from the Federal Government but from other sources, public and private. A high level of autonomy in system operation and utilization of funds must be assured at all levels.
- The national Child Advocate's office would be under the control of a national policy board which would establish operating policies and priorities. A similar structure would operate at the state and local levels.

- The national policy committee would include representatives from the parent and youth categories, as well as representatives of cultural, ethnic, racial, and sex categories.
- The method of selecting the national policy committee must ensure that most members will not be political appointments of the national administration but will *primarily* include members selected in a democratic process so that members represent divergent interests and positions.

We recommend a new organizational form, such as a neighborhood resource and service center, to coordinate all community programs that can help families meet the needs of their children. Resources and services should be designed to eliminate those conditions that limit the nurture of a healthy sense of identity and the development of positive self-concepts. Such a center would have liaison with the local welfare department and make available public health, recreation, Veterans Administration, and other services [like] those provided by churches and private social agencies.

Neighborhood centers would be community controlled and locally autonomous. Services would be easily accessible and available to all on demand, on a 24-hour-a-day basis. The center would provide·

- Information and referral to all social services through a nationwide computer input system.
- Escort, transportation, and supportive relationships to enable individuals to use specialized services and resources not available within the center.
- One staff person as a citizen advocate with various bureaucratic systems.
- Training to develop indigenous resource personnel.

Comprehensive resources and services such as medical, dental, nutrition, psychological, public welfare, education, parent education, and training are essential fcr the feeling of well-being that generates and sustains one's sense of self-direction, dignity, and self-respect. These feelings and attitudes can be encouraged through programs that seriously consider social-emotional development curriculum, talent development activities, the development of family communication skills, and support for cultural diversity and identity. Deliberate efforts will be made to eliminate stereotypic racial, ethnic, and sexual roles in mass media, toys, and other program facilities.

The center's structure should be determined by the needs of the community served. A competent staff should be recruited and provisions made for career development of the indigenous members interested in this area of work. These personnel would represent all age levels, sexes, ethnic, and racial backgrounds.

Models from which these centers can be developed include: parent and child centers; comprehensive health centers; comprehensive mental health centers; new careers; neighborhood information centers; social services in Head Start; Lincoln Hospital, New York; Institute for Personal Effectiveness in Children, San Diego, California; Tom Gordon's Parent Effectiveness Training; Community Controlled Health Center, Cincinnati, Ohio; Institute for Training in Program Development, Los Angeles, California.

We recommend the establishment of a national commission to strengthen and enhance cultural pluralism within an independent child advocacy agency (or other appropriate agency). The charge of the commission would be: to strengthen, enhance, and make visible the pluralism that exists in our society; and to give tangible expression to the positive value of each individual's identity.

The goals of the commission are:

- To recognize the way each culture expresses itself through the arts and other outlets
- To utilize these diverse artistic forms and other expressions to strengthen each individual's identity and to bridge the existing gaps between different groups
- To protect the right of each individual and each group to maintain those differences that make ours a pluralistic society
- To create a climate in which social institutions assume a pluralistic character
- To take necessary steps to remove all oppressive actions of special interest groups, institutions, or governmental agencies which, for religious, political, or monetary gain, currently destroy or distort the identity of members of specific groups such as the American Indians.

The commission should include, on a policy-making level, professionals representing the wide spectrum of disciplines and individuals within our pluralistic society.

Selection of the commission will be the responsibility of the office of the Child Advocacy Agency (or other designated agency).

Suggested programs and services include:

- Supporting legislation on Federal, state, and local levels designed to further the purposes of the commission.
- Providing cultural exchange programs.
- Establishing and utilizing a "cultural voucher" system or "culture bank" on a national and regional basis.
- Providing short-term experiential programs, such as a children's exchange program, among children of varying backgrounds.
- Providing advisory and consultative services to mass media such as television, films, radio, and press to ensure a valid portrayal of any group within our society.

- Assisting individuals and groups seeking funds from private or governmental agencies for purposes related to the commission's goals. In achieving these purposes, the rights of persons or groups required to participate must not be violated.
- Providing the instruction and other resources required to develop and reward those kinds of giftedness valued by specific cultural groups.

We recommend that a multifaceted approach be used to convey information on human development and family relations to parents and parents-to-be and to others who interact with infants and young children.

Approaches should provide "how to" information and techniques for day-to-day child-rearing, and should provide the parents understanding of how a child's healthy and functional identity emerges. The rights and responsibilities of parenthood must also be conveyed.

Providing, at different levels, courses in child development and family relations should be a primary goal. These educational courses should help individuals appreciate the development processes of children in ways which will aid more creatively both the child in his struggle for identity and those who assume parental roles, either full-time or part-time, in their key responsibility for strengthening a child's sense of identity.

Two key avenues to follow in implementing parenting education are schools and the mass media.

Required courses in human development and family relations should be made available for girls and boys in both junior and senior high school.

It is anachronistic to consider adhering to the traditional nine-month school year at any level, including elementary. By using existing facilities throughout the entire year, greater flexibility can be achieved in existing curricula, and new programs may be introduced and implemented. Federal monies must be available to develop appropriate curricula on human development and to develop methods for use in the courses and in training qualified teachers.

Consideration could be given to developing work-study programs involving individuals in human development courses and day care centers (child development centers).

Colleges should provide required courses in human development and family relations at the undergraduate level.

In-service training composed of a core of courses should be required for teachers preparing to teach human development and family relations in any of a variety of educational settings.

The following areas of adult education should be made available:

- In-service training for interested and concerned adults (teachers and/or parents) in human development and other related courses in early childhood education. Expectant parents might, for example, be encouraged to take advantage of existing programs in community hospitals and, in smaller communities, individual programs offered by community medical clinics.
- Teachers and teacher assistants in day care or nursery schools (public, private, church) must have opportunities to take courses in child development and family relations.
- Vocational education, using materials and concepts embodied in training programs for child development assistants, should be incorporated in curricula of vocational and community colleges to serve the needs of post high school students or older adults.

The prescribed training programs should be offered by qualified instructors and an appropriate number of credit hours must be awarded and recognized upon completion. And participants graduating as salaried assistants to various human development professionals will find employment in programs such as day care, nursery school, hospital playrooms, day activity centers for mentally retarded children, and kindergartens.

Optimal time, effort, and funds are essential for research and development of program content and format and subsequent televising of resulting programs. The goal of these programs would be effective communication with parents and parents-to-be on:

- Positive and unique aspects of our pluralistic society
- Constructive approaches for children handicapped by blindness, deafness, birth deformities, mental retardation, physical injury, and emotional disturbance
- Resources for aiding intellectually gifted and creative children and children with outstanding talent in music, visual arts, dramatics, writing, and the like
- The fact that human beings are remarkably similar in their basic concerns for the welfare of all children

Long-range funding of the parents' television workshop would be derived from government, business, industry, labor, and private foundations.

Creative spot announcements should inform the public about all agencies and services that have existing programs for children and families or about special events pertaining to particular topics, for example, pregnancy and nutrition, childbirth, breast feeding, and discipline.

The Office of Child Development (OCD) must effectively serve as a clearing house and/or evaluator of all publications pertaining to child development and family relations.

The OCD should recognize and utilize expertise in the scientific and commercial community on how to increase the public appeal and utilization of such publications. For example, Madison Avenue advertising strategies must be used to prepare and disseminate UNICEF-quality material.

The OCD must underwrite the production of an evaluative "Consumer's Report" that deals with all literature pertaining to human development.

The OCD must ensure that all literature given a high rating is valid and free from racial, cultural, and sexual prejudices.

We recommend that child-oriented environmental commissions be established at national, state, and local levels to ensure that children's needs are not neglected by city planners, architects, building contractors, and others who influence how homes and neighborhoods are constructed.

Only recently has active concern been expressed about what might be called ecological child psychology. In his recent book, Barker pointed out that a common view among psychologists is that "the environment of behavior is a relatively unstructured, passive, probabilistic arena of objects and events upon which man behaves in accordance with the programming he carries about within himself." Barker, however, proposes that the environment be viewed as "highly structured, improbable arrangements of objects and events that coerce behavior in accordance with their own dynamic patterning." Barker and his associates have found that they can predict some aspects of a child's behavior more adequately from behavior settings (drug stores, playgrounds, classrooms) than from knowledge of the behavior tendencies of the particular child.

The child's environment consists of those things, events, and persons who help the child define, establish, and maintain his identity. Prominent among these influences are parental and other adult model figures, ethnic customs, and the special environment in which the child develops. As we strengthen the value and meaning of these things, events, and persons in the child's life, we strengthen his identity.

An optimum physical environment would allow the child to successfully manipulate his surroundings at any age and would also provide a variety of sensual experiences. Children, however, have little say in structuring their environments, and the world remains essentially adult-centered.

A child-oriented environmental commission, possibly a division of Health, Education and Welfare or a child advocacy agency financed by Federal and local funds, could be composed of parents, pediatricians, educators, engineers, architects, and builders; it could operate at a national, state, or local level. The commission would advise, help plan, inspect, and approve construction and renovation of homes, apartments, public buildings, parks, day care centers (child development centers), and streets to meet the needs of children. For example, before the construction of a new shopping center, the commission would be responsible for consulting and advising the architects, merchants, and financiers about incorporating into the actual design of the center physical surroundings that are more stimulating to children, such as innovative flooring material whose color and texture make it more interesting for children to walk on, small-scale furniture, low-level displays which are either "child proof" or may be touched by a child without being damaged. It would also advise merchants on using their stores as learning experiences for children. A shoe store, for example, may display various types of leather which children would be invited to touch and investigate.

To further expand or improve a child's environment:

We recommend organizing a children's cultural committee to help expand a child's environment to include parks, zoos, museums, libraries, and other facilities of the larger community. A directory listing all available child-oriented activities—parks, zoos, libraries, clubs, and municipal buildings—could be collated by local, civic, or religious groups, publicized by volunteer media and advertising, and distributed by municipal outlets and interested commercial patrons.

Community centers should provide a variety of materials for children to explore and enjoy. Existing, but unused, schools or buildings can become community warehouses supplied with mechanical devices, scrap wood, clay, paper, and wheels, obtained through donations. The center could be supervised by day care centers, parents, or youth organizations.

Public health clinics could conduct seminars in how families can best utilize space in terms of identity formation—stressing the importance of privacy to a child and the need for a child to have his own place, no matter how small. Public health nurses and agencies should make such information available to crowded city dwellers.

The traditional conception of the family fails to accommodate the many other family forms now being recognized; and also fails to recognize that many families change over time. Because family membership in whatever form is a major environmental influence on children, we support Forum 14 in urging that the variability of family forms be recognized, that a presidential commission investigate legislation for its effect on family form and its discrimination against family structure, that an institute be created to study variant family structure and to support programs for basic family needs.

The editors of home furnishing and building magazines should be encouraged to consider child development more carefully in presenting home construction or decorating ideas, such as giving attention to children's play and traffic patterns.

Information should be amassed and disseminated on how families can make the best use of their environmental resources, and the availability of free materials and recreational facilities should be made known. Special attention should be given to making available resources for developing outstanding or unusual talents of families, especially among families living in poverty.

The preservation of green areas, playgrounds, parks, and living space in city planning and in neighborhood projects should be encouraged.

A concern for, and interest in, the preservation of the ecology should be developed in both children and parents.

The recommendations which have evolved from this 1970 White House Conference on Children are but a beginning. From here it becomes the responsibility of the delegates and other Conference participants to help set into motion the implementation of these recommendations. Furthermore, the Conference staff should devote their energies to setting up the means by which this may be done.

Nor should the process stop here. As we continue to evaluate our efforts, each state organization should begin to think toward the next conference. If these state organizations are included in the preliminary planning, the next conference can be developed with much greater delegate participation and much greater articulation between the state organizations and the forum task force groups. The Conference itself can then become a tool for tying together these concerns and for actually setting up the structures by which they may be met. As we go from this Conference with our concerns for meeting the needs of children, let us begin *now* to think of 1980.

The Dissolution of the Training Schools in Massachusetts

ANDREW RUTHERFORD

Andrew Rutherford is an associate professor, Department of Criminal Justice Studies, University of Minnesota.

Reprinted from "The Dissolution of the Training Schools," by Andrew Rutherford, from pamphlet published by The Academy for Contemporary Problems, Columbus, Ohio.

PREFACE

In 1969 provisions for young offenders in Massachusetts were not in any marked respect different from those which exist today throughout most of the United States and Western Europe. They were characterized by the reformatory heritage of the nineteenth century, and by a very limited array of alternatives for the court. The institutions tended to brutalize both staff and youngsters, and the few community programs that did exist offered nothing more than a mediocre level of supervision. The dramatic changes that occurred during the next three years comprise one of the most significant and hopeful events in the bleak history of corrections. By rejecting rather than reforming the old system Massachusetts developed a very wide range of services for youngsters in trouble. It was the abrupt closing of the training schools that caught the attention of people throughout the United States and beyond. This event has taken on a symbolic significance, and perhaps because of this there has not often been a close scrutiny of what has actually taken place in Massachusetts. This report is an attempt to provide a concise and up-to-date account of the Massachusetts Department of Youth Services.

The study represents part of a larger comparative description and analysis of correctional change in several states. This is being prepared for the Group for the Advancement of Corrections, comprised, in the main, of a number of correctional administrators from across the United States who are brought together by the Academy for Contemporary Problems. I am grateful to several people for their helpful comments on earlier drafts of this report: in particular to John Conrad, Lloyd Ohlin, David Ward, and Juliet Rutherford.

THE 1969 LEGISLATION AND THE MANDATE FOR CHANGE

During the 1960's youth corrections in Massachusetts had been characterized by continued scandal and mismanagement. There were a series of inquiries into the operations of the Division for Youth Services and the Youth Services Board. Following a number of critical state investigations came the most devastating of all, the report by the Children's Bureau of the Department of Health, Education, and Welfare in August, 1966. A further study was conducted during 1967 by the Massachusetts Committee on Children and Youth and by a special committee of the Senate which reported in June of that year. Most of the reports were in agreement as to the general direction of the changes required. There was considerable comment in the press, and a growing demand for a more humane approach to children in trouble. On becoming Governor in early 1969, Francis Sargent strongly identified himself with this demand. He stated, "Simply caging children is not the way of an enlightened society." Following the growing public outcry against the Division's leadership, pressure was brought to bear on the director, Dr. John Coughlin, to resign in March, 1969. Two months later a committee set up by the Massachusetts Conference on Social Welfare called for further resignations and for institutional closures. Sargent gave his backing to legislative moves to bring about important administrative changes. With support from the Governor and some key legislators, and with the constant urging of the media, especially the *Boston Globe*, the legislation, which had been debated for two years, moved easily through the House and Senate.

The legislation, expressed in Chapter 838 of the 1969 Acts, was signed into law by Governor Sargent in August, 1969. It contained several important features:

(1) The Division for Youth Services and Youth Services Board were transformed into a Department of Youth Services, which was placed under a commissioner within a newly created super agency, the Department for Human Services;

(2) The commission was empowered to select four assistant commissioners;

(3) The Department's spending flexibility was greatly increased, including the authority to purchase services from outside sources;

(4) The Department was empowered "to establish necessary facilities for detention, diagnosis, treatment, and training of its charges including post-release care." It was given full control over the juvenile institutions which had formerly been somewhat autonomous;

(5) The Department was given the authority to place children in any institution or program.

A blue-ribbon search panel was set up to find a commissioner. After Coughlin's departure in May, 1969, Frank Maloney, formerly of the Boston University School of Social Work, was appointed as acting commissioner. Governor Sargent would have been prepared to confirm Maloney who had managed to calm the institutions down by giving strong support to staff. To some extent the political heat had been lifted from the agency, but Sargent had agreed to accept the choice of the committee. Dr. Jerome Miller, an associate professor of social work at Ohio State University, had seen the job advertised and was one of eighty applicants. At the interview he made it clear he had a bias against institutions. Prior to his teaching work he had had several years experience developing services for the children of Air Force personnel stationed in England. Following the committee's recommendation, Miller was appointed commissioner on October 28, 1969.

THE MORAL CRUSADE FOR CHILDREN, 1969–1972

The humanizing of the institutions was an obvious goal, given Miller's stance as the advocate for the children committed to the Department. The decision to close the training schools was preceded by an attempt to make them a better place for children to live. Miller had a number of advantages. He was from out of state and was more easily able to present himself as the agent of change. He arrived on the scene in the wake of considerable public disquiet as to the manner in which youth institutions were run, and a solid legislative framework had been created. Miller possessed considerable ability in dealing with the media and was able to clearly and dramatically present his message. He built upon the active commitment already established by the *Boston Globe* and made good use of whatever television coverage came his way. He had the ability to quickly grasp the political complexities of Massachusetts. He made a point of establishing some firm allies from the start. These included Tom Winship, editor of *The Globe;* David Bartley, Speaker of the House of Representatives; Maurice Donahue, then President of the Senate; Mrs. Jessie Sargent, wife of the Governor; and John McGlynn, Chairman of the Joint Legislative Committee on State Administration and the chairmen of several other legislative committees. Although Miller had a number of persistent political enemies he was able to use their opposition to magnify the polarization of the issues in such a way as to gain support from various groups. A great deal of his time was spent either on television or radio, or speaking to groups, large and small, throughout the state. On many of these occasions he was accompanied by youngsters who echoed his dismay at the system as it existed and stated the need for immediate change. The presence of these youngsters, often articulate and persuasive, dramatically strengthened Miller's basic message that the issue was not one of young hoodlums and offenders but of kids who had been battered by an inefficient and corrupt system for too long.

This may well have been one of Miller's greatest achievements. He significantly modified the public image of the young offender throughout the state. He demonstrated the havoc and destruction caused by institutions on the lives of countless youngsters over the years. Throughout his crusade, he had the vocal encouragement of such varied groups as the Lifers' Group of Walpole Prison and the League of Women Voters. It should be noted that it was the groups composed of lay people, such as the League of Women Voters, which were to provide consistent support to the agency throughout the fundamental changes. A similar level of support was not generally forthcoming from professional social work and established penal reform organizations, which maintained a somewhat ambiguous position during the period of change. Miller was very aware that there would be considerable resistance to meaningful change, some of it from those groups with a vested interest in arrangements as they existed. This resistance, which took a number of forms, was countered by a solid base of informed public support for reform.

Miller set out to humanize the training schools in a forceful and direct manner. He developed open lines of communication with youngsters by talking with them on his visits to the institutions, encouraging them to write or call him. There were, in fact, occasions when youngsters left the training school and made their way to his office. He was aware that there were considerable difficulties in upgrading the quality of staff. Although superintendents could be replaced, the state civil service regulations made it virtually impossible to remove line staff, even if they were highly unsuited for work with young people. Attempts were made to train staff in new techniques and in a broader understanding of the needs of youngsters. Consultants used for such training sessions included Dr. Maxwell Jones, one of the originators of the therapeutic community concept, and Dr. Harry Vorath, who had developed group techniques with young offenders in Minnesota. Miller's attempts to improve institutional settings were not pursued for long at the segregation unit which the agency maintained at the Bridgewater Correctional Institution. He was appalled by the conditions that existed at this eighty-bed unit, known as the Institute for Juvenile Guidance. He had on one occasion visited the facility with the Governor's wife, and they had together witnessed staff assaulting some youngsters who had attempted to abscond. The difficulties that followed in attempting to discipline the staff involved in this incident and the persistently punitive character of the Bridgewater unit convinced Miller that the only appropriate action was to close it down completely, and this was accomplished by September, 1970. A little over a year later Miller was to apply much the same reasoning to the training schools themselves.

During his first year in office Miller was joined by a number of former associates from Ohio and from the United States Air Force. They were not, on the whole, people with experience in working with youngsters who had been before the courts. They came to Massachusetts to be a part of Miller's crusade for children in trouble. Expertise in penology and experience in working within correctional bureaucracies were less valuable qualifications than a high degree of commitment to change. Miller and his associates were very conscious of the high level of staff sabotage of the attempts to humanize the institutions, including the creation of incidents in the schools to undermine the credibility of the new administration. Apart from coping with active staff opposition, they also attempted to confront the tendency of any institutional program, even the most carefully designed, to slide back into a deadening routine. Miller and his colleagues, however, became increasingly impressed that there was no way of maintaining the impetus for change and growth within the institutional setting. By the time he had been in office for a year Miller was convinced that humanizing the institutions could be no more than a short-term solution. It simultaneously became clear that some of the more effective programs that Miller had developed would be still more appropriate in a community setting. As a result of reducing the length of time youngsters remained in the training schools Miller had already brought about a drop in the institutional population.*

*In 1971 there was a daily average of 465 youngsters in training schools.

By the end of 1971 he was convinced that it would be politically feasible to move all the youngsters out of the four training schools. He possessed the administrative authority to transfer youngsters to any program but did not have the authority to totally close the schools. The training school buildings and many of the staff, for the time being at least, had to remain. Miller was certain that the best strategy would be a rapid rather than a gradual approach, which would have produced heavy resistance.* He established task forces within the agency to develop plans and it was clear the regional structure which had already been established would play an increasingly significant role. The seven regional offices, however, lacked the experience and resources to fully develop the potential that Miller was convinced existed in the community for a wide array of programs. Given the political context, the process had to be swift if it was to succeed, and the main thrust had to come from the central office. Time did not permit the full preparation of the regional offices for the rapid de-institutionalization that took place.

The main effort to empty the institutions took place in January, 1972. The population had been reduced at the Shirley Industrial School; those boys remaining were transferred to the Lyman School. An original and effective device was used to de-institutionalize the residual group at Lyman, which became known as the University of Massachusetts Conference. The boys remaining at Lyman moved to the campus at Amherst where they participated in a one-month National Conference on Juvenile Delinquency Prevention and Treatment Program. About 100 youngsters, including girls from the Lancaster School, were involved and they were joined by a similar number of college students. Joint student-youth groups were established with guidance from agency staff to develop community placements for the youth involved. The idea of using a university in this novel manner was conceived only a month or so before, and the final decision to go ahead was made on very short notice. The decision to remove the youngsters from the training schools was made completely within the agency, and there were no consultations with either the Secretary of Human Services or the Governor. Miller, however, was correct in his calculation that he would receive support from these two offices, and Governor Sargent visited Amherst to participate in some of the proceedings. It was a good time to move. The period between semesters was convenient to the University and the legislature was in recess. Because of the short notice, there were some difficulties of coordination between central office, the regional offices, and the conferees at Amherst, but despite these problems the device proved to be effective. The conference was run in a rather less formal manner than had originally been intended and a study by the

---

*Attempts to gradually phase out the Shirley Industrial School during 1971 had been thwarted by staff resistance, which included the encouragement of runaways.

Harvard Center for Criminal Justice noted: "Advocates and 'their kids' did their own thing and for the most part this appeared to work out rather well."* Two thirds of the youngsters were placed at their own homes, foster or group homes, and the remaining twenty (eleven ran away from the conference) were held by the agency pending a placement decision. The Harvard paper indicates some of the points of learning that arose from the experience. There is considerable promise in its replication with a number of possible variations.

The agency was able to develop a wide range of new programs, which included arranging services for youngsters who resided at home. Many of these services were purchased rather than directly provided, and it was soon very clear that the process of de-institutionalization had radically altered the whole character of the agency. There was a movement of decision making from the central to the regional offices, and many of the staff found that they were less involved in direct contact with youngsters and were instead involved in the tasks of selecting and monitoring services provided by groups outside the agency.

CONSOLIDATION 1973-1974

Dr. Miller left Massachusetts in January, 1973, his moral crusade completed. He considered that his essential work was accomplished and that the task of consolidation was better in the hands of someone else. The new commissioner did not have to carry the full weight of all the opposition that Miller had generated. Although Joseph Leavey was seen as one of Miller's people, having been deputy commissioner with responsibility for the development of the regional structure, he was from Massachusetts and would be more able than Miller to improve agency relations with such groups as the juvenile court judges.

During his first year in office, Leavey was concerned with strengthening the regional offices which now have complete responsibility for placement within the community. It is planned that the regional offices will have responsibility for detention placements and, probably in the long run, Intensive Treatment placements. The other crucial task facing Leavey was to develop an administrative and budgeting structure which would support the massive move in the direction of purchased services. For much of 1973 the agency faced a series of financial crises, but considerable progress was made in developing sound procedures both within the agency itself and with related parts of the government machinery. During the 1973 fiscal year one third of the agency's budget was used for the purchase of serv-

---

*R. B. Coates, A. D. Miller and L. E. Ohlin, "Strategic Innovation in the Process of De-institutionalization: The University of Massachusetts Conference," in *Closing Correctional Institutions*, edited by Yitzhak Bakal, Lexington, Mass.: D. C. Heath, 1973.

ices, with plans to increase this to half the budget in 1974. By the Fall of 1973, the worst of the financial crisis was over. More effective administrative methods had been developed by the agency and within other government departments to accelerate payments to programs. The changed financial situation has greatly improved the relationship between the Department and the various groups with which it does business.

Staff salaries are still being paid and other costs borne by the agency at the former training schools which continue to be part of the Department's responsibility. There are indications that this double cost, borne by the agency since its transition from institutions to community programs, will not continue much longer. Increasing attention is being given to contract-making with the private groups that provide services for youngsters. At the same time, more attention is being given to evaluation of programs, both by regional staff who have responsibility for placements and by evaluation teams which are based within the central office and visit each program periodically. This process will be refined as evaluation procedures become more sophisticated and the standard setting develops greater precision.

It is not surprising that some of the staff who felt closely identified with Miller and the crusading phase have left. Some of these in fact have joined Miller in Illinois, where he is presently Director of Children and Family Services. Leavey has assembled his own team of senior staff and has recognized that the phase of consolidation requires a different style of administration. The main political battles appear to be over; substantial work remains to be done on developing and refining procedures, and there is considerably less staff contact with the youngsters themselves. Some staff failed to recognize that the agency faced new tasks and misinterpreted structural changes within the agency as regressive developments. The phase of consolidation is likely to be a search for consensus rather than a further polarization of the issues. The change in relationship with youngsters also poses problems for staff. Now that agency staff is essentially concerned with initiating, facilitating, coordinating, and evaluating programs, they are perceived by youngsters in programs as playing a controlling rather than a helping role, as compared with program staff who receive a more positive rating.* This change of role for many agency staff may be just as difficult as that which faced institutional staff three or four years ago. Given these changes in the agency task and structure, it can still be said that the central office of the Department must be one of the most informal headquarters of a corrections agency in the world. It has an exceptionally young staff who tend to be casually attired and who work with an

---

*Lloyd E. Ohlin, Robert B. Coates, Alden D. Miller, "Radical Correctional Reform: A Case Study of the Massachusetts Youth Correctional System," *Harvard Educational Review*, 44(1) 1974.

unusual degree of open communication between the different sections. A small number of youngsters, committed or referred to the agency, work at central office on a part-time basis. The headquarters is characterized by its ease and informality, and a visitor is left in no doubt that the staff's basic concern is the youngsters served by the agency.

FACTS AND FANTASIES CONCERNING DEVELOPMENTS IN MASSACHUSETTS

There has been widespread circulation of rumor throughout the United States concerning the consequences of the removal of youngsters from training schools in Massachusetts. There is no doubt that it was a very threatening event to many correctional administrators across the country. They and others have been only too anxious to hear some of the rumors. Fifty-eight of the sixty participants at the 1973 Annual National Conference of Superintendents of Training Schools and Reformatories, it seems, intended that their endorsement of the so-called Manwell Report be regarded as a censure of Miller. This report (compiled by a former training school superintendent from Ohio) presents a fairly straightforward account of the agency. The closest, however, that Manwell came to a criticism of the agency was his conclusion that: "Granted that in the Massachusetts program there is much that is innovative, creative, and progressive, this preliminary survey indicates also many flaws and weaknesses, due in part to the haste in which the program was constituted."* The forthcoming findings of the Harvard team, and of the comparative study by the University of Michigan's National Assessment of Juvenile Corrections (Massachusetts is one of the sixteen states in the sample receiving intensive study), will greatly assist the serious consideration of what has taken place.

The most prominent of the rumors are:

(1) *The training schools have been quietly re-opened.* With the exception of Lancaster (the former girls' school), it can be categorically stated that there are no agency youngsters at any of the former training schools. The situation is as follows:

- *Bridgewater Institute for Juvenile Guidance:*
  Closed September 1970 and not used by the Department since.
- *Shirley Industrial School:*
  Closed January 1972. The facility houses some drug programs operated by the Department of Corrections.

---

*The text of this report is printed in the April 1973 issue of *Impact* (Raleigh, N. C.). The subsequent issue of *Impact* (Vol. 1, No. 6) contained a very detailed survey by Richard Coleman of the Massachusetts situation, which specifically rebutted a number of rumors.

It has also been used by a private agency that has a drug program, but not involving agency youngsters. It was officially handed over to the Department of Corrections in January 1974.

- *The Lyman School:*
  Closed January 1972 and has held no agency youngsters since. It currently houses computers for the Department of Public Welfare.
- *Oakdale:*
  Closed June 1972 and now used as an administration office.
- *Lancaster School for Girls:*
  Closed August 1972. Cottages at this facility are used for several purposes. Up to ten girls are held there for placement in community programs; a cottage is used as a regional girls detention center. Other cottages are used by private groups for their own programs.

There is certainly no intention by Leavey and his colleagues to reopen the training schools. He is anxious to transfer total administrative responsibility for them to other government agencies as soon as he can, both on economic grounds and to reduce the chance that facilities may revert to their former use.*

(2) *An increasing number of youngsters are being sent to adult state and county facilities.* This is the stated belief of a number of people in and beyond Massachusetts. It is a view commonly expressed, for example, by some juvenile court judges, who believe that this is the case because they are aware of an increase in the number of youngsters bound over by their court to the adult court. It is difficult to form a conclusion as to an increase in bind-overs because figures on a state-wide basis do not exist. It is clear, however, that not all such bind-overs result in the imposition of a custodial sentence. In perhaps the majority of cases, the youngster is placed on adult probation. Other cases are passed back to the juvenile court for a disposition. The important point here is that a bind-over is not synonymous with committal to an adult facility.

The latest published figures on youngsters in adult facilities appeared in an Information Bulletin, issued by the Department of Corrections, on May 30, 1973. These fig-

---

*It should be noted that the three county training schools were closed during the winter of 1972-1973 following the failure of the legislature to appropriate the required funding. Miller and others in the agency had campaigned actively for their closure. For an excellent account of a county training school and its political environment see the novel by John Hough, Jr., *A Two-Car Funeral*, Boston: Little, Brown and Company, 1973.

ures exclude committals to the psychiatric prison at Bridge-water. It should be noted that the cut-off age for the analysis is 17, whereas courts currently have power to commit youngsters to the Department of Youth Services who are 16 or younger. It is expected that the maximum age of commitment to the Department will be raised from 16 to 17 during 1974.

Between January 1972 and March 1973, 56 (4.2%) of the 1326 persons sentenced to state adult institutions were 17 or younger, compared with a percentage of 4.3% for the previous six years. As of August 1 there were one 16 year old and fourteen 17 year olds in adult state institutions.* While there was no increase in number of youngsters going to state institutions, there was a slight increase in the percentage going to county facilities. The actual number of committals has not increased, but the rate for youngsters has not followed the declining pattern that has characterized committals as a whole. There are no figures available for 1973. On the basis of these figures, there is no evidence to support the contention of certain judges and others that more youngsters are now being committed to adult institutions because of the closing of the training schools.

**Number and percentage of persons committed to
state prisons and county jails by year and age**

Adult State Institutions				County Jails			
Year	Total Committed	Age 17 and Under		Year	Total Committed	Age 17 and Under	
1966	826	39	(4.7%)	1969	8990	275	(3.1%)
1967	739	32	(4.3%)	1967	8550	263	(3.1%)
1968	855	42	(4.9%)	1968	8467	263	(3.1%)
1969	875	30	(3.4%)	1969	8108	247	(3.0%)
1970	859	38	(4.4%)	1970	8119	287	(3.5%)
1971	1091	47	(4.3%)	1971	6474	240	(3.7%)
1972	1127	50	(4.4%)	1972	5449	252	(4.6%)
1973*	199	6	(3.0%)	1973	No Figures Available		
Total	6571	284	(4.5%)	Total	54207	1847	(3.4%)

*First three months only.

---

*Source: Research and Planning Division, Massachusetts Department of Corrections.

(3) *The Department places many youngsters out of state.* The suggestion has been made that the agency has simply rid itself of difficulties by moving large numbers of children to institutions or programs in other states. Selective use is made of some particularly good programs, such as an outward bound camp in Maine. The allegation that large numbers of youngsters are simply moved out of state is without any basis. Of some 2,600 active cases during 1973, a daily average of 65 were placed in programs outside Massachusetts.

(4) *Dr. Miller was forced to resign.* There is no evidence for this rumor; in fact both the Governor and the Secretary of Human Services attempted to persuade Miller to remain in Massachusetts. Miller made the decision to go to Illinois as Director of Children and Family Services with some reluctance, as he felt that he was needed in Massachusetts for several more months. He was, however, convinced that in the long run his deputy, Joseph Leavey, would be more able to take the agency through the period of consolidation.

SOME CONTEMPORARY ISSUES

(1) The number of youngsters in secure facilities

The question as to how many agency youngsters are held within secure facilities is complicated by program definitions. Intensive treatment might mean confinement to a program characterized by tight security or one where there is a high staff-youth ratio and an intensive program is in operation. There are a small number of youngsters confined to psychiatric hospitals (where the services purchased are considerably more expensive than those provided once by the training school).* The main provision for fairly close security at present is the Andros program, which is a purchased service in a part of the Judge Connolly Youth Center in Roslindale, Boston. This program usually accommodates about thirty-five boys, with an average stay of nine months. There is general consensus within the Department that the number of Intensive Treatment placements will have to be increased. Current planning is to increase the number available from 35 to 109; this reflects the difficulty in placing certain youngsters in the existing range of services. These new Intensive Treatment programs will probably develop within the detention facilities at Worcester and Westfield. Considerable thought is being given, within the agency, to their program content. It is unlikely that they will rely on total physical security; instead they will place more reliance upon sound relationships with staff and a purposeful program. During 1974 a priority in the allocation of federal was the development of these

---

*On December 1, 1973, there were twelve youngsters who had been placed by the agency in psychiatric hospitals.

units, with particular attention to the provision of a wider range of services for girls.

Unlike the practice in most states, the state agency, rather than county authorities, has the responsibility for those youngsters detained pending their court hearing. The regional director has the responsibility to decide the form of detention. The Department has been able to reduce the number of youngsters held in secure detention by developing some creative alternatives. On December 1, 1973, the Department was responsible for 219 youngsters in detention. Of these, 70 were in secure facilities, 118 in shelter care detention and 31 in temporary foster home detention. Secure detention is provided within a purchased program at the Roslindale facility and at the Worcester and Westfield detention centers. The agency would like to completely abandon Roslindale which is a bleak and barren place, and it is hopeful that further reductions can be made in the number of youngsters held in secure detention. There are seven shelter detention programs throughout the state, consisting of a short-term residence without physical security for about ten youngsters. They are purchased programs, and two of them are located within YMCA buildings. Temporary placement in foster homes while in detention status is the least used of the options. The agency is planning to extend its strategy of purchasing rather than directly providing services for detained youngsters.

(2) The budget for the department of youth services

The agency's budget has increased from $7.2 million in 1969 to $16.3 million for the fiscal year 1974. The agency is still meeting the cost of maintaining the training schools and paying the salaries of about 200 institutional staff positions. These items, for which the agency hopes soon to lose responsibility, amount to $2.7 million. In addition there are 150 positions which the agency would like to abolish but the very strict civil service laws in the state have so far prevented this. It is also necessary to take into account the impact of inflation and the large increase in the agency's caseload. The new pattern of services has resulted in some additional costs, such as the establishment of regional offices and evaluation teams. The agency has also firmly resolved to provide a comprehensive range of services, and in some cases these are very expensive. Leavey would like to see a greater emphasis on the use of foster homes and on non-residential services. One consequence of this would be a reduction in the overall cost of purchased services. Because the agency has had to bear the double cost of the old and new systems it is not yet possible to conclude, in the context of the total budget, that the expenditure for each youngster has decreased since 1969. Within the next two or three years some or most of the unwanted line items on the budget are likely to be removed.* The agency's budget and staff complement should then

---

*Budget details are provided in the *Annual Report of the Department of Youth Services*, 1973.

match its new tasks. Evaluative research data will also be available by then to enable the assessment of comparative costs to take into account data on recidivism.

(3) The purchase of services

The agency either purchases individual placements or makes a contract for the entire program. During 1973 many of the groups that provided services, and in particular foster parents, were put to very severe financial strain with the agency being on many occasions unable to pay for the services it had purchased. This occurred, in the main, because the financial mechanisms had not developed at the same pace as the other major structural changes in the agency. The Department was still bearing much of the cost involved in the upkeep of the training schools, while at the same time greatly increasing its expenditure on purchased services. Neither the agency nor the other parts of state government (such as the Rate Setting Board, which sets the rate for each program) had adjusted to the new and increasing demands resulting from this dramatic organizational change. Furthermore, federal funding was extensively used in the early stages of service purchasing, but as the procedures became routinized state finances were increasingly required.

The level of strain on individual programs caused by these financial difficulties was in part determined by the resources of the program or its parent organization. There did, however, appear to be certain differences in response to the crisis that were not simply a function of financial reserves. A visit to eight community programs in August 1973, just after the worst of the financial crisis, suggested that there might be three broad responses:

- An exclamation of shocked outrage at the way in which change had occurred in the state. A number of statements such as "the real victims are the kids" and "no one was in favor of the old training institutions" were accompanied by protestations about the lack of professionalism of agency staff. The financial situation was seen as evidence that the agency did not know what it was about and as proof that it failed in its mission to provide an alternative system. Those who took this position tended to come from the more established agencies and were mainly outraged at the challenge to their prescriptive approach to the offender and at the apparent removal of sanctions that had in the past made their job seem easier. As professional social workers they had developed a particular perspective on the offender and operated comfortably within a system that had shaped offenders to respond to its needs. They were now, however, being asked to make difficult adjustments at both a personal and organizational level. With the easing of the financial situation, such conflicts are likely to become more visible.

- A response of strained tolerance. Most programs were concerned with providing a good service, but remained very anxious as to whether the program could continue to operate effectively at a high level of frustration and uncertainty.
- A determined commitment to overcome the challenges of a new situation. The people involved in these programs were less likely to see themselves in professional social work terms and were more closely identified with the youngsters. Financial security, although welcome, was not an essential part of their lives. The program staff was likely to share the problem with the youngsters and to work out a joint method of tackling it. This was seen as part of the process of being involved in the program, and on one occasion staff members and youngsters took part in a sleep-in at the agency headquarters to focus attention on their situation. Although such confrontation tactics were used, the staff expressed a great deal of sympathy for the agency and placed the blame on factors beyond its control.

(4) Philosophy and content of services

The purchase of services approach has allowed the agency to place youngsters in a wide variety of programs. As of December 1, 1973, the agency was responsible for 2,602 youngsters in over 200 programs (not including 219 detention cases).* They were to be found within these broad categories:

	Committals	Referrals
Residential Services		
Group Homes, Boarding Schools, etc.	379	199
Foster Care	136	63
Non-Residential Services		
Street Programs, Day School, etc.	368	294
Parole	1163	—

---

*It is interesting to compare the 1970 and 1973 situation. In 1970 the agency was responsible for 932 youngsters (average daily count). They were distributed as follows:

Institutions: 507	Group Care: 125
Detention: 238	Foster Care: 30
Forestry: 25	Non-Residential: 7

Exact parole figures are not available for 1970. It is estimated that there were approximately 1200 youngsters on parole status, but most of these were receiving minimal services.

Specialized services which were not part of the residential situation were also provided to 71 youngsters placed in residential programs. There were also 837 youngsters with an inactive parole status.

The residential programs include a variety of types of group homes, placement in boarding schools, and very exceptionally in a psychiatric hospital. The agency itself is responsible for a small forestry camp at Cape Cod. Most youths can expect to stay at a group home for three to four months. Placement in other residential programs, and in foster care, is likely to be for longer periods. Some interesting research is being collected by the Harvard team which indicates that youth placed in group homes have a considerably higher regard for the staff of these programs than did the youngsters for staff in training schools three years ago. There are two particular pertinent issues concerning programs:

(a) Alternatives to the medical model   Miller hoped that it would be possible to develop programs that would avoid moving from penal to medical definitions. In relation to the emerging changes in Massachusetts, he wrote:

> In terms of ideology, the question of correctional reform is not whether we can break out of previous definitions to more up-to-date definitions. It is rather whether we can (1) effectively break the vicious circle of definitions calling for institutional arrangements which, in turn, revalidate the definitions and (2) build into new definitions (since they will come) enough categories that show the social and psychological strengths and life-span of those defined as delinquent or criminal.*

Many of the programs, however, still operate within a prescriptive frame of reference with assumptions about personal pathology very much to the fore. There is considerable room both to extend the choice that youngsters have as to the program they enter and also to allow youngsters more opportunity to shape program design and operation. Leavey and his staff intend to give more time to the development of standards that would prompt program design to experiment with alternatives to the medical model.

(b) The meaning of "Community Corrections."   Deinstitutionalization did not mean that all youngsters went home. A number of the residential programs are situated a considerable distance from the youngsters' homes. The need to link the residential program with the youngster's own community, to which he will be returning, is as critical as it was in the training school.

---

*Jerome Miller, "The Politics of Change: Correctional Reform," in *Closing Correctional Institutions,* edited by Yitzhak Bakal, Lexington, Mass.: D. C. Heath, 1973.

Some of the residential and all the non-residential programs are situated within the youngster's own community, and continued attention is being given to program design that has immediate relevance to the young person's needs. A related and key question concerns whether decisions about such crucial issues as placement should be made by a state agency or the court. It can be argued that the court is closer to the local scene than the regional office of a state agency. One result of this, however, might be considerable discrepancies in the qualities of services provided across the state. Without careful safeguards, a further consequence might be the reappearance of youth institutions in Massachusetts. Leavey is very conscious of the role that the agency plays both in maintaining the level of services and in offsetting pressures toward reinstitutionalization.

(5) The implications of referrals to the department

One of the factors that contributed to the agency's budgetary problems was the increase in the number of youth served. This was partly the result of an unanticipated increase in the number of youngsters referred by the courts to the agency. In December 1973 referrals represented a little over 21 percent of the total of the agency's active caseload, excluding detention. The purpose of referral is to avoid the stigma of commitment and to ensure that the youngster receives adequate services. A referral requires the voluntary agreement of the youngster, his attorney, his parents, and the judge. A key role is usually played by the agency's Court Liaison Officer.* One reason for the increase in referrals during 1973, which is interesting given the critical stance of many judges toward the agency, is that the courts have been more impressed by the quality of services that youth receive through the agency than with services arranged by the Department of Public Welfare. The agency, however, does refuse to accept a large number of referrals, and by the end of 1973 was taking active steps to reduce the referral rate. The acceptance of referrals by the agency raises important issues quite apart from additional financial strain that results. A central concern is the possibility that the process widens the correctional net to include youngsters who might not otherwise have penetrated so far into the criminal justice system. How this issue is resolved will depend a great deal on the way in which the agency is perceived by youth and the public in general. Given a widespread reduction in the stigma attached to the agency, and continued provision of high quality services, the referral method of intake can be justified. It is clearly a matter that requires careful research and continual review.

An associated issue is the agency's policy to retain youngsters on an inactive parole status after the provision of services has been

---

*It should be noted that Court Liaison Officers, who are employees of the Department, have played a key role in improving the relationship with the courts.

terminated.* This is done so that the agency can be an advocate for the youngster if such an occasion arises, and a strong defense of the practice can be made. If, however, the agency were less benign, it would be under considerable pressure to make a clear parole termination. This points to some central issues which the agency must face concerning the rights of all youngsters, whether committed or referred. These include the opportunity for the youngster to protest a program placement at any time, and to be given a hearing as to parole termination should he request one. During the crusading phase, when the task was to get the youngsters out of the institutions, such issues did not arise. The grievance was seen as the old system and the agency as the advocate of change. This advocacy role will continue to be important, but it should not be allowed to obscure the development of procedures that provide the young person with the means of redress concerning decisions made about him by the agency, however benign in intent they might be.

(6) Evaluation

Mention has been made of the teams sent out from central office to evaluate programs. This process is growing in sophistication, and plays an important part in the establishment of standards. Four programs have been terminated and others modified as a result of these inspections. The agency has undertaken a small research program, and its organization of data requires considerable refinement. It is particularly fortunate that a major research study commenced in 1969 under the direction of Professor Lloyd Ohlin of the Center for Criminal Justice at the Harvard Law School. The Harvard study, which is financed by the Law Enforcement Assistance Administration, and by the Governor's Committee on Law Enforcement and Administration of Criminal Justice, has five main components:

1   An organizational study of the agency during this period of radical change in shape and function.
2   A study of the political arena within which the changes occurred.
3   Subculture studies within institutions and group homes.
4   Program evaluation. The focus here is on general strategies rather than particular programs. This is the closest that the Harvard study comes to action research.
5   The cohort study. Successive admissions are being followed through the system, within two regions at any one time. The data that is generated by the cohort study will answer the question as to the recidivism of those youngsters who went through the institutional system as compared with those who went through the system after the training schools were closed.

---

*The Department can retain responsibility up to the age of 21.

A number of papers have already been prepared and many others will appear during the next few years, including two or three major publications.* The Harvard research is important in a number of respects. In particular, it will provide an objective account and analysis of a significant landmark in correctional change. The Harvard study started before the training schools were closed, and its findings will throw light on a development that no part of the United States has been able to ignore. In the meantime, the quarterly and other reports from the Harvard study should enable the Department to avoid becoming trapped with new panaceas. This regular flow of information and the constant stream of visitors to the agency should encourage staff to think through the implications of the considerable feedback material that is available. Youth served by the system should also have input into these deliberations. David Rothman in his book, *The Discovery of the Asylum*, has clearly expressed the required note of warning: "Proposals that promise the most grandiose consequences often legitimate the most unsatisfactory developments . . . *(But)* we need not remain trapped in inherited answers. An awareness of the causes and implications of past choices should encourage us to greater experimentation with our own solutions."†

THE POLITICAL CONTEXT OF CORRECTIONAL CHANGE IN MASSACHUSETTS

When Miller arrived in Massachusetts, there was little political support for the status quo, and the legislation enacted in 1969 was clearly a mandate for meaningful change. Such change had the very strong backing of the Governor, a number of influential legislators, and a large number of groups across the state. Much of the media had played an important part in drawing attention to the inequities of the old system, and the press continued to provide Miller with considerable support. His crusading style allowed the issues at stake to be dramatically polarized and neatly articulated by the press and television; people were either for or against kids. The removal of children from the training schools took place within this context, and although Miller was to face considerable opposition from some legislative committee members and certain segments of the media, he was never in deep trouble. By the beginning of 1973, the closing of the training schools had ceased to be a political issue. None of the opponents whom Sargent may face in the 1974 gubernatorial election is likely to use youth corrections as an issue. During 1973 some judges

---

*The most complete report available to date is in Lloyd E. Ohlin, Robert B. Coates, Alden D. Miller, "Radical Correctional Reform: A Case Study of the Massachusetts Youth Correctional System." *Harvard Educational Review*, 44 (1) 1974.

†David Rothman, *The Discovery of the Asylum*, Boston: Little, Brown and Company, 1971, page 295.

expressed concern about the limited options they had for the more serious offender. In September a number of them gave testimony to a Commission on Children in which they went on record as calling for legislation which would give courts the power to determine the length of institutional sentences. Leavey and his staff have had a number of meetings with judges, and there is little likelihood of such regressive legislation being enacted. Much of the criticism of the Department of Youth Services during 1973 arose from the budgetary situation, and this in part reflected the very real concern of many personnel in the programs affected. A Post-Audit Committee of the Legislature undertook a very detailed investigation of the administration of the agency but the committee's report is not expected to create much of a furor. Given the improvement in the agency's financial position, the report will probably seem out of date.

In January 1972 John Boone was appointed commissioner of the Department of Correction, and a continuing series of controversies deflected some of the political heat away from the youth corrections. This was particularly so in the case of certain legislators and a daily newspaper, *The Boston Herald American.* Boone had arrived in the state with apparently bipartisan support for an overhaul of the adult prison system. Some important prison reform legislation, in the main developed before his appointment, was enacted in July 1972, pointing adult corrections in the direction of the community. Boone, however, was to find himself involved in upsets and crises involving one prison after another each of which was used by some legislators and segments of the media as justification for demanding his resignation. The adult corrections scene was to a large degree shaped by correctional officers' unions, which together with the increasing organization of prisoners, created a highly volatile situation. There is little doubt that Sargent backed meaningful change in adult corrections for longer than narrow political considerations suggested was wise. It was with considerable reluctance that Sargent decided, in June 1973, that Boone had to go. The presence in Massachusetts of this liberal Republican Governor (both Houses are controlled by the Democrats) in part explains why during 1972–1973 Massachusetts was the most interesting state to watch in relation to both youth and adult corrections.

The changes that have taken place in youth corrections in Massachusetts have implications for every state in the Union and beyond. No agency for young offenders can ignore the fact that Massachusetts has now existed without training schools for two years. The process of deinstitutionalization is, throughout the Western world, taking place over a wide range of areas of social concern. It implies not the ready solution of problems, but the creation of opportunities to face them more realistically. The Massachusetts experience, one of the major correctional events of our time, has enhanced our ability and confidence to take the creative leap forward that is needed in the development of more humane and effective approaches to social problems.

"The Youth Ain't Criminal, the Institution Is": Alternative Programs for Juvenile Delinquents

DEXTER WAUGH

Dexter Waugh is a newspaper journalist in the San Francisco area.

A word of caution. The development of these alternatives, designed to divert offenders from institutions by means of community alternatives, should not be controlled by those presently in command of conventional correctional systems. Decisive participation by the private sector is indispensable. True alternatives are competing alternatives: the correctional establishment is poorly prepared, both by tradition and ideology, to nurture its own replacement. The surest way to defeat such a program would be to place it under the control of those who have been unable either to acknowledge or to correct their own fundamental errors.

–RICHARD KORN

Dr. Korn's statement in 1971 to Senator Birch Bayh's Senate Subcommittee to Investigate Juvenile Delinquency has been virtually ignored. The funding process for most alternative programs, originating in Washington and funneled through the states and then to the counties or regions, has insured a subtle, but unmistakable, degree of control. Alternative programs not controlled in some manner by existing correctional systems are rare indeed. In the San Francisco Bay Area, the geographical focus of this study, there has been, from the mid-sixties to the mid-seventies, a trend toward control over alternative methods of dealing with offenders by those officers of the existing institutional systems. Although activities in the San Francisco region during that decade may not be typical of the national experience, programs were put into practice there that addressed the problem of juvenile delinquency among various ethnic groups.

Among the forty or fifty different language and ethnic groupings found in San Francisco, there are Chinese, Japanese, blacks, Chicanos, Samoans, and Koreans. Although court-ordered school busing distributes San Francisco's youth across the city during school hours, the various minority groups tend to dwell in specific neighborhoods. They come from homes and neighborhoods where ties among people of similar backgrounds are stronger than that in the city as a whole. During the decade under discussion, these various neighborhood interest groups began to vie for funds to remedy specific juvenile problems that were not being addressed by the bureaucracy. While official responses to these entreaties tended to keep neighborhood groups in competition with one another, attempts were made to form citywide coalitions to compete more strategically for the limited funds available for programs dealing with juvenile offenders. The successes and failures of these attempts gave a dynamic spin to the routine processes surrounding distribution of funds—"seed money"—flowing from Washington during the sixties.

Several instances illustrate how control over juvenile offenders evolving since the late 1890s was maintained. These include Real Alternatives Program (RAP), which began in San Francisco's multiracial, Latino-dominated Mission District in 1969, and, later, the San Francisco Youth Services Bureau. RAP was one of a handful of alternative, community-based programs that resisted absorption by the traditional systems. This resistance was grounded both in philosophical and personal commitments, although the founder of RAP, Jim Queen, stated that the personal differences stemmed from an intellectual analysis of the traditional correctional system. Queen was to insist that "the youth ain't criminal, the institution is," which became a RAP slogan that was emblazoned on its posters. RAP's unyielding approach predictably led them into a direct confrontation with the juvenile court judge of San Francisco and the judge's chief juvenile probation officer (CJPO)—a clash that lasted over five years.

The alternative viewpoint embraced a conflict analysis of the juvenile justice system, and a belief that it is a fundamental mistake to attempt rehabilitation of youths toward a system which they perceived had failed them in the first place. The judge and the CJPO, on the other hand, embraced an ordered approach, which encouraged gradual, controlled change in the system, rather than relinquishing jurisdiction to community groups. This difference in viewpoint meant that RAP and others in the Free Youth Coalition* were denied the access to juveniles, which was available to other community-based groups that did not openly challenge the legitimacy of the judge and the court structure.

The services offered by alternative, community-based programs are substantially different than services offered through juvenile hall. Alternative programs do not follow a service model in the traditional sense. They are rather "organizing" models, in which wards of the court and other youths are "organized," first to understand the contradictions in the system and then to work toward institutional change. The community organization acts as a representative of the youth's community. It operates on the premise that the youth can-

---

*The Free Youth Coalition was a shifting coalition of six to ten youth groups, including, at various times, community agencies of Potrero Hill, Hunters Point, the Western Addition, and Chinatown—all minority-dominated groups that were pro-community and anti-establishment.

not afford high-priced attorneys, will get little or no help from the institution's staff, and will be placed in lock-up unless the community organization convinces the staff to release the youth in its care.

There is an implicit understanding that the community group acts as a surrogate for the judicial system, suggesting a degree of co-operation between the community group and the court probation system. The groups usually insist that cooperation means one-way co-optation, and that the youth has a right to remain in his own community to be "treated" by his own peers, including people from his own environment as well as youthful "veterans" of the judicial system. In this, the community groups remind that the juvenile court began as a surrogate for a parent who was absent or was unable to handle parental responsibilities. Once given that legal responsibility, however, the court today argues that it cannot release its hold on the child as easily as the parent.

If the youth is released into the care of community groups, he is required to make regular contacts with its workers, and take part in various community programs. He will have a chance to serve on youth committees, and to become involved in attempts to organize community members around various issues, such as securing jobs for the community, better housing, and improved or alternative schooling. The key to the alternative approach is to instill in the youth a sense of responsibility to both himself and to the community against which he transgressed. RAP and other groups in the Free Youth Coalition were viewed with abhorrence by the court because they stressed the inadequacy of the court system, and encouraged youths to oppose it, repeatedly advocating alternatives based on the premise that neighborhood matters should be controlled by those in the neighborhoods. An example of the education a youth experiences at RAP was described by Queen: "These kids come out of YGC [the Youth Guidance Center, or juvenile hall] bragging about how many times they've been there. We tell him, that's cool, his parents have to go down there each time he gets thrown in jail and beg to get him out. We tell him if he thinks that's slick, that's together, to have your parents begging to get your ass out of jail, right on, but don't come to us. A lot of kids really flashed on that."

Numerous studies during the sixties showed that the nation's court system was failing to rehabilitate youthful offenders. Of some six thousand youths taken to juvenile hall each year in San Francisco during the early 1970s, over four thousand were released at intake. Virtually none of these youths was followed up, either by probation staff or alternative groups, to determine his or her needs. Studies meanwhile showed that some of San Francisco's alternative, community-based youth programs had been more effective when compared with institutionalizing youths; they showed higher success rate at less cost. These limited evaluations often suggested that the programs could be even more effective if given an adequate chance.

However, alternative programs were rarely allowed time to prove themselves. Members of the Free Youth Coalition asserted that juvenile hall should be closed down and replaced by neighborhood councils, consisting of adults and youths, to which the youth would be taken in lieu of a trip to juvenile hall and court. Resources and programs would be developed by these councils within San Francisco neighborhoods, using existing talents. This system never got off the ground, primarily because it required transferring authority and jurisdiction from the court and probation department to community lay-people. The principle behind the system was introduced at the state level, although it was not passed into law. It would have established youth boards in every senior high school attendance area to deal with errant youths both before and after they encounter the juvenile justice system, with the majority of each board consisting of adults and high school students elected from each area.

Something similar to that did come into being in East Palo Alto, a primarily black community of about twenty thousand, located thirty miles south of San Francisco. Since East Palo Alto is an unincorporated area serviced by the San Mateo County sheriff's department, youths from there have traditionally been taken to juvenile hall and adjudicated in a system dominated by white judges and probation officers, and placed in institutional programs with mostly white youths, since the rest of the county is predominantly white. East Palo Alto residents considered this system unsatisfactory. The Community Youth Responsibility Program (CYRP) evolved after years of residents being "victimized by the law enforcement agencies, the courts," according to CYRP's director, Ralph Trivers. While he and others saw a need for transferring control into the hands of East Palo Alto residents, the transition process was difficult to accomplish. It was ultimately accomplished because it was successful in what it sought to do, and because it was absorbed as a distinct part of the county probation system. East Palo Alto could be compared with an African colony that is grudgingly given a semblance of independence by a European colonizer. However, the East Palo Alto youth program was intricately interwoven with the county probation network; it depended on having wards referred to it from other agencies of the county's juvenile justice system.

"It was a new concept," said Trivers. "The law enforcement agencies were wary, the community people were unsure. They initially saw us as an extension of the existing system." After several public hearings, the East Palo Alto municipal council approved the new program. It developed a rocky on-again, off-again rapport with the sheriff's department, the probation department, and other criminal agencies in the county. Originally funded through federal Law Enforcement Assistance Administration (LEAA) money, the CYRP—like the youth bureau in nearby Pacifica—is now funded by the county of San Mateo using a formula based on the savings of diverting youths away from the more expensive court-probation process.

The CYRP was one of the first alternative programs in the county to utilize a panel of youth peers to sit in judgment in lieu of a juvenile court judge. Though the program was voluntary, the vast majority of East Palo Alto youths who encountered the justice system opted for the CYRP rather than the traditional process. The panel functioned in a predictable way, not substantially different from the normal court process, as is illustrated by the case of Carol, a thirteen-year-old who was caught shoplifting in nearby Palo Alto, a largely white community, home of Stanford, one of California's largest private universities. It was a Thursday night, and Carol, who appeared before the panel with her mother, was one of four youths whose cases were being considered.

"Is this the first time you ever shoplifted?" asked Tony Bishop, a college student who was a member of the panel.

"No," responded Carol.

"Do you know how much money they pay people to watch kids, especially black kids, when they come in stores?" asked David Butler, a high school student also on the panel. "Have you ever heard of Hillcrest [the county juvenile hall]?" Butler continued. "Do you know that if this program wasn't here, they'd probably put you in Hillcrest, and maybe the next time they will? You're thirteen, you should get yourself together rather than going this route. Else you are going to get a big fat record that'll follow you everywhere. So you ought to think about that."

"You may have people coming to your home and confronting you with something you didn't do, just because you have a record," added Kenneth Perkins, an East Palo Alto high school graduate.

"I hesitate to believe you didn't know what you were going to do when you went in that store," said Mrs. Johnnie Price, the chairperson of the panel. "Because if you were going to buy something, you would have taken along some money. And remember, your last referral to us was for a similar incident."

Willie B. Bowser, the tall, sixty-four-year-old CYRP investigator, told the panel he had visited Carol's home. "There's no reason for her to steal. She lives in an adequate home. It's up to snuff."

Carol's mother commented, "She's just not settled. She has a lot of peer pressure."

Although Carol was usually talkative with her peers, she had little to say in the face of the panel. In many ways her experience reinforced a statement by Queen, in support of turning over the control process to community people: "A council composed of your peers would be a hell of a lot more strict than the court with a kid who had messed up. If the kid is in the community, we're going to see him on the street every day, and we're going to give him shit if he's jiving around. And besides being stricter, we'd also be more supportive. How can a probation officer, who sees him maybe once a month, do that?"

Carol and her mother left the room while the panel deliberated.

Mrs. Price told the others that Carol had been referred to the CYRP on a prior occasion by her mother, who had found stolen articles in the home. This time Carol had been caught in the act by authorities. Through an agreement with the Palo Alto police and the Sheriff's department, juveniles from East Palo Alto who commit minor offenses were handled by the CYRP. Now the panel was deliberating her "sentence."

Tony Bishop suggested that "her mother may have summed up the girl's predicament. She's going through a lot of peer pressure. I think she's just asking for attention."

"She likes clothes; maybe she could learn to sew over at the girls' club," said Cheryl Hall, an eighteen-year-old college student, and, like the others, a resident of East Palo Alto.

After perhaps fifteen minutes of discussion, the panel agreed on a three- to four-month "involvement" for Carol with the CYRP. When Carol and her mother returned, Carol's mother requested that the panel increase it to six months. The "involvement" meant that Carol would meet with a CYRP counselor at least once a week. The counselor would decide, after consultation with Carol, what sort of program to recommend. The counselor would not be the same as a probation officer, in terms of how she (or he) would be perceived by Carol. Trivers, although in fact a probation officer on loan from the county probation department, was careful not to use the word "probation"; youths were told they were being "involved" in CYRP's program. In that way, he said, the stigma, and glory, of being on probation were removed.

Mrs. Price, the chairperson, told Carol she would be given a work task, to be selected by the counselor after talking with Carol. She concluded by giving a little speech: "I hope during this time you will think, get your head in the right direction; else you will be taken away from the community next time. Each time you tell us you're sorry; but you've got to prove you're sorry. This is the Community Youth Responsibility Program, and you've got to take responsibility for your acts."

The panel never assumed guilt, even though youths were usually referred by the sheriff's department or probation. This second-level safeguarding of rights was an important value of the CYRP. In cases where there was a dispute, Mr. Bowser arranged to have all personnel involved come to testify—school principals or deans, sheriff's deputies, or citizens. The same night Carol appeared, the panel also heard the case of a seventeen-year-old boy, charged with assault and battery on a teacher. Since the boy's testimony, coupled with Bowser's findings, suggested that the teacher might have been the aggressor, the panel postponed the case two weeks until the teacher could come in to testify.

Some eight hundred youths went through the CYRP between 1970 and 1975, most of them with an "involvement" of six months. Recidivism was measured each year between 14 and 18 percent (after six months), a much lower rate than for youths going through the conventional county justice system.*

A similar project operated during the same time in Pacifica, a largely white community in San Mateo County. The police chief and the juvenile officer there praised the Youth Services Bureau (YSB), which they view as being essentially an adjunct of their department. One of nine pilot projects begun in the late 1960s by the state of California, the Pacifica Youth Services Bureau is now funded by the county, and operates under a unique joint powers agreement among the city council, the school district, the delinquency prevention commission, and the county board of supervisors. The cornerstone of the Pacifica YSB is family counseling. Its director, Mark Savage, stated that the bureau had never been successful when counseling involved only the youth. He cited the case of a boy, a junior in high school, to illustrate the necessity of parental involvement in working out a youth's problems. "School was a pain in the neck to this kid, and he was a pain in the neck to the schoolteachers. He would do outrageous things in the classroom so he'd get kicked out." The youth was referred to the YSB, where a counselor convinced the youth's father to accompany him to the sessions. After a few consultations, a deal was struck between father and son. The father, a foreman on a loading dock, would allow the youth to quit school and work on the dock. In return, the youth agreed to pay for tutoring out of his earnings. "It was a beautiful solution," said Savage. "But it wasn't one we could have arrived at. We didn't know the dad could get him a job on a loading dock for $5.83 an hour. Eight months later, the youth had his GED [high school diploma equivalent]. Can you imagine if the kid had come in here himself and then gone home and said, 'Dad, the counselor says I ought to quit school.' His dad would have come down here so mad he would have torched the place."

Pacific police praised the YSB because they saw it as nonthreatening and cooperative. "When we take a kid in there they know we have done all we can," stated the police juvenile officer. After four years, the Pacifica police were referring about one-tenth of their total juvenile cases to the YSB. Over half of the youths counseled by the YSB had experienced emotional, family, or school problems. Like East Palo Alto, Pacifica is a small, isolated, and homogeneous community, but compared to East Palo Alto, the gap between its citizens and the managers of its criminal justice system is not as great. It experienced some of the problems typical of California's bedroom

---

*In the summer of 1976, San Mateo County officials terminated funding support for CYRP, after it failed to receive the increased number of youth referrals that had been projected for it by county personnel, using the cost-savings formula employed when the county had originally picked up support of the program. There were some allegations, particularly by the mayor of East Palo Alto, that the county's move was "racist," since the county at the same time launched several new youth service bureau programs elsewhere in areas where the population was predominantly white

542

suburban communities in the late 1960s, receiving a great deal of local publicity concerning increased drug use by youths. The YSB was viewed in some ways as an alternative method of tackling this and other juvenile problems. When it began, the YSB allowed several youths under the age of eighteen to serve on its board. But a few citizens pointed out that this violated state law, which excluded minors from public servitude. After consulting city and county attorneys, the Pacifica directors acquiesced, changing the bureau's bylaws to exclude youths.

In contrast to the experience of Pacifica, when San Francisco began its YSB in 1975, it chose to challenge the same state law. An amendment was passed into law by the state legislature, allowing minors to serve on the policy making bodies of publicly supported agencies that serve youths. Youth membership on the San Francisco YSB board was an issue from the outset, essentially involving the same antagonists who had been involved in previous skirmishes between court and community-control advocates. The YSB had been planned and established by the mayor's Criminal Justice Council (MCJC), the local planning body for Law Enforcement Assistance Administration grant funds. Under the MCJC plan, eleven ex officio members were automatically seated on the board. These consisted of the heads of all existing agencies dealing with youths, including the juvenile court judge, his chief juvenile probation officer, and the heads of the police juvenile bureau, parks and recreation, the school district, and so on. In addition, the MCJC plan provided for ten community representatives to be seated, which gave the ex officio members a one-vote edge.

A citizens committee, an outgrowth of the earlier Free Youth Coalition and involving many of the same people and groups, pressured for an election. The community representatives, they said, should be elected from each of the five districts outlined in the earlier, community-based "council" plan. The elections were held, and three members were elected from each district. Ultimately, the YSB bylaws were amended to allow the seating of fifteen community members, three from each of the five districts. The strongest opposition to expansion of the board came from the Chief Juvenile Probation Officer, who objected that the board would become dominated by community people. He suggested that both young people and other community agency workers were motivated by a desire to control the board, and that the court and probation department could not legally abdicate their authority and jurisdiction. The community people, some of whom were aligned with the RAP forces, argued successfully that programs serving and affecting youths should have meaningful youth involvement at the policy level, and that youths could gauge their own problems and needs better than adults. The same argument had been used at the state level during the legislative process of amending the law to allow minors to serve on such program boards. A majority of the board voted for expansion, seating fifteen community representatives, including five minors. The expanded board then elected a seventeen-year-old high school senior as its chairman over the only other candidate, who was also seventeen.

It was clear from the outset, however, that the board's authority stemmed directly from the MCJC, which was dominated by the same justice system officials who comprised the ex officio element of the YSB board. The main focus over the following months involved cutting off direct ties to the MCJC, and adopting bylaws that would give more power to the community element. There was disunity among the community members, and much effort was expended on internal bickering rather than concentrating on developing a comprehensive plan for delivering services to San Francisco youths. As previously noted, the community was not initially unanimous in support of a community-based and controlled system. Some community representatives had philosophical difficulties in accepting the YSB, since it had been planned from the top down, rather than originating within the communities. Others, long denied access to the traditional process, were ready to become part of it.

It remained to be seen how successful the community aspect of the YSB board would be in diverting the correctional system from its traditional path. However, the YSB was the first significant convening of people with differing ideologies and attitudes. Most of the traditional system recognized the value of YSB attempts to accommodate youths and community agency workers. The handwriting was already starting to fade from the wall when San Francisco's system managers finally met with their critics on a superficially equal basis. This did not occur entirely of their own volition, of course, but largely in response to federal and state encouragements that such Youth Service Bureau boards reflect the populations they serve. Soon after this, Jim Queen and several other long-time critics from around the state were appointed to the state Council on Criminal Justice. Queen and the others began raising questions about various regional grant applications, such as those from San Francisco's MCJC, which had been prepared without community review. At the same time, the YSB hired as its first executive director a young man who from the outset stated his approval of the concept of diversion, and criticized the traditionally closed planning process. Everything considered, it seemed that the gap between the community and those managing the system was being narrowed even further.

The history of the relationship of the court and the community groups, as well as later development of the YSB illustrates how managers of the existing system attempted to maintain control of the processing and treatment of juvenile offenders in the face of mounting local and national pressure for alternatives to institutionalization. The chief juvenile probation officer at the time of this writing came to San Francisco in 1970, at a time when the juvenile hall was grossly overcrowded. He relieved the situation by simply releasing a greater number of youths into the care of community-based programs, which had begun to develop in the late 1960s, following the report of the President's Commission on Crime. These emerging programs were used, but the CJPO was careful to maintain a vigil for the slightest erosion of the court's jurisdictional and legal powers. This approach was lauded by traditionalists and criticized by reformists.

Although in the early 1970s the MCJC began bringing together the heads of the various public agencies who regularly dealt with youths, interagency conflicts emerged. In some ways, the MCJC and its various task forces tended to exacerbate conflicts by bringing together these professional public servants. For instance, when the San Francisco Police Department launched a new diversion program of its own design for juveniles early in 1975, it received only grudging cooperation from the juvenile court judge and probation officers. The program, which focused primarily on first offenders, used an objective score sheet to determine whether a youth was "divertible." Some twenty-eight offenses or conditions were listed, which automatically excluded youths from the program, ranging from murder to traffic citations, or whether the youth was a current or prior diversion client. The MCJC youth task force, consisting of the same ex-officio members as the YSB board, cancelled the program's second-year LEAA funding, diverting it to the new YSB. The police officers, who had worked for nearly a year to set up their diversion program, protested vehemently, concerned both by the loss of their proprietary rights over the program and by legitimate questions concerning the role of the new YSB.

The police diversion program did have some positive side effects. Despite initial conflicts between police and probation officers, good relations were established after the program was launched. The police valued this relationship, since often they did not have records of youths referred to probation by non-police sources. In addition, police and probation officers cooperated on a neighborhood drop-in center, where parents and youths could meet one night a week to discuss their cases. This was a pilot project similar to that suggested in the MCJC's proposal for the new YSB, which envisioned the eventual formation of YSB teams consisting of a probation officer, a police officer, a mental health worker, a social worker, a community referral representative, a learning specialist, and an attorney. These teams, situated in three to five districts around San Francisco, would be similar to the citizen committee's five-district peer council system. But they would differ in that they would be based on the traditional treatment model, and would be legal arms of the existing system, maintaining official control over youngsters in the various districts. The citizen committee's proposal was based on the premise that the peer councils would be quasi-legal, distinct from the court, elected within the various districts, and accountable only to the districts' constituencies.

A version of the YSB team proposal had been tried unsuccessfully by the court in 1970–71, when the Free Youth Coalition managed to block an attempt by the CJPO to establish a probation out-post in the Mission district. Resistance rose out of the fact that the probation department planned to dispatch a white, English-speaking probation officer into a district heavily populated by Latinos and Chicanos—another attempt by the established system to undermine the community-controlled, noncorrectional model. Their resistance was successful. But the court's attempts to establish quasi-alternative decentralized systems was successful in the fall of 1974, when the CJPO secured a federal grant to start a remedial school program for sixty dropouts and offenders at three locations in the city. Since they lacked the facilities to establish separate, new facilities, the probation department, with the cooperation of the school district, set them up at existing community youth centers.

Although the community agencies grumbled privately that the program was imposed upon them, they complied for several reasons. First, with the program there rather than at juvenile hall, the community could exercise some degree of control over it. Second, the program added another component to their own structures, giving them a sense of legitimacy. Finally, they believed in the essential worth of the program. (Members of the Free Youth Coalition, which by then had evolved into the Citizens Committee, were not asked to participate.) The three agencies that participated were able to exercise control over the program at their respective sites. The teachers, who had previous affiliations with the agencies, largely determined the curriculum. Left on their own to adapt the class format to the students, the innovative teachers grew pleased with the results, seeing youths with long truancy records attending classes each day. Beyond securing the initial grant, however, the probation department and the school district reportedly did little to provide on-going support, leaving it up to the teachers to secure their own class supplies. The following year the program was left totally in the lurch. Although funding was available, the various bureaucracies fiddled and faddled so long that the program, due to resume in the fall of 1975, did not begin until March 1976. One of the teachers, who remained on the school district's payroll for much of this time, was given no assignment during the six-month period. He stood by helplessly as his former students, reassigned to regular schools, began losing interest and dropped out once again.

This lack of commitment from the existing system was not unexpected. Alternative group programs were used by the court-probation system when expedient, but little was done to help them survive. Of over three hundred community youth programs in San Francisco dealing with both specialized and generalized problems affecting minors, over half went out of business for lack of funds between 1969 and 1975. The paid staffs of these programs were usually small, and the executive director often spends up to half his time, during a given year, solely concerned with seeking financial assistance for the program. The competition for funding weeded out both private programs that were failures, and those that had success with the youths in their care. The survival of such programs has often depended on the imagination of their directors.

One well-known streetwork program for boys in San Francisco, for instance, devised an ingenious method to extend its LEAA funding after its first three-year grant ran out. It simply started again, this time focusing entirely on girls, enabling it to qualify as a new program. Other programs in San Francisco have bypassed the dead-end street of federal funding by avoiding it altogether: RAP, for instance, started with a private foundation grant, and later received funds from United Way, a charitable program requiring annual renewal. In 1976, United Way placed RAP on probation because of what it perceived as a "bad relationship" with YGC. RAP workers blamed this on a member of the probation department staff who served on United Way's budget committee, and countered that their only bad relations were with YGC administration, not the probation officers and other line personnel.

Energy, a program serving mainly white youths in a predominantly white area of San Francisco, managed to secure federal revenue-sharing money when its LEAA funds ran out. Energy now goes through the same annual budget process that other city departments go through, which has made them as skillful in this area as many city hall bureaucrats. The experience of Energy demonstrates that even white groups must use ingenuity in dealing with the white power structure. In the early days of the RAP coalition, Energy experienced internal changes, adopted a new executive director, a new board of directors, and a new direction of toning down its role as public adversary, but maintaining its advocacy of alternatives. It was taken on as a project by a local bank, which provided volunteer, daily help, as well as executive expertise. These executives were initially helpful in 1974, when Energy requested $100,000 in federal revenue-sharing funds that had been portioned out to the San Francisco mayor's office for distribution to various agencies and programs. Although Energy had received $50,000 of such funds with little trouble the previous year, in 1974 the funds were eliminated from the mayor's budget.

Energy subsequently spent four months working to get the funds restored to the mayor's budget. The staff mounted a meticulously mapped out campaign, involving lobbying and gathering support from virtually every city agency that dealt with juvenile delinquency. It involved such fine touches as getting one of its board directors, who had a season opera seat next to that occupied by the city's chief administrative officer, to line up a meeting to explain Energy's program and needs. The campaign, which began in January, reached virtually every influential person in San Francisco, and did not end until the group finally met in April with a close associate of the mayor. This owner of a San Francisco hotel prevailed upon the mayor to restore the $50,000 in the mayor's budget. When the appropriation finally reached the Board of Supervisors, it was increased to $83,000.

Energy's change in direction helped it stay alive but weakened the Free Youth Coalition, since there was now one less member group in the alternative systems coalition. While Energy successfully proceeded to financially renew itself, two other coalition groups in predominantly black sections of the city failed to secure funding, and went out of business.

Energy, although following a course of peppering away from inside rather than sharp public opposition, was the most verbal opponent of the MCJC, when in 1975 it attempted to institute stricter evaluative procedures over community groups that were receiving federal LEAA funds. The MCJC wanted to track such groups' youth clientele in a way that the staff of Energy and every other youth group felt would violate the confidentiality of the youths served. This conflict was being experienced all over the country, but in San Francisco, it centered around the fact that, despite the obvious need for proper evaluation and accountability, such a hard look had never been required of the conventional court-probation system. The probation department, for instance, had never even released recidivism statistics to the state, contending that it did not have the capability to compile them.

The issue of accountability was discussed in a 1975 study for the Bar Association of San Francisco by a criminologist, Robert Mintz. Although mainly concerned with a proposed pretrial diversion program for adults charged with misdemeanors, he summarized well the viewpoint of alternative, community-based programs:

> Community agencies are distrustful and apprehensive about being used by the criminal justice system. Our survey of agencies showed that they were torn between their need to survive and their reluctance to be a part of a possibly punitive criminal justice program. They expressed concerns about confidentiality of records and case "tracking," remuneration for services to be provided, and the additional strain of already overcrowded caseloads.

Mintz's complaints about diversion programs were virtually the same as those that began surfacing in the mid-seventies at every conference of juvenile court judges, district attorneys, public defenders, probation officers, and others in the juvenile justice field. Mintz noted that:

> Diversion is a rationalization of an irrational and discriminatory system. It fails to address the basic inequities which it purports to alleviate, while reinforcing [by abdication] those aspects of the administration of criminal justice which are in need of more fundamental reform.

Mintz noted that police arrest far too many people, and do not sufficiently use citation procedures in lieu of taking youths into cus-

tody. He said that diversion is used on a limited portion of the arrested population and that these tend to be "low risk" misdemeanants
rather than so-called "high risk" youths:

> Diversion has been shown to represent an "expansion of the
> justice system to a neo-justice system" where many of those
> diverted would not have been placed under supervision had
> there been no diversion law. Most would have been placed on
> court probation or would have had their cases dismissed for
> lack of evidence.

In a similar vein, Rutgers University sociologist Paul Lerman found,
in a 1975 study of the California Youth Authority's (CYA's) treatment programs, that juveniles selected for CYA non-institutional
community programs tended to experience more supervision than if
they had simply been incarcerated.

Finally, Mintz pointed out that "diversion is criminal prosecution, albeit without a determination of guilt or innocence," and suggested that funding would be better directed toward correcting
inequities in the existing system rather than toward diversion programs. Some community youth groups in San Francisco were reluctant to participate in the police department's diversion program
because of the lack of due process. The officers who ran the program
insisted that the diversion program was entirely voluntary, and that
every effort was made to remove coercive elements from official deal-
ings with youths. But youths who encountered officers and were told
of the diversion program were invariably presented with an either/or
situation. Either he went through the normal court-probation process, or agreed to be diverted and take part in a community agency
program (for which the agency received no remuneration), thereby
implicitly admitting guilt.

Alternative programs for juveniles have always involved diversion, but usually only after the juvenile had already encountered the
justice system. Thus, diversion programs have not been true alternatives, since, despite claims to the contrary, they are involuntary.
Youths diverted to community programs are still on probation, regardless of whether it is referred to as something else, like "involvement," as in the East Palo Alto program. In the San Francisco police
diversion program, juveniles could be diverted only once.

A true alternative system would seem to involve something
along the lines of the system proposed by the Free Youth Coalition.
Such a system should assess youths' needs and respond to them at a
community level, without the intervention of the criminal justice
system. This would also have involuntary aspects, in being spread
across the board and across the map. But it would avoid the discrimination of the current system, which disproportionately affects
minority and low-income youths, and carries such youths further
along in the system, while dislodging white youths and those from
wealthier families earlier. While most of those who advocate alterna-

tives that return control to the community recognize that there will probably be a "hard core" of incorrigible offenders needing secure detention, they assert the number of such youths is significantly small. Tim Dupre, the first director of the YSB, who began working toward the development of district councils along the lines of the Free Youth Coalition plan, said:

> "The community must be the key in planning and needs assessment. Too long have guidelines and planning requirements descended from the administrative level of institutions or branches of government. . . Community participation in needs assessment is imperative and district councils should be [the] mechanism."

It still remains to be seen whether such an alternative system would be more effective than the present juvenile justice system. The alternative groups have offered something which at least is contradictory to the traditional treatment model. Alternative agencies stress that society is largely responsible for juvenile "acting out" because of racism and oppression. Their view contrasts with that traditionally disseminated by courts, probation departments, and school systems, which insist that all is well with society, and that it is the individual who is ill and must undergo correctional adjustment. San Francisco's most outspoken community groups are often not on good terms with upper-echelon probation staff, they may have to deal with youths who have been referred to them only after encountering the system, and they often must depend on funding sources controlled by the conventional system managers. But in spite of this, their efforts show they can succeed and function on a daily, working basis with probation officers. Community groups have served in large part as mere arms of the justice system, doing little beyond relieving superficial problems, such as overcrowding at juvenile hall.

This is due largely to managers in the conventional system, who view treatment only in a certain way, and are unwilling to accept change unless it is in line with their own concepts. In addition, they are members of a bureaucracy in which fundamental change is possible only when a sufficiently large mandate for change arises outside the system, such as that in Massachusetts in 1969. But the example of Massachusetts also illustrates the trauma that accompanies such change, showing the necessity for careful, coordinated planning lest the change be for naught. Closing down institutions will not eliminate the large numbers of juveniles who must, according to society, be handled, treated, or disposed of. Society has not reached the point where it can once again accept the responsibility it abrogated to the court nearly eighty years ago—the responsibility of handling its own children on an individual basis, father to son, neighbor to neighbor.

The experience of San Diego between 1974 and 1975 underscores the need for coordinated, long-range planning. The CJPO and considerable citizen action in San Diego County, California, was instrumental in changing policy in August 1974, such that juvenile status offenders would no longer be detained at juvenile hall. Although citizen groups had also pressed for an adequate screening and referral service for status offenders, ensuring that they would be sent to proper placement facilities, the money was never budgeted for this. A year later there was utter confusion because these status offenders, of which some five thousand had been housed at juvenile hall during the previous fiscal year, had not been tracked. Assuming that a comparable number would have been housed at juvenile hall between August 1974 and August 1975, authorities should have gathered some information on them. Since none was, no one can say with certainty what happened to the assumed five thousand status offenders between 1974 and 1975. Some observers have suggested that police officers dealt with status offenders by elevating the charges against them to 602s—delinquents. These observers suggest that in the past officers may have ignored more serious charges when mitigating circumstances intervened, and booked them at juvenile hall on a 601 (status offender) charge. Since juvenile hall in 1975 was no longer dealing with status offenders, the assumption is that officers may not have been so inclined to ignore other charges as they had in the past. Although statistics do not prove this assumption, San Diego's juvenile hall records show that after a sudden drop in enrollment, the facility climbed back to capacity, and a year after the policy decision juvenile hall was again jammed with 602s. This occurred simultaneously to a political shift on the San Diego Board of Supervisors, in which a majority of supervisors began supporting a conservative, lock-them-up approach to treatment of juveniles. No money was allocated to provide status offenders with either referrals or treatment services.

The future of treatment of juveniles—whether or not you favor Jim Queen's preference of referring to them as "oppressed" youth—is related to Dr. Korn's view that "the surest way to defeat such a program [of alternatives] would be to place it under the control of those who have been unable either to acknowledge or to correct their own fundamental errors." In San Francisco such control has ensured the failure of alternatives. Authorities fear a shift in power and control from the public to the private sector, and from the established institutional system to a community-controlled system. Such a shift would involve either a loss of jobs, or a fundamental change for many who are accustomed to working in a certain way, under certain conditions. Some also contend that the creation of new bureaucracies in place of the old would merely mean that today's advocates for reform would become managers of the conventional system of tomorrow. This contention reflects a rather static, ordered view of society, which encompasses no concern for its disenfranchised members.

Future approaches should recognize that conflict and constantly shifting power blocs are inherent to this society, and community-controlled models would be subject to change. Communities are not static; we should expect struggle, change, flux, and always a certain amount of insecurity. A community model may sacrifice efficiency (as anyone who attended meetings of citizen boards during the days of the poverty program will testify), but perhaps efficiency and orderliness are not the most crucial values needed to help youths in trouble. The current managers of the system, because of their training, background, and ideology, are ill equipped to manage a community model.

Advocates for change, even those who support a community model, may also eventually become arrogant, distant, and unresponsive to changing community needs. However, a model based on democratic citizen input and control, which can adapt to changing public concerns, would be better able to insure that an unresponsive manager or council member is soon replaced. Since the current system is under the sole authority of the juvenile court judge, who is selected by a committee of other judges, such actions are presently unlikely. If one day the various community councils established on the neighborhood level should become a string of little bureaucracies, then they will also be subject to reform efforts. Then, as now, it will depend on the desires and concerns of the parents and youths themselves. The difference between the system today and tomorrow will revolve around the degree of democratic control today's advocates for change are able to secure.

Confinement in the Community: A Selective Assessment of Paul Lerman's Community Treatment and Social Control: A Critical Analysis of Juvenile Correctional Policy

SHELDON L. MESSINGER*

Reprinted, with permission of the National Council on Crime and Delinquency, from *Journal of Research in Crime and Delinquency*, January 1976, pp. 82-95.

I

For years "evaluation research" in corrections has almost exclusively meant assessment of the effectiveness of programs in stemming the renewed delinquencies and crimes of persons exposed to them. Critics of such research have pointed out that asserted causal links have been seldom demonstrated, criteria of effectiveness often confused or biased, methods frequently faulty, and theories usually weak or absent. Paul Lerman has contributed to this tradition, his widely-known 1968 paper counseling correctional evaluators to look to their criteria and methods unless they wanted to continue to mislead themselves and the more unwary among the rest of us.[1]

With that same paper, however, Lerman became one of the few critics plainly to state that correctional programs might reasonably be expected to be "effective" in other ways as well; for example, they might be expected to be humane and fair. Indeed, Lerman suggested, evaluation in terms of these and like standards seems particularly important in view of the persistent finding that correctional programs are about equally useful in coping with recidivism. We should be concerned with humane care and fairness for themselves; also, the capacity of correctional programs to achieve these values appears to be among the few bases for choosing among them.

Happily Lerman has taken his own counsel in this assessment of two famous California programs, the "Community Treatment Pro-

*My thanks to Allen F. Breed, Ted Palmer, Robert L. Smith, and Philip D. White, all of the California Department of the Youth Authority, for making unpublished comments on Lerman's book available. And to Paul Lerman for bringing the book to my attention and patiently answering some impertinent inquiries about it. None of these persons should be held responsible for any but the true, agreeable and insightful statements that follow.

ject" and "State Aid to Probation Services" (better known as "Probation Subsidy"). Both have been widely understood as exemplars and harbingers of a new correctional strategy designed to lead to more "effective" ways of handling offenders for less money with less confinement. Lerman finds the programs variously wanting in these respects. He questions the benefits of the broader strategy as currently pursued. The result is a creative and thought-provoking treatise —that some will find simply provoking.

Everything in Lerman's book deserves scrutiny. It is not only time constraints which move me to focus mainly on his assertions about the continued growth of institutionalization. These seem to me the most important from a policy standpoint and the most challenging to some emerging conventions among correctional professionals and those of us who study and write about them.

II

The "Community Treatment Project" was initiated in 1961 within the California Youth Authority. Two groupings of juvenile court commitments were to be created by random assignment, the "experimentals" and the "controls." Members of each grouping would spend about four weeks in a diagnostic center. Then experimentals would be exposed to a special program of eight months of "intensive-treatment" in their own communities before being eased into a regular parole case-load. Controls would receive the Authority's standard program at the time: about eight more months of institutionalization, then parole in a regular case-load. These procedures were to test the proposition, among others, that many juvenile commitments could be handled satisfactorily within their own communities without the standard period of institutionalization.

By the late 1960s, the Project's program was being hailed as more effective in curbing renewed delinquency, more economical per correctional-career, and considerably less dependent on institutionalization. Reanalyzing Project reports, Lerman comes to quite another set of conclusions. He holds that the Project did not demonstrate its program to be more "effective." Nor was it less expensive. And, although experimentals were confined for less time than controls during their correctional-careers, the Project used confinement more than is commonly appreciated and for highly questionable reasons. Moreover Lerman suggests that the Project's lasting effect on its host the Youth Authority may well have been to increase rather than reduce dependence on institutionalization.

Now it should be emphasized that Lerman does not hold that experimentals were institutionalized for more time than controls. It should be emphasized partly because Lerman sometimes writes as if he does. But there is a more important reason for emphasis. At bottom, Lerman is not interested in comparing the Project's program with the regular Authority program. He is willing to concede—well, almost—that it was an improvement, at least so far as confinement is concerned. He wants to ask two other questions: What did the project actually deliver to juveniles in the name of "intensive-treatment in the community"? And, of the things it delivered, which might one expect the correctional enterprise to adopt? To ask such questions is to treat the present as history—a difficult, but rewarding and needed exercise, all too rare.

Lerman notes, for one thing, that the Project quickly extended the period of intensive-treatment for experimentals from eight to about 36 months. This extension may have been a factor in the considerable use of out-of-home placements, two-thirds of the first 72 experimentals being so-placed. Lerman does not count such placements as "institutionalization," but he does mention in passing that many juveniles appear to find them another form of deprivation of liberty. Lerman's main concern is reserved for the use of "short-term detention"—the Project practice of confining experimentals in a Youth Authority institution or a county detention facility for relatively brief periods of time. It is mildly ironic that in this 1968 article Lerman mentioned short-term detention as a Project procedure possibly worth imitation because it involved much briefer periods of institutionalization, typically, than parole revocation. Further thought and a closer look, however, revealed that short-term detention was not only, and possibly not mainly, a *substitute* for parole revocation; instead it was used by Project parole officers *in addition* to revocation. And it was used on occasions when revocation probably would not, and in any case probably should not, have been sustained. Thus the Project reported that short-term detention was used frequently to deal with "such relatively nondelinquent offenses as missing a group meeting, 'sassing' a teacher, showing an uncooperative attitude, or a threat of an emotional explosion (protective custody)." (Quoted by Lerman on p. 37 from a Project report.)

Data of this order led Lerman to speculate about the possibility that detention was the main element of "intensive treatment" as developed by the Project. To see, he constructed two "ratios of detention," comparing days of short-term detention experienced by experimentals with days of "direct service" they could have received from Project parole officers. Schedules showed that Project parole officers could have delivered no more than two hours per week of direct service to each experimental. On the other hand, the average experimental was confined 2.8 times, for 20 days each time, in a 16-month period reported by the Project; 1.75 of these experiences were for status and technical offenses. Thus the first "ratio of detention" works out to 9.8:1; 9.8 days of short-term detention for each day of direct service. The second shows each experimental receiving 6.1 days of short-term detention for status and technical offenses only for each day of direct service. Lerman's conclusion: the primary program element actually delivered by the Project was short-term confinement—not intensive-treatment services.

One can think of other ways of computing a "ratio of detention," to be sure (thus, experimentals who avoided parole revocation experienced about nine nondetention days for each detention day). But the ratios, like the other data presented, do suggest some things that need to be taken into account about "intensive-treatment in the community." The phrase may gloss a considerable amount of institutionalization, strictly conceived. The assumptions undergirding "intensive-treatment"—assumptions about the "causes" of renewed delinquency and the value of "intensive-treatment" in relieving them—may well encourage institutionalization for reasons having little to do with delinquency as ordinarily understood. When subjects fail to comply with the norms of the intensive-treatment regime, or even when a program agent believes subjects might fail to comply, then, as they say in intensive-treatment circles, detention may be indicated. Both of these features, and the extensive use of out-of-home placements as well, suggest that the term "community," like the term "intensive-treatment," may come to have a very special meaning in programs designed to deliver "intensive-treatment in the community."

Still, the Project's program did involve considerably less confinement for experimentals than controls. As mentioned, Lerman does not contest this point. What he does contest, at least implicitly, is that the Project furnishes any solid reasons for believing that sponsoring state agencies will adopt those features of programs like the Project's that result in eliminating routine institutionalization. The Project does give reason to think, on the other hand, that practices like short-term detention for "treatment purposes" will be adopted by sponsoring agencies. This seems to have happened in 1968 when the use of short-term detention for treatment purposes (and administrative purposes) was authorized for *all* Youth Authority parole officers. In 1967, less than 8 percent of those received by the Youth Authority from the courts, through parole revocation, or through short-term detention came via the latter route, presumably from the Project and other special programs. By 1969, 18 percent were received through short-term detention. By 1971, the percentage reached close to 35, and figures for 1974 suggest that the proportion is remaining about the same. At the same time, the mean length of stay in Youth Authority institutions was rising.

Regular parole agents have begun to use short-term detention frequently to deal with wards who have not in the main received the abbreviated institutional stays given to Project experimentals. At the same time, the rate of parole revocation has begun to decline. To the extent that short-term detention is being used as a substitute for revocation, this may mean less confinement; data available to Lerman did not permit him to learn whether it was being used as a substitute (nor was he able to learn the average stay in short-term detention for non-Project wards). Authority publications noted by Lerman suggest caution about any such conclusion, however. They reveal that wards locked up via short-term detention were not given the hearing required for those facing revocation; indeed, finding a way to avoid such hearings may have been one reason for the adoption of the practice by the Authority. And the Project's use of short-term detention raises a serious question about the proportion of occasions for short-term detention which would, or should, justify revocation.

In Lerman's view, then, the Community Treatment Project should serve to forewarn us about several matters. Programs designed as "alternatives" to state incarceration may themselves involve a considerable amount of incarceration. Such programs may use incarceration on occasions that lack legal and perhaps rational justification. (Which is not to say, given current statutes, that it is illegal to use incarceration in this fashion—but that is another topic.) The lasting heritage of such programs may be not intensive-treatment in the community (whatever its faults), but parole programs which tack short-term detention onto already long and perhaps increasing periods of incarceration in state institutions.

III

Initiated in 1965, "Probation Subsidy" pays counties for reducing their rates of commitment to state institutions below the rates for certain earlier years. Payments are earmarked for the support of county probation units meeting such "special" administrative standards as case-loads of 50 or less. Any probationer, not just the diverted, may be supervised in a special unit. Theoretically, the money for Subsidy payments is "offset" by what the state would have spent to service and house the diverted offenders.

Although from the standpoint of its promoters the main aim of Subsidy is to expand and strengthen county probation services, it has been widely understood as a financially sound way of diverting offenders from state institutions. Lerman does not doubt that it has resulted in diversion. What he does challenge, along with the claim that but for Subsidy the state would have spent more for corrections, is the inference that such diversion has necessarily resulted in a reduction in institutionalization. He invites us to consider, indeed, whether Subsidy might not be having an opposite effect.

He begins by noting that the mean length of stay in state correctional facilities for the young has increased from about eight months in 1964, pre-Subsidy, to over 11 months in 1972. The Youth Authority, which operates the facilities, has not hidden the increase; it has argued its justification in terms linked to Probation Subsidy. It is the justification with which Lerman takes issue.

The Youth Authority receives commitments from both the juvenile court and the criminal court, the latter sending persons over 17 and under 21 years of age. Subsidy has apparently induced not only a rate-reduction in juvenile court commitments, but a reduction in absolute numbers as well. As one result, the Authority has been receiving a larger proportion of older, criminal court commitments.

Such persons have traditionally received longer terms from the Authority, on the average, than younger, juvenile court commitments. The reasons for this tradition are doubtless many. Its justification, on the other hand, has typically been that Authority "standards" call for it. Additionally it is assumed that Subsidy is having a "screening" effect. Easier to manage offenders are ostensibly being diverted away from state facilities to the county systems. Proportionately more "difficult, 'hard core' youths, who pose greater problems of control and more acute treatment needs," who "are seen as requiring longer periods of institutionalization" are being sent on. (Quoted by Lerman on pp. 131-132 from an Authority document.) The somewhat greater proportion of offenders against persons in the Authority's new "mix" are among the sorts of data used to support this judgment.

Lerman's response is that extant Authority data fail to support either its traditional "standard" for older, criminal court commitments, or its inference that those shoved through the "screen" of Subsidy require longer periods of confinement. Reluctantly using parole revocation data, Lerman shows that the rates of revocation are less for older, criminal court Youth Authority commitments than for younger, juvenile court commitments. They are less for offenders against persons (and drug offenders) than for property offenders. Post-Subsidy parolees apparently do not commit violent offenses at a higher rate than pre-Subsidy parolees. There is no evidence that increased periods of confinement reduce recidivism in any case.

At the state level, there is no argument over whether institutional (and parole) terms have been lengthened in response to Subsidy-induced changes; the argument is over the justification for increased terms. At the county level, the situation is more complex. Subsidy proponents have held that post-adjudicative facilities have been used less—or no more—since the advent of Subsidy, usually citing average daily population figures or percent of capacity used. Lerman argues that these facilities are being used to confine a larger proportion of the juvenile population since the advent of Subsidy. He shows that there were more facilities in 1970, after five years of Subsidy, than 1965. A larger proportion of the juvenile population was newly admitted to them in 1970 than 1965. He also compares the two periods 1960-1965 and 1965-1970 to show pre- and post-Subsidy changes in the pace of construction of such facilities and of rates of new admissions to them. Both slowed down in the 1965-1970 period, the new admission rate rising 56 percent from 1960 to 1965 and 23 percent from 1965 to 1970. Lerman concludes that Subsidy has not resulted in a reduction of the number of such facilities or in the rate of new admissions to them, but that it was associated with a slow-down in the increase of both. Whether the slow-down was a result of Subsidy or, if so, how, is not made apparent.

Next, confinement in juvenile halls—the county counterparts of jails for adults—is examined. Subsidy proponents for the most part have simply not discussed such confinement, the implication being that the program is most unlikely to affect it one way or the other. Lerman disagrees, at least tentatively. He argues that responses to Subsidy, particularly by the police, may well have increased the use of juvenile halls. He also argues that Subsidy proponents should be concerned with controlling the use of juvenile halls. Detention in such halls accounts for the confinement of by far the largest proportion of juvenile lockups—and this has probably been the case for much of this century. To the extent that Subsidy proponents would reduce institutionalization in the state, this important source must not be overlooked; the Subsidy program should be restructured to control it.

Data on the number of halls are not presented. The rate of admissions to juvenile halls was higher in 1970 than in 1965. Moreover, the percentage increase in the rate was much larger in 1965-1970, while Subsidy was operating, than in the earlier five-year period. The latter fact, especially, leads Lerman to look at other rates and percentage changes in rates of official actions toward juveniles to see what light they may throw on whether Subsidy is implicated in this increase. The discussion is too complex to summarize briefly, but the nub of Lerman's conclusions can be stated. Although it is possible that the marked increase in the rate of detention admissions from 1965-1970 might have occurred without Subsidy, there is a decided possibility that Subsidy had a good deal to do with it. The rate of police referrals to probation rose precipitously during the period— about the same amount as the detention admission rate—and there is reason to think that this may express police resentment of the effort to reduce commitments to state facilities (a published letter from the Los Angeles Chief of Police is quoted). Probation officers seem to be responding to police pressures by detaining more juveniles. Further, Subsidy-supported increases in probation staffs may have increased their capacity to notice juvenile misconduct and their willingness to respond with detention, possibly for "treatment purposes" as in the Community Treatment Project.

Finally, Lerman looks at the institutionalization of juveniles for the state as a whole, adding up rates of new juvenile admissions to state and county correctional facilities and all admissions to juvenile halls for 1960, 1965 and 1970, and comparing the percentage changes in rates for the two five-year periods. He also calculates "institutional youth days" by multiplying admission rates by estimated average stays. All admission rates were higher in 1965 than 1960; the percentage change in the summed rates was about 11 percent. The rate of new juvenile court admissions to the Youth Authority for 1970 was lower than for 1965, but the other two rates were higher. The summed rate was about 43 percent higher in 1970 than 1965, mainly because the rate of detention increased so much. "Youth days" showed a similar pattern, but the percentage increase was much less from 1965-1970 than from 1960-1965, the drop in the number of

Youth Authority days in 1970 almost compensating for the rise in the other two rates.

Subsidy, too, should serve to forewarn us. At a minimum, but crucial, there is no reason to assume that a strategy of diversions constructed like Subsidy will result in a decrease of institutionalization. The Subsidy program offers inducements to county officials not to commit adjudicated offenders to state institutions. This seems to work. But critical decision-points affecting institutionalization are left uncontrolled by Subsidy—and the "logic" of Subsidy—its presumed "screening" function—may move officials at all levels to increase, rather than decrease, institutionalization. At the state level, the supposedly "hard core" cases committed under Subsidy may receive longer terms. A larger proportion of the diverted may be committed to county facilities—for county officials, too, must now deal with "hard core" offenders who would otherwise have been sent to state institutions. It may even be that this "logic" will seem illogical to some lower officials, like the police, breeding resentment. They will refer greater proportions of the arrested to probation officers and press for detention. Then one may see the pace of institutionalization quicken and not just continue to increase, particularly for alleged offenders not destined for adjudication at all. All of this has happened under Subsidy in California according to Lerman, making the gains from the program difficult to identify.

IV

It is a tribute to Lerman that it is difficult adequately to summarize —much less criticize—his main arguments and conclusions even when one focuses on only those related to institutionalization. I do not want entirely to neglect his other main findings, however, because they contribute to his overall judgment about the programs and strategy, a judgment that calls for a weighing of various costs and benefits, not just one kind. I hope that a few, very brief comments will prove suggestive rather than confusingly cryptic, and that they will encourage those more interested in these issues than in institutionalization to read Lerman's book for themselves. I shall then return to the issue of institutionalization.

As I have noted, Lerman concludes that the Community Treatment Project was no better in stemming renewed delinquencies than the regular Authority programs. His analysis of the weaknesses of the Project's main measure of "effectiveness" is brilliant; surely he is right that the rate of parole revocation more clearly reflects official policy with respect to what warrants revocation than it does ward behavior. His own measure, however, based on police arrests as recorded in parole suspension reports, is almost surely faulty for related reasons. The Project may well have been more "effective" than he allows.[2]

In arguing that the career-costs of juveniles in the Project were as high or higher than the costs in the regular program, Lerman presses a point that is not now in contention.[3] This is a small matter. But in connection with this discussion, Lerman proposes generally that "alternative" programs should cost fewer dollars than traditional ones, or at least no more. Why should they? Corrections have never been very liberally endowed; why should extant programs provide a standard? On the other hand, it seems correct to ask what will be bought for the dollars and how they might otherwise be used, with which Lerman agrees.

Lerman also holds that Subsidy expenditures have not been "offset" by funds that the state would have spent but for the Subsidy-induced diversion. That this hasn't been recognized is due in part, he holds, to the flawed method used by Subsidy proponents to calculate what the state might have spent. They have multiplied the number of offenders diverted each year by each year's rising per offender correctional career-costs, without ever stopping to consider whether, and in what proportion, these rising costs might be due to Subsidy itself. Lerman holds that policy changes at the state level, especially lengthened institutional terms, account for most of the rise in career-costs; he proposes substitution of an inflation-adjusted version of the career-costs at the time Subsidy was initiated.

I agree that proponents have miscalculated in the way Lerman criticizes. Whether the adjustment for inflation he would allow is sufficient—he could use the Consumer Price Index—is arguable. I think not; the cost of services of all kinds has been rising much faster than consumer items. But however that may be, I think Lerman overlooks a more important point. Should per capita career-costs be used for such calculations at all? Although I suggest it with the considerable diffidence only proper for one who has thought so little about such matters, using career-costs to make such calculations seems to me to leave intact the fantasy that the operating expenses of correctional institutions are tightly tied to the numbers of persons serviced. I think this must be wrong; within wide limits, the operating expenses of all institutions, not just state lockups and parole units, are quite inelastic.

These are all, one might say, sins of commission. Two sins of omission might be mentioned too, although I think the first hardly even venial. Those devoted to the Community Treatment Project and to Probation Subsidy, I know, besides having other (well, let's say) negative thoughts about Lerman's work, feel that he has overlooked or given short-shrift to aspects of these programs that deserve much fuller consideration. He spends little time discussing the quite elaborate diagnostic scheme employed by the Project or the ideas developed in connection with this scheme about appropriate forms of treatment for different types of offenders. He discusses the Subsidy-induced changes in county probation departments hardly at all. In other words, he selectively assesses these programs. Frankly I think that's all right for a variety of reasons, the most important being that his main interest was in the "social cost" of such programs as parts of a broader strategy of community treatment. It is fitting, therefore, that he should focus on those aspects of the programs best illustrating the general features of this strategy. He might, indeed, have been even more selective.

The second omission I regard as more important. One kind of "social cost" is measured, in part, by the coerciveness of correctional programs; institutionalization is an example. Another, quite different, is related to not institutionalizing adjudicated offenders. Whatever else it does or does not do, institutionalization does tend to insure that those persons, anyway, will not visit depredations on the community while they are institutionalized (although they may visit them on institution staffs and other inmates, which is all too frequently forgotten). How shall we measure this social cost? The Project practice of comparing the "recidivism" of experimentals and controls during equal periods in the community, whatever else its faults, leaves completely out of account the fact that experimentals were in the community for a more substantial portion of the time they were under the jurisdiction of the Youth Authority than controls were. This should be taken into account in weighing the social cost of the two regimes, in my opinion. And Subsidy has apparently resulted in the presence in the community of thousands of adjudicated offenders during periods when they would otherwise have been institutionalized. One need not be "for" institutionalization to suggest that we should measure the relative social cost of this fact too.

V

My enthusiasm for Lerman's analysis of the possible implications for institutionalization of the new strategy of corrections in the community is not meant to suggest that I have no reservations. Lerman seems much more eager to pursue data and interpretations when the programs appear to be increasing confinement than when they appear to be on the way to reducing it. I have already mentioned his tendency at times to write as if Project experimentals were institutionalized for longer periods than controls. He makes a smaller effort, it seems to me, to see whether the Project's scheme for skipping routine institutionalization made any headway with the Authority than he does to see if its short-term detention practices did so. Relative to Subsidy, the large percentage rise in the rate of detention admissions between 1965 and 1970, compared to 1960 and 1965, receives much attention; the much smaller rise in the rate of new admissions to county correctional facilities in the later period compared to the earlier one gets much less. Further, Lerman's discussion of the various rates and percentage changes in these rates is often confusing. As one example among many, it is confusing to read that it is "readily apparent" that the overall juvenile arrest rates "are not changing" (p. 147), when the yearly rates have increased, by Lerman's calculations, an average of 3.6 percent between 1960 and 1970. Apparently what is meant is that the percentage changes in the rates were the same—18 percent—in 1960-1965 and in 1965-1970. A calculation error compounds the confusion: the rate increased 22 percent from 1965 to 1970.

Flaws of omission occur here too. It is not evident that *new* admissions to county and state correctional facilities give a fair picture of changes in the volume of incarceration of juveniles each year, particularly since, as Lerman has shown, short-term detention has become an important source of admissions to state facilities. Parole revocation is also important. Together they have come to outweigh the court as a route from the street to a Youth Authority lockup. Perhaps the same is true at the county level. Also, I think one should give more warning to readers about the ambiguities of the kinds of rates which extant data permit constructing than Lerman has provided. Yearly rates of admission per 100,000 juveniles are not, strictly speaking, accurate indicators of the proportions of juveniles admitted; they necessarily overestimate this proportion since some juveniles are locked up more than once in a year. And Lerman's estimates of "youth days" in lockup—a fascinating idea—are based on very tenuous estimates of the average length of stay in county facilities; moreover, estimates which provide for no changes over time at all.

A more general reservation goes to Lerman's attempt to distinguish between "treatment" and "social control," a distinction reflected in his title. I found the attempt difficult to follow; I also think it is misguided. It is difficult to follow because Lerman confuses the harshness, restrictiveness and painfulness of measures of social control with whether these measures undertake to remedy some assumed defect in those subjected to them. It is misguided insofar as it could serve to mask the enduring connection between "treatment" in a correctional context and the state. The connection suggests to me, at least, that all measures used by correctional agencies, whatever the assumptions on which they are based, are best conceived as "social controls."

Also I think Lerman is less sensitive than he might have been to the costs perhaps necessarily associated with reversing the long-embedded policy of institutionalization. The reports of the Community Treatment Project, some of which I have read, make quite clear the resistance to keeping troublesome juveniles out of state institutions. Some of the resistance comes from the "community"; some comes from the state correctional apparatus itself, including parole officers. Extended periods of "intensive supervision" coupled with short-term detention may be part of the price required to reduce this resistance. Whether intensive supervision reduces "recidivism" may be a less important issue than whether it provides "assurances" to involved parties; and short-term detention for unacceptable reasons can be curbed in ways that Lerman suggests (and that the Project, without his prompting, apparently adopted as time went by).

Similarly, it is not instantly evident that the promoters of Subsidy would have been wise, much less successful, had they attempted to control commitments to county correctional facilities and juvenile halls right from the start. The probation departments and courts were being asked to modify or reverse an entrenched policy of commitment to state institutions. Whatever the reality of their fears about a negative "community" reaction—and Lerman's inferences about police responses suggest he would agree there was some reality—such fears probably had to be addressed. The continued, if slowing, increase in commitments to county correctional facilities, even the quickening pace of detention may be part of the price for addressing these fears.

In the same vein, I should be less reluctant than Lerman to credit Probation Subsidy for helping reverse or defer plans to build still more state institutions for juveniles. Such plans may very well have been unfounded in reason, as Lerman holds. Without Subsidy and the kind of thinking it represents, those ill-founded plans would likely have been implemented in full if past experience in California be any guide. Credit aside, moreover, it would be worth trying to discern how Subsidy may have helped reverse this steel and concrete tide.

VI

To sum up: Paul Lerman has produced a volume worthy of the serious, close attention of every student of corrections, academic or practical. He has demonstrated how an empirically-guided concern with the evaluation of programs can come to grips with correctional policies. He has shown the value of secondary analysis of official documents within a conceptual framework that encourages the analyst to move beyond conventional questions and to see corrections as a system, however loosely coordinated. In the process, he has turned attention to one of the most understudied problems in "criminology": how official actions and organizations change and resist change.

This is very much to have accomplished, but it is not all that Lerman has done. The results of his analysis challenge the emergent wisdom about the thrust of the correctional enterprise and the meaning of the changes now in train. "Deinstitutionalization" has become a byword. But is it a fact? Lerman's findings suggest that it is not a fact for juveniles in California. Whether it is a fact for adults in California, or for anyone elsewhere, we simply won't know until we stop taking intentions for outcomes, stop using inadequate measures, stop looking so fixedly at state and federal institutions without looking where most of the institutionalization is taking place—and probably always has taken place.

NOTES

1   Paul Lerman, "Evaluative Studies of Institutions for Delinquents: Implications for Research and Social Policy," *Social Work*, 13, 3 (July 1968) 55-64.

2   Ted Palmer, "The Youth Authority's Community Treatment Project," *Federal Probation*, 38, 1 (March 1974) 3-14.

3   *Ibid.*

Laundry, New York House of Refuge

THE AMBIGUITY
OF SOCIAL REFORM

CHAPTER 9

Today there are few friends of the juvenile court. The special "children's court" celebrated as the most progressive reform of the Progressive Era attracts a variety of critics. Their critiques of the juvenile justice system are important, because they present a wide range of reform proposals for the prevention and treatment of juvenile delinquency. Critiques of the juvenile court rest upon several assumptions concerning the nature of our society, the causes of delinquency, and the extent of change needed to improve the operation of the juvenile justice system. From these assumptions (or biases) flow the social policy implications which structure public debate over the future of juvenile justice. In this chapter we summarize our own assumptions and spell out some of the policy alternatives flowing from this analysis.

One group of critics complains of the leniency of juvenile justice dispositions. The court's treatment philosophy is seen as inapplicable to hardened youth who commit serious crimes. This view assumes that when delinquents commit crimes, they calculate the relative costs and benefits of their acts. Some observers charge that the alleged leniency of the juvenile court actually encourages crime, since youngsters feel they can "get away with murder." Such observers feel the court should not assume the role of parents, but rather that parents should be made to live up to their responsibilities. These critics feel that delinquency reflects the growing permissiveness of society, and that the juvenile justice system contributes to the lack of respect for law and authority. They promote stiffer penalties for juvenile offenses, as well as swift and certain punishment for all delinquent acts.

Other critics of the juvenile court essentially support its philosophy, while underscoring the lack of adequate resources to properly conduct the court's business. They suggest reforms ranging from improved training of judges, and better diagnosis facilities, to development of a wider range of treatment alternatives. In their view, the court fails because it is overloaded by large caseloads, and, as a result, processes wayward youth in an impersonal, bureaucratic manner. This group usually attributes delinquency to biological and psychological factors, requiring time for correct diagnosis and treatment. These observers applaud the wide discretionary powers of the court, and support the flexibility of court operations.

An increasingly popular criticism of the juvenile justice system decries the lack of adequate legal protection for children. Some in this group suggest that children should possess all the constitutional protections available to adults in criminal trials. They call for jury trials, full adversary proceedings, and broad protections against illegal searches, and self-incrimination. The "due process" school, for example, would argue that children should have their own attorneys, since their legal interests often differ from those of their legal guardians. Of particular concern to this group are the status offenses, which especially place juveniles in legal jeopardy. There is criticism that juvenile law overreaches into the areas of morality and private conduct. The "due process" proponents attack the looseness of court procedures, and the apparent arbitrariness of court dispositions. In their view, the quasi-legal character of court operation increases youthful cynicism about our system of justice, and sometimes inappropriately stigmatizes children with negative labels encouraging future delinquency.

Another common criticism employs the terminology of systems analysis, pointing to a lack of connectedness among various components in the juvenile justice system due to the competing goals of police, judicial, and correctional agencies. The juvenile process is criticized for its irrationality and inefficiency. This group neither suggests specific causes of delinquency, nor openly attacks the philosophy of the juvenile court. Criticism is couched in terms of improved "needs assessments," improved planning, and resource allocations. They propose no solution to the value conflicts except to recommend that conflicts be clarified and reconciled within the framework of political realities. Their reforms include the use of computers, improved data processing methods, new mechanisms of coordination among juvenile justice agencies, and the use of statistical decision making models in court operations. Much has been written documenting the irrationalities, inefficiencies, and inequities of the juvenile justice system. But these criticisms lack a convincing explanation of the problems, beyond merely blaming workers within juvenile justice agencies for the faults of the system. We do not dismiss the contributions to inefficiency and injustice made by system workers exercising broad powers of discretion over youth. But a thorough understanding of the problems of our system of handling juvenile delinquents must take account of forces in society influencing the actions of individual workers. Policemen, judges, and probation officers do not invent the values that guide their daily activities. Rather longstanding preconceptions, methods of operation, and stereotypes about delinquents affect the functioning of the juvenile justice agencies. Social inequalities created and perpetuated by larger political and economic structures intersect with and penetrate the daily occupational life of law enforcers, judges, court functionaries, and professional healers.

To state the obvious—the juvenile justice system operates within society. Its efforts and consequences are circumscribed and guided by the social arrangements of that particular historical, material, and cultural context which is *society*. Many critics of the juvenile court point up obvious problems and contradictions, but fail to relate these observations to broader social factors. Disregard of the effect of social structure on juvenile justice creates the impression that agencies, rules, and professional roles exist in a sociopolitical vacuum. Such a conception clearly would make little sense if the focus of our attention was the family, the educational system, or the political process. Any study of those social institutions that ignored the workings of class, status, and power would be bad sociology, and would produce findings that would be illusory and, perhaps, propagandistic.

The trick of disassociating juvenile justice from the larger societal context often is accomplished by ignoring history. Few texts on juvenile justice contain much historical information. History that is presented in traditional works tends to downplay the influence of political and material forces, portraying the legacy of juvenile justice as a steady march of ideas toward more humane and enlightened conceptions of childhood and delinquency. This romanticized version of history, which is used as an ideological defense of the present juvenile court, obscures the real relationships that have determined the development of various methods of handling wayward youth. Our own historical approach emphasizes changing social structures, and changes in social institutions. Often, we analyze class conflicts, and political and economic events that gave impetus to new social arrangements. This approach is stimulated by Anthony Platt's study, *The Child Savers, The Invention of Delinquency*, which encouraged a renaissance of historial research on juvenile justice.

In their classic study of the evolution of punishment in 1939, Georg Rusche and Otto Kirchheimer examined the forms of punishment in particular historical periods; social, economic, and political changes; and the related development of penal ideologies. They concluded:

> Punishment is neither the simple consequence of crime, nor the reverse side of crime, nor a means which is determined by the end to be achieved. . . . The transformation in penal systems cannot be explained only from changing needs of the war against crime, although this struggle does play a part. Every system of production tends to discover punishments which correspond to its productive relationships. It is thus necessary to investigate the origin and fate of penal systems, the use and avoidance of specific punishments, and the intensity of penal practices as they are determined by social forces, above all economic and then fiscal forces.[1]

Our brief presentation of the history of juvenile justice in America supports the Rusche and Kirchheimer hypothesis. The importance of social, political, and economic forces was demonstrated in the emergence of houses of refuge, the treatment of slave children, and the rise of post–World War Two gang-busting programs, among other historical developments. Dislocations in the social structure—whether due to labor conditions, alterations in status arrangements, or power struggles—shape the way those in power respond to challenges by the powerless.

The history of juvenile justice needs further study and refinement. Future research will likely reveal more about the treatment of children in colonial America, the handling of rebellious slave children, and the methods used to control urban youth in the nineteenth century. But even current research reveals that the history of penal practice weighs heavily upon the modern juvenile justice system. In order to break the chains of the past, we need to creatively interpret this legacy of penal ideology. A thoughtful historical analysis will promote consideration of alternative approaches to delinquency. Such an analysis encourages a detached assessment of our current system, which can be supplemented by further study of juvenile justice in various contemporary social systems. Though comparative research on juvenile delinquency is quite limited, expansion of these studies will expand our capacity to critically assess contemporary juvenile court operations, as well as reform proposals.

We have presented commentary and readings about juvenile court statutes, as well as the administration and enforcement of these laws. It becomes clear that laws governing juvenile justice agencies give license for widespread discretion. Police, probation, and court decisions are often made without significant parental or community input. Practices and procedures are so flexible that they allow gross distortions of cherished precepts of justice, including due process and equal protection of law. Another significant finding is that children of the poor predominate in the juvenile justice process. Since they lack the necessary resources to protect themselves against state intervention, children of the poor are subject to virtually unlimited authority of the juvenile justice system. Empirical studies verify that poor children receive more severe treatment than children from more privileged families.

The contemporary juvenile justice system contains an imposing maze of conflicting rules and bureaucratic routines that defy easy categorization. Few lawyers possess sufficient knowledge of juvenile court practice to adequately defend their clients. The role of the defense counsel in juvenile court is still ambiguous and subject to considerable debate. Questions continually arise as to whether the child's attorney should act as advocate or guardian, who should decide when the child's legal interests differ from that of parents or a legal guardian, and how states will provide adequate legal defense for predominantly indigent juvenile defendants.

The great hopes that the juvenile court would provide benevolent and personalized treatment of delinquent youth are unfulfilled in actual court practice. Juvenile justice in large urban areas exhibits the same assembly line style of justice that characterizes adult misdemeanant courts. In the more rural areas juvenile judges are likely to have neither legal training nor demonstrated skill working with children. Diagnostic facilities are often limited and treatment alternatives are scarce, resulting in reliance on traditional probation supervision and incarceration. Detention, or the jailing of children, is a persistent feature of juvenile court practice.

Despite a series of liberal Supreme Court decisions mandating greater attention to the legal rights of juveniles, juvenile justice reform has been imperceptible. Dissatisfaction with the snail's pace of reform has led many to advocate diversion programs that direct children away from the juvenile court at early stages. But, preliminary studies of diversion show that these programs tend to expand the network of state control over an even larger pool of youngsters.[2] Distinctions of class, race, and sex in juvenile justice programs have led to inequities and injustice for many youths.

Our review of law and court practice, together with accumulated social science research, further supports our contention that social forces circumscribe juvenile justice. One discovers institutionalized racism, sexism, and class discrimination built into the bureaucratic routines of juvenile justice agencies. Tests, decision making criteria, and perceptions of appropriate and inappropriate youthful demeanor are laden with biases that reflect the privilege structure of society. The contemporary juvenile justice system is characterized by the same stereotypes and oppressive social relationships inherent in society. The juvenile justice system, along with welfare, penal, educational, and mental health agencies enforce conformity to conventional morality and punish youthful rebelliousness, giving support to the status quo.

REFORMS AND SOCIAL POLICY

Few current social policies aimed at reducing delinquency are grounded in the societal perspective we have taken. Most contemporary proposals assume that the social order is basically healthy, and suggest only limited tinkering with existing laws, personnel, and routines. Rarely do suggested reforms seek to redistribute power and resources throughout society. Increased use of diversion and community-based corrections are currently fashionable reform ideas. These reforms are relatively easy to implement, since they weed out youngsters who probably do not deserve the harsher treatment they would receive in the traditional juvenile justice system. Such programs have appeal for politicians who seek cheaper methods of dealing with crime and delinquency. Diversion and community-based corrections programs are not fundamental threats to the ideology of the juvenile court.

Reforms calling for decriminalizing both status offenses and the possession of marijuana have met with considerable resistance from the court, police, and legislators. Similarly, the quest for increased legal rights for children has made little headway among juvenile justice personnel and state lawmakers. It seems highly unlikely that those who participated in the construction and maintenance of the present system will readily accept an entirely new justice structure. Reform developments are as subject to societal power and status configurations as the conditions they seek to remedy.

Critics of piecemeal reforms charge that diversion, decriminalization, community corrections, and more legal protection for children are neither new nor likely to succeed. Alex Liazos suggests the need for wholesale social reform to produce significant changes in the juvenile justice process:

> America has many institutions to channel people to undesirable positions; the juvenile justice system is one such institution. Its victims can be liberated only if the entire structure of that class society is destroyed. Anything short of such destruction may seem to improve things somewhat, or in fact it may bring a slight temporary improvement, but, as the history of juvenile justice shows, in time it too will crumble.[3]

One need not accept this classic radical position to acknowledge the urgent need for fundamental social reform in America. Recall the observation of William Healy, founder of the child guidance clinic movement, that the solution to delinquency may lie in radical social and economic changes. Virtually all national commissions on crime, delinquency, and the status of children and youth for the last four decades have concluded that there is a need for major social reform. Unfortunately the authors of these reports often have down-played the seriousness of their messages by suggesting untested, short-run programs as partial answers to grave societal contradictions. When narrow reforms are implemented, initial waves of optimism about solving the "delinquency problem" are soon followed by disappointment, and, in some cases, severe pessimism. This leads many to conclude that delinquents are becoming more dangerous and less amenable to treatment, and, as a result, require more repressive penal measures.

Given the failure of most traditional juvenile justice programs and the lack of meaningful reform proposals, it would be easy to fall back into a "knowing cynicism," supporting only those proposals that appear to limit state authority over youth. Edwin Schur has summarized this view as radical nonintervention, which envisions restricting court jurisdiction, ending the rehabilitative ideal, and frankly recognizing that some delinquent acts should be severely punished. Schur maintains hope that expanded efforts by the legal profession will restore principles of justice to the juvenile process. But, if we consider the barriers to effectively providing due process to juveniles, and that lawyers often have social biases against the poor, people of color, women, and the young, it is clear that Schur's position is just a pipe dream. "Leaving kids alone" may solve some problems, but it fails to resolve the real suffering of children who come into contact with the juvenile justice system. Nonintervention may result in little more than "benign neglect" of inadequate educational programs, needed medical care, and deteriorating living environments.

One possible direction is suggested by a review of the history of juvenile justice in America. At several points there were calls for community-based *prevention* programs, but these were always co-opted by the system, leading to a return to the usual methods of processing wayward youth. From the Cincinnati Social Unit Experiment of 1917 to the Chicago Area Project of the 1930s and the Mobilization for Youth in the 1960s, the idea was advanced that community residents could best design their own programs to prevent delinquency. Although these programs differed in their analysis of the nature of the political economy, their common view about localized control of community life posed serious threats to existing concentrations of political and economic power. In two instances, state representatives denigrated these programs as "communist-inspired," and succeeded in restricting funding.

The community-controlled approach to delinquency emphasizes placing power and resources at the disposal of those people closest to the needs and problems of youth. Community programs generally seek to assist children in their growing-up process through support and encouragement. Since such programs recognize the contributions of poverty, racism, and sex discrimination to delinquency, they challenge the existing structure of privilege on behalf of youth. Misbehavior by children is treated firmly, but with the compassion nurtured by a communality of persons who view the child as an individual.

Such programs ideally are aimed at increasing the quality of life for all community residents; they are not hampered by the need to defend the ideological integrity of a distant political-economic elite.

Although the community-controlled approach to delinquency prevention presents interesting possibilities for action, it also raises several potential problems. For instance, is it realistic to expect communities to take over social service programs? Perhaps only the more wealthy and organized communities can effectively support their own youth programs. What of disorganized communities that need community-controlled programs, but do not have the resources to bolster and sustain adequate community organization? In addition, the community-controlled approach may not solve inequities of justice stemming from differences in wealth. And there is the danger of the potential balkanization of juvenile justice. Under a community-controlled model, what mechanisms would ensure equity of treatment and uniformity of rules?* Community juvenile justice systems might prove more amorphous and arbitrary than the current justice process. There exists little data on the kinds of interests that dominate localized prevention efforts and the nature of their operations. And finally, there is no guarantee that decentralized programs will necessarily promote grassroots democracy.

Despite the grave problems inherent in the community-controlled model of juvenile justice, however, an argument can be made for experimenting with this approach. As we have noted, although the community approach has never been given a fair testing, its theory remains sound and worthy of careful evaluation. This approach to delinquency prevention recognizes the contradictions posed by power concentrations, and proposes to deliver services desired by communities in response to their stated needs.

Programs for youth organized and directed at the community level run the gamut of human services. Results of delinquency research suggest we should encourage the healthy development of all youth. Delinquency prevention cannot be isolated from broad-based attempts to improve the quality of life for all people; separation of delinquency prevention from attention to human needs creates a false distinction. Reducing crime, improving the quality of education, promoting mental health, and supporting family life are several sides to a common, if complex, human service enterprise.

It would be easy to construct rationalizations fashioned from various theories of delinquency for particular programs, but our knowledge of the specific causes of delinquency is quite limited and imprecise. For example, there is evidence that a comprehensive program of prenatal and postnatal care would reduce the number of children suffering retardation and brain damage, which might prevent

---

*Some argue that such diversity of practice is desirable so long as it is responsive to the needs of children. Besides, studies document widespread discrepancies in practice both within and among current juvenile court jurisdictions.

certain cases of delinquency. But adequate health care should be provided to expectant mothers as a matter of course, since such care is a human right, not a special privilege. Every member of society should be entitled to the best health care currently available. Similarly, employment programs should be created because of a social responsibility to provide work for all who seek jobs, not primarily because jobs will reduce the delinquency rate by a certain amount.

Local centers that provide a wide range of services might form the core of a community delinquency prevention model. Such multiservice centers could offer educational and counseling programs in the areas of health, nutrition, mental health, welfare, parent-effectiveness, and employment. Staffed by community people and professionals, neighborhood-based service centers could provide a vehicle for community organization efforts such as public forums on delinquency and related problems. By administering and delivering human services at a level close to those who use them, reform efforts could be more attuned to local conditions, resources, cultural differences, and diverse lifestyles. Community programs help to bridge the gap between people and the social institutions of community life. Visible centers of community aid and activity provide citizens with opportunities to participate in defining issues for collective action. Maximum citizen involvement, coupled with vigorous efforts to provide meaningful youth participation, is one way to avoid the inadequacies of youth programs designed and conducted by those living outside the immediate world of program clients.

Beyond decentralizing social services through neighborhood centers, we also need to break down the walls that exclude people from all public institutions. Schools would be an important place to begin. Many delinquency theorists have pointed to the crucial role of schools in promoting or preventing delinquency. In many communities there is a growing sense of distrust and isolation between educators, students and parents. Some observers believe that this growing alienation contributes to truancy, vandalism, and other delinquency acts on school grounds. As schools become further isolated from other aspects of community life, students increasingly perceive the curriculum as irrelevant, and begin to doubt the legitimate authority of school officials.

There are various ways in which schools can reverse their isolation from the communities. School officials must incorporate a much broader definition of education—a definition that expands the scope of the curriculum, as well as the assumptions about who should be involved in the learning process and where education takes place. For example, it is too often assumed that schooling takes place only on school grounds or within school buildings. This view ignores the growing number of community programs that encourage study and offer opportunities for academic attainment in day-care centers, recreation centers, businesses, religious organizations, community organizations, and the home. Schools might enter into agreements to expand learning facilities in the community. School personnel could offer training programs and seminars; educational materials could be made available to community groups and agencies that collaborate on educational programs with school officials. New programs could experiment with flexible scheduling and creative use of existing facilities to maximize opportunities for community participation in the learning process.

Community residents could serve as instructors, teaching aides, and resource persons within schools. For example, local artisans or craftspersons could be invited to lecture to students, or field trips could be taken to their places of work. Community residents could be involved in decision making in such school operations as curriculum development and program evaluation. Students should be encouraged to participate in internships and field placements as part of the regular school curriculum. Teachers should direct their students to view their communities as learning resources: local museums, libraries, universities, scientific establishments, and businesses can become places of instruction and study. Central to this concept of education is a firm, cooperative relationship between school personnel and various segments of the community. The schools must view their role as serving the entire community, and the community must believe that school personnel and resources are available to them.

We could give numerous illustrations of the range of possible programs permitting people fuller participation in the social institutions affecting their lives. This new participation may not be warmly received by those professionals who have traditionally controlled education, health care, recreation, and welfare agencies. The "pros" will need to explain their bureaucratic routines, and they can expect basic operating assumptions to be questioned and challenged. Increased flexibility for meeting public needs will require new methods of conducting public business. Community residents may need to become more organized, to demand services, and to become more responsive to the needs of their youth. While change is often painful, the potential rewards to people and the possibility of strengthening the social fabric make the effort worthwhile.

THE AMBIGUITY OF SOCIAL REFORM

Delinquency theories suggest two broad strategies of prevention. The first approach assumes that juvenile crime is concentrated among the lower classes—the policy implication flowing from this assumption is that steps should be taken to improve the lives of the underprivileged. This approach calls for equalizing social opportunities and rewards in order to promote greater conformity and law-abiding behavior among the poor. The second approach to prevention assumes delinquency is a product of the basic values of society, and that the entire structure of the society must be reformed to reduce crime and delinquency. Adherents of this second position often cite the widespread criminality reported in self-report delinquency studies. Moreover, there is evidence that delinquents use rationalizations taken from the values of the dominant society to explain their criminal behavior.

We do not know the exact nature of the political or economic transformations needed to accomplish either of these broad strategies of delinquency prevention. Clearly, the community control approach in itself cannot compete with the power concentrations of multinational corporations and established political interests, or with institutionalized social prejudice. Our knowledge of how the powerful maintain control of public agencies and organizations is incomplete. It is even more difficult to know how to return power to victims of social injustice. The scarcity of genuinely critical perspectives to assist our intellectual and political liberation makes it especially difficult to make sense of the social contradictions around us.

The profound changes that are needed mean that many people will have to live differently than they do at present. The same values that promote social injustice and delinquency—the values expressed in the pursuit of material possessions, the competition of the marketplace, an emphasis on personal freedom and individualism, on meritocracy, and on traditional sex and age relations—are values cherished by important segments of the population. The ambiguity of social reform surrounds the decision to forfeit presumed benefits of existing social arrangements in order to reduce the social costs of delinquency, mental illness, divorce, or racial conflict. For example, while banning violence on television might well reduce delinquency, such an approach would pose the problems of censorship and restraint of free speech. Each step toward fundamental social change necessitates trade-offs in existing values and modes of living. The real costs and future benefits of social reforms are rarely obvious, and there are always risks that reforms will backfire, producing unanticipated consequences that are worse than the original conditions.

Adopting a critical perspective is one way of responding to the ambiguity of social reform. To paraphrase historian William Appleman Williams: a critical perspective offers no answers per se. It only offers an opportunity for people to use their own minds to make their own history. The point of a critical perspective is to encourage people to become aware of their society, to evaluate its fairness and humanity, and to seek more liberating social arrangements. Do various juvenile justice reforms only bolster existing inequities, or do they work toward the healthy and full development of all children? Good intentions and sincerity on the part of reformers are poor predictors of future outcomes. Better benchmarks include the questions of whether power and resources are more evenly distributed, whether decisions are made more democratically, and whether people are given more rights to participate. Reforms based solely on arguments of expediency, reduced fiscal expenditures, vacuous behavioral science theories, or the alleged dangerousness of the Children of Ishmael, are likely to portend more contradictions and failures within our social structure.

578

NOTES

1   Georg Rusche and Otto Kirchheimer, *Punishment and Social Structure* p. 5.
2   See Malcolm Klein, *Final Report: Pivotal Ingredients of Police Juvenile Diversion Programs*; and Donald Cressey and Robert McDermott, *Diversion From the Juvenile Justice System.*
3   Alexander Liazos, "Class Oppression and the Juvenile Justice System," p. 23.

BIBLIOGRAPHY

Cressey, Donald, and McDermott, Robert. *Diversion From the Juvenile Justice System.* Ann Arbor: University of Michigan, 1975.

Klein, Malcolm. *Final Report: Pivotal Ingredients of Police Juvenile Diversion Programs.* Washington, D.C.: National Institute of Juvenile Justice and Delinquency Prevention, 1975.

Liazos, Alexander. "Class Oppression and the Juvenile Justice System." *Insurgent Sociologist* 1(1974): 2-24.

Rusche, Georg, and Kirchheimer, Otto. *Punishment and Social Structure.* New York: Russell and Russell, 1968.

INDEX

Abrahams, Roger, 246
Adams, Stuart, 423-25
Addams, Jane, 26, 28
Adjudication hearing, 74-76
Adler, Mortimer J., 187
Age, 3, 65-66; segregation by, in
   lower class, 148; as social category
   in industrial society, 219-27, 262-
   63; and rates of delinquent behavior
   and arrest, 314-15, 320, 323, 332
Aichhorn, August, 460, 462
Alternative programs for treating juvenile delinquents: and control by
   existing agencies, 535, 543-46, 550-
   51; funding conflicts and, 535-36,
   546; community involvement in,
   536-37, 542-43, 548-51; criticized
   by correctional establishment, 542-
   48; criteria of effectiveness, 552,
   559-61; and resort to institutionalization, 554-59, 561-62; costs of,
   560, 561, 562-63
American Bar Association, 59-60
American Law Institute, 41

Amsterdam House of Correction, 8
Andrews, R. Hale, 382
Anomie: and deviance, 157, 163,
   164n3, 168, 170-71, 203; and
   decline of Protestant Ethic, 233; as
   product of cultural crisis of capitalism, 242
Appeal in juvenile court, 72-73
Apprenticeship, 12, 18
Armstrong, Gail, 277
Arrests, juvenile: statistics, 3; police
   behavior and, 63, 64-65, 81, 83,
   84-85, 90-92; alternatives to, 83-84;
   race, sex, and social class bias in,
   85-90, 333-44 passim; and demeanor, 87-88, 89-90. See also
   Delinquent behavior; Social class
   discrimination in administration of
   juvenile justice system
Augustus, John, 20
Authoritarianism: police as exhibiting, 79; ambivalent attitude of
   lower class culture toward, 146-47;
   youth restiveness with, 240

579